THE INTERFACE BETWEEN INTELLECTUAL PROPERTY RIGHTS AND COMPETITION POLICY

The purpose of this book is to examine the experience of a number of countries in grappling with the problems of reconciling the two fields of competition policy and intellectual property rights. The first two parts of the book indicate the variation in legislative models as well as the wide variety of judicial and administrative doctrines that have been used. The jurisdictions selected for study are the three major trading blocks with the longest experience of case law, the EU, the USA and Japan, and three less populous countries with open economies, Australia, Ireland and Singapore. By setting out the legislative and judicial and administrative alternatives available in those constituencies with some experience of dealing with the interface, this research study provides a reference work which can be used as a resource to throw light on how the two fields of law can be adapted to create a coherent whole in the particular circumstances of any one legal system.

In the third part of the book a number of issues closely related to the interface between competition law and intellectual property rights are examined. Separate chapters analyse: (i) the issue of parallel trading and exhaustion of IPRs, a system of legal rules that creates its own interface with the exercise of IPRs alongside the competition rules, (ii) the issue of technology transfer showing the important differences between international IP licensing and foreign direct investment as well as highlighting how limits on technology spillover are set in bilateral investment treaties, and (iii) the economics of the interface between intellectual property and competition law to suggest how economic thinking may find a way of interacting with legal argument in this field.

D1395066

THE INTERFACE BETWEEN INTELLECTUAL PROPERTY RIGHTS AND COMPETITION POLICY

Edited by
STEVEN D. ANDERMAN

CAMBRIDGE UNIVERSITY PRESS

Cambridge, New York, Melbourne, Madrid, Cape Town, Singapore, São Paulo

Cambridge University Press
The Edinburgh Building, Cambridge CB2 8RU, UK

Published in the United States of America by Cambridge University Press, New York

www.cambridge.org
Information on this title: www.cambridge.org/9780521863162

First published 2007

Printed in the United Kingdom at the University Press, Cambridge

A catalogue record for this publication is available from the British Library

ISBN 978-0-521-86316-2 hardback

CONTENTS

v

511- 516
- patents

NOTES ON CONTRIBUTORS

STEVEN D. ANDERMAN is Professor of Law at the University of Essex. He has been an expert on competition policy to the Economic and Social Committee of the European Union since 1984. He is currently advising the IP Academy and the Intellectual Property Office of Singapore on the interface of IP with the new Singapore competition law while also advising the Singapore Competition Commission on the implications of the new Competition Act and the preparation of Block Exemption Regulations and Guidelines.

MIRANDA FORSYTH is a Lecturer in Law at the University of the South Pacific where she teaches criminal law and is currently developing a course in intellectual property law in the South Pacific. She studied at the University of Melbourne, and as a postgraduate at the University of Connecticut. She is currently completing a PhD at the Australian National University on the relationship between the customary justice system and the state justice system in Vanuatu.

FRANCES HANKS is Senior Fellow in the Faculty of Law, University of Melbourne. She is an expert on competition law. She is a member of the trade practices committee of the Law Council of Australia, a body which advises the government on proposed changes to competition law. Recent publications include: 'The Benefits and Costs of Copyright: An Economic Perspective', 'The Treatment of Natural Monopoly under the Australian Trade Practices Act: Four Recent Decisions' and 'Intellectual Property and Price Discrimination: A Challenge for Australian Competition Law'.

CHRISTOPHER HEATH studied at the Universities of Konstanz, Edinburgh and the London School of Economics. He lived and worked in Japan for three years, and between 1992 and 2005 headed the Asian Department of the Max Planck Institute for Patent, Copyright and Competition Law in Munich. He is now a Member of the Boards of Appeal at the European Patent Office in Munich. He is the editor of the Max Planck Institute's

Asian Intellectual Property Series and the Asian editor of the Max Planck Institute's publication *IIC*.

ROHAN KARIYAWASAM is a Lecturer in Law, Director of the Program in Information Technology, Media and E-Commerce Law, and Member of the Human Rights Centre at the University of Essex. He qualified as a technology lawyer with Denton Hall (Denton Wilde Sapte) and has worked as a consultant with several global law firms, and as an external consultant to the United Kingdom's Department for International Development and Office of Telecommunications, and also Cable & Wireless.

IMELDA MAHER is Sutherland Professor of European Law, University College Dublin. She was Director of the Centre for Competition and Consumer Policy, Regulatory Institutions Network, at the Australian National University. She has published extensively on competition law and EU law and is author of *Competition Law: Alignment and Reform* (1999). Recent publications include 'Innovation, Competition, Standards and Intellectual Property' (co-edited with Peter Drahos, 2004) and 'The Interface of EC Competition Law and Intellectual Property Rights: The Essential and the Innovative' (2005).

BURTON ONG is a member of the Faculty of Law at the National University of Singapore. His current research interests include the anti-competitive consequences of expanding intellectual property protection to include industry standards and other new subject matter. He is a Fellow of the Singapore IP Academy where he teaches Patent Law and Antitrust Law in its Graduate Certificate in Intellectual Property Programme, and has given public seminars to civil servants, legal professionals and non-lawyers in and around Singapore.

RUDOLPH J. R. PERITZ is Professor of Law and Director of the IProgress Project at New York Law School. Before entering the legal profession, he was a software engineer and programmer for mainframe computer systems. He has been Visiting Professor at LUISS, Rome, and at the University of Essex, and lectures regularly in Europe and the United States. He has written on competition law as well as intellectual property rights and cyberlaw. He is currently at work on an IP project entitled *The Political Economy of Progress*.

PIERRE RÉGIBEAU is a Reader in Economics at the University of Essex. He has been on the faculty of the Sloan School of Management (MIT), Kellogg School of Management and Institute for Economics (Barcelona). He is a fellow of the Centre for Economic Policy Research. His research interests include the economics of technology and intellectual property, the internal organisation of firms, competition policy and international trade policy. He is the Managing Editor of the *Journal of Industrial Economics*.

KATHARINE ROCKETT is a Senior Lecturer at the University of Essex. She has previously served as a visiting Assistant Professor at the Institut d'Analisi Economica, in Barcelona and an Assistant Professor at Northwestern University. Her interests are in the field of industrial organisation, particularly the economics of new technologies. More specifically, her work has been in the areas of licensing strategy, the economics of patents, the interface between intellectual property and competition policy, and organisational issues raised by new technologies.

WARWICK A. ROTHNIE practices intellectual property law, having spent ten years at Mallesons Stephen Jaques in Melbourne as a Senior Associate and Partner, and, since 2002, as a barrister. He teaches patents in the postgraduate program at the University of Melbourne, having previously taught copyright and designs. Publications include *Parallel Imports* (1993) and, with Valentine Korah, *Exclusive Distribution and the EEC Competition Rules* (2nd edn, 1992).

HEDVIG K. S. SCHMIDT is a Lecturer in Law at the University of Southampton where she teaches courses in EU law and European and international competition law. She has previously worked as a research fellow at BIICL, which included organising and teaching at a seminar for national judges in competition law sponsored by the European Commission. In 2005 she received an award to visit the Max Planck Institute for Intellectual Property, Competition and Tax Law in Munich and further her research into the interface issues of intellectual property and competition law.

PREFACE

This work owes its origin to the Singapore IP Academy, which was established in January 2003 as a result of a national initiative. Acknowledging the value and importance of intellectual assets and creativity as primary sources of wealth and competitive advantage, the broad objective of IP Academy is to contribute to the building of a thriving culture that encourages the management and harnessing of innovation, and the resultant IP rights for the achievement of success in this global, knowledge-driven economy. Although at present it is largely funded by the Singapore Government, it is an independent body.

Professor Gerald Dworkin and Associate Professor Loy Wee Loon were IP Academy's founding directors from January 2003 to December 2004. They have been succeeded by Professor David Llewelyn as director and Ms. Ng Lyn as deputy director.

One aspect of the IP Academy's work is training. A broad range of courses, of varying lengths, are being provided for all those who can benefit from an understanding of intellectual property. At one extreme are university-based courses. For example, the Graduate Certificate in Intellectual Property provides a foundation course suitable for those seeking to qualify as registered patent agents in Singapore, and the MSc in IP Management is targeted at mid to senior management, executives and professionals with a background in science, technology or engineering who wish to specialize in the management of IP in a technology-related business. At the other extreme are a stream of short courses, for example Negotiating Skills for IP-Related Technology Transactions and Performing Arts Management: Copyright and Performing Rights for Practitioners.

The other major aspect of IP Academy's work is 'Thought Leadership', namely the promotion of research. Its research projects take on a multi-disciplinary focus straddling management, social, economic and legal perspectives. The research faculty supports both local and regional development of best practices in IP policy and endeavours to improve the ability of businesses, professional research institutions and other creators of IP to exploit and commercialise their IP.

Shortly after the IP Academy began its work, the government announced that it was proposing to introduce a framework of competition law for

Singapore. Because of the close relationship between competition and intellectual property law, this development provided an excellent opportunity for the IP Academy to promote its research programme and to assist those responsible for determining the nature of such legislation.

The IP Academy was fortunate in enlisting Professor Steve Anderman to lead an internationally based team to provide an examination of this interface between competition and intellectual property rights in different legal systems. It was hoped that the outcome of the study would produce findings and set out policy options of relevance to those responsible for the drafting and implementation of competition legislation in Singapore; an opportunity to provide customised national legislation in its broader international context.

As the policy formulation and draft legislation proceeded, some of the research work and the experts involved fed in their own contributions, at the very least to better inform and assist the decision makers. Thus, in the early stages, there was an expert Roundtable meeting: 'Issues at the Interface between Intellectual Property and Competition Law: Dealing with the Residual Conflicts'. This was followed by a conference for the Singapore legal profession and others: 'The New Competition Bill and its Implications for Intellectual Property Rights'.

The Singapore Competition Act is now in place. It is hoped that the IP Academy played a useful role in assisting the way in which the legislation was framed. The IP Academy is most grateful to Steve Anderman and to all his colleagues who embarked upon the project with such enthusiasm. It is to be hoped that the work which they have done will be of interest and of value to a wider international audience.

The competition law/IP 'interface': an introductory note

STEVEN D. ANDERMAN

I. Introduction

Competition policy and intellectual property rights (IPRs) have evolved historically as two separate systems of law. Each has its own legislative goals and each its own methods of achieving those goals. There is a considerable overlap in the goals of the two systems of law because both are aimed at promoting innovation and economic growth.[1] Yet there are also potential conflicts owing to the means used by each system to promote those goals. IP laws generally offer a right of exclusive use and exploitation to provide a reward to the innovator, to provide an incentive to other innovators and to bring into the public domain innovative information that might otherwise remain trade secrets. Competition authorities regulate near monopolies, mergers and commercial agreements with the aim of maintaining effective competition in markets. This regulation occasionally results in limits being placed on the free exercise of the exclusive rights granted by IP laws.

In recent decades, competition authorities and courts have prohibited conduct by intellectual property owners which was otherwise lawful under intellectual property rights legislation, because it contravened the rules of competition law. This has occurred in four main spheres of activity of IP owners. First, cases have been brought by the competition authorities in the USA, the EU and Japan to place limits on the anticompetitive commercial conduct of individual owners of IPRs where they protect a market standard or de facto monopoly.[2] The competition issue presented in these cases has generally been the IP owner's exclusionary conduct towards innovators and potential competitors on markets which are secondary to and dependent upon an IPR protected industrial standard or de facto monopoly. The anti-competitive conduct has tended to take the form of a 'refusal to deal', 'refusal to license', 'refusal to provide proprietorial software interface codes', or a 'tie-in' or illegal 'bundling', but the act is prohibited because it is viewed as an attempt to 'lever' the IP reinforced market power in the 'primary' market into exclusionary conduct in the secondary market.[3] Secondly, the competition authorities in the USA, the EU and Japan have created a detailed framework of regulation for certain terms of bilateral IPR licensing agreements, whether by means of official guidelines or legislation. Thirdly, the practices of collecting societies, R&D agreements and patent and technology pools have raised the issue of the appropriate treatment of cooperation between competitors in IP related fields under the competition rules. Finally, in the field of mergers and acquisitions, the owners of intellectual property rights have found that competition authorities have intervened on occasion to limit IPR owners from acquiring competing technologies[4] as well as to require compulsory licences of IPRs to third parties as a condition of merger approval.

As modern commercial practices involving the use of intellectual property rights have encountered these forms of 'second tier' regulation by competition authorities, concerns have been raised about the nature of the accommodation between the two systems of law.[5] First, to what extent and on what basis do the competition authorities and the courts have authority to limit the exercise of intellectual property rights in these ways? If IPRs are granted by laws which have their own elaborate system of checks and balances, why is it necessary for competition law to add a second layer of legal regulation to the exercise of IPRs? It appears as if the competition authorities in a number of jurisdictions take the view that their role is a form of public law regulation while the exercise of an IPR is essentially the exercise of a private property right. Certainly, in the USA and the EU, the competition authorities have at times described IPRs as 'essentially comparable' to any other form of private property for the purposes of the competition rules.[6] To what extent do legislation and judicial decisions support the competition authorities in that view?

Secondly, despite the use of this description, when competition law is actually applied to the exercise of IPRs, in these same jurisdictions, concessions are often consciously made *within the competition rules* to the unique nature of intellectual property rights: to their legislative and, in the USA, their constitutional basis as well as to their contributory role in the process of innovation. Indeed, the compatibility between the aims of the two systems tends to ensure that the normal exercise of the prerogatives of intellectual property rights is consistent with the competition rules. The competition rules applied to IPRs, either explicitly or implicitly, almost inevitably acknowledge a form of 'comity' between the two systems of law. Yet, the forms of comity developed within the competition rules in different legal system have tended to differ from system to system.

A third issue raised by the emergence of an extra layer of regulation of IPRs by the competition authorities is to what extent could and should the various IPR laws themselves, the patent, copyright, and design rights laws be reformed in order to reduce the extent of the 'external' regulatory role now played by competition law. To what extent does the experience of interface cases suggest that the IP laws can enhance the nature and degree of comity by embarking upon a process of 'internal' reform? Some issues of reform that have been considered are: (i) the optimum width and duration of patent and copyright protection; (ii) the issue whether industrial copyright laws should provide for compulsory licensing where innovation is improperly obstructed by IP owners along lines similar to patents; (iii) the extent to which industrial copyright such as software programs and databases should be subject to interoperability obligations under IP law; and (iv) the extent to which IP laws can and should acknowledge when the IPR itself creates a monopoly and place limits on the scope of the IP protection. Underlying these enquiries is perhaps the largest policy issue of all: what is the most appropriate relationship between competition policy and IPRs in a growing industrial economy?

If we look at the major legal systems with extensive experience of the coexistence of the two fields of law, the EU, the USA and Japan, we can see considerable variation in their chosen forms of accommodation. The major legal systems have generally accepted that there are cases where the market maintenance concerns of competition law can prevail over the exercise of IPRs associated with substantial market power. However, the nature of this accommodation varies considerably with each system; both in terms of method and where the line is drawn. Moreover, the experience of these countries makes it plain that the true extent of variation cannot be appreciated by a cursory examination. To see it clearly and accurately requires a look in some depth. For example, in Japan, at first sight its competition law gives an extensive legislative immunity to intellectual property rights; the Japanese Antimonopoly Act exempts intellectual property rights from the scope of its application. Yet, on closer examination, the provision has not been interpreted as an overall exemption to all exercises of intellectual property rights but can be limited in cases of private monopolisation or undue restraint of trade (See Chapter 4). In the EU and US, in contrast, there are no explicit legislative immunities in the competition rules of Articles 81 and 82 of the European Treaty or Sections 1 and 2 of the Sherman Act. Instead, the general competition rules in both legal systems have been given judicial and administrative interpretations that result in their application to the exercise of IPRs in extreme cases. Both systems have created wide general norms of competition law which if not modified can apply to limit the exercise of IPRs. Yet, on closer examination, the application of the general competition rules in the US and the EU has resulted in the evolution of judicial and administrative doctrines which apply special rules and even self-denying ordinances acknowledging to a considerable extent the sui generis nature of IPRs, their constitutional foundations in the USA and their legislative foundations in the EU. Sometimes these forms of comity are given expression in special rules explicitly designated for IPRs. One example is offered by the 'exceptional circumstances' test devised by the European Court of Justice when applying Article 82 to an issue of abusive refusal to licence by an IP owner. More often, there are powerful partial immunities or safe havens built into the logic of the general competition rules when they are applied to the acts of the conduct of the IP owner. Often this is the logical outcome of the two systems of law pursuing similar aims. For example, both US and EU competition law make it clear that if a company grows by internal investment in R&D and IPRs to a position of significant market power that is perfectly lawful under the competition rules. Moreover, if the owners of IPRs wish to charge high prices for their successful products protected by IPRs, the risks of investment ex ante will be respected by the competition rules in each legal system albeit in different ways. The normal exercise of IPRs is by judicial doctrine viewed as lawful under the competition rules but each system has its own line where the exercise of an intellectual property right is not viewed as normal under the competition rules.

The purpose of this book is to examine the experience of a number of countries in grappling with the problems of reconciling the two systems and dealing with interface issues. The book is divided into three parts. The first two parts of the book indicate the variation in legislative models as well as the wide variety of judicial and administrative doctrines that have been used to attempt to deal with problems raised at the interface between intellectual property rights and competition law. The jurisdictions selected for study are the three major trading blocks with the longest experience of case law: the EU (Chapter 2), the USA (Chapter 3) and Japan (Chapter 4) and three less populous countries with open economies, Australia (Chapter 5), Ireland (Chapter 6) and Singapore (Chapter 7).

In these parts, the intent is not to attempt to arrive at a definitive model of reconciliation between the systems of legal regulation or even a recommended 'best practice'. The examination in depth of the different jurisdictions makes it plain that each system must determine its own appropriate accommodation. It is true that recently, efforts have intensified in different jurisdictions to find the most appropriate basis upon which to combine the two policies into a coherent whole for the purposes of innovation policy. In the USA the Antitrust Division of the Department of Justice and the Federal Trade Commission have held extensive hearings on the interface issue.[7] In the EU the Technology Transfer Block Exemption Regulation has recently been significantly reshaped and a series of conferences have been held with the aim of obtaining a clearer idea of the best way to apply competition law to the commercial exercise of intellectual property rights.[8] In Australia the Intellectual Property Review Committee was established both to review IP laws from the standpoint of competition and to recommend a reform of the width of the exemption the Trade Practices Act gave to the exercise of intellectual property rights. In many countries with new competition laws which have already enacted IP legislation, such as India, China, Singapore and Hong Kong, there is a need to shape the overall system to deal with the inevitable conflicts that can arise when the exercise of IPRs runs into the buffers of the competition rules. Finally, in the USA, EU and Japan, the interest in the interface has been whetted by the growth of digital multi-media technology and the potential legal roadblocks in the new technological environment. Nevertheless, it seems almost inevitable that the optimum method of reconciliation will differ for each national system depending upon its legal culture and its state of economic development.

Hence the overall aim of this book is the more modest one of setting out the array of options on offer, the legislative and judicial and administrative alternatives available in those constituencies with some experience of dealing with the interface. The intention is to produce research findings in sufficient depth so that the experience of the selected legal systems can be understood and used as points of reference by competition authorities and the parties involved in interface disputes. This is a research study that should be viewed as a reference work and a resource to be adapted to the particular circumstances of any one legal system.

In the third part of the book we look at a number of issues closely related to the interface between competition law and intellectual property rights. Chapter 8 analyses the issue of parallel trading and exhaustion of IPRs, a system of legal rules that creates its own interface with the exercise of IPRs alongside the competition rules. Chapter 9 discusses the issue of technology transfer showing the important differences between international IP licensing and foreign direct investment as well as highlighting how limits on technology spillover are set in bilateral investment treaties. Finally, Chapter 10 examines the economics of the interface to suggest how economic thinking may find a way of interacting with legal argument in this field.

II. A note on the compatibilities between the two systems of legal regulation

Even without a legislative immunity for IPRs, the case law interpreting the competition legislation in the countries studied demonstrates that the competition rules create certain self-denying ordinances to ensure that there is an extensive reconciliation between the two systems of legal regulation. This is entirely to be expected since, within each legal system, the different means used by intellectual property rights legislation and competition law operate in many ways in conjunction rather than in conflict with each other. IP laws, such as patent and copyright laws, confer an exclusive right to exploit an invention or creation commercially for a limited period as an incentive to creation and innovation. These rights are essentially 'negative' rights; they prevent copying of the protected innovations. They do not ensure profitability but if the IPR is combined with a successful product, the legal exclusivity provides a stimulus to innovation by acting both as a reward to the inventor/creator and as an incentive to innovation more generally. In the case of patents, without the protection of exclusivity, firms may choose to keep their innovative ideas secret as opposed to disclosing them in their patent claims. This stimulus to the spread of information is also a stimulus to innovation resulting in new products and processes entering existing markets and creating new markets. In these ways, intellectual property rights can actually enhance the forces of competition.

Moreover, each IP law, as well as competition policy, strikes its own balance between protecting early innovators and protecting the claims of 'follow on' innovators. IP laws, such as patent and copyright laws, strike an 'internal balance' between the rewards for 'the improvements on earlier invention by later innovators', and the rewards to 'early innovators . . . for the technological foundation they provide to later innovators'.[9] As Merges and Nelson have pointed out: 'Ultimately it is important to bear in mind that every potential inventor is also a potential infringer. Thus a strengthening of property rights will not always increase incentives to invent; it may do so for some pioneers, but it will also greatly increase an improver's chances of becoming enmeshed in litigation.'[10] In copyright, the idea/expression dichotomy operates to ensure that copyright contributes to common knowledge while protecting the originator or creator from copying the expression of his or her work. In other words, IP laws usually attempt to strike a balance between providing sufficient incentives to innovation by the creator/inventor and avoiding the protection of any single innovation operating as a disincentive to cumulative 'follow on' innovation.

At the same time, the basic doctrines of modern competition law work in conjunction with IP laws by acknowledging their positive role in the process of innovation in at least five major respects. First and foremost, both the US and the EU competition laws accept that the achievement of an economic monopoly by means of investment R&D and intellectual property rights is a legitimate course of conduct for a firm, a form of 'competition on the merits'. Secondly, and relatedly, both EU competition law and US antitrust law acknowledge that the pricing of IPRs, even by dominant firms, must include a return which *adequately* reflects the reward/incentive function of IPRs as well as the ex ante investment risks of their owners. Thirdly, the competition laws in both systems *in most cases* give recognition to the right of IPR owners to prevent copying even if the exercise of this right denies access to markets to competitors. Fourthly, the competition laws in both systems no longer automatically assume that the legal monopoly conferred by IP laws, such as patent and copyright legislation, automatically amounts to an economic monopoly or even confers market power. That issue is left to be established empirically. Finally, in their analysis of IP licensing agreements both systems of competition policy work with the presumption that the licensing of IPRs is in general pro-competitive in its effects.

Nevertheless, as we have seen, modern competition policy, does act in reserve to prevent the excesses of private property owners in order to maintain effective competition on, and access to, markets,[11] operating as a 'second tier' of regulation of intellectual property rights.

It is also worth noting that the Agreement on Trade Related Intellectual Property Rights (TRIPS) spells out at various points that there is a role for competition policy to supplement the intellectual property rights policy of the Treaty. In formal terms, it does not require such laws. It permits them. For example, Article 8 (2) TRIPS states that 'Appropriate measures, provided they are consistent with the provisions of this Agreement, may be needed to prevent the abuse of intellectual property rights by right holders . . .' Article 8 also makes it clear that in principle Member States may enact legislation to prevent practices by the right holder that adversely affect the international transfer of technology. Moreover, in Article 40, the TRIPS agreement specifies the types of licensing practices or conditions relating to intellectual property rights which restrain competition and impede the transfer and dissemination of technology including exclusive grant-back conditions, coercive package licensing and clauses preventing challenges to the validity of the IPR. Nevertheless, as this note and the following studies will show, it is wise not to have a system of IPR legislation which is unaccompanied by a system of competition law.

III. The changing nature of the interface between the exercise of IPRs and competition policy in the major competition law systems

From the early years of the twentieth century, the conflict between the exercise of IPRs and competition policy tended to be exaggerated by judicial and administrative doctrines initially in the USA and later in the EU. During these and later decades, patents were equated with monopolies[12] and patent licensing was subject to tight restrictions by competition law, initially following a doctrine of patent misuse,[13] and latterly by the regime of the 'Nine No-Nos' in the USA and its counterpart in the EU.[14] Since the 1970s, a new antitrust legal framework has emerged in both trading blocks with a greater appreciation of the economic benefits of IPRs and a move away from any automatic association of real market power with exclusive IP rights.[15] This change was prompted in part by judicial and administrative acceptance of the law and economics analysis of the 'Chicago School',[16] initially in the USA and later in the EU. Yet the Chicago School's initial success in restoring greater economic realism has been followed by a 'post-Chicago School' view emerging both in the USA[17] and in the EU[18] that acknowledges that not all IPRs are monopolies but recognises that some can be. There are cases where IP owned assets make a right holder dominant in a product market in established sectors of industry and such cases can be found not infrequently in the 'new economy', particularly in the copyright protected information technology, media and telecommunications sectors. Moreover, patent protected products and processes in the biotechnology sectors may also be potentially subject to the limits of this competition policy/intellectual property law interface.[19]

The concern of competition authorities with IPR protected dominant market power in the form of industrial standards particularly in the sectors of the 'new economy' can be traced to two developments. First, there has been an unprecedented expansion of IPR protection to a whole new range of products in the knowledge economy.[20] Existing protection regimes such as patent and copyright have been extended to accommodate new technology such as biotechnology in the EU Biotechnology Directive, and information technology in the new EU Copyright and Related Rights Directive for the Information Society, as well as the Digital Millennium Copyright Act in the USA. Copyright and patent protection have been extended to new areas such as computer software and business methods. Sui generis protection has been extended to databases and semiconductors.

This expansion of functional coverage of IPRs in recent decades has been fuelled by an increased awareness in the US and EU of the role of intellectual property rights in information goods as a significant source of wealth creation and a basis for success in international competition[21] as well as an increased concern to protect such informational rights against the ease of illegal copying of such goods.[22] The arguments of certain scholars, particularly but not exclusively in the USA, for acceptance of a stronger 'property rights' conception of IPRs have contributed to a wider acceptance of this concept.[23] During the last two decades, the US judiciary have made a number of decisions resulting in greater ease of obtaining patents[24] and greater ease of enforceability of IPRs,[25] as well as a wider view of protected subject matter in copyright.[26] In the USA, a new Federal Court of Appeals specialising in patent and other IPR matters was established in the 1980s[27] and during its period of tenure the number of patents granted in the USA has risen at a steep rate.[28] The decisions favouring a wider IP protection over other balancing contentions have not been unanimous,[29] but the accretion of landmark cases widening intellectual property protection in the USA have amounted to a noticeable judicial pattern, even if there are cases going the other way.[30] By and large the EU has followed suit by widening its definitions of patentability and copyright, if not quite so extensively as the USA.[31]

Along with this expansion of their functional coverage, IPR protection regimes have also been extended geographically as minimum standards through the medium of the TRIPS agreement within the framework of the World Trade Organisation (WTO). The impetus for this globalisation of IPR legislation has come from the large IP owning corporations wishing to protect their investments in R&D from copying, particularly in developing countries with weaker IP legislation. The emergence of TRIPS has been described as 'a process whereby the wish lists of various intellectual property lobby groups are inscribed into public international law'.[32] In the 1980s, the US Government brought IP protection within the GATT and used its s. 301 procedure to obtain bilateral agreements to protect US IPRs. By 1993, the USA, supported by the EU and Japan, was able to secure a TRIPS agreement as part of the WTO agreement of 1994. These highly developed countries had accepted the economic arguments that the return to such investments by the larger corporations helped to maintain the growth and development of their economies in the face of world competition.[33] The TRIPS agreement imposes high minimum standards[34] upon its members for all forms of IPRs based on the Berne and Paris Conventions as well as most of the rights.

The second development, particularly in the highly industrialised countries, is that the expansion of IPR protection, along with its increased incentives for R&D investment, has also produced certain risks to cumulative innovation in the high technology sectors. There has been a noticeable tendency for particular markets in the USA, EU and Japan to be characterised by individual market leadership reinforced by IPR protected industrial standards.[35] The phenomenon of a product achieving such a market position normally calls for careful monitoring by the competition authorities.[36] The risks from a competition policy point of view arise from the possibility that the market power inherent in a market standard might be abused to preclude access to downstream related markets. In such situations, the owner of the 'system' which has achieved the status of an IP protected industrial standard tends to look proprietorially at the development of improvements and new products relating to the 'system'. As Ordover and Willig put it, in a situation where the incumbent market leader has high sunk investments and is confronted by risks of leaks to free-riding competitors, there is a tendency to look more closely at a strategy of capitalising on vertical integration to develop modular applications related to the market standard.[37] In the recent US *Microsoft* case, for example, the Federal District Court that tried the case accepted that the market share of the Windows operating system was 94 per cent of all Intel chip PCs worldwide. In respect of modular applications, MS Word had fended off Word Perfect to gain about 90 per cent of the word processing market and Microsoft's Internet Explorer had captured more than 80 per cent of the web browser market from the previously dominant Sun Microsystem's Netscape Navigator (50 per cent).[38]

It is true that some vertical business strategies can, on balance, be pro-competitive where they are based on genuinely innovative products.[39] Moreover, they can help to create and maintain useful industrial standards in related markets. Yet, in network industries where the incumbent enjoys a monopoly, with substantial 'network effects' and a large installed base of users, the possibility of anticompetitive strategies cannot be ruled out.[40]

Similarly, where a base product such as a biotechnological patent gets into a strong position to control follow-on research and development of related products, competition concerns may arise.[41]

The strategies of owners of IPR protected industrial standards can take the form of vertical foreclosure by exclusive contracts, the tying-in of one product with the sale of another, or 'bundling', and refusals to deal or license, all means by which the owner of the industrial standard can lever its monopoly on an upstream market into a monopoly on the downstream/dependent market.

The vertical foreclosure of downstream markets by owners of industrial standards in upstream markets entails two risks to innovation. The main risk is that the process of further innovation will be restricted to the R&D of the owner of the upstream industrial standard and thereby deprive a wider circle of developers from contributing to the next stages of innovation.[42] A second risk is that the 'network effects' barrier to entry can result in technologically inferior products 'tipping' certain downstream markets and technologically superior products being lost.[43]

Some economists, such as Schmalensee and Evans, have objected to this type of competition concern claiming that the process of competition in markets in the new economy is different in kind to that in the old because it takes the form of different technological systems competing *for* the market rather than the traditional form of competition *in* the market.[44] Competition in high technology markets, they say, consists of a rivalry between products designed to replace one another rather than remain in competition in the same market and these forces make monopolies fragile and transitory.[45] They describe this form of competition as 'dynamic competition', or 'Schumpeterian' competition, because it involves a process of 'creative destruction' which strikes 'not at the margins of the profits of existing firms but their foundations and their very lives'.[46] There has even been a suggestion that these forces of competition can make markets self-regulating.[47] In the IT field there is undoubtedly some evidence of dynamic competition, i.e. succeeding generations of products achieving industrial standard status only to disappear and be replaced by competitors: Wang and dedicated word processors gave way to CP/M and Wordstar. Wordstar in turn was ousted by MSDOS/Word Perfect and Lotus 1-2-3, which in turn was displaced by MS Windows, MS Word and MS Excel, etc.[48]

It is misleading, however, to portray copyright and patent protected industries as presenting a picture of endless winner-take-all races.[49] In the first place, we can see a pattern of protracted competition between IP protected products in systems in a number of highly concentrated industrial sectors: mobile telephones, computer games, PC hardware, ISPs on the Internet, pay TV, motion pictures and music recordings.[50] In these sectors, there is still competition, albeit reduced to a few suppliers, between firms *in* the market. The pattern of highly concentrated industries can be seen both at national and international levels.[51] Secondly, there are sectors where there are market standards, some persisting through several generations. Microsoft has maintained its Windows operating system/middleware from Windows 3.0 to Windows XP and now accounts for more than 90 per cent of Intel chip driven PCs worldwide. Intel microchips have provided several generations of Pentium processors that now power almost 90 per cent of all PCs worldwide. Far from copyright protected innovation producing life-threatening dynamic competition on 'new economy' markets, the picture seems to be a familiar one of highly concentrated industries and industrial standards. Despite the undoubted consumer benefits created by these industrial standards, and the stimulus to investment in technological development provided by IPRs, the ownership of industrial standards in the new economy can also confer inordinate market power. In other words, it is difficult to accept uncritically that every transaction which is viewed as anticompetitive in the short run can be justified by reference to its long term effects where the long term benefits are difficult to predict and the costs of restrictions on competition are tangible and immediate.[52]

Moreover, this type of individual market dominance can be prolonged by the presence of a new type of demand side barrier to entry in the form of 'direct network effects'[53] and 'indirect network effects', sometimes referred to as 'network externalities'[54] in the sale of complementary products in 'systems'.[55] 'Direct network effects' are the effects on demand for a 'system' product, or network, by the purchase of a network product by more users. The inherent interoperability of the product means that the more buyers of the product there are, the more attractive it will be to all users, new and existing. A good example of this is the fax machine, ATM machines,[56] mobile telephone or even software such as Word or Lotus 1-2-3.[57] Direct network effects can operate as a barrier to entry when one product has become an industrial standard simply because they raise the ante for entry. The new entrant faces the task of generating a comparable critical mass of customers *for their product* as a condition of entry.[58]

'Indirect network effects' or 'network externalities', arise from the effect a larger network has on the production of *complements*. Some innovative system products experience a lift off in their rivalry with other products as an increase in demand for one or more of their cluster of 'complementary' products sets off an increase in the demand for their core product in a mutually reinforcing way. Werden has persuasively argued that indirect effects 'may pose more formidable entry obstacles than direct ones because an entrant may find it difficult to enlist the support of essential complementers'.[59] It has been suggested by economists that indirect network effects were a major factor allowing MS-DOS to dislodge the previously dominant CP/M as Microsoft and independent application developers created so many applications that users preferred MS-DOS to its rival, although the disparity in cost and bit technology between the two were also important factors.[60] In the *Microsoft* case in 1996, the US District Court found that the network effects of applications compatible with Windows on PC users created an 'applications barrier to entry' to other PC operating systems.[61] The network effects barrier to entry is enhanced by 'switching costs'[62] and the difficulties of new entrants obtaining support from unreceptive, existing producers of complementary products, particularly when they 'must enlist multiple independent complementers'.[63]

In situations where systems achieve the status and power of market standards and are IP protected the issue arises for all economically mature legal systems – what is the appropriate method to reconcile the respective concerns of competition and IP policy? How should competition policy and IPR policy apportion responsibility to ensure open access to market standards for modular applications makers, who seem to be indispensable to cumulative innovation in systems industries with an industrial standard? To what extent should competition law operate as a default mechanism when IP laws facilitate rather than limit an abuse of market power?

IV. The relevant principles of IP law and innovation

IPR specialists have often stressed the importance of IPRs as an incentive to innovation because of their reward to invention and creativity.[64] Without adequate incentives, the proponents of the traditional IPR view assert, research and development investment would decline and with it the innovative capacity of an economy.[65] The classic empirical case for this comes from the pharmaceutical industry where the millions of pounds, dollars and euros of expenditure on research and development would not occur unless the companies making the investment could be certain of exclusive rights to returns and protection from competitors for a period of time sufficient to recoup their investment and gain a profit.[66] This model of IP legislation as catalyst for innovation by the inventors of novel products or processes, however, offers an unduly narrow perspective of both the process of innovation and the role of intellectual property rights. We can see this by looking more closely at patent and copyright laws.

A. Patent laws

As is well known, patent law provides an exclusive right to exploit, i.e. make, use and sell, a novel invention[67] for a limited period both as a reward to the inventor and as a wider incentive to investment in research and development. Yet, the wider incentive to investment in research and development is not synonymous with the reward to the pioneer inventor. All patent laws have built into their design a demonstrable interest in encouraging further generations of innovation as well.[68] In the first place, the time limit for exclusivity of 20 years is established to ensure that after a limited period for profit taking, the invention can be replicated and used more generally. Perhaps equally importantly, the disclosure obligations in the patent claim are meant to release information about the patented invention to expand knowledge within the technological community and stimulate research *during the protected term of the patent.* Economists such as Kenneth Arrow[69] and Robert Merges[70] have conceptualised the patent as a trade off of the exclusive right for both its incentive effects and its disclosure of information on technological change.[71] Cornish, a noted IP legal academic, cautions against exaggerated expectations but accepts that '[p]atents do make available a large quantity of information about the latest technical advances and they are regularly consulted by those concerned with development in many industries'.[72] Article 29.1 of TRIPS, reflecting the majority of patent systems, emphasizes this function of the disclosure obligation: 'disclosure must be sufficiently clear and complete for the invention to be carried out by others'.[73]

Moreover, the scope of the exclusive right conferred by a patent is limited by the statutory defences to infringement, including the 'experimental' use defence which is designed to prevent the patent right being used to inhibit scientific development,[74] the 'prior use' right and the 'personal use' right.[75] Furthermore, as we shall explore later in this chapter, where the scope of patents is defined narrowly this can help to ensure that a balance is struck between the protected product and subsequent streams of innovation.[76]

Consequently, the theory behind the award of a patent can be seen not only to be to provide a reward to the pioneer inventor and create an incentive merely for a pattern of serial invention. The initial grant of exclusive rights has a wider remit; it is shaped to encourage other, cumulative streams of innovation to flow as a result of any individual invention, along with the original inventor's own development of its protected product.[77]

In addition, many patent laws in Europe and elsewhere in the world, along with policies of excluding certain fields of technology, and Crown use,[78] have long had a policy of compulsory licensing in extreme cases where exploitation of the intellectual property right inter alia operates to block the development of other technology.[79] Under the UK Patent Act, 1977, as amended in the light of the TRIPS agreement, for example, the comptroller has a discretionary power, upon application by an aspiring licensee,[80] to grant a compulsory licence where, inter alia, a refusal to grant a licence on reasonable terms has the effect of impeding the exploitation of other new technology. In such a case it is possible for third parties to obtain a compulsory licence subject to an obligation to cross-license their own patent on reasonable terms.[81] A second ground for a compulsory licence is the fact that a patent is not being worked at all and it can be shown that there is demand within the

UK for a patented product.[82] A third basis for a compulsory licence arises when a report of the Competition Commission has decided that the patentee is engaging in an anti-competitive practice against the public interest. In such a case, the appropriate minister is given the power to apply to the comptroller to have the patent endorsed as a licence of right.[83] This offers an example of the links between the internal checks and balances of patent law and the external tier of regulation provided by competition law.[84]

Applications for a compulsory licence are in fact rarely made, and even more rarely granted,[85] partly because applicants face the double burden of proving a statutory ground and then convincing the comptroller to exercise his discretion, but a claim for a compulsory licence can be used as a bargaining chip for a cross licence and the grounds for compulsory licences must be taken into account by patentees in their commercial decisions.

The legislation on the Community Patent[86] also contains provisions for compulsory licensing which 'are designed to provide guarantees against abuses of the rights conferred by the patent'. It too is based on the requirements of Article 5 of the Paris Convention and Article 27(1) and Article 31 of the TRIPS Agreement.[87]

The Community Patent's provisions allow the Commission to grant a compulsory licence of a Community patent:

(i) When licensing is needed to use a second patent involving an important technical advance of considerable economic significance in relation to the invention claimed in the first patent, subject to an obligation to cross-license;

(ii) In times of crisis or extreme urgency, or to remedy a practice determined by judicial or administrative process to be anticompetitive.[88]

Consequently, the Community Patent provides an explicit basis for the competition authorities to intervene in an extreme case where a patent is used to block subsequent innovation by other inventors.

A further example[89] of this concern is offered by the Biotechnology Directive in its new regime for compulsory licensing and cross-licensing of technological inventions. The compulsory licensing rules are concerned with the relationship between the use of patents and the use of plant variety rights. Under Article 12(1) where plant breeders cannot acquire or exploit a plant variety without infringing a prior patent, they may, after a failure to secure a voluntary licence, apply for a non-exclusive, compulsory licence to use the invention, subject to the payment of an appropriate royalty and the offer of a cross-licence on reasonable terms. Under 12(2) the same rules apply mutatis mutandis where the owner of a patent concerning a biotechnological invention cannot exploit it without infringing a plant variety right. Both rights also presuppose that the applicant can show that the target IPR for which they wish a compulsory licence constitutes 'significant technical progress of considerable economic interest' by comparison with their own IPR (Art. 12(3)(a)(b)). The policy underlying these compulsory licensing provisions is to prevent IPR protection from blocking further innovative development by other innovators.

The TRIPS agreement[90] also endorses a compulsory licensing regime, subject to a number of conditions: that the applicant must first have applied unsuccessfully to the right holder for a voluntary licence on reasonable commercial terms;[91] and the right holder must be paid adequate remuneration in the circumstances of each case taking into account the economic value of the authorisation (Art. 31(h)).

Under Article 31 a compulsory licence may be authorised to permit the exploitation of a patent ('the second patent') which cannot be exploited without infringing another patent ('the first patent') provided that: (i) the invention in the second patent 'involves an important technical advance of considerable economic significance in relation to the invention claimed in the first patent'; (ii) the owner of the first patent is entitled to a cross-licence on reasonable terms to use the invention claimed in the second patent; and (iii) the use authorised in respect of the first patent shall be non-assignable except with the assignment of the second patent.

Furthermore, under Article 31(k) specific authorisation is given for legislation to provide for a compulsory licence 'to remedy a practice determined after judicial and administrative process to be anti-competitive'. In such cases, certain preconditions are waived and termination of the compulsory licence can be refused if the authorities consider that the conditions which led to the compulsory licence 'are likely to recur'.

Finally Article 30 of the TRIPS treaty states that Members may provide limited exceptions to the exclusive rights conferred by Article 28 subject to conditions that reflect the delicate balance that must be struck between private ownership rights and public interests in drafting and implementing the exceptions provisions. These exceptions must not *unreasonably* conflict with the *normal* exploitation of the patent or *unreasonably* prejudice the legitimate interests of the patent owner, taking account of the legitimate interests of third parties.

On its face, the TRIPS treaty appears to strike a reasonable balance between the two dimensions of innovation: reward of limited exclusive rights to inventors and originators and protection for follow-on invention and origination. Moreover, it appears to offer help to developing countries in the areas of pharmaceuticals, education, traditional knowledge and the patenting of living organisms. As is gradually becomingly better understood, however, there is a huge gap between the rights allowed in the language of the Treaty and the experience in practice in developing countries.[92]

The balance in TRIPS between first generation and later generation innovation requires consideration of yet another factor. The TRIPS agreement spells out at various points a role for competition policy to supplement the overall intellectual property rights policy of the treaty. Thus Article 8(2) states that: 'Appropriate measures, provided they are consistent with the provisions of this Agreement, may be needed to prevent the abuse of intellectual property rights by right holders.' Article 8 also makes it clear that in principle Member States may enact legislation to prevent practices by the right holder that adversely affect the international transfer of technology. Moreover, in Article 40, the TRIPS agreement specifies the types of licensing practices or conditions relating to intellectual property rights which restrain competition and impede the transfer and dissemination of technology including exclusive grant-back conditions, coercive package licensing and clauses preventing challenges to the validity of the IPR.

In these ways, TRIPS embodies a view of property rights that on its face combines IP rights with restrictions and responsibilities for IP right holders. It also projects a view of innovation policy that allows Member States to strike a balance between protection of invention, public health concerns and diffusion of inventive ideas by a combination of intellectual property rights legislation and competition policy. The balance struck in the words of the TRIPS agreement cannot be read in isolation from its geopolitical context. The TRIPS package of high minimum protection in respect of patentability (Art. 27), patentee rights (Art. 28) and a minimum term of 20 years (Art. 33) has had a dramatic effect on developing countries, placing them under considerable pressure to invest their limited resources in legislation and enforcement machinery to implement the increased standards of protection.[93]

B. Copyright laws

In copyright law, too, there is also a balance struck between protection against overt copying and use by follow-on innovators of the inventive or creative idea, but this balance differs in nature from patent law. First and most fundamentally, even during the copyright terms, most systems of copyright tend to endorse the idea/expression dichotomy, that is they do not protect the idea underlying a work but only the original mode or form of expression of that underlying idea, leaving open to other innovators and creators free access to and use of the underlying idea.[94] Secondly, copyright law contains a doctrine of 'fair use', or 'fair dealing', that permits some use for reporting for news, educational and research purposes, criticism or review as well as some personal use.[95] Further, the copyright term is also limited although the 70 years plus life duration, recently extended from 50 years, seems more suited to literary than informational copyright protection.[96]

In the new economy of information technology, there are specific adaptations of the general copyright rules to computer software and databases that strike their own type of balance between idea and expression.[97] The EU

Computer Software Directive endorses the general principle that 'ideas and principles which underlie any element of a computer program, including those which underlie its interfaces are not protected' (Art. 1(2)). The US Copyright Act 1976 s. 102(b) recognises a similar dichotomy: 'In no case does copyright protection for an original work of authorship extend to any idea, procedure, process, system, method of operation, concept, principle, or discovery, regardless of the form in which it is described, explained, illustrated or embodied in such work.'[98]

The EU Computer Software Directive[99] also requires Member States to recognise four exceptions to the scope of exclusive copyright protection: first, acts by a lawful acquirer of a copyright computer program which are necessitated by use of the program for its intended purposes; secondly, to allow the making of backup copies by lawful users; third to permit the studying and testing of a program; and fourth, the decompilation of programs. These exceptions are regarded as so significant that the Directive does not permit the parties to contract out of any of them.[100]

The Directive introduces a decompilation right to assist interoperability of software programs where the program maker neither publishes information about access codes nor licenses it.[101] Under Article 6(1), lawful software users[102] are entitled to reproduce and translate the form of a software program even without the right holder's authorisation when such acts are 'indispensable to obtain the information necessary to write and produce a new program which will be interoperable with the protected program but will be independent of it'. This provision permits unauthorised 'decompilation' of a program for the limited purpose of creating a new program, i.e. one which when completed would not infringe the rights of the owner of the original program.[103] Moreover, it offers some protection to the right holder by requiring the decompiler under Article 6(2)(c) to obtain authorisation from the right holder when the interface codes are to be used 'for the development, production or marketing of a computer program substantially similar in its expression'.[104]

The decompilation right is universally applicable to software in the sense that it applies independently of a finding that the software product has achieved market dominance.[105] Moreover, even where patent protection applies to a software program, Article 6 will apply. Hence, it can be viewed as an inherent limit to the scope of IPR protection in computer programs. Yet, that said, it is important to note that such an inherent limit does not have the same effect as a provision for a compulsory licence because there is no enforcement process incorporated in the decompilation right to gain compulsory access to interface codes where they prove elusive. It operates at the level of a defence to an action for infringement.[106] Thus far there has been no litigation over Article 6. Nevertheless, it is clear to computer program developers as well IPR owners that it offers an alternative, albeit a sometimes time-consuming and difficult alternative, to licensing. Article 6 also provides an incentive to the owners of copyright in computer programs to make available the source codes so that decompilation ceases to be lawful. Finally, there is evidence of some owners taking a commercial strategy of providing interfaces specially designed to allow third parties to interoperate with the program without access to the IP protected core codes they wish to protect. Whether this is in response to the legislation implementing the directive or a response to the possible threat of competition remedies of compulsory code provision is difficult to say but the design of Article 6 is to promote inter-operability by a measure within intellectual property law.

The Community's Database Directive[107] introduces two tiers of protection for databases: a sui generis form of copyright protection of 15 years for the contents of databases, if there has been a substantial investment in either the obtaining, verification or presentation of them;[108] and a copyright for the structure of the database itself, if the selection or arrangement of the contents is the author's own intellectual creation. In both cases, after initially producing a draft contemplating an IPR based right of interoperability, the Commission opted for a different approach to the limits on possible misuse. In contrast to the Computer Software Directive, the Database Directive provides a limited exception for use of the database for the purposes of access to and use of the contents of the database where a person already has a right to use it.[109] It thus provides an extremely limited research and private study defence subject to the condition that 'the source is indicated'.[110] The Database Directive, however, contains no exception for decompilation; nor does it provide for compulsory licences. Instead, in Article 13 it states that the provisions of the Directive are subject to the 'laws on restrictive practices and unfair competition'.

Recital 43 explains this provision as follows:

> in the interest of competition between suppliers of information products and services, protection by the *sui generis* right must not be afforded in such a way as to facilitate abuses of a dominant position.

A similar formula has been adopted in the Regulation on Community Plant Variety Rights (2100/94); the Directive on the Legal Protection of Biological Inventions (98/44/EC); and the Directive on the Legal Protection of Designs (98/71/EC).[111]

There is thus a striking contrast between the way copyright and patent laws in their 'internal' systems of checks and balances strike a balance between protection of initial innovation and further invention and creativity. Patent law uses both the device of limiting the scope of protection and providing for a possibility of compulsory licences in cases inter alia where a patent can be shown to block further inventive development. In this respect, patent law anticipates some of the 'vertical' or downstream consequences of the patent decision.

Copyright law limits the scope of protection by its exceptions for fair use and its idea/expression dichotomy. It also allows decompilation or reverse engineering rights to some extent although it contains no provision for compulsory licensing as such where the copyright coincides with an industrial standard, apart from the special cases of collecting societies. In principle, if copyright in computer programs were to provide a legal device to ensure widespread interoperability, there would be little scope for competition law remedies. The existing decompilation right offers a potential way forward as a general norm for interoperability of software programs but, in its current form, it offers no assurance of the supply of code information to competitors facing market standard owners with strategies of control in applications markets. In such cases software developers are left with no option but to invent around the protected software or turn to competition law measures for a remedy to the 'external' effects of IP protection in appropriate cases.[112]

C. The limits of the patent and copyright internal balance

The traditional model of the patent as a stimulus to innovation is based on the notion that the patent confers an exclusive property right that in economic terms is a barrier to entry offering the inventor the incentive of a monopoly return. This incentive to invention is necessary because inventive knowledge requires a fixed investment to create it, whereas the marginal cost of its transmission is low, its consumption does not exhaust it and charging for its use is difficult to arrange.[113] Without the right to exclude people few would invest in the research and development to create inventions. The overall loss, or 'deadweight loss', caused by the monopoly is seen by economists as being the price of obtaining the invention in the first place as well as the disclosure of information about the invention.[114] The early theory of patents and possibly copyright was based on a 'one property right per marketable work' image of things.[115] This view was later elaborated to extend the IPR to something more than residing in a marketable product. By drawing attention to the way IPRs created a market for information, Kenneth Arrow showed that IPRs could not be viewed simply as coextensive with economic markets for final (tangible) products.[116]

Far from amounting solely to an argument for expanding the borders of the exclusive right, however, this insight also raises the issue of how property rights are to be allocated among sequential innovators in various industries.[117] Where a market, whether old or new, consists of complex 'systems' of products, and if in such systems, the development of the technology involves an accumulation of incremental improvements, the traditional model of the patent as incentive to single product invention may not be appropriate as the sole model of innovation.[118] While in the context of pharmaceutical inventions, investment in research and development might not take place without the incentive of an exclusive right, it is less clear that the individualistic incentive benefits outweigh the innovation costs in product markets involving cumulative technology and systems of products.[119]

In such situations, some adjustment of patent granting decisions may be called for. Some specialists have argued that it would be appropriate to adjust the *length* of the patent term in cases where the social benefits are exceeded by the social costs of the invention.[120] Unless we are prepared to accept a government agency as an appropriate authority to subject each and every patent award to a public interest audit and award protection of varying lengths depending upon the results, however, we are left with the 'one size fits all' length of patent terms, except where legislators are prepared to assign different length terms for special categories of protection, e.g. medical process patents in India.

That being the case, the spotlight must shine on decisions of the patent authorities' in respect of the *width* of each patent.[121] On the one hand, to grant a wide patent claim in a cumulative technology industry entails a risk that the social and economic costs of the IP protection for one product will exceed its benefits because it forecloses too many avenues to future improvement and innovation by later innovators.

Merges and Nelson[122] have underlined this point in the following observation:

> When a broad patent is granted … its scope diminishes incentives for others to stay in the invention game, compared again with a patent whose claims are trimmed more closely to the inventor's actual results. This would not be undesirable if the evidence indicated that control of subsequent developments by one party made subsequent inventive effort more effective. But the evidence, we think, points the other way.[123]

In the new economy of cumulative technology industries, as in the old sectors of systems products such as motor vehicles and aeroplanes, it has been argued by economists that there are often palpable innovative advantages if a substantial number of different participants try different approaches simultaneously. On the whole, the obstacles of complexity of system products and qualitative uncertainties inherent in the innovative process are normally best overcome by a variety of approaches and numerous participants rather than single innovators coordinating the efforts of a closed system.[124]

This may explain why it is that many new industrial standards are being created by a collective and collaborative process such as joint ventures, patent pools and cross-licensing arrangements. Recent inventions such as DVDs and certain semiconductors required wide collaboration with either a pooling of IP or a generous policy of cross-licensing to achieve their finished form. In such cases, there may be a pro-competitive motive for, as well as effect of, this horizontal collaboration that may make such forms of cooperation between competitors more acceptable to competition authorities in the EU and the USA.[125]

To preserve a variety of approaches in innovation, in defining the scope of *individual* patents in the new economy, as in the old, there is a need for patent authorities to be aware of the potential anti-innovative effects of overly wide patents, i.e. patents that allow a single party to obtain and maintain control of multiple components of a system. A wide patent entails the risk of limiting the possibility of diverse approaches to improvements of a system. As well, it can allow the patent holder to block or delay through litigation innovations elsewhere in the system which threaten the long-run value of the package of components which the patent holder controls.[126]

The significant feature of such blocking tactics is that they may not necessarily be designed to increase returns on the investment in the original innovative product; rather they may be aimed at controlling the development of the system product and its ownership to favour the value of the components under the patent holder's control.[127] This can result in a distortion of the innovation process by limiting the innovative contribution of competitors. It can also lead to the practice of predatory product innovation, i.e. creating succeeding generations of market standards which do not interoperate with each other.[128]

However, there is the complication that other economists have strongly argued that *wide* patents offer advantages to innovation. For example Kitch, in presenting his 'prospect theory', has argued that patents which are wide allow their owners to 'mine' them more effectively by 'offering their holder a secure opportunity to orchestrate in an orderly fashion the subsequent development of the original idea'[129] and this increases the incentives to invest in patents. There may well be occasions where market standard owning firms can go on to further develop a superior standard internally rather than in a competitive environment for their derivative products in downstream markets.[130]

Other research suggests, however, that there is a real risk that too wide a patent may actually limit the further development of a standard or its modular applications. In cumulative technology industries, unduly centralised control might in fact have the effect of hindering the development of improved standards. The existence of diverse suppliers of various components of the system interacting with users may be a more desirable pattern for the best development of a standard and this appears to be the case particularly in the software field.[131] There are occasions when the owner of an industrial standard can itself adopt such a strategy by establishing an open system. For example, Sun Microsystems consciously developed a predominantly open system for its technical workstations, deciding that greater profits would be generated by the larger market offered by an open system than by inter-system rivalry between closed proprietary systems. (See too the contrasting fortunes of Apple Macintosh and Microsoft as a consequence of one adopting a closed system and the other, at least in its early stages, an open system.) But genuinely open systems can never be guaranteed by reliance on commercial strategies in all markets.

Instead, it seems clear that the implications for innovation policy are that once a technical standard becomes industry wide, and there is no longer any inter-system competition, there are risks that the standard owner may choose to engage in conduct that gives it private advantages at the expense of a potentially richer overall development of the technology. This may not be inevitable. However, for strategic business reasons, the owners of industrial standards may find it tempting to close off avenues of innovation that represent a threat to the profit potential of the standard by reducing the degree of modularity of the components of the system or by reducing the possibilities of competitors to achieve compatibility at certain points within the system.[132] This may not always result in a technologically inferior product, and indeed it may sometimes produce a technologically superior product, but it creates the risk that the favoured alternative of the standard owner may not be the best technological solution. The cases involving Microsoft in the US and in Europe offer good examples of such conduct. Microsoft 'customised' the Java language it supplied with Windows so that it could not interoperate with other operating systems. This customising made it impossible for licensees to use Java to bypass Windows and access the Internet via Netscape. Alternatively, owners of industry wide technical standards may be tempted to engage in 'predatory product innovation' by bringing in new generations of the system that are incompatible with the old.[133]

Whether or not patent authorities take these issues into account, their definitions of patent scope can have 'vertical' consequences, one of which might be to inhibit the process of innovation.[134] There are fewer controls on copyright and neighbouring rights at the time of conception. However, in infringement actions, courts can be made aware of the vertical consequences of their copyright enforcement decisions.

A major problem for patent authorities therefore is the extent to which they are able to take into account the potential anti-innovative effects of patents *at the point of conferring a patent*. At that stage, it is difficult to differentiate between 'good' and 'bad' innovation. It might seem clear that, in most cases, the narrower the width of a patent, the less will be the opportunity for an owner of an industrial standard to control a large proportion of the components of a system and thereby to control the pace and direction of further development of the original idea in the product or process.[135] In cumulative innovation industries narrower patents will have the advantage of allowing more scope for related research by a wider group of researchers.

However, the claim is also made that the narrower the width of a patent, the greater the risk that the inventor will be 'invented around' and this may reduce the reward and the incentive effects of patents according to the traditional model. Moreover, US economists such as Heller and Eisenberg, have mounted a case based on the risks of too narrow a definition of patent scope, arguing that unduly narrow patents will result in fragmentation and claiming that each 'upstream patent allows its owner to set up another toll booth on the road to product development, adding to the cost and slowing down the pace of downstream biomedical innovation'.[136]

My own view is that while their use of metaphor is imaginative, they damage their case by making no comparison with the costs of allowing upstream patent owners to own broad patents. The most important such cost to consider is to what extent in the particular sector a broad patent would discourage further innovation, either because of the scope of the patent or the threat of litigation because of the unclear implications of the wider patent claim. Without a comparison of such costs, we are left with a not particularly helpful partial picture.

Moreover, while it is also true that holders of narrow patents in recent years have a track record of erecting a 'patent thicket' around their original invention[137] and multiple patents have been more frequently resorted to in recent years, nevertheless their effect is not necessarily to allow their owner to achieve the same degree of control over downstream innovation as a wide patent. An extensive empirical study of the semiconductor industry in the United States by Hall and Ham suggests that the main aim of firms investing in multiple patents is not to gain exclusive control of stand-alone inventions, but to ensure that they have a 'legal bargaining chip' for cross-licensing agreements which enables them to get 'access to external technologies on more favourable terms of trade'.[138] With large sunk costs in manufacturing facilities and a need to draw on process and product technologies invented (and patented) by a diverse array of parties, managers amass large patent portfolios of their own largely to avoid being excluded or 'held up' by other parties.[139]

A cross-licensing culture has much to recommend it as a platform for innovation.[140] Cross-licensing agreements it should be remembered do not always conform to the stereotype of 'closed' joint ventures between parties bound by strict non-competition clauses. They can also take the form of reciprocal agreements not to bring infringement actions against 'licensees' in the course of their separate research and development.

Inevitably however there will be limits to the extent that control of the width of a patent can ensure that inter-firm downstream competition can flourish in a situation where the IPR right coincides with an industrial standard. The patent authorities do not have the degree of law and economics weaponry to make these sorts of decisions at the time of granting a patent. And the courts, at least in the EU, do not seem to have the doctrinal wherewithal to strike the necessary law and economics balance within the confines of patent or copyright law.

As we have mentioned, it is possible to amend IP laws to make the prospect of competition remote. Narrowing the scope of the protected product, offering the possibility of compulsory licences and providing for interoperability obligations within the IP laws themselves would have such an effect. However, insofar as IP laws allow wider protection with blocking potential even when the IP is associated with significant market power,[141] it can fall upon competition authorities to apply competition policy measures to maintain access to relevant markets. The competition rules tend to operate essentially as a default. And, indeed, the experience thus far suggests that under most existing IP law regimes the competition rules will continue to have some role to play because the competition authorities tend to look more often at the conduct of the IP owner long after the IPR has been granted, whereas with few exceptions such as compulsory licences etc. the IP authorities concern themselves with the qualification for the grant and the issues of enforcing its exclusivity in infringement actions.

Yet, as has been mentioned, there is considerable variation in the way different systems operate as a default system to the exercise of intellectual property rights. It is that degree of variation which is the subject of the following chapters of this book.

Notes

1. See e.g. *Atari Games Corp.* v. *Nintendo of America Inc*, F. 2d. 1572 (Fed. Cir. 1990).
2. See e.g. *Microsoft Corporation* v. *United States* 253 F. 3d 34 (D.C. Cir.) cert. denied 122 S.Ct. 350 (2001).
3. See e.g. the Microsoft cases in the EU and Japan.
4. See e.g. *Tetra Pak Rausing SA* v. *Commission* (Tetra Pak I) [1990] ECR II-309.
5. See e.g. Federal Trade Commission, 'To Promote Innovation: The Proper Balance of Competition and Patent Law and Policy' (2003).
6. See US Department of Justice and Federal Trade Commission Antitrust Guidelines to Intellectual Property Licensing 1995.
7. DOJ/FTC Hearings on Competition and Intellectual Property Law and Policy in the Knowledge Based Economy: Comparative Law Topics, 22 May 2002, Washington, D.C.
8. See e.g. 10th Annual EU Competition Law and Policy Workshop, 'The Interaction Between Competition Law and Intellectual Property Law', 3–4 June 2005, Florence, Italy.
9. S. Scotchmer, 'Standing on the Shoulders of Giants: Cumulative Research and the Patent Law' (1991) 5 *Journal of Economic Perspectives* 29–30.
10. R. Merges and R. Nelson, 'On the Complex Economics of Patent Scope' (1990) 90 *Columbia Law Review* 839, at 916.
11. The modern phase of competition law which began with the US Sherman Act in the 1890s has to be seen as a reaction to the experience in the USA with

widespread trusts creating monopolies and cartel and market sharing arrangements in the decades after the Civil War. R. Peritz, *Competition Policy in the United States* (Oxford: Oxford University Press, 1998).

12. See e.g. *E. Bement & Sons* v. *National Harrow Co.*, 186 U.S. 70, 91 (1902); *United States* v. *Masonite Corp.*, 316 U.S. 265, 280 (1942).

13. See e.g. *Motion Picture Patents Company* v. *Universal Film Company Manufacturing Company*, 243 U.S. 502 (1917).

14. See discussion in H. Johannes, 'Technology Transfer under EEC Law – Europe between the Divergent Opinions of the Past and a New Administration: A Comparative Law Approach' (1982) *Fordham Corporate Law Institute* 65.

15. See the principles of the US Department of Justice and Federal Trade Commission, 'Antitrust Guidelines for the Licensing of Intellectual Property' (6 April 1995).

16. See R. Bork, *The Antitrust Paradox* (New York: Basic Books, 2nd edn, 1978); R. Posner, *Antitrust Law: An Economic Perspective* (Chicago 1976).

17. See e.g. the US Department of Justice and Federal Trade Commission, 'Antitrust Guidelines for the Licensing of Intellectual Property' (6 April 1995).

18. See *Deutche Grammophon GmbH* v. *Metro-SB-Grossmärkte* [1971] ECR 487 para. 16; *Volvo AB* v. *Veng (UK) Ltd.* [1988] ECR 6211 para. 8; *RTE, ITV and BBC* v. *Commission* [1995] ECR I-743, paras. 45–7. See discussion in S. Anderman, *EC Competition Law and Intellectual Property Rights* (Oxford: Oxford University Press, 1998) Ch. 12.

19. See e.g. Report of the Royal Society, 'Keeping Science Open: The Effects of Intellectual Property Policy on the Conduct of Science' (2003) 9–10.

20. See discussion in the report of the Commission on Intellectual Property Rights (CIPR), 'Integrating Intellectual Property Rights and Development Policy' (2002) 2. See too I. Rahnasto, *Intellectual Property Rights, External Effects and Antitrust Law* (Oxford: Oxford University Press, 2002) 49–62.

21. See e.g. OECD, *Competition Policy and Intellectual Property Rights* (Paris, 1989).

22. See discussion by W. Cornish and D. Llewellyn. *Intellectual Property: Patents, Copyright, Trademarks, and Allied Rights* (London: Sweet & Maxwell, 4th edn, 2000).

23. See e.g. H. Demsetz, 'Towards a Theory of Property Rights' (1967) *American Economic Review* 347; R. Posner, *An Economic Analysis of Law* (New York, 1998); M. Lehmann, 'The Theory of Property Rights and the Protection of Intellectual and Industrial Property' (1989) 16 *IIC* No. 5 525.

24. The adoption of the presumption of validity and the lowering of the standard for the test of non-obviousness. See R. Merges, 'As Many as Six Impossible Patents for Breakfast: Property Right for Business Concepts and Patent System Reform' (1999) 14 *Berkeley Technology Law Journal* 578.

25. E.g. the modification of the doctrine of equivalents by the US Supreme Court in *Warner Jenkinson Co.* v. *Hilton Davis Chemical Co.* 520 U.S. 17 (1997) (an accused product infringes only if it has 'all elements' of a claimed invention)

and *Boyden Power-Brake Co.* v. *Westinghouse*, 170 U.S. 537 (a patent for a 'pioneer invention' is entitled to a broad range of equivalents); see further discussion in Rahnasto, *Intellectual Property Rights* p. 54.

26. See e.g. *Lotus Development Corp.* v. *Borland Int'l Inc.*, 49 F. 3d 807 (1st Cir. 1995); *Sony Corp.* v. *Universal Studios Inc.*, 464 US 417 ('monopoly privileges that Congress may authorize are neither unlimited nor primarily designed to provide a private benefit').

27. See M. Adelman, 'The New World of Patents Created by the Court of Appeals for the Federal Circuit' (1987) 20 *University of Michigan Journal of Law* 979.

28. See Merges, 'As Many as Six Impossible Patents for Breakfast'.

29. See e.g. *Whelan* v. *Jaslow* F.S.R. 1 (C.A. 3rd Cir. 1987) (dental lab program); *Computer Associates* v. *Altai*, 982 F. 2d 693 (C.A. 2d Cir. 1992) (computer job scheduling); *Sega Enterprises Ltd* v. *Accolade Inc.* 977 F.2d 1510 (9th Cir. 1992) (reverse engineering as fair use).

30. See e.g. *Diamond* v. *Chakraubarty*, (1980) 447 U.S. 303; *State Street Bank & Trust Co.* v. *Signature Financial Group*, 149 F 3d 1368 (C.A. Fed. Cir. 1998).

31. See Cornish and Llewellyn, *Intellectual Property*; L. Bently and B. Sherman, *Intellectual Property Law* (Oxford: Oxford University Press, 2001).

32. P. Gerhart, 'Why Lawmaking for Global Intellectual Property is Unbalanced' (2000) *European Intellectual Property Review* 309.

33. J. Braithwaite and P. Drahos, *Global Business Regulation* (Cambridge: Cambridge University Press, 2000) 61–3.

34. If a country fails to implement the standards of the agreement, another member may make a complaint to the WTO and thereby initiate the WTO dispute resolution procedure that can result in trade sanctions until that country amends its legislation to conform to TRIPS. The actual impact of TRIPS on the national legislation of the highly developed members has been small since these countries had already implemented the relevant conventions. This procedure has been brought against both developed and developing countries but the TRIPS agreement operates most forcibly upon the poorer developing countries. The UK Commission on Intellectual Property Rights has made the point that inadequate thought has been given to the appropriateness of the application of Western substantive legal concepts to developing countries: CIPR, *Integrating Intellectual Property Rights and Development Policy* (2002) p. 2. The main effect of TRIPS on EU members has consisted of some modification to their compulsory licensing laws. See e.g. M. Hodgson, 'Changes to UK Compulsory Patent Licensing Law' (1992) *European Intellectual Property Review* 214.

35. See e.g. D. Evans and R. Schmalensee, 'Some Economic Aspects of Antitrust Analysis in Dynamically Competitive Industries', www.nber.org/books/innovation2/evans 5-1-01.pdf.

36. See e.g. S. Anderman, *EC Competition Law and Intellectual Property Rights: The Regulation of Innovation* (Oxford: Oxford University Press, 2000).

37. J. Ordover and R. Willig, 'An Economic Definition of Predation: Pricing and Product Innovation' (1981) 91 *Yale Law Journal* 8, 13.

38. See C. Ahlborn, D. Evans and A. Padilla, 'Competition Policy in the New Economy; Is European Competition Law up to the Challenge?' (2001) *European Competition Law Review* 156, 160.

39. See e.g. D. Balto and R. Pitofsky, 'Antitrust and Competition in High Technology Industries: The New Challenge' (1998) 43 *Antitrust Bulletin* 583, 596.

40. A. D. Melamed, 'Network Industries and Antitrust', Federalist Society Eighteenth Annual Symposium on Law and Public Policy: Competition, Free Markets and the Law, www.usdoj.gov/atr/public/speeches/2428.htm.

41. The Royal Society Report gives as one example the patent held by Myriad Genetics Inc. on diagnostic testing for mutation in 'breast cancer genes'. *Keeping Science Open: The Effects of Intellectual Property Policy on the Conduct of Science* (2003) 9–10; see too Wadman, 'Testing Time For Gene Patents as Europe Rebels' (2002) *Nature* 413, 433.

42. See e.g. R. Nelson and S. Winter, 'In Search of a More Useful Theory of Innovation' (1977) *Research Policy* 5: 36–7; R. Langlois and P. Robertson, 'Networks and Innovation in a Modular System: Lessons from the Micro-Computer and Stereo Component Industries' (1992) 21 *Research Policy* 297.

43. The Betamax/VHS rivalry offers a good example of the phenomenon of 'tipping' followed by ejection of a rival product in a competition between 'closed systems' of products, i.e., products which are not interoperable with products of another system. In that rivalry as we know, Betamax was completely ejected from the consumer market. See e.g. B. Arthur, 'Competing Technologies, Increasing Returns, and Lock in by Historical Events' (1989) 99 *Economic Journal* 116; see too R. Peritz, 'Towards a Dynamic Antitrust Analysis', Paper presented to the American Antitrust Institute Annual Conference, 1 July 2002, Washington D.C. This conclusion has been disputed. See e.g. S. Liebowitz and S. Margolis, 'Are Network Externalities a New Source of Market Failure?' (1995) 17 *Research in Law and Economics* 1. However, it has also been acknowledged as a theoretical possibility. See e.g. J. Church and N. Gandal, 'Complementary Network Externalities and Technology Adoption' (1993) 11 *International Journal of Industrial Organization* 239.

44. R. Schmalensee, 'Antitrust Issues in Schumpeterian Industries' (2000) 90 *American Economic Review* (Papers and Proceedings) 192, 193; D. Evans and R. Schmalensee, 'Some Economic Aspects of Antitrust Analysis in Dynamically Competitive Industries', www.nber.org/books/innovation2/evans 5-1-01.pdf.

45. Ibid.

46. J. A. Schumpeter, *Capitalism, Socialism and Democracy* (Harper Collins, 1984) p. 82.

47. See e.g. D. Teece and M. Coleman, 'The Meaning of Monopoly: Antitrust Analysis in High Technology Industries' (1998) *Antitrust Bulletin* 801.

48. Liebowitz and Margolis, 'Are Network Externalities a New Source of Market Failure?'
49. See e.g. G. Ramello, 'Copyright and Antitrust Issues' (2002) 114 *LIUC Papers in Economics*.
50. Ibid.
51. Ibid.
52. W. Tom, 'Background Note' *OECD Competition Policy and Intellectual Property Rights* (1998) 23.
53. This phenomenon of positive 'direct network effects' can apply to particular components of a system as well as a system as a whole. See e.g. *Lotus Development Corp.* v. *Borland Int'l Inc.*, 49 F. 3d 807 (1st Cir 1995).
54. G. J. Werden, 'Network Effects and Conditions of Entry: Lessons from the Microsoft Case' (2001) 68 *Antitrust Law Journal* 87. This mutually reinforcing process has been described as a 'positive feedback loop'. In certain cases, this mutually reinforcing process created by network externalities can gather momentum or 'snowball' to the point where the product and its applications, i.e. the product system, eventually 'tips' a market and becomes the market standard. In the event competing products or systems can end up being either ejected from the market or reduced to low market shares irrespective of their technical superiority.
55. Products in the new economy more frequently consist of complex 'systems' of products rather than individual products as in the old. It is true that cars, aeroplanes and other types of engines were effectively 'systems' of products. However, the more common feature of the old economy was the single independent product while the more common feature of the new is a 'system' of complementary products as exemplified by the 'systems' of software or mixed software/hardware products. In a 'system' of products any one product can only function in conjunction with other complementary products. In the relationship between PC hardware, operating systems or middleware such as Windows and applications such as word processing software or web browsers, for example, no one product has full functionality independently of one or more of the others.
56. G. Saloner and A. Shepard, 'Adoption of New Technologies with Network Effects: An Empirical Examination of the Adoption of Automatic Teller Machines' (1995) 26 *Rand Journal of Economics* 479.
57. See *Lotus Development Corp.* v. *Borland Int'l Inc.*, 49 F. 3d 807 (1st Cir. 1995).
58. Werden, 'Network Effects and Conditions of Entry: Lessons from the Microsoft Case'.
59. Ibid., at p. 33.
60. See e.g. N. Gandal, G. Greenstein and D. Salant, 'Adaptations and Orphans in the Early Microcomputer Market', (1999) 47 *Journal of Industrial Economics* 87.
61. *United States* v. *Microsoft Corp.*, 84 F.Supp. 2d 9, 20 (D.D.C. 1996).

62. W. E. Cohen, 'Competition and Foreclosure in the Context of Installed Base and Compatibility Effects' (1996) 64 *Antitrust Law Journal* 535, 541.
63. Werden, 'Network effects and Conditions of Entry: Lessons from the Microsoft Case' at 92–3.
64. See e.g. I. Govaere, *The Use and Abuse of Intellectual Property Rights in EC Law* (Sweet & Maxwell, 1996).
65. See e.g. K. Arrow, 'Economic Welfare and the Allocation of Resources to Invention', in R. Nelson (ed.), *The Rate and Direction of Inventive Activities* (Princeton: Princeton University Press, 1962).
66. The empirical case has not been entirely conclusive. See F. Scherer and D. Ross, *Industrial and Market Structure and Economic Performance* (Houghton Mifflin, 3rd edn, 1990) p. 637.
67. Sometimes this is called a 'first generation' product. See B. Dumont and P. Holmes, 'The Scope of Intellectual Property Rights and their Interface with Competition Law and Policy: Divergent Paths to the Same Goal?' *Economics of Innovation and New Technology* (2002) 11(2) 149–62.
68. See e.g. Scotchmer, 'Standing on the Shoulders of Giants: Cumulative Research and the Patent Law'.
69. Arrow, 'Economic Welfare and the Allocation of Resources to Invention'.
70. R. Merges, 'Institutions for Intellectual Property Transactions: The Case of Patent Pools', in R. Dreyfuss, D. Leenheer Zimmerman and H. First (eds.), *Expanding the Boundaries of Intellectual Property: Innovation Policy for the Knowledge Society* (Oxford: Oxford University Press, 2001) 123 at 124.
71. Arrow also called attention to the disclosure of information in the patent claim as facilitating licensing since it offers potential buyers an indication of the invention. See Arrow, 'Economic Welfare and the Allocation of Resources to Invention'.
72. Cornish and Llewellyn, *Intellectual Property*.
73. See too Articles 27 and 28 of the European Patent Convention.
74. See discussion in Bently and Sherman, *Intellectual Property Law* pp. 506–9.
75. See e.g. s. 60(5)(b) of the UK Patent Act 1977 and Article 27(b) of the Community Patent Convention. See W. Cornish, 'Experimental Use of Patented Inventions in European Community States' (1998) 29 *IIC* 735. Cf. the 'regulatory exception' or 'Bolar' provision in Article 8 of TRIPs which allows use of patented inventions by the manufacturers of generic drugs to obtain marketing approval from public health authorities before the expiry of the patent so that they can market their versions as soon as the patent expires. See 'TRIPS and pharmaceutical patents', WTO OMC Fact Sheet, April 2001.
76. See e.g. Merges and Nelson, 'On the Complex Economics of Patent Scope'.
77. See e.g. discussion in Rahnasto, *Intellectual Property Rights* p. 3. The increasing interdependency between companies suggests a shift from a 'serial model' to a 'simultaneous model of innovation'.
78. There is also an important policy of Crown use in the UK legislation.

79. The Paris Convention of 1881 allowed compulsory licensing as well as exclusion of fields of technology from protection.
80. Three years after a patent has been granted.
81. Patent Act 1977 (PA) s. 48(3)(d)(i),(iii) and (e).
82. PA s. 48(3)(b). A third ground is where a patent is not being worked within the UK or another EC Member State. This may be a ground for a compulsory licence. The policy behind this provision is to induce the actual working of the patent within the home territory. EC law has required the concept of the home territory to extend to anywhere within the EC.
83. See PA s. 51.
84. It is worth noting that the old defence to infringement actions when non-patented matter was 'tied' in licences of patented inventions in PA s. 44 was repealed by the Competition Act 1998, presumably because that practice was now covered by the 1998 Act.
85. According to the Banks Report (Cmnd. 4407, 1970) between 1959 and 1968 there were about 14 applications for a compulsory licence of which two were granted.
86. Proposal for a Council Regulation on the Community Patent, COM (200) 412 final, 1 August 2000 (OJ C 337 E/278, 28 November 2000).
87. See Explanatory Memorandum.
88. The compulsory licence must be non-exclusive and may be cancelled when the circumstances which led to its granting cease to exist and are unlikely to recur. Member States may not grant compulsory licences in respect of a Community patent (Article 22).
89. There are compulsory licensing provisions in the Design Rights legislation as well.
90. The TRIPS treaty prefers to use the term 'other use without authorisation of the right holder' to allow for Government use.
91. This requirement is waived in cases of 'circumstances of extreme urgency' (Art. 31(b)).
92. See e.g. P. Cullet, 'Patents and medicines: the relationship between TRIPS and the human right to health' (2003) 79 *International Affairs* Vol. 1 139–60.
93. One result has been to deprive many third world countries of a development strategy used by many highly developed countries such as the USA, the UK, Japan, Switzerland and Holland who consciously restricted IPR protection to foreign IPR owners during earlier stages of their development. Many of the recently developed East Asian countries such as Taiwan and Korea also used IPR restrictions as a spur to their development. Now with TRIPS providing a one-size-fits-all set of IPR standards worldwide, developing countries lose considerable autonomy in devising their own development policy.
94. See Article 2 Berne Convention incorporated in the TRIPS treaty by Article 9.
95. See e.g. Article 9 of the Berne Convention; Article 2bis, Article 10 (educational utilization) and Article 10bis (press, broadcasting and wire services to the

public), Chapter III ss. 29–30 of the Copyright, Designs and Patents Act 1988 (CDPA).

96. See e.g. the arguments in the *Eldred* case about the increased time limits giving inadequate consideration to the 'rights' of follow on innovation. *Eldred* v. *Ashcroft* (US Supreme Court No. O1-618, decided 2003); see too S. Breyer, 'The Limits of Copyright' (1970) 84 *Harvard Law Review* 281.

97. Cf. TRIPS Treaty Article 10.

98. See e.g. *Whelan* v. *Jaslow*, F.S.R. 1 (C.A. 3rd Cir. 1987) (dental lab program) *Computer Associates* v. *Altai*, 982 F. 2d 693 (C.A. 2d Cir. 1992) (computer job scheduling). See e.g. *Lotus Development Corp.* v. *Borland Int'l Inc.*, 49 F. 3d 807 (1st Cir., 1995); *Sony Corp.* v. *Universal Studios Inc.*, 464 U.S. 417 ('monopoly privileges that Congress may authorize are neither unlimited nor primarily designed to provide a private benefit').

99. 91/250/EEC.

100. See e.g. CDPA 1988, s. 296A(1)(c).

101. See Articles 5 and 6 of Directive 91/250/EEC.

102. A 'licensee or … another person having the right to use a copy of the program', Article 6(1)(a).

103. Compare the judicial view in some US cases that some reverse engineering may be 'fair use' under Sections 102 and 105 of the US Copyright Act in *Sega Enterprises Ltd.* v. *Accolade Inc.*, 977 F. 2d 1510 (9th Cir. 1992).

104. Under Article 6(3) this right is specifically subject to the three step test that (i) it must be limited to special cases, (ii) it must not conflict with a normal exploitation of the work, and (iii) it must not unreasonably prejudice the legitimate interests of the author.

105. This can be compared with the telecommunications field where interconnection rights arise only in the case of Significant Market Power or dominance as defined under the EU Framework Directive.

106. Compare the defence of 'fair use' offered in the USA by the case of *Sega Enterprises Ltd.* v. *Accolade, Inc.* 977 F.2d 1510 (9th Cir. 1992).

107. Reg. No. 96/9/EC.

108. Note that there is no originality requirement; 'sweat of the brow' compilations of data are sufficient as long as they involve substantial financial investment. Cf. the rather different approach in the USA.

109. Database Regs. 8 and 9. This probably extends to a right to download a database in the memory of a computer in the course of searching a database without infringing.

110. Database Reg. 8(1); see too CDPA s. 29(1) and 1(A).

111. See too Regulation on the Legal Protection of Industrial Designs and Models, in particular 'as regards the creation and distribution of new products and services which have an intellectual, documentary, technical, economic or commercial added value; whereas therefore the provisions of this Directive are without prejudice to the application of Community or national competition rules'.

112. See e.g. Rahnasto, *Intellectual Property Rights*.
113. Arrow, 'Economic Welfare and the Allocation of Resources to Invention'.
114. Ibid.
115. See e.g. Merges, 'Institutions for Intellectual Property Transactions: The Case of Patent Pools', 123 at 124.
116. Arrow, 'Economic Welfare and the Allocation of Resources to Invention'.
117. Merges and Nelson, 'On the Complex Economics of Patent Scope', 888–93.
118. R. Langlois, 'Technological Standards, Innovation, and Essential Facilities' (1999) University of Connecticut Working Papers 1999–07.
119. See e.g. Merges and Nelson, 'On the Complex Economics of Patent Scope', 916.
120. L. Kaplow, 'The Patent–Antitrust Intersection: An Appraisal' (1983) *Harvard Law Review* 1813, 1823–9.
121. See Merges and Nelson, 'On the Complex Economics of Patent Scope', 888–93; see too Scotchmer, 'Standing on the Shoulders of Giants: Cumulative Research and Patent Law'.
122. Merges and Nelson, 'On the Complex Economics of Patent Scope', 916.
123. Ibid.
124. Nelson and Winter, 'In Search of a More Useful Theory of Innovation'; Langlois, 'Technological Standards', p. 207.
125. See e.g. C. Shapiro, 'Setting Compatibility Standards: Cooperation or Collusion' in Dreyfuss, Zimmerman and First (eds.), *Expanding the Boundaries*.
126. (1994) 62 *Tennessee Law Review* 75.
127. Langlois, 'Technological Standards', p. 208.
128. See e.g. Ordover and Willig, 'An Economic Definition of Predation: Pricing and Product Innovation'.
129. E. Kitch, 'The Nature and Function of the Patent System' (1977) 20 *Journal of Law and Economics* 265–90.
130. This certainly corresponds to the Schumpeterian view of innovation. Yet the Schumpeterian view applies to the real world in a meaningful way only where there is *actual* competition between systems in an industry and real competitors to replace incumbents through the introduction of a superior innovative product. Where there are no real inter-system competitors, a purely theoretical *potential* competitor to an established industrial standard is a poor candidate to produce the features of dynamic competition suggested by Schumpeterian enthusiasts.
131. Langlois has drawn attention to this idea as an approach to standard setting in the field of software: 'Technological Standards' p. 219.
132. Ordover and Willig, 'An Economic Definition of Predation: Pricing and Product Innovation', 13.
133. Ibid.
134. See e.g. C. Matutes, P. Regibeau and K. Rockett, 'Optimal Patent Design and Diffusion of Innovations' (1996) 27 *Rand Journal of Economics* 60.

135. See e.g. R. P. Merges and R. R. Nelson, 'Market Structure and Technical Advance: The Role of Patent Scope Decisions', in T. Jorde and D. Teece, (eds.) *Antitrust, Innovation and Competitiveness* (New York: Oxford University Press, 1992) 244; see too G. Stiglitz, Address to the US FTC Hearings on Global Competition and Innovation, (1996) FTC Report, Ch. VI, p. 6.

136. M. Heller and R. Eisenberg, 'Can Patents Deter Innovation? The Anticommons in Biomedical Research'(1998) 280 *Science* 698, 699.

137. R. Merges, 'Intellectual Property Rights and Bargaining Breakdown: The Case of Blocking Patents' (1994) 62 *Tennessee Law Review* 75; Heller and Eisenberg, 'Can Patents Deter Innovation? The Anticommons in Biomedical Research'.

138. B. H. Hall and R. M. Ham, 'The Patent Paradox Revisited: Determinants of Patenting in the US Semi-conductor Industry', Working Paper 7062 NBER, March 1999, 4.

139. Ibid.

140. Cf. J. Ordover, 'A Patent System for Both Diffusion and Exclusion' (1991) Vol. 5, No. 1 *Journal of Economic Perspectives* 430.

141. My thanks to Professor Peritz for raising the 'copyright improvements' issue.

PART I

Intellectual property rights and competition law
in the major trading blocks

2

EC competition policy and IPRs

STEVEN D. ANDERMAN AND HEDVIG SCHMIDT

I. Introduction

EC competition policy and intellectual property rights (IPRs) are widely recognised to be complementary components of a modern industrial policy. Both pursue a common aim of improving innovation and consumer welfare although they do so by using rather different means. Intellectual property legislation such as patents, copyright and design rights laws pursue this aim by offering a period of exclusive rights to exploit to IP right holders as a reward and incentive to innovation and R&D investment. Modern competition policy attempts to keep markets innovative by maintaining effective competition on markets by preventing foreclosure of markets and maintaining access to markets. At first sight there seems to be a potential clash between the methods used by the two systems of legal regulation to achieve their common aims; the concern to maintain access to markets appears to be implacably opposed to the concept of exclusive rights to make, use and sell a product. And indeed, historically there was a period when the misunderstanding of the economic effects of IPRs led EC competition policy to attempt to place overly strict limits on the exercise of IP rights particularly in the field of patent licensing. Today, however, EC competition policy treats the economic effects of IPRs more realistically. It no longer assumes that the legal monopoly conferred by IP laws, such as patent and copyright legislation, to make and sell a particular product or process automatically amounts to an economic monopoly or even confers market power. Its view is that this issue must be left to be established empirically. Equally importantly, EC competition law gives explicit recognition to the positive contribution that IPRs make to competition as well as innovation and has made a number of significant adjustments within its doctrines to accommodate the exercise of IPRs.

The forms taken by this accommodation are not as obvious as the full or partial legislative immunity given for the exercise of IPRs in Japan and Australia.[1] The EC 'immunity' is offered on occasion in the form of an 'exceptional circumstances' test for IP protected products. More often, however, it takes the form of an accommodation within the general doctrines of competition law, as interpreted by the Community Court judges and by the regulations, guidelines and notices issued by the Directorate General of Competition within the European Commission. A close reading of the case law together with these regulations and notices suggests that EC competition law, in its own way, gives an extensive, albeit limited form of immunity to the exercise of IPRs.

Underlying this judicial and administrative accommodation is the extensive recognition given by EC competition law and policy to the contribution that IP laws make to innovation and competition. In the first place, it is now openly accepted that the incentives to innovation created by IPRs produce new competitors on existing markets and indeed create new products which open up entirely new markets. Secondly, it is presumed that the licensing of IPRs is in general pro-competitive as well as pro-innovative in its effects and helps to ensure that IPRs are more widely diffused throughout the common market. IP licensing also adds new products to markets which either add new competitors to existing markets or form new markets. The EC competition authorities also acknowledge that too heavy a regulatory burden on the exercise of IPRs could discourage investment in IPRs in the European Union (EU).

Even in this more enlightened era when competition law may generally accord a favoured position to the exercise of an IP by a firm because of its contribution to innovation, there are still rare situations where conduct by an IP owner which is lawful under IP legislation, can be viewed as unlawful under competition law. In such cases, EC competition law does not confer immunity upon the exercise of an IPR simply because it is consistent with the rules of IP legislation. Instead, it tends to reserve a right to intervene in extreme cases.

Certain safeguards are embedded within the logic of competition law which ensure that this intervention is in fact kept to exceptional cases. For example, EC competition laws accept that the achievement of an economic monopoly by means of investment R&D and intellectual property rights is a legitimate course of conduct for a firm, a form of 'competition on the merits'. EC competition law also *in most cases* gives recognition to the right of IPR owners to prevent copying even if the exercise of this right denies access to markets to competitors. Further, EC competition law acknowledges that the pricing of IPRs, even by dominant firms, must include a return which *adequately* reflects the reward/incentive function of IPRs.

However, in extreme cases where IPRs are used unjustifiably by their owners to exclude competitors from markets, EC competition policy reserves a right to intervene to limit their exercise. It tends to view intellectual property rights as any other form of private property rights at this point and to restrict their use when that use amounts to prohibited conduct under the rules of competition law. This can apply to the unilateral exploitation of an IPR by its owner as well as to an agreement between the IP owner and a licensee to exploit the IPR in a particular territory.

Today, in fact, there are four main spheres in which EC competition policy may be said to act as a 'second tier' of regulation of intellectual property rights and intervene in extreme cases. First, competition policy under Article 82 of the EU Treaty has, in extreme cases, been used to restrict the abusive commercial conduct of *individual* owners of IPRs, particularly where the IPR protects a market standard or de facto monopoly. This form of regulation has extended to excessive pricing,[2] but has been more frequently focused on the IPR holder's conduct towards innovators who are 'downstream' of an IPR protected industrial standard including refusals to deal, refusals to license, refusals to provide proprietorial software interface codes and tie-ins. Secondly, competition policy regulates certain terms of bilateral IPR licensing agreements, i.e. technology transfer agreements, under Article 81 of the EU Treaty, and a block exemption regulation. Thirdly, competition policy regulates cooperative relationships between competitors in joint ventures and multilateral agreements including patent pools, multilateral cross-licensing agreements and standardisation agreements.[3] Finally, in the context of mergers, competition policy has intervened on occasion to limit IPR owners from acquiring competing technologies[4] as well as requiring compulsory licences as a condition of merger approval. This chapter will concentrate on the first two fields of regulation of IPRs

II. Article 82 and IPRs

A. *Introduction*

The role of Article 82 in the system of EC competition law is to regulate undertakings, usually individual undertakings but occasionally two or more undertakings acting jointly, which have been found to occupy positions of dominant market power, such as monopolies or near monopolies. Its aim is not merely to prohibit 'exploitive' pricing or limitations of output which are the more traditional methods of monopolists. It is also concerned with the use of market power to damage effective competition in markets by preventing access to markets or driving out existing competition. It has been interpreted to prohibit anticompetitive or 'exclusionary' abuses such as refusal to supply without justification, predatory pricing, exclusive dealing, tie-ins and discriminatory dealing. It can also extend to retaliatory or reprisal abuses in which a dominant firm disproportionately penalises an existing customer.[5] Unlike Article 81, Article 82 of the EU Treaty only regulates the conduct of undertakings which have already achieved market dominance. If a firm falls below the threshold of dominance (and is not part of a collectively dominant position), it is not affected by Article 82.

The framework for the rules regulating undertakings in a dominant position is established by the general prohibition in Article 82 of the Treaty:

> Any abuse by one or more undertakings of a dominant position within the common market or in a substantial part of it shall be prohibited as incompatible with the common market insofar as it may affect trade between Member States.

Article 82 then goes on to list four examples of abuse:

> Such abuse in particular may consist in:
> (i) directly or indirectly imposing unfair purchase or selling prices or unfair trading conditions;
> (ii) limiting production, markets or technical development to the prejudice of consumers;
> (iii) applying dissimilar conditions to equivalent transactions with other trading parties, thereby placing them at a competitive disadvantage;
> (iv) making the conclusion of contracts subject to acceptance by the other parties of supplementary obligations which by their nature or according to commercial usage, have no connection with the subject of such contracts.

The analysis of abuse under Article 82 involves three stages. First the 'market' in which the alleged abuse occurred must be defined. Secondly, there must be a determination of whether or not the firm allegedly committing the abuse was 'dominant' in a market, whether or not it is in the market in which the abuse occurred. Thirdly, the conduct complained of must be analysed to determine whether or not an 'abuse' was committed.

From the IP perspective, it is worth noting at the outset that a legal monopoly created by a patent or other IPR is not assumed by EC competition law to confer market power or dominance. There must be hard evidence that the actual market share of a product, whether or not protected by an IPR, actually reflects significant market power amounting to a dominant position. Moreover, under the prohibition of Article 82 the mere achievement of dominance is not itself unlawful. The judicial interpretations of Article 82 have accepted the principle that monopoly power is not unlawful if it is lawfully acquired. A firm may lawfully grow to a position of dominant market power on a particular market owing to superior productive efficiencies, quality and competitive pricing which reflects those efficiencies. Embedded in Article 82's concept of legitimate competition is recognition of innovative efficiencies brought about by investment in research and development and IP protection. Even if a firm creates an economic monopoly in a product or a group of firms create an industrial standard, and this is propped up by possession of an intellectual property right, this as such does not constitute abusive conduct. Under Article 82 by definition, the mere possession of extensive market power, if lawfully acquired, does not amount to an abuse.

Finally, Article 82 confers upon dominant firms, whether IP protected or not, a position of 'special responsibility' not to use their dominant market power anticompetitively to further weaken the already weakened state of competition on markets caused by their dominance.[6] However, a dominant firm may continue to compete against competitors as long as it only uses means which are 'competition on the merits'. Hence, in principle, it may continue to use its superior efficiencies created by its investments in R&D and the normal exercise of its intellectual property rights to reduce the market shares of competing firms by pricing products based on its lower total costs created by productive and other efficiencies. On the other hand, the concept of abuse has been defined by European Court of Justice (ECJ) judgments to ensure that a dominant firm may not use its market power *unfairly* either to exploit consumers or to deny competitors access to markets which are affected by its dominant market power. These rules can apply irrespective of whether or not the market power of the dominant firm is propped up by an IPR. Where an IPR reinforces a dominant position, the rules of abuse make certain significant concessions to the exclusionary rights of the IPR owner. Broadly, one can talk of an 'exceptional circumstances' test under Article 82, which operates to limit its application to the exercise of IPRs quite explicitly in the case of the abuse of refusal to supply and implicitly in the case of the abuse of excessive pricing.

For IP owners, the logic of Article 82 requires two specific points to be established. Firstly, when does the ownership of an IPR coincide with, or place a company in, a dominant position in a particular market? Secondly, in what situations will the use and exploitation of an IPR by a dominant company create an abuse of a dominant position? If the mere ownership of an IPR, even one which has become an industrial standard, is seen as non-abusive and a form of legitimate competition, when, if ever, will the exercise of an exclusive right amount to an abuse of a dominant position?

B. Dominance, relevant market and IPRs

1. The determination of the relevant market

Before the Commission can decide whether an IPR owner has a product with a position of dominance on a particular market, it must first define what that market is both in terms of the cluster of products in the market and its geographical reach. It does this by taking the product, whether goods or services, of the firm complained of and investigating whether other products are substitutable or interchangeable with that product. Close enough substitutes can act as competitive restraints and influence the capacity of an undertaking to price freely. Once the relevant market is identified, it can be used as the base to calculate the market share and degree of dominance of the undertaking alleged to have committed an abuse.[7] Defining the relevant market can therefore be described as a tool of competition policy used to determine market power, a tool which is used not only for Article 82, but for Article 81 and merger control policy.

The European Commission's Notice on the Definition of the Relevant Market[8] states that it uses an economic approach to define the relevant market. Paragraph 7 states that 'a relevant product market comprises all those products and/or services which are regarded as interchangeable or substitutable by the consumer, by reason of the products' characteristics, their prices and their intended use'. The Commission starts by defining the 'product' produced by the company complained of and then applies a test of substitutability to determine whether other products are in the same market. If the product produced by the company complained of is a single product, say a banana[9] or a rubber tyre[10] or Vitamin A[11] then the Commission can move on to test for substitutes. If, however, the product is a complex product, there is an element of discretion in deciding the relevant product with which to begin the investigation. For example, in *Hilti* v. *Commission*,[12] Hilti produced nail guns, cartridges and nails and sold them in a commercial package which it called a Power Activated Fastening System (PAFS). Hilti held a patent for the gun and one for the cartridges strips, but none for the nails. The Commission decided that the relevant market was not the wall construction market in which the PAFS was one product. Instead, it chose to define each part of the package as a separate product and found that there were three separate markets.

To the extent that the Directorate General for Competition opts to start its market definition with components as separate products rather than 'systems' of products, it defines markets narrowly and naturally makes it easier to find dominance. In the *Hilti* case for example, since there were separate markets for cartridge strips and nails, and the cartridge strips were a patented product, the patent contributed to Hilti's market power on the cartridge market by allowing Hilti to legitimately exclude competition. Indeed, this definition of markets not only influenced the issue of dominance; it also influenced the issue of abuse. The tie-in with the unpatented nails was caught by Article 82 as a case of attempted leveraging of the patent protection going beyond the scope of the patent. This also occurred in *Hugin*,[13] a case dealing with new spare parts for Hugin cash registers. It also occurred in the *Volvo*[14] case where 'new Volvo spare front wing parts' were held to be a relevant market. The Commission's practice of defining markets narrowly is not directed solely at IPR owning giants. It is part of a wider tendency to regulate essential infrastructures which create dependency relationships or 'lock ins' in 'after markets' such as maintenance markets, spare parts markets, consumable markets and complementary markets. The Commission's actions, as it openly argued in the *Magill* case,[15] however, are in part prompted by a desire 'to use Article 82 to supervise effective competition in markets in the new economy of information technology and telecommunications'. In its definition of markets, the Commission has increasingly acknowledged the existence of 'technology markets' and the possibility that IPRs such as patents or copyright can confer dominance or reinforce market standards in such markets.[16] It has also been prepared to define informational goods such as TV programme listings and databases as sufficiently separate entities to amount to separate 'markets' or facilities when they create market power which can extend to their 'after markets'.[17]

When determining the relevant market both the ECJ and the Commission also requires consideration of its geographical reach. Often the geographical reach of an IPR-based product is limited to a single country but the test is an empirical one. The starting point for analysis for a product protected by a national patent for example could be the exclusive right of the patentee to produce or sell this product within the borders of a particular country. However, if in fact the market is subject to regular parallel imports from other countries owing to exhausted patent protection that may widen the geographic market.[18]

Paragraph 8 of the Commission Notice defines the relevant geographic market in the following manner:

> The relevant geographic market comprises the area in which the under-takings concerned are involved in the supply and demand of products or services, in which the conditions of competition are sufficiently homogeneous and which can be distinguished from neighbouring areas because the conditions of competition are appreciably different in those areas.

The geographic market is identified in relation to the area in which the product in question is marketed. Factors which can help distinguish one geographic market from another are cost of transport, the nature of the product and legal regulation. The latter is the most significant for IPRs and has often been applied by the ECJ and the Commission as a justification for defining the geographic market narrowly without taking into consideration the degree of interpenetration of trade features in their analysis.

In practice, the ECJ has often identified the geographic market as the whole of the Common Market or a Member State, but even a small region of a Member State or a port[19] or air route[20] has qualified for the competition authorities' test. From an IP perspective, the competition authorities have too readily accepted the state monopoly as the boundary of the relevant geographic market, thus not giving much prominence to potential economic substitutes,[21] and resulting in an easier finding of dominance. It should be noted, however, that the Commission and the Community Courts do not always agree with each other. In *Tetra Pak II*,[22] the Court of First Instance (CFI) rejected the Commission's finding that significant price differences in different Member States were relevant to the definition of the relevant geographic market.

2. The concept of dominance under Article 82 and IPRs

Dominance under Article 82 can take two forms: single firm dominance and joint or collective dominance. The Commission's assessment of single firm dominance starts with an estimation of the market share of the product in its market, but market shares by themselves are merely the starting point. They only create a presumption of market power. It is necessary to go on to measure the market shares of competitors in the market, the presence of potential competition outside the market and the extent of barriers to entry, such as IPRs and access to supply and distribution. The Court has also indicated that pricing experience is part of the investigation of market power. Persistent high pricing suggests dominance[23] whereas responsiveness by a firm with a high market share to lower prices by competitors suggests an absence of dominant market power.[24]

For the purpose of understanding the Article 82/IPR interface, it is important to distinguish between two types of single firm dominance: dominance of a market with real competitors existing in that market and dominance in the form of few if any real competitors, i.e. a near monopoly. A firm can, in the first category, be dominant with a market share as low as the 50 per cent level and in very unusual cases as low as 40 per cent. In an extreme case, in the second category, dominance can take the form of a de facto monopoly in which there are no actual competitors in the 'market'. Examples are offered by markets where dominance takes the form of an industrial standard such as the MPEG component in DVD chips or Windows operating systems for Intel powered PCs.

If a firm has a de facto monopoly in a particular market consisting of a near 90–100 per cent market share, it is still necessary to see whether there are 'barriers to entry' for potential competitors, i.e. possible new entrants to the market. One such barrier can be intellectual property protection reinforcing exclusive use of the product by the incumbent firm. The mere existence of an IPR is not presumed to be a barrier to entry. Since a market consists of goods that are substitutes for each other, it is only where the market is a single good market, i.e. a market standard, that the IPR constitutes an absolute barrier to entry.

In other cases, the IPR might be empirically shown to be merely a financial impediment to entry in the sense of raising the costs of entry. In such cases it will be viewed as equivalent to any other type of financial barrier to entry, such as the capital costs of entry ('sunk costs') or the marketing costs of entry, that is the added costs of entry compared to the operational costs of the incumbent. In other words, IPRs as such, in these situations, are not singled out for different treatment merely because they take the form of exclusive rights or 'monopolies' in a legalistic sense.

There is a further demand side barrier to entry, one created by other complementary products in a 'system' which is demonstrated by the analysis of indirect network effects. In the Microsoft case[25] in the USA for example, the high market share of Microsoft's Windows operating systems in the Intel chip PC market was reinforced by an 'applications barrier to entry' caused by the fact that tens of thousands of applications interoperated with Windows and a new entrant would have the added difficulty of convincing the makers of complementary products to interoperate with its new product. In other words, the demand for the main product in a system is influenced by the demand for the products with which it interoperates.

A key issue in determining the legal responsibilities of IPR owners under Article 82 is to assess whether the high market share of its IP protected product, whether patent, copyright or design right, coincides with a de facto monopoly which is also an 'essential facility'.[26] To meet this test, the IPR protected product must not merely make its owner dominant in a market, it must also be: (1) a real 'monopoly' with no substitutes; and (2) an 'indispensable' input to a product or products in a secondary product market or after market.

In *Oscar Bronner* v. *Mediaprint*,[27] the ECJ insisted on a strict indispensability test. Even if an IPR owner had a monopoly, that monopoly had to be indispensable to access to a market, i.e. 'refusing a third party in an after market access to an essential facility would only amount to an abuse when . . . (iii) the service in itself is indispensable to carrying on that person's business, inasmuch as there is no actual or potential substitute in existence'.[28] In addition, the aspiring entrant had to show that without access to the incumbent's service, it would be completely excluded from the market.[29]

The test of indispensability, however, was carefully defined. The claimant must show that even if its resources were comparable to the incumbent in the primary market, it would still not be able to create a facility that would allow it entry to the secondary market.[30] 'For such access to be capable of being regarded as indispensable, it would be necessary at the very least to establish . . . that it is not economically viable to create a second home delivery scheme for the distribution of daily newspapers with a circulation comparable to that of the daily newspapers distributed by the existing scheme.'[31]

This was the Court's response to Oscar Bronner's argument that they were too small to replicate the Mediaprint home delivery system. In other words, it would be necessary for a complainant wanting access to a dominant product to show that even if he had the economic resources of the facility's owner he could not duplicate it.

The ECJ made it clear that following *Magill*, this reasoning applied to IPRs where the conditions were met.[32] This reinforces the view of the case law that suggests that dominance must consist of the attributes of a de facto monopoly which is also an indispensable input to another product to create the first step in the test of 'exceptional circumstances'. This tends to restrict the possibility of such complaints under Article 82 to cases of IP protected products for which no substitutes could be found owing to the IP protection, a prime example of which would be an IP protected industrial standard.

In addition to individual dominance, Article 82 applies to joint or collective dominance. This category of dominance is more relevant to cross-licensing relationships and technology or patent pools.[33] The method of assessing whether collaboration among IP owners amounts to joint dominance requires, first, to find whether there are demonstrable links between the undertakings amounting to a joint endeavour;[34] secondly, if the links are there, whether the group hold a dominant position, as determined by the criteria used in cases of single firm dominance.[35] If in such cases the collective entity is dominant, then it will be subject to the prohibitions against abusive conduct established by Article 82 and its interpretation by the courts and Commission.

C. The concept of abuse under Article 82

1. The concept generally

Once an undertaking achieves a position of dominance it has a special responsibility 'not to allow its conduct to impair genuine undistorted competition on the common market'.[36] Any literal reading of the abuses listed in Article 82 suggests that these responsibilities consist first and foremost in a duty by the dominant firm not to unduly exploit its customers or consumers by extracting monopoly rents from them by such practices as excessive pricing, limiting markets, tie-ins, etc.[37] Insofar as that is the case, they are not likely to impinge upon the exercise of IPRs except in a marginal way. Competition law has long recognised that the pricing of IPRs included a reward element that could take it above price levels which would apply in more normal competitive markets. Moreover, the Court has also accepted that the logic of the exclusive right allows its holder to eliminate competition from unauthorised manufacturers and sellers of the protected product.

The problem for IPR holders is that the definition of abuse extends more widely to require dominant firms not to engage in 'anticompetitive' abuses directed against competitors, both in primary and related markets. A dominant IPR owner, particularly one in an enhanced dominant position, can be restrained from acquiring other firms with competing technology.[38] It may be required in exceptional cases to supply or license the protected products or processes to competitors in secondary markets.[39] Its pricing and product bundling decisions may be found to be unlawful because of their effect on existing competitors in secondary markets.[40] In some cases, the IP owner is restricted with little differentiation made between IP owners and non-IP owners; the issue is abuse of dominance under Article 82 and the IPR is seen simply as a factual element in the assessment of constituent elements of dominance and abuse. In other cases, such as excessive pricing, special note is taken by the competition authorities of the existence of the IPR and in the case of the abuse of refusal to supply, the IP owner's exercise of its IP right is curbed only in 'exceptional circumstances'.

The ECJ interpretation of the language of Article 82 to apply to anticompetitive abuse is directed against conduct by a dominant firm causing damage to the competitive structure of markets already weakened by the presence of its dominance on a market. In other words, it has been interpreted to protect competitors as well as consumers and customers. However, an anticompetitive abuse has a second dimension. In *Michelin* v. *Commission*,[41] the Court stated that 'Article [82] covers practices which are likely to affect the structure of a market where, as a direct result of the presence of the undertaking in question, competition is weakened *and which through recourse to methods different from those governing normal competition in products or services based on traders' performance* has the effect of hindering the maintenance or development of the level of competition still existing in the market.'[42]

A finding of anticompetitive abuse under Article 82 therefore requires not merely conduct which is likely to weaken the structure of a market by restricting competition, i.e. driving out existing competitors or denying entry to new firms, which are prima facie abusive; but also that the methods used to achieve this effect are different from those which govern competition on the basis of performance.[43]

However, the concept of legitimate competition by performance is not to be taken as merely normal commercial practice; it is a product of competition policy analysis. For example, in *Hilti*[44] and *Tetra Pak II*,[45] the dominant undertakings argued that their practice of product bundling was normal commercial usage. Yet, neither Commission nor Court were prepared to accept commercial usage as an objective justification for a practice which had the likely effect of excluding existing competitors from and preventing entrants to the market. The concept of legitimate competition by performance clearly extends to the use of internal economic efficiencies to grow and compete with other firms by passing on those economic efficiencies in the form of lower prices. For example, in *AKZO* v. *Commission*,[46] a case concerning alleged predatory pricing, the Court held that charging prices which were lower than average total costs could be presumed to be anticompetitive and pricing below average variable costs was per se anticompetitive. The clear implication of these presumptions was that, as long as a dominant undertaking priced above average total cost, it could pass on its efficiencies in the form of low prices and legitimately compete with and weaken competitors remaining in the market without acting abusively.

Similarly, the development of a competitive edge through innovation is legitimate competition by performance which can be translated into practices which result in the elimination of competitors, either those who attempt to copy the protected product or those who are forced out of the market owing to the superior quality of the innovation in relation to their products. For example, in *Volvo*,[47] the Court acknowledged that the dominant manufacturer of spare parts could eliminate competition from other manufacturers of spare parts by using its design right.[48] However, the Court qualified that right in respect of the supplying of spare parts to secondary markets, such as maintenance markets.[49]

The issue of whether or not a firm is engaging in competition by performance is a constituent element of the Article 82 abuse in the sense that the competition authority must at least make out a prima facie case that it is not part of the dominant firm's conduct. If that test is met, the burden of proof shifts to the dominant firm to show a defence of objective justification. For example in *Commercial Solvents*,[50] the Commission was able to show that the decision to refuse to supply Zoya was not compelled by necessity; ICI had sufficient capacity to supply itself and Zoya. Kallaugher and Venit suggest that 'there is a legitimate presumption that a dominant firm will supply any customer that is willing and able to pay the purchase price for its goods and services. Thus in the special case of refusals to supply, a burden could be put on the dominant firms to rebut the presumption by showing that it had a good reason for refusal.'[51] Moreover, in *United Brands*,[52] the Court indicated that a proportionality principle was manifestly not applied in United Brands' decision to discontinue deliveries to its distributor for selling competing bananas and taking part in its competitor's advertising campaign. The decision implied that a less severe sanction in response to the action of the distributor may have been justified.

Under Article 82, the concepts of competition on the merits and objective justification apply to a dominant undertaking's relationships with customers. For example, in *Hoffman La Roche*,[53] the Court made it plain that if the dominant firm offered discounts to customers based on quantities ordered, as opposed to 'loyalty rebates', this would be normal competition on the merits and objectively justified. Similarly, in *Hilti*[54] and *Tetra Pak II*,[55] the Court was prepared to accept in principle that issues of safety and hygiene and quality control were legitimate grounds for tie-ins as long as these could be shown to be objectively justified.

Furthermore, Article 82 also incorporates a legitimate means test by applying a limiting principle of proportionality. The dominant undertaking may act as efficiently as it wishes in its attempts to gain profits and improve its market position but only by employing methods which are necessary to pursue its legitimate aims, i.e. methods which limit competition no more than is necessary.[56] Finally, in some cases self-defence, under Article 82, can be an objective justification.[57]

In the next sections we shall look at three specific abuses largely in terms of their application as limits to the exercise of IPRs.

2. Excessive pricing and IPRs

2.1 Article 82(a) generally   Under Article 82(a), a dominant firm is prohibited from 'directly or indirectly imposing unfair purchase or selling prices or other unfair trading conditions'. From an early stage, the European Court of Justice has held that in principle, a particularly high price, unjustified by any objective criteria, may be an abuse of a dominant position.[58] In *United Brands*,[59] the Court described the abuse in terms which suggested close regulation by the competition authority. It defined the abuse as attempting to reap trading benefits which are higher than an undertaking would have reaped if there had been normal and sufficiently effective competition in the market.[60] Similarly in *SACEM II*,[61] the Court stated that there could be an abuse under article 82(a) if prices were 'appreciably higher' than a competitive level, a standard which suggested close scrutiny gradations in prices.

At first glance, these statements appear to call into question the entitlement of an IPR owner to a just reward for its innovation because of the effect on competition of the exclusive right. However, this must be reconciled with the fact that the ability to charge higher than competitive prices for a protected product, and to restrict competition, is 'the very essence of patents'.[62] In acknowledgement of the need for 'comity' with IP law, the Court of Justice has accepted that there must be considerable room for a high return on IPRs based on the amounts which right holders have invested in order to perfect the protected right.[63] Moreover, the collecting societies have received careful treatment by the Court and Commission. Indeed, the regulation of the pricing of IPRs in the case law on Article 82(a) offers a good example of special treatment of IPRs under general competition norms.

Moreover, there are two features of the case law interpreting Article 82(a) more generally, that suggest that the actual application of Article 82(a) to the facts of cases has resulted in a test of unfair pricing which is far less interventionist. In its recent decisions, the Commission has been clear about the relatively high legal standard required to prove that prices are excessive. Thus in *Scandlines Sverige* v. *Port of Helsingborg*,[64] the Commission rejected a claim by ferry operators that the port fees charged by the port owners for services provided on the Helsingborg/Helsinør route were excessive. The Commission indicated that recognition should be given to the entitlement of an entrepreneur who invests in an advantageous asset to charge higher prices based on the comparative advantage it offers, 'the intangible value of which is represented by the advantageous location of the ferry port which must be taken into account as part of the assessment of the economic value of the service provided by HHAB, and which is not reflected in the costs actually incurred by HHAB'.[65]

Secondly, the Court has tended to apply the article only to demonstrably excessive prices, as if acknowledging that its oversight of pricing under

Article 82(a) must be kept to the more extreme cases. The Commission has long taken a similar line. In its 1994 Report on Competition, it stated:

> The existence of a dominant position is not itself against the rules of competition. Consumers can suffer from a dominant company exploiting this position, the most likely way being through prices higher than would be found if the market were subject to effective competition. However, the Commission in its decision-making practice does not normally control or condemn the high level of prices as such. Rather it examines the behaviour of the dominant company designed to preserve its dominance, usually directed against competitors or new entrants who would normally bring about effective competition and the price level associated with it.[66]

In applying the standard of Article 82(a), the Court has resorted to more than one test to determine whether pricing is abusive. What is quite striking in the case law however is that whichever test has been used, the facts tend to reveal that the pricing practice must be demonstrably excessive to come within the Article 82(a) prohibition. In *General Motors*,[67] for example, the Court stated that when prices are set which have no reasonable relation to the 'economic value' of the product, there is an abuse under Article 82(a). In that case the basis for a finding of excessive pricing was that General Motors Continental charged double for the same certificate in Belgium for cars imported from other member states. In *United Brands*,[68] the Court amended the criterion slightly to, 'charging a price which is excessive because it had no reasonable relation to the economic value of the product supplied'. The method to be used when asking whether the sales price exceeded the economic value of a product was to compare sales prices with production costs to determine the profit margin. If that difference appeared excessive, the next step was to decide 'whether a price has been imposed which is unfair itself'. The Court also endorsed in principle a third test that emphasised a comparison of product prices with other competing products[69] including those in other geographic markets. Yet what was significant about *United Brands* was that the Court rejected the Commission's finding of unfair pricing based on comparison of costs in other member states as unduly simplistic. There was a need for careful consideration to be given to the cost structures and other conditions in the local market that could influence profit margins.[70]

While in *United Brands* the Court overturned the Commission's finding of excessive prices based on the comparative prices test, it did not reject the comparative price method as such. It merely insisted that if a comparison of prices was to be used, it should be based on adequate evidence that the lower prices actually covered costs. The Court recognised that there were difficulties entailed in: working out production costs which may sometimes include a discretionary apportionment of interest costs and general expenditure and which may vary significantly according to the size of the undertaking, its object, the complex nature of its set up, its territorial area of operations, whether it manufactures one of several products, the number of its subsidiaries and their relationship with each other.[71]

The contrast with US practice under the Sherman Act is instructive here. Under US antitrust law, it is recognised that the regulation of pricing is so demanding an exercise that it requires the establishment of a specific regulatory commission.[72] In interpreting Article 82(a) to potentially involve hands-on regulation of excessive pricing[73] the Court may have underestimated the handicap of not having dedicated regulatory institutions to carry out the type of sophisticated analysis of prices and costs which are needed in most cases to substantiate a charge of excessive prices.

It would appear to be implicit in the evaluation of efficiency in an assessment of excessive pricing that the Commission and Court must define the legitimate rewards to firms whose growth has come about through greater efficiency and reduced production costs. If the gap between costs and prices is used as the sole yardstick, there is the possibility that the more efficient firms could be penalised by the regulatory standard. One problem here is that the test appears to make little allowance for the way the dominant position was acquired. If a firm achieves dominance through efficiencies and maintains that dominance through continued internally generated efficiencies, it could nevertheless be penalised for its pricing decisions as excessive and exploitive. One would expect the defence of legitimate competition by performance to apply to such a position should it ever arise in practice.

2.2 Article 82(a) and individual IPRs   The difficulties of measuring unfair pricing in general under Article 82(a) are intensified when an assessment must be made of a fair return to innovators exploiting their IPRs. In *Parke Davis*, the Court held that 'higher sale price for a patented product as compared with that of an unpatented product ... does not necessarily constitute an abuse'.[74] This suggested that in principle the concept of a higher than competitive return could be a fair return where intellectual property is concerned partly because of the costs of innovation, including the need to reward the individual firm for its investment in research and development. As the Court noted in *Maxicar*,[75] the higher price for components sold by the manufacturer as compared to those sold by the independent producers 'does not necessarily constitute an abuse, since the proprietor of protective rights in respect of an ornamental design may lawfully call for a return on the amounts which he has invested in order to perfect the protected design'.[76]

This case also gave some indication that the principle of a return on amounts invested does not necessarily embody a narrow cost-plus approach. In *Maxicar*, Advocate General Mischo stated that 'the inventor is entitled to recover not only his production costs in the strict sense and a reasonable profit margin but also his research and development expenditure'.[77] Moreover, as Korah has pointed out, 'the concept of costs can be reconciled with providing incentives to investment provided that factors for the risk of failure and delay in obtaining a return are included in the costs that can be recovered before prices are considered unreasonable'.[78]

Furthermore, the principle of return on amounts invested allows some flexibility in assessing a fair return for different types of IPRs. For example, R&D costs are particularly applicable to IPRs such as design rights and patents and perhaps informational copyright.[79] In the case of other rights such as trade marks, the costs can include the expense involved in promotion, advertising, and systems of quality control.[80] There is room to develop a separate type of calculation under Article 82(a) depending upon the particular character of the IPR.

Nevertheless, the concept of fair pricing as based on a fair return on costs under Article 82(a) may not always give full recognition to the reward function of the grant of the IPR. Even though the Court has recognised that charging a higher than competitive price is legitimate competition by performance, this does not go so far as to allow IP owners always and under all conditions to attempt to appropriate the full value of their IPR as that value is conceived under national law.

Even within the framework of competition law, there are strong arguments for a high return on products or processes protected by IPRs. The return is not simply a reward to the individual inventor; it is also designed to act as an incentive for other inventors or originators to invest in innovation.[81] It also includes an element to compensate for the failures of other efforts at commercial exploitation.[82] From an intellectual property point of view, this incentive function of 'just reward' results in a figure which is established by what consumers and customers are willing to pay for the added value the IPR confers on a product compared with another product which does not incorporate that right, in other words what the market will bear. As Friden has pointed out, it represents not the possibility to charge reasonable prices and obtain reasonable profits but rather the possibility, for the holder of an exclusive right, to charge whatever the market will pay, one of the main justifications being the need to give the innovator an incentive to bear the risk of innovation which he might refuse to do if only promised a reasonable profit.[83] Moreover, economists have made the point that the methodological difficulties of measuring what is a reasonable or unreasonable reward are so great that it is best left to a regulation of the duration of the period of the grant of the exclusive right.[84]

Nevertheless, the Court has not been willing to stretch the logic of Article 82(a) to entitle the right holder in all circumstances to charge 'what the market can bear' during the period of the patent or design right. Article 82(a) requires a differentiation between dominant and non-dominant undertakings, including undertakings whose position coincides with, or is reinforced by, ownership of an IPR. Non-dominant firms can charge what the market will bear. Dominant undertakings however are entitled only to fair return, not an excessive one.[85] The Court must work within the framework of Article 82(a).

The implication of the above analysis is that Article 82(a) could potentially impose a limit on the pricing of IPRs. In practice, however, this is not likely to affect IPR owners unless their conduct is egregiously and demonstrably excessive in the light of their own previous conduct.[86] Moreover, there is considerable room for IPR owners to price at high levels to obtain a return on their intellectual property investment.[87] As the Advocate General expressed it in Maxicar, 'the proprietor of protective rights ... may lawfully call for a return on the amounts which he has invested in order to perfect the protected design'.[88] Furthermore, prices charged by an IP owner which are considerably higher than those charged by competing independents are not necessarily abusive because of this right of return.

However, Article 82(a) is not solely concerned with purely exploitive excessive pricing. Excessive pricing which has the effects of excluding competitors can also be abusive under Article 82(a).[89] This is a point of conflict between a just reward for the IPR under IP legislation and the need to prevent a weakening of competition often in a secondary market under competition law. In Maxicar, the Court referred to the fixing of prices at an unfair level as an alternative abuse to refusing to supply spare parts to an independent repairer.[90] In that case, the Court's concern was with a pricing practice that was so high that it had the effect of discouraging independent repairers in a secondary market from ordering supplies and therefore functioned as a virtual refusal to supply (see next section).

Moreover, there was some indication that in analysing the fairness of prices in a secondary market like spare parts, the reward can be reduced because of the consideration that profits had been recouped on the sale of the original manufactured product. In Maxicar, the Advocate General stated that in the case of 'bodywork components sold as spare parts the problem displays an unusual aspect in so far as part of that expenditure has probably already been recovered from the sale of new cars. It is therefore necessary, when fixing the prices of spare parts, to take due account of that factor.'[91]

In practice, the issue of pricing in the two market context is likely to arise if at all if there is an order of a compulsory licence on reasonable and not discriminatory terms under Article 82(b) rather than as an issue of excessive pricing under Article 82(a) (see next section). Insofar as commentators consider the regulation of the pricing of IPRs to be 'unworkable',[92] they can quite legitimately point to the methodological difficulties facing courts and indeed the Commission dealing with a complaint under Article 82(a). Nevertheless, Article 82(a) must be taken into account in pricing decisions along with the limits on discriminatory pricing imposed by Article 82(c).

2.3 Collecting societies and the EU competition rules   Collecting societies manage and enforce copyrights for music on behalf of their members. They give collective permission for the use of members' work, often in the form of block licences; they set rates for royalties for licensees such as broadcasting authorities, cable TV companies and discos etc. on behalf of members; they collect royalty fees and enforce their IPRs in case of detected infringement. Their justification is that it is only by acting collectively in this way that most artists can get a reasonable income for their work and hence the collecting societies provide the economic foundation for a valuable cultural and entertainment sector. Moreover, by offering copyrights collectively, they enable much more copyright material to be used than if licences were left to individual negotiation. They are, however, usually dominant on a national market and hence subject to Article 82 generally[93] and Article 82(a) specifically.

The case law defining abusive pricing under Article 82(a) suggests a reluctance by the Court and Commission to intervene actively in the price setting decisions of the collecting societies. In the most important case of *SACEM II*,[94] the operators of French discotheques complained of excessively high prices. The evidence suggested that the royalties were high by comparison with other member states such as Germany and the UK and more than four times higher than the European average. The Court accepted that the comparative royalty test was applicable and even articulated the relevant standard as 'appreciably higher than those charged in other member states, the rates being compared on a consistent basis'.[95] Yet even in such a case, there was no abuse per se. Instead, the Court stated that the burden of proof shifted to the collecting society to justify the difference by reference to dissimilarities in the respective copyright management regimes.[96] Although the Court noted that the rates seemed high, it refused to rule on the issue of whether the rates were abusively high leaving that to the national court. In later cases, the Commission too has shown a marked disinclination to intervene in detail in the detailed assessment of prices.[97]

3. The abuse of refusal to supply: Article 82(b)

Over the years, the ECJ has chosen to reconcile the entitlement of dominant firms to compete on the merits with the prohibition in Article 82(b) by allowing firms to enjoy the essence of their IPR protection by liberally exercising their exclusive rights in the market in which they are dominant, i.e. 'primary markets.' However, the Court has also been more cautious in accepting that the exercise of exclusivity by dominant firms in 'secondary' markets, or 'after markets', i.e. those which are dependent on the product in the primary market, can be as free as in the primary market. This distinction has become increasingly important in industries where systems of complementary products have become widespread.

This guideline to the interpretation of Article 82 was introduced by the ECJ in *Volvo*,[98] a case which was triggered by Veng's infringement of Volvo's design right for its front wing panels in the UK by importing cheaper copies. When Veng was enjoined from importing the infringing wing panels, he claimed as a defence that Article 82 required Volvo to supply or license him to make panels. The ECJ, on a reference from the UK court, held that there were three separate markets: the market for cars, the market for Volvo spare parts and the market for repair and maintenance of Volvo cars. Volvo was not dominant in the car market but was dominant in the spare parts market for Volvo front wing panels. Moreover, by virtue of its design right and the nature of the product, this was a monopoly with no substitutes and the product was indispensable to the repair market. The Court held that in the primary market for which Volvo had a monopoly owing to its design right, there was no duty to supply competitors or to license them to make or sell the IPR protected product. The exclusive right to make or sell was the very purpose of the IPR protection. As the ECJ put it:

> It must also be emphasized that the right of the proprietor of a protected design to prevent third parties from manufacturing and selling or import-ing, without its consent, products incorporating the design constitutes the very subject-matter of his exclusive right. It follows that an obligation imposed upon the proprietor of a protected design to grant to third parties, even in return for a reasonable royalty, a licence for the supply of products incorporating the design would lead to the proprietor thereof being deprived of the substance of his exclusive right, and that a refusal to grant such a licence cannot in itself constitute an abuse of a dominant position.[99]

However, while a refusal to grant a licence in a primary market is not itself unlawful under Article 82, this does not mean that all conduct by an IPR owner in a primary market in which it holds a dominant position is exempted from the competition rules. For example, in primary markets, the Court has found it to be abusive conduct for a dominant firm to acquire control over potentially competing innovative technology by another firm[100] because this type of conduct would foreclose access to the competing technology to that market. Underlying this decision is the concept that while it is acceptable to grow organically to monopoly, it is not competition on the merits to grow to monopoly or extend a monopoly by mergers and acquisition. The concept of 'competition on its merits' in EU competition law does not apply to the use of its market power by the dominant firm to buy out competition; it only applies to cases where the dominant firm beats competition by unilateral efficiencies.

Moreover, while pricing of IPRs by a dominant firm is normally viewed as incorporating room for the IPR owner to recover costs and make a profit on its investment in the IPR, in exceptional circumstances Article 82 can be used to find excessively high pricing to be abusive because it is exploitive of the dominant position.[101] In such cases, the presence of an IPR requires a special reconciliation of Article 82 with the costs and risks attached to the R&D investment that led to the high prices. Other forms of unfair pricing are viewed as abusive because they are anticompetitive in nature. They are essentially attempts to use dominant positions to foreclose markets. These abuses include excessively low or predatory pricing[102] and discriminatory pricing.[103]

Nevertheless, following the *Volvo* case, in the 'primary' market for the product there is normally no requirement for a dominant firm to license competitors to make or sell its IP protected product. However, the Court went on to indicate that in the 'secondary' and dependent market for Volvo spare parts, Volvo as the occupier of a dominant position in the spare parts market, could not always refuse to supply to competitors. Nor could it price so high as to make supplies of the protected product inaccessible to the secondary market. The concern of Article 82 was to maintain access and prevent abusive use of dominance in one market to foreclose competitors in secondary markets. As the Court put it:

> It must however be noted that the exercise of an exclusive right by the proprietor of a registered design in respect of car body panels may be prohibited by Article [82] if it involves, on the part of an undertaking holding a dominant position, certain abusive conduct such as the arbitrary refusal to supply spare parts to independent repairers, the fixing of prices for spare parts at an unfair level or a decision no longer to produce spare parts for a particular model even though many cars of that model are still in circulation, provided that such conduct is liable to affect trade between Member States.[104]

The concept of abuse in the secondary market is that a firm that is dominant in a primary market is prohibited from 'leveraging' its market power in a secondary market to exclude existing competitors and to deny access to new entrants to that market.[105] The implication of the Volvo judgment was that in exceptional cases where a dominant firm refuses to supply as a device to prevent competition on secondary markets, competition authorities may have the authority under Article 82 to order compulsory supply of or reduced prices for supply even of an IP protected good. The case proved to have far reaching implications for IP owners whose concept of exploitation of IPRs increasingly extended to systems of complementary products in after markets, such as spare parts, consumables and applications of software programs etc.

These implications of paragraph 9 of the *Volvo* case were considerably extended by the landmark case of *Magill*.[106] Magill was a compiler of a comprehensive weekly TV guide combining the contents of the three individual weekly TV guides sold separately by the respective TV companies. After losing a copyright infringement action at the national level, Magill successfully complained to the Commission that the TV companies' refusal to license the program listings was abusive conduct under Article 82 and won an order for a compulsory licence of the listings material from the TV companies to produce its comprehensive TV guide. The case, a cause célèbre, went to the CFI who affirmed the Commission's order. On further appeal to the ECJ, the TV companies were supported in their arguments by the Intellectual Property Organisation (IPO), representing software makers internationally. The appeal resulted in a lengthy opinion by the Advocate General recommending reversal on the grounds that the intellectual property right should be protected against competitors in secondary markets as well as primary markets. The ECJ however decided that the order for a compulsory licence should stand. The Court held, citing Article 82(b) as authority, that copyright itself did not justify a refusal to license in the 'exceptional circumstances' where there was consumer demand for the new product, where the TV companies had a de facto monopoly over the listings by virtue of their scheduling of TV programs, where a license of the listings was an indispensable input for the comprehensive TV guide and where they were not themselves supplying the product to consumers:

> The appellants' refusal to provide basic information by relying on national copyright provisions thus prevented the appearance of a new product, a comprehensive weekly guide to television programmes, which the appellants did not offer and for which there was a potential consumer demand. Such refusal constitutes an abuse under heading (b) of the second paragraph of Article 86 of the Treaty.[107]

The Court went on to say that an owner of a de facto monopoly over a product such as TV listings for which there were no substitutes and which was indispensable to the provision of another product in a secondary market could not use its monopoly in one market to eliminate competition in the second market reserving that second market for itself.

> .... finally, as the CFI also held, the appellants, by their conduct, reserved to themselves the secondary market of weekly television guides by excluding all competition on that market (see the judgment in Joined Cases 6/73 and 7/73 Commercial Solvents v Commission [1974] ECR 223, paragraph 25) since they denied access to the basic information which is the raw material indispensable for the compilation of such a guide.[108]

After *Magill*, the 'exceptional circumstances' in which an IPR holder could commit an abuse under Article 82 seemed initially as if it might extend to at least two different types of cases. First, an IPR holder, who enjoyed a de facto monopoly of an indispensable input, and who used its IP protected product to block innovation by unjustifiably refusing to supply or license a competitor seeking to introduce a new product on a secondary market could be acting abusively. This would apply even where the owner of the IP protected product had no previous dealing with the new entrant because it would have the effect of foreclosing access to a secondary market of that new product.

Secondly, where a dominant firm with an IPR protected de facto monopoly in the form of an indispensable input refused to supply or license a competitor in a second dependent market with whom it had been dealing with a view to reserving that secondary market for itself, that might constitute an abuse even in the absence of a new product by the third party. This conclusion derived from earlier cases such as *Commercial Solvents*[109] which involved a cutting off of supplies and/or licences to existing customers, but its inclusion in *Magill* made it possible to regard it as extending to a refusal to supply to or possibly even license a new customer or competitor. There was some language in the case suggesting that both these conditions were cumulative and not separate[110] but it was not entirely clear whether this was because of the facts or was the view of the Court about the minimum requirements of the exceptional circumstances test more generally. In other words, it was not entirely clear whether or not the unlawfulness of a dominant IPR owner reserving a secondary market to itself applied to a case on new entrants with 'me too' products as well as those with 'new products'.

Moreover, the *Magill* case itself offered little guidance to the question of what defence the IPR holder could put forward to this abuse. In its treatment of the issue of 'justification' for refusal to license, the ECJ in *Magill* made clear that the mere ownership of an IPR would not as such justify a refusal to license in 'exceptional circumstances'. However, this was in response to the litigation strategy of the IPO on appeal which limited its justification defence to a blanket right to exercise an IPR at the owner's will. The Court also indicated that the mere fact that the owner had never dealt with the competitor before was not such a justification. However, it offered no guidance about the positive grounds for justification for a refusal to supply or license which has the effect of blocking a downstream market. It only made clear that the IPR to exclusive use as a reward to invention did not apply automatically in the second market as it did in the first.

The obvious contenders for justification under the reasoning of other Article 82 cases were where the firm seeking compulsory access was a credit risk, where there were objective grounds to worry about quality control and where there were health and safety risks, all sound commercial objections which would need to be proved to be well-founded,[111] in the sense that the grounds were established as factual and that the resort to refusal was proportionate to the threat.[112] What remained unclear was whether a dominant IPR owner was justified in refusing to license new entrant competitors in secondary markets when those competitors offered only the same or largely similar products to the IPR holder.

In the subsequent case law, the ECJ and the CFI did little to clarify this issue but made it a point to reiterate that a refusal to license by a dominant firm would only be abusive in the strict conditions of the dominance element of the 'exceptional circumstances' test as articulated in *Magill*. Thus, in *Oscar Bronner* v. *Mediapoint*,[113] as we have seen, the ECJ stressed the need for a special test of dominance in cases of alleged abuse of refusal to supply, one which incorporated a test equivalent to that of the criteria for a finding of an 'essential facility'. Yet this raised another question – whether a finding of essential facility is sufficient or whether it is only necessary to meet the test of exceptional circumstances:

> In *Magill*, the Court found such exceptional circumstances in the fact that the refusal in question concerned a product (information on the weekly schedules of certain television channels) the supply of which was indispensable for carrying on the business in question (the publishing of a general television guide), in that, without that information, the person wishing to produce such a guide would find it impossible to publish it and offer it for sale (paragraph 53), the fact that such refusal prevented the appearance of a new product for which there was a potential consumer demand (paragraph 54), the fact that it was not justified by objective considerations (paragraph 55), and that it was likely to exclude all competition in the secondary market of television guides (paragraph 56).
>
> Therefore, even if that case-law on the exercise of an intellectual property right were applicable to the exercise of any property right whatever, it would still be necessary, for the *Magill* judgment to be effectively relied upon in order to plead the existence of an abuse within the meaning of Article 86 of the Treaty in a situation such as that which forms the subject-matter of the first question, not only that the refusal of the service comprised in home delivery be likely to eliminate all competition in the daily newspaper market on the part of the person requesting the service and that such refusal be incapable of being objectively justified, but also that the service in itself be indispensable to carrying on that person's business, inasmuch as there is no actual or potential substitute in existence for that home-delivery scheme.[114]

The ECJ held that where a newspaper proprietor asked for access to another proprietor's home delivery service, a finding of abusive refusal of access using *Magill* as a precedent for the limits to the exercise of any property right, including an IPR, could not be made unless (i) the refusal of the service in the home delivery market would be likely to eliminate all competition in that market on the part of the person requesting the service, (ii) there was no objective justification for the refusal, and (iii) that the service in itself was indispensable to carrying on that person's business, inasmuch as there is no actual or potential substitute in existence for the home delivery scheme.

In *IMS Health Inc* v. *Commission*,[115] three years later, the issue was raised whether, in a case of an IP protected industrial standard, the 'new product' condition was essential to a finding of 'exceptional circumstances' in which a compulsory licence could be obtained. In *IMS* the Commission ordered a compulsory licence of information contained in a database, consisting of an '1860 brick structure' which provided a format for storing regularly updated information about the sales of pharmaceutical products in Germany region by region. The beneficiaries of the compulsory licences were firms started by former senior management to market regional sales data services based on the brick structure database. The Commission distinguished between the brick structure database, which it found to be copyright protected, and the related market of regional sales data services. It then found that the IMS 1860 brick structure was an essential facility because it had become a market standard demanded by customers including the wholesalers as well as the pharmaceutical companies and that it was not economical for competitors in the second market of selling regional sales data services to reproduce it. It found that the refusal to license was abusive because once the tests of essential facility and dependent product were met, it was not necessary that the competitors in the 'after market' were offering a product which was new in relation to the product offered by IMS. IMS appealed to the CFI which stayed the order of compulsory licence pending the result of the appeal because there was a serious doubt that the decision would be upheld on appeal in part because the Commission had proceeded on the supposition that the new product requirement was not an indispensable condition of the exceptional circumstances test.

The President of the CFI emphasised that the Commission had mistakenly proceeded on the supposition that 'the prevention of the emergence of a new product for which there is potential consumer demand is not an indispensable condition of the "exceptional circumstances" developed by the Court of Justice in *Magill*.[116] The Commission has now withdrawn its order for a compulsory license in the *IMS* case because in August 2000 the Frankfurt Regional Court decided that the data base should not have been protected by copyright.

The Commission's original *IMS* decision offers a reminder inter alia[117] of the type of risks that arise from a reading of the IP/competition law interface that is skewed because a competition authority has failed to give sufficient weight to the nature of the balance struck by the 'exceptional circumstances' test in *Magill*. The precondition that a new entrant to an 'after market' who wishes to have compulsory access to an IP protected industrial standard must offer something more than a 'me too' product or 'clone' of the IP owner's product is not an optional condition. It is essential to meet the test of Article 82(b) of limiting technical development.

Moreover, the fact that the new product must also be one for which there is demonstrable unmet consumer demand is also required by the language of Article 82(b). It is then and only then, following *Magill*, that 'exceptional circumstances' exist to justify a compulsory licence for a new entrant to a market under Article 82. In *IMS*, the Commission seemed to make the assumption that an IP protected industrial standard could be treated as if it were any other type of physical 'essential facility', with an obligation to supply to all firms in a secondary dependent market. In *IMS* the Commission gave a reductionist interpretation of the exceptional circumstances test in *Magill* and thus misread the judicial authority. During the period that the CFI was giving its interim decisions, the Frankfurt Regional Court dealing with the IMS case, separately referred a series of questions to the European Court of Justice. The Court of Justice held that the three main conditions of the *Magill* 'exceptional circumstances' test were cumulative, i.e. that in order for a refusal to license new entrants to a market dependent upon an indispensable IP protected input, to be abusive, the refusal must meet three conditions:

  (i) the undertaking which requests the licence intends to offer, on the market for the supply of data in question, new products or services not offered by the copyright owner and for which there is potential consumer demand;
 (ii) the refusal is not justified by objective considerations;
(iii) the refusal is such as to reserve to the copyright owner the market for the supply of data on sales of products in the Member State concerned by eliminating all competition on that market.

This interpretation of the 'exceptional circumstances' test based on *Volvo* and *Magill* could be seen as offering in its own right an intriguing reconciliation between competition law and IPRs based on their mutual interest in innovation by stressing that the 'exceptional circumstances' for a compulsory licence for new entrants to a market is limited only to cases of new products or 'follow up' innovation and not 'me too' competition.

Even this apparently narrow type of test of 'exceptional circumstances', however, leaves a number of issues to be resolved in future litigation: how different must a new product be from the one offered by the owner of the IP protected industrial standard? How strong must the potential unmet consumer demand be to qualify a new entrant to a compulsory licence? Presumably, following Article 82(b), the *Magill* criteria require a look at the issue of whether a product is a new product as much in terms of whether there is genuine unmet consumer demand for it as in terms of a straight comparison of the features of the two products, i.e. the product offered by the new entrant and the product offered by the incumbent. Must the new entrant show that the new product has been developed to the point that it simply requires the indispensable component supplied by the IPR owner, or can it ask for access in order to do more work on its own product? At this point, because of the need to show unmet consumer demand, it is probable that the new product offered by the new entrant must be almost fully developed.

Furthermore, how important is the extent of the investment by the IP owner? Should there be some weight given to the fact that the IP protects a product which entailed considerable investment and involved considerable risk, as opposed to an IP protected product such as that in *Magill* which was essentially a by-product of the investment in TV programs? Finally, how much weight should be given to the fact that the incumbent IP owner claims with some evidence that it intends quite soon to offer a similar product itself? In some cases, this should be a genuine objective justification, particularly in the period shortly after the acquisition of the IPR. This assertion should never, however, be viewed as an automatic justification for a refusal to license since the easy availability of such a defence would be likely to act as a deterrent to new innovation. A careful reading of the exceptional circumstances test for new entrants to a market suggests that even the new product requirement alone implies a balancing test that can shift with different circumstances as long as certain essential preconditions are met.

3.1 Refusals to licence and supply information   To what extent does the ECJ's definition of 'exceptional circumstances' in *Magill* establish the outer limits of that category? In principle, Article 82(b) relied on by the Court in *Magill*, prohibits as abusive conduct by dominant firms where it limits technical development of markets to the detriment of consumers. Limiting technical development is a wider concept than the particular factual circumstances and conditions of the *Magill* case. In its *IMS* judgment, the Court seemed to make it a point to indicate that the *Magill* conditions did not offer an exhaustive definition of the test of 'exceptional circumstances'. It carefully referred to *Magill* as a case in which 'such exceptional circumstances were present'.[118] The Court also held 'that "it is sufficient" (rather than "it is necessary") to satisfy the three *Magill* criteria in order to show an abusive refusal to license'.[119] That proposition would seem to follow from the purpose of Article 82(b). Hence, both the language of Article 82(b) and the ECJ judgment in *IMS* offer good grounds for concluding that other types of abuse can also fall within the category of 'exceptional circumstances'.

3.2 Refusals to continue to licence or supply interface information on an 'after market'   A second category of 'exceptional circumstances' in which Article 82 can apply to IPR owners can occur where a dominant firm with an IPR protected monopoly in the form of an indispensable input refuses to supply or license a competitor in a second dependent market *whom it had been supplying* with a view to obtaining that secondary market for itself. In the *Microsoft* decision of 23 March 2004, the Commission found that Microsoft had abused its near monopoly in the Windows 2000 operating system by deliberately restricting interoperability between the Windows operating systems (OS) and non-Microsoft work group servers such as those operated by

Sun Microsystems.[120] The remedy imposed by the Commission for the refusal to supply interface information was to require Microsoft to divulge all necessary interface information to allow non-Microsoft workgroup server OS to achieve full interoperability with Windows PCs and Microsoft workgroup servers even if copyright protected. In such a case, Microsoft would be entitled to 'reasonable remuneration' for its compulsory licence. The Commission also required Microsoft to update the disclosed information each time it brings to the market new versions of its relevant products. Moreover, the Commission indicated that it planned to appoint a Monitoring Trustee to oversee that Microsoft's interface disclosures are complete and accurate. Finally, the Commission imposed a fine of 497.2 million Euros for the infringement.[121] Microsoft has paid the fine and appealed against the decision to order the disclosure of the interface information. The Commission suspended its order pending the outcome of the appeal to the CFI.

How does Article 82 apply to such cases of exclusionary conduct by a dominant firm when it uses its control over interface information to disrupt its supply of such information or uses its copyright to refuse to license an *existing* contractor/competitor in the secondary market with whom it has been dealing in respect of earlier versions of its product and with the apparent purpose of evicting competitors from that market? How relevant is it that the existing competitor is an innovator in the product market, such as the Netscape Navigator in the web browser market or in the Sun Microsystems (Sun) Solaris server in the low end workgroup server operating system market?

Article 82(b) as interpreted by the European Court of Justice suggests that there are two approaches to the category of 'exceptional circumstances' that may be relevant to this set of facts. One approach is a variation on the innovation test of *Magill* which emphasises that the firms whose supplies are cut off are themselves engaged in the technical development of the market. The second is that the emphasis should be placed on the historical relationship between the dominant firm and the after market and the obligations which accrue to a dominant firm to continue to supply or licence on the dependent 'after market.'

This second category of cases was introduced by *Commercial Solvents*,[122] a case involving a US dominant supplier of chemical raw materials to an Italian firm making those chemicals into a pharmaceutical product. After a period of supply, the US firm making the 'essential raw material' for the pharmaceutical product decided belatedly to enter the pharmaceutical product market itself and as part of that vertical integration decision stopped supplying its downstream competitor. The ECJ upheld the Commission's finding of abuse on the principle that the refusal of a dominant firm to continue to supply, where there were no alternative sources of supply and where it had sufficient capacity to continue to supply the competitor and its own subsidiary in the after market was conduct unjustifiably intended to eliminate its major competitor in the market.

In the information technology field, this principle has been extended to IPR owners of industrial standards who have been compelled by the European competition authorities to supply or license or provide proprietorial information about interface codes on 'reasonable' terms.[123] The starting point for the imposition of this second category of competition law restriction on the conduct of copyright protected industrial standards was the IBM undertaking of 1984.[124] The Commission had initiated proceedings against IBM based upon Article 82 as early as 1980, claiming that IBM was dominant in the markets for the supply of the main memory and basic software for IBM System 370 Central Processing Units and had abused its dominant position by tying or bundling memory and software to the purchase of its Central Processing Units (CPU) and discriminating against other manufacturers of memory and software by delaying the supply of changes in interface codes to them even though they had taken orders for the supply of the CPUs. This created an artificial advantage for itself in the downstream markets by denying competitors an opportunity to adapt their products to the new IBM products. At this stage, the Commission did not explicitly use essential facility reasoning; it relied on the dependence of the peripheral product makers on the IBM System 370 CPUs owing to the high costs of 'switching' to other mainframe computers.

In 1984, IBM negotiated with the Commission to accept its unilateral undertaking to provide other manufacturers with technical interface information needed to permit competitive products to be used with IBM's System 370 mainframe computers. IBM agreed to provide interface information to software developers in a timely manner and to announce changes affecting interoperability in advance of general availability. The information could be supplied in source code or special documents setting out interface information specifically. This information was to be freely available to any relevant company doing business in the EU and any fees were to be reasonable and non-discriminatory. IBM was required to support international standards for open system interconnection for products, systems and networks of different manufacturers.[125]

What was noteworthy about the IBM undertaking in the mid-1980s was that it applied the obligation of interoperability more widely than *Commercial Solvents*. It applied it to all competitors, existing and new entrants. The Commission gave little weight to the right of IBM as the inventor of the mainframe system to prevent competing manufacturers of peripheral applications for the IBM system from enjoying the position of 'free riders' who had not contributed to the costs of researching and developing the system. It gave priority to interoperability over reward-incentives to innovation, seeking only to ensure that IBM as the owner of the essential infrastructure received a fair and reasonable return for any licences.

A decade later, Microsoft was charged with unlawfully 'leveraging' its Windows 95 monopoly against competitors[126] both in the USA and in Europe. In June 1993, the Commission received a complaint from Novell that Microsoft's licensing practices were abusive under Article 82 because they foreclosed competitors from the market for PC operating systems software. The Commission found that Microsoft was dominant in the disk operating system (DOS) market by virtue of its Windows 95 product and engaged in tying and discrimination in its pricing, rebates and licensing in the graphical user interface (GUI) market and software application markets. The charge against Microsoft both in Europe and the USA was that it used its dominance to raise barriers to entry and foreclose innovation to competitors in the primary market of PC operating systems. The tactic it used was to charge the original equipment makers (OEMs) a royalty for the Microsoft Windows and MS-DOS for each PC sold (a 'per processor licence') even when the OEMs did not load the Microsoft software. The practice did not preclude OEMs from pre-installing other operating systems, as for example an exclusive contract might have done. However, it meant that if an OEM did install a competing operating system, the cost would be higher since consumers would have to pay for two operating systems even though one was to be used. This anti-innovative practice raised concerns under US antitrust law as well as EU competition law. After negotiations between Microsoft, the US Department of Justice and the European Commission, a settlement was reached whereby Microsoft undertook inter alia to end its 'per processor' licensing practices for its current versions of Windows and MS-DOS and use only 'per copy' licences.

Then in 1996 a case was brought against Microsoft by the US Department of Justice and eighteen states under the Sherman Act for using almost identical tactics by employing its Windows 98 OS monopoly to promote its web browser product Internet Explorer against Sun's Netscape Navigator.[127] In this case, Microsoft was found guilty of monopolising in the OS market for Intel powered PCs by using its market power in the Windows 98 OS market to limit access to Netscape Navigator in the web browser market by, inter alia, the device of per processor licences and withholding code information about its applications protocol interfaces.[128] The European Commission stood by as the US government made its case against Microsoft.[129]

3.3 The *Microsoft* case in Europe and 'exceptional circumstances' In 2000 and 2001, however, the European Commission[130] itself investigated Microsoft after a complaint by Sun Microsystems, one of Microsoft's most important competitors in the work group server market. Sun complained that Microsoft was leveraging its Windows 2000 and Microsoft's Office Suite monopoly to obtain a further monopoly for Microsoft's workgroup server operating system in the workgroup OS market. Sun stated that Microsoft provided inadequate information about interface codes for Sun to equip its servers to interoperate smoothly with Microsoft's 'integrated' package of Windows 2000, Office Suite and workgroup server operating system because it refused to disclose how the integration between Windows, Office Suite and its server operating system worked. This refusal had the effect of preventing Sun from offering certain services to Windows-based users of its non-Microsoft workgroup server. The Commission in a decision issued on 24 March 2004 found that Microsoft had abused its near monopoly in the Windows operating system by deliberately restricting interoperability between the Windows OS and non-Microsoft work group servers such as those operated by Sun Microsystems.[131]

The remedy imposed by the Commission for the refusal to supply interface information was to require Microsoft to divulge all necessary interface information to allow non-Microsoft workgroup server OS to achieve full interoperability with Windows PCs and Microsoft workgroup servers within 120 days. This was to enable rival vendors to compete on a level playing field in the work group server operating system market. Insofar as this information is copyright protected, the Commission indicated that it would require a compulsory copyright licence to be given to competitors in the workgroup server market, but Microsoft would be entitled to reasonable remuneration. The Commission also required Microsoft to update the disclosed information each time it brings to the market new versions of its relevant products. The Commission also indicated that it planned to appoint a Monitoring Trustee to oversee that Microsoft's interface disclosures are complete and accurate.[132]

The Commission's finding that Microsoft had abused its near monopoly in the Windows operating system by deliberately restricting interoperability between the Windows OS and Sun Microsystems work group server operating systems was based on an 'entirety of the circumstances' test which asserted that its decision must be based on the results of a comprehensive investigation and not be bound by an exhaustive checklist of exceptional circumstances. Yet in choosing to adopt a formula labelled 'the totality of the circumstances' to describe its test it may have underestimated the ways the factual nexus of the *Microsoft* case could be fitted into an 'exceptional circumstances' framework.

There was little doubt that Microsoft met the threshold test of a monopoly which was an indispensable input to a secondary product.[133] There was little doubt as well that Sun Microsystems was offering an innovative product for which there was substantial and demonstrable demand. The Sun work group server OS was not a 'me too' product of the Microsoft server and may in fact have preceded it in the market. The Commission could therefore legitimately impute to Microsoft the exclusionary motive of using its control over the PCOS market to evict an innovating competitor, i.e. conduct which amounted to an abuse of 'technological' leveraging of its dominance.[134] If a dominant firm with a monopoly of an IP protected product which is an indispensable input, chose to 'compete on the merits', it would have to continue to license the relevant interface information to its innovating competitors and compete directly in that secondary market on the basis of quality and price, etc. For a dominant firm with a de facto monopoly which is an indispensable input to other products to be allowed to use its power in any other way would have a 'chilling effect' on innovation by competitors in the dependent after market and limit technical development in that market, conduct which is characterised as an abuse by Article 82(b). Without access to interface information, competitors in the work group server market would be gradually deprived of their opportunity to develop servers with new or added functionality that Microsoft does not offer to the consumer.[135] This would place the facts of the Microsoft case squarely within the 'exceptional circumstances' test of Article 82(b) because the conduct of the dominant firm unjustifiably limits the technical development of the market.

In addition, it is important to see that embedded in the *Microsoft* facts is the further circumstance, not present in *Magill*, which could significantly change the calculus in, and thereby expand, the 'exceptional circumstances' test. Following the authority of the reasoning of *Commercial Solvents*, and subsequent ECJ decisions,[136] if a dominant firm has been engaged in a course of dealing with a contractor in an after market and suddenly chooses directly to compete with it by vertically integrating its operations and introducing its own product on that market, it has an obligation to continue to 'supply', i.e. license or inform its existing customers (now competitors) in the downstream market, unless it can offer a justification for that refusal. To fail to do so would mean that the dominant firm was not 'competing on the merits' in an already weakened market. By initially opting for an open system as a strategy to grow and achieve dominance, the owner of an IP protected industrial standard has created expectations and under EC competition law would have difficulties refusing to continue to supply downstream contractors under Articles 82(b) and possibly 82(c) for discriminating between its own subsidiary and competitors, particularly where there are no capacity restraints. In such a case, a dominant firm can be found to be acting abusively by refusing to continue to supply information or to license a firm with which it has been dealing where its motive is self-evidently one of using its dominance to evict that competitor from the market.

In other words, the 'exceptional circumstances' in which a compulsory copyright licence can be awarded by a competition authority would include refusals to supply interface code information or license existing innovative downstream operators with predatory intent. In such cases, the Commission would be relying on the authority of Article 82(b) but with a theory that, in the IT sector, Article 82(b) can be infringed when a company such as Microsoft with an industrial standard limits technical development by refusing to continue to share interface information and thereby prevents competitors on related markets from developing their interoperable systems. If Microsoft had opted for a closed system in the way, say, of Apple Mac initially, the circumstances may have been different because the company would have achieved its dominance on the basis of originally integrated products and it would normally have been entitled to continue to compete on that basis. To hold otherwise would be to make dominance itself unlawful. However, having built up its dominant position on the basis of interoperating with downstream applications makers, it seems arguable that Microsoft cannot freely resort to a policy of 'closing up' interoperability by withholding interface information once it establishes its Windows OS as an industrial standard. That type of commercial strategy would be viewed as predatory under Article 82 rather than 'competition on the merits' and even if the interface information were copyright protected, the Commission would be entitled to order a resumption of the supply of such information. The compulsory licence of the copyright protected information was essentially to ensure the resumption of that supply.

One point that makes its appearance at the margins of the Microsoft case is the argument suggested by Microsoft that Sun's right to reverse engineer through decompilation under article 6 of the EC Computer Program Directive made the Article 82(b) complaint unnecessary. Yet, in principle, Article 82(b) of the Treaty and article 6 of the Computer Program Directive are separate and independent laws even if they reach to certain types of overlapping conduct. The EC Computer Program Directive does not only promote interoperability in the form of a limited decompilation right in Article 6 and a reminder of the idea/expression dichotomy in Article 1; Recital 26 of the Directive also states: 'Whereas the provisions of this Directive are without prejudice to the application of the competition rules under Article 85 (now 81) and 86 (now 82) if a dominant supplier refuses to make information available which is necessary for interoperability as defined in this directive.'

In the *Microsoft* case, Sun seems to have given evidence to make it plain that the decompilation option was not adequate to meet the need for full interoperability in the circumstances, if for no other reason than that the reverse engineering process was so complex that it handicapped them in their efforts to provide software compatible with a new Windows version in sufficient time for the new version of Windows OS. The Commission's view, which is a legitimate interpretation of Article 82, is that Article 82 offers a source of authority which may exist alongside but applies independently of Article 6 of the Computer Programme Directive. It is worth noting, however, that if IP law were to take a form offering a more extensive guarantee of interoperability of interface information for software, then the effect would be that Article 82 would be called upon even more rarely to adjudicate cases of non-supply of interface information.

A second point raised by the *Microsoft* case is, why does competition law have the authority to override IPR protections in the EU? Why are firms like Microsoft not justified objectively in refusing to disclose or license interface information?

In the *Magill* case, the Court of Justice established that the mere ownership of an IPR as a property right would not as such offer either an immunity or a defence of justification for a refusal to license in secondary markets.[137] The Court first observed that '[w]ith regard to the issue of abuse, the arguments of the appellants and IPO wrongly suppose that where the conduct of an undertaking in a dominant position consists of the exercise of a right classified by national law as "copyright", such conduct can never be reviewed in relation to Article [82] of the Treaty'.[138]

It later added: 'There was no objective justification for the refusal of the TV companies to licence Magill, either in the activity of television broadcasting or in that of publishing television magazines.'[139]

A similar argument for unlimited intellectual property rights was put forward by the Microsoft Corporation in the antitrust case brought against its licensing practices in relation to Windows 98 and web browsers. The US government alleged that Microsoft had engaged in anticompetitive licensing restrictions. Microsoft argued that the licensing restrictions were legally justified because its was simply 'exercising the rights of valid copyrights'. 'If intellectual property rights have been lawfully acquired, their subsequent exercise cannot give rise to antitrust liability.' The Federal Circuit rejected the argument as bordering upon the frivolous. It quoted precedent to the effect that 'intellectual property rights do not confer a privilege to violate the antitrust laws'.[140]

In the European *Microsoft* case, the Microsoft Corporation produced a variation on the theme that their refusal to supply interface information to Sun was objectively justified owing to their property rights in the information requested. They argued firstly that they were justified in refusing to supply on the grounds that it would eliminate their incentives to innovate.[141] They also complained that providing the interface information to Sun 'would make it relatively easy for competitors to clone new features in the Windows family of operating systems'.[142]

The Commission refuted both contentions on the facts and went on to introduce a balancing test to justification. It started with the reminder that it was necessary to take into account the effect on the market if Microsoft's anticompetitive behaviour was allowed to remain unfettered[143] and there was a risk that Microsoft would succeed in eliminating all effective competition in the work group server operating systems market.[144] The Commission then concluded that on balance the possible negative impact of the order to supply on Microsoft's incentives to innovate was outweighed by its positive impact on the level of innovation of the whole industry (including Microsoft).[145]

The Commission could legitimately treat the justification test as a balancing exercise under Article 82(b) but it could equally legitimately raise the barriers to justification to a high level because of the serious anticompetitive effect of the conduct. As the Commission put it the refusal to supply would 'have the consequence of stifling innovation in the impacted market and of diminishing consumers' choices by locking them into a homogeneous Microsoft solution. As such it is particularly inconsistent with the provisions of Article 82(b) of the Treaty.'[146]

This was effectively an endorsement of a view of innovation which suggests that technical development in the IT industry is best promoted by a number of different firms innovating rather than one. It is consistent with the philosophy underlying the interoperability provisions of the Computer Software Directive.

Finally, it is useful to ask why the judges in the European Court of Justice consider it legitimate for EC competition law to restrict the conduct of the owners of IPRs where their market power equates to that of an industrial standard or a de facto monopoly which is an indispensable input to a secondary market. There are two main reasons for this hierarchical relationship between these two legal regimes in the EC. The first is that competition law has been given a central role in the EC treaty while intellectual property legislation in the EC has been based mainly on national law.[147] The second is the fact that competition laws are viewed as public law norms whereas the exercise of an intellectual property right is viewed as an exercise of a private property right.

The general view of competition law is that the exercise of any property right, whether one related to intellectual property or tangible property, must be circumscribed to allow the public interest in effective competition on markets to be maintained. Modern competition policy, having arisen as a reaction to the excesses of use of the freedom of contract by large organisations systematically creating monopolies and cartels in unregulated markets, has been designed to impose public law limits on the freedom of contract and the autonomy of private property owners in order to maintain effective competition on, and access to, markets.[148]

Competition law offers only one example of the responsibilities which public law places on private ownership. In general private property is dependent for its existence upon legal institutions and may be seen as a bundle of legally created responsibilities as well as rights.[149] Intellectual property is also a legally created mix of rights and responsibilities with its rights to exploitation dependent upon legal institutions. An owner of tangible private property cannot do entirely as she wills with it where the exercise can cause harm to others. The owner of a Ferrari sports car, despite her property right and the purpose for which she acquired it, cannot lawfully drive it above 20 miles an hour on a road in front of a school entrance if that is the speed limit for that stretch of road.

In the case of intellectual property rights, the claim of intellectual property owners to an untrammelled autonomy to exploit their property is more specifically at odds with the laws that create them. Patents and copyright, with their balance of time limited rights, exceptions and array of responsibilities inter alia to disclose information, are more akin to carefully defined leaseholds or licences as opposed to absolute property rights. IPRs have been explicitly created for utilitarian purposes by legislators in the form of limited exclusive rights and to argue otherwise is to distort the foundations for their creation.[150] In Europe, most if not all patent laws view patents as conferring temporary market exclusivity in return for the commercial investment in the R&D leading to the invention and as making publicly available the knowledge on which it is based. It is true that some Continental systems of copyright protection, and indeed Article 6*bis* of the Berne Convention, stress the moral rights to copyright and this on occasion has been portrayed as a natural right but this classification does not remove copyright from the 'rights/responsibilities' balance. In any case, moral rights are more concerned with protecting the author's rights to identification as the originator of the work[151] and the right to object to derogatory treatment of the work,[152] rather than making a bid for IPRs to be viewed as absolute rights when they enter the economic arena.

IPRs are more appropriately viewed as a form of 'licence' or leasehold conferred by the state to innovators for a limited period to pursue the ends dictated by the legislation that give them their protected status. This licence has certain checks and balances within it but those exercising the licence are still bound by regulatory legislation such as environmental laws, health and safety laws, product liability and drug safety laws that restrict the free exercise of intellectual property rights in the public interest.[153] It is true that there is an important public interest in the incentive effects of IPRs but this must be reconciled with, and cannot automatically trump, these other public interest concerns. The inherent weakness of the property rights theoreticians in this area of law is that private property is always subject to public law norms. Moreover, their analysis offers little help in the essential task of striking an appropriate balance between the protection of limited exclusive rights to pioneer innovators and the rights of access of information and ideas of follow-on innovators,[154] particularly where that task is performed by competition policy.

One implication of this analysis is that when the point is reached that IPR laws are comprehensively EC-wide in their grant, EC competition law may well remain a default 'regulator' of the exercise of IPRs.

4. Tie-ins (Article 82(d))

Under Article 82(d) 'tie-ins' are defined as 'making the conclusion of contracts subject to acceptance by the other parties of supplementary obligations which, by their nature or according to commercial usage, have no connection with the subject of such contracts'.[155] The prohibited abuse of tying overlaps with the commercial practice of bundling two products together to create a commercial package to offer the consumer. Much bundling is perfectly lawful. It is only when the bundling takes on the characteristics of tying as defined in Article 82(d) that it becomes unlawful.

From the perspective of the IPR owner, bundling products together is simply one method of exploiting the IPR. However, if the legal monopoly of the IPR owner coincides with market power amounting to dominance, tie-ins create the risk that an IPR owner may use them either to force customers to choose products they would rather not have or to exclude competitors and eventually foreclose competition in a second related market as the tie creates a competitive advantage for the IPR owner, compelling competitors to have access to both markets if they are to compete on equal terms with the IPR owner.

Nevertheless, in many cases, bundling may have a clear commercial logic, especially in high technology industries, where the bundling often introduces a 'new generation' of products. For example, in the mobile phone industry – first generation: mobile phones; second generation: mobile phones with camera; third generation: phones with video link and music. Moreover, one of the main reasons for Microsoft's tying of its Windows Media Player with its Windows platform was to maintain a strong position in the market for downloading content such as music.[156] By bundling Windows and its Media Player, Microsoft wanted to ensure that its Media Player would be installed on more PCs than any other media player and thus persuade programme makers for multimedia players to write for Microsoft's Media Player.[157] Nevertheless as a firm in a dominant position in the PC operating systems market, Microsoft's conduct was subject to the test of Article 82(d), whether its conduct had the object or effect of leading to foreclosure of the media player market.

The case law of Article 82(d) suggests that five constituent elements must be established before the bundling conduct can be shown to be abusive tying:[158]

  (i) Is there a 'tied' product separate from the 'tying' product?
 (ii) Is the seller of the tying product dominant?
(iii) Is there coercion by the dominant firm?
 (iv) Is there an effect on competition in the tied product?
  (v) Is there is no proportionate and objective justification for the tying?

4.1 Separate tied product The first requirement is to show that there were two separate products, a tied and a tying product at the time the products were sold. The Commission's practice of narrow market definition tends to facilitate such a finding. The main criterion of the Commission in analysing whether two products are separate or integrated is user or consumer demand. For example, in *Napier Brown* v. *British Sugar*, the Commission found that the delivery of British Sugar's sugar was a separate distinct market from the actual sugar market.[159] In *Hilti* v. *Commission*,[160] Hilti was a company producing nail guns, cartridge strips, and nails and selling them in a package as a power activated fastening system (PAFS). Hilti had a patent both for the gun and cartridges strips, but not for the nails. Along with Hilti, there were some small independent manufacturers producing nails compatible with Hilti's gun cartridges. Hilti applied a number of practices to make sure that its customers, who bought the cartridges, also bought its nails rather than the nails from the independent manufacturers. One such practice was making the sale of the patented cartridges dependent on purchase of a specified number of nails. Eurofix and Bauco, two independent manufacturers, complained to the Commission. The Commission found firstly that there were three separate markets, one for the nail guns, one for the cartridge strips and one market for the nails rather than, as Hilti had argued, one single market for the power activated fastening system.[161] One important basis for the finding of three separate product markets was the existence of independent nail manufacturers.[162] The CFI stated that 'in the absence of general and binding standards or rules, any independent producer is quite free, as far as Community competition law is concerned, to manufacture consumables intended for use in equipment manufactured by others, unless in doing so it infringes a patent or some other industrial or intellectual property right'. In *Telemarketing*,[163] the independent TV marketing firm had established a separate product from the TV broadcasting company. In the *Microsoft* case, there was a separate market for media players before Microsoft decided to come out with its own media player and sell it as an integrated product with Windows. If a complex product is presented as 'integrated' from the start, before the owner of the combined product becomes dominant, it will be more difficult for independents later to claim that the components are separate products.

However, both the Commission and the ECJ have not proved willing to treat claims of product 'integration' too differently from contractual bundling. In *IBM*,[164] the Commission challenged the fact that IBM had integrated a memory device into its Central Processing Unit. The case was settled when IBM promised to deliver a version of its CPU without the memory device or with the minimum capacity required for testing.[165]

4.2 Establishment of dominance The second requirement in the case of an alleged tying abuse is to establish that the seller is dominant in the tying market; otherwise article 82(d) will not be applicable. Any analysis of dominance is dependent upon a prior finding of relevant market and, as we have seen, the Commission is not averse to defining markets narrowly and separating components of a system of products into separate products. If an undertaking selling a product in a system can be shown to hold a dominant position, its practice of bundling that product together with another product in a dependent market can be subject to Article 82(d). Thus in *Hilti*, when the PAFS system was deconstructed into three products, and the Hilti firm was found to be dominant in the gun cartridge market. In *Télémarketing*,[166] a Belgian TV broadcasting company entered into the related market of television marketing by bundling its services and displaying only its new subsidiary's telephone number in its TV advertising. It simultaneously terminated its agreement with an independent contractor Télémarketing and withheld advertising time from its new competitor. The TV company was held dominant in the TV market for its programmes by virtue of its monopoly at the time.

In *Microsoft*,[167] Microsoft was investigated by the Commission for having bundled its Media Player into Windows, using its 'near monopoly' (95 per cent market share of the desktop operating system market) to harm its competitors in the market for audiovisual players, such as RealNetworks' RealPlayer and Apple Computer QuickTime.[168] Microsoft was found to be dominant on the operating system market due to its high market share amounting to a de facto standard operating system product for client PCs.[169] This high market share was reinforced by the network effects barriers to entry enjoyed by Microsoft. The Commission stated that '[i]n industries exhibiting strong network effects, consumer demand depends critically on expectations about future purchases. If consumers expect a firm with a strong reputation in the current (product) generation to succeed in the next generation, this will tend to be self-fulfilling as the consumers direct their purchases to the product that they believe will yield the greatest network gains. Even customers who do not immediately plan to migrate their client PCs to newer versions of Windows will factor in their anticipated platform in their current purchase decisions concerning complementary . . . software.'[170]

4.3 Coercion   The third requirement, in common with US cases, is to establish coercion by the dominant firm. The coercion may be contractual as in *Hilti* or *Tetra Pak* or it may be financial by prohibitive discounts or by removing certain benefits, again as in *Hilti* where Hilti refused to honour guarantees if customers had used a third party nail in their guns. The Commission argued that Hilti's policies 'leave the consumer with no choice over the source of his nails and as such abusively exploit him'.[171] Alternatively, it may consist of technical bundling. Thus, in *Microsoft*, Microsoft refused to offer Windows and its Windows Media Player separately. As a result, OEMs and consumers were compelled to take the Windows Media Player.[172] The licence for Windows covered Windows Media Player and the software was pre-installed with Windows.[173]

4.4 Anticompetitive effects   Thus far, there has been little clear indication from the Courts on the extent to which it is necessary to show that the tie has an anticompetitive effect. In *Napier Brown* v. *British Sugar*, the Commission did not even assess whether the tying had foreclosed or had any anticompetitive effect upon the transport market. The fact that British Sugar had 'reserved for itself the separate activity of delivering sugar' was evidence enough to establish the requirement of anticompetitive effect.[174] A similar analysis was applied in *Télémarketing*,[175] the ECJ stating only that Télémarketing reserved to itself 'an ancillary activity which might be carried out by another undertaking as part of its activities on a neighbouring but separate market, with the possibility of eliminating all competition from such undertaking'.[176] In *Hilti*, the Commission considered the actual tying as abusive exploitation because it prevented customers from having a choice of the source of nails.[177] It added, 'these policies all have the object or effect of excluding independent nail makers who may threaten the dominant position Hilti holds'. On the strength of these cases, it was reasonable to conclude that factual evidence of foreclosure is not needed as a constituent element of tying under Article 82(d). It was enough to show tying conduct with a possibility of foreclosure. In *Microsoft* however, the Commission suggested that it would be more concerned with analysing the factual basis for likely effects in tying cases. It found that Microsoft's conduct potentially risked foreclosure in the future,[178] and pointed to the tendency of tipping in a market with network effects.

4.5 Objective justification   If the Commission meets the first four requirements, the burden of proof of objective justification for the tying shifts to the defendant. For example, in *Hilti*, the dominant company argued that safety and quality reasons objectively justified its requirement that customers bought Hilti nails rather than nails from other manufacturers because their nails were incompatible with Hilti's nail gun.[179] The CFI rejected the defence because it found that Hilti's conduct was not consistent with its assertion. If Hilti had really had concerns about Hilti compatible nails produced by independent manufacturers it would have taken steps to prevent their sale by warning users or notifying the appropriate UK authorities to stop the sale of dangerous products. The CFI found Hilti's conduct was that of a company merely acting to protect its commercial position.[180] Tetra Pak's justification for its tying of carton filling machines to sales of cartons was that there was a natural link between the cartons and the filling machines and therefore the tie was based on commercial usage.[181] Both the CFI and ECJ rejected this argument stating that other companies on the market for non-aseptic cartons did not produce the machinery, hence the 'commercial usage' justification was not proven.[182] It is worth noting that these companies had only a 12 per cent market share.[183] The Court added: 'Moreover and in any event, even if such a usage were shown to exist, it would not be sufficient to justify recourse to a system of tied sales by an undertaking in a dominant position. Even a usage which is acceptable in a normal situation, on a competitive market, cannot be accepted in the case of a market where competition is already restricted.'[184]

In *Microsoft*,[185] the dominant company's attempt to justify its tying was based on the concept that the two products were technically integrated and that taking the Media Player out of Windows would weaken the program or 'break' it. This is very similar to the argument Microsoft made in the US courts in relation to its integration of Internet Explorer into Windows.[186] The Commission rejected the integration argument, favouring a policy of hindering a full foreclosure of the media player market, as the Commission found evidence that the market had already started tipping to the advantage of Microsoft's Windows Media Player.[187] One argument that could be accepted as an objective justification is that the tie is being used as an alternative to royalties or fees simply to 'meter' the application of a product or process, in which case it is legitimate competition.[188]

III. Article 81 and agreements between firms

A. Article 81 generally

1. Introduction

Article 81 prohibits '. . . agreements, decisions and concerted practices between undertakings' which have the *object or effect* of preventing, restricting or distorting competition. Such agreements are prohibited in particular where they (a) directly or indirectly fix purchase or selling prices or any other trading conditions; (b) limit or control production, markets, technical development, or investment; (c) share markets or sources of supply; (d) involve discriminatory dealing; or (e) concern tie-ins. In the intellectual property rights context, for example, Article 81(1) has been held to apply widely to individual licensing agreements; to R&D joint ventures; to concerted practices involving licensing agreements;[189] to assignments of IPRs to third parties;[190] to trade mark delimitation agreements;[191] and to cross-licensing agreements arising out of patent settlements[192] and patent or technology pools.[193] Moreover, in principle Article 81(1) applies to vertical agreements, i.e. agreements between non-competitors as well as to horizontal agreements, i.e. agreements between competitors.[194] It is worth noting that the Court has repeatedly stated that an IPR licensing agreement, as such, is not a 'restriction on competition',[195] but may fall within the scope of Article 81(1) whenever it is 'the subject, the means or the consequence of',[196] or 'serves to give effect to',[197] a commercial practice which has as its object or exercise the prevention, restriction or distortion of competition in the common market.

Under Article 81(1), an agreement is only prohibited if it meets all of the provision's three main conditions. The first condition in Article 81(1) is that there must be evidence of *agreement or other form of collaboration between two or more 'undertakings'*. Insofar as the conduct of an intellectual property right holder consists of unilateral enforcement of such a right under national law, it will not be caught by Article 81(3) though it might be regulated by Article 82.

The concept of an 'undertaking' in Article 81(1) though not defined in the Treaty has been held to apply widely to individuals, partnerships, joint ventures, and companies. The Court of Justice has defined it as 'any entity' engaged on a commercial activity.[198] Public authorities are caught if they are engaged on a commercial or economic activity but are excepted if they are acting as a public authority.[199]

However, an undertaking has also been defined as being a wider 'economic unit' consisting of a group of companies. Under EC competition law, the group rather than the individual company may be the 'undertaking'. The Court of Justice has stated that the concept of undertaking is not identical with the question of legal personality for the purposes of company law. The corporate veil can be lifted to show the underlying economic and commercial reality.[200] If a licensing agreement is made between two companies within the same corporate group it may fall outside Article 81(1) because, despite the corporate form, the agreement is viewed as an internal allocation of functions between members of the same economic unit, not one between separate undertakings.[201] If, however, the reality is that a subsidiary has a measure of independence in determining its commercial policy, then the subsidiary will be viewed as a separate undertaking for the purposes of Article 81(1).[202] The effect of this jurisdictional condition is to offer to companies the option of avoiding the regulatory effects of Article 81 by acquiring the licensor, or vertically integrating, rather than obtaining a licensing agreement.[203] This may, however, place them within the scope of Article 82.

The requirement of collaboration between two or more independent undertakings has also meant that certain categories of dependent relationships are not caught by Article 81(1). For example, some types of commercial agents and certain types of manufacturing–subcontractor relationships have been excepted from Article 81(1) by Commission Notice.[204]

The second major jurisdictional condition of Article 81(1) is that it applies only to agreements, decisions, and concerted practices which have an 'appreciable' quantitative effect on interstate trade. This condition is essentially a jurisdictional test for the application of the system of EC competition law in two important respects. It first establishes a territorial point: whether an agreement made inside or outside the EC is caught by EC competition law by virtue of its effects. Secondly, it defines the jurisdictional borderline between EC competition law and the domestic competition law of the Member States.

The third test is that the agreement has the object or effect of preventing, restricting or distorting competition. If a licence agreement is made between independent undertakings and has an appreciable effect on interstate trade, it is still necessary to show that it has as its object or effect the prevention, restriction or distortion of competition before it is contrary to Article 81(1). This test is jurisdictional in the sense that it constitutes a precondition to the application of Article 81(1). Yet it also involves a preliminary substantive assessment of the pro- or anticompetitive nature of the licensing agreement. On its face, the concept of a restriction of competition could have been interpreted as *on balance* restrictive of competition. However, in part because of the 'rule of reason' test in Article 81(3) and in part because of a concern with market integration, the Commission and to a lesser extent the Court tended historically to interpret the concept of restriction of competition in Article 81(1) strictly, resulting in the equation of certain contractual restraints such as exclusive territoriality with restrictions of competition without applying a balancing test.

At an early stage in the case of *Consten Grundig* v. *Commission*,[205] the Court was concerned with territorial exclusivity and suggested a concept of restriction of competition that resulted in a contractual restraint on the freedom of action of the parties in the market being equated to a restriction of competition without any reference to the actual process of competition in the market or the effects of the agreement on that process.[206] In other words, if a contractual restraint restricted the rivalry between licensor and licensee or between one of them and a third party that contractual restraint amounted to a restriction of competition under Article 81(1) of contractors and third parties associated with the contract.

The Court of Justice, however, always maintained that the concept of restriction of competition, whether under the object test or the effects test,[207] must be accompanied by a second stage test of 'appreciability' particularly in the case of vertical agreements.[208] The appreciability test referred in part to quantitative appreciability which in more recent years has taken the form of a de minimis test explained in the Commission Notice on Agreements of Minor Importance. The concept of 'qualitative appreciability' was developed in a series of cases by the ECJ which created specific exceptions to its wide and otherwise uneconomic definition of restriction of competition. These cases have been somewhat loosely grouped together as 'the rule of reason' cases under Article 81(1).[209] On closer inspection, the case law of appreciability could be interpreted more accurately as subscribing to a doctrine concept of 'ancillary restraints'.[210] In fact, however, during much of the period since *Grundig*, as a result of the Court and Commission's strict interpretation of restriction of competition in Article 81(1), the parties to exclusive commercial agreements have made use of the process of exemption – either individual exemption or, when available, block exemption.

2. Exemption under Article 81(3)

If an agreement is caught by Article 81(1), it can nevertheless be saved from non-enforceability by being exempted under Article 81(3) if it meets its four conditions. Article 81(3) formally recognises the pro-competitive value of innovative agreements by stipulating that an agreement must contribute 'to improving production and distribution of goods and promoting technical progress' as a necessary condition of exemption. However, it goes on to require three other conditions to be met. First, the agreement must allow consumers a fair share of the resulting benefit. Secondly, the agreement must not contain restrictions on competition which are not 'indispensable to the attainment' of the above objective. Thirdly, the agreement must not afford the parties to it 'the possibility of eliminating competition in respect of a substantial part of the products in question'.

Under Article 81(3) therefore the Commission has the task of balancing the innovative benefits of an agreement against any risks that it might deny access to a particular market to existing competitors and new entrants. Exemption can be obtained in two possible ways: (a) qualification under one of the group or block exemptions issued by the Commission, or (b) convincing a national court or competition authority that the agreement is exemptible by applying the block exemption regulation by analogy with the help of the relevant guidelines accompanying the regulation. Block exemptions automatically exempt certain categories of agreements from the prohibition of Article 81(1). If an agreement fits within the scope of the block exemption, it is deemed to have met the conditions stipulated in Article 81(3) unlike individual exemptions which can require an elaborate examination of the pro-competitive and anticompetitive effects of an agreement before a finding that an agreement is exempted or exemptible. Block exemptions may be useful to help lawyers, courts and competition authorities to apply the conditions of Article 81(3) under the new modernisation regulation, although their usefulness has changed under the modernisation reforms.[211]

Block exemption regulations   With the modernisation of competition policy in 2004, the European Commission lost its previous monopoly of interpretation of Article 81(3) and now shares that competence with national competition authorities and national courts to determine how Article 81 as a whole applies to any one case. The previous 'monopoly' was accompanied by two features, the requirement for parties to pre-notify agreements caught by Article 81(1) to the Commission and the procedure for individual exemption by the Commission. Both are now abolished. Yet even after the modernisation process of 2004, the Commission retains its competence to design block exemption regulations for various categories of agreements. However, as part of the modernisation process, the Commission has begun to take a new and more economic approach to the assessment of agreements under Article 81(3) and has changed the nature of the block exemptions. It has moved away from a legalistic and form-based approach to a more economic and effects-based approach to the regulation of agreements, taking into greater account the economic analysis of possible costs and benefits, or 'efficiencies', of certain restrictions and recognising the different economic effects of vertical and horizontal agreements respectively. This could be seen in the main characteristics of the Commission's reforms of vertical distribution agreements, such as exclusive and selective distribution and franchising (the Vertical Agreements Block Exemption Regulation (BER) (EC 2790/1999)) and horizontal agreements, such as the Research and Development BER (EC 2659/2000) and Specialisation Agreements BER (EC 2658/2000). These have been accompanied by guidelines which help parties to understand both the BERs and the ground-rules for the application of Article 81(3) outside the safe haven of the block exemptions themselves. There is also a revised Notice on Agreements of Minor Importance which do not appreciably restrict competition under Article 81(1), the so called 'De Minimis Notice'.[212] Furthermore, the Commission has rewritten its procedure in its Regulation 1/2003 on the implementation of the rules of competition laid down in Articles 81 and 82.[213] Finally, even if an agreement is exempted under Article 81, whether by individual exemption or block exemption, the conduct of the parties to the agreement is still subject to the parallel prohibitions in Article 82.[214]

The parties to IP licensing agreements continue to enjoy the possibility of shaping an agreement to fit within a block exemption regulation, in particular the new Technology Transfer Block Exemption Regulation 240/96 (TTBER). However, with market share limits inserted into block exemptions, they must also prepare for the possibility of their agreement losing the benefits of a block exemption should their product's market share exceed the limits set by the block exemption.

If an agreement falls outside the safe harbour of a block exemption it is no longer presumed to be legally invalid under Article 81(2). Nor is it presumed to be legally valid. Its legal status can only be determined by an assessment of its contents in the light of a two-step test: applying the criteria of the scope of Article 81(1) and applying the balancing test in Article 81(3). This process requires a form of self-assessment by legal advisors and parties. Only if they have engaged in this process of 'self certification', will the parties be in a position to face any challenges to the lawfulness or enforceability of an agreement.

If the prohibition in Article 81(1) applies to an agreement, even if only because it contains a 'hard core restriction' and it cannot be exempted, the agreement as a whole will be automatically void and unenforceable under Article 81(2) in national courts as well as the Community courts. In the event, either party to the agreement can treat it as no longer binding upon them.[215] Article 81(2) can operate as a 'Euro-defence' to any action in a Member State court to enforce an agreement.

IV. IP licensing and competition law

A. Introduction and background

One of the most important areas of regulation of IP licensing agreements is the Commission's block exemption regulation for technology transfers, TTBER, which has recently been revised as part of the modernisation process. The revision offered the Commission an opportunity to re-evaluate its policy towards IP licensing agreements as part of a wider EC industrial policy as well as part of the modernisation process. The industrial policy dimension requires a careful balance of the innovative benefits of IP licensing with its potential risks to competition.

The test of an effective regulatory framework is to strike an appropriate balance between allowing the process of technology licensing room to 'breathe', so that the parties can shape their own agreements according to their needs, and protecting the public interest in workably competitive markets by minimising the risks of market sharing, market foreclosure and market isolation. If the limits created by the regulation are too tight, the incentives to the parties to enter into agreements will be significantly reduced and the benefits obtained from the process of technology transfer will be reduced because firms will license to territories outside the EU and export in instead of locating manufacturing establishments in European countries. Competition policy has a chilling effect on investment in technology transfer. Of course, if the restrictions are too loose, there will be greater risks of anticompetitive practices. In view of the many economic benefits of the process, and the economic costs of overly restrictive regulation, however, the onus should lie upon the regulators to carefully calibrate their restrictions.

Technology transfer, essentially the process of technological intellectual property licensing, is on balance a highly pro-competitive activity. One effect of the process is to raise the level of technology throughout the EU by creating incentives for the introduction and diffusion of means or inclination to exploit the product in the new territories. Because a licensing agreement invariably requires some degree of manufacture as well as sale, it results in a technological lift to the licensee that would not occur if the licensor merely manufactured elsewhere and exported the finished product into the EU for distribution. Technology licensing agreements also introduce new products to existing markets, adding to competition and in some cases actually creating new markets. By adding to competition and innovation, as empirical studies have shown, IP licensing also enhances competitiveness in world trade.

In the course of drafting the IP licensing agreement, the parties must inevitably place certain contractual restrictions upon each other to achieve the object of the agreement. Many licensees will be reluctant to undertake the risks of manufacture and sale of a new product without the protection of an exclusive licence that limits competition from the licensor and other licensees within the licensed territory. Most licensors will not give an exclusive licence without the quid pro quo of a 'minimum royalties' clause. In addition they will not license their IP without an array of clauses designed to protect the integrity and value of their IP once it is licensed to the licensee. They will, for example, insist on certain obligations of confidentiality in respect of know-how, limits on sublicensing, quality controls on materials used, and limits on the use of the licensed IP once the licensing agreement has expired. They may also insist on obligations by the licensee to grant back licences for improvements and not to exploit technologies that compete with the licensor as well as an obligation not to challenge the validity of the licensed IPR. Many of these may be viewed as commercially indispensable to induce licensors to license their technology in the first place. Many of these contractual restrictions do not amount to restrictions on competition but some may take a form that raises competition concerns.

On occasion, contractual restrictions can be used as a device to create competitive restraints. Some royalty arrangements can help to underpin a price-fixing scheme. In some technology transfer agreements the exclusive territorial protection needed by licensees or output restrictions can, on occasion, be used by clever draftsmen as a cover for market sharing agreements. In a European perspective, they can also reinforce the isolation of national markets from the single market by excessive territorial protection. Moreover, some IP licensing agreements have the potential to create conditions of dominant market power in the licensed market and foreclose competitors from entering that market. However, licensing agreements rarely have this result, particularly when they are agreements between non-competitors like an agreement between an inventor/licensor and a manufacturer/licensee. Nevertheless, IP licensing agreements have been the subject of detailed competition block exemption regulations since the early 1980s.

B. The evolution of the regulatory framework for IP licensing in the EC

The first EC block exemption regulation regime for IP licensing was the Patent Licensing Regulation in 1984 which was followed by the Know-how Licensing Regulation in 1989. These were replaced in 1996 by a single TTBER applying both to pure or mixed patent licensing and know-how agreements. The scope of the new unified block exemption was slightly wider because it defined certain other IPRs like utility models, semi-conductor topographies and plant breeder certificates to be 'patents' for the purpose of the Regulation. If, however, a licensing agreement included other IPRs, such as trademarks and copyright protection, as part of the package, the Regulation only allowed the licensing agreement to be exempted if such IPRs were 'ancillary' to the main purpose of the agreement which had to be that of licensing patents and/or know-how.[216]

The legal framework for technology transfer created by TTBER 1996 was form-based and legalistic in the sense that certain clauses were either exemptible or non-exemptible depending almost entirely on their form. To qualify for exemption the parties were required to draft an agreement which was consistent with the Commission's threefold categorisation of numerous restraints in licensing agreements: its 'white' list of twenty-six clauses, the clearly exemptible clauses under the block exemption,[217] and its 'blacklist' of seven clauses which consisted of clearly non-exemptible clauses. If a clause was blacklisted, the *agreement* as a whole was non-exemptible and unenforceable. There was no severance policy for blacklisted clauses. Instead, there was a third category of 'grey' clauses (all those which are not whitelisted or blacklisted). These clauses could be approved or non-opposed under a 'quick look' procedure subject to a deadline of four months for the Commission.

This Commission's threefold characterisation encompassed a wide variety of typical clauses in licensing agreements: territorial restraints, customer allocation, field of use, output restrictions, price restrictions, non-compete obligations, tying grant-backs and no-challenge clauses. It somewhat controversially subjected the contractual restrictions on territorial restriction to micro regulation more for political concerns to promote market integration than for conventional competition reasons.

The Commission claimed in the TTBER 1996 that it recognised that the EU's ability to draw abreast of its competitors in the rest of the world depended upon the capacity of European industry to devise new technologies and to spread them throughout the member states of the Community. It acknowledged that its licensing policy as incorporated in TTBER was designed to play a pivotal role in the development of innovation within the EU economy and in contributing to the competitiveness of businesses operating in the Community (para. 9). It also asserted in Recital 3 that it wished to 'encourage the dissemination of technical knowledge in the Community and to promote the manufacture of technically more sophisticated products'.

Yet, although the 1996 regulation allowed industry to transfer the more conventional technology, on the whole, sufficiently freely and with legal certainty within the EU, it also created a regulatory structure that did not display a light touch. Its draftsmen never tackled the task of differentiating between genuinely vertical and horizontal agreements. Their concern with the political–economic problems of maintaining intra-brand competition and integration of the Member States into a single market led them to give less than optimum incentives to technology licensing agreements from a purely economic competition point of view. In particular, their strict rules for territorial exclusivity, even where the economic costs and benefits, or 'efficiencies', suggested little competition risk, meant that the needed incentives for second and subsequent waves of licensees could be greatly reduced. The Commission itself has openly acknowledged that its territorial restrictions have been imposed 'because of the added market integration objective which EC competition policy has'.[218]

On the other hand, TTBER 1996 facilitated licensing by not setting market share limits to the safe harbour of the block exemption. Instead, it left high market share agreements to be regulated by Article 82 or the possibilities of a 'withdrawal procedure' whereby the benefits of the block exemption could be formally withdrawn by the Commission or the competition authority of a Member State in carefully defined cases. This approach was adopted in the final draft of the Regulation after a strong campaign by industry throughout Europe was waged against a Commission proposal to introduce market share limits to the 1996 block exemption.

By 2001, the Commission had decided that there was a clear need to change its policy towards technology transfer agreements even before Regulation 240/96 was due to expire in April 2006. This was caused partly by the change in the Commission approach to the regulation of vertical agreements more generally under Article 81. It had begun to move away from a legalistic and form-based approach to a more economic and effects-based approach to the regulation of other types of agreements, taking into greater account the economic analysis of possible costs and benefits, or 'efficiencies', of certain restrictions and recognising the different economic effects of vertical and horizontal agreements respectively. This could be seen in the main characteristics of the Commission's reforms of vertical distribution agreements, such as exclusive and selective distribution and franchising (the vertical agreements block exemption (EC 2790/1999)) and horizontal agreements, such as research and development (EC 2659/2000) and specialisation agreements (EC 2658/2000). The new vertical agreements block exemption introduced a more flexible regulatory approach by widening its scope to include a variety of categories of agreement. It also abandoned white and grey lists of clauses, retaining only an outright prohibition upon a limited number of 'hard core' restrictions. This easing of the regulatory straitjacket allowed the parties greater freedom to draft their agreements but the benefits of the safe haven offered by the block exemption were restricted by a market shares limit of 30 per cent built into the block exemption as part of a more economic approach to regulation.

The new regulatory framework placed a premium upon self-certification by the parties in cases where their market shares exceeded the limits. To offer assistance in this endeavour, the Regulation was supplemented by guidelines.

At a more technical level, the reform of the Commission resulting in the replacement of Regulation 17 by the new Regulation 1/2003 gave the courts and competition authorities of the Member States the power to apply Article 81(3) directly. This not only ended the need for precautionary notification of agreements; the Commission decided that it also meant that the opposition procedure or quick look facility for grey clauses would have to be abandoned and clauses would 'either be covered by the block exemption or treated as hardcore'.[219]

A second important factor was the publication of the Commission's Evaluation Report on the Technology Transfer Regulation[220] which evoked a response from Member States and the licensing community that strongly favoured reform. The Report stressed that the 1996 Regulation had a number of shortcomings.

First, because of its legal formalism and narrow definitions of scope, the Regulation was described as creating a 'legal straitjacket' in the sense that companies often had to redraft their commercial agreements to fit within its confines. Secondly, Regulation 240/96 was too narrow in scope, covering only a limited number of exclusive licensing arrangements, mainly to pure and mixed patent and know-how licences. Other criticisms related to the lack of economic realism of the regulatory framework. The Regulation was too restrictive in the sense that the blacklist covered items that were not always anticompetitive and could have efficiency enhancing effects. On occasion, restrictions with different legal form but with similar economic effects on markets were given different treatment.[221] Finally, some exempted clauses had the potential for economic harm.

These criticisms were taken on board by the Commission in its decision to reform the regulatory framework for technology transfer. In choosing the form of a new technology transfer regulation, the Commission used the Vertical Agreements Block Exemption regulation as a role model and gave priority to a harmonising TTBER with its other block exemption regulations as part of its preparation for competition policy in the post-modern world of twenty-five Member States.

C. The main features of the new Technology Transfer Regulation and Guidelines

The European Commission has proclaimed that the new TTBER's assessment of IP licensing agreements takes 'due account of the dynamic aspects of technology licensing ... in particular' and that it makes 'no presumption that intellectual property rights and licence agreements as such give rise to competition concerns'.[222]

Within the safe haven itself, the new BER offers many advantages: It applies to a wider array of IPRs; it offers greater flexibility and longer periods of protection. It also reduces the list of non-exemptible 'hard core restraints' which, if included in a licensing agreement, make it void in its entirety. The shorter blacklist, particularly for vertical licensing agreements, leaves a wider scope for exemptible clauses. There is also a short list of excluded restrictions which are unenforceable under the TTBER but which can be severed from a licensing agreement without affecting its overall enforceability within the BER.

One problem with the introduction of market shares is that they have made the application of the 'safe haven' unpredictable ex ante, i.e. at the time when an IP licensing agreement is signed. The market shares of IP protected products, often new and often based on extensive R&D, tend to be volatile. The Commission is willing to accept that the designation of the parties as competitors or non-competitors can be settled at the time the agreement is made and in the absence of the effects of the licence itself. Thus if the parties start off as non-competitors, the agreement remains an agreement between non-competitors, even if they later become competitors during the course of the agreement.[223]

However, the Commission has been unwilling to offer any such ex ante assurance in respect of market shares. If the market share increases during the course of the agreement beyond the market share limits, the agreement will no longer benefit from the block exemption. At that point, the agreement is not invalid but it no longer enjoys the benefit of the 'safe haven'. The Commission offers the reassurance that above the market share thresholds, there is no presumption of illegality.[224]

The procedure of the Commission has been reformed by Regulation 1/2003 so that there is no longer a need to submit a precautionary notification to the Commission to ensure provisional validity to a licensing agreement. Its validity stands or falls depending on its contents at the time it is challenged. Thus, if an agreement is caught by Article 81(1) and falls outside the block exemption, it is no longer automatically void under Article 81(2). Its legal status can be analysed by analogy with the contents of the Regulation and Guidelines to determine whether it is exemptible under Article 81(3).

The Commission envisages that the Guidelines taken together with the list of hard core restrictions and conditions, as well as the Regulation and Guidelines by analogy, can be used as a form of 'self assessment' by the parties to determine whether or not their licensing agreements are exemptible if they fall outside the scope of the safe harbour.

The Commission seems to be encouraged by the fact that this method is similar to that in use in the USA under the IP Licensing Guidelines of the FTC and the Antitrust Division of the Justice Department. However, the introduction of this new method of self-certification within the EC calls for a rather radical change in legal practice in a sensitive area of commercial life. The move ultimately to self-certification may be inevitable in a decentralised and modernised world of competition policy but it introduces an abrupt change in European legal practice in this field.

The new regulatory framework can perhaps best be described under five main heads: (1) the new wider scope and duration for IP licensing; (2) the new distinction between 'horizontal' and 'vertical' licensing agreements; (3) the new market shares limits; (4) the prohibited restrictions; and (5) the new way of assessing licensing agreements and restrictions.

1. The scope and duration of the Regulation

The Regulation extends to a wide range of IPR licensing agreements and assignments: pure and mixed patent[225] and know-how agreements have been expanded to include software copyright licensing agreements and design rights licensing agreements. All these IPRs are viewed as the 'core' technology to be licensed.[226]

The Regulation also allows a wider variety of IPRs to be included in the licensing[227] package along with the core 'technology' as long as they are 'ancillary' provisions.[228] To meet the test of 'ancillarity', they must (i) not constitute the primary object of the agreement and (ii) be directly related to the manufacture or provision of the contract products. This formula is clearer than its predecessor. The test is whether the other IPR is included essentially to enable the licensee to better exploit the core licensed technology. If it appears that licensing the 'ancillary' IPR, say a trademark, is the real purpose of the agreement, it will not be exempted under TTBER.

The Regulation offers both a wider, and more clearly defined, scope for IP licensing than its predecessor. Moreover, although the Regulation itself does not extend to copyright licensing other than software licensing, the Guidelines state that the principles set out in the Regulation and Guidelines will apply to traditional forms of copyright by analogy.[229] The Guidelines are less positive about pure trademark licensing; they state that the Regulation is not intended to extend to pure trademark licensing, even by analogy.[230]

The application of the block exemption is also conditional upon the fact that the licensing agreement must be concluded for the 'purpose of producing contract products', i.e. products incorporating or produced with the licensed technology.[231] Licences contained in agreements which are primarily for reselling or distribution purposes are excluded and parties to such agreements will have to look to the vertical distribution agreements exemption regulation for exemption. In respect of sublicensing, agreements by licensees to sublicence the licensed technology are covered but pure sublicensing agreements are not exempted by TTBER although the principles of the

Regulation will apply by analogy to such agreements.[232] Finally, since the Regulation only deals 'with agreements where the licensor permits the licensee to exploit the contract products, it should not deal with licensing agreements for the purpose of sub-contracting research and development'. Recital 5 indicates that the exemption could apply to exploitation by the licensee in the form of manufacturing and selling 'possibly after further research and development by the licensee'.[233]

The exemption conferred by the Regulation has a potentially longer duration than its predecessor; it can last 'as long as the intellectual property right in the licensed technology has not expired, lapsed or been declared invalid or, in the case of know-how for as long as the know-how remains secret'. If the know-how becomes publicly known as a result of action by the licensee, the exemption will continue to apply for the duration of the agreement. The block exemption will apply separately to each licensed property right covered by the agreement but will continue in effect until the date of expiry, invalidity or the coming into the public domain of the last intellectual property right which constitutes core 'technology' as defined by Article 1 of TTBER. The BER itself expires in 2014 so contracts cannot be expected to remain block exempted after that date. On the other hand licensing agreements which are self-certified as exempted can last longer than ten years, the limit imposed by TTBER 1996 on know-how, if the know-how remains secret or the patent remains valid.

2. The distinction between 'horizontal' and 'vertical' licensing agreements

The 1996 version of TTBER persisted with the view that most IP licensing agreements should be treated as potentially 'horizontal' agreements between competitors in part because the licensee often evolves into one as a result of the experience with manufacturing the new technology. Yet the overwhelming evidence is that at the time a licensing agreement is signed, most are actually 'vertical' agreements between non-competitors. The economic realism of the new Regulation has resulted in a division of licensing agreements into two categories – agreements between non-competitors or agreements between competitors – and a recognition that the regulatory concerns are considerably greater in the case of horizontal agreements. This has resulted in a re-evaluation of prohibited restraints in the case of vertical licensing agreements and the creation of a deservedly more benign regulatory regime. This reform is far-reaching because it applies not only within the confines of the safe haven but also up to a point where the parties' market shares may be as high as 40–50 per cent as long as they fall below dominance.

Moreover, the Regulation gives an expansive definition of vertical 'agreements'. It applies not only to the paradigm vertical case of an agreement between an inventor and a manufacturer but also to an agreement between two manufacturers as long as they are not competitors in respect of the licensed product. In 'product markets' competitors are defined as 'actual' competitors, i.e. competing undertakings who in the absence of the technology transfer agreement would have been active on the relevant product and geographic markets on which the contract products are sold without infringing each other's intellectual property rights.[234] The one complication is that in product markets, 'competitors' also includes a narrow category of 'potential' competitors who realistically are in a position to undertake the necessary investments and accept the switching costs of entering the same market had the price of the product been raised.[235] In 'technology markets', the definition of competitor is limited to 'actual' competitors.[236]

A further feature of the Regulation that is important for IP licensing is that it defines the parties as 'competitors' or 'non-competitors' at the time the contract is made and will not allow the natural competition that may develop out of the licensing agreement as the manufacturing expertise of the licensee matures to affect the designation of the contract. Thus, if the parties are non-competitors at the time the agreement is made, they will not be re-designated for the purposes of the exemption during the duration of the agreement unless the agreement is materially amended.[237] The distinction between horizontal and vertical agreements is particularly noticeable in two regulatory contexts: the market share limits to the BER[238] and the types of hard core restrictions in licensing agreements.[239]

3. The market share limits

The Regulation may have been helpful to IP licensing in these respects, but it has created complications for IP licensing by introducing a system of market share limits to its scope to harmonise it with the regulatory methods used in the design of the Vertical Agreements BER. By introducing a new legal regime whereby its 'safe harbour' is limited by market share limits, the TTBER radically alters the nature of the block exemption and the overall legal framework for IP licensing. Under the guise of giving greater recognition of the economic realities of IP licensing, it creates legal uncertainty for the parties in volatile new technology markets. For licensing agreements between non-competitors, or 'vertical' licensing agreements, the block exemption will not apply where the licensed product exceeds 30 per cent of the relevant market because such agreements normally impose a lower risk to competition. For the parties to agreements between competitors or 'horizontal' licensing agreements, the exemption will not apply where the licensed product exceeds a 20 per cent market share. In defining the market for the licensed product, both actual and potential competition are relevant. If the agreement is to license technology only actual competition will be considered.

If the product which is the subject of a technology transfer agreement exceeds the market share ceiling at any time during the course of the contract, it will lose the benefit of the block exemption, after a transitional period of two years. The Regulation makes no other concession to the volatility of relationships during the term of the licensing agreement as it did in respect of the status of the parties as competitors or non-competitors.[240] If an agreement loses its exemption under the BER, it will not be automatically prohibited by Article 81(1); nor will any notification be required to the Commission. Indeed, the agreement may still be exempted by self assessment, i.e. an analysis of Article 81(3) as it applies to the agreement using the Guidelines and the case law of the Community Courts and Commission. However, to lawyers accustomed to the old style block exemption regulation, the legal security offered by self assessment seems more precarious than the legal security of the safe harbour of the block exemption.

4. The hard core restrictions

The new Regulation places considerable emphasis upon a narrow blacklist of prohibited 'hard core' restrictions whose presence in a licensing agreement make it 'unexemptible' under the BER but also almost always unenforceable under Article 81 generally. The hard core restrictions have been drafted on the supposition that they are 'almost always anti-competitive'.[241] They have been defined differently depending upon whether the licensing agreement that contains them is between competing undertakings or between non-competing undertakings.

4.1 Restrictions on agreements between competitors   Where the licensee competes with the licensor at the time the agreement is concluded, the Regulation contains four main hard core restrictions. The first three are basic anti-cartel competition rules, bans on price fixing,[242] reciprocal output limitations[243] and market allocation clauses.[244] The fourth is a prohibition on licensors restricting the licensee's ability to carry out R&D and exploit its own technology.[245]

Perhaps in partial recognition of this strict regulatory regime, the Regulation provides that where the agreement between competitors takes the form of a non-reciprocal licensing agreement, the licensor is allowed under an exception to Article 4(1)(c) to offer an exclusive licence, that is a licence to produce and sell the contract products without the licensor himself producing goods in that territory or selling the contract goods from that territory. In such a case, the licensee will merely be doing what the licensor was entitled to do and hence that restriction, on its own, cannot be viewed as anticompetitive. Indeed, it may even be argued that Article 81(1) does not apply to a simple exclusive licence between licensor and licensee as long as the agreement involves no third parties such as other licensees.[246]

A second analogous exception consists of field of use provisions. A field of use restriction limits the exploitation of the licensed technology by the licensee to one or more particular fields of use, leaving untouched the licensor's ability to exploit the licensed technology in another field. A good example is offered by a maize seed variety which is licensed for animal food only, with the licensor retaining exclusive rights to exploit the seed variety for human foodstuffs. Field of use restrictions may be 'exclusive' or 'sole' and are treated for competition purposes as analogous to exclusive or sole territorial licences. Again, as long as the field of use obligation is limited to the licensing agreement, it is little more than a sub-division of the licensor's own powers and may not even be caught by Article 81(1).

4.2 Restrictions on agreements between non-competitors For agreements between non-competitors,[247] the hardcore restrictions are more varied in their concerns. They include price fixing and they extend to territorial restrictions and to restrictions of active and passive sales to end users by a licensee who is part of a selective distribution system.

The territorial restriction prohibition is contained in Article 4(2)(b) which states that an agreement may not be exempted if it has as its object, '(i) the restriction of the territory into which, or of the customers to whom, the licensee may sell the contract products'.

It then provides a limited list of exceptions consisting of permitted territorial restrictions, including obligations on licensees not to sell *actively* into the exclusive territory of another licensee, not sell at all into the exclusive territory of the licensor, requiring the licensee to manufacture or provide contract products only for its own use, etc.

The Commission has acknowledged the indispensability of protection against *passive* sales for licensees. '[I]t is unlikely that licensees would not enter into the licence without protection for a certain period of time against passive (and active) sales into the exclusive territory of a licensee by other licensees.'

This statement recognises the strategic importance of passive sales protection as an incentive in the technology transfer agreement and the Regulation provides that licensors can provide every licensee with protection for two years from the sale of the licensed product in its territory against passive sales by other licensees manufacturing the same licensed product in other territories. The theory is that the two years should be sufficient for each licensee to familiarise itself with the production process to achieve the efficiencies to allow it to catch and compete on equal terms with other licensees.[248]

Excluded Restrictions
The Commission has also created a short list of prima facie excluded restrictive conditions in Article 5 which, unlike hard core restrictions, are only void in themselves; they will not affect the remainder of the agreement. The Commission has in effect introduced a severability rule for such clauses.

Whilst they cannot be exempted as part of the block exemption process, they can be exempted individually if they meet the four conditions of Article 81(3). There are four main excluded restrictions: (a) any direct or indirect obligation by the licensee to assign or to grant an exclusive licence in respect of its own several improvements to the licensed technology; (b) any direct or indirect obligation by the licensee to assign or to grant an exclusive licence in respect of its own several improvements to the licensed technology; (c) any direct or indirect obligation on the licensee not to challenge the validity of the IPRs held by the licensor; and (d) in a vertical licensing relationship, any direct or indirect obligation limiting the licensee's ability to exploit its own technology or limiting the ability of any of the parties to the agreement to carry out research and development unless indispensable to prevent the disclosure of the licensed know-how to third parties.

5. The new methods of assessing individual restraints in licensing agreements outside the safe harbour of the TTBER

The new Guidelines offer a general methodology for the economic and legal analysis of licensing agreements and individual restrictions under Article 81 both within and outside the safe haven of the TTBER. In view of the differences in the risks of anticompetitive harm from agreements between non-competitors as compared with agreements between competitors, the Guidelines' general methodology creates a rather different framework of regulation for each type of agreement.

Before looking more closely at these differences of treatment, it is helpful to examine the criteria the competition authorities use to differentiate between licensing agreements between competitors and those between non-competitors.

5.1 The distinction between competitors and non-competitors under the TTBER and the Guidelines   The modernisation reform has resulted in an important change to the treatment of licensing agreements by drawing a careful and more enlightened distinction between agreements between competitors and those between non-competitors. Historically the BERs rather crudely distinguished between 'vertical' and 'horizontal' agreements. Vertical agreements were defined as agreements between undertakings each of which operates at a different level of the production or distribution chain. Horizontal agreements were defined as agreements between undertakings operating at the same level of the production and distribution chain. While relatively easy for lawyers to apply, this distinction meant the vertical agreements were defined narrowly and horizontal agreements too widely and as a consequence, competition concerns were incorrectly aimed at agreements between non-competitors.

As part of the Commission's new economic approach, the Guidelines on Vertical Agreements stress that the test should be whether the relationship between the parties operating *for the purposes of the agreement* is at a different level of the production and distribution chain. This means that there could be a 'vertical agreement' between firms on the same level, i.e. two manufacturers, as long as they are manufacturing products which are not in competition with each other. The Guidelines on Vertical Agreements stated that an undertaking could be 'active at more than one stage of the production and distribution chain'.

The TTBER and the Commission's Guidelines to Technology Transfer Agreements have also adopted a more economically enlightened view of the distinction between the two types of agreement, adhering to the spirit if not the letter of the Vertical Agreements Guidelines. The test in TTBER is whether the parties would have been actual or potential competitors *in the absence of the agreement*. If without the agreement, the parties would not have been competitors, they will be deemed to be non-competitors.[249] This requires a careful understanding of the two parties as well as the commercial nature of the markets in which they operate.

The TTBER draws a distinction between 'product markets' and 'technology markets'[250] and defines 'competing undertakings' differently in each market. Under the TTBER, the licensor and licensee can either be actual or potential competitors in the product market but only actual competitors in the technology market.

The licensor and licensee will be viewed as actual competitors when in the absence of the agreement they: '. . . are both active on the same *relevant product market and the same geographic market(s)* or the same technology market[251] without infringing each other's intellectual property rights'. Consequently, the existence of blocking patents will be important in the analysis.[252]

The licensor and licensee will be viewed as potential competitors on the relevant product market and geographic market(s) if, in the absence of the agreement and without infringing the intellectual property rights of the other party, it is likely that they would have undertaken the necessary additional investment to enter the relevant market in response to a small but permanent increase in product prices within a short period such as a year or two.[253]

Finally, the Guidelines make special provision for 'breakthrough' products such as drastic inventions which make the competitor's technology obsolete.

A good example is offered by the US Licensing Guidelines Example 5: 'AgCo, a manufacturer of farm equipment, develops a new, patented emission control technology for its tractor engines and licenses it to FarmCo, another farm equipment manufacturer. AgCo's emission control technology is far superior to the technology currently owned and used by FarmCo, so much so that FarmCo's technology does not significantly restrain the prices that AgCo could charge for its technology. AgCo's emission control patent has a broad scope. It is likely that any improved emissions control technology that FarmCo could develop in the foreseeable future would infringe AgCo's patents.'

Note that they are not actual competitors in emission control technology despite both being manufacturers of emission control technology. Note also that they are not likely potential competitors in emission control technology because of the blocking patent.

A second feature of TTBER is that if the parties are non-competitors *at the time the agreement is concluded*, they will continue to enjoy the more liberal regime of hard core restrictions for the duration of the agreement unless the agreement itself is materially altered.[254] This will be true even if the licensees and licensors become actual competitors at a later date because 'the licensee starts licensing out his technology or the licensor becomes an actual or potential supplier of products on the relevant market'. This was a concession made by the Commission which had originally intended a reassessment at any time that commercial conditions called for one. Outside the TTBER the position is more complex and we shall come back to it in context.[255]

5.2 The new concept of 'restrictions on competition' Once the status of the parties as competitors or non-competitors at the time the contract is made is determined, the next step in the analysis of licensing agreements under Article 81(1) outside the TTBER is to decide whether the licensing agreement as a whole or any provision within it constitutes a *'restriction on competition'* under Article 81(1).

Under the old regime, as we have seen, the interpretation of Article 81(1) was very wide and despite the case law of appreciability, the issue of analysing Article 81(1) closely to avoid the reach of Article 81 altogether was rarely on the practitioner's agenda since the parties tended to accept that the BER was the main source of legal salvation. Under the new regime, in contrast, the status of the agreement under Article 81(1) is more important to analyse because there is a greater prospect that the agreement and its provisions can be assessed as not constituting 'preventions, restrictions or distortions of competition'. In such a case, the issue of 'exemptibility' may never arise. The key reason for this is that while many IP licensing agreements by their very commercial nature will contain contractual 'restrictions' on licensors and licensees, under the new methodology fewer contractual restraints will be restrictions on competition.

Article 81(1) prohibits agreements which either by object or effect prevent, restrict or distort competition.

Under the new methodology, the prohibition of licensing agreements with anticompetitive objects under Article 81(1) is still exemplified by the provisions listed as hard core restrictions in Article 4 of the TTBER. However, the concept of a hard core restriction under Article 4 has changed from that of the blacklisted provisions in the 1996 TTBER. Formerly the test whether the provision was restrictive in nature was elaborately defined and this resulted in seven blacklisted restrictions. Now the test has been modified so that it also asks whether the restriction is so likely to lead to anticompetitive harm that detailed economic analysis of effects is required.[256] In consequence, the hard core restrictions are now limited to price fixing, output limitations and market allocation, and do not extend to territorial restrictions and sales restrictions. These latter provisions are now classified as exceptions to hard core restrictions in Article 4 which indicates that they are not anticompetitive in their object and are now left to be evaluated mainly on the basis of their economic effects. The beneficiaries of this analysis are agreements between non-competitors and non-reciprocal agreements between competitors.

Under the new framework, if an agreement (or a restriction within it) is not restrictive of competition by its object, there is still a need to assess whether in fact it has the effect of restricting competition. This assessment has more of an economic dimension.

There are three highlights in this new test of effects:

- First, in order to determine whether or not an agreement (or a restriction within it) has the economic effect of restricting competition, much will depend on whether the licensor and licensee were competitors or non-competitors before the contract was made.[257] Thus, as Guideline 12(a) asks, does the license agreement restrict actual or potential competition that would have existed *without the contemplated agreement*? And, as Guideline 12(b) asks, does the agreement restrict actual or potential competition that would have existed *in the absence of the contractual restraint(s)*?
- Secondly, the test of effects will be radically different for agreements between non- competitors and those between competitors.
- Thirdly, the test of economic effect of restricting competition will apply both to competition between licensor and licensee (inter-technology competition) and competition between different licensees of the same technology in different territories (intra-technology competition).

6. Licensing agreements between non-competitors

6.1 Inter-technology competition   In the case of agreements between non-competitors, there is normally no inter-technological competition either actual or potential at the start of the agreement. Hence the fact of the agreement itself will not restrict competition unless the market power of the licensee threatens consumer harm through foreclosure of competition.[258] Consequently, the test will concentrate on whether any provision within the licensing agreement is a restriction of competition by effect.

Where a licensing agreement is made between non-competitors, whether actual or potential, many restrictions on the conduct of licensor and licensee inter se in the licensing agreement will not constitute a restriction of competition under the new framework.[259]

For example, many non-territorial clauses between licensors and licensees will be regarded as ancillary restraints and therefore 'almost always *not* restrictive of competition within the meaning of Article 81(1)'.[260]

Some examples of such restrictions are those which are indispensable to achieving the main purpose of the licensing agreement. These include:

(a) confidentiality obligations;
(b) obligations on licensees not to sublicence;
(c) obligations not to use the licensed technology after the expiry of the agreement, provided that the licensed technology remains valid and in force;
(d) obligations to assist the licensor in enforcing the licensed intellectual property rights;
(e) obligations to pay minimum royalties or to produce a minimum quantity of products incorporating the licensed technology; and
(f) obligations to use the licensor's trade mark or indicate the name of the licensor on the product.

Moreover, certain territorial restrictions *as between licensor and licensee* can be viewed as not *restrictive of competition* under Article 81(1).

Where a licensor offers a sole and exclusive license to the licensee, if the parties were not competitors before the contract was made, a pure obligation on the licensor not to appoint another licensee in the territory or not itself to exploit the licensed product in the territory might be restrictions but they would not be 'restrictions on competition' for the purpose of Article 81(1).[261]

A similar analysis can be performed for contractual restraints such as field of use restrictions. What is important to note here is that the new methodology recognises that the IP owner can sub-divide its powers of exploitation by contractual restriction and not be caught by Article 81(1) under the analysis of restriction on competition rather than the scope of the patent or limited licence doctrines which stem from IP law. Consequently, in the case of agreements between non-competitors, the new methodology gives a wide scope for contractual restrictions between licensor and licensee not to be caught by Article 81(1) in the first place.

6.2 Intra-technology competition   The second process of competition that is relevant for article 81(1) is the process of intra-technology competition, normally the competition that can exist between different licensees producing the same product.[262]

Under EC law, since the *Consten Grundig*[263] case, there have been specific competition concerns with restrictions on intra-technology competition such as provisions placing obligations on licensees not to sell directly into the territories of other licensees. From the Commission's point of view since such obligations are viewed as restricting the potential competition that could have existed between the licensees in different territories in the absence of such obligations, they are regarded as a restriction of competition for the purposes of Article 81(1). A more universal example of restrictions on intra-technology competition would be a price restraint placed on all licensees by a licensor.[264] Insofar as a licensing agreement between non-competitors contains a restriction on intra-technology competition, it will be necessary to resort to the analysis under Article 81(3) to decide whether such restrictions of competition in the licensing agreement are acceptable under Article 81 as a whole.

For example, an obligation placed by the licensor upon the licensee not to sell directly into the territory of another licensee will be caught by Article 81(1) because it restricts intra-technological competition but will be exemptible under the TTBER in respect of *active* sales for the duration of the contract and in respect of *passive* sales for two years. This shows a particularly improved understanding of the need to encourage investment in IP licensing because every licensee gets protection against rivals' licensees and the licensor itself for a minimum of two years from the time it first markets the product in its territory. The thinking is that the licensee gets an initial period to tool up to match the efficiencies of production of its rivals. In previous BERs there was no such guarantee because the period of five years of allowed protection against passive sales in any one territory was dependent on the time left after the product was put on the market by any licensees. Hence 'second' and 'third wave' licensees could end up with less than two years' protection which might discourage investment at that stage and hence inhibit further diffusion of the technology throughout the single market.

Even if the market share of the licensee exceeds 30 per cent and the two years of the TTBER do not automatically apply, the factual analysis of the indispensability licensees need for such protection could lead to a two-year period of protection, or, in the case of particularly complex and expensive technologies, possibly an even longer period of protection for licensees. In other words, even outside the TTBER, Article 81(3) offers a relatively benign treatment of licensing agreements between non-competitors. First it asks whether there will be any pro-competitive benefits arising from the provision; whether the benefits were objectively necessary (or indispensable) to achieve those benefits and whether or not competition in the market would be eliminated – note eliminated – not merely reduced.

One feature of the new framework which needs careful attention is the assessment of competition between licensor and licensee outside the safe harbour of the TTBER. In principle, once outside the TTBER, a reassessment must be made at that stage whether the agreement is one between competitor and non-competitor. The TTBER offers a special ex ante treatment of the status of the contractual relationship within the safe harbour for the purpose of applying the hard core restrictions in Article 4(3). This provision was a concession made by the Commission during the course of the final draft and it constitutes special recognition of the dynamic aspects of technology licensing.[265] To what extent does this ex ante analysis continue outside the scope of the safe harbour of the TTBER?

In the General Framework for the Application of Article 81, the Guidelines specifically mention a case where the parties become competitors subsequent to the conclusion of the agreement because the licensee develops and starts exploiting a competing technology.[266] They state that it must be taken into account that the parties were non-competitors at the time the agreement was made and that the Commission will therefore mainly focus on the impact of the agreement on the licensee's ability to exploit its own (competing) technology and the hard core restrictions will continue to apply to the parties as if they are non-competitors unless the agreement itself is materially amended after the parties have become competitors. If the reassessment is made in this way it should take sufficient account of the inherent dynamic of the licensing relationship, i.e. the fact that almost every IP licence creates potential technological competition after the licensee has mastered the technology but while the contract remains in existence.

Since the technology is inevitably transferred at the early stages of the contract, licensors view as an indispensable inducement to give an *exclusive* licence of its technology the assurance of a return for the period of the contract. That is why the licensor inserts a 'minimum royalty' clause. Moreover, that is also why it inserts a non-compete clause *in respect of the technology transferred*. The non-compete clause in respect of *inter-technological* competition between the parties at the start of the contract cannot limit the licensee's independent development of its own R&D. Some limits can be placed on its exploitation of that R&D during the period of the contract owing to the incidental effect of the minimum royalties clause.

What must be guarded against is the use of the competition rules to allow licensees opportunistically to opt out of a contractual commitment when they are ready to do so instead of respecting the contractual obligation. If the new legal framework were to have this effect, this would cause investors either to think twice about investing new technology within the EU or insist on a premium rate upfront as a guaranty. In either case the effect of the competition rules will be to chill investment in IP licensing into the EU and limit the diffusion of technology transfer. The Guidelines seem to offer a reassurance that this will not happen by conceding that the designation of the parties as competitors or not will take adequate account of the ex ante relationship. Even though in principle the reassessment is ex post it seems that it will be accepted that the contractual non-compete clause continues to operate as a contractual block on potential *intra-technology* competition during the course of the agreement.[267]

7. Licensing agreements between competitors

The treatment of licensing agreements between competitors is on the face of it much harsher than agreements between non-competitors largely because of the greater competition concerns with 'horizontal agreements'. At the Article 81(1) level, there will be more restrictions by object and there will be little argument that many other territorial restrictions in the agreement can be said not to be restrictions of inter-technology competition. The longer list of hard core restrictions is accompanied by lower market share thresholds of 20 per cent. Access to the safe haven of the TTBER is clearly less open to licensing agreements between competitors.

Yet, it is wrong to conclude that the competition authorities are entirely hostile to licensing agreements between competitors. The Commission has clearly felt that it had inadequate knowledge and experience of the permutations of pro-competitive licensing agreements between competitors to regulate them in the TTBER with the light touch approach they used to regulate licensing agreements between non-competitors. Moreover, the Commission was only too aware that this type of agreement is the source of the most serious risks of anticompetitive licensing agreements even if that is true in only a minority of cases. As a consequence, the Commission has left the application of the full range of Article 81(3) to such agreements to the second tier of the Guidelines.

Moreover, there are important concessions to this tighter approach to licensing agreements between competitors. One such is the creation of the special category of *non-reciprocal* licensing agreements between competitors.[268] Both within and outside the TTBER they are treated as honorary agreements between non-competitors.[269]

The application of Article 81(3) to licensing agreements between competitors is further ameliorated outside the TTBER and above the 20 per cent market share by a 'second safe harbour' where there are at least four other poles of independently controlled technologies and no hard core restrictions in the licensing agreement.[270]

However, under the new methodology, licensing agreements between competitors are generally more easily caught by Article 81(1) because restrictions, even ancillary restrictions, are usually *restrictions of competition* under Article 81(1) and the permitted scope for provisions is carefully regulated by Article 4(1) of TTBER.

If a licensing agreement between competitors is reciprocal and its contents or market share take it outside the TTBER, the legal status of the agreement must be assessed on the issue of the balancing test of the four conditions of Article 81(3). At this point there will be a need to argue both that the provision contributes significant pro-competitive benefits and that those benefits could not be obtained by a less restrictive provision particularly one that was not restrictive by object. This indispensability test will not require a fine toothcomb and will not place the Commission in the position of pointing to less restrictive alternatives. Of course, in practice, as the Commission reminds us, it is only exceptional that the hard core restriction will fill the four conditions of Article 81(3) and in particular its indispensability condition. However, there is a possibility for the parties to justify their licensing agreements between competitors under Article 81(3) outside the safe harbour of the TTBER. This is a major change from the old legal framework. Today, licensing agreements between competitors which fall outside the comfort zone of the BER owing to a hard core restriction in the agreement may still obtain exemption under the balancing provisions of Article 81(3) if their pro-competitive effects outweigh their anticompetitive effects. The hard core restrictions, unlike the blacklists of the 1996 BER, do not deliver a knock-out blow to exemption. As the Commission states in its Guidelines, 'even license agreements that do restrict competition may often give rise to pro-competitive efficiencies, which must be considered under Article 81(3) and balanced against the negative effects on competition'.[271]

V. Remedies

A. Article 82

The newly introduced Council Regulation 1/2003[272] lays down the powers of the Commission for the enforcement of the competition rules.[273] The purpose of the new enforcement regulation is to ensure effective enforcement on the one hand and simplification of administration on the other.[274] Moreover it seeks to improve on the experience learned from the application of the old regulation and the developments of competition within the Common Market.

The remedies at the Commission's disposal include the power to take final decisions ordering found infringement to terminate,[275] taking procedural decisions during the investigation process, and introducing interim measures[276] to prevent irremediable harm occurring before the Commission can draw a final conclusion.[277]

Chapter VI of 1/2003 allows the Commission to impose penalties in the form of fines and periodic penalty payments for any breaches of either Article 81 or 82.[278] The Commission may charge fines of up to 10 per cent of the annual turnover in the preceding business year of the undertakings involved in the infringement.[279] In addition, the Commission may impose fines of up to 5 per cent of the average daily turnover for every day that an undertaking is in breach, in order to compel it to terminate an infringement.[280]

In the old Regulation 17,[281] Article 3(1) stated only that the Commission in its finding of an infringement could require the involved undertakings to bring the infringement in question to an end. It did not give detailed examples of the specific powers at the disposal of the Commission to order the parties to take positive steps to end the infringement. The Commission integrated the wide language of Regulation 17 to conform its broad powers in several cases and these decisions were confirmed by the European Court of Justice. In *Commercial Solvents*,[282] the ECJ ruled that Article 3 of Regulation 17 must be applied in relation to the infringement which has been established and may include an order to do certain acts or provide certain advantages which have been wrongfully withheld as well as an order prohibiting the continuation of certain actions, practices or situations which are contrary to the Treaty.[283] In this particular case, Commercial Solvents had refused to supply a raw material to another undertaking. Commercial Solvents was ordered by the Commission to resume supplying a *former customer*. Similarly in *Magill*[284] three broadcasting companies were ordered to license their TV listing to each other and third parties after having refused to supply these to a company that wished to make a comprehensive television guide. The actual remedy chosen by the Commission was a compulsory licence on terms which were 'reasonable and non-discriminatory'. It chose this remedy only because an order to supply the information in the listings would not have allowed their use and therefore would not have ended the infringement. The only way the Commission could be sure that Magill could publish the new product in the secondary market and the parties to end the infringement was to require a licence to publish along with the supply of the listings.

Furthermore, the Commission has not only restricted itself to finding certain conduct unlawful, but has also prohibited similar conduct in the future. This form of remedy has been confirmed by the ECJ, for example in *Tetra Pak II*[285] and *Steel Beams*.[286] Tetra Pak had among other things tied the purchase of cartons together to its lease of machines for packaging milk. The Commission ordered Tetra Pak to delete certain abusive clauses in its leasing agreements and furthermore inform any customer purchasing or leasing a machine of the specifications which packaging cartons must meet in order to be used on its machines in order to bring the infringement to an end.[287] The Commission added that 'Tetra Pak shall refrain from repeating or maintaining any act or conduct described in Article 1 and from adopting any measure having equivalent effect'[288] thereby ensuring that future equivalent action by Tetra Pak would be deemed illegal. The ECJ upheld the Commission's decision.

The remedies laid down in *Tetra Pak II* show that the Commission with the blessing of the ECJ has the power to restrict future conduct even where the illegal conduct has already been brought to an end.

In the information technology field the attitude to remedies has been more strongly influenced by the imperative of interoperability. In the *IBM* settlement in 1984, the Commission insisted on undertakings by IBM to provide full interface information to all applications makers comparable to that provided to its own subsidiary operating in a downstream market. The purpose of that settlement was to ensure that the dominant firm, particularly where it operated in a downstream market, adhered to the principle of fair and non-discriminatory treatment of competitors in that market. In the later *Microsoft* cases the issues of shaping a competition law remedy to ensure interoperability became more controversial.

In the *Microsoft* case in the USA, after the District Court judge's remedy of compulsory division of Microsoft into two companies was overturned by the Circuit Court, the Department of Justice together with half of the litigating states negotiated a consent decree with Microsoft which stipulated that Microsoft had to cease a number of monopolistic practices. The decree also placed three positive obligations upon Microsoft to assist dependent competitors to achieve full interoperability with Microsoft products. First, Microsoft was required to supply to ISVs, Internet Access Providers and Original Equipment Manufacturers, among others, the Application Protocol Interfaces (APIs) and related documentation used by Microsoft middleware to interoperate with a Windows Operating System product in a timely manner. Secondly, there was an obligation to license to third parties, on reasonable and non-discriminatory terms, any communications protocol implemented in a Windows Operating System product when it is installed on a client computer and used to interoperate 'natively,' i.e. without the installation of additional software code, with a Microsoft Operating System product. Finally, Microsoft agreed to give a compulsory licence to ISVs etc. of any IPRs owned or licensable by Microsoft that was required to exercise any of the options or alternatives expressly provided to them under the final judgment on reasonable and non-discriminatory terms.[289]

The difficulty was that these obligations were subject to a wide proviso on security to the effect that Microsoft would not be required to disclose or license to third parties portions of API documentation or layers of communications protocols inter alia 'if their disclosure would compromise the security of a particular installation'.[290]

Taking the ECJ judgments and the Commission's decisions into account when shaping the new provisions in Regulation 1/2003, the article replacing Article 3 of Regulation 17 (Article 7(1)) states:

> Where the Commission, acting on a complaint or on its own initiative, finds that there is an infringement of Article 81 or of Article 82 of the Treaty, it may by decision require the undertakings and associations of undertakings concerned to bring such infringement to an end. For this purpose, it may impose on them any behavioural or structural remedies which are proportionate to the infringement committed and necessary to bring the infringement effectively to an end. Structural remedies can only

be imposed either where there is no equally effective behavioural remedy or where equally effective behavioural remedy would be more burdensome for the undertaking concerned than the structural remedy. If the Commission has a legitimate interest in doing so, it may also find that an infringement has been committed in the past.

Consequently, when dealing with remedies under the new rules of Regulation 1/2003 one should distinguish between behavioural and structural remedies. All examples of remedies discussed above fall under the category of behavioural remedies. The inclusion of structural remedies in Article 7(1) was thoroughly debated because Regulation 17 did not provide for such remedy.[291] The application of the structural remedy is however restricted to situations where there is no equally effective behavioural remedy or where the structural remedy would be less burdensome for the undertaking than the behavioural.

Commercial Solvents offers an example where the Commission could have applied a structural remedy instead of a behavioural remedy. In this case the infringement was however brought to an end by forcing Commercial Solvents to supply its former customer, even though it had a daughter company in the downstream market which competed with the customer. In a similar situation where a vertical integrated company like Commercial Solvents continued the abuse by discriminating in various ways against the downstream competitors a structural remedy of breaking up the company would be possible according to this new provision. Recital 12 of Regulation 1/2003 clarifies that the application of a structural remedy should only take place if 'changes to the structure of an undertaking as it existed before the infringement was committed would only be proportionate where there is a substantial risk of a lasting or repeated infringement that derives from the very structure of the undertaking'.

B. Article 81

Cases under this article either deal with contracts or cartels between companies which infringe by their nature and hence should be brought to an end. An example is the *Welded Steel Mesh* case, a cartel case, where the Commission decided that 'the undertakings ... which are still involved in the welded steel mesh sector in the Community shall forthwith bring the said infringement to an end (if they have not already done so) and shall henceforth refrain in relation to their welded steel mesh operations from any agreement or concerted practice which may have the same object or effect'.[292] However, there are limits to the extent of the remedies which can be enforced upon a company. In the *Langnese-Iglo* case,[293] the ECJ held that the Commission could not order a company not to enter into future 'exclusive purchasing agreements', due to the fact that these types of agreements can in certain circumstances be pro-competitive and hence could be exempted under Article 81(3). This is opposite to the remedies applied under Article 82. Another important contrast between the two articles is that they have a different purpose. Article 81 prohibits agreements and hence the Commission can instruct them to be terminated; a refusal to supply a customer is not in itself unlawful under Article 81 and thus a company cannot be ordered to supply under this article.[294] In *Automec II*,[295] BMW had informed Automec that it was not going to renew their contract to supply vehicles and spare parts. Automec complained to the Commission and requested the Commission to take a decision ordering BMW Italia and BMW AG to bring the alleged infringement to an end and continue the contract. Automec complained about the potential dealers losing their commission and added that since it was being boycotted by BMW it had become impossible for it to purchase vehicles from Italian and foreign BMW distributors, even though vehicles were available. Consequently, it had recently been unable to meet several orders which it had received.[296] The Commission held that 'since freedom of contract must remain the rule, it cannot in principle be considered to have among the powers to issue orders which it has for the purpose of bringing to an end infringements of Article 85(1) [later to be article 81(1)] of the Treaty the power to order an undertaking to enter into contractual relations, since in general it has appropriate means at its disposal for requiring an undertaking to terminate an infringement'.[297] Hence the Commission decided that it had no powers under Article 81 (then 85) to issue the requested order. This decision was upheld by the CFI. In *Automec*, the Commission was strict as to how far its powers extended. However, in *Atlantic Container Line*,[298] it went one step too far in what it held would be necessary for putting an end to the infringement. The case dealt with a horizontal agreement, which fixed prices in maritime transport. Fifteen liner shipping companies were parties to a trans-Atlantic agreement. It covered several aspects of maritime transport laying down, among other things, the prices of the tariffs applicable to maritime transport and 'intermodal'[299] transport.[300] The Commission annulled the agreement and ordered the conduct to cease. It also required that the companies party to the agreement should inform their customers that the rates were now open for renegotiation. It argued that the renegotiation 'is intended to prevent the applicants from continuing to enjoy the benefits of long-term contracts entered into on the basis of a price-fixing agreement regarded as unlawful. Although these contracts are not themselves void, customers must be entitled to renegotiate them under normal conditions of competition.'[301] The CFI held, however, that this clause was not obviously necessary to bring the infringement to an end and furthermore the CFI pointed out that the clause did not fit in with previous Commission decisions.[302] Finally the CFI felt that the Commission had failed to establish the need for the contested clause and hence it decided to annul it.[303]

In relation to the licensing of intellectual property rights the Commission has taken much of the same approach as with other types of agreements. Thus in *Sega and Nintendo*[304] the Commission ordered the involved parties to delete certain clauses in their licensing agreement for computer software with publishers of video games, because it felt that Sega and Nintendo through these clauses could control the market for video games.[305] A similar remedy was ordered against Microsoft in the *Microsoft Internet Explorer* case.[306] Microsoft had included a minimum quantity on the distribution of its Internet Explorer browser and imposed a ban on advertisement of its competitors' browsers in its licensing agreements. The Commission ordered Microsoft to remove this from the agreement in fear that these would foreclose the market for competitors.[307] In general, minimum quantity requirements are allowed for in licensing agreements since they are not considered harmful to competition.[308] However, the Commission was concerned that in this particular situation the clause would harm competitors.

C. Mergers

Mergers are regulated under the EC Merger Regulation.[309] Articles 7 and 8 deal with the decision powers of the Commission to either suspend or declare the merger compatible or incompatible with the common market. These two rules also provide the Commission with powers to dissolve a merger or enforce measures of equivalent effect, such as divesting part of an existing undertaking. Moreover, Articles 14 and 15 allow the Commission to issue fines and periodic penalty payments, equal to the articles in Regulation 1/2003. For IPRs the main area of interest is the power of the Commission to insist upon licences or cross-licences as a precondition for approval of a merger.

The Commission has issued a notice on remedies acceptable under the EC Merger Regulation,[310] pointing several general principles in its approach. Firstly, the notice defines a 'remedy' in relation to mergers as a 'modification', with the object of reducing the merging parties' market power and restoring conditions for effective competition which is in jeopardy of being distorted as a result of the merger creating and strengthening a dominant position.[311] Hence, a remedy in relation to mergers can be a means to achieve the merger which would otherwise raise competition concerns. If the remedy is enforced to the Commission's satisfaction, the merger can gain clearance. It is not a form of penalty as such, since no illegal conduct has occurred. Rather it is a form of prevention. Secondly, the Commission shows preference to such structural remedies when dealing with mergers because these do not require medium or long term monitoring.[312] As the CFI stated in *Gencor*: 'Since the purpose of the Regulation is to prevent the creation or strengthening of market structures which are liable to impede significantly effective competition in the common market, situations of that kind cannot be allowed to come about on the basis that the undertakings concerned enter into a commitment not to abuse their dominant position, even where it is easy to check whether those commitments have been complied with. Consequently, under the Regulation the Commission has power to accept only such commitments as are capable of rendering the notified transaction compatible with the common market. In other words, the commitments offered by the undertakings concerned must enable the Commission to conclude that the concentration at issue would not create or strengthen a dominant position within the meaning of Article 2(2) and (3) of the Regulation.'[313]

One example of such a remedy is the sale of a subsidiary since it can be implemented effectively within a short period of time, but remedies will be construed on a case-by-case basis.[314] The Commission Notice also lays down different types of remedies that the Commission can apply in order to make a merger comply with the Merger Regulation. Firstly there is divestiture, which is seen as the most efficient means of re-establishing effective competition. The divested activity must be a viable business, which can exist on a 'stand-alone' basis, independent from the merging parties.[315] A divestiture is applied when the merger will cause an overlap horizontally or in some cases with vertical integration and hence effecting competition. The aim is to separate the conflicting business parts of the merging companies from the merger. In relation to IPRs a part of a business which includes the right to a patent or other key technology can be divested, if that would help it fulfil the conditions of a 'stand-alone' undertaking. This was the case in the *Allied Signal/Honeywell* merger,[316] where the companies had overlapping businesses in the Airborne Collision Avoidance Systems (ACAS) and on the market for Terrain Awareness Warning Systems (TAWS), where Allied Signal before the merger held a monopoly. The Commission feared that the merger would foreclose the access to the TAWS market. Moreover, this market was strongly linked to the so-called next generation of Integrated Hazard Surveillance Systems (IHAS), which was a key technology held by Honeywell. The Commission's remedy was that the parties had to sell their overlapping ACAS business and furthermore supply third parties with open interface standards in the TAWS market.[317]

Where divestiture is impossible,[318] or there are specific features which cause concern for effective competition such as existing exclusive agreements, network effects, and the combination of key technology such as know-how or patents,[319] the notice suggests that other remedies are applicable. One optimal remedy is ensuring access to the necessary infrastructure or key technology as in *Allied Signal/Honeywell*. Rather than selling off a part or parts of the companies the remedy for achieving efficient competition can be to establish competition through licensing agreements. As the Commission notes in its Notice it will accept 'exclusive licences without any field-of-use restrictions on impeding efficient, on-going research'.[320] This approach was employed in *Glaxo/Wellcome*[321] involving a merger between two UK based pharmaceutical companies. The merger was found to affect three markets: the anti-emetics, the systemic antibiotics and the anti-migraine treatments market. Only in the last market did the Commission find that there was a threat to effective competition, because both Glaxo and Wellcome had several products on this market in competition with each other. Moreover, both were carrying out extensive research on this market. Glaxo possessed a near monopoly on one of its anti-migraine products, 'Imigran', due to its special features.[322] Wellcome had been carrying out clinical trials on a similar product, which would when available on the market be in strong competition to Imigran. The Commission therefore requested that Glaxo when merging with Wellcome would license to third parties either Wellcome's 3IIC or Glaxo's Naratripan.[323]

Finally, once a remedy has been ordered and established the parties are not entitled to obtain the divested business again or revoke the licence granted, unless the structure of the market has changed significantly, so the holding of such business or licence no longer constitutes a threat to effective competition on the market.[324]

VI. Conclusion

Within EC framework, much of the accommodation between competition law and IPRs tends to occur within the general doctrines of competition law rather than via mechanisms whereby IPRs are singled out for special treatment. There are some limited examples of IPRs being treated as a special form of property. The most striking example is the 'exceptional circumstances' test embedded within the abuse of refusal to supply under Article 82.[325] This test represents an important acceptance by competition law that IPRs are not the same as all other forms of property rights even while maintaining that the exercise of IPRs must be subject to the regulatory limits of competition policy. This doctrine includes the corollary proposition that the 'normal' exercise of IPRs will not abuse a dominant position. Hence only in the most extreme cases, where IPRs are used unjustifiably by their highly dominant owners to exclude competitors from markets, does EC competition policy reserve a right to intervene to limit the exercise of IPRs.

Article 82 also provides an example of the more typical form of accommodation to the exercise of IPRs in the logic of its concept of dominance. As we have seen, the attainment of dominance as such is not unlawful. EC competition law accepts that the achievement of market dominance by organic growth[326] including investment in R&D and intellectual property rights protection is a legitimate course of conduct for a firm. Once dominant, a firm must accept 'special responsibilities', but only if it engages in abusive conduct will it be behaving unlawfully. Yet, these special responsibilities do not preclude it from growing at the expense of its competitors by conduct that is 'competition on the merits'. This is an example of how IPRs can benefit from the logic of an ordinary doctrine of EC competition law rather than one specifically dedicated to IPRs.

This observation offers a good perspective for viewing the relationship between Article 81 and IP licensing under the new post-modernised legal framework. The accommodation with IPRs in the new TTBER and Guidelines occurs almost entirely within the logic of the doctrines of competition law. The 2004 IP Guidelines do not state explicitly that IP protected products are treated as any other form of property rights, as did the US Guideline in 1995,[327] but an analysis of the new methodology makes it plain that there is little special treatment for IPRs under Article 81. Most of the accommodation takes place through the incidental benefits of the logic of the ordinary interpretation of Article 81 under the modernisation programme. In the Guidelines and Recitals there is evidence that the competition authorities have made a considerable effort to understand the nature of IPRs and IPR licensing. Thus, they acknowledge that the creation of IPRs often entails substantial investment and that it is often a risky endeavour. They state plainly that '[i]n order not to reduce dynamic competition and to maintain the incentive to innovate, the innovator must not be unduly restricted in the exploitation of the IPR that turns out to be valuable'. In particular, they must be able to seek compensation for successful projects that takes failed projects into account. The Commission also acknowledges that technology licensing may require the licensee to make considerable sunk investments in the licensed technology and production assets necessary to exploit it.[328] Moreover, the Guidelines have accepted that the great majority of licensing agreements are pro-competitive and compatible with Article 81.[329]

In spite of all these acknowledgements, the nature of the accommodation chosen by the Commission is broadly to fit the assessment of licensing agreements into the modernised framework of Article 81 rather than to offer much in the way of special treatment such as could be found in the 1996 TTBER. As the Guidelines confidently proclaim '[i]n assessing licensing agreements under Article 81, the existing analytical framework is sufficiently flexible to take due account of the dynamic aspects of technology licensing'. Nevertheless, even under the Commission's new methodology it is possible to point to a number of accommodations that have been made. For example, the great gain of the new economic approach is the separation of the real 'verticals' from the real 'horizontals', providing enlightened definitions of each and providing a more lenient treatment of the former. Secondly, there is special treatment for IPRs in the way the competitive relationship between licensor and licensee at the time the agreement is made is frozen for the duration of the agreement barring material modifications of the agreement. That this special treatment is contained within TTBER and carries over outside the safe harbour of the TTBER signals a sensitivity to the dynamics of technology licensing by the competition authorities.

It cannot have escaped attention that the new paradigm for Article 81 has produced considerable convergence with that in the USA. This may simply constitute a recognition that on the issue of competition analysis of vertical agreements in general, and licensing agreements in particular, the US approach offers a useful legal framework. However, it is stretching things too far to assume that the same convergence will necessarily be in the EU's interest in respect of Article 82 and mergers.

Notes

1. See Chapters 4 and 5 in this volume.
2. See, for example, *United Brands* v. *Commission* [1978] ECR 207.
3. For a study of the treatment of these forms of collaboration under Article 81 see S. Anderman and J. Kallaugher, *Technology Transfer and the New EC Competition Rules: Intellectual Property Licensing after Modernisation* (Oxford: Oxford University Press, 2006) Ch. 9.
4. See, for example, *Tetra Pak Rausing SA* v. *Commission (Tetra Pak I)* [1990] ECR II-309.
5. See, for example, *United Brands* v. *Commission* [1978] ECR 207.
6. *Michelin* v. *Commisssion* [1983] ECR 3461.
7. Case 6/72, *Europemballage Corp. and Continental Can Co. Inc.* v. *Commission* [1973] ECR 215, [1973] CMLR 199.
8. Commission Notice on the definition of the relevant market for the purpose of Community competition law [1997] OJ C372/5, [1998] 4 CMLR 177. This notice is not legally binding, and is 'without prejudice to the interpretation which may be given by the European Court of Justice or the European Court of First Instance' (para. 6). Nevertheless, it offers guidelines for undertakings themselves to assess their situation as well as setting out the Commission's views upon the issue.
9. *United Brands* v. *Commission* [1978] ECR 207.
10. *Michelin* v. *Commission* [1983] ECR 3461.
11. *Hoffman La Roche* v. *Commission* [1978] ECR 1137.
12. *Hilti* v. *Commission* [1994] ECR I-667.
13. *Hugin Kassaregister AB* v. *Commssion* [1979] ECR 1869, [1979] 3 CMLR 345.
14. *AB Volvo* v. *Erik Veng* [1988] ECR 6211, [1989] 4 CMLR 122.
15. [1991] ECR II-485.
16. See, for example, *IBM Undertaking* [1984] 3 CMLR 147; *Digital/Olivetti* [1994] OJ L 294/10; *Shell/Montecatini*, Commission Decision 94/811/EC of 8 June 1994, Case IV/M. 0269, OJ L 332/48 (22 November 1994).

17. *RTE, ITV and BBC* v. *Commission* [1995] ECR I-743 and Case C-418/01 *IMS Health GmbH & Co. OHG* v. *NDC Health GmbH & Co KG*, judgment of 29 April 2004.

18. See Chapter 10 in this volume.

19. *Sealink/B&I Holyhead: Interim Measures* [1992] 5 CMLR 255.

20. *British Midland* v. *Aer Lingus* [1992] OJ L96/34 4 CMLR M17 and *London European-Sabena* [1988] OJ L31/47, [1989] 4 CMLR 662.

21. S. Anderman, *EC Competition Law and Intellectual Property Rights, the Regulation of Innovation* (Oxford: Oxford University Press, 1998) 166.

22. *Tetra Pak Rausing* v. *Commission* [1994] ECR II-755, [1997] 4 CMLR 726.

23. *United Brands* v. *Commission* [1978] ECR 207.

24. See for example *Hoffman La Roche* v. *Commission* [1978] ECR 1137.

25. *United States* v. *Microsoft Corp*, 253 F.3d 34 (D. C. Cir.), cert. denied 122 S.Ct. 350 (2001).

26. See for example *B&I Line* v. *Sealink Harbour* [1992] 5 CMLR 255.

27. *Oscar Bronner GMbH & Co. KG* v. *Mediaprint* [1998] ECR 1–7791.

28. Ibid. para. 41.

29. Ibid. para. 41; see too *European Night Services* v. *Commission* [1998] ECR II-3141.

30. I. Forester, 'Compulsory Licensing of Intellectual Property Rights in Europe: a Rare Case of Aberrant Intellectual Property Rights', Paper presented to DOJ/ FTC Hearings on Competition and Intellectual Property Law and Policy in the Knowledge Based Economy: *Comparative Law Topics* (May 22, 2002) 15.

31. *Oscar Bronner*, note 27 above, para. 46.

32. Ibid. para. 41.

33. The participants in a technology pool might be regarded as jointly dominant in a technology market on the basis that the pool members are appearing on the market as a single entity. Where there are several complementary pools in a market, the pools (and their constituent members) might be regarded as jointly dominant on the basis of oligopolistic dominance.

34. Demonstrable links can be established by (i) joint ownership or contractual links that give each of them a significant competitive advantage over firms outside the group; (ii) joint control by otherwise independent firms of an essential facility that gives each of them an advantage in the downstream market; (iii) the firms presenting themselves on the market as a group, as was the case of the liner shipping; (iv) 'oligopolistic dominance' where the firms in a market are interdependent as a result of the market structure. See Anderman and Kallaugher, *Technology Transfer*, Chapter 10.

35. See *Shell/Montecatini* decision, note 16 above.

36. *Michelin* v. *Commission* [1983] ECR 3461.

37. See Joliet, *Monopolization and Abuse of a Dominant Position: A Comparative Study of American and European Approaches to the Control of Economic Power*

(The Hague, 1970). See too Temple Lang, 'Monopolisation and the Definition of Abuse of a Dominant Position under Article 86 EEC Treaty' (1970) 16 *Common Market Law Review* 345.

38. *Tetra Pak* v. *Commission* [1990] ECR II-309 *[Tetra Pak I].*
39. *RTE, ITV and BBC* v. *Commission* [1995] ECR I-743.
40. *Hilti* v. *Commission* [1994] ECR I-667.
41. *Michelin* v. *Commission* [1983] ECR 3461.
42. Ibid. (italics are the author's own).
43. *Hoffman La Roche* [1979] ECR 461.
44. [1994] ECR 1–667.
45. [1997] 4 CMLR 662.
46. Case C-62/86 *AKZO Chemie BV* v. *Commission,* [1991] ECR I-359.
47. Case C-238/87 *AB Volvo* v. *Erik Veng* [1998] ECR 6211, [1989] 4 CMLR 122.
48. *Volvo,* note 14 above, para. 8.
49. Ibid., para. 9.
50. Joined cases C-6 and 7/73 *Commercial Solvents* v. *Commission* [1974] ECR 223.
51. J. Venit and J. Kallaugher, 'Essential Facilities: A Comparative Law Approach' (1994) *Fordham Corporate Law Institute* 315 at 328.
52. *United Brands* v. *Commission* [1978] ECR 207 para. 301.
53. *Hoffman La Roche* [1979] ECR 461.
54. *Hilti* v. *Commission* [1994] ECR I-667.
55. *Tetra Pak Rausing* v. *Commission* [1994] ECR II-755.
56. For example, in *United Brands* v. *Commission* [1978] ECR 207 para. 301, the Court declared that a prohibition imposed by a dominant undertaking upon the resale of green bananas by its customers was abusive because its effects went beyond the object to be attained. See too *BRT* v. *SABAM and Fonier,* [1974] ECR 51 in which the Court held that conditions imposed by a copyright-management association in contracts intended to protect members' rights were abusive because they encroached more severely on members' freedom to exercise their copyrights than was necessary to protect its rights. Implicit in this decision was a view that measures requiring members to assign their present and future rights on a global basis could be justified by a test of necessity or indispensability.
57. As the Court of Justice said in *United Brands*: 'the fact that an undertaking is in a dominant position cannot disentitle it from protecting its own commercial interests if they are attacked, and that such an undertaking must be conceded the right to take such reasonable steps as it deems appropriate to protect its said interests'. [1978] ECR 207, para. 189; see too *AKZO* v. *Commission* [1991] ECR 1–3359.
58. *Sirena* v. *Eda* [1971] ECR 3169.
59. Above, note 52.
60. *United Brands* v. *Commission* [1978] ECR 207 at para. 249.
61. *Ministère Public v. Tournier* and *Lucazeau v. SACEM* [1991] 4 CMLR 248.

62. See, for example, F. Machlup, *An Economic Review of the Patent System, Study of the Committee on Patents, Trademarks and Copyright*, Senate Judiciary Committee, US 85th Congress, Study no. IS, Washington, DC (1958) at p. 12.

63. *Parke Davis* v. *Probel* [1968] ECR 55.

64. *Scandlines* v. *Port of Helsingborg* (HHAB) COMP/A36.568, 23 July 2004.

65. Ibid., para 235.

66. XXIVth Report on Competition Policy (Commission 1994), p. 207.

67. *General Motors Continental* v. *Commission* [1976] ECR 1367 at 1379.

68. [1978] ECR 207.

69. *British Leyland* v. *Commission*, [1986] ECR 3263, illustrates that the charge of excessive prices may be proved by evidence of the dominant undertaking's own previous pricing conduct, particularly where there is a huge discrepancy.

      In that case, British Leyland had sole authority under British law to issue certificates of conformity for traders of left-hand drive Metros wanting access to the British market. After a period of charging a single fee of £25 for both right- and left-hand drive vehicles, it raised its fee for left-hand vehicles to £150 for dealers and £100 for consumers. The Court found that British Leyland had abused its dominant position in respect of the supply of certificates of conformity by refusing to approve certificates and by charging excessive fees.

70. In *United Brands*, the Commission had found that United Brands had charged excessive prices based on a comparison of the price in Ireland with that in other countries. This was the 'comparative cost' method borrowed from German jurisprudence. The Commission had found that the price in Belgium was 80 per cent higher than in Ireland and ordered United Brands to reduce its prices wherever they were higher than the Irish baseline. The Court found that the failure of the Commission to refute United Brands' contention that the Irish price was making a loss meant that it was operating from a false base.

71. [1978] ECR 207 at 302.

72. As Fox has described it 'American law rests on the principle that price should be controlled by the free market unless Congress has in effect determined that the market cannot work and has established a regulatory commission.' E. Fox, 'Monopolization and Dominance in the United States and the European Community: Efficiency, Opportunity, and Fairness' (1986) 61 *Notre Dame Law Review* 981 at 993.

73. EC law rejects the concept of US antitrust policy which holds that if a firm attains monopoly on its competitive merits and prices at monopoly levels, the high price itself will invite new entry and market forces would gradually wear away the monopoly power. See T. Kauper, 'Article 86, Excessive Prices and Refusals to Deal' (1991) 59 *Antitrust Law Journal* 441.

74. [1968] ECR 55 at para. 73.

75. [1988] ECR 6039.

76. [1988] ECR 6039 para. 17.

77. Ibid.
78. V. Korah, 'No Duty to License Independent Repairers to Make Spare Parts: The Renault, Volvo and Bayer Henneke Cases' (1988) *European Intellectual Property Review* 381 at 383.
79. See, for example, I. Govaere, *The Use and Abuse of Intellectual Property Rights in EC Law* (London: Sweet & Maxwell, 1996) Chapter 2.
80. G. Tritton, *Intellectual Property in Europe* (London: Sweet & Maxwell, 1995).
81. Machlup has described this as the monopoly-profit-incentive theory of patent protection, emphasising its incentive for innovation. See Machlup, note 62 above.
82. See, for example, V. Korah, *EC Competition Law and Practice* (Oxford: Hart Publications, 5th edn) at p. 99.
83. G. Friden, 'Recent developments in EEC Intellectual Property Law: The Distinction Between Existence and Exercise Revisited' (1989) 26 *Common Market Law Review* 193 at 211.
84. Machlup has suggested that since 'it is the very essence of patents to restrict competition and permit output to be kept below, and price above, competitive levels, it is difficult to conceive economic criteria by which one could judge whether output is less than reasonably "practicable" and price is "unreasonably high". See note 62 above.
85. See for example *Sirena* v. *Eda* [1971] ECR 3169 at para. 17: 'A higher price for a trademarked product does not per se constitute sufficient proof of abuse but it may nevertheless become so, in view of its size, if it does not seem objectively justified.' [1971] ECR 3169 at para. 17.
86. See for example *British Leyland* v. *Commission* note 69 above.
87. [1988] ECR 6039 para. 16.
88. Ibid., para. 17.
89. In *British Leyland* v. *Commission*, for example, a finding of abusive pricing under Article 82(a) was based on its exclusionary effects, where the pricing policy was linked to a policy of discouraging competitors by refusing to approve.
90. Note 87 above.
91. Ibid., para. 63.
92. See for example Govaere, note 79 above at p. 260.
93. See for example *BRT* v. *SABAM* [1974] ECR 51. See discussion in D. Goyder, *EC Competition Law* (Oxford: Oxford University Press, 4th edn 2003) 312–14.
94. Note 61 above.
95. Note 93 above.
96. *Lucazeau et al.* v. *SACEM et al.* [1989] ECR 2811 at para. 29.
97. See for example *Tremblay* v. *Commission* [1996] ECR I-5545.
98. Note 14 above.
99. Ibid. para. 8.

100. See, for example, *Tetra Pak* v. *Commission* [1990] ECR II-309.

101. See, for example, *United Brands* v. *Commission* [1978] ECR 207 para. 301 (a price which is excessive because it had no relation to the value of the product supplied).

102. See, for example, *AKZO* v. *Commission* [1993] 5 CMLR 215.

103. See, for example, *Hoffman La Roche* v. *Commission* [1979] ECR 461.

104. Note 14 above, para. 9.

105. See *ICI and Commercial Solvents* v. *Commission* [1974] ECR 223; see too *Tetra Pak International* v. *Commission* [1994] ECR II-755.

106. Joined cases C-241/91P and C-242/91P *RTE, and ITP* v. *Commission* [1995] ECR I-743.

107. Ibid. para. 54.

108. Ibid., para. 56.

109. Note 122 below.

110. Ibid. at para. 57 'In the light of all those circumstances the Court of First Instance did not err in law in holding that the appellants conduct was an abuse of a dominant position.'

111. See for example *Tetra Pak International* v. *Commission* [1996] ECR-1–5 951 para. 37.

112. See, for example, *Sega and Nintendo*, EC Commission 1997.

113. *Oscar Bronner GMbH & Co.KG* v. *Mediaprint* [1998] ECR 1–7791.

114. Ibid. para. 40–41.

115. Case T-184/OIR (2001).

116. See para. 91. The appeal against the suspension of the Commission's compulsory licence was dismissed by the President of the ECJ on 11 April 2002.

117. The case has raised other issues on appeal to the ECJ such as the need for *two* separate markets and the nature of the indispensability test. See Advocate General Tizzano's Opinion of 2 October, 2003 Case C – 418/01 *IMS Health GmbH & Co. KG* v. *NDC Health & Co. KG*.

118. Case C – 418/01 *IMS Health GmbH & Co. KG* v. *NDC Health & Co. KG*.

119. See analysis by John Kallagher, 'Recent Developments under Article 82', talk given to IBC Conference London, 30 April 2004.

120. See Press Release, Conclusion of Microsoft Investigation, 24 March 2004, IP/04/382.

121. Ibid.

122. *Commercial Solvents* v. *Commission* [1974] ECR 223; see too *Centre Belge d'Etudes de Marché (CBEM)* v. *Télémarketing* [1985] ECR 3261. Compared to *Otter Tail* in the USA.

123. See, for example, *IBM Personal Computer EC* Comm. Doc. 84/233 (1984); *Microsoft IP* (94) 643 [1994] 5 CMLR 143.

124. *IBM Personal Computer* EC Comm. Doc. 84/233 (1984).

125. [1984] 3 CMLR 147.

126. *Microsoft IP* (94) 643 [1994] 5 CMLR 143.

127. *United States* v. *Microsoft Corp*, 253 F. 3d 34 (D. C. Cir.) cert. denied 122 S.Ct. 350 (2001).

128. Ibid.

129. See Chapter 3 in this volume for more about the US case.

130. Case COMP/C-3/37.792. This statement of Objections also alleged that Microsoft may have acted illegally by incorporating its new Multi Media Utility Media Player into its Windows PC operating system. See S. Anderman, 'Microsoft in Europe' in *International Intellectual Property Law and Policy* (Juris Publications 2002).

131. See Press Release, Conclusion of Microsoft Investigation, 24 March 2004, IP/04/382.

132. Ibid.

133. Judging from the statement of objections and the recent Press Release, the Commission revealed its acceptance of the network effects analysis of barriers to entry in high technology markets that had influenced the US Justice Department and Federal Trade Commission in the US Microsoft case.

134. Compare this with Chapter 3 in this volume.

135. See M. Dolmans and N. Levy, *EC Commission v Microsoft: Win, Lose or the Tie?* (Brussels: Cleary, Gottlieb, Steen & Hamilton).

136. See for example *Centre Belge d'Etudes de Marché (CBEM)* v. *Télémarketing* [1985] ECR 3261.

137. *RTE, ITV and BBC* v. *Commission* [1995] ECR-I 743 para. 55.

138. Ibid. para. 51.

139. Ibid. para. 55.

140. See *United States* v. *Microsoft Corp.*, 253 F.3d 34 (D. C. Cir. 2001) 62–3.

141. EC *Microsoft* Commission Decision para. 709.

142. Ibid. para. 713.

143. Ibid. para. 724.

144. Ibid. para. 725.

145. Ibid. para. 763.

146. Ibid. para. 782.

147. S. Anderman, *EC Competition Law and Intellectual Property Rights: The Regulation of Innovation* (Oxford: Clarenden Press, 1998).

148. The modern phase of competition law beginning with the US Sherman Act in the 1890s has to be seen as a reaction to the experience in the USA with widespread trusts creating monopolies and cartel and market sharing arrangements in the decades after the Civil War: see R. Peritz, *Competition Policy in the United States* (Oxford: Oxford University Press, 1998).

149. See for example J. Harris, *Property and Justice* (Oxford: Clarendon Press, 1996); I. Rahnasto, *Intellectual Property Rights, External Effects and Antitrust Law* (Oxford: Oxford University Press, 2002).

150. See, for example, the language of Article 1 Clause 8 of the US Constitution.

151. The right of paternity. See, for example, CDPA section 77.

152. The right of integrity. See, for example, CDPA section 80.

153. See for example EU Biotech Directive, recital 14.

154. Compare with the excellent discussion by I. Rahnasto, *Intellectual Property Rights*, pp. 49–62.

155. It should be noted that this is the exact same example as the one given in Article 81(e), suggesting that tie-ins can be caught under both Articles.

156. D. Rushe, 'Microsoft Braced for Big Fines by EU', *Sunday Times* 21 March 2004.

157. R. Stillman, 'Review of the Microsoft Decision', Speech at 'Opening Windows: The Economics of the Microsoft Case', Lexecon, Conrad Hotel Brussels, 19 May 2004.

158. M. Dolmans and T. Graf, 'Analysis of Tying Under Article 82 EC: The European Commission's MICROSOFT Decision in Perspective' (2004) 27(2) *World Competition* 225; compare with Ahlborn et al., Winter 2003, p. 31–32.

159. *Napier Brown* v. *British Sugar*, Commission Decision 88/519/ EEC, [1988] OJ L284, 41 at 46.

160. C-53/92P *Hilti AG* v. *Commission* [1994] ECR I-666; [1994] 1 CMLR 590.

161. T-30/89 *Hilti* v. *Commission* [1991] ECR II-1439, [1992] 4 CMLR 16, para. 68. However, AG Jacobs questions the found market definitions by noting that if there is significant degree of substitutability between the PAF system and others, thus Hilti might not be dominant: AG Jacobs' opinion [1994] 4 CMLR 614, at 624. The ECJ, however, decided not to look further into the relevant market definition, since the CFI already had accepted the Commission's findings and found as well that it was not its responsibility as an appellant court, C-53/92P *Hilti AG* v. *Commission* [1994] ECR I-666; [1994] 1 CMLR 590, para. 11–16.

162. T-30/89 *Hilti* v. *Commission* [1991] ECR II-1439, [1992] 4 CMLR 16, para. 67.

163. Note 166 below.

164. European Commission, 'Fourteenth Report on Competition Policy', point 94 [1984] 3 CMLR 147.

165. Shortly after it became industry standard to offer the memory device integrated into the CPU.

166. C-311/84 *Télémarketing* v. *CLT* [1985] ECR 3261; [1986] 2 CMLR 558.

167. Commission Decision of 24 March 2004, Case COMP/C-3/37.792 Microsoft.

168. D. Lawsky, 'EU Set to Rule Against Microsoft', Reuters, 23 March 2004 (www.reuters.com).

169. *Microsoft* Commission Decision, para. 472.

170. Ibid., para. 438.

171. *Eurofix-Bauco/ Hilti* Commission Decision [1988] OJ L65/19, [1989] 4 CMLR 677, para. 75.

172. Note 170 above, para. 841.

173. Ibid., para. 239.
174. *Napier Brown* v. *British Sugar*, Commission Decision 88/519/ EEC, [1988] OJ L284, 41.
175. Note 166 above.
176. C-311/84 *Tele-Marketing* v. *CLT* [1985] ECR 3261; [1986] 2 CMLR 558, para. 27.
177. *Eurofix-Bauco/Hilti* Commission Decision [1988] OJ L65/19, [1989] 4 CMLR 677, para. 75 and Ahlborn et al. p. 36.
178. *Microsoft* Commission Decision, para. 842.
179. *Hilti* v. *Commission* [1991] ECR II-1439, [1992] 4 CMLR 16, para. 102–14.
180. Ibid. para 102–119.
181. *Tetra Pak International SA* v. *Commission* [1996] ECR I-5951, [1997] 4 CMLR 662, para. 34.
182. *Tetra Pak Rausing* v. *Commission* [1994] ECR II-755, [1997] 4 CMLR 726, para. 82.
183. Ibid.
184. Ibid., para. 137.
185. EC *Microsoft* Commission Decision
186. D. M. Smith, 'EU Antitrust Ruling won't affect Microsoft or its Customers', 17 March 2004, Gartner Research (http://www4.gartner.com/Display Document?doc_cd=120139 (24/03/04)).
187. EC *Microsoft* Commission Decision, paras. 1019 and 1071.
188. See for example *Vaassen/Moris* Commission Decision 79/86, IV/C-29290, OJ L19/32, [1979] 1 CMLR 511.
189. See, for example, *Lucazeau* v. *SACEM* [1989] ECR 2811.
190. See, for example, *Sirena* v. *Eda* [1971] ECR 3169.
191. See, for example, *Ideal Standard* [1994] ECR 1–2789.
192. See TTBER Guidelines paras. 204–9.
193. Ibid. 210–35.
194. *Consten Grundig* v. *Commission* [1966] ECR 299.
195. See, for example, *Coditel 11* [1982] ECR 3381 at para. 14; see too *Parke Davis* v. *Probel and Centrafarm* [1968] ECR 55, [1969] CMLR 47.
196. See, for example, *Deutsche Grammophon Gesellschaft* [1971] ECR 489 at para. 6.
197. See, for example, *Coditel II* (note 195 above) at para. 14.
198. See for example *Polypropylene* [1988] 4 CMLR 34 para. 99.
199. *Corinne Bodson* v. *Pompes Funèbres des Régions Libérées SA* [1985] ECR 2479; [1989] 4 CMLR 984.
200. It can also be lifted to establish the jurisdiction of EC law over the foreign parent of a subsidiary within the EC (see for example *Commercial Solvents* v. *Commission* [1974] ECR 223) or when holding a parent company attributable for the guilty conduct of the subsidiary (see, for example, *Johnson and Johnson* [1981] 2 CMLR 287).
201. Compare with *Commission* v. *Bayer* Case C-3/01 P.

202. See, for example, *Commission* v. *Solvay and La Porte* [1985] 1 CMLR 481. The issue of autonomy is raised again in the context of the relationship between parents and joint ventures.

203. After *Grundig* (note 194 above) for example, Grundig simply acquired Consten and integrated it within the Grundig organisation.

204. Commission Notice, Guidelines on Vertical Restraints, OJ C 291, 13.10.2000, 1–44.

205. Note 193 above; see too *XXIII Report on Competition Policy* (1993) Com (94) 161 final, p. 212.

206. This mode of analysis took no account of the actual economic effects of an agreement or provision, let alone basic economic arguments that strong inter-brand competition in the final product market can operate to curb the effects of anticompetitive restrictions within a vertical chain of manufacturing and distribution. The analysis consisted of an examination of the terms of agreements to determine whether they limit, or are intended to limit, the freedom of action of the parties to the agreement or third parties in the market. See C. Bright, 'Deregulaton of EC Competition Policy: Rethinking Article 85(1)' and I. Forrester, 'Competition Structures for the 21st Century' in (1994) *Fordham Corporate Law Institute* at 505 and 405 respectively.

207. Ibid.

208. Even at the time of the *Grundig* decision, the Court of Justice had the conviction that the freedom of action concept should not apply as comprehensively to vertical agreements as it should to horizontal agreements. Having insisted in *Grundig* that Article 81 applied to vertical agreements as well as horizontal agreements, and accepted that a version of the freedom of action test was applicable, the Court was equally insistent that the test of restriction should be subject to a qualitative as well as a quantitative appreciability test.

209. See, for example, R. Whish and B. Sufrin, 'Article 85: The Rule of Reason' [1987] *Oxford Year Book in European Law*; Forrester and Noralt 'The Laicisation of Community Law Self Help and the Rule of Reason' [1984] 21 *Common Market Law Review* 11.

210. See, for example, D. Gonzales, 'Some Reflections on the Notion of Ancillary Restraints under EC Competition Law' [1995] *Fordham Corporate Law Institute* 325 at 350–4.

211. Regulation 1/2003, [2003] OJ 1/1, 4.1.2003.

212. Commission Notice on agreements of minor importance which do not appreciably restrict competition under Article 81(1) of the Treaty establishing the European Community ('De Minimis'), OJ C 368, 22 December 2001, pp. 13–15.

213. Regulation 1/2003, [2003] OJ 1/1, 4.1.2003.

214. *Compagnie Maritime Belge* [2000] ECR I-1365 para. 130.

215. See, for example, *Crehan* v. *Courage* [2001] 5 CMLR 1058 (automatic voidness under Article 81(2) does not preclude a damages action by an injured party to the contract. Moreover, severance may be allowed under national law.).

216. Recital 6: see too Articles 1(1) and 5(1)(4).
217. In fact they consisted of a mix of cleared clauses, i.e. those not caught by Article 81(1) and exemptible clauses, i.e. those caught by Article 81(1) but automatically exempted under Article 81(3).
218. See Evaluation Report para. 55; see too Guidelines on Vertical Restraints, point 7.
219. Commission Evaluation Report on the Transfer of Technology Block Exemption Regulation No. 240/96, 'Technology Transfer Agreements under Article 81' at p. 6.
220. COM (2001) 786 final, 20.12.2001.
221. For example territorial and customer restrictions were treated differently.
222. Guidelines para. 9.
223. Article 4(3).
224. Guidelines paras. 24 and 131.
225. 'Patents' are widely defined to include utility models, designs, topographies of semiconductor products and plant breeder's certificates (Article 1(1)(h)).
226. Article 1(1)(b).
227. Guidelines para. 53.
228. Article 1(1)(b).
229. Guidelines para. 51.
230. Guidelines para. 53.
231. Article 2; Guidelines para. 41.
232. Guidelines para. 42.
233. Guidelines para. 44.
234. Article 1(j)(ii); Guidelines paras. 24 and 31.
235. Article 1(j)(ii).
236. Article 1(j)(i).
237. Article 4 (3); Guidelines para. 31; see too paras. 32–3.
238. Article 3.
239. Article 4.
240. Article 3.1; Guidelines para 31.
241. Guidelines para. 74.
242. Article 4(1)(a); Guidelines paras. 79–80, 156.
243. Article 4((1)(b); Guidelines paras. 82–3, 175.
244. Article 4(1)(c); Guidelines para. 84.
245. The one exception is where the restriction is indispensable to prevent the disclosure of the licensed technology. Article 4(1)(d).
246. Compare with article 4(2) of Regulation 17/62.
247. Article 4(2).
248. See discussion in Guidelines paras. 107–16.
249. Article 1(j)(ii).
250. Outside the safe harbour of the TTBER, potential competition can be taken into account to some extent in technology markets: Guidelines para. 66.

251. A 'technology market' is defined under Guideline 22 as consisting of the technologies which are rivals to the technology of the licensor. If any technologies would be substitutable for licensees faced with a SSNIP ('Small but Significant and Non-transitory Increase in Price'), then those technologies are in the same market. Guideline 23 suggests that an alternative approach is to calculate the shares of the technology by reference to the market share of its licensed product on the relevant product market. See TTBER Article 3(3).

252. If the parties own technologies that are in a one-way or two-way blocking patent position the parties are considered to be non-competitors on the technology market. A one-way blocking position exists when a technology cannot be exploited without infringing upon another technology. This is for instance the case where one patent covers an improvement of a technology covered by another patent. In that case the exploitation of the improvement patent presupposes that the holder obtains a licence to the basic patent. A two-way blocking position exists where neither technology can be exploited without infringing upon the other technology and where the holders thus need to obtain a licence or a waiver from each other. In assessing whether a blocking position exists the Commission will rely on objective factors as opposed to the subjective views of the parties. Particularly convincing evidence of the existence of a blocking position is required where the parties may have a common interest in claiming the existence of a blocking position in order to be qualified as non-competitors, for instance where the claimed two-way blocking position concerns technologies that are technological substitutes. Relevant evidence includes court decisions including injunctions and opinions of independent experts. In the latter case the Commission will, in particular, closely examine how the expert has been selected. However, other convincing evidence, including expert evidence from the parties that they have or had good and valid reasons to believe that a blocking position exists or existed, can also be relevant to substantiate the existence of a blocking position (para. 32).

253. However, in individual cases longer periods can be taken into account. The period of time needed for undertakings already on the market to adjust their capacities can be used as a yardstick to determine this period. The parties are for instance likely to be considered potential competitors on the product market where the licensee produces on the basis of its own technology in one geographic market and starts producing in another geographic market on the basis of a licensed competing technology. In such circumstances, it is likely that the licensee would have been able to enter the second geographic market on the basis of its own technology, unless such entry is precluded by objective factors, including the existence of blocking patents.

254. Article 4(3). In some cases it may also be possible to conclude retrospectively that even though the licensor and the licensee produced competing products at the time the agreement was made, they are nevertheless non-competitors on the relevant product market and the relevant technology market because

the licensed technology represents such *a drastic innovation* that the technology of the licensee is rendered obsolete or uncompetitive. This classification can be made at any stage when it becomes clear that the licensee's technology has become obsolete or uncompetitive on the market. Guidelines para. 33.

255. See, for example, Guidelines para. 31.

256. Guidelines to application of Article 81(3). Compare to TTBER Guidelines para. 75, 'based on the nature of the restriction and experience showing that such restrictions are almost always anti-competitive'.

257. The Guidelines indicate that the agreement must affect actual and potential competition to such an extent that on the relevant market negative effects on product, innovation or variety of goods and services can be expected with a reasonable degree of probability. These effects must be appreciable, i.e. not insignificant (Guidelines to Article 81(3) para. 24). The assessment of the effects of a licence agreement must be made on the basis of a proper market analysis. The burden of proof that an agreement restricts competition will be on the Commission or competition authority.

258. The new methodology assumes that market shares are a proxy for market power. It provides a first safe haven at 30 per cent, a second safe haven with four other poles of competition, below dominance and dominance as meaningful stages of market power for the purpose of the Guidelines.

259. However, one cannot argue that all provisions within a contract between non-competitors will not have a competitive effect. A clause in a licensee's contract that obligates him or her not to directly sell into the territory of another licensee would be one example.

260. Para. 155. Compare with Article 81(3) Guidelines para. 29. It is useful to revive the distinction between non-restrictive and exemptible clauses in licensing agreements. The white lists in previous regulations tended to combine contractual restraints not caught by Article 81(1) with those that were so caught but nevertheless exempted in a single white list of clauses. For parties engaged in self-certification today it is wise to make such distinctions clearer.

261. The Guidelines are more cautious: 'For instance, territorial restraints in an agreement between non-competitors may fall outside Article 81(1) for a certain duration, if the restraints are objectively necessary for a licensee to penetrate a new market.'

262. See in this respect, for example, judgment in *Consten Grundig* v. *Commission* [1966] ECR 429.

263. Note 193 above.

264. See TTBER article 4(2).

265. The Commission has pointed out that Article 4(3) will apply even if the licensees and licensors become actual competitors at a later date because 'the licensee starts licensing out his technology or the licensor becomes an actual or potential supplier of products on the relevant market'.

266. See Guidelines para. 31.

267. Further evidence of non-competitor status during the course of the contract will be offered by the licensee's use of the licensor's trade mark.

268. See definitions in TTBER Article 1(1)(c) and (d). Are the parties cross-licensing competing technologies or technologies which can be used to produce competing products? See too the special position of one-way or two-way blocking patents (Guidelines para. 32) and 'drastic innovations' (Guidelines para. 33).

269. A similar more lenient treatment is given to reciprocal agreements between competitors where a restriction on output is imposed only on one of the licensees. See, for example, Article 4(1)(b).

270. Guidelines para. 131.

271. Guidelines para. 9.

272. Council Regulation 1/2003 on the implementation of the rules on competition laid down in Articles 81 and 82 of the Treaty.

273. It replaced the old Council Regulation 17/62, 1 May 2004.

274. Regulation 1/2003, recital 1–3.

275. Council Regulation 1/2003 on the implementation of the rules on competition laid down in Articles 81 and 82 of the Treaty, Article 7(1).

276. Council Regulation 1/2003 on the implementation of the rules on competition laid down in Articles 81 and 82 of the Treaty, Article 8.

277. A. Jones and B. Sufrin, *EC Competition Law, Text, Cases, and Materials* (Oxford: Oxford University Press, 2001) p. 850.

278. Note there is a separate regulation for mergers, which also deals with fines and penalties for mergers not compatible with the Common Market.

279. Article 23(2).

280. Article 24(1)(a).

281. Council Regulation 17/1962, First regulation implementing Article [81] and [82] of the Treaty, [OJ Sp. Ed. 1962, No. 204/62, p. 87] as amended by Regulation (EC) No 1216/1999 of 10 June 1999 [OJ 1999, No. L148/5]. Note this regulation is no longer in force.

282. C-6, 7/73 *Instituto Chemioterapica Italiano SpA and Commercial Solvents Corp.* v. *Commission* [1974] ECR 223, [1974] 1 CMLR 309.

283. Ibid., para. 45.

284. *Re Magill TV Guide/ ITP, BBC, and RTE*, (Commission Decision 89/205) [1989] OJ L78/43, [1989] 4 CMLR 757 and C-241–242/91P; *Radio Telefis Eireann* v. *Commission* [1995] ECR I-743, [1995] 4 CMLR 718.

285. C-333/94P *Tetra Pak International SA* v. *Commission* [1996] ECR I-5951, [1997] 4 CMLR 662.

286. Commission Decision 94/215, [1994] OJ L116/1, [1994] 5 CMLR 353.

287. Article 3 of Commission Decision *Tetra Pak II* 92/163, OJ L72 (18.03.92), [1992] 4 CMLR 551.

288. Ibid.

289. See Second Revised Final Proposal of 6 November 2001, III D–F.

290. Ibid., III J.
291. R. Whish, *Competition Law* (Oxford: Oxford University Press, 5th edn, 2003), p. 255.
292. *Welded Steel Mesh*, [1989] OJ L260/1, [1990] 4 CMLR 13.
293. Cases T-7 and 9/93, *Langnese-Iglo & Schöller Lebensmittel* v. *Commission* [1995] ECR II-1533, [1995] 5 CMLR 602, upheld by the ECJ in Case C-279/95P *Langnese-Iglo & Schöller Lebensmittel* v. *Commission* [1998]ECR I-5609, [1998] 5 CMLR 933.
294. Whish, *Competition Law*, p. 254.
295. Case T-24/90 [1992] ECR II-2223, [1992] 5 CMLR 431.
296. Ibid., para. 8.
297. Case T-24/90 [1992] ECR II-2223, [1992] 5 CMLR 431.
298. Case T-395/94 *Atlantic Container Line AB v Commission* [2002] ECR II-875, [2002] 4 CMLR 1008.
299. 'A door-to-door transport, includes, in addition to maritime transport, the inland carriage of maritime containers between the coast and inland locations. The price of an intermodal transport service is made up of two elements, one relating to the maritime service, the other to the inland service. Thus, [the trans-Atlantic agreement] established, in addition to a maritime tariff, a tariff for the inland transport services operated in the territory of the Community in the context of an intermodal transport operation.' Para. 27.
300. Note 297 above, para. 27.
301. Ibid., para. 405.
302. Ibid., para. 415.
303. Ibid., para. 415–16.
304. Commission's XXVII Report on Competition Policy (1997), point 80 and pp. 148–9.
305. Whish, *Competition Law*, p. 743.
306. Commission's XXIX Report on Competition Policy (1999), points 55–6 and p. 162.
307. Whish, *Competition Law*, pp. 743–4.
308. In the old Block Exemption Regulation on Technology Transfer Agreements (240/96) OJ [1996] L31/2, Article 2 consisted of a so-called 'white list' which included clauses that are normally found in licensing agreements and normally do not restrict competition. The minimum quantity requirement was on this list. However, in the new Technology Transfer Block Exemption Regulation there is no 'white list'; anything that is not specifically blacklisted in the provisions is now permitted. Minimum quantity requirements are not included.
309. Council Regulation (EC) No 139/2004 of 20 January 2004 on the control of concentrations between undertakings, OJ L 24 (29.01.2004), pp. 1–22.
310. Commission Notice on remedies acceptable under Council Regulation (EEC) No. 4064/89 and under Commission Regulation (EC) No. 447/98, (OJ 2001, No. C68/03).

311. Commission Notice on acceptable remedies, para. 2.

312. Commission Notice on acceptable remedies, para. 9.

313. Case T-102/96 [1999] ECR II-753, [1999] 4 CMLR 971, paras. 317–18.

314. *Gencor*, para. 319 and Commission Notice on acceptable remedies, paras. 9–10.

315. Commission Notice on acceptable remedies, para. 14.

316. COMP/M. 1601, *Allied Signal/Honeywell*, Commission Decision of 1 December 1999.

317. Commission Press Release IP/99/921, 'Commission authorises Allied Signal/ Honeywell merger, subject to substantial conditions', Brussels, 1 December 1999.

318. This was the case in *Boeing/McDonnell Douglas* IV/M.877, where the Commission found that there was no purchaser for the Douglas Aircraft Company.

319. Commission Notice on acceptable remedies, para. 26.

320. Commission Notice on acceptable remedies, para. 29.

321. *Glaxo/Wellcome* IV/M.555, Commission Decision of 28 Feb. 1995, OJ C 65 (16.3.1995), p. 3.

322. Ibid., para. 23.

323. Ibid., para. 29.

324. Commission Notice on acceptable remedies, para. 49.

325. This doctrine includes the corollary proposition that the 'normal' exercise of IPRs will not abuse a dominant position. Only in extreme cases where IPRs are used unjustifiably by their highly dominant owners to exclude competitors from markets does EC competition policy reserve a right to intervene to limit the exercise of IPRs. It defines the special responsibilities of a dominant firm towards weakened competition so as to allow the dominant IPR owner to compete by preventing copying even if the exercise of this right denies access to primary markets to competitors. The test of 'exceptional circumstances' requires evidence of leveraging conduct in 'after markets'.

326. Growth to dominance by mergers and acquisitions is treated as fundamentally different.

327. The US Guidelines state: '2.0 (a) for the purpose of antitrust analysis, the Agencies regard intellectual property as being essentially comparable to any other form of property and apply to conduct involving IP on the same basis as to conduct involving any property tangible or intangible. IP has different characteristics . . .' but add, 'These characteristics can be taken into account by standard antitrust analysis and do not require the application of fundamentally different principles': (para 2.1).

328. Guidelines para. 8.

329. Guidelines para. 9. See too para. 17 in which the Commission sets out the pro-competitive potential of licensing agreements.

3

Competition policy and its implications for intellectual property rights in the United States

RUDOLPH J. R. PERITZ

Introduction: innovation and competition

At the federal level of US law, both intellectual property protection and antitrust policy share a common goal of encouraging innovation. But observers agree that this common goal is achieved by different approaches – antitrust policy by fostering competition and patent and copyright policies by granting rights to exclude rivals. Still, this distinction of means is not absolute: antitrust permits some exclusionary strategies and intellectual property policy fosters some competition. In consequence, both approaches must be understood as balancing property protection and competition, exclusion and access and, ultimately, private rights and public benefits.

The several states provide a second level of intellectual property protection: each state protects intellectual property through its own trade secret and trademark laws. In contrast to the European Union, whose federalism is informed by a policy imperative to harmonise the laws of individual states with those of the Union, federalism in the United States is not guided by one clear imperative. On the one hand, the US Constitution's supremacy clause means just that: where federal and state laws conflict, federal law is supreme. On the other hand, federal law often leaves room for state law, regardless of policy conflict, and sometimes invites states to regulate. In the domain of trademark protection, federal law does even more – the Lanham Act was passed to supplement state laws. But in other areas of overlap, such as federal patents and state trade secrets, policy differences sometimes call for limitations on state law rights.

This chapter examines federal antitrust law as well as federal and state intellectual property protection.[1] Each body of law has developed its own approach to competition and its own conception of property rights. In this light, an evaluation of the impact of competition policy on intellectual property rights must proceed in two stages. First, within each applicable body of law, the internal relations between the particular competition policies and intellectual property rights must be examined. Second, the results of the internal analyses must then be compared to determine whether there are conflicts and, if there are, how to reconcile them.

Accordingly, this chapter is organised in three sections. The first describes US intellectual property law, beginning with its historical and economic foundations. It then examines the federal copyright and patent systems and, finally, the largely state law regimes of trade secret and trade name protection.

The second section presents an overview of US antitrust law. After a very brief introduction to its historical and economic foundations, the section analyses the statutory, regulatory and judicial components of the national antitrust regime.

These overviews of US intellectual property protection and antitrust law provide the analytical framework for the third and final section, which examines antitrust regulation of intellectual property rights (IPR). The section takes a transactional approach, scrutinising antitrust treatment of particular strategic conduct such as licensing practices, joint ventures, and stock or asset purchases.

I. US intellectual property rights and innovation: the competition policies within

This section begins with an introduction to the purposes guiding IPR protection in the United States, noting how the constitutional foundations for patent and copyright differentiate their goals in significant ways from those of common law trade mark and trade secret. Next, the copyright and patent regimes are described and compared. The section concludes with a discussion of trade mark and trade secret laws, including their relationships with copyright and patent. Throughout, special attention is given to the interplay between property protection and competition policy in shaping IPR.

A. The purposes of intellectual property rights

On the heels of two centuries of contentious debate over copyright in England, consensus over the nature of copyright, as well as patent, was reached rather quickly in the United States by adopting the resolutions reached in England. US trade name and trade secret protection, however, has continued to reflect somewhat unsettled foundations. Broadly speaking, policy debate over IPR in the United States has addressed two related issues: First, the differences between tangible and intellectual property; and second, the justifications for protecting intellectual property.

Certainly there is a fundamental difference between tangible property, whether goods or land, and intellectual property in the work of writers and inventors. First and foremost, because tangible property is a physical thing, its use or ownership is understood as 'rivalrous' or exclusive – for example, while

I use my mobile phone or possess my freehold, you do not. Moreover, my use depletes the store of tangible property available. Fundamentally, private ownership of tangible property has come to mean the right to exclude others.[2] In this light, enforcing ownership rights provides a system for settling disputes over private property use and avoids the 'tragedy of the commons', the waste attributed to overuse of public property.[3]

But with intellectual property, possession and use need not be exclusive or rivalrous. Any number of people can simultaneously read copies of the same poem or run copies of the same software algorithm without stopping anyone else's use. Moreover, an expression or the idea behind an invention does not wear out with increasing use (though popular expression risks decay into dismal cliché). Indeed, widespread use can sometimes increase the value of an invention or expression. Why then protect IPR? Four justifications have emerged, some of them applicable to tangible property as well.

First, there is the tenet often associated with the English writer John Locke that government protection of private property, including IPR, preserves a person's natural right to the product of her labour, whether a poem or an acre of corn. Although this labour theory of property ownership has certain limits, its foundation is the moral precept that a person should own what he produces.

A second justification emerged out of the German philosophical tradition. Traced back to the writings of Kant and Hegel, this view emphasises the importance to personhood of some kinds of property. It distinguishes between property's value to personal identity and its functional value. In this light, a poem or web page design would merit greater IPR protection than a customer list or a trade secret. A prohibition against film colourisation would be more worthy than a right against film copying.[4]

The third and most influential justification for IPR in the United States is found in the constitutional clause granting Congress authority to enact patent and copyright legislation. The clause begins with the justification: 'To promote the Progress of Science and the useful Arts.'[5] Explicitly instrumentalist, the clause has been uniformly interpreted as calling for Congress and the courts to shape and enforce private rights in order to maximise the public benefit of encouraging innovation. As the Supreme Court has stated: 'The immediate effect of our copyright law is to secure a fair return for the author's creative labour. But the ultimate aim is, by this incentive, to stimulate artistic creativity for the general good.'[6] Copyright and patent are both regarded as the private means to accomplish a public end. In consequence, both overprotection and underprotection can pose dangers to the general good. Copyrights to derivative works and broadly described patents, for example, can amount to overprotection of computer software, where cumulative or add-on innovation is a significant competitive factor.[7]

In the latter half of the twentieth century, market economics has been applied to the task of determining 'the general good'. To begin, there is the consensus that IPR remedies a market failure that results from the 'public goods' characteristics of inventions and expressions.[8] By privatising the benefit of intellectual activity, IPR seeks to stop the diversion of profits and other benefits from the creator that stems from the ease of copying and misappropriation of a non-rivalrous good. Thus IPR is viewed as creating an incentive to engage in intellectual activity that produces progress in science and useful arts. Yet, despite the consensus, there is the fundamental problem that the very efficacy of IPR as an engine for innovation lacks sound empirical ground. In the shadow of this empirical uncertainty, policy debate has emerged over the metes and bounds of 'the general good'. Some have expressed concern about underprotection, arguing that maximising IPR maximises incentives to innovate. Others have focused on harms of over-protection, pointing to the heightened entry barriers to first-stage innovation, especially in markets evidencing network effects.[9] Nonetheless, policy analysts and legal decision makers in the United States rightly persist in seeking to cast 'the general good' in the constitutional mould of encouraging progress in science and the useful arts.

The constitutional mandate has been interpreted as requiring a careful balancing of property rights and competitive effects. Because competition is seen as an important spur to invention, the mandate is closely linked to IPR's fourth and final justification. The last rationale is IPR's role in efficient markets, whether promoting fair competition on the merits or improving market information. For example, trade name protection can produce market efficiencies when it dispels consumer confusion or otherwise decreases information search costs. So too does the strict patent filing requirement of description and enablement address informational asymmetry, by making public the knowledge of novel and useful inventions and, in consequence, improving conditions for further innovation.

The overviews that follow show how thoroughly competition policy has suffused IPR protection in the United States. Indeed, the approach taken to encouraging progress in science and useful arts cannot be understood without recognising the fundamental commitment to competition as an engine for driving innovation.

B. Constitutional origins: copyright and patent protection

Copyright and patent protections share a common constitutional origin whose clearly stated purpose has informed congressional legislation and federal case law for the past 200 years. The Copyright and Patent clause of the US Constitution is a model of concise drafting: Congress is granted power 'to promote the progress of science and the useful arts, by securing for limited times, to authors and inventors, the exclusive right to their respective writings and discoveries'. Parallel ordering of references in the clause is instructive: Copyright involves 'Science . . . authors . . . writings'. Patent applies to 'useful arts . . . inventors . . . discoveries'. And both grants were intended 'to promote progress . . . by securing for limited times . . . exclusive right[s]'.[10] The drafters left to Congress the tasks of determining the standards for protection, the term of years, and the nature of the rights, guided nonetheless by the explicit goal of promoting progress. Although there is some debate about the meaning of 'progress', all agree that it involves the public dissemination of knowledge, as evidenced by the traditional requirements of publication. Most would also agree that 'progress' includes two kinds of development: first, the research and development of inventions to improve people's lives; and second, the development of a public domain of knowledge to inform and spur further innovation. In both senses of development, innovation is seen as best served by the right mix of private property rights and competitive markets.

Three years after the Constitution's adoption, Congress passed the twin Patent and Copyright Acts of 1790. Following two centuries of congressional legislation and judicial construction, copyright and patent have come to differ somewhat despite their common origin. The differences have sometimes raised questions about their proper relationship, especially in markets where information goods can qualify for protection of both invention and expression. To address the thorny issues raised in such markets, this section pays special attention to copyright and patent protection of computer software.

1. Patent protection and competition policy

The Patent Act provides that anyone who 'invents or discovers any new and useful process, machine . . . or composition of matter, or any new and useful improvement thereof, may obtain a patent therefor'. Patent prosecution begins with the filing of an application in the Patent and Trademark Office (PTO) and, if successful, concludes with the grant of a right to exclude others from making, using or selling the patented invention for a term of 20 years.[11] It should be noted that patent grants are not affirmative rights to practise patented inventions. They are subject, for example, to antitrust limitations or, in the case of medications, to approval by the Food and Drug Administration. Moreover, prior patents owned by others might interfere with a patent holder's rights to employ the invention – calling for cross-licensing agreements.

To be successful, the application must satisfy the PTO that four statutory requirements are met: the specifications must reflect patentable subject matter, utility, novelty and non-obviousness. Moreover, the application must describe the invention in a way that would enable others to make and use the invention. The resulting patent grant reflects the constitutional goal of encouraging innovation in three ways: when the patent is granted, the invention is disclosed in the PTO records, giving public access to new knowledge; next, the patent holder is given exclusive control over the invention as the incentive to exploit it by developing new and improved products for public use; and finally, after the patent expires, the invention becomes part of the public domain, making it freely available to all.

In construing patent legislation, courts have sought to balance private rights to exclusive use and public rights to a commons of knowledge available for research and development of competing products and services. It should be noted that Congress, in passing the 1790 statute and its successors, largely adopted the language and sentiments of the English Statute of Monopolies (1624), enacted by Parliament to limit the royal prerogative to grant patent monopolies.[12] In short, it outlawed all crown grants except those based on true inventions. The 1624 statute and the circumstances of its passage remind us of competition policy's central role in a utilitarian formulation of incentives to encouraging invention. Indeed, competition policy has been no less important to the US approach. It is in this light that the section first describes the well-known requirements for patentability, then the elements of an infringement claim and, finally, the major defences to such claims.[13]

The statutory elements of patentability   Patent Act sections 101 and 102 as glossed in decisions of the federal courts delineate the subject matter, utility, novelty and non-obviousness requirements; section 112 specifies the standard for sufficient description of the invention. Subject to oversight by the Secretary of Commerce, the PTO is responsible for examining applications, for granting and issuing patents, and for disseminating to the public information regarding patents granted. Applicants have statutory rights to seek re-examination of adverse decisions of examiners and, if unsuccessful, to appeal to the Board of Patent Appeals and, further, to the Court of Appeals for the Federal Circuit.[14]

Patentable subject matter
Applicants can seek patent protection for 'any process, machine, manufacture, or composition of matter, or ... any improvement thereof'. In the landmark *Diamond* v. *Chakrabarty*[15] decision, a deeply divided Supreme Court concluded that 'a live, human-made micro-organism is patentable subject matter'. Emphasising that the claim was to 'a non-naturally occurring manufacture', the majority opinion pointed to congressional committee reports accompanying the Patent Act, reports stating that Congress intended to 'include anything under the sun that is made by man'. In the court's view, its expansive interpretation of the statute was supported by broad language, particularly the adjective 'any' that modifies 'composition of matter'.[16]

Despite this expansive view of patentable subject matter, the federal courts have developed several limiting doctrines, most notably the rule against patenting 'abstract ideas'. Based on the traditional notion that a patent is intended to cover physical products of the useful arts, the doctrine holds that an 'idea of itself is not patentable, but a new device by which it may be made practically useful is'.[17] The practical impact of the doctrine attaches to determinations of patent scope. The broader a patent claim the more closely it approaches the underlying idea. The danger in overbreadth, whether with patents or copyrights, is its power to pre-empt competitive innovation. Clearly, the extreme case of overbreadth would be patent protection for an abstract idea underlying an invention.

The 'abstract idea' limitation was addressed in the early cases dealing with computer software patents. In the well-known *Gottschalk* v. *Benson* decision,[18] the Supreme Court, in denying patentability, stated: 'Phenomena of nature, ... mental processes, and abstract intellectual concepts are not patentable, as they are the basic tools of scientific and technological work.' Viewing software as abstract concepts in the form of algorithms, the Court concluded that a patent on such claims 'would wholly pre-empt the mathematical formula and the practical effect would be a patent on the algorithm itself'. But when, as in *Diamond* v. *Diehr*,[19] the application characterised the software as part of 'an industrial process', the combination was seen as falling outside the 'abstract idea' doctrine and hence into the category of patentable subject matter.[20] The Supreme Court reasoned that such processes are more than abstract ideas when they produce some physical or chemical transformation. The consequence of tying the software to a physical process was a narrowing of the patent claim, a movement away from abstract ideas, and an expansion of the free range for later innovation to compete with the patented software.

More recent decisions in the Federal Circuit such as *State Street Bank & Trust*,[21] however, have expanded the scope of software patents by declaring patentable as a process any software that produces a 'useful, concrete and tangible result' including mathematical calculations. In *State Street Bank*, the tangible results were computed share prices. No longer was a physical transformation necessary. These decisions rang the death knell for the mathematical algorithm exclusion. In extending patentable subject matter to purely mathematical algorithms and thus closer to the realm of abstract ideas, the Federal Circuit has significantly narrowed the area for later innovation to subservient patents for improvements that will see the light of day only in the event that the dominant patent holder finds the improvement attractive enough to enter into a cross-licensing agreement. The result is a more confined range for new product innovation and inter-patent competition, and an expanded space for incremental innovation and intra-patent cooperation.[22] The Supreme Court has not disapproved of the Federal Circuit's expansive view of software patentability. After some resistance, the PTO has adopted the Federal Circuit's view, resulting in an explosion of patents granted to computer software applications. But the Court has expressed disagreement and reversed Federal Circuit in other aspects of patent law. Perhaps we have not yet heard the last word on software patentability.

Utility

The most fundamental and yet the least demanding requirement for patentability is usefulness. Whether an invention 'be more or less useful is a circumstance very material to the interest of the patentee', Justice Story wrote in *Lowell* v. *Lewis*,[23] 'but of no importance to the public. If it be not extensively useful, it will silently sink into contempt and disregard.' In short, the value of an invention is a matter left to the market mechanism of competition. On the one hand, this view grants patent protection to minimally useful inventions. On the other, it allows early public access to new technology, increasing the public domain of knowledge and, with it, improving the conditions for subsequent innovation.

Computer software is designed to produce a particular result and, in consequence, does not raise questions of utility. In the fields of biotechnology and chemistry, however, the utility requirement has sometimes raised a barrier to patentability. In the influential *Brenner* case[24] for example, the Supreme Court affirmed the PTO examiner's denial of a process patent for a 'failure "to disclose any utility" for the chemical compound produced by the process'. 'Potential usefulness ... under investigation by serious scientific researchers' was not enough because a 'patent system must be related to the world of commerce'. In partial dissent, Justice Harlan called for a more lenient standard to serve the public benefit, like that described by Justice Story above, of 'achieving and publicizing basic research' in the sciences such as 'chemistry [which] is a highly interrelated field'. Consistent with its expansive view of patentable subject matter, the Federal Circuit has adopted a lenient standard of utility closer to Justice Harlan's view than to the majority's position in *Brenner*. Indeed, the Federal Circuit opinion in *In re Brana*[25] ignored *Brenner* entirely in reversing the PTO's denial of a patent for a compound with claimed anti-tumour effects but without proof of success in actual treatment of the disease in live animals.

Note on novelty and non-obviousness

Though independent of one another, the requirements of novelty and non-obviousness delineated in sections 102(a) and 103(a) go hand in glove, both of them calling for evaluations of the claimed invention's relationship to 'prior art'. They require the PTO to compare the invention to the current state of technology as reflected in the 'references' listed in section 102 (a), which include 'such documentary materials as patents and publications, as well as evidence of actual uses or sales of technology in the United States'.[26] Section 102 (a) allows patents only to inventions not 'known or used by others'. Hence, novelty can be understood as calling for a preliminary determination that the claimed invention was not earlier known or used. If the invention satisfies the novelty requirement, then the non-obviousness inquiry under section 103 (a) proceeds, asking whether the claimed invention is a non-trivial extension of 'prior art'.

Novelty

Together with non-obviousness, novelty defines the very essence of invention and is, fittingly, the heart of the patent system. Economist Joseph Schumpeter portrayed 'the new' as the 'perennial gale of creative destruction' that drives economic progress. Demanding novelty serves two important goals of the patent system. First, it maintains a public domain of knowledge and tech-nology to foster a competitive environment for further research and devel-opment. Second, it encourages knowledge of the field and discourages duplicative research efforts by motivating researchers 'to turn first to libra-ries, not laboratories, in order to gain needed technology'.[27]

Section 102 deals with two separate aspects of prior art: 'statutory bars' that penalise some delays in filing, and previous inventions.

Statutory bars

The most common bars to patentability are printed publication, public use, or sale of the invention more than one year prior to filing the application.[28] The Federal Circuit has described the purposes served by the statutory bars:

> First, there is a policy against removing inventions from the public which the public has justifiably come to believe are freely available to all as a consequence of prolonged sales activity . . . . Next, there is a policy favour-ing prompt and widespread disclosure of new inventions to the public. A third policy is to prevent the inventor from commercially exploiting the exclusivity of his invention substantially beyond the statutorily authorised [20]-year period. The 'on sale' bar forces the inventor to choose between seeking patent protection promptly following sales activity or taking his chances with his competitors without the benefit of patent protection. The fourth and final identifiable policy is to give the inventor a reasonable amount of time following sales activity (set by statute as 1 year) to deter-mine whether a patent is a worthwhile investment. This benefits the public because it tends to minimize the filing of inventions of only marginal public interest. The 1-year grace period provided for by Congress in § 102(b) represents a balance between these competing interests.[29]

The printed publication bar is quite severe. For example, the Federal Circuit found prior publication in the filing of a doctoral thesis indexed only in a special dissertations card catalogue in the Freiburg University Library in the Federal Republic of Germany.[30] Other bars are equally severe. The 'on sale' bar, for example, includes offers for sale. According to the Supreme Court, the offered invention need not have been completed or built. It need only 'be ready for patenting'.[31] The Federal Circuit has even applied the bar to sales by a third party who had stolen the invention from the inventor.[32] The 'public use' bar includes secret use by the inventor, according to Judge Learned Hand, because it allows the inventor to 'extend the period of monopoly' beyond the statutory term.[33] Moreover, the practice frustrates the goal of public dissemination of knowledge to inform competitive innovation.

There is, however, one defence to the statutory bars to patentability – the experimental use exception – which permits the inventor additional time to file beyond the one-year grace period. The Supreme Court's decision in *City of Elizabeth* v. *Pavement Company*[34] remains both an influential and controversial statement of the exception. In the case, an inventor filed for a patent on 'a new and improved wooden pavement' after six years of continuous use. The Court accepted the inventor's claim that the 75-foot length of pavement 'adjoining to a toll-gate' in Boston was used only to test 'the effect on it of heavily loaded wagons, and of varied and constant use; and also to ascertain its durability; and liability to decay'. Noting testimony that the inventor examined the pavement almost daily and observing that long-term durability was a plausible concern, the Court concluded that the inventor's use was experimental rather than commercial. More recently, the Federal Circuit has articulated an approach that looks at the surrounding circumstances to determine whether the use is experimental, emphasising that the testing must relate to technical rather than commercial viability of the invention.[35] In sum, the PTO and courts must be persuaded that the inventor's procrastination in filing for the patent was not a strategy to delay public access to the knowledge reflected in the invention or surreptitiously to extend the statutory grant of a 20-year monopoly. The statutory bars reflect the importance to innovation of the information flow from prompt filing and of the competition that follows strictly limited patent terms.

Previous inventions
The second step of the novelty inquiry requires the PTO to examine once again its body of references, this time to determine whether the invention itself is new in comparison to prior art. In *Rosaire* v. *National Lead Co*[36] for example, the isolated commercial use of a method for oil prospecting, although not a matter of public knowledge, was enough to include the method in prior art because the prospecting was openly done by a large company and, presumably, a matter of knowledge in the industry.

When the application includes computer software claims, special problems can arise. First, 'in the field of ... computer programs, much that qualifies as prior art lies outside the areas in which the PTO has traditionally looked. Many new developments in computer programming are not documented in scholarly publications at all.'[37] Second, even those programs that are found in the reference materials offer little usable information to examiners when prior software patents were granted without a requirement to disclose source code and flow charts.[38] This matter is discussed in the section below on description and enablement. But it should be noted that the inadequate description of invention defeats the most valuable public benefit expected in exchange for patent grants – the public disclosure of new knowledge and technology needed to inform and inspire subsequent inventors.

Non-obviousness

After determining that an invention passes the novelty test, the PTO must return yet again to its body of reference materials to ascertain whether the invention was obvious in light of the prior art.[39] Section 103(a) denies a patent 'if the differences between the [invention] and the prior art are such that the [invention] ... would have been obvious at the time the invention was made to a person having ordinary skill in the art'. Although the section, enacted in 1952, clarified the courts' uneven standards for non-obviousness, questions remain about its application. The Federal Circuit court has taken clear positions on several of those issues. One intensely debated point involved the proper approach to inventions that were combinations or integrations of formerly independent products or processes. The court's *Rockwell* opinion[40] declared that the 'invention must be considered as a whole' not as a combination of elements. Thus, for example, Microsoft's long-held strategy of integrating applications programmes, such as the Internet Explorer browser, into the Windows operating system would likely not be compared to prior art in stand-alone browsers and operating systems. Rather, the integration would more likely be compared to other integrations or even published viewpoints toward integrating browsers and operating systems.[41] Commercial success attributable to a surprising or unanticipated integration would strengthen the non-obviousness claim – presumably even if the applicant has an economic monopoly.[42]

Inventions involving computer software raise difficult questions in determining non-obviousness for the very reasons they pose problems in the novelty stage of comparing an invention to prior art. The uneven and incomplete data base of prior art, and rampant unfamiliarity with standard programming techniques, has led to patents for the obvious. Scholars have criticised the explosion of patents granted for obvious inventions with a software component, not only on account of the prior art problem but also because of the Federal Circuit's expansive interpretation of *Diamond* v. *Diehr* and, thus, its lenient approach to software patentability. Examples include the *Rockwell* decision, discussed above, and *In re Zurko*,[43] in which the Federal Circuit held an invention non-obvious despite the PTO's determination that each of the elements was found in prior art and their combination was an obvious step. In the critics' view, the standard for non-obviousness is far too lenient.[44] The criticisms echo a largely ignored Supreme Court decision,

Dann v. *Johnson*,[45] which applied a stricter test of non-obviousness in the computer industry, one that assumed that someone 'reasonably skilled in [the software programming] art . . . would have been aware both of the nature of the . . . data processing systems in the banking industry and of the [non-computerized] system encompassed in' the invention. Putting them together by computerising the system, the Court concluded, should have been obvious. Despite scholarly criticism and Supreme Court precedent, the Federal Circuit has not turned back on its lenient approach to non-obviousness. The costs of leniency, according to several economic studies, include an incentive shift to the short term and away from the long term research that brings more significant innovation.[46]

Description and enablement

Section 112 requires that the patent application adequately describes the invention and that the description enables skilled technicians or artisans to make use of the invention.[47] A description is adequate if it shows that the applicant is 'in possession of' the invention itself rather than 'a wish, or arguably a plan, for obtaining' it.[48] A patent grant extends only as far as the inventor's work is 'enabled' in the 'embodiments' described. Thus, for example, Samuel Morse successfully claimed the telegraph but not 'all forms of communicating at a distance' using electromagnetic waves because his description did not (and could not) anticipate later embodiments such as telephony or microwave technology. An adequate description gives competitors proper notice of the invention and the patent monopoly and, at the same time, allows rivals to avoid the costs of duplicative research and development.

The associated requirement of enablement is intended to assure that rivals and other interested parties 'skilled in the art' are able to make and use the invention without extended experimentation. The Supreme Court denied a patent to an inventor in *The Incandescent Lamp Patent* case[49] because 'the description [was] so vague and uncertain that no one [could] tell, except by independent experiments, how to construct the patented device'. The patent grant must give proper notice to 'competing manufacturers and dealers of exactly what they are bound to avoid' to allow them to compete without infringing the patent. In short, competition by further innovation depends upon the enablement that results from an adequate description of the invention.

The Federal Circuit's recent easing of the description requirement is illustrated in the *Lockwood* decision.[50] The court concluded that the plaintiff's software patent failed the novelty requirement because it was obvious in light of prior art, which included American Airlines' SABRE software system for online air travel information and reservations. SABRE was included in the prior art even though crucial aspects of the software code were secret and, thus, inaccessible to programmers and designers interested in learning about it. In the court's estimation, 'Americans' public use of the high-level aspects of the SABRE system was enough.' The Federal Circuit paid scant attention to the impact of its low disclosure threshold on the source materials for determining 'prior art' and on building the knowledge commons necessary to inform competitive innovation.[51]

Patent infringement At the core of the patent grant is the power to exclude others from making, using or selling the invention. The metes and bounds of that power are defined by the claims in the application that are ultimately retained in the grant. When a patent holder files an infringement suit, typically seeking injunction and damages, the court must begin by interpreting the claims. Like any other effort to give effect to a legal document, this one is informed by doctrines – some of them canons of construction and others substantive rules, together forming the framework that shapes the legal rights in question. The section begins with the interpretational issues surrounding the doctrines of literal infringement and equivalents, and concludes with those revolving around direct and indirect infringement.

Interpretation of claims
Section 271(a) of the patent statute states: 'Except as otherwise provided in this title, whoever without authority makes, uses, offers to sell, or sells [or imports] any patented invention . . . during the term therefore, infringes the patent.' It should be noted that patent rights empower holders to restrain others from practising their patents. They are not affirmative grants of rights to practise patented devices, which remain subject, for example, to antitrust limitations or, in the case of medications, to approval by the Food and Drug Administration. Moreover, prior patents owned by others might interfere with a patent holder's rights to employ the invention – calling for cross-licensing agreements in order to employ the patent.

Infringement is not limited to devices that are literally identical to the patented invention. The courts have developed a 'doctrine of equivalents' to stop a competitor from employing a device that is not identical but that 'performs substantially the same overall function or work, in substantially the same way, to obtain substantially the same overall result as the claimed invention'.[52] Reflecting the importance of public information to further innovation, the Supreme Court has declared that failing to protect the patentee from 'unscrupulous copyists [who] introduce minor variations to conceal and shelter the piracy . . . would foster concealment rather than the disclosure of inventions, which is one of the primary purposes of the patent system'.[53]

Literal infringement
In contrast to the Federal Circuit's holistic approach to the question of non-obviousness, discussed above, courts have evaluated claims of literal infringement by comparing the patent to the accused invention on a claim-by-claim,

element-by-element basis. In *Laramie Corp.* v. *Amron*,[54] for example, the court granted a summary judgment of non-infringement because the patent claim described the plaintiff's water gun as having a water tank *in* a case while the accused 'SUPER SOAKER' claim described the tank *atop* the case. Successful literal infringement claims are rare, particularly in software patents. But in *Computrol Inc.* v. *Lowrance Electronics Inc.*,[55] the court found that the plaintiff made a sufficient showing that the accused 'side-looking fish detection software' literally infringed its patent.

The doctrine of equivalents
More often, patent holders claim infringement by the doctrine of equivalents. Here too the patent owner must prove that the accused product has a 'substantial equivalent' of every element in the patent claims. In the *Laramie Corp.* decision discussed above, the court rejected a claim of equivalents in finding that the use of an external water tank was not only different from the tank element of the patented water gun but a significant improvement. The competitor's water gun did not infringe the patented product because it was found to embody a new and innovative element.

Even though the requirements for obtaining software patents have eased, courts in infringement cases have construed software patent claims narrowly. In *Weiner* v. *NEC Electronics Inc.* for example,[56] the Federal Circuit affirmed the trial court's determination of no equivalence between two programs employing the same data for the same purpose because the data were arrayed and accessed in somewhat different ways. In *Digital Biometrics, Inc.* v. *Identix, Inc.*,[57] the Federal Circuit again construed a software patent claim narrowly on account of differences in the intermediate steps taken to store a fingerprint image. In light of currently low thresholds for novelty and non-obviousness, this narrowing of the patent monopoly can be seen as a mechanism for adjusting the balance between protection and access, for expanding the scope of competition in software development.

In the closely related issue of equivalence between successive technologies, the Federal Circuit has not followed a steady course. Where a patented process was not computerized and an accused competitive process performed the same function with computer assistance, the doctrine of equivalents has yielded inconsistent conclusions. In *Hughes Aircraft Co.* v. *U.S.* for example,[58] the court determined that the use of on-board computers to control satellites infringed an older patented system which controlled satellites deploying ground telemetry. But in *Alpex Corp.* v. *Nintendo of America*,[59] the court concluded that Nintendo's new video game technology did not infringe the plaintiff's microprocessor patent for a very similar video game because the two inventions processed data in substantially different ways. The equivalence issue in cases involving competition between new technologies runs parallel to the question of non-obviousness seen in decisions such as *Rockwell*, discussed above. But there, the Federal Circuit declared that the 'invention must be considered as a whole' not as a combination of elements. Both the equivalence and non-obviousness issues raise the fundamental question of how to judge whether a difference amounts to an innovative step. The *Texas Instruments* case[60] involved the pioneering patent in integrated circuits, an example of 'a wholly novel device' and thus 'entitled to a broad range of equivalents'.[61] Nonetheless, the Federal Circuit concluded that major improvements in the patent's elements, including redesign of the invention and use of metal oxide semiconductor transistors rendered the accused pocket calculators non-infringing.

At the margin, the problem is even more difficult. Where the patented invention is not pioneering and the accused product is a lesser improvement, the outcome reflects a choice between incentives for innovation. Given the inconclusive research regarding the incentive value of patents, any decision about equivalence at the margin is the product of an assumption made about the better incentive for encouraging innovation – whether slightly greater patent protection or slightly stronger commitment to competition policy.[62]

Direct and indirect infringement

A patent owner can assert a claim not only against direct infringers – those who have practised the invention without authorization, but also against indirect infringers – third parties who have encouraged or helped them.[63]

Direct infringement

Claims of direct infringement are themselves straightforward. The infringer's state of mind, for example, is entirely irrelevant. A patent holder need only prove that the defendant has made, used, sold or offered to sell, or imported the patented invention. However, questions of claim interpretation and asserted defences often complicate the claims. For example, in *Eolas Technologies Inc. v. Microsoft Corp.*,[64] the 'plaintiffs allege that certain aspects of Microsoft's Internet Explorer ("IE") infringe their software patent, and consequently, they accuse Microsoft products which integrate or incorporate IE'. A simple accusation. But the trial court has published eight opinions to resolve pre-trial motions that Microsoft has filed seeking summary judgment on patent claims elements and asserting affirmative defences.

Indirect infringement

Since the 1952 patent statute codified judicial doctrines of infringement, indirect infringement has taken two particular forms. Their common ingredient is the requirement that direct infringement first be proved. In other respects, their elements differ. Section 271(b) states only that a claim of active inducement to infringe a patent is itself infringement. Taking from prior judicial doctrine, courts require the patent holder to prove that the accused infringer knowingly helped another directly infringe the patent by, for example, designing and supplying the plans for an infringing device. The 'knowingly' element does not require proof of 'specific, knowing intent'. Circumstantial evidence can suffice. To prove the requisite intent, courts have required plaintiffs to show, first, that the accused infringer knew of the patent and, second, that he knew that his activities would lead to infringement.[65] Requiring such strong evidence of intent makes good sense given that active inducement can create liability in someone who is sparking competition and has not made, used, sold, or imported the patented device.

Section 271 (c) defines a contributory infringer as anyone who imports, sells, or offers to sell a component of a patented device or a product specially made to infringe the patent when the accused knows it to be unsuitable for any substantial non-infringing use. The Federal Circuit requires as well that the contributory infringer knew that the component was specially designed for a device that would infringe a patented invention.[66] At a recent summary judgment hearing held in a pending software infringement case, the court was faced with a difficult issue arising out of Microsoft's well-known strategy of integrating others' application software into Windows: 'Can Microsoft escape liability for contributory infringement by combining additional software applications with the patented applications and calling the result a "staple article or commodity of commerce suitable for substantial non-infringing use?"'[67] Because the accused components were part of a large and complex software program, the court determined that the issue was a question of fact to be resolved at trial. Although it makes sense generally to treat the issue of substantial non-infringing use as a question of fact, such treatment in cases of large scale software integration raises troubling policy questions about the incentives that result. Allowing such integration diminishes patent protection of applications software and, with it, shortens incentives to innovate because others are permitted to appropriate the patented software as long as they integrate it into a large enough suite of software. Moreover, by condoning the free riding, the accused infringer has no incentive to develop competing applications software. Given the harmful effects on all incentives to innovate, perhaps such integration should be treated as per se infringement.

Defences to infringement

Not all unauthorised practices of patented devices give rise to liability. Some uses are permitted because the conduct itself produces a public benefit. The experimental use defence falls into this category. Other uses are infringing but are shielded from liability because the patent holder has engaged in conduct seen as improperly extending the statutory grant. The most prominent example – indeed the leading defence to infringement – is patent misuse.[68] Each defence is informed by a commitment to competition policy and several overlap antitrust doctrines, most notably the misuse and exhaustion defences. That discussion is deferred until the antitrust laws have themselves been explained later in the report.

Patent misuse

The Supreme Court in *Motion Picture Patents Co.* v. *Universal Film Manufacturing Co.*[69] first adopted the defence, which bars patent holders from relief in an infringement action when they have misused the patent. Misuse has a wavering history that includes both judicial and congressional action. But in general terms, misuse has always been construed as conduct that improperly extends the patent monopoly. This section does not parse the history but turns directly to the current state of the misuse doctrine.[70]

Even though congressional legislation has largely given shape to the misuse defence, court doctrine remains important in several respects. The *Morton Salt Co.* v. *G. S. Suppiger Co.*[71] opinion still provides the most extensive statement of the defence and its underlying policy. In that decision, the Supreme Court concluded that *Morton Salt* had misused its patent by leasing its patented machines on condition that licensors use only Morton's unpatented salt tablets. When misuse is proved, the Court declared, relief should be denied in patent infringement suits because the patent holder 'exceeded its monopoly' by restraining competition in the sale of unpatented products. Attempts to secure an exclusive right beyond the patent grant disserve the constitutional goal of encouraging progress in the useful arts. Once the offender has abandoned the practice and the effects have subsided, the patent can once again be enforced.[72]

In addition to the tying strategy seen in *Morton Salt*, courts have found patent misuse in conduct such as price fixing, prohibiting the manufacture of competing products, extending licences beyond the patent term, and basing royalties on total sales rather than sales involving only the patented invention. But tying has been far and away patentees' favoured strategy to exploit their grants. It is easy to see why. Since the *Motion Picture Patents* case, patent owners have sought to extend their control from the patented invention to complementary products and services. But this strategy to increase revenues has usually run headlong into efforts of others to compete in those complementary markets. To restrain this competition, patent holders have filed lawsuits seeking to characterise such conduct as contributory infringement and calling for injunctions and damages. The accused infringers have responded by claiming that the patent holders were misusing their grants by seeking to 'extend the patent and thus monopolise the market for the unpatented component'.[73]

Section 271 defines the most significant aspects of the misuse defence, including the treatment of tying. Although it is not explicitly stated, the courts have construed section 271(c) and (d)(1) to permit patent holders to tie a patented product to another product 'especially made or adapted for use [with it] ... and not a staple article'. In *Motion Picture Patents*, for example, tying the lease of its patented film projector mechanism to the use of its film, assuming the film was unsuitable for any substantial non-infringing use, would not be patent misuse. Moreover, the patent holder could sue other sellers of compatible film for contributory infringement, again if the film was unsuitable for any substantial non-infringing use. Section 271(d)(5) further provides that it is not misuse for a patent holder to tie a patented product to *any* other product when the holder does not have market power in the market for either the patent or the patented product. In *Morton Salt* for example, tying the lease of its patented machines to unpatented salt tablets would not be misuse unless Morton had market power in the patent or the patented machinery. Sanctioning these strategies extends the patent grant and, in consequence, lessens the opportunities for competition. The doctrine reflects good policy if the tie can be justified as an ex ante incentive to innovation which would not otherwise occur. In the absence of such justification, the doctrines in section 271(c) and (d) would reflect an ill-advised extension of property rights and restraint of competition that injure the public interest in promoting innovation.

First sale or exhaustion
Like its copyright counterpart, the exhaustion of patent rights by first sale has long been recognised and recently endorsed.[74] But again like its copyright analogue, the exhaustion defence has been severely limited. While the Supreme Court has not spoken to the issue, the Federal Circuit has consistently permitted an action for infringement where the sale or licence of the patented device was conditional, the first sale doctrine notwithstanding. In *Mallinckrodt* v. *MediPart*[75] for example, the Federal Circuit endorsed the doctrine but gave effect to a 'label licence' affixed to a patented medical device, the label stating that only a single use was authorised. The same court in *B. Braun Medical Inc.* v. *Abbott Labs. Inc.*[76] narrowed the exhaustion doctrine even more: the doctrine 'does not apply to an expressly conditional sale or licence [because] it is more reasonable to infer that the parties negotiated a price that reflects only the value of the "use" rights ... As a result, express conditions accompanying the sale or licence of a patented product are ... upheld ... [unless they] violate some law or equitable consideration.' The reference to 'some law' certainly includes antitrust. The other reference includes the equitable doctrine of misuse. Indeed, the court proceeded to describe misuse as a limit on the restraints that survive the exhaustion defence: 'Using a patent ... to restrain competition in an unpatented product [by tying in violation of section 271(d)(5)] or employing the patent beyond its [20]-year term would constitute misuse. In contrast, field of use restrictions ... are generally upheld', subject to anti-trust scrutiny.[77] This view has attenuated the exhaustion doctrine, leaving it with little practical impact on the kinds of conditions a patentee can impose.

Experimental use

Although the experimental use defence is seldom asserted and even more rarely successful, it is worth a moment of attention because of its implications for competition policy and the scholarly debate it has engendered. It was Justice Story's opinion in *Whittemore v. Cutter*[78] that first articulated the defence, declaring that 'it could never have been the intention of the legislature to punish a man, who constructed ... a machine merely for philosophical experiments, or for the purpose of ascertaining the sufficiency of the machine to produce its described effects'.[79] For the past two centuries, courts have not strayed from Justice Story's narrow path. In *Roche Products Inc. v. Bolar Pharmaceutical Co.* for example,[80] the Federal Circuit concluded that experiments by a generic drug manufacturer made solely to prepare for the FDA approval process were infringements. The court determined that such tests were motivated by business purposes and thus outside the experimental use exception. Congress very quickly amended the Patent Act to overrule *Bolar Pharmaceutical*, adding section 271(e)(1) to exempt such testing from infringement claims.[81] More recently, the Federal Circuit denied the experimental use defence to Duke University in an infringement suit brought by a former research professor. Despite its non-profit status, Duke did not 'sanction and fund research projects ... to satisfy idle curiosity, or for strictly philosophical inquiry'. In consequence, the use did 'not qualify for the very narrow and strictly limited experimental use defence'.[82]

The meagre experimental use defence should be contrasted with the generous experimental use doctrine that can extend the one-year grace period to file patent protection if the PTO and courts are persuaded that the inventor's use of the device was experimental. Recall the *City of Elizabeth* decision which allowed the inventor six years of testing even though the invention was certainly intended for patent application long before. Why the different treatment of inventors and potential competitors? The difference can be justified if one believes that an inventor should have broad discretion in determining when her device has successfully embodied the underlying idea and, at the same time, if one believes that allowing a broad experimental use defence to infringement would give competitors a head-start which would effectively shorten the 20-year period of exclusivity. On the other hand, it can be argued that the broad discretion to inventors effectively lengthens the period of exclusivity, as does a denial of a broad experimental use defence. In both instances, doubts, if any, are resolved in favour of strengthening the grant based, presumably, on a tacit assumption that more innovation is expected to result from the expanded period of exclusive rights than would result from an expanded period of competition. It should be emphasised that the assumption is unexpressed in the doctrine and is just that – an assumption rather than an empirically based determination.[83]

2. Copyright protection and competition policy

Before Congress passed the Copyright Act of 1790, it was state law that
provided protection for authors' work.[84] Until the 1909 amendment, only
books, maps and charts were protected and, until 1976, only published and
registered writings qualified for IPR.[85] In 1980, Congress crossed the traditional boundary between expression and function by explicitly extending
copyright to include computer software despite its functional character.[86]
Additional amendments in the past 20 years have added a form of moral
rights, extended the copyright term, and granted copyright owners controversial powers of enforcement.

Requirements of original work and fixation   The current copyright statute
protects 'original works of authorship fixed in any tangible medium of
expression'.[87] Congress has stated that the originality standard 'does not
include requirements of novelty, ingenuity, or aesthetic merit'.[88] Federal
courts have long recognised that original authorship 'means little more
than a prohibition of actual copying'.[89] Nonetheless, copyright does not
reward all works of authorship but only those that show some originality. In
its well-known *Feist Publications* v. *Rural Telephone Service*[90] decision, the
Supreme Court affirmed this proposition in denying copyright protection to
the information in a telephone directory. Nor are other compilations of facts
protected unless they reflect some originality in their selection, coordination or
arrangement. In language that reflects on data base and, perhaps, software
protection, the Court made clear that 'copyright protection may extend only
to those components of a work that are original to the author . . . [C]opyright in
a factual compilation is thin . . . [A] subsequent compiler is free to use the facts
contained in another's publication to aid in preparing a competing work.'[91] The
Feist Publications opinion recognised that private property rights of the copyright holder are limited by the benefits of a public domain and its importance
to competition, even when the copying seems to be an appropriation of
someone else's labour. In short, the private right extends only far enough to
encourage the public benefits of encouraging innovation. Without proof that
the work reflects innovation and thus merits copyright protection, it is public
ownership and competition that best serve the public interest in progress.

    The Copyright Act also requires that the work be fixed in a 'tangible medium
of expression'. Section 101 defines a fixed work as one that 'can be perceived,
reproduced, or otherwise communicated, either directly or with the aid of a
machine or device'.[92] Fixation can play a role in claims of infringement because
a 'copy' is further defined as a 'material object . . . in which a work is fixed'. The
issue has been hotly contested in some infringement cases involving 'RAM
copies', which are temporary electromagnetic copies that appear as a matter of
course each time a computer program or file is used.[93]

Exclusive rights and their limits   The Act grants copyright owners exclusive rights in their works, including rights to make copies, distribute them, prepare derivative works, and authorise others to do so.[94] Anyone who violates any of these rights, or assists or encourages someone to violate them, is liable for copyright infringement.[95] The most obvious limit on these exclusive rights is the term of protection. Congress has power to grant protection only for 'limited times' as stated in the constitutional provision. The 1790 statute granted a fourteen-year term with possible renewal by one additional term. Plaintiffs in the recent *Eldred* v. *Ashcroft*[96] case argued that the Sonny Bono Copyright Term Extension Act exceeded congressional power in several respects. In deferring to Congress, the Court rejected the argument that a potential 120-year term crossed the constitutional boundary of 'limited times'.[97]

Perhaps the most elusive limitation is expressed in the doctrine that copyright protects original expressions but not the ideas found in those expressions. In short, ideas fall into the public domain.[98] Despite the inherent difficulty of distinguishing between an idea and its expression, courts must locate the hazy line because it is the only way to reconcile copyright's 'two competing societal interests . . . namely, rewarding individual ingenuity, and nevertheless allowing progress and improvements based on the same subject matter by others than the original author'.[99] Copyright's distinction between ideas and expressions rises out of the fundamental belief in a marketplace of ideas and the corollary that progress depends upon public access to the ideas and other knowledge embodied in protected expressions.

Drawing the boundaries of copyright protection for computer software raises special difficulties because a program is fundamentally a utilitarian process or system. Since the 1980 amendment to the Copyright Act, there has been no question that computer programs are copyrightable material.[100] Nonetheless, some software, in whole or in part, may be ineligible for copyright protection because they lack originality or because the limited ways of embodying an idea brings the merger doctrine into play. Software can lack originality in two ways. First, the entire programs may be so simple or so common that it does not satisfy the *Feist Publications* level of minimal originality. Second, the source code in programs components may reflect industry standard routines or modules such as operating system interfaces that are not original.

Indeed, despite the 1980 addition of section 117, software by its very nature seems to overstep the traditional boundary of copyright protection now found in section 102(b), which denies protection to a 'process', 'system', or 'method of operation'. In seeking to mediate this tension, courts have recognised that software designers and programmers usually have numerous ways to accomplish a given task.[101] This creates a space for creativity, which results in a work that has some elements of originality embedded in a process or

system. It is those elements that merit copyright protection. The leading decision is *Computer Associates International* v. *Altai*,[102] in which the Second Circuit
Court of Appeals called for a process of filtering out the unprotectable elements
of the software. Those elements can include, at one extreme, ideas instant-
iated in the program's design and, at the other extreme, the *scènes à faire* –
standardised modules or stock protocols of machine code – employed by the
programmers.[103]

The right to make copies   The exclusive right to copy includes more than
protection from the making of identical duplicates such as photo or digital
copies. It also prohibits others from making 'substantially similar' reproductions, whether 'by imitation or simulation'. The expansive scope of the right
to copy has required courts to resolve two issues when determining whether
copying has occurred.

First, courts must determine whether copies were actually made because
even identical musical compositions or software routines, for example, could
have been produced independently. In the absence of direct proof of copying
such as the infringer's admission or eyewitness testimony, the decisions turn
on circumstantial evidence. 'If there is evidence of access and similarities
exist, then the trier of fact must determine whether the similarities are
sufficient to prove copying.'[104]

Second, if copying is established, courts must then decide whether the copy
included enough material from the protected work to constitute 'unlawful
appropriation'.[105] In order to resolve this issue, the protected work must be
parsed by separating the elements that are protected expression from those
that are not. Courts have found, for example, that the *scènes à faire* doctrine
excludes from copyright protection the stock elements of 'computer software
that have been dictated by external factors, such as hardware standards and
mechanical specifications, software standards and compatibility requirements, computer manufacturer design standards, target industry practices
and demands, and computer industry programming practices'.[106]

Moreover, one court has recognised 'that the *scènes à faire* doctrine may
implicate the protectability of interfacing and that this topic is very sensitive
and has the potential to affect widely the law of computer copyright'.[107]
Although no court has addressed this question directly, the well-known *Sega
Enterprises Ltd.* v. *Accolade Inc.* decision[108] involved reverse engineering and,
with it, copying in order to identify application program interfaces (APIs)
which the defendants needed to write game programs that would run on the
SEGA system. The court determined that Accolade's copying did not infringe
SEGA's copyright in the operating system, noting that Accolade's games competed directly with those of SEGA and its licensees. These and other limitations
on the exclusive right to copy reflect the crucial importance of access to
information for encouraging add-on innovation produced by competitors.

The right to distribute copies   As a practical matter copying must precede distribution of copies. But the two rights are independent and, as a result, either duplication or distribution alone can constitute infringement. A separate right of distribution allows for contributory or vicarious infringement claims against third parties who need not themselves have made copies. In *A&M Records* v. *Napster Inc.*[109] for example, the court held that plaintiffs established a prima facie case of contributory and vicarious infringement by showing that Napster knowingly made it possible for its users to infringe copyrights by copying MP3 files of protected musical performances. Napster itself engaged in no copying.

Nonetheless, there are limits to the exclusive right to distribute copies,[110] particularly when distribution takes the form of performance or display. In addition to limited rights given to educational, religious and charitable organisations, Congress has imposed compulsory licensing in limited circumstances, including some cable and satellite transmission, and 'cover' recording rights to some musical compositions that have been previously recorded. It must be emphasised that compulsory licensing in the United States is limited to very narrow confines.[111]

First sale or exhaustion doctrine
First endorsed in the Supreme Court's *Bobbs-Merrill Co.* v. *Straus*[112] decision and then codified in section 109(a) of the 1976 Copyright Act, the 'first sale' or 'exhaustion' doctrine appears to be the most significant limitation on the distribution right. The doctrine states that the first sale of a protected work exhausts the copyright, entitling the buyer of the particular copy to 'sell or otherwise dispose of possession of' the copy without the copyright holder's permission. As we show later in this chapter, the exhaustion doctrine coincides with US antitrust policy's limitations on manufacturers' rights to control distribution of their goods. Moreover, in the recent *Quality King Distributors Inc.* v. *L'Anza Research International Inc.* decision,[113] the Supreme Court applied the exhaustion doctrine to deny a copyright owner the ability to prohibit unauthorised imports. But the exhaustion doctrine itself has a severe limitation: when a transaction takes the form of a licence rather than a sale, courts have declared that the copyright is not exhausted because there has been no 'sale'.[114] In practice, then, virtually all agreements to transfer information goods – software licensing agreements are the best example – escape the strictures of the 'first sale' doctrine simply because they are usually drafted as licences rather than sales.

The right to create derivative works   The right to distribute sometimes implicates the independent right to create derivative works. In *Mirage Editions* v. *Albuquerque A. R. T.*,[115] for instance, the defendant scissored images of an artist's work out of a copyrighted book, glued them onto ceramic tile, and distributed them for sale in shops. The court found that the decorative tiles were derivative works that infringed the copyright even though no copies had been made.[116] But some commentators and courts have rejected the approach taken in *Mirage Editions*. The *Lee* v. *A.R.T. Inc.* decision,[117] for one, has read the Act's section 101 definition of 'derivative works' to require the addition of new copyrightable material to the original work. In its view, the decorative tiles did not add new copyrightable material and thus were not derivative works but only permissible displays of the original work.[118]

This disagreement over the nature of derivative works can be understood as a conflict in views of the proper balance between the property rights and competition policies underwriting copyright protection. On the one hand, extending copyright to include the exclusive right to produce the tiles and to gain profits made from the tiles, especially when they do not reflect creativity, recognises that the tiles' value derives from the spark of originality seen in the artist's copyrighted book. Should the benefit not go to the original artist as part of the ex ante incentive structure to encourage just such creative work? On the other hand, do such benefits, likely unanticipated and certainly attenuated, really produce ex ante incentives? Can such benefits be expected to have had any impact on the artist's earlier creative activity? If not, then shouldn't the profits go as ex post incentives to the tile producer and to others who make and sell new artefacts that attract buyers' dollars? Does this activity harm the artist by allowing a competitor to free ride on his originality? It seems that there is free riding but no harm to the artist from introducing products to a market that the artist had no intention of entering. Is not this harmless free riding an important part of the public benefit expected from copyright protection? The disagreement in a nutshell: what is it that encourages innovation in these situations – the ex ante incentives of private property rights or the ex post of competitive markets? The *Mirage Editions* decision results in an extended IPR, while the *Lee* decision broadens the scope of the public domain and, with it, incentives to compete.[119] At least on these facts, the *Lee* decision seems more sensible.

Courts have reached divergent conclusions in video game cases involving claims of derivative works. In *Midway Manufacturing Co.* v. *Arctic International Inc.*,[120] for example, the owner of copyrights in video games brought an infringement action against the seller of printed circuit boards for use inside the owner's video game machines, alleging that the defendant's sale of two circuit boards that sped up the rate of play of copyrighted video games infringed the plaintiff's copyrights in such video games by altering the characteristics of the displays. The Seventh Circuit Court of Appeals concluded that the speeded-up video game was a derivative work and held that selling the defendant's circuit boards infringed the plaintiff's copyrights. In the course of the opinion, the court expressed concern that the new circuit boards displaced the originals and, hence, competed directly with them, thereby depriving the owner of revenues rightly derived from the copyright. In a similar case, *Lewis Galoob Toys Inc.* v. *Nintendo of America Inc.*,[121] the manufacturer of copyrighted game cartridges brought an infringement suit against the manufacturer of 'Game Genie', a piece of hardware placed between the game device and the game cartridge, which enabled the player to alter features of the manufacturer's copyrighted games. But here, the Ninth Circuit concluded that audiovisual displays created by 'Game Genie' were not derivative works. As a result, the copyright owner did not have a claim to the revenues produced by the new hardware middleware.[122] The court put great weight on the fact that 'the Game Genie cannot produce an audiovisual display; the underlying display must be produced by a Nintendo Entertainment System and game cartridge'. In sharp contrast to the *Midway Mfg.* decision, this court determined that Nintendo was not entitled to profits from a device produced to work with its video game hardware.

Perhaps the two decisions can be rationalised by the nature of the allegedly derivative work. In *Midway Manufacturing*, the new circuit boards were permanent components of the game machines that displaced the originals while in *Lewis Galoob Toys*, the new hardware was temporary, supplementary and did not replace any original components. Extending the copyright monopoly in the latter case would restrain all competition in add-on innovation that connected to the game machine and would amount to something more akin to a blocking patent, whose broader scope is consistent with patent law's more rigorous requirements for protection. Indeed, recognizing the fact that it was the video display images that were protected suggests that the *Midway Manufacturing* decision might have extended copyright protection to subject matter more appropriately placed under the patent law regime.

Nonetheless, the two decisions illustrate the uncertainty engendered by copyright infringement claims involving both hardware and software goods, uncertainty resulting from difficult questions about the proper ratio of protection to access. The questions are difficult because courts are asked to shape, based upon deeply imperfect information, IPR protection that will best encourage innovation first by parsing the factual circumstances of the case to determine the innovation incentives at issue and then by balancing ex ante incentives of private property rights with ex post incentives of competitive markets in light of the circumstances.

Defences to infringement claims   The Copyright Act sections 107–118 and 507 enumerate a series of defences, most prominent among them the fair use doctrine found in section 107. In addition, there are a number of non-statutory defences.[123] This section addresses the statutory defence of fair use and the evolving judicial doctrine of copyright misuse.

Fair use

The most prominent defence to copyright infringement is the fair use doctrine, which originated in the courts and was codified in the 1976 Copyright Act. The doctrine holds that unauthorised copying is permissible when the material is used in certain limited ways. Fair use is not a compulsory licence because no royalties must be paid. Rather, activities such as news reporting, teaching and research that make unauthorised use of copyrighted materials are permitted because they are seen as producing important public benefits. Courts are instructed to determine fair use by considering a specific set of factors.[124] Two well-known cases involved excerpts from President Gerald Ford's memoirs for critical commentary in *The Nation* magazine and borrowing of characters and scenes from *Gone with the Wind* for retelling from a slave's perspective in *The Wind Done Gone*.[125]

Still it is the lesser-known cases about new duplication technologies that have produced broad legal and financial ramifications. In *Sony Corp. of America* v. *Universal City Studios Inc.*, for example,[126] Sony was accused of contributory infringement by selling its VCRs. Sony avoided liability because the Supreme Court declined to find direct infringement in Sony customers' private videotaping of television programmes at issue. Although unauthorised, the home videotaping constituted fair use when done for the purpose of time-shifting.[127] The Court reasoned that the benefit of increased public access required 'the copyright holder to demonstrate some likelihood of harm' – something plaintiffs failed to do. Analogising to patent cases, the divided Court 'recognised the critical importance of not allowing the [copyright holder] to extend his monopoly beyond the limits of his specific grant', noting that a successful infringement claim and injunction in those circumstances would likely lead to 'a continuing royalty pursuant to a judicially created compulsory licence'. The four dissenting Justices insisted that Sony was a contributory infringer because 'the primary purpose or effect' of the VCR was to enable direct infringement. The majority's approach took into account the public benefit of increased dissemination and rightly created a presumption of fair use that called for the plaintiffs to prove economic harm. The dissenters, in contrast, seemed to apply a Lockean notion of property rights out of step with the instrumentalist conception embodied in the constitutional and statutory provisions.

Sony of course would become an insignificant player when the VCR market tipped toward the competing VHS format technology, leaving Sony's Betamax machines on the shelf. Tipping can occur when incompatible systems such as VHS and Betamax or sponsors of rival networks such as Internet Explorer and Netscape Navigator users compete in markets that tend toward winner-take-most outcomes. Such markets tip when a network of linked users or a system of complementary products becomes more attractive as its user base increases in size. A larger telephone network, for example, is more attractive than a smaller rival to both current and potential users simply on account of its size. Sony Betamax machines lost consumer appeal because both VHS machines users and pre-recorded tape renters increased more quickly than their Betamax counterparts. The market process created a positive feedback loop that made each element of the system – the pre-recorded tapes and the VCRs – increasingly more attractive to current and prospective users as demand for the other element expanded. Although consumers benefit from the innovation produced in the standardised environment of a common platform such as Internet Explorer, VHS format or Windows operating system, the impact of system and network effects on both property rights and market competition raises several difficult questions about the fair use doctrine. The questions emerge because customers are to some extent locked in to the system as the result of the perceived costs of switching to the rival system. Switching from VHS to Beta format pre-recorded tapes, for example, would require the purchase of a Beta format VCR. The high switching costs would tend to lock in the customer base, which would likely increase the revenues of IPR holders far beyond those gained from sales that do not involve networks of linked users or systems of complementary products.[128]

Both courts and commentators have recently addressed questions about the proper scope of fair use doctrine in cases involving computer software. In the *Accolade* decision,[129] for example, the influential Ninth Circuit Court of Appeals concluded that Accolade's duplication of copyrighted game programs in order to reverse engineer Sega's Genesis game console was fair use under the circumstances. It was fair use because Accolade's purpose was to study the decompiled software in order to develop original game programs that were compatible with Sega's Genesis game console. What other alternative, the court asked, did the program developers have to learn the interface requirements? Although there was substantial copying, the court was persuaded that fair use permitted the reverse engineering needed to engage in the competitive activity of creating new games. The games themselves did not include portions of Sega's protected work. The decision can be understood as allowing access to the interoperability information needed to encourage the innovation that leads to intra-system competition. In light of the network and system effects involved, denying access to the information presented the danger of overcompensating Sega, overprotecting the copyright and, as a result, an incentive to overinvest in the system and its components. A corollary danger would be an entry barrier to intra-system competition leading to underinvestment by independent game producers. Finally, IPR overcompensation would send signals soliciting overinvestment in inter-system competition because potential rivals to Sega's Genesis system would view the possibility of higher returns from broad IPR protection in network industries as a rationale for taking greater risks. The ultimate public cost would be misallocation of capital resources in affected innovation and technology markets, adding air to speculatory bubbles of the sort seen in the 1990s.

Copyright misuse

Unlike its patent counterpart, copyright misuse is entirely a creature of the courts. Although the twin misuse doctrines differ in some respects, they share the fundamental rationale that an owner's strategies to extend his IPR beyond the statutory grant can constitute misuse. As with patents, when a court finds copyright misuse, the remedy is an injunction against enforcement of the IPR until the misuse is abated and its effects eliminated.

It is important to note that unlike patent misuse, the copyright doctrine is not uniformly recognised. The Fourth Circuit's *Lasercomb America*[130] decision was the first to endorse copyright misuse doctrine, followed some years later by two sister circuit courts of appeal.[131] The court concluded that an overly broad non-competition provision forbidding the licensee to develop any competing software for 99 years, whether or not it infringed the copyright, would be an 'egregious' extension of the statutory IPR. The provision was seen as an attempt to restrain competition beyond the bounds of copyright exclusion. The decision raises two points of particular interest. First, the court ordered the injunction despite the defendants' flagrant infringement and fraudulent practices to conceal the conduct. Given circumstances supporting equitable defences of 'unclean hands' all around, it was surprising that the court nonetheless granted equitable relief. Second, even though the court recognised that the plaintiff's non-competition clause might offend the antitrust prohibition against leveraging monopoly power, the opinion explicitly distinguished between copyright misuse and antitrust violations. The upshot was the court's refusal to interject antitrust's 'rule of reason' into misuse doctrine. In this respect, the resulting misuse doctrine imposes stricter constraints than antitrust on strategic behaviour to exploit IPR.[132]

The *Lasercomb* decision remains the most influential statement of the copyright misuse defence.[133] Nonetheless, because the defence is still developing, it is useful to pause long enough to note the scholarly debate provoked by the opinion's view of copyright misuse as entirely independent of antitrust. One side has criticised the *Lasercomb* decision, pointing to patent misuse doctrine as the appropriate approach. As discussed in the report's patent section above, Congress enacted legislation to conform the patent doctrine to antitrust, at least so far as the requirement that the defence is available only when the misuse is shown to have anti-competitive effects. This makes sense, it is argued, because misuse doctrine is intended to limit the IPR and its exclusion of competition to its statutory bounds. Misuse then should call for some evidence of impermissible restraint of competition. Indeed, Congress amended the Patent Act in 1954 by adding precisely that requirement. The other side agrees with the *Lasercomb* approach, arguing that copyright misuse and antitrust reflect different concerns about the competitive process. Copyright misuse calls for close scrutiny of strategies to extend a limited statutory grant of exclusionary power because of the clearly instrumentalist character of copyright. The access to knowledge and use of ideas that constitute the public benefit of copyright must be closely guarded from the harms of overextending the private rights of exclusion. Moreover, a strong misuse doctrine minimises the public cost of overinvestment that follows overcompensation in well-functioning markets. Indeed, the bright-line doctrine and limited remedy of an injunction against enforcing the copyright combine to create a clear disincentive to those copyright holders who would engage in conduct seeking to extend their statutory grant.

Throughout both patent and copyright doctrines, notwithstanding their differences, the constitutional foundation for these intellectual property rights calls for an approach toward encouraging innovation that recognises the importance of both exclusive rights and public access. Certainly, the relative weights accorded private rights and public access reflect differences in kind between copyrightable expressions and patentable functions – patent's strong description and enablement requirements and its constricted doctrine of misuse, copyright's minimal requirement of originality and its expansive doctrine of misuse, patent's more substantial originality requirement and copyright's recognition of a fair use defence, and copyright's thinner coverage but lengthier term. Throughout, Congress and the courts have been authorised by the Copyright and Patent Clause of the US Constitution to shape and allow the grant of exclusive rights that provide public access to the knowledge produced and that limit competition no more than necessary to encourage innovation.

C. Common law origins: trademarks and trade secrets

The common law origins of trademark and trade secret protections are reflected in their goals, which differ markedly from those of patent and copyright. The Copyright and Patent Clause of the US Constitution mandates that congressional legislation 'promote the Progress of Science and the useful Arts,' although some court opinions and congressional legislation have raised doubt about their fidelity to the Constitution's utilitarian ethic. The common law protections, in contrast, have always been associated with a variety of public policies. For example, both trade secret and trade name rights have sometimes been characterised not in terms of property protection but rather by a moral rubric of wrongfulness associated with the common law tort of unfair competition. Moreover, many states have adopted statutes that typically codified the pre-existing common law. Finally, there is a federal statutory overlay: the Lanham Act of 1946 supplements state trademark laws and the Economic Espionage Act of 1996 renders trade secret misappropriation a federal crime.[134]

1. Trade secrets and competition policy

Each of the United States protects trade secrets. Protection originated in the common law tort of misappropriation, which is reflected in the still influential Restatement of Torts (1939) sections 757 and 758. Today, approximately forty state legislatures have enacted the Uniform Trade Secrets Act (1979).[135] Yet another cited source of doctrine and policy is the Restatement (Third) of Unfair Competition (1994). Although these three renditions of trade secret principles differ in some respects, they are all in agreement that a trade secret claim has three elements. First, to be eligible for trade secret protection, the information must have some economic value to the claimant. Note that a claimant need prove neither novelty nor non-obviousness, distinguishing trade secrets, at least in theory, from copyright and patent protections. Second, the claimant must show that the defendant misappropriated the information. Misappropriation can be shown in two ways – either by a breach of a confidential relationship or by a wrongful act such as deception or theft. It is this element that establishes trade secret protection as a tort of unfair competition. Third, the claimant must establish that reasonable precautions were taken to prevent disclosure of the secret. The secrecy element obviously conflicts with the public policies of disclosure associated with patent and copyright protection.

This section begins with discussion of the public policies underlying trade secret protection and then goes on to a description of eligible subject matter and conduct of misappropriation. As we shall see, the differing views taken of public policy underlying trade secret protection have had significant impact on the extent of protection and kind of remedy granted to claimants.

The public policies underlying trade secret protection   The US Supreme Court has been called upon to apply state trade secret laws in numerous cases. On two of those occasions, the Supreme Court has described trade secret protection as promoting two different goals. The prominent *Kewanee Oil Co.* v. *Bicron Corp.*[136] opinion observed that the property rights reflected in 'trade secret law will encourage invention in areas where patent law does not reach'.[137] But in the often cited *E. I. DuPont & Co.* v. *Masland*[138] decision, the Court observed that 'the law makes some rudimentary requirements of good faith ... Therefore the starting point for the present matter is not property ... but that the defendant stood in confidential relations with the plaintiffs.'[139] Judge Richard Posner has written that these alternative tort and property conceptions of trade secret protection 'are better described as different emphases. The first emphasises the desirability of deterring efforts that have as their sole purpose and effect the distribution of wealth from one firm to another. The second emphasizes the desirability of encouraging inventive activity by protecting its fruits from efforts at appropriation that are ... not productive activities.'[140]

Despite the frequent articulation of two policies, the incentive to invent is better understood as merely coincidental to trade secret protection because claimants are not required to prove innovation. Rather, they must prove only commercial value or business advantage, which can result from any number of activities, including but not limited to invention. It is more correct then to say that encouraging innovation is a desirable by-product of trade secret protection, which expresses a primary commitment to a Lockean conception of property as the rightful result of one's labour and thus the necessary condition for fair competition. In contrast to copyright and patent protection, courts and policy makers are not called upon to determine a level of protection that optimises ex ante incentives to invent. Rather, they are asked to make an ethical determination whether an accused party is a free rider in the extreme case – someone who has engaged in conduct akin to theft, fraud, or abuse of trust.

There are times when state protection of trade marks or trade secrets overlaps federal protection of copyrights or patents. At those junctures, questions of federal pre-emption can arise. Under the Supremacy Clause of the US Constitution, state laws are invalidated when they interfere with the goals of patent, copyright or other federal regulation. 'States may not offer patent-like protection to intellectual creations which would otherwise remain unprotected' under the patent statute.[141] The tension is greatest in the relationship between trade secrets and patents because encouraging concealment of potentially patentable inventions conflicts directly with patent policy's principal goal of encouraging dissemination of knowledge. The upshot is a patent law that disfavours trade secrets. This attitude can be seen, for example, in the judicial doctrine that permits a later inventor to patent the subject matter of a prior inventor's trade secret.[142]

Even in cases where federal regulation does not control the entire field, courts have often found an implied congressional intent to leave the area free of all regulation. State attempts to regulate in those areas are thus invalid.[143] But state protection of intellectual property does not always conflict with its federal counterparts. In *Kewanee Oil Co.*, for example, the Supreme Court upheld a trade secret law that prohibited disclosure of the plaintiff's industrial device which was no longer eligible for patent protection.[144] As the remainder of this section describes, common law rights and their statutory supplements play important roles in US intellectual property protection. Indeed, a study in 1994 showed that trade secret protection is especially important for small businesses.[145]

Eligible subject matter   The prominent *Fourtek* opinion,[146] written by a federal circuit court judge to determine state law, provides a good discussion of the requirements for trade secret protection. Beginning with the Texas courts' reliance on the Restatement of Torts section 757, the court declared that the trade secret claimant must first prove secrecy by showing reasonable efforts to maintain the information's confidentiality. Then, the opinion continued, the court must balance three 'equitable considerations' taken from evidence presented by the claimant: the information's value, its cost of development and, finally, the flagrancy of the misappropriation. The *Fourtek* court concluded that 'it seems only fair that one should be able to keep and enjoy the fruits of his labour . . . [T]his is an area of law in which simple fairness still plays a large role.' Echoing the Supreme Court's *Masland* decision, this modern opinion is more clear than most on the Lockean justification for trade secret protection and, by implication, on the importance of fairness to the process of competition.[147]

(i) Secrecy

Claimants must make reasonable efforts to protect the secrecy of their information or ideas from competitors and others. The court in *Rockwell Graphic Systems Inc.* v. *DEV Industries Inc.* for example,[148] observed that '[P]erfect security is not optimum security.' In that case, Judge Posner concluded that legends stamped on each item and confidentiality agreements, although unevenly enforced, could reflect a reasonable effort to maintain secrecy, even though 'tens of thousand of copies . . . [were] floating around outside Rockwell's vault'.[149] Certainly it has long been recognised that computer hardware and software are eligible for trade secret protection. Regardless of the *Fourtek* and *Rockwell Graphics* holdings that public sale need not compromise secrecy, however, courts have disagreed over the impact of public sale on software secrecy.[150] Those cases reflect the difficulty of determining the extent to which commercial circumstances can defeat claims of secrecy.

Two recurring sets of circumstances that can negate secrecy in computer software cases involve knowledge that is ascertainable from inspection of commercially available goods and information that is generally known or easily ascertainable to competitors in an industry.

As for knowledge that is ascertainable from inspection of commercially available goods, computer software raises special questions because software is even more difficult to inspect than a physical object like a DVD drive, an LCD monitor, or an ergonomically designed chair. In *Data General Corp.* v. *Grumman Systems Support Corp.* for example,[151] the court upheld a jury verdict of misappropriation of trade secrets contained in object code form of the claimants' software because object code 'is essentially unintelligible to humans' and thus not ascertainable from inspection.[152] The conclusion was that the defendants, who had no authorisation to access the information, must have misappropriated it.[153] The holding suggests that distributing object code widely does not itself compromise secrecy. If the claimant instead distributes the source code – that is, the lines of code written in a particular programming language and therefore intelligible by computer programmers – then the decision would be more difficult. In such circumstances, some reasonable effort to maintain secrecy would more likely be required because inspection would yield the software's secrets to someone knowledgeable in the particular source language. With reasonable precautions taken, it would be conduct of misappropriation rather than any novelty or non-obviousness that would inform an entitlement to trade secret protection. In these circumstances, it is less the value of the misappropriated scheme than the unfair method of competition that would persuade a court to protect the claimant's system.

Nor can a trade secret consist of information that is readily ascertainable or generally known to competitors in an industry.[154] One court has held that the basic organisational concepts for a computerised price quote system were entitled to trade secret protection if the particular organisation was not generally known in the industry.[155] This circumstance presents an implicit question about the relationship between secrecy and uniqueness or novelty. On the one hand, an idea that occurred to someone else or even one that is being used by another does not negate secrecy. On the other hand, a trade secret, according to one court, must 'possess at least that modicum of originality which will separate it from everyday knowledge'.[156] Another court has suggested that a 'trade secret may be no more than "merely a mechanical improvement that a good mechanic can make"'.[157] Apparently, a trade secret need not be unique or novel so long as it is not common knowledge. In this light, trade secret protection takes on the appearance of a tort of unfair competition by misappropriation rather than a property right to spur competition by invention.

(ii) Commercial value

If a trade secret claimant need not prove novelty or non-obviousness, how does she establish commercial value or business advantage? One commentator suggests that 'value is seldom a practical issue in trade secret cases . . . [because] . . . the high cost of enforcing [them] suggests that plaintiffs will only commence litigation concerning information of considerable value'.[158] Where value has been an issue, plaintiffs have offered either direct evidence of the information's value or, failing that, evidence of development costs or even efforts to maintain secrecy.[159] In the *Fourtek* case, already discussed, the claimant offered both sorts of evidence – not only that its zinc recovery process produced higher quality carbide from cobalt carbide drilling bits but also that the development costs were high. The *Rockwell Graphics* opinion, also mentioned above, observed that the greater the efforts to maintain security, the more valuable the secret. In this light, it is clear that both decisions promote investment rather than invention. Certainly it was proof of investment that was called for.

The question of commercial value also arises in the remedy stage of a misappropriation suit. What should the court award a successful claimant? Here courts have applied a consistent standard, whether awarding royalties, damages or injunctive relief. That standard follows the so-called 'head-start' theory. In *K-2 Ski Co.* v. *Head Ski Co.* for example,[160] the court limited the term of an injunction to the period of time it would have taken the misappropriator, 'either by reverse engineering or by independent development, to develop its ski legitimately without use of the K-2 trade secrets'. Monetary damages, limited to the lead time advantage lost by the claimant, have been awarded to equal either the loss suffered or the gain realised, whichever is greater.[161]

But a controversial issue has appeared in contract cases involving trade secrets that have fallen into the public domain. In *Warner-Lambert Pharmaceutical Co.* v. *John J. Reynolds Inc.*[162] for example, the pharmaceutical company sought a judgment declaring void its 1881 agreement to pay royalties for the 'Listerine' formula, once but no longer a trade secret. The company argued that trade secrets were limited, just as patents and copyrights, to their terms. For a trade secret, the term is the period of secrecy. The court rejected the argument, stating that 'parties are free to contract with respect to a secret formula or trade secret in any manner which they determine is for their own best interests'.[163] As a result Warner-Lambert was obliged to continue royalty payments for a formula that 'has gradually become a matter of public knowledge'. Here, the court insisted on the importance of freedom of contract to commercial enterprise, regardless of the disappearance of commercial value to one of the parties. But other state courts have agreed with Warner-Lambert's position; and the newest Restatement of Unfair Competition suggests that such agreements should be unenforceable.[164] It should be recalled that federal courts have held agreements to extend a patent or copyright beyond its term misuse and thus illegal per se because such agreements 'project . . . monopoly power beyond the patent [or copyright] period'.[165] As we saw in both the patent and copyright sections, however, courts have permitted parties to 'contract around' another boundary of federal grants – the exhaustion doctrine and thereby extend exclusionary rights beyond the first 'sale.' It is evident that courts have not been consistent in their views of the relationships between public policies reflected in intellectual property protection and those expressed in individual freedom of contract. That inconstancy is seen again in court attitudes toward anti-trust law, which are discussed later in the report.

Misappropriation

At the core of trade secret protection is an ethical judgment about fair competition: Gaining a commercial advantage by unfair means corrupts the process of competition and undermines its goals. Misappropriation through wrongful conduct can occur in two situations. First, a trade secret may be learned by someone who has no relationship with the trade secret holder. In such cases, courts will grant a remedy when the accused obtained the trade secret by improper means. Second, a trade secret may have been disclosed to the accused misappropriator in the course of employment or in a commercial relationship. If the accused then uses the properly obtained information to his own commercial advantage, he will be subject to liability for misappropriation if the court finds that he has breached an obligation of confidentiality.

(i) Improper means

Certainly trade secret laws condemn criminal acts such as fraud, theft, wiretapping as well as tortious forms of industrial espionage. But courts have taken a much broader view of trade secret acquisition by improper means, a view that takes in conduct calculated to overcome reasonable efforts to maintain secrecy. In the leading case on the subject, *E. I. duPont de Nemours & Co.* v. *Rolfe Christopher*,[166] the court determined that aerial photography of plant construction was an improper means because it fell 'below the generally accepted standards of commercial morality and reasonable conduct ... [O]ur ethos has never given moral sanction to piracy.' The evidence of improper means need not be direct. In *Pioneer Hi-Bred International* v. *Holden Foundation Seeds Inc.* for example,[167] the court found misappropriation based on evidence of strict confidentiality procedures and three scientific tests of genetic similarities whose results were offered to show a low probability that the accused infringer's hybrid seeds had been developed independently.

But not all unauthorised acquisitions or disclosures are improper. There are a number of proper ways for competitors to acquire trade secrets, most notably by reverse engineering.[168] This behaviour is seen as fair competition, according to the Restatement of Torts, section 757(1), when 'starting with the known product and working backward to find the method by which it was developed. The acquisition of the known product must ... be by a fair and honest means, such as purchase of the item on the open market.' Although reverse engineering usually requires more ingenuity than acquisition by, for example, industrial espionage, there is still a faint odour of unethical conduct. Why permit it? Some have explained the reverse engineering defence as an incentive for inventors to choose patent protection, which does not allow reverse engineering nor most experimental use.[169] Favouring patent over trade secret protection would reflect, in this view, a preference for public disclosure and a 20-year period of exclusivity to secrecy and an unlimited term. Each form of protection reflects its own balance between the incentives to innovation embodied in exclusivity and competition, private rights and public access.

(ii) Confidential relationship

Even if the trade secret has been properly obtained, it may still be misappropriated if it is improperly used or disclosed. Perhaps the most extreme statement of the tortious nature of misappropriation by violating a confidence is
found in *Franke* v. *Wiltschek*: 'It matters not that the defendants could have
gained their knowledge from a study of the expired patent and plaintiffs'
publicly marketed products. The fact is they did not. Instead they gained it
from the plaintiffs via their confidential relationship, and in doing so
incurred a duty not to use it to plaintiffs' detriment. This duty they have
breached.'[170] Duties can arise from promises made in the course of confidential relationships. Even if there is no express promise, courts are predis-
posed to 'find' an implied promise in certain kinds of relationships, including
employment relationships and those with customers or joint venturers. In the
influential *Dravo Corporation* decision,[171] the court found that an implied
duty of confidentiality with respect to secret blueprints and patent applications arose out of negotiations to sell a business. The prospective buyer
breached the duty and misappropriated the information when he used it to
start a competitive business.[172]

Courts have had greatest difficulty resolving claims of misappropriation by
current or former employees. In a high-tech industry, the typical written
employment agreement includes the employee's promises to assign ownership of inventions to the employer, not to disclose confidential information,
and, upon departure, neither to compete with the employer nor to recruit
other employees. For the employer, the thread of concern running through
these provisions is the danger of losing a competitive advantage, often in the
form of trade secrets. In such cases, courts must balance 'competing public
policies'. On one side is a recognition that the court should protect the
'business person ... from unfair competition stemming from usurpation of
trade secrets', and on the other the belief that the court should also permit 'an
individual ... to pursue unhampered the occupation for which ... she is best
suited'.[173] In consequence, courts are careful to assure that the agreements are
no broader than necessary to protect the employer's interests – much like the
limitations imposed on licensing agreements.[174] Yet again, courts are seeking
to balance the property rights of trade secret holders and the public interest in
market access and competition.

2. Competition policy and protection of trade marks and trade names

Like its trade secret counterpart, trade mark protection[175] finds its origins in
the common law tort of unfair competition. It is not surprising, then, that
both common law protections do not exist outside the domain of competition. A device is not eligible for trade secret protection unless the claimant
can show commercial or business advantage and, to obtain a remedy, some

injury to that competitive advantage. Neither can a trade mark exist outside commercial activity because a mark to identify goods has no function absent the sale of goods. 'Palming off' goods can occur only if other trademarked goods are being sold in competition. '[T]he right to a particular mark grows out of its use, not its mere adoption', declared the Supreme Court in *United Drug Co.* v. *Theodore Rectanus Co.*,[176] 'and it is not the subject of property except in connection with an existing business.'[177]

Trade mark protection has more recently been justified as a mechanism to correct market failure by decreasing consumer search costs – in particular, by preventing mistake, confusion, and deception regarding the origin of goods. Stated more broadly, trade marks help consumers in estimating the nature and quality of goods before purchase – a particularly important function with goods that cannot be easily inspected. A by-product of this public benefit is the private benefit to business owners of protecting their commercial good-will. As markets expanded in the last century, especially as mass retailing displaced most face-to-face exchange, courts have come to view the functions of trade marks more expansively, to include not only an indication of origin but also a marketing device and a guarantee of quality.[178] In consequence, trade mark law is seen as protecting both sellers and buyers, as serving both private rights and public interests. The buyer's interest is shared by the seller to the extent that a competitor's trademark infringement harms the seller by misleading or confusing the buyer. Yet when the competitor's conduct does not confuse or deceive a buyer but still harms a seller, interests diverge and may conflict. A good example of this 'propertisation' of the seller's trade mark rights is protection of the seller's investment in promotions that have failed or that have just begun. Here, the seller's rights have nothing to do with decreasing buyers' search costs or protecting them from tortious conduct that causes confusion. It is property protection of the seller's investment plain and simple.

Unlike the public policies underwriting patent and copyright protection, none of the justifications for trade marks includes the encouragement of innovation. The Supreme Court observed long ago that a trade mark does not 'depend on novelty, invention, discovery, or any work of the brain. It requires no fancy or imagination, no genius, no laborious thought.'[179] But like trade secret law, trademark protection can be seen as encouraging investment – here, in product advertising and promotion, and perhaps product quality.[180]

Since the pioneering work of economist Edward Chamberlin, economists in the United States have disagreed about the effects on competition of brand differentiation and, thus, of trade mark protection. Chamberlin offered the strongest criticism, arguing that trade mark rights were barriers to competition that artificially differentiated products, raised costs, and created power to raise prices for products that were often functionally identical. In this view, advertising and other forms of brand differentiation harm consumers. More recently, a number of economists have come to believe that advertising communicates useful information to consumers. Because advertising can accomplish both purposes, it should come as no surprise that dissensus persists regarding the economic role of trade marks and their impact on competition.[181] The latter portion of this report will show that this ambivalence is not reflected in the antitrust laws, which permit great latitude to firms engaging in interbrand competition.

Acquiring state and federal protections 'The United States has a "dual" system of trade mark law. A firm can secure trademark protection under state law, usually under state common law, or it can seek federal rights, under . . . the Lanham Act, or both. The two are independent of one another.'[182] In most respects, the federal and state protections share the same requirements, the most basic being that the claimant actually use the mark in commerce. Still, there are differences that make the federal trade mark law more than simply a national registration system. The most significant are the national reach of federal trade mark protection, trademark incontestability after five years and, under section 43, a federal law of unfair competition that goes beyond trade mark protection to prohibit false statements, conduct diluting famous marks, and Internet cybersquatting of marks.

Establishing trade mark rights At common law and under the federal system, two conditions must be met for trade mark appropriation. First, the party claiming the mark must prove that she was the first commercial user of the word, name, phrase, symbol, device, or logo. The second condition is the mark's distinctiveness. The federal system also requires registration with the Patent and Trade Mark Office, a procedure in which an examining attorney evaluates the application to determine whether the mark meets statutory requirements.[183]

Priority of use
Under both the common law and the Lanham Act, a business person can lay claim to a trade mark by priority of use. While the first use must be in commerce, it need not be widespread because the 'concept of priority is applied . . . on the basis of the equities involved'. That said, courts have reached strikingly disparate views of the equities in different cases. For example, the Third Circuit Court of Appeals in *Natural Footwear Ltd.* v. *Hart, Schaffner & Marx*[184] announced a bright-line test requiring sales to no fewer than 50 customers and the Seventh Circuit in *Schaffner & Marx, Zazu Designs* v. *L'Oréal S.A*[185] found inadequate a small number of sales over the counter by a small retailer, the court concluding that a large firm's subsequent mass sales of goods with the same mark deserved protection on

account of substantial unpublicised investments in product development. But the Second Circuit in *Blue Bell Inc.* v. *Jaymar-Ruby Inc.*[186] suggested that even one bona fide use would be sufficient and the District Court for the Southern District of New York in *G. D. Searle & Co.* v. *Nutrapharm Inc.*[187] found that shipments to an independent testing laboratory established use in commerce. In a sharp departure from the common law, the Lanham Act section 1(b), a 1989 amendment, permits federal registration of trade marks when the applicant persuades the PTO that there is a 'bona fide intent' to use the mark. Congress amended the statute to protect firms that have invested heavily in developing and designing a mark only to discover that another firm had already used it in commerce.

Both a lenient judicial standard for determining trademark use and the 1989 amendment can be justified as incentives to invest in trade marks. But it must be recognised that this sort of 'propertisation' has nothing to do with the traditional common law concern over consumer confusion and deception, or with the modern economic justification of decreasing consumer search costs. Nor does it seek to protect a business from unfair competition. But there may be another rationale in certain limited circumstances. In cases like *Zazu Designs*, a more lenient standard might have protected a start-up or small business whose early trade mark use was necessarily more confined, from claims by a large firm seeking protection for exploratory investments in product development that frequently do not see the light of day. There does not seem to be a justification either in economics or in equity to prefer the large firm, particularly in light of Lanham Act section 1(b), which invites registration in those very circumstances. Indeed, both the economics and the equities point toward protecting a trade mark based on the small firm's bona fide use in commerce.

Distinctiveness

The value of a trade mark is its distinctiveness, its ability to differentiate the marked product's origin from those of its competitors. Distinctiveness is a measure of the relationship between the product and the mark that is affixed. A mark is inherently distinctive when it communicates no direct information, or very little, about the product itself. In this case, the mark's sole function to the public is identification of the origin – the brand name, such as Kodak or Exxon. If, on the other hand, the mark simply describes the product – as Bread or Wine, for example – then distinctiveness is entirely lacking and the mark is deemed generic. Between the extremes of inherently distinctive and generic marks are those that are somewhat descriptive but that can gain distinction through public recognition after extended use. The policy underlying the requirement of distinctiveness for trademark eligibility ultimately rests on the importance of market access and fair competition: the more descriptive a mark, the more likely merchants will need it to describe their product, leading to the conclusion that no single merchant should be granted a monopoly on the mark.

Courts have developed a typology for placing marks along a continuum of distinctiveness. As stated in the landmark *Abercrombie & Fitch* (1976) opinion, 'The cases . . . identify four different categories of terms with respect to trade mark protection. Arrayed in an ascending order which roughly reflects their eligibility to trade mark status and the degree of protection accorded, these classes are (1) generic, (2) descriptive, (3) suggestive, and (4) arbitrary or fanciful. The lines of demarcation, however, are not always bright.' Generic terms can never attain trade mark status and always remain in the public domain. Descriptive terms can become eligible for trade mark protection if the claimant proves that the term has developed a secondary meaning that is stronger than the informational value – that is, the public has come to recognise the term as a brand rather than as a description of the product. Even misdescriptive terms such as Black & White for Scotch whisky, so long as they are not deceptively misdescriptive, can develop a secondary meaning and trade mark eligibility.

One distinction with particular legal significance is the line between suggestive and descriptive terms because a suggestive term is protected on first use but a descriptive term must develop a secondary meaning to attain trade mark status. Although, for example, the trade mark Coppertone suggests that product use can result in a coppery skin colour, it does require an imaginative step, if not a leap, to connect the brand name on the label with the skin-tanning product in the bottle. Yet the spray deodorant Hour After Hour has been held a descriptive term. The renowned Judge Learned Hand described best the subjectivity of this important distinction: '[I]t is quite impossible to get any rule out of the cases beyond this: that the validity of the mark ends when suggestion ends and description begins.'[188]

Moreover, a descriptive term is subject to its own fair use defence. In the *Zatarain's Inc.* v. *Oak Grove Smokehouse Inc.* case,[189] the Fifth Circuit Court of Appeals found 'Fish-Fri' and 'Chick-Fri' to be descriptive terms that had acquired a secondary meaning and thus had become distinctive enough to merit trade mark protection. However, competitors, actual and potential, were permitted fair use of highly similar terms such as 'fish fry' and 'chicken fry' to describe the characteristics of their goods. '[O]nly the penumbra or fringe of secondary meaning is given protection. Zatarain's has no legal claim to an exclusive right in the original, descriptive sense, so long as such use will not tend to confuse customers.'[190]

Perhaps of even greater significance than the distinction between suggestive and descriptive terms is the porous boundary between descriptive and generic terms because generics can never attain trademark status. Indeed, that is the very argument made by the accused infringer in the recent case filed by Microsoft claiming infringement of the Windows trade mark by the defendant's use of Lindows as the name for its form of the LINUX operating system. The Lindows product competes directly with Windows, whose name is registered as a trade mark with the PTO.

In response to Microsoft's motion seeking a temporary injunction to block the use of Lindows, defendant argued that, although registered and thus prima facie valid, Windows was a generic term used in the industry at the time of registration and thus incapable of developing a secondary meaning. The trial court judge denied Microsoft's request for injunction after finding the accused infringer's proffered evidence sufficient to rebut the presumption of trade mark validity. Whether Windows retains trade mark status will likely depend on the term's categorisation as generic or descriptive.[191] Judge Richard Posner has written that to 'allow a firm to use as a trade mark a generic word . . . would make it difficult for competitors to market their own brands of the same product. Imagine being forbidden to describe a Chevrolet as a "car" or an "automobile" '.[192] Some twenty years after its initial use, Windows seems not descriptive or generic but imbued with secondary meaning. Nonetheless, the current perception may turn out to be entirely irrelevant. The current perception should be irrelevant if the term was generic at the time of trade mark registration, courts and scholars agree, because the monopolisation of such a term is precisely what the generic category's underlying competition policy of market access is intended to prohibit.

The Lindows case demonstrates that trade marks can be particularly important in computer markets and other industries where compatibility with established standards is crucial for product acceptance. Because network effects make inter-system competition so difficult in markets that have tipped to a dominant standard such as Windows, the importance of marking one's product as compatible should not be underestimated. In *Creative Labs. Inc.* v. *Cyrix Corp.*[193] the very meaning of compatibility was at issue. Claiming false advertising under section 43(a), the plaintiff persuaded the court to issue a preliminary injunction prohibiting the defendant from describing its product as 'compatible with Sound Blaster', the plaintiff's sponsored industry standard, because 'only' 184 of 200 programs tested ran properly. Moreover, in a side show to the featured government antitrust litigation against Microsoft, Sun Microsystems has filed its own suits claiming antitrust violations, breach of contract, and copyright and trade mark infringement of its Java middleware. Java is the de facto industry standard, written to run on fifteen operating systems. At one point, the court in the trademark litigation issued an injunction prohibiting Microsoft from using the 'Java-compatible' mark because the Microsoft version of Java, revised to run more efficiently with Windows, was divested of its capacity to run on other operating systems, rendering it Java-incompatible. Sun characterized the conduct as unfair competition to lure and lock Java users into an incompatible system that would impose high costs on them to switch back to the standard Java. The court agreed that Microsoft's use of the 'Java-compatible' mark would likely mislead users into believing that the Microsoft version of Java was compatible with the standard software. Shortly thereafter, Microsoft agreed to pay Sun $20 million in settlement and to cancel the licensing agreement.[194] With Sun's antitrust and copyright claims still pending trial, the court clearly viewed the trade mark issue in terms of unfair competitive practices that would mislead consumers into believing that Microsoft Java was compatible with the industry standard Java.

Note: Trade dress and computer software
In addition to trade mark protection, merchants can also protect a product's 'total image and overall appearance'. In *Two Pesos Inc., v. Taco Cabana Inc.*[195] the Supreme Court found that the trade dress of a restaurant – the config-uration of its decor, sign, servers' uniforms, menu and equipment – could be inherently distinctive and thus immediately protected under Lanham Act section 43(a). Trade dress protection has been asserted in a growing number of cases to protect the look and feel of computer software. To assert trade dress claims, however, plaintiffs must overcome a significant hurdle, parti-cularly for computer software: the item's functional features are not protect-able subject matter. In several cases, trade dress protection has been asserted for the software's graphical user interface (GUI).[196] The scope of trade dress protection depends largely on decisions regarding the functionality of trade dress, decisions which courts make by looking at the product's configuration. The scope of copyright protection, by contrast, turns not on the product con-figuration but on scrutiny of each individual element of the GUI to determine whether functional considerations dictated the element's design.[197] Despite the Supreme Court's configuration approach in *Two Pesos*, an element-by-element analysis might make more sense for determining trade dress protection in the software context for two reasons. First, because many elements, such as desktop icons, are functionally conceived; and second, because it is only in the key elements of a GUI that infringers need to match a competitive product's look and feel.

The Supreme Court has expressed concern in other contexts that expansive trade dress protection might restrain fair competition. 'Where an item . . . is unprotected by a patent, "reproduction of a functional attribute is legitimate competitive activity".'[198] In the recent *TrafFix Devices Inc.* v. *Marketing Displays Inc.*,[199] the Court was asked to determine 'whether the existence of an expired utility patent forecloses the possibility of the patentee's claiming trade dress protection in the product's design'. Even in the absence of patents, *Two Pesos* teaches that trade dress protection may not be claimed for product features that are functional. The Court in *TrafFix* concluded that a prior patent creates a presumption of functionality that imposes on the claimant 'a heavy burden of showing that the feature is not functional [but] merely an ornamental, incidental, or arbitrary aspect of the device'. The Court denied trade dress protection to the springs, though distinctive in appearance, because they were designed and used to keep outdoor road signs upright despite windy conditions. 'Functionality having been established, whether [the] dual-spring design acquired secondary meaning need not be considered.' Once the patents expired, the springs fell irretrievably into the public domain. In short, trade dress protection could not extend the patent term to exclude copying by competitors.

The *Sears, Roebuck & Co.* v. *Stiffel Co* opinion[200] captures the priority given federal patent policy. The district court had held Sears liable under state unfair competition law, finding a likelihood of confusion because the lamp was copied from Stiffel's unpatented lamp and, in consequence, the two looked exactly alike. The court enjoined Sears from producing and selling the lamp. 'Of course there could be "confusion" as to who had manufactured these nearly identical articles', the Supreme Court observed. 'But mere inability of the public to tell two identical articles apart is not enough to support an injunction against copying or an award of damages for copying that which the federal patent laws permit to be copied. Doubtless a State may, in appropriate circumstances, require that goods, whether patented or unpatented, be labelled or that other precautionary steps be taken to prevent customers from being misled as to the source, just as it may protect businesses in the use of their trademarks, labels, or distinctive dress in the packaging of goods so as to prevent others, by imitating such markings, from misleading purchasers as to the source of the goods. But because of the federal patent laws a State may not, when the article is unpatented and uncopyrighted, prohibit the copying of the article itself or award damages for such copying.' As the Second Circuit Court of Appeals remarked in another trade dress case, 'imitation is the lifeblood of competition'.[201]

Infringement   Traditional trade mark protection reflected concern about consumer confusion or deception regarding a product's source in its explicit requirement that the infringement create the likelihood of confusion over the product's source. But consumers no longer know or care very much about a product's actual source, given modern networks of distribution and sale, which have etiolated links between product names and producers. Rather, when consumers show a preference, it is more often for the trade mark itself, perhaps because advertising has persuaded them of its quality or simply because the mark itself has value. The modern expansion of trade mark protection reflects the value of marks apart from any goods to which they might be affixed. By recognising claims for trade mark dilution without regard to whether the infringing activity creates consumer confusion about the source of the marked product, the courts and the Lanham Act protect the owner's investment in the mark itself, which creates value in the owner's commercial goodwill or reputation.

Thus modern trade mark infringement claims take two forms. The first is a tort of unfair competition whose harm is the likelihood of consumer confusion and, as a consequence, injury to the trademark holder. The second is a property right to protection against dilution of a trade mark's value without explicit regard to consumer harm.

Likelihood of consumer confusion

The crux of the matter is 'whether concurrent use of the two marks is likely to confuse the public'. When the accused infringer directly competes for sales, proof that the marks are 'sufficiently similar', without more, gives rise to an inference that 'confusion can be expected'.[202] But when the goods are related though not competitive, a series of factors are taken into account. The factors include the mark's strength, the similarities of the marks and of the underlying goods, and the variety of goods to which the marks are affixed.[203] One factor that has become more important as trade mark protection has grown is the likelihood that either the senior or junior user will expand his product line into competition with the other. If a likelihood of expansion is found, then current use will be considered infringement, even though the likelihood of consumer confusion is purely hypothetical. Both the doctrines of expansion and dilution encourage an owner to invest in the mark itself by granting a right to enter another market and make use of the good reputation or goodwill embodied in the trade mark. The impact on competition depends on the circumstances.

A new source of infringement litigation is the unauthorised use of trade marks as 'metatags' on Internet web pages. Metatags are strings of characters, self-chosen key words that are invisible to users but are used by software search engines to determine web site content. Some web site owners have started using competitors' trade marks or just popular trademarks such as 'NY Yankees' or 'Playboy' in their metatags to draw unwitting visitors to their sites.[204] The rationale for extending protection to invisible labels is found in protecting consumers from being lured to a site that, at least initially, would be confused with the desired destination. It is the deliberate nature of the conduct that throws it into the category of unfair competition even though such confusion is quickly dispelled. In general, if the web site owner is not a competitor, courts are more likely to find innocent intentions and, with them, a legitimate reason for using the metatag.[205]

Dilution

The second prong of trade mark infringement is justified not by the prevention of consumer confusion but rather the preservation of a trade mark's uniqueness. Thus, non-confusing uses of a protected trade mark are still infringing uses when they 'water down, erode or weaken the cachet and magnetism of a strong trade mark'.[206] An amendment to the Lanham Act in 1996 and its corollaries in most state laws extend the dilution doctrine only to 'famous' or 'highly distinctive' trade marks, reflecting a concern that extending the dilution doctrine to less-than-famous marks would grant property status to so many marks that competition would be unduly restrained.[207]

Dilution claims were originally conceived as protection against infringing uses that do not compete with the trademarked product.[208] If there were actual or likely competition, then the cause of action would be infringement based on a likelihood of consumer confusion. But when there is no competition, there is no danger of confusing the origins of the rival products. Nonetheless, the value of the famous trade mark could be impaired because dilution 'reduces the public's perception that the mark signifies something unique, singular, or particular'. In this light, claims of infringement by trade mark dilution have taken two forms: dilution by tarnishment and by blurring.

Dilution by tarnishment protects a famous trade mark 'from negative associations through defendant's use'.[209] Tarnishment claims typically arise out of commercial uses that the trade mark owner views as unsavory or lurid. Occasionally, there have been claims that tarnishment resulted from trade mark use on low quality goods.[210] But most dilution claims allege that a non-competitive use diluted the mark's distinctive quality by 'blurring' its product identification. The classic example is the British *Kodak* case,[211] in which the court issued an injunction against using the famous Kodak name on bicycles, even though there was no evidence of low quality goods or unsavoury circumstances. The logic of blurring goes something like this: If the trademark owner of Kodak could not enjoin the use of the famous mark on bicycles or boots or baby food, then, at some point, the Kodak mark's relationship with photographic equipment would blur, losing 'its distinctiveness and hence impact'.[212]

Since the development of the Internet as a commercial sphere, domain names have become more important and thus more valuable. Early in this development, speculators saw the value and registered famous trade marks and valuable generic terms as domain names. While there have been no lawsuits challenging the registration of generic terms – for example, 'baseball' as baseball. com – an avalanche of cases were filed by trade mark owners claiming that registrations amounted to trademark infringement by dilution. Perhaps the most useful generalisation that can be made about those cases is that the trade mark owners always won. To begin, courts have declared that merely registering another's trade mark as a domain name amounts to a commercial use. Moreover, even when a court could not fit the claim into the dilution categories of blurring and tarnishment, they were not deterred. Simply investing 'great resources in promoting its service mark was enough.' The Ninth Circuit Court of Appeals in *Panavision International, L.P.* v. *Toeppen*[213] did not feel compelled to do more than remark that dilution was not limited to blurring and tarnishment.[214] Trade mark dilution has become the theory of choice for suing such speculators as 'cyberpirates' without the need to prove harm of any sort. The conduct is viewed as illegal per se, something akin to theft.

Defences to infringement   The accused infringer has available a series of defences. Some find their sources in doctrines already discussed. As mentioned in the Lindows discussion, there is the defence of 'genericness.' The trade dress discussion introduced the doctrine that denies protection to functional configurations. In its 1998 amendments to the Lanham Act, Congress included functionality as a reason to refuse registration.[215] Since use is a requirement for protection, abandonment of trade mark use is a defence. Each of these defences implicates a fundamental policy underlying trade marks. Allowing trade mark protection of generic terms would harm both consumers and competitors by denying public use of a fundamentally useful word or symbol in the public domain; indeed, allowing monopoly of a generic term would confuse consumers and harm competition for no justifiable reason. Protecting a functional configuration would grant patent-like protection outside the federal patent system and thus without its requirements of novelty and non-obviousness, limited term, and public benefits of description and enablement.

In addition, there is a bundle of fair use defences. Their fairness derives from the incidental use of the mark for purposes other than those normally made of the trademark. First, there is no liability for non-commercial use. Second, non-trade mark or nominative use is permitted – for example, a newspaper's identification of a singing group, whose name was a registered trademark, as the subject of a public opinion poll.[216] The court pointed out that there was no reasonable alternative to calling the singing group by its name. Next, a cluster of fair uses reflect values found in First Amendment Speech rights. The Lanham Act section 43(c)(4) permits unauthorised use of a famous mark in 'all forms of news reporting and news commentary' as well as in 'comparative commercial advertising or promotion to identify the competing goods or services of the owner of the famous mark'. Recognising fair use in advertising serves not only the constitutional rights associated with commercial speech but also the recognition of the informational value of advertising to competition. At common law, parodic use of a trade mark is allowed. In the well-known *L. L. Bean* case,[217] the court permitted a two-page article that presented a 'prurient parody of Bean's famous catalogue', concluding that the infringer's use in an adult erotic magazine was artistic rather than commercial. There is, however, no additive principle: It is not fair use when the parody is used to promote competitive goods or services.[218]

Even more than copyrighted works, trade marks by their essentially commercial nature place them at the intersection of markets for goods and services and the marketplace of ideas. In that busy intersection, trade mark protection offers a particularly clear picture of how concerns about regulating strategic commercial conduct and creating investment incentives interact to produce intellectual property rights in the United States.

II. Overview: US antitrust law and innovation

This part of the report introduces the four cornerstones of US antitrust law: antitrust economics, the statutes, judicial doctrine, and the federal regulatory agencies.[219] Since the Congressional debates over the Sherman Act of 1890, antitrust policy makers have sought to find a balance between competition policy and private property rights. Theoretically the two policies are complementary. Private property rights enable people to enter into transactions to buy and sell goods. Competition policy seeks to ensure that these transactions result in a fair price for buyers and a fair profit for sellers. However, in reality, these two propositions tend to conflict when competition policy requires government regulation of private contracts in the form of antitrust law in order to promote an efficient marketplace.[220] Although both policies aim to maximise wealth by producing what consumers want at the lowest cost, without some level of government regulation sellers may exploit market imperfections to increase profits and reduce consumer welfare.[221] Antitrust law protects against such exploitation by seeking to strike a balance between the two policies.

A. Antitrust economics

In one of the best-known passages of antitrust doctrine, Judge Learned Hand offered an elegant rationale for permitting monopoly in an antitrust regime of competition. He encapsulated the rationale in a phrase – 'Finis opus coronat.'[222] The end crowns the work. In essence, he asked the following question: encouraged to compete, how can we punish the success that follows? Certainly, this sense of fairness is strikingly attractive. But it is not the only justification for monopoly that has been heard over the last century. Since Congress passed the Sherman Antitrust Act of 1890, antitrust policy makers have given four rationales for determining whether to permit monopoly or, more generally, whether to permit the exercise of market power in an antitrust regime dedicated to promoting competition. Each new rationale has reflected the emergence of a new antitrust economics. To quickly summarise the last century of antitrust economics, the remainder of this section examines the rationales for evaluating the exercise of market power.

As we shall see, each new rationale emerged from a new model of market economics. Unlike new scientific paradigms or new technologies whose 'perennial gales of creative destruction' typically overthrow their predecessors, newer models of market economics have not displaced older approaches. Rather, each one has supplemented its antecedents. As a result, a four-firm rivalry flourishes in the policy market for antitrust economics.

Classical economics   In the same year Congress passed the Sherman Act of 1890, Alfred Marshall launched the 'marginalist revolution' with his *Principles of Economics*. But Marshall's market economics of marginal cost and marginal revenue did not begin to influence antitrust doctrine in America until some thirty years later. Instead, lawyers argued and judges judged within the framework of classical economics. Classical economics is not market economics as we know it but, rather, a political economy of competition founded on freedom of contract. According to this view, competition follows as a logical inference from freedom of contract – the more freedom of contract, the more competition. The less freedom of contract, the less competition. Thus, the antitrust question for classicists was whether a particular practice unreasonably restrained freedom of contract. At the turn of the twentieth century, the common law of trade restraints and then a comparable Sherman Act jurisprudence sought to answer that question.

When the first great antitrust case reached the Supreme Court in 1896, lawyers for the Trans Missouri Railroad Association insisted that their cartel was a reasonable restraint of trade. In support of their claim, they made two arguments, one which the Justices addressed and one which they did not. All nine Justices considered a common law argument about reasonable restraints; a majority of five rejected the familiar classical economic argument and the railroad lost the case. But none of the Justices dealt with an unfamiliar argument about charging reasonable prices in the face of ruinous competition. The economic argument about ruinous competition called for an understanding of what we today would call high sunk costs, steady or declining marginal costs, and declining average total costs in the railroad industry. The railroad attorneys' arguments were likely informed by market studies that had begun some ten years earlier, even before Lord Marshall's book. By the late 1880s, the new American Economics Association and others had already published articles about the cost structure of American industry and its significance. But the Court did not have a framework for making sense of arguments outside the classical paradigm.[223] They thought of competition as a logical inference from freedom of contract.

Neo-classical price theory   In the 1920s, federal judges began to apply the neo-classical approach, beginning with the tenet that market share reflects economic power. But their early understandings of market share were surprisingly bifurcated. That bifurcation can be seen in their approach to monopolies. In the *United States Steel* case (1920), for example, the Supreme Court treated competitive markets and monopoly markets as mutually exclusive conditions. In short, markets that were not dominated by one firm were declared competitive. They envisioned nothing between the two extremes. In that view, even an 80 per cent market share did not amount to monopoly power. In a long series of trade association cases throughout the first half of the twentieth century, the neo-classical approach informed the court's attempts to grapple with difficult questions of information exchange and its effects on market prices. During the Great Depression years, the Supreme Court began to emphasise the central importance of the market as a price mechanism. It should be understood that neo-classical price theory focuses on price and output in particular markets. The theory is powerful in its simplicity. First and foremost, market participants are assumed to make decisions based purely on price. Goods and services are treated as fungible. To facilitate this treatment, notions of cross-elasticity developed to quantify in terms of price and output the extent to which non-identical products can be treated as substitutes. Nonetheless, all macro-economic variables are assumed to hold constant variables such as the value and supply of money, changes in taste and income, and the quality of alternative goods and services. As a result, market changes are attributed entirely to changes in market price and output regardless of exogenous factors. In the landmark *Socony Vacuum* case (1940),[224] Justice William O. Douglas declared competitive pricing the 'central nervous system' of the economy. Price fixing cartels were the economy's worst affliction and, thus, antitrust's greatest sin – a view that still holds today in the United States.

Post-classical economics   While neo-classical price theory reigned supreme in the federal courts, most market economists in the United States were already shifting their analytical framework, based largely on the work of Harvard economist Edward Chamberlin. By the late 1930s, his book, *The Theory of Monopolistic Competition* (1932), had persuaded most market economists that neo-classical price theory's limitations should be addressed because its assumptions were too confining to apply to the workings of most markets. Chamberlin's theory can be understood as relaxing two counter-factual assumptions – one that price is the sole motivation for market trans-actions and the second that markets are either monopolistic or competitive, with nothing in between. As to the first assumption, his concept of product differentiation presented a language and an analytical structure for the non-price strategies deployed in most markets but unseen through the lens of neo-classical price theory. After all, how many of us make purchasing decisions based only on price? If that were the case, brand names and perceived quality differences would be immaterial. Advertising would deal only with price. In short, the model of competition by product differentiation reflects the reality that, given a choice, sellers seek to avoid price competition, preferring instead to develop customer brand loyalty through advertising and other forms of non-price competition.

As to price theory's second assumption, Chamberlin's oligopoly theory recognised that most markets were neither perfectly monopolistic nor per-fectly competitive but a third species. His theory showed why market structure should be an important part of determining the full range of incentives and strategies available to managers. Despite some influential scholarship that misguided antitrust policy in the mid-twentieth century, oligopoly theory is best understood as a primordial game theory that preceded the mathematic models and strategic business planning that have recently emerged in the fourth approach to antitrust economics. In sum, Chamberlin's twin theories raised questions about the centrality of price competition and developed an approach to understanding the importance of market structure.

Neo-classical price theory reprise   The influence of oligopoly theory grew after the Second World War, becoming the economic logic that supported the Supreme Court's special solicitude toward small businesses, especially in its merger jurisprudence of the 1960s and 1970s. The jurisprudence followed the 1950 amendment to the antitrust merger statute, which was intended to slow the perceived growth of industrial concentration. This impulse toward Jeffersonian entrepreneurialism was attacked by Chicago School price theorists, including Robert Bork and Richard Posner, as anti-efficiency and, thus, as against the greater public good. By the late 1970s, the price theory rhetorics of allocative efficiency and consumer welfare[225] had convinced the Supreme Court that oligopoly theory and its Jeffersonian sentiments were bad economics. A few years later, the Jimmy Carter and Ronald Reagan administrations would embark on deregulation programmes intended to allow businesses to cut costs and compete more freely. Neo-classical price theory was seen as the best way to produce a minimalist antitrust policy that would encourage firms to increase output and lower prices. Reagan appointees to the federal agencies and federal bench especially tended to be adherents to the resurrected price theory. In consequence, agency enforcement policies and court opinions typically evaluated market strategies by examining commercial purposes and effects through the rather narrow lens of price and output.

It was a caricature of Chamberlin's oligopoly theory that provided the target for the Chicago School's revival of neo-classical price theory, which emerged to dominate antitrust jurisprudence in the 1980s. In the mid-1970s, then-Professor Richard Posner attacked oligopoly theory – more particularly, the simplified version portrayed by Harvard professor Donald Turner in his influential Harvard Law Review article about the nature of agreement under Sherman Act section 1.[226] Turner argued that consciously parallel conduct such as industry-wide pricing changes or standard gas station leases should not be an antitrust violation because the defendants were acting as economically rational oligopolists: it made no sense for oligopolists to compete on price because a lower price by one firm would be immediately recognised and matched by the others. Industry prices would fall and everyone would be worse off. This economically rational behaviour should not and, as a practical matter, could not be enjoined. The only economically rational solution, according to Turner, was to deconcentrate the industry, to change the structure and, with it, alter the economic logic. Posner attacked Turner's structural logic, insisting that there remained the same incentives to compete on price, regardless of structure. But both Turner and Posner got it wrong, even though Posner's view has largely prevailed. Turner got it wrong because Chamberlin, correctly, never claimed a structural logic in oligopoly industries that compelled certain conduct, only the importance of market structure to gauging rational reactions to strategic choices. Sometimes, price competition would make sense. Sometimes it would not. The answer was not a matter of structural logic but one of expectations informed by actual experience. Posner got it wrong because the incentives to compete on prices were indeed different in concentrated industries. As the strategic marketing literature has shown us, structure is important though not controlling. Again, the answer is not a matter of some universal imperative to compete but a factual question of oligopolists' rational expectations informed by experience. Hence, the signalling behaviour of, for example, the commercial airlines over their common computerised reservation system.[227]

Dynamic approaches to antitrust economics   Nonetheless, competition has long been understood as involving more than price competition. Alfred Marshall recognised it. Indeed, since the early twentieth century, Austrian economist Joseph Schumpeter argued the primary importance of dynamic competition by innovation, insisting that the static economics of price competition misses the larger point. In the mid-twentieth century, other economists began to view market statics as inadequate for an entirely different reason.[228] They saw strategic behaviour in markets, behaviour that came in under the radar of a neo-classical price theory. The model, on its own terms, was not capable of registering, describing, or analysing the conduct. Dynamic approaches were needed to understand and evaluate the behaviour in many markets. In the last decade of the twentieth century, two dynamic approaches have developed out of scholarly work of economists and the practical needs of business managers – innovation economics, and strategic marketing and management.

Innovation economics
Joseph Schumpeter's view of market dynamics has become most influential in America. It is competition by innovation, he wrote, that truly improves social welfare. It is 'perennial gales of creative destruction' that uproot monopoly and improve society. In the mid-twentieth century, market economists were particularly interested in testing Schumpeter's claim that innovation called for large dominant firms, which are not at immediate risk from the day to day pressures felt by firms in highly competitive markets. Are large dominant

firms better situated to produce useful research and development? The research has been inconclusive.

Despite attention to innovation as an antitrust policy concern since the late 1950s, it did not begin to gain prominence until the mid-1980s, when Congress passed special legislation to limit the antitrust liability of firms engaged in research and development joint ventures. At about the same time, antitrust economists began to take up Schumpeter's call for attention to dynamic efficiency, particularly in the context of information and high technology industries. That attention led to a spate of writing about the special characteristics of network industries, whether about physical networks such as telephone systems or virtual systems such as the Windows operating system customer base. In network industries, the value of the product increases as the network grows. Once a network market tips toward one industry standard, it makes little sense for a potential customer to choose, for example, Mac OS or Linux rather than Windows, even if Windows is more expensive, less efficient and less stable because Windows supports more application programmes and Microsoft is least likely to fail. For the same reasons, application software companies choose to develop products for the industry standard. This positive feedback loop tends to produce winner-takes-all results in network industries whose standard protocols or specifications are not compatible with alternatives. Thus, there is a logic to firms' developing aggressive strategies to increase their market shares. In these circumstances, aggressive behaviour can raise new antitrust questions, particularly about industry standard-setting organisations and single firm strategies to gain or maintain dominance.

Strategic marketing and management
The second piece of a dynamic antitrust analysis that looks beyond the statics of price and output is game theory or strategic market behaviour. Attempts to understand, model, and evaluate strategic behaviour are not entirely new to antitrust policy or to market economics. As I mentioned earlier, Edward Chamberlin's oligopoly model, rightly understood, is not a structuralist logic of causation but an intuitive approach to modelling strategic marketing in concentrated markets with fungible products. Unfortunately, the overlay of static price theory has obscured the strategic kernel of Chamberlin's approach, which requires a temporal dimension. A temporal dimension is required to comprehend Chamberlin's view that oligopolists' trust and interdependence take time to develop.

The implication for antitrust, of course, is that stable markets, especially oligopolies, are likely to produce cooperating firms who act on their common interests and seek to avoid price competition. The prediction is familiar to students of antitrust but the analysis is not. Game theory, in its broadest sense, calls for a particular state of mind, an approach to transactions founded on the fundamental importance of predicting and seeking to shape the other parties' reactions to one's actions. In the United States, the game theoretic approach dominates marketing and management scholarship, and suffuses mainstream micro-economics, both inside and outside the academy. But in antitrust economics, its influence is just developing.

How might a game theoretic approach inform antitrust analysis? How might it extend antitrust economics to commercial conduct whose purposes and effects are not well understood by students of antitrust? Widely influential studies, some written for business school courses and others for marketing managers, counsel readers that 'bidding for customers' (i.e. price competition) makes little sense. Why? Because there are numerous 'hidden costs'. For one, the other firm might retaliate. In other words, price competition might break out. For another, a bad precedent is set: other customers will want the same lower price. Moreover, this game produces winners and losers amongst sellers. Or just losers. 'Lowering your competitor's profits isn't necessarily smart . . . . If you lower your rival's profits, he then has less to lose and every reason to become more aggressive . . . In contrast, the more money your rival is making, the more he has to lose from getting into a price war.'[229]

The marketing literature stresses that there are strategies that promise only winners. What is a win-win strategy? Smart strategies invite 'good' imitation rather than the 'bad' imitation of price competition. One example is the airline frequent flyer and credit card programmes to develop a base of loyal customers who have incentives to stay with one airline to accumulate credit. Another strategy is meeting-competition and most-favoured-customer clauses, which tend to lower the pressure to cut prices. If such clauses are adopted industry wide, market studies show, prices tend to be higher.

These dynamic approaches allow market analysis to register change and, thus, to account for behaviours, purposes, and effects that escape detection under the lens of the earlier approaches, with the partial exception of Chamberlin's product differentiation theory, rightly understood, which does take some kinds of change into account.

Each approach, in its own way, has sought to mediate the tensions between competition policy and private property rights. Current antitrust law in the United States is best understood in light of the four economic logics that have entered judicial opinions and regulatory guidelines since the late nineteenth century. While innovation economics is at the forefront of competition policy, the other approaches to market economics continue to inform and influence courts and competition agencies in their production of antitrust decisions.

B. The antitrust statutes in historical context

Federal antitrust law in the United States is statutory in origin and common law in character. Since the passage of the Sherman Antitrust Act of 1890,

Congress has enacted two additional statutes and several amendments. But the courts have taken the common law language of the Sherman Act as licence to reshape doctrine to new economic insights and changing commercial circumstances.[230]

The Sherman Act was passed in the late nineteenth century, an era of common law sensibility, a time when the courts had few statutes to make use of but significant economic changes to regulate. Whether the rise of labour unions or the cartelisation of industry, courts turned to common law doctrines as the tools of regulation. England and the several states had common law doctrines of 'restraints of trade' and 'monopoly' to regulate commercial conduct that exploited buyers and excluded rivals. That era's Congress turned to the common law as a familiar source of language and policy for the first federal antitrust statute. The Sherman Act was drafted in two sections, each one an echo of the common law. Substantially unchanged today, section 1 prohibits 'every contract, combination . . . or conspiracy, in restraint of trade or commerce'. Section 2 prohibits conduct that 'monopolise[s], or attempt[s] to monopolise any part of trade or commerce'. In the two decades following the statute's enactment, the Supreme Court treated as per se illegal all violations of the statute. But with the landmark *Standard Oil* decision (1911), the Court began a long march toward the more flexible jurisprudence that is now termed the rule of reason.[231] Today, courts usually apply the rule of reason, looking at the purposes and competitive effects of the conduct, as well as the actors' market power, to judge whether the conduct in question is a reasonable restraint in the circumstances.

Shortly after publication of the *Standard Oil* opinion, Congress began deliberations over new antitrust legislation, in large part because of the widespread view that the announced 'rule of reason' resulted in too much judicial discretion in the interpretation of the Sherman Antitrust Act. After three years of deliberation, Congress enacted two statutes, each one a different reaction to the rule of reason and judicial discretion. The Clayton Act of 1914 was drafted in the form of a laundry list of specific offences that were declared anticompetitive. The statute outlawed tying, exclusive dealing, and stock mergers 'where the effect . . . may be to substantially lessen competition or tend to create a monopoly in any line of commerce'.[232] A significant amendment, enacted in 1950, extended the merger provision, section 7, to include asset acquisitions and non-horizontal mergers.

A second noteworthy amendment to the Clayton Act, passed in 1976, added section 7A, which requires firms meeting the statutory size standard to file pre-merger notification documents with the Federal Trade Commission and Department of Justice, Antitrust Division. The notification process has changed the very nature of antitrust merger regulation in the United States, a change from a litigation regime to a less adversarial regulatory practice under the agencies' joint *Horizontal Merger Guidelines*.

Liability under the Sherman and Clayton Acts in private causes of action includes the possibility of treble damages and attorneys' fees, as well as injunctive relief.[233]

The Federal Trade Commission (FTC) Act of 1914 and its later amendments reflect an entirely different approach. Congress created an independent agency to regulate conduct found to be 'unfair methods of competition ... or ... unfair or deceptive acts or practices' under FTC Act section 5. The FTC was given extensive investigative powers and broad authority to formulate policy under the general language of the statute. The Supreme Court declared early on that the agency's discretion was subject to judicial oversight. As a general matter, remedies are limited to cease and desist orders, and there is no private cause of action under the statute. The FTC has concurrent authority with the Department of Justice, Antitrust Division, to enforce the Clayton Act.

C. Judicial interpretation of the statutes

From the *Standard Oil* opinion's announcement in 1911 of the rule of reason until the mid-1970s, judicial interpretation of the statutes reflected a bifurcated jurisprudence. Courts approached allegedly anticompetitive conduct in one of two ways. Some conduct was categorised as illegal per se and other conduct was evaluated more extensively under a rule of reason.[234] Conduct in the per se category includes agreements among competitors to fix price, reduce output, rig bids or divide geographic markets or customer bases.[235] In a tying case brought under Sherman Act section 1, the Supreme Court explained the rationale for a per se doctrine:

> [T]here are certain agreements or practices which because of their pernicious effect on competition and lack of any redeeming virtue are conclusively presumed to be unreasonable and therefore illegal without elaborate inquiry as to the precise harm they cause or the business excuse for their use. This principle of *per se* unreasonableness [not only creates a bright-line rule but] avoids the necessity for an incredibly complicated and prolonged economic investigation ... in an effort to determine at large whether a particular restraint is unreasonable.[236]

If judicial experience with the conduct under scrutiny did not call for per se illegality, courts applied a fact-intensive rule of reason analysis to determine and then balance the competitive benefits against the competitive harms.[237] The conduct was deemed reasonable when the competitive benefits outweighed the harms.[238] Potential competitive harms include higher prices and lower output, lower quality and less product diversity, as well as decreased innovation and greater danger of collusion. Potential competitive benefits reflect the harms' opposites – for example increased innovation, as well as improved market efficiencies such as better information flow or lower transaction costs.

Before explicating the nuances of current antitrust jurisprudence, it is useful to describe the underlying statutory framework. Under Sherman Act section 1, some agreements in restraint of trade are illegal per se. Price fixing cartels and market allocation agreements fall into the per se category. Most agreements, however, are judged under the rule of reason, which calls for a fact-intensive evaluation of purpose, power and competitive effects. Under Sherman Act section 2, claims of monopolisation and attempts to monopolise are always judged under the rule of reason. Purpose is inferred from a limited set of conduct identified as predatory, including certain pricing below cost and unjustified refusals to deal. For monopolisation, the power element is typically satisfied by evidence of market share of 70 per cent or more. For attempts to monopolise evidence of 30 to 50 per cent market shares has been adequate; but attempt claims include an additional requirement that calls for proof of a dangerous probability that the attempt will succeed. The Clayton Act offences, which include price discrimination, mergers, tying and exclusive dealing, call for proof that the conduct under scrutiny may substantially lessen competition. Here, too, market power and anticompetitive effects are evaluated.

There had long been signs that the wide array of conduct subject to antitrust scrutiny required more flexibility than the two extremes permitted. Most significant was the common law doctrine of ancillary restraints. If a restraint such as price fixing and market allocation is the main purpose of an agreement, then it is per se illegal. When, however, the restraint is ancillary to the main purpose of an agreement, then it is judged under a rule of reason. Perhaps the most common example of an ancillary restraint is a covenant not to compete in a contract to sell an ongoing business. The doctrine of ancillary restraints is usually traced back to Judge William Taft's opinion in *United States* v. *Addyston Pipe & Steel Co.*[239] and informs the federal enforcement agencies' current 'Guidelines for Competitor Collaboration', discussed later in this chapter. But even when the Supreme Court found the main purpose of an agreement to be price fixing, pure per se treatment did not always follow. For example, the court's *United States* v. *Trenton Potteries Co.*[240] decision had applied what might be called a modified per se approach in holding that price fixing cartels with significant market power are per se illegal. Even the *Socony Vacuum*[241] opinion, generally viewed as the most strident expression of per se illegality, discussed the cartel's anticompetitive effects and other aspects of the factual circumstances before declaring that the price fixing cartel was illegal per se.

In the late 1970s, the Supreme Court began in earnest to dissolve the categorical distinction between per se and rule of reason approaches. The most important decision in that enterprise was *Broadcast Music*, a case involving the blanket licensing of performance rights to copyrighted music. Plaintiff Columbia Broadcasting argued that the bundling was a price fixing scheme and thus per se illegal under Sherman Act section 1. The Supreme Court announced that a court should precede per se treatment with a 'quick look' at the restraint to determine whether it 'facially appears to be one that would ... almost always tend to restrict competition and decrease output'.[242] If anticompetitive effects do not obviously follow the restraint, then the court should apply a more intensive analysis of power or of less restrictive alternatives to evaluate competitive harms and efficiencies and, if both occur, to determine the net result. In *Broadcast Music*, a quick look showed that significant transactional efficiencies resulted from the joint marketing, monitoring and pricing of the blanket licences. Moreover, the Court determined that the non-exclusive nature of the licences permitted individual negotiations and thus mitigated the anticompetitive effects. The Court concluded that the case called for rule of reason analysis and remanded to the trial court. In jurisprudential terms, the case instructed lower courts to take a 'quick look' at the circumstances and likely effects before assigning the case to the per se or rule of reason category.

In *Arizona* v. *Maricopa County Medical Society*,[243] the Supreme Court evaluated a maximum fee schedule that members agreed to charge patients insured by the foundation. Defendants argued that their arrangement was pro-competitive because it limited physicians' charges and thus benefited patients. The Court declared that a price agreement among competitors without integration of their operations was facially anti-competitive and, moreover, the claimed benefits could be achieved in less restrictive ways. The Court concluded this 'quick look' by assigning the restraint to the per se category.[244] Thus the holding was per se illegality but the analysis was enhanced beyond simply determining whether the conduct occurred.

NCAA v. *Board of Regents of University of Oklahoma*[245] involved an agreement between the National Collegiate Athletic Association, representing major colleges and universities, and two national television broadcast networks to set prices for and limit output of televised college football games. The Supreme Court determined that a rule of reason analysis was appropriate to this joint pricing agreement because some degree of cooperation was needed simply to organise and market the product. That is, the pricing provisions were seen as ancillary to the main purposes of the NCAA. But the analysis required was something less than a full rule of reason. Just as the facial inquiry in *Maricopa County* enhanced the per se approach, this rule of reason analysis was truncated. Here, the integrated nature of the joint venture, a feature missing in *Maricopa County*, took the case out of the per se category. A truncated rule of reason allowed the Court to ask whether the integration was likely to produce efficiencies and whether the joint pricing was necessary to achieve the efficiencies. Affirmative answers to both questions would call for a more extensive analysis.[246] After observing that the output limitations imposed on both national and local broadcasts were not

necessary to achieve the organisational and marketing efficiencies gained by
the joint venture, the Court concluded that 'no elaborate industry analysis is
required to demonstrate the anticompetitive character' of the NCAA's agreement.[247] The practical effect of the new approach was on the plaintiff's
burden of proof: There was no need to go through the elaborate and expensive process of defining the relevant market and proving market power, as
would have been required in a full-blown rule of reason analysis.

In its most recent treatment of collaboration among competitors, *California
Dental Association v. FTC*[248] a sharply divided Supreme Court removed the last
brick supporting the categorical distinction between per se and rule of reason
approaches. The FTC had held illegal those provisions of the Association's code
of ethics requiring members to comply with restrictions on advertising that
was neither false nor misleading. The Association claimed that the advertising
restrictions were pro-competitive because they improved the quality of information provided to patients. The FTC concluded that the restrictions on price
advertising were per se illegal. The FTC concluded, alternatively, that restrictions on both price and non-price advertising were illegal under a truncated
rule of reason analysis because the likely informational benefits were too small
to outweigh the restraints on competition on price and quality, given the
finding that the Association had significant market power. The Ninth Court
of Appeals affirmed the FTC's order under a quick look analysis. The Supreme
Court vacated the order and remanded because the quick look analysis was
found inadequate. In particular, the Court determined that more weight
should have been accorded the Association's claims that the advertising
restraint would tend to correct the market's information failures.[249]

The opinion in *California Dental Association* offered the FTC and lower
courts little instruction for determining when a truncated analysis would be
appropriate or how truncated the analysis should be:

> [T]here is generally no categorical line to be drawn between restraints that
> give rise to an intuitively obvious inference of anticompetitive effect and
> those that call for more detailed treatment. What is required, rather, is an
> enquiry meet for the case, looking to the circumstances, details, and logic of
> a restraint. The object is to see whether the experience of the market has
> been so clear, or necessarily will be, that a confident conclusion about the
> principal tendency of a restriction will follow from a quick (or at least a
> quicker) look, in place of a more sedulous one.[250]

With these generalities, the Court left federal judges and enforcement agencies without guidance for placing an inquiry along the continuum between
pure per se treatment and a full-blown rule of reason. The likely reaction from
pragmatic judges, not wanting to be reversed on appeal, will be to push cases
toward the full-blown rule of reason, a result that discourages private plaintiffs from bringing actions and is arguably in conflict with the antitrust policy
of encouraging enforcement by 'private attorneys general.'

Writing for the four dissenters in *California Dental Association*, Justice Breyer argued that the FTC's treatment actually satisfied the majority's standard. Moreover, Breyer stressed the importance of structuring the inquiry by paying close attention to the 'allocation of the burdens of persuasion'. Such structure reflects a gradual evolution within the courts over a period of many years. That evolution represents an effort carefully to blend pro-competitive objectives of the law of antitrust with administrative necessity. It represents a considerable advance, both from the days when the Commission had to present and/or refute every possible fact or theory, and from antitrust theories so abbreviated as to prevent proper analysis. The former prevented cases from ever reaching a conclusion and the latter called forth the criticism that the 'Government always wins'.[251]

The Court majority responded to Justice Breyer's dissent in a disarmingly affirmative way: 'Had the Court of Appeals engaged in a painstaking discussion in a league with Justice Breyer's . . . its reasoning might have sufficed to justify its conclusions.'[252] In this light, Justice Breyer's structured approach seems to reflect a truncated rule of reason that could satisfy not only the four dissenters but also the five Justices in the majority. It is quoted at some length because of its potential influence:

> I would break [the] question down into four classical, subsidiary antitrust questions: (1) What is the specific restraint at issue? (2) What are its likely anticompetitive effects? (3) Are there offsetting pro-competitive justifications? (4) Do the parties have sufficient market power to make a difference? . . .
>
> Commission found a set of restraints arising out of the way the Dental Association implemented this innocent-sounding ethical rule in practice, through advisory opinions, guidelines, enforcement policies, and review of membership applications . . .
>
> The FTC found that the price advertising restrictions amounted to a 'naked attempt to eliminate price competition' [and] that the service quality advertising restrictions 'deprive consumers of information they value and of healthy competition for their patronage' . . .
>
> In the usual Sherman Act § 1 case, the defendant bears the burden of establishing a pro-competitive justification . . . And the Court of Appeals was correct when it concluded that no such justification had been established here . . .
>
> I shall assume that the Commission must prove one additional circumstance, namely, that the Association's restraints would likely have made a real difference in the marketplace . . . The Commission . . . found that the Association did possess enough market power to make a difference.[253]

The preceding description of current antitrust jurisprudence and its unsettled condition have been extracted from cases of competitor collaboration under Sherman Act section 1. In other doctrinal precincts, the Supreme Court has not allowed the complexities to dissolve the categorical distinction between per se and rule of reason treatment. For example, in merger cases, whether judicial doctrine under Clayton Act section 7 or agency evaluation of pre-merger notification documents, the approach taken has consistently been a full-blown rule of reason, including market definition and market share determination. The same holds for vertical price fixing – per se illegality unless maximum price setting and then, full rule of reason. Monopolisa-tion and attempts to monopolise are always evaluated under a full rule of reason. Yet the Court has not addressed the doctrinal disparity between the complexities of evaluating competitor collaboration and the bifurcated juris-prudence still employed to evaluate other conduct that attracts antitrust scrutiny.

The only exception to this widespread bifurcation is tying doctrine, which often includes proof of market power and, of course, the burdensome pre-requisite of market definition. Market power is a material issue because courts accept it as indirect evidence that buyers are forced to take the tied products and proof of forcing pushes the tie into the category of (enhanced) per se illegality.[254] With proof of forcing, a tie is unlawful without further evidence of its purpose or effects. Without proof of forcing, tying arrange-ments are evaluated under a full rule of reason. The exceptional nature of tying jurisprudence carries heightened importance in this report because intellectual property owners have favoured tying arrangements as a strategy to exploit their exclusionary rights.

D. The regulatory agencies

Although several agencies have some antitrust authority in defined areas such as maritime shipping, telecommunications and banking, it is the Department of Justice, Antitrust Division, and the Federal Trade Commission that have primary authority to enforce the federal antitrust laws. They have overlap-ping statutory authority to enforce the Clayton Act, which most often comes into play with review of pre-merger notifications filed under section 7A. Given the large number of notifications processed annually, the agencies cooperate on a variety of projects including issuance of joint guidelines and they coordinate activities to assure that each merger is reviewed by only one agency. Over the years, each has developed special expertise in particular sectors and typically takes up the mergers and other investigations that fall into those areas of expertise. Both agencies have subpoena and discovery powers that aid in the investigative process, and both have the power to reach settlements that may later be enforced by the courts.[255] Although the agencies rarely share results of their investigations, the FTC did send its files to the Antitrust Division when the FTC Commissioners deadlocked on the decision whether to proceed against Microsoft in 1994.

In 1933, President Franklin D. Roosevelt created a separate Antitrust Division within the Department of Justice, although the agency had primary authority for enforcing the Sherman Act since its enactment in 1890. The Antitrust Division's responsibilities include investigating antitrust violations and initiating enforcement proceedings in federal courts under the Sherman and Clayton Acts, including criminal proceedings under the Sherman Act. The Division acts as a competition advocate in both federal regulatory hearings and private antitrust litigation. The Antitrust Division also invites requests for Business Review Letters 'with respect to proposed business conduct'.[256] Although a favourable response does not guarantee that no future action will be taken, the agency has rarely investigated a venture after review. Finally, the Division has entered into enforcement agreements with some European and other counterparts, and has cooperated with State Attorneys General in investigations and proceedings, most notably in litigation of the recent *Microsoft* case.

The Federal Trade Commission Act of 1914 created the FTC to act as an independent bureau to regulate competition. The FTC has power to enforce the statute and its 1914 sibling, the Clayton Act, with cease and desist orders.[257] The agency has authority to investigate and issue reports about 'the organisation, business, conduct, practices, and management [of persons] engaged in or whose business affects commerce'.[258] The FTC will also respond to requests for comment letters if the subject matter is novel.[259]

State Attorneys General also have a role to play. In addition to their long-recognised standing to sue under the federal statutes, Clayton Act section 4C since 1976 has authorised them to sue as *parens patriae* on behalf of citizens. As they did even before passage of the Sherman Act in 1890, the states can bring actions under their own statutes and common law. Multi-jurisdictional actions are brought through the National Association of Attorneys General (NAAG).[260] The NAAG enables multiple states to combine the investigative and enforcement efforts of their typically small antitrust enforcement departments.

The federal statutes do not pre-empt state law. Nor is there any legislative imperative in the United States for the kind of harmonisation that is fundamental to the institutional framework of the European Union.[261] In order to avoid duplicative investigations and actions, the federal enforcement agencies have adopted a protocol for collaboration with State Attorneys General in the evaluation of pre-merger notifications.[262]

E. Agency guidelines

The Department of Justice and Federal Trade Commission have issued a series of joint guidelines in recent years.[263] Two significant guidelines are summarised below: the *Horizontal Merger Guidelines* and the *Competitor*

Collaboration Guidelines. Discussion of the *Licensing Guidelines* is deferred until this chapter's final section.

Horizontal merger guidelines The *Merger Guidelines* set out a five-step analysis that the reviewing agency will follow to determine whether a merger presents the likelihood of substantially lessening competition or tending to create a monopoly in any line of commerce or in any section of the country, as prescribed by Clayton Act section 7.[264] First, relevant product and geographic markets are defined in order to determine market concentration. Second, actual and potential market participants are identified. Third, the agency applies the Herfindahl-Hirschman Index (HHI) to denote market concentration.[265] The Guidelines define three ranges of the HHI to reflect low, medium and high levels of market concentration. Proposed mergers in markets that fall into the low range of post-merger concentration pass without further investigation. Review of those that fall into the upper ranges proceeds through the remaining steps, unless the merger produces only an insignificant increase from the pre-merger to the post-merger HHI. Fourth, the agency assesses the actual and potential competitive effects of the merger. Fifth, the reviewing agency performs an analysis of barriers to market entry to determine the likelihood, timeliness and impact of potential entrants. The merging parties are given the opportunity to respond to the agency's determinations and to raise additional rebuttals, including claims of specific efficiency gains and proof that the acquired firm is a failing company whose loss would not affect competition.

In 1992, the *Merger Guidelines* were divided into two documents, one to address horizontal mergers and one to address non-horizontal mergers.[266] In 1997, the *Horizontal Merger Guidelines* were revised to expand consideration of a proposed merger's efficiency-enhancing effects. The agencies will consider only merger-specific efficiencies that could not be practically achieved absent the merger and only those that have been verified and that do not arise from reductions in output.[267]

Although the pre-merger review process does not shield the merging parties from private or state civil action,[268] it creates a safe harbour from future enforcement by the federal agencies. Because many mergers involve multiple states, the NAAG issued *Horizontal Merger Guidelines* in 1993[269] and a voluntary pre-merger notification system in 1994.[270]

Competitor collaboration guidelines In 2000, the Department of Justice and Federal Trade Commission issued guidelines for evaluating collaboration among competitors (Guidelines).[271] The Guidelines broadly define conduct as collaborative if two or more competitors combine assets to engage in economic activity such as research and development, production, distribution, sales or purchasing. Information sharing and trade association activities might also involve collaboration among competitors.[272] Collaboration is evaluated under the rule of reason, as prescribed by *California Dental Association* and other applicable case law. Competitors, actual or potential, who are considering collaboration, are invited to request business review or comment letters from one of the enforcement agencies. To be approved, the collaboration must be reasonably necessary to achieve the benefits. The parties need only show that there are no practical, less restrictive means of achieving their goals. In general terms, the reviewing agency applies a rule of reason to evaluate the business purpose, scope and potential competitive effects of the collaboration.[273] Simply coordinating price, output or general business decisions does not fall into the Guidelines' definition of collaboration and may be per se illegal.

The Guidelines recognise the potential benefits of collaboration, such as creating cheaper, more valuable goods that can be brought to the market more quickly and allocating resources more effectively.[274] To promote such efficiency-enhancing collaboration, the Guidelines describe two safety zones. The first shields competitor collaborations when the market shares of the collaboration and its participants collectively account for no more than 20 per cent of any market affected by the agreement.[275] The second safety zone applies to research and development collaborations in innovation markets. The agencies will not generally challenge the collaboration when, in addition to the collaboration under scrutiny, there are three or more independently controlled research efforts which possess the required specialised assets or characteristics and the incentive to engage in research and development that is a close substitute to the research and development being done.[276] Experience suggests that large-scale ventures are most likely to seek agency review and that give-and-take during the review process has led to changes in the shape of some joint ventures and, ultimately, approval that allowed the collaborations to proceed with some measure of confidence.

A note on extra-territorial reach

The antitrust statutes apply to personal or corporate transactions that affect interstate or foreign commerce.[277] Their reach in foreign commerce extends to foreign conduct that affects domestic trade or commerce and, even if not, if it affects a person in such trade or commerce. For example, in *Zenith Radio Corp.* v. *Hazeltine Research*,[278] a US exporter brought a claim against a Canadian patent pool whose conduct had the effect of reducing the plaintiff's export sales from the USA to Canada. Jurisdiction was grounded on the fact that the anti-trust injury occurred in the USA, even though the conduct was legal under Canadian law. In *Hartford Fire Insurance Co.* v. *California*,[279] the Supreme Court held that a United Kingdom company, operating in the United Kingdom, could be subject to US anti-trust law if the purpose and effect of the foreign activity is to hurt US competition. The Supreme Court's 'purpose and effects' test has been adopted in the Guidelines for International Operations, issued by the Department of Justice and Federal Trade Commission.[280] These Guidelines address comity and conflict of law issues as well as a series of factors considered in determining whether to enforce the US antitrust laws against foreign actors. Moreover, the Guidelines are used in conjunction with the licensing and merger guidelines when they are applied to foreign firms.[281]

III. The impact of antitrust on intellectual property rights

This chapter began with the familiar view that antitrust and intellectual property rights, at the federal level, share a common goal of encouraging innovation. The preceding sections have shown that trade secret and trade name protections at the state level complicate matters because their main goals are not to promote innovation. Moreover, each body of law, whether federal or state, has an internal competition component.

At the federal level, it has long been recognised that antitrust and intellectual property rights encourage innovation but by different means which can conflict. In simplest terms, they can conflict because copyright and patent protection grant monopolies and antitrust promotes competition. Moreover, their methodologies proceed from sharply different assumptions about market forces: to the extent that antitrust is concerned with price and output, its policy focuses on short-term effects of strategic conduct. Copyright and patent, in contrast, are intended to encourage innovation over the longer term. The methodological difference is significant because even the antitrust policy to encourage innovation is typically implemented by a statics analysis.

Tying doctrine illustrates the potential gap between policies to further static and dynamic efficiency. The traditional antitrust concern underlying tying is leverage – using power in one product market as a lever to gain power in a second market. The theory is dynamic because it recognises the strategy as working over time to achieve a future result. But neo-classical price theory advocates such as Robert Bork have persuaded many federal judges that traditional leverage theory makes no economic sense because a monopolist can already obtain the profit maximising price in the monopolised market. If the monopoly is extended into the second market as well, according to statics logic, then the double monopolist must still charge the same total price for the two products or lose those customers who refuse to pay more for the tied products than they pay for them separately. In short, statics analysis holds that the profit maximising price for the tied products still equals the sum of the prices for the separate products. With a higher price for the tied products, the demand functions for the two products determine the extent of lost customers and revenues. This view makes some sense within the static, short-run model of price theory.[282]

But if a dynamic, long-run view is taken, the logic changes drastically. Indeed, Louis Kaplow observed some 20 years ago that traditional leverage theory had long reflected concerns about what are now termed dynamic effects such as market foreclosure, reputation effects, strategic positioning, and market share, effects that are not visible in the static model of neo-classical price theory which has influenced so many antitrust decisions in the last 30 years.[283] Traditional leveraging doctrine is undoubtedly dynamic in its explanatory theory that the monopolist has adopted a strategy that foregoes current profits, if necessary, in the pursuit of future gains. The debate about traditional leveraging doctrine is significant because it creates uncertainty over the impact of antitrust on an intellectual property owner seeking to tie or bundle.

After antitrust scrutiny, whether static or dynamic, intellectual property policy calls for a second analytical step because antitrust and intellectual property policies focus on different time periods in the competitive life cycle of innovation. Antitrust policy is mainly concerned with the circumstances ex post, after the invention is in the stream of commerce, and asks whether the particular conduct, on balance, is anticompetitive: do the harms of foreclosing market access or otherwise restraining competition, including innovation by others, outweigh the benefits of the conduct being assessed, including com-mercialisation of the intellectual property?[284] After resolving this question, the court must turn to the intellectual property inquiry, which focuses on the earlier time period of invention: was the expectation of exploiting the intellec-tual property right in this way a necessary incentive, ex ante, to encourage the innovation and its exploitation? After answering that question, the court must determine whether there is a conflict between ex post and ex ante incentives and, if there is, resolve it with an extended rule of reason analysis.

Against this background, the remainder of this chapter examines the ways that antitrust courts and agencies have actually evaluated conduct to exploit intellectual property rights. Most of the decisions have involved copyright and patent protection. The small number regarding trade secret and trade name protection has raised somewhat different questions, particularly when the underlying policies were seen as conflicting with the copyright and patent regimes. The section first introduces the current approach to antitrust analy-sis of intellectual property rights by setting out the major court opinions and the federal enforcement agencies' intellectual property licensing guidelines. In that framework, the main body of the section takes a transactional approach and examines antitrust treatment of particular strategic conduct to exploit intellectual property rights: enforcing intellectual property rights, licensing practices, refusals to license and exclusive dealing, standard setting and other joint ventures, and mergers and asset acquisitions.

A. Framework: judicial and regulatory approaches

Before describing the judicial and regulatory approaches to evaluating aggressive conduct to exploit intellectual property rights, it is useful to review the underlying statutory framework. Under Sherman Act section 1, some agreements in restraint of trade are illegal per se. Price fixing cartels and market allocation agreements are treated as illegal per se. Most agreements, however, are judged under the rule of reason, which calls for evaluation of purpose, power and competitive effects. As we discussed in the antitrust section of this chapter, that evaluation can range from a 'quick look' to a full-blown rule of reason, depending upon the strength of preliminary evidence regarding the conduct's competitive effects. Under Sherman Act section 2, claims of monopolisation and attempts to monopolise are always judged under a full-blown rule of reason. Purpose is inferred from a limited set of conduct identified as predatory, including certain pricing below cost and unjustified refusals to deal. For monopolisation, the power element is typically satisfied by evidence of market share of 70 per cent or more. For attempts to monopolise evidence of 30 to 50 per cent market shares has been adequate; but attempt claims include an additional requirement that calls for proof of a dangerous probability that the attempt will succeed. The Clayton Act offences, which include price discrimination, mergers, tying and exclusive dealing, call for proof that the conduct under scrutiny may substantially lessen competition. Here, too, market power and anticompetitive effects are evaluated.

1. The courts: antitrust scrutiny of intellectual property rights

As a general matter, aggressive competition does not violate the antitrust laws. Nor do most strategic uses of intellectual property. There are a few clear exceptions – for example, naked price fixing is seen as inherently anticompetitive and thus illegal per se. But because the competitive effects of most conduct are indeterminate a priori, the analysis of most aggressive competition takes a fact-intensive approach to determine whether the resulting restraints are reasonable in the circumstances. The inquiry into competitive effects employs market definition to plot the boundaries of the effects analysis and market power determinations to help gauge their severity. For the most part, antitrust scrutiny of strategies to exploit intellectual property rights follows a rule of reason analysis to determine whether the strategy oversteps the proper bounds of the grant and, if so, whether the strategy unreasonably restrains competition by harming consumers.

With regard to patents and copyrights, courts have articulated an exception to the antitrust laws. In *Simpson* v. *Union Oil Co.*,[285] the Supreme Court declared that 'the patent laws . . . are in pari materia with the antitrust laws and modify them pro tanto'. The influential *SCM* decision (1981) held that 'where a patent has been lawfully acquired, subsequent conduct permissible under the patent laws cannot trigger any liability under the antitrust laws'. The often-cited *Data General Corp.* opinion (1994) states that 'an author's desire to exclude others from use of its copyrighted work is a presumptively valid business justification for any immediate harm to consumers'.[286] There is, however, some disagreement over the strength of the exception, a topic taken up in the report's section on refusals to license.

It is worth noting that the Federal Trade Commission has recently published a lengthy report entitled *To Promote Innovation: The Proper Balance of Competition and Patent Law and Policy (2003)*.[287] While the document exceeds 300 pages and offers many recommendations, one fundamental concern is the decline in standards for patentability. The FTC report has taken the position that innovation policy would be better served if the courts and the PTO would adopt measures to decrease the number of questionable patents. Specific recommendations include tightening the non-obviousness standard for patentability, easing the requirements for contesting a patent grant, increasing PTO funding, and enacting legislation to require publication of all patent applications 18 months after filing. Overall, the recommendations break little new ground but they do accumulate a large number of individual criticisms and recommendations that have been heard over a number of years. The report can be expected to have some impact on the future shape of patent law and agency practices.

There have been few court opinions evaluating the interaction between trade secret protection and the antitrust laws. Although trade secrecy conflicts with the goals of patent law and thus appears less worthy of antitrust deference, *Perfumer's Workshop* v. *Roure Bertrand du Pont*,[288] the leading case in the area, held that monopoly power acquired through trade secret protection does not violate the antitrust laws. The relationship between patent and trade secrecy did arise in the *United States* v. *Pilkington plc*[289] decision, which held that trade secrecy to extend the term of an expired patent does state a cause of action for antitrust liability. But as a general matter, trade secrets are seen as 'not inimical to free competition'.[290]

Trademark protection has been asserted as a justification for restraints on competition since the *Dr. Miles* decision,[291] which dismissed the argument as nothing more than a claim of business necessity. But the Supreme Court in *White Motor Co.* v. *United States*[292] recognised the value of inter-brand competition and, by implication, the product differentiation made possible by trademark and trade name protection. Since that decision, improving one's position in competition against other branded manufacturers has become broadly accepted as a justification for manufacturers' restraints on the distribution and sale of their branded products. Still, courts and the regulatory agencies have remained somewhat sensitive to the dangers of product differentiation, aided by trademark protection, in highly concentrated markets where brand marketing can strengthen incentives to avoid price competition.[293]

2. Guidelines for the licensing of intellectual property (1995)[294]

Jointly issued by the FTC and the Justice Department, the Guidelines stand on three principles. First, intellectual property is comparable to other forms of property – an approach at odds with the case law that creates an intellectual property exception. While all property shares the essential power to exclude others, critics of the Guidelines have pointed out that different forms of property reflect different capacities to exclude.[295] Hence, in evaluating the competitive effects of licensing arrangements, the Guidelines would likely take into account, for example, that copyright prohibits derivative works but patent does not; that intellectual property in general raises more serious free rider questions than tangible property; and that intellectual property rights in network industries raise special questions about dominance and barriers to entry. Second, the Guidelines recognise that intellectual property does not necessarily create market power.[296] A pioneering patent might create monopoly power in a product market. But many patented products compete with differentiated substitutes, some of which might also be patented. In this light, the Guidelines identify three types of markets that licensing agreements can affect: those for goods, technology, and innovation.[297] The Guidelines' third principle holds that combining complementary factors of production by licensing is generally pro-competitive. They observe that 'the intellectual property laws and the antitrust laws share the common purpose of promoting innovation and enhancing consumer welfare'.[298] Nonetheless, licences can raise competitive concerns, both vertical and horizontal. Licences can raise vertical concerns when they involve products or activities in a complementary relationship. Competitive harms include foreclosing access to important inputs or raising rivals' costs. Where the licensing parties are actual or potential competitors, there is a horizontal component that can raise concerns about licences 'if they are likely to affect adversely the prices, quantities, qualities, or varieties of goods and services either currently or potentially available'.[299]

Still, most licensing arrangements will likely fall into three 'safety zones' provided by the Guidelines. The regulatory agencies will not question a licensing agreement if a restraint is not facially anticompetitive (a price fixing agreement, for example) and if one of three additional criteria is met: (1) for goods markets, if the licensor and its licensees collectively account for no more than 20 per cent of each relevant market significantly affected by the restraint; (2) for technology markets, if there are at least four independently controlled substitute technologies; (3) for innovation markets, if there are at least four additional independently controlled entities capable of conducting research and development that would be a close substitute for the licensing parties' activities.[300] Unless a licence falls into one of the 'safety zones,' the Federal Trade Commission or the Department of Justice Antitrust Division will generally apply a rule of reason analysis to determine its legality.

B. Transactional analysis: antitrust scrutiny of intellectual property rights exploitation

The common thread in the analysis that follows is antitrust's function as sentry at the boundary between rights to exclude and duties to provide access for competitors. The report has already described the internal interplay between exclusionary rights and competition within the domain of intellectual property – for example, the requirement that a patent application include a description of the device sufficient to enable someone knowledgeable in the field, likely a competitor, to construct and use the device. Failure to meet the requirement means denial of the patent grant and loss of its power to exclude others from using the device during the 20-year term. The antitrust sentry imposes a second set of limits on the patent holder's exclusionary power, under threat of treble damages, injunctive relief and, in some very limited circumstances, compulsory licensing.[301]

1. Enforcement of intellectual property rights

Although enforcement of intellectual property rights generally does not lead to an antitrust violation, there are a few exceptions. The most notable risk of antitrust liability stems from attempts to enforce a patent procured by fraud on the PTO. First articulated by the Supreme Court, the *Walker Process* doctrine holds that this course of conduct together with proof of sufficient market power can give rise to a claim of monopolisation under Sherman Act section 2.[302] In the more recent *Nobelpharma AB* case,[303] the Federal Circuit applied the doctrine and held that fraudulent non-disclosures to the PTO, together with a suit to enforce a patent known to be invalid, established monopolising conduct.[304]

Such sham litigation can violate not only Sherman Act section 2 but also section 1 if the lawsuit involves collective action. In the *Buspirone Patent Litigation*, for example,[305] 30 states, numerous private plaintiffs and several public interest organisations filed antitrust claims against Bristol-Myers Squibb for improperly listing a patent in Buspirone prescription drugs with the Food and Drug Administration in order to obtain an unwarranted 30-month stay on FDA approval of generic substitutes. Bristol-Myers Squibb was also charged with conspiring with two generics manufacturers to restrain trade by wrongfully settling a patent infringement suit. Plaintiffs asserted that the settlement was a sham used to cover up an unlawful anticompetitive arrangement under which the generics makers agreed to stay out of the Buspirone market and help maintain a public perception that the disputed patent was valid in return for $72.5 million, even though both parties knew that the patent was not valid. The decision was the first to apply the *Walker Process* doctrine outside the context of a PTO filing. In a related case entitled *In re Bristol-Myers Squibb*,[306] the Federal Trade Commission filed a complaint under FTC Act section 5 that alleged 'unfair competition' in the same course of conduct, which improperly extended exclusive rights under not only Buspirone but also two additional patented drugs. The matter was concluded with a consent order denying Bristol-Myers the right to obtain automatic 30-month delays in FDA approval of generic versions of those and other related drugs.

In *Professional Real Estate Investors* v. *Columbia Pictures*,[307] Columbia Pictures brought an infringement suit against a group of hotel operators for renting copyrighted videodiscs to its hotel guests. The hotel responded with an antitrust counterclaim alleging that the suit was part of a conspiracy to monopolise and to restrain trade under the Sherman Act. Columbia asserted immunity from any counterclaim because filing suit is a constitutionally protected right to petition government. The hotel responded that the suit was a sham and thus not worthy of constitutional protection. The trial court denied Columbia's copyright infringement claim on summary judgment. The Supreme Court rejected the antitrust counterclaim, declaring that the infringement suit, though dismissed at the summary judgment stage, was not a 'sham' because it was not 'objectively baseless'. The result was Columbia's immunity from antitrust liability. The consequence, more broadly, is the heightened difficulty of winning an antitrust counterclaim based on wrongful enforcement of an intellectual property right. The increased difficulty, even if compelled by constitutional right, conflicts with both antitrust and copyright policies to the extent that it shields from liability wrongful conduct that threatens the public benefits identified with those policies.

Of course litigation is not the only means of enforcing intellectual property rights. More frequently, parties resolve conflicts among themselves, often by entering into licensing agreements. Although courts typically enforce licences, they have looked with some scepticism on agreements that extend patent terms through licensing of trademark or trade secret rights.[308] We defer discussion of licensing agreements for the moment. But it is useful to pause for a quick look at the antitrust consequences of another extra-judicial effort to enforce licences.

When licensing fails, some intellectual property owners have collaborated to enforce their rights in a confrontational manner. Such extra-judicial efforts have largely run afoul of the antitrust laws. The classic case is *Fashion Originators Guild of America* v. *FTC*,[309] in which an organisation of fashion clothing designers and manufacturers organised an elaborate system to monitor their retailers in order to assure that they did not deal with 'style pirates'. FOGA insisted on an exclusive dealing agreement and blacklisted any retailers discovered purchasing dresses made from stolen designs. The Guild argued that it was protecting members' property rights under state unfair competition laws. The FTC termed the conduct a group boycott, ignoring the claim that the system was 'necessary to protect the manufacturer, labourer, retailer and consumer against devastating evils growing from the pirating of original designs'. The Supreme Court affirmed the FTC's holding of per se illegality and declared that 'even if copying were an acknowledged tort under the law of every state, that situation would not justify petitioners in combining together to regulate and restrain interstate commerce'. The decision carries the implication that the anticompetitive effects ex post of boycotts always outweigh the intellectual property rights incentives ex ante because such conduct is a wrongful extension of those rights, deserving of no protection even when intended to stop property misappropriation.

2. Industry standardisation

Industrial history is filled with examples of rivals agreeing on product standardisation for reasons of utility, safety, or cartelisation. Often collaborative standardisation programmes were adopted under the aegis of a trade or professional association. Less frequently, industry standards resulted without agreement from the dominance of a particular product complement and its sponsors. Standardisation will almost always have some advantage for consumers and other users in eliminating repetitive search costs or simplifying compliance with standard protocols. In the landmark *Broadcast Music* decision for example,[310] the Supreme Court determined that ASCAP and BMI's blanket licensing of copyrighted works, despite its virtual elimination of price competition, was a reasonable restraint and thus legal because the two organisations created enormous efficiencies in sales, monitoring and collection for use of thousands of copyrighted works. The Court majority was not persuaded by Justice Stevens' dissenting opinion, which argued that the collaboration was an impermissible extension of copyright protection. Stevens observed that the market efficiencies could have been accomplished by the less restrictive means of a clearinghouse without pricing authority. But the Court majority viewed the blanket licence as a new product that, in essence, created a new market that left the old market for individual negotiation in place because the licence was non-exclusive. The decision can be read as consistent with the determinations that ex post competition were not restrained and that licensing and enforcement practices were improved to comport more closely with optimal ex ante incentives for composers.

In some instances, as in standardisation of railroad track or football field dimensions, or of personal computer component interfaces or Internet message protocols, industry-wide compliance has been crucial to growth and progress. Nonetheless, collaborative efforts to standardise products can chill the competition to provide variety. Moreover, by making the relevant

product more homogeneous, standardisation agreements can facilitate cartelisation or interdependence that produces higher prices. Finally, standardisation agreements are sometimes accompanied by mechanisms to suppress
products or exclude rivals that do not meet the standards; and while such
exclusion may sometimes improve safety or protocol compliance, exclusion
does eliminate competition.[311] The dangers of exclusion are intensified in
network industries, which set into motion the dynamic of demand side
economies that tend to reward firms with larger customer bases. Customer
demand intensifies as the base increases in size and moves closer to a tipping
point, even if the switching costs are small.[312] Once the market has tipped,
new products or services, even if superior or cheaper, that are not compatible
with the dominant system or network standards face sharply higher barriers
to buyer acceptance.

Some clear examples of standardisation effects come out of the information technology sectors. Internet protocols were developed as open and
minimal standards to allow for efficient interfacing and diversity of usage
clustered at Internet portals.[313] The result is a network of networks that has
spawned enormous innovation. The Unix operating system eventually
became an open standard and spawned Linux some years later. Linux is a
successful contender in the operating system markets for network servers and
other spoke computers that are more powerful and larger than personal
computers. In recent years, large corporate sponsors have formed joint
ventures to market PCs with Linux operating systems. While their success
is still in doubt, they remain viable though marginal competitors.

In sharp contrast, Windows software and its hardware complement, Intel
microprocessor chips, have always been proprietary technologies. Their
product qualities, intellectual property rights, positive feedback between
system components, network effects, and ingenious marketing strategies
have combined and interacted to create and reinforce market dominance.
As a result, they have both become de facto industry standards. Government
antitrust suits against Microsoft and Intel have attacked some of the strategies
used to maintain their dominance and, in Microsoft's case, strategies to
leverage dominance into new markets. The antitrust implications of those
strategies are examined later in this chapter. But it is worth mentioning now
that Microsoft has been largely successful in using integration strategies to
leverage its Windows standard in ways that have passed antitrust scrutiny.
Microsoft has continually produced new versions of Windows, as well as its
industry-standard Microsoft Office suite of applications software, that customers have adopted in part because of improvements and in part because
Microsoft stopped supporting earlier versions. As these new versions have
become the standards, changes and additions have also become standard. In
the United States, few questions were raised about adding functions such as
file compression and multimedia player to Windows or a photo editor to the

Office suite. Nor were challenges posed when Microsoft introduced Windows 95, which integrated the DOS operating system with the original Windows graphical user interface, thereby eliminating the need for independent DOS software.[314] Moreover, despite the government antitrust suit, discussed at several junctures below, Microsoft's integration strategy has also made Internet Explorer the industry standard web browser in a market that had been dominated by Netscape Navigator.

When an industry standard results from a single firm's success and industry dominance rather than a standard-setting organisation of industry members, antitrust questions have also been posed about that firm's duty to disclose information to market participants. In the landmark *Berkey Photo* decision (1979),[315] the Second Circuit Court of Appeals rejected the claim of a competitor in a derivative market for complementary products that Eastman Kodak, a monopoly in the primary market, owed Berkey a duty to pre-disclose new products in order to permit Berkey to make its products compatible. The Court concluded that Eastman Kodak had a right to its competitive advantages of size and vertical integration and, moreover, that a disclosure rule would be unworkable.

More recently, the Federal Trade Commission challenged Intel's refusal to provide technical information necessary for customers to produce complementary products compatible with Intel's microprocessor chips, which dominated the market and were thus the de facto industry standard. Intel stopped sharing the information with customers seeking to protect their intellectual property rights against Intel.[316] The case was settled with a consent decree in which Intel agreed not to withhold information in such circumstances. Nonetheless, the antitrust laws do not prohibit an intellectual property owner, even a dominant firm, from withholding information for a legitimate business reason.

The issue of information disclosure was revisited in the government's monopolisation case against Microsoft. The district court found, for example, that 'Microsoft tried to convince IBM to move its business away from products that themselves competed directly with Windows and Office. Microsoft leveraged the fact that [IBM] needed to licence Windows at a competitive price and on a timely basis, and the fact that the company needed Microsoft's support in many more subtle ways. When IBM refused to abate the promotion of those of its own products that competed with Windows and Office, Microsoft punished the IBM PC Company with higher prices, a late licence for Windows 95, and the withholding of technical and marketing support.'[317] In particular, Microsoft refused to share information that IBM needed to conform its products with the announced Windows 95 operating system because IBM would not acquiesce to Microsoft's demands, including an insistence that IBM stop promoting its competing OS/2 Warp operating system. As a result of IBM's refusal to accede, it was scheduled to pay almost $50 million more in annual royalty payments than its favoured rivals. Moreover, without pre-release access to the technical information needed for compatibility with Microsoft's industry standard operating system, IBM was unable to conform to its products in time to compete with its rivals until the crucial initial selling season had passed. In consequence, IBM lost several hundred millions of dollars in sales and Microsoft sacrificed the associated royalties by withholding pre-release information. The trial court determined that those coercive refusals to share information were part of Microsoft's monopolising course of conduct to maintain barriers to entering the operating market for Intel-compatible PCs.[318]

Antitrust issues can also arise when industry standardisation results from collaborative efforts. The *Addamax*[319] case involved antitrust claims against a joint venture to standardise computer software that evolved from the Unix operating system. AT&T developed the Unix operating system as a proprietary product for mainframe computers but faced antitrust challenges to entering computer software markets in 1969. AT&T decided the next best strategy was to give it away to universities. In this way, Unix began as an open standard and, over a period of 30 years, fragmented into a variety of not entirely compatible operating systems. Linus Torvald, for example, developed the Linux operating system out of Unix.

A group of large computer manufacturers formed a non-profit foundation, the Open Software Foundation (OSF), to establish an operating system to compete against an AT&T–Sun Microsystems product that had emerged as the industry standard for Unix operating systems.[320] OSF put out a 'request for technology' for bids on security software to integrate into its version of Unix. Two bids were submitted. Some time later, the losing bidder, Addamax, decided to phase out its security software entirely. Addamax then sued OSF and two sponsors, Hewlett-Packard and Digital Equipment, claiming that they conspired to force down the price of security software, driving Addamax out of the business. The Court stated that

> Addamax alleges that [OSF] forced competitors to offer their products at below-market prices and under disadvantageous conditions. The loser sees his technology left out of a new system that automatically becomes an industry standard. A firm that fails in an OSF bid loses the chance to sell its product, not only to OSF, but to all OSF members. In this way, Addamax claims, OSF functions as a . . . buyers' cartel. Addamax maintains that OSF extracts major concessions from its suppliers in terms of both price and conditions-of-sale. Addamax claims that OSF's strategies secure software at a fraction of its market price, and in some instances at prices below those necessary to recoup research and development costs.

Addamax also alleged that by announcing an OSF standard, the defendants 'sought to paralyse the industry and deter users from committing to other systems'. The Court declined to apply per se scrutiny to the joint venture and, moreover, denied the plaintiff's motion for summary judgment. The venture was too complex, the Court concluded, and the competitive effects too speculative in light of competition from Microsoft to support such peremptory treatment.[321]

For the most part, collaborative standard setting has been viewed as a reasonable restraint of trade. The greatest danger of antitrust liability lies in conduct that is seen as an abuse of the standard setting process. In *Allied Tube & Conduit Corp.* v. *Indian Head Inc.*,[322] the leading case in the area, an excluded competitor brought an antitrust claim against a non-profit standard setting organisation that formulated building and safety codes which were adopted nationwide. A standard setting committee would not endorse the plaintiff's new plastic insulation technology for electric conduit after a representative of metal conduit manufacturers (metal being the industry standard) convinced them to vote down the new product. The fact that one member convinced the committee to exclude the product of potential competitor did not violate antitrust law; rather it was the manner in which the petitioning member achieved that goal. In order to exclude the new technology, the member recruited commercially interested parties to become members of the organisation and paid their fees and expenses to ensure attendance and a favourable vote at the standard setting meeting. It was this behaviour that triggered antitrust scrutiny. However, courts will uphold industry standard setting efforts when the purpose is to adopt reasonable measures to respond to existing problems.

Two recent Federal Trade Commission cases have involved abuse of standard setting initiatives. In *FTC* v. *Dell Computer*,[323] the patent holder failed to notify the standard setting association that it held patents for the VL-bus, an important computer component. The association did compel disclosure of participants' intellectual property rights – not an unusual requirement in standard setting organisations. Only after the association chose that technology to be the industry standard did Dell disclose its patents. The FTC filed an enforcement action which was settled, with Dell agreeing not to enforce its undisclosed patents, but without much guidance either to standard setting organisations or participants about the scope of their disclosure duties.

In the pending *In re Rambus Inc.* case,[324] the FTC issued a complaint in a standard setting situation much like the one in *Dell*. The Commission alleged that Rambus did not disclose relevant patents and patent applications to an industry organisation considering standards for DRAM, a common type of computer memory. Despite organisation rules requiring disclosure, the Commission claimed, Rambus intentionally concealed patents and pending applications until the standards had been approved. Shortly thereafter, Rambus entered into licensing agreements with seven major manufacturers, instituted infringement suits against others, and stood to gain royalties in excess of $1 billion per year. In one of the suits, *Infineon Techs.* (2003), the

trial court summarily dismissed Rambus's infringement claim.[325] The Court
also upheld in part a jury verdict on the accused infringer's counterclaim that
Rambus engaged in fraud for failure to disclose the patents and pending
applications. The Federal Circuit reversed the fraud ruling because it found
that the disclosure policy was vague and thus 'Rambus's mistaken belief ...
does not substitute' for the evidence required to prove that it had a duty to
disclose.[326] Given the FTC's pending action against Rambus, the law regarding disclosure in standard setting organisations is currently unsettled. The
approach most consistent with both patent and antitrust policies would call
for full disclosure and penalties for refusals to disclose because the patent
holder is the least-cost provider of the information. Disclosure of information is consistent with patent policy, which is premised on the exchange
of publication for exclusionary rights. It is consistent with antitrust policy,
which seeks to promote competitive markets and which has long recognised
informational asymmetry as a significant market failure.

3. Duty to license

As a general matter, the US antitrust laws do not impose on individual firms,
even monopolies, a duty to do business with anyone or otherwise to make
their facilities available. Although there have been a small number of decisions over the years – sometimes termed essential facility cases – imposing
duties to deal or decreeing compulsory licences, none has resulted solely from
ownership of an intellectual property right. They have all required some
additional exclusionary conduct. Consistent with this approach, it should
be recalled, both the Patent Act and traditional common law contract doctrine as a general matter authorise owners to refuse to license or use their
creations. The report has already mentioned a disagreement among federal
courts about the limits of the refusal right. In this section, we take a closer
look at the doctrinal disagreement and its implications.

On a few occasions, antitrust courts have imposed on dominant firms a
duty to deal with customers, suppliers or competitors. The earliest instance
was the Supreme Court's decision in *Terminal Railroad Association* (1912),
which required a group of railroads which jointly owned the only railroad
switching yard across the Mississippi River at the important City of St. Louis
hub to give access to non-members. The Court determined that, 'in view of
the inherent physical conditions', no practical alternative was available. In
Lorain Journal (1951), the Court characterised the only newspaper in a region
of northern Ohio an 'indispensable medium' of advertising. Despite regulatory oversight by the Federal Power Commission, the Court in *Otter Tail
Power Co. v. United States*[327] required an electrical utility to make available its
transmission lines to wheel electrical power from other utilities to its former
customers. Through the course of such decisions was born the 'essential
facilities' doctrine and the accompanying remedy of compulsory access. It

should be noted that the doctrine has long been used by federal courts and antitrust scholars but has never been explicitly adopted by the Supreme Court.[328]

More recently, the Eighth Circuit Court of Appeals compelled AT&T to allow cable television operators to string their cables on its poles because the operators were 'actual competitors'.[329] The courts have been consistent in their view that the doctrine applies only to competitors. In the recent *Intergraph* case,[330] the plaintiff sought injunctive relief, arguing that Intel had an affirmative obligation to continue supplying it with chips, technology and interoperability information because Intel products were the de facto industry standard and thus 'essential facilities' needed to do business in the industry. Intel dominated the market with well over an 80 per cent share of microprocessor chip sales. In consequence, Intergraph asserted, the refusal to deal was monopolising conduct in violation of Sherman Act section 2. The district court determined that Intergraph's claim was likely to succeed at trial and so granted a preliminary injunction against Intel. But the Federal Circuit vacated the order on the grounds that the essential facilities doctrine applies only when the facility owner and the user compete in a downstream market that requires access to the facility.[331] Intel and Intergraph were not competitors. Intergraph was one of several customers who were asserting intellectual property rights against Intel, who refused to deal with Intergraph and other customers until they agreed to withdraw their claims.

The *Intergraph* court's approach was consistent with that taken in other circuit courts. In *MCI Communications* v. *American Telephone & Telegraph Co.*, for example,[332] the Court enumerated the elements of liability under the 'essential facilities' theory as '(1) control of the essential facility by a monopolist; (2) a competitor's inability practically or reasonably to duplicate the essential facility; (3) the denial of the use of the facility to a competitor; and (4) the feasibility of providing the facility'. The Federal Circuit in *Intergraph* concluded: 'The courts have well understood that the essential facility theory is not an invitation to demand access to the property or privileges of another, on pain of antitrust penalties and compulsion; thus the courts have required anticompetitive action by a monopolist that is intended to "eliminate competition in the downstream market".'[333]

Imposing an obligation to deal in a case involving intellectual property rights raises special concerns because an equitable remedy would amount to a compulsory licence outside the narrow circumstances explicitly defined by Congress.[334] In that light, some courts have announced patent and copyright exceptions to any obligation to deal imposed by laws of general applicability such as antitrust. Several decisions, following the logic of the influential *Data General Corp.* decision,[335] have given the patent exception more weight than its copyright counterpart. The *Data General Corp.* court observed that Congress amended the Patent Act, but not the Copyright Act, to provide under section 271(d) that 'no patent owner otherwise entitled to relief for infringement ... shall be denied relief or deemed guilty of misuse or illegal extension of the patent right by reason of [a] refusal to license or use any rights'. In the government's most recent *Microsoft* suit, the Circuit Court of Appeals wrote that 'copyright law does not give Microsoft blanket authority to license (or refuse to license) its intellectual property as it sees fit'.[336] But the difference in treatment of copyright and patent holders should not be overestimated because both must withstand antitrust scrutiny of refusals to deal under the Sherman Act's rule of reason.[337] The Supreme Court in *Kodak* (1992) emphasised that power gained through some natural or legal advantage such as a patent, copyright, or business acumen can give rise to liability if 'a seller exploits his dominant position in one market to expand his empire into the next'.[338]

Although Patent Act section 271(d) applies explicitly only to patent misuse, its implications have sparked a disagreement over its breadth between the Federal Circuit, which has statutory authority over all patent cases, and the Ninth Circuit, which has territorial jurisdiction over California and thus hears a great number of suits involving intellectual property rights in high tech industries. The Ninth Circuit in *Kodak* (1997) has construed section 271(d) narrowly, as creating only a presumption in favour of the patent owner: 'the desire to exclude others from its [protected] work is a presumptively valid business justification for any immediate harm to consumers'.[339] The presumption, however, was overcome in that case and the plaintiff won its monopolisation claim that Kodak's practice of refusing to sell patented parts to independent service providers was an unreasonable restraint of trade that violated Sherman Act section 2. The Federal Circuit, however, has interpreted congressional policy expansively to mean that a refusal to license a patent, or copyright, can never violate the antitrust laws.[340] This approach takes its direction from an expansive reading of *Simpson Oil* (1964), which declared that 'the patent laws ... are in pari materia with the anti-trust laws and modify them pro tanto'.[341] Still, there are limits, even in the Federal Circuit. In *C. R. Bard* v. *M3 Systems*,[342] the Court held that a patent does not shield from antitrust scrutiny changes in a medical needle system designed to create incompatibility with a competitor's product.[343] Such conduct has been termed predatory innovation – that is, product change whose primary purpose is to raise rivals' costs and lock-in customers, and whose modifications do not benefit consumers. Neither patent nor antitrust policy supports such conduct.

A very recent Supreme Court decision has raised doubts about the viability of cases that adopt an 'essential facility' rationale or that otherwise require a dominant firm to deal with competitors. In *Verizon Communications Inc.* v. *Trinko*,[344] plaintiff class sued the incumbent local telephone monopoly for refusing to share its local exchange facilities with other providers, as required under the Telecommunications Act of 1996. The complaint asserted that plaintiffs were harmed because Verizon provided lower quality lines to their provider. Writing for the Court, Justice Antonin Scalia found no antitrust violation. Viewed most narrowly, the decision stands on the rationale that the antitrust laws will not supplement statutory duties to deal, as glossed by regulatory agency oversight, even though plaintiffs made a strong argument that Congress did intend antitrust laws to apply. In this light, antitrust would not impose greater obligations than those imposed under the supervisory authority of a regulatory agency, here the Federal Communications Commission. Viewed more broadly, the decision is a repudiation of the essential facilities doctrine and similar rationales. Certainly there is language in the opinion to support this broader view, including dismissive references to *Aspen Skiing*[345] and other cases that have been characterised as essential facility cases. But questionable readings of earlier cases and very broad statements in Justice Scalia's opinion suggest that the reach of *Trinko* is an open question.

4. Licensing of intellectual property

The *Kodak* (1992) approach is reflected in the federal agencies' Licensing Guidelines, which treat intellectual property no differently from other kinds of property and which, for the most part, evaluate both licences and refusals to license under a rule of reason. Economic theory views licensing in a positive light because the practice permits the intellectual property owner to transfer the right to the most productive users, thereby employing market transactions to help determine the most efficient means of commercialising the invention. Moreover, licensing permits the owner to increase its reward from the invention in a manner consistent with reasonable expectations ex ante. As a general matter, antitrust doctrine treats licences no differently from other agreements intended to create efficiencies. Further, the agencies' Licensing Guidelines observe that licensing can 'benefit consumers through the reduction of costs and the introduction of new products'. They can protect 'the licensee against free-riding on the licensee's investments'.[346]

Although the Guidelines favour licensing agreements, they do recognise that 'antitrust concerns may arise when a licensing arrangement harms competition among entities that would have been actual or likely potential competitors . . . in the absence of a licence'. A licence may 'facilitate . . . market division or price fixing' or it may foreclose access to an adjacent market.[347] *Palmer* v. *BRG*[348] is a good example of using a licence as a subterfuge to divide markets. BRG and HBJ were the two main competitors in providing review courses for the bar examination in Georgia. They entered into an agreement that gave BRG an exclusive licence to market HBJ's copyrighted materials in Georgia and to use its trade name 'Bar/Bri'. The parties agreed that HBJ would not compete with BRG in Georgia and that BRG would not compete with HBJ outside of Georgia. The licence included a provision in which BRG would pay HBJ $100 per student and BRG raised its price from $150 to $400. The trial court granted summary judgment for defendants and the Court of Appeals affirmed. The Supreme Court in a short *per curiam* opinion reversed, concluding that the revenue-sharing formula coupled with the price increase that took place immediately after the parties agreed to cease competing with each other indicated that the licensing agreement was 'formed for the purpose and with the effect of raising' the price of the bar review course. The Court held that the agreement to divide markets was 'unlawful on its face'. The restraint was not evaluated under a rule of reason even though the main purpose of the licence was arguably to acquire materials on account of BRG's loss of a royalty-free licence from another source. The decision reflects the Supreme Court's strong antipathy toward price fixing and market allocation, even when such an agreement between competitors appears in an otherwise legitimate licence for intellectual property.

A number of lower court cases have taken the same approach. In *A&E Plastik Pak Co.*, for example,[349] the Ninth Circuit Court of Appeals observed: 'The critical question in an antitrust context is whether the restriction may fairly be said to be ancillary to a commercially supportable licensing arrangement, or whether the licensing scheme is a sham set up for the purpose of controlling competition while avoiding the consequences of the antitrust laws.' The Court determined that plaintiff should be given the opportunity to prove that a trade secret licence was a 'subterfuge enabling the participants to divide markets and fix prices'.[350] In a series of cases following the Second World War, courts struck down complicated worldwide networks of cross-licensing agreements as subterfuges enabling the participants to divide markets and fix prices while avoiding antitrust laws. The courts found that true trade secrets were either absent or insufficiently substantial to support restraints of such magnitude. The parties' intent, principally to restrain competition, was regarded as a critical factor.[351] Certainly, licensing of true trade secrets would be judged under a rule of reason and found reasonable in most circumstances.

Tying provisions in licensing agreements   Tying claims can fall under three statutory sections. If litigated under Sherman Act section 2 as conduct evidencing a purpose to monopolise, for example, the courts have uniformly taken a rule of reason approach.[352] When brought under Sherman Act section 1 or Clayton Act section 3, the doctrine is more complex because tying provisions can sometimes be per se illegal. In the leading case, *Jefferson Parish Hospital*,[353] the Court declared that tying falls into the category of per se illegality upon proof of three elements: first, that there is a tie-in of two separate products (or services); second, that 'the seller has some special ability ... to force a purchaser' to accept the tie-in; third, that the arrangement forecloses a substantial volume of commerce. This enhanced or modified per se approach requires plaintiff to prove more than simply the fact that the restraint occurred but less than a full rule of reason burden of purpose, power and anticompetitive effects.

In the recent *Microsoft* (2001) monopolisation case, however, the D.C. Circuit Court of Appeals carved an exception out of the per se treatment of forced tying. The integration of the Windows 98 'platform' and Internet Explorer was not accomplished by licensing agreement. Rather, the two software programs were 'technologically tied' by interlocked and shared software modules. In consequence, users were not able to separate them. The Court determined that such integration of platform and applications software created technical issues whose evaluation should begin with great deference to the producer. In consequence, such integration should always be evaluated under a full rule of reason. Moreover, the Court held that Microsoft's integration was prima facie lawful as long as the products could be disintegrated.[354]

Returning to the Supreme Court's *Jefferson Parish* opinion, the majority prescribed an approach that sometimes called for per se treatment and other times a rule of reason. This bifurcated approach seeks to distinguish pro-competitive bundling from anticompetitive tying. Bundling can be pro-competitive in a number of ways. For example, a manufacturer can gather and assemble RAM, processor chips, motherboards, storage devices and other components to produce a personal computer more efficiently than individual consumers. But combining products can also restrain competition and harm consumers. For example, a tie might promote oligopolistic behaviour when all firms in parallel fashion adopt the same tie. The *Kodak* (1992) case involved circumstances that suggested this harm: with Kodak, Xerox and IBM together controlling over 90 per cent of the market in photocopiers and microcopiers, each tied the sale of patented replacement parts to repair of its leased machines.[355]

The Court articulated a three-step approach to assess tying. It begins by asking whether there was evidence that consumer purchasing behaviour reflected separate demand for the two products in the absence of the tying arrangement. If not, then the product bundle was deemed pro-competitive. While the test makes sense, its application requires a prior time period of separate demand to characterise the bundling. For Kodak, there was such a period and the Court found separate markets. Indeed, Kodak continued to sell replacement parts to large customers with their own repair staffs. But Xerox and IBM always bundled replacement parts and repair. Should Kodak be penalised on that account, without regard to the practices of its competitors? Or should Kodak's change to bundling be viewed as an oligopolist joining the parallel conduct of its rivals? The *Kodak* opinion does not give a clear answer to these questions and can be read as consistent with either one.

This separate products element of the *Jefferson Parish* test presented a particularly difficult question in each of the government's two *Microsoft* cases. In the first, the Department of Justice sought to block the bundling of Windows 95 operating system software with the Internet Explorer web browser. In interpreting the consent decree at issue, the D.C. Circuit Court of Appeals interpreted the language of the decree to determine whether the bundling fell into a provision permitting Microsoft to integrate software or whether the bundling was a prohibited tie-in. Relying to some extent on antitrust precedent, the Court did not adopt the consumer demand test of *Jefferson Parish* but took a new approach to determine that the integration was permitted because Microsoft could make a 'plausible claim' that the integration 'brings some advantage' to consumers.[356] Dissenting Judge Patricia Wald alluded to the ignored mandate of *Jefferson Parish*, writing that 'the courts must consider whether the resulting product confers benefits on the consumer that justify a product's bridging of two formerly separate markets'.[357] In the second *Microsoft* case,[358] the federal and state government plaintiffs prevailed in their complaint that Microsoft maintained its Windows 98 monopoly in the operating system market for Intel-compatible PCs by engaging in a course of predatory conduct that artificially maintained barriers to market entry. One related claim involved the enhanced integration of Internet Explorer and the operating system. Here, the D.C. Circuit explicitly rejected the *Jefferson Parish* test as the exclusive inquiry for determining whether there was separate demand for the two products because the Court believed that this backward-looking test would not give 'a fair shake' to the first producer who integrated two separate products. The Court was persuaded by Microsoft's argument that an exclusively static test would 'chill innovation to the detriment of consumers'.

If the court finds a tie-in, it proceeds to the second element of the *Jefferson Parish* test, to determine whether the arrangement will be analysed under the rule of reason or the per se approach. Per se treatment applies when the plaintiff shows that the seller has the power to force the buyer to take the tied product. Direct evidence of actual forcing would be enough. In the alternative, indirect proof could proceed by inference from evidence of market power. Early cases seemed to require significant market share approaching monopolisation. *Jefferson Parish* called for proof of 'substantial' market power and refused to make an inference from the hospital's 30 per cent market share. Moreover, the Court discounted evidence of market imperfections that facilitated the hospital's exercise of power, including evidence of poor consumer information that hurt their ability to evaluate the quality of care. *Jefferson Parish* also carried forward the doctrine that patent or copyright grants evidenced substantial market power and, thus, provided sufficient evidence of forcing to treat the tying as illegal per se.

Subsequent developments have called two aspects of the *Jefferson Parish* forcing inquiry into question. First, the Supreme Court's *Kodak* decision

(1992) attributed great weight to market imperfections, particularly informational asymmetry, in the process of defining a separate primary market for photocopiers and secondary markets for replacement parts and for repair. The upshot was a determination that Eastman Kodak could have monopoly power in aftermarkets without substantial power in the primary market. In a section 1 case, per se treatment of the tying arrangement is likely to follow this approach to market definition. In contrast, the Licensing Guidelines, tilting away from per se treatment, embody a second shift from *Jefferson Parish*. They have rejected the view that intellectual property rights produce monopoly power and, in consequence, they evaluate licences that are not facially anticompetitive under a rule of reason. Under the Guidelines, agency evaluation of tying arrangements is more lenient than judicial treatment that accords with *Jefferson Parish*. It remains to be seen, of course, whether the Supreme Court will adopt the currently prevailing approach reflected in the Guidelines, an approach taken in *Jefferson Parish* by Justice O'Connor's concurring opinion.[359]

With evidence of forcing, the plaintiff must satisfy only the minor third element that the arrangement affects a 'not insubstantial' amount of commerce in the tied-product market – for example, the punch cards in *IBM* or Internet Explorer in *Microsoft*. This element is itself insubstantial and has been interpreted as a mechanism to filter out isolated and inconsequential transactions. Without evidence of forcing, however, the plaintiff faces a full rule of reason. In short, the plaintiff must then prove anticompetitive effects in the tying product market – for example, the card machines in *IBM* or operating systems for Intel-compatible PCs in *Microsoft*.

In the absence of intellectual property rights, a firm with substantial market power is not permitted to leverage that power into an adjacent market by refusing to sell one product to buyers unless they also take the forced product. Such tying arrangements are illegal per se.[360] The enforcement mechanism for forced tie-ins is a refusal to deal. But in intellectual property licences, tie-ins, enforced by refusals to deal on other terms, are viewed quite differently. As a general matter, courts have accorded great latitude to bundling of patent or copyright licences. This chapter has already described the *Broadcast Music* decision's approval (1979), in a duopolistic market, of nonexclusive blanket licences to perform copyrighted music. The Supreme Court had long before affirmed the validity of block licences for hundreds of patents and patent applications in *Hazeltine Research* (1950).[361] But there were limits to the courts' permissive attitude toward intellectual property licences. Notably, when patent holders sought to tie patented machines with staple products – for example, salt Lixator machines with salt – the Court held them illegal per se as unlawful attempts to extend a patent monopoly into a second market. They were held illegal per se even when the licensing agreement included a provision stating that a rival's lower price would be matched.[362]

Moreover, even when the tied product was a non-staple, when it could be used only with the tying product, early court decisions prohibited the arrangement. Indeed, a modern decision in the Eleventh Circuit Court of Appeals held that block-booking of television shows was per se illegal as a tie-in. The Court in *MCA Television Ltd.* relied on old Supreme Court precedent that treated block-booking of movie films as per se illegal. But no reference was made to the more recent *Hazeltine* or *Broadcast Music* decisions. Both cases, however, can be distinguished from *MCA*. *Hazeltine* involved patents rather than patented products and, thus, justifies greater leniency because the licensing was an early step in dissemination and commercialisation of the patented ideas. *Broadcast Music* involved blanket licences that were non-exclusive – that is, they allowed individual copyright holders to negotiate their own deals with prospective licensees. In contrast, *MCA* involved an exclusive licence for films. Moreover, the films were products well beyond the invention stage. Finally, the licence provided for liquidated damages which sometimes resulted in double royalties. Copyright incentives ex ante do not anticipate double royalties and no claims were made that the exclusive licence under scrutiny produced transactional or other efficiencies that would legitimately improve ex post incentives to innovate.

In recent years courts have shown no hesitation in prohibiting licensing provisions for tying a patented device to a staple item – that is, to an item that can be used with products other than the patented device. Examples include standard printer paper to be used with all computer printers or standard CDs with all CD players. The *Tricom Inc.* case[363] illustrates the point. In it, the Court found an actionable tying agreement in a provision conditioning the lease of software for computer-assisted design (CAD) to the purchase of time sharing on the software provider's mainframe computer. The tied product was a staple product: The mainframe computer had uses other than running the CAD software. Moreover, the buyer was a competitor in the market for mainframe time-sharing. Explicitly separating the refusal to license from the tie, the Court stated that the intellectual property holder could refuse to license the copyrighted software but could not use it as leverage to sell time sharing on its computer system. The decision is consistent with the view that ex ante copyright incentives for authors do not include anticipated revenues from unrelated products. It also serves competition policy by freeing a competitor from a restraint that has no offsetting public benefits ex post.

At the same time, antitrust courts have been more solicitous of licensing provisions tying a patented product to a non-staple. For example, one well-known justification for tying finds its origins in *Jerrold Electronics*.[364] The Court approved the practice of selling cable antenna systems only in conjunction with a service contract when the patented technology was still in its infancy. The practice was justified because the technology patent owner's 'reputation and growth of entire industry was at stake during development

period'. The Court rightly rejected claims of both patent misuse and monopolisation because ex ante incentives plausibly included the expectation that
the patent holder could choose to control the technology's development and
commercialisation. The Court was careful to state that the tying arrangement
could not continue into the industry's maturity, presumably when competition would provide ex post incentives to improve the technology or lower
prices. This analysis is consistent with more recent tying doctrine, including
the *Kodak* case, discussed earlier, which prohibited a patent holder from
refusing to sell patented replacement parts to independent service companies
in a mature industry.

Exclusive dealing provisions in licensing agreements   Exclusive dealing and
tying are sibling arrangements when they are forced upon the acquiescing
party – typically the buyer.[365] Both arrangements gain their force from a
refusal, whether express or implied, to do business on other terms. Both
condition the transaction on a measure of exclusivity that restrains the
buyer's freedom to deal with competitors. In at least one respect, they differ:
exclusive dealing provisions may be more restrictive because they foreclose
all inter-brand competition for the dealer, whereas a tying provision's
restraining effects depend upon the extent of the dealer's purchases of the
tied product. In that light, exclusive dealing can restrain competition more
effectively than tying arrangements.

  Although both tying and exclusive dealing offences come out of precisely
the same statutory language, whether Clayton Act section 3 or the Sherman
Act, exclusive dealing doctrine is not as well-developed as tying, largely
because cases that could be characterised either way have generally been
litigated as tying cases. The underlying concern, however, is the same for
both offences: that the exercise of market power will foreclose market entry.
With exclusive dealing arrangements, licensing agreements can prevent the
licensee not only from acquiring competing technology from competitors but
also from developing new technology itself. Hence the possible foreclosure
effects can be both vertical and horizontal, restraining the licensee from
becoming a competitor's customer and from becoming a competitor. The
horizontal effects raise greatest concern when the licensing parties are already
competitors – as is frequently the case in cross-licensing and litigation
settlement agreements.[366]

  As a general matter, courts have applied the rule of reason to evaluate
exclusive dealing arrangements and, for the most part, have found them to be
reasonable. The old Supreme Court cases focused on the extent of market
foreclosure, typically by determining the defendant's market share.[367] The
Supreme Court had an opportunity to sharpen the doctrine in *Jefferson Parish
Hospital*[368] but limited its analysis to tying. The concurring opinion
addressed the exclusive dealing issue but did little more than observe that

the defendant's 30 per cent market share should not satisfy the 'substantial foreclosure' requirement. More recently, lower courts have required proof that the arrangement foreclosed a substantial percentage of the market. In *Omega Environmental* v. *Gilbarco Inc*, for example,[369] the Ninth Circuit determined that the defendant's 38 per cent share was insufficient to show substantial market foreclosure because the contracts were short-term – one year or less and many of them terminable on 60 days notice. While *Omega Environmental* is representative of Sherman and Clayton Act jurisprudence, the Federal Trade Commission has been more sceptical. In *In re Beltone Electronics Corp.*,[370] the FTC found that the leading firm, with a 20 per cent market share of an oligopoly market, employed exclusive dealing provisions and other restraints that foreclosed a substantial share of the market. The FTC took 'into account not only the market share of the firm but the dynamic nature of the market in which the foreclosure' occurred. In particular, the combination of restraints, adopted in parallel fashion by firms in the market, satisfied the substantial foreclosure requirement under FTC section 5, which subsequent courts have equated with the Clayton and Sherman Act standards.[371]

In the *Microsoft* (2001) monopolisation case, plaintiffs asserted exclusive dealing claims under Sherman Act sections 1 and 2. The district court concluded that Microsoft had not engaged in unlawful exclusive dealing under section 1 because the evidence did not 'demonstrate that Microsoft's agreements excluded Netscape altogether from access to roughly 40 per cent of the browser market'.[372] But the Court held that Microsoft's exclusive dealing provisions did violate section 2. The D.C. Circuit affirmed, declaring that 'a monopolist's use of exclusive contracts, in certain circumstances, may give rise to a section 2 violation even though the contracts foreclose less than the roughly 40 per cent or 50 per cent share usually required in order to establish a section 1 violation'. More specifically, the Court found that 'closing to rivals a substantial percentage of the available opportunities for browser distribution, Microsoft managed to preserve its monopoly in the market for operating systems'. The Court's evaluation added a final step: 'Plaintiffs having demonstrated a harm to competition, the burden falls upon Microsoft to defend its exclusive dealing contracts ... by providing a pro-competitive justification for them. Significantly, Microsoft's only explanation for its exclusive dealing is that it wants to keep developers focused upon its APIs – which is to say, it wants to preserve its power in the operating system market ... That is not an unlawful end, but neither is it a pro-competitive justification.'[373] The Court's shifting burdens of proof are consistent with current rule of reason jurisprudence in other areas.

Royalty payments   Antitrust policy generally views monopoly pricing simply as the monopolist's reward. As Judge Learned Hand put it in the *ALCOA*[374] case: 'Finis opus coronat.' Patent and copyright policy, rightly understood, takes a more measured view of monopoly profits as the maximum price needed to produce the public benefit of progress in the useful arts and science. Given the instrumentalist foundations of copyright and patent, scholars have engaged in a long standing debate about the pecuniary reward that would create an optimal incentive to innovate. It should come as no surprise that antitrust cases reflect concern about royalty payments only when they are perceived as exceeding the bounds of the intellectual property grant. For example, the Supreme Court in *Brulotte v. Thys Co.*[375] held that a provision in a patent licence calling for royalty payments beyond the patent term was per se illegal. In a recent opinion, Judge Richard Posner has criticised the opinion, characterising such provisions as simply altering the timing of payment – a practice that would allow more investment in development during the early years of the term.[376] If, however, one assumes that Congress would reasonably take a patent's life cycle into account, then the patent term's length would already reflect Judge Posner's observation.

The Court in *Hazeltine* held unlawful royalty payments based on sales of products that did not include the patented device; but the opinion did suggest that the practice might be lawful when 'the convenience of the parties rather than patent power dictates'.[377] The *Hazeltine* question about non-metered royalty payments arose in the government's first *Microsoft* case. Microsoft's licence for Windows 95 called for royalties from manufacturers based on PC unit sales, regardless of the operating system installed. The Department of Justice attacked the provision as anticompetitive because double payment of royalties for machines shipped with other operating systems created a disincentive to license competing systems. Microsoft agreed to stop using the non-metered royalty as part of the case settlement.[378]

Licensing restrictions   Licences often include specific restrictions that range from pricing practices to cross-licensing. As a general matter, courts evaluate them under a rule of reason and begin with a presumption that they are legal. Both the courts and the enforcement agencies' Licensing Guidelines recognise the benefits of intellectual property licensing but look more closely at licensing restrictions in concentrated industries. The more common licensing restrictions are discussed below.

Price restrictions
The Licensing Guidelines section 5.2 reminds us that since the *Dr. Miles*[379] decision resale price maintenance is per se illegal when 'commodities have passed into the channels of trade and are owned by dealers'. Moreover, the first sale doctrine has led the Supreme Court to hold per se illegal provisions in intellectual property licences that fix a licensee's resale price of products embodying the intellectual property.[380] However, there is uncertainty about the treatment of price restrictions on account of the *General Electric*

decision,[381] which held per se legal a licensing agreement fixing the resale price of patented products sold by Westinghouse, General Electric's sole licensee and sole competitor. Subsequent decisions and scholarly criticism have limited the decision but it still stands. On two occasions, the case was upheld, both times by equally divided courts. Some view the case as limited to circumstances when the licensor also manufactures the product and consigns it for sale. Further, the significance of the sale versus consignment distinction remains a mystery. On the one hand, the influential *Sylvania* decision[382] announced the end of the distinction in antitrust analysis of vertical non-price restraints. On the other, a subsequent decision, *Business Electronics Corp.* v. *Sharp Electronics Corp.*[383] seemed to revive it, at least in the context of resale price maintenance. Again in an antitrust analysis of vertical restraints, the Court's decision in *Simpson* v. *Union Oil Co.*[384] limited *General Electric*'s rule of per se legality to patent licences. Finally, the Supreme Court has disallowed price restraints that were part of industry wide licensing schemes, schemes with a significant horizontal component. The *U.S. Gypsum* decision[385] held illegal a patentee's actions 'in concert with all members of an industry, to issue substantially identical licences to all members of the industry under the terms of which the industry is completely regimented'. The *Line Material* opinion[386] applied the same limitation to cross-licensing agreements that fixed prices for competing products.[387] In summary, while *General Electric* remains good law, it has been limited on numerous occasions because of concerns about restraints on competition, especially price competition and horizontal effects, in concentrated markets. In cases that are found to fall outside the *General Electric* doctrine, price restraints ancillary to licensing agreements are judged under a rule of reason. Finally, licences claimed to be pretexts for price fixing would be evaluated under an enhanced per se or truncated rule of reason, consistent with *California Dental Association*, discussed in this chapter's introduction to US antitrust law, and the Licensing Guidelines.

Quantity restrictions
The purposes and effects of restricting output are similar to those of price fixing and market division. Restrictions on maximum output allow the licensor to adjust its own output and thus control industry output to reach the level of profit maximisation. Given the recognised right to charge a monopoly price directly, allowing licensing with such provisions can be understood as permitting the licensor to take advantage of opportunities to lower costs and increase product dissemination. Nonetheless, courts have given more lenient treatment to non-price restraints involving intellectual property licences, as they have more generally to vertical non-price restraints. In the small number of antitrust cases addressing the issue, courts have upheld quantity restrictions on patented items produced by the licensor.

When, however, a licence for a patented process has been found to limit the quantity of unpatented product output, the decisions have been inconsistent because of differing views regarding the extent of the patent monopoly.[388]

Customer allocation

A similar concern about industry-wide restraints was voiced in *General Electric*, with the Department of Justice claiming 'that GE has entered into anti-competitive [licences] with more than 500 hospitals that are among GE's most significant actual or potential competitors in the servicing of medical imaging equipment . . . In exchange for the licence . . . GE has required each hospital to agree not to compete with GE in servicing any other facilities' medical imaging equipment.' The Court concluded that the licences 'could have been agreements to allocate customers that were *per se* illegal. The manufacturer and hospitals were competitors or potential competitors in the servicing of medical imaging equipment. The restraints were not ancillary to legitimate transactions.'[389] The approach reflects concerns about horizontal restraints articulated in the Licensing Guidelines at sections 3.4 and 5.1.

Territorial restrictions

The Patent Act permits exclusive licensing 'to any specified part of the United States' and the courts have extended the permission to export restrictions.[390] Moreover, the *Sylvania* decision, mentioned above, holds that non-price restraints imposed on distribution of all products falls under the full rule of reason. In this light, territorial restrictions imposed by licensors without substantial market power will be found reasonable in most circumstances. But courts on occasion have struck down licences viewed as pretexts for market division among competing licensors or licensees.[391]

Field-of-use restrictions

The Supreme Court in *General Talking Pictures Corp. v. Western Elect. Co.*[392] upheld licensing provisions that restrict the licensee's use of a patented invention to specified fields, concluding that such restrictions are reasonably within the reward that a patent grant contemplates, as announced in *General Electric*. But it should be noted that the Court declined an opportunity to reaffirm the *General Talking Pictures* opinion, an attitude consistent with its broader ambivalence toward *General Electric*. Nonetheless, subsequent decisions in the lower courts have generally upheld field-of-use restrictions, sometimes under the dubious logic that a patent owner's right to exclude all competition includes the lesser right to restrict the licence's field of use.[393] The logic is dubious in its assumption that other public policies never intervene to prohibit a lesser restriction, making all lesser restrictions per se legal. A better analysis would begin with a determination whether the restriction seeks to extend the scope of the intellectual property right[394] and, if it does, whether it unreasonably restrains competition. Finally, here as elsewhere, the first sale doctrine exhausts the licensor's right to impose restrictions on resale, including field-of-use and territorial restrictions.[395]

Pooling and cross-licensing

The Licensing Guidelines have usefully defined cross-licensing and pooling as 'agreements of two or more owners of intellectual property rights to licence one another or third parties'.[396] The rights may be 'transferred directly by patentee to licensee or through some medium such as a joint venture, set up specifically to administer the patent pool'.[397] Regardless of their structure, however, all intellectual property pools are grounded on agreements between owners to waive exclusive rights for the purpose of granting rights to one another and/or jointly to others. Pools can differ in the ancillary restrictions imposed, including any of those discussed above and others such as grant-back provisions. In consequence, the competitive effects of pools can vary widely, especially when the separately owned intellectual property would have generated competitive goods or technologies. The Licensing Guidelines section 5.5, which addresses cross-licensing and pooling, gives as the example of pro-competitive licensing the arrangement in *Broadcast Music*, the copyright case discussed in the Industry Standardisation section, above. Recall that the Supreme Court applied a 'quick look' or truncated rule of reason to conclude that 'the cooperative price was necessary to create' the transactional efficiencies that spawned a new product market. As a general matter, the legality of intellectual property pools turns on the reasonableness of the licensing restraints, with *Broadcast Music* as the standard for reasonableness.

Intellectual property pools can offer unique benefits in addition to the general benefits that result from licensing of intellectual property. Pools can reduce transaction costs, facilitate settlement of conflicting claims and, in the case of patent pools, unblock blocking patents and link complementary technologies. But pools can also restrain or even eliminate competition between goods, technologies or independent researchers and developers. The anticompetitive effects are magnified in concentrated markets. The Licensing Guidelines and judicial doctrine both reflect the significance of market concentration in evaluating the competitive effects of pooling arrangements. That is not to say that pooling raises only questions of horizontal effects. Pools can raise barriers to entering downstream markets through use restrictions; they can increase costs uniformly to buyers in adjacent markets; they can introduce price discrimination that disadvantages some buyers in those markets. Finally, pools can dampen incentives to innovate, particularly when the arrangement includes a grant-back provision and royalty allocations that do not reflect the newer patents' proportional value in the pool.

With the exception of the *Broadcast Music* copyright case, antitrust scrutiny has largely involved patent pools. In consequence, the remainder of the discussion will address patent pools, which have typically stemmed from efforts to settle three sorts of conflicts among blocking patents: (1) Two separately owned patents covering complementary steps in a process to produce a particular product cannot be practised together without cross-licensing. (2) Nor can improvement patents and dominant patents be practised without cross-licensing. (3) Finally, pooling agreements can settle claims involving patents of questionable validity short of litigation. As a general matter, claim settlements and other pooling agreements to cross-license competing patents in concentrated industries have met with the strongest hostility from courts and, more recently, from agency enforcement under the Licensing Guidelines. Cross-licensing of patents for complementary products has typically passed antitrust evaluation.

The landmark Supreme Court decision in *Line Material Co.* held that patent pools with price fixing provisions fall outside the *General Electric* doctrine of per se legality for such provisions in an individual licence. The challenged pool centred around three product patents, which controlled about 40 per cent of worldwide production and all of domestic production of certain insulation for electrical circuitry. 'It is not the cross-licensing to promote efficient production which is unlawful', the Court declared. 'The unlawful element is the use of the control that such cross-licensing gives to fix prices' in a concentrated industry. The arrangement was held per se illegal. But in the absence of price fixing, the Court has applied a rule of reason to a cross-licensing provision in an agreement that settled a case disputing the validity of blocking patents for petroleum cracking technology.[398]

In *Northrop Corp. v. McDonnell Douglas*,[399] two major manufacturers in a highly concentrated market entered into a joint venture to develop military aircraft for which neither alone had sufficient expertise. The agreement contemplated joint ownership of the patents and other intellectual property developed, and included a field-of-use restriction that limited Northrop to selling land-based planes and McDonnell to selling planes designed for air-craft carriers. When McDonnell started selling land-based planes, Northrop sued to enforce the agreement. McDonnell answered that the restriction was unenforceable because it violated Sherman Act section 1. The trial court held the restriction per se illegal. But the court of appeals reversed, finding that a truncated rule of reason applied because the joint venture combined firms with complementary skills and brought efficiencies to the research and development enterprise. The Court determined that the restriction was crucial to forming the joint venture. In applying a truncated rule of reason, the Court concluded that neither firm would have entered the market alone and, thus, that the two firms would not have competed in the market for land-based planes. In short, the field-of-use restriction had no anticom-petitive effect. The Court applied what is now the standard joint venture analysis.[400]

Since issuance of the Licensing Guidelines in 1995, the Department of Justice has issued three significant business review letters regarding patent pools: the MPEG-2 Business Review Letter, the DVD Business Review Letter, and the 3G Business Review Letter.[401] According to these letters, one important factor held in favour of patent pools is the degree of complementarity among the patents and one factor held against patent pools is the extent of substitute or rival patents assembled. In the MPEG-2 Business Review Letter, the Department approved a pool of 27 patents involving video compression technology, which was cross-licensed among nine large companies. An independent administrator determined which patents were essential to the technology and, thus, to be included in the pool. The agreement provided for five-year blanket licences for set royalties. The Letter set forth guidelines for probable approval of pooling arrangements: (1) the patents must be valid and still effective; (2) the pool should not aggregate competitive technologies and fix a single price for them; (3) an independent expert should determine which patents are essential; (4) the pool must not disadvantage rivals or facilitate collusion in downstream markets. Although the Letter seems to call for efficiency justifications and minimise dangers of anticompetitive effects, it has been criticised as a 'collectively enforced monopoly over a fundamental communications standard'.[402]

In a pair of more recent Review Letters, the Department has whittled the inquiry down to two fundamental issues: first, 'whether the proposed licensing programme is likely to integrate complementary patent rights'; second, 'if so, whether the resulting competitive benefits are likely to be outweighed by competitive harm posed by other aspects of the programme'. It is not at all clear whether the two-step inquiry would have changed the outcome in the MPEG-2 Letter. The new inquiry asks, at bottom, whether the blanket licences and set royalties are consistent with the Supreme Court's *Broadcast Music* standard. Comparing the Letter to the standard, both joint ventures created significant transactional efficiencies. Yet there are two salient differences between the MPEG-2 and the *Broadcast Music* pools. First, the copyright pool in *Broadcast Music* involved a non-exclusive licence which, at least in theory, provided for an alternative source and thus competition. That suggests that the exclusive licence in MPEG-2 restrained competition more severely. Second, the two copyright pools controlled by Broadcast Music and ASCAP aggregated virtually all of the competitive copyrights. The MPEG-2 pool aggregated only essential complementary patents, which suggests that its anticompetitive effects were less severe. Yet given the unlikelihood of actual competition in *Broadcast Music*, the MPEG-2 pool would seem to present significantly less danger of anticompetitive effects. On balance, the MPEG-2 pooling arrangement should meet the *Broadcast Music* standard reflected in the Licensing Guidelines. If the trend continues, agency review under the Licensing Guidelines will be the initial framework for determining the legality of large patent pools and other licensing arrangements with antitrust implications.

5. Unilateral acquisition of intellectual property rights

The Supreme Court in *Automatic Radio Mfg. Co. v. Hazeltine Research Inc.*[403] declared that '[t]he mere accumulation of patents, no matter how many, is not in and of itself illegal'. However, unilateral acquisition of patents and other intellectual property from third parties are subject to antitrust review under Sherman Act section 2 and Clayton Act section 7.[404] The discussion begins with monopolisation under Sherman Act section 2.

As a general matter, Sherman Act section 2 imposes under the rule of reason constraints on dominant firms that do not apply to others. The report has already examined the section's application to conduct that seeks to enforce invalid patents. Acquisitions that take the form of exclusive licences also raise questions of monopolisation or attempts to monopolise, particularly when courts determine that the licences are part of a broader scheme to maintain a monopoly. For example, the *Kobe*[405] decision is frequently cited for the proposition that needlessly stockpiling patents by a firm with monopoly power, together with other predatory conduct to intimidate customers and potential rivals, constitutes unlawful monopolisation.

The landmark *United Shoe*[406] opinion by District Court Judge Wyzanski recognised the anticompetitive effects of a dominant firm's acquisition of more than 2000 patents in a course of predatory conduct. The Seventh Circuit Court of Appeals in *L. G. Balfour Co. v. FTC*[407] held that when a firm with monopoly power acquires exclusive licences that cover technology needed to compete and competitors therefore cannot procure the needed licences, the accumulation itself may constitute monopolisation. In the *Transparent-Wrap* decision,[408] the Supreme Court warned that as 'patents are added to patents a whole industry may be regimented. The owner of a basic patent might thus perpetuate his control over an industry.' Accordingly, there is some basis for the proposition that patent acquisitions, without more, can constitute predatory conduct by a firm with monopoly power.[409]

The Licensing Guidelines address unilateral acquisitions of intellectual property when they take the form of exclusive licensing arrangements.[410] An acquisition is considered exclusive if the licence as a whole is exclusive or if it has any one of a number of provisions such as exclusive territories or fields of use. The rule of reason is applied to evaluating the purposes and effects of the licence in light of the licensing party's market power. As a general matter, non-exclusive licences do not raise antitrust concerns.

The Licensing Guidelines state: 'Generally, an exclusive licence may raise antitrust concerns only if the licensees themselves, or the licensor and its licensees, are in a horizontal relationship.' A recent FTC action illustrates treatment of an exclusive licence that raised concerns about its effects on competition. The Commission investigated Biovail, a manufacturer of both branded and generic pharmaceutical products.[411] One of its most popular brands is Tiazac, a prescription drug used to treat high blood pressure and chronic chest pain. When Andrex Pharmaceutical filed an application with the Food & Drug Administration to market a generic version of Tiazac, Biovail sued for infringement. Under the terms of the Hatch–Waxman Act, the suit automatically delayed the generic's entry into the market.[412] Andrex prevailed but Biovail sued again, this time for infringement of a different patent, which Biovail had acquired by exclusive licence from DOV, another pharmaceutical company. The FTC asserted that Biovail had acquired the exclusive licence in order to protect its monopoly in the branded and generic markets for Tiazac rather than develop it into a commercially viable product. Moreover, the FTC alleged that Biovail engaged in predatory conduct to maintain its monopoly by wrongfully listing the acquired patent with the FDA as covering Tiazac and by making misleading statements to the FDA in the course of the listing process. The case was settled under a consent order which required Biovail to divest part of the exclusive licence back to DOV; to desist from taking any action that would trigger additional statutory delays in the final FDA approval of a generic form of Tiazac; and to refrain from wrongfully listing patents with the FDA for already approved applications. Given the fraudulent conduct, it is perhaps surprising that the FTC did not seek 'disgorgement of ill-gotten profits' under FTC Act section 13(b).

Grant back clauses   The Licensing Guidelines define a grant back as 'an arrangement under which a licensee agrees to extend to the licensor of intellectual property the right to use the licensee's improvements to the licensed technology'.[413] They follow the teaching of *Transparent-Wrap*, which evaluated grant backs under the rule of reason, with the caveat that a pattern of patent accumulation with grant backs and other provisions to regiment 'a whole industry' can amount to predatory conduct to maintain a monopoly.[414] The trade-off in grant back clauses is conceived as stimulating licensors' first-generation innovation at the cost of discouraging licensees' innovation in improvements or in competitive first-generation innovation. The licences' exclusivity and substantial market power held by the licensor will prompt closer scrutiny of a grant back provision's likely effects on licensees' incentives to invest in research and development.

Asset acquisitions and mergers   Section 7 of the Clayton Act is the merger provision that prohibits acquisition of any company, stock or asset where it is likely to lessen competition substantially. Courts have viewed copyrights and patents as assets subject to merger review and there is no reason to believe that other intellectual property rights would be treated differently. Moreover, under Clayton Act section 7A, parties to exclusive licences valued at

$50 million or more must file pre-merger notification documents with both the FTC and Department of Justice, assuring agency review under the Horizontal Merger Guidelines.

The Horizontal Merger Guidelines have provided a remedial flexibility that is illustrated in the Department of Justice approach to the 1992 merger between Borland and Ashton-Tate, the then-largest suppliers of relational data base management software.[415] Of roughly equal size, neither was dominant but together they maintained a 60 per cent market share. Both software packages were copyrighted, although Ashton-Tate claimed protection only of the 'look and feel' of its dBASE software. In consequence, there were enough dBASE clones that the underlying technology was edging toward becoming the industry standard. Not surprisingly, Ashton-Tate was prosecuting infringement against the clones in seeking to appropriate the value of the network externalities that could tip the market toward dBASE as the de facto standard. Rather than blocking the transaction, the Department negotiated a settlement that permitted the merger to proceed. The Department conditioned the corporate acquisition on Borland's agreement to withdraw the dBASE copyright litigation, which would of course weaken the copyright in dBASE and open competition in the market for relational data base management software. The resulting market equilibrium followed the rule of unintended consequences. After the consent decree, Microsoft entered the market with a compatible software package that was acquired from Fox Software, one of the dBASE clones accused of copyright infringement and let off the hook by the consent decree. A few years later, Microsoft became the dominant firm in the market. It can of course be argued that prohibiting the merger could have opened the market to similar results.

An earlier case reflects federal court practice before development of the innovation economics that currently informs analysis of information and technology markets. In *SCM Corp.* v. *Xerox Corp.*,[416] a competitor sued Xerox under both Sherman Act section 2 and Clayton Act section 7, claiming that Xerox's acquisition of fundamental patents and subsequent refusals to deal allowed it to monopolise the photocopying industry. Although the Court did recognise the possibility that patent acquisitions could substantially lessen competition and thus violate the statute, the claim was rejected out of hand because the patents were acquired before there was a market for photocopiers. Current agency guidelines might call for a different approach, if the evaluation proceeded under the Licensing Guidelines, which provide for examination of competitive effects in markets not only for goods but also for technology or innovation. But Clayton Act section 7A requires registration under the Horizontal Merger Guidelines, which provide only for goods (and services) markets. How would the enforcement agency proceed?

Two recent FTC cases suggest that there is sufficient room under the Horizontal Merger Guidelines for consideration of competitive effects beyond current markets for goods. In *Ciba-Geigy/Sandoz*, the FTC framed its complaint in terms of a market for the development of gene therapy products, apparently because there were no FDA-approved products available at the time. The complaint observed that commercial products would not be available for three years but that within ten years of their appearance annual sales could reach $45 billion. The FTC alleged that the anticompetitive effects of the merger would be felt in broadly defined markets for research and development and manufacture and sale of a number of gene therapy treatments. Although research and development of gene therapy treatments was widespread among numerous firms, the Commission asserted that Ciba-Geigy and Sandoz together dominated the research and development in the important sense that other firms felt compelled to enter into joint ventures with one or the other. In creating Novartis, the merger would therefore eliminate the competition between Ciba-Geigy and Sandoz that was producing joint ventures and development contracts on reasonable terms. Novartis as the newly dominant firm would appropriate the value of such joint ventures, leading to a substantial decrease in joint research and development.[417] The FTC was concerned that Novartis would not licence its intellectual property broadly enough to enable other firms to engage in substantial research and development and thereby to compete with Norvartis. But the Commission did not block the merger. Instead, it settled the case with a consent order that required Novartis to licence crucial technology and patent rights to Rhone-Poulenc Rorer, a large firm whose research and development capacities, together with the patent licences, returned the innovation market to its pre-merger structure of a duopoly with numerous fringe firms.[418]

Whereas the *Ciba-Geigy* case raised concerns about horizontal effects, *Silicon Graphics*[419] posed questions about vertical foreclosure at two market levels. With revenues of $1.4 billion, Silicon Graphics maintained a 90 per cent market share for entertainment graphics workstations, servers, and supercomputer systems. The merger would have combined Silicon Graphics with Alias and Wavefront, two of the three dominant developers of entertainment graphics software that run on the Unix-based workstations. The FTC asserted that the merger would threaten innovation in both markets. In the workstation market already dominated by Silicon Graphics, competitors could not compete effectively if Alias and Wavefront designed their software to be compatible with only Silicon Graphics workstations. In the market for entertainment graphics software inhabited by Alias and Wavefront, rival software developers would be foreclosed from 90 per cent of the market if Silicon Graphics closed its open software interface to allow compatible software designed only by Alias and Wavefront. Again, the Commission did not block the merger. Instead, it negotiated a consent order with Silicon Graphics to preserve workstation competition. Silicon Graphics was required to enter into a 'porting' agreement with workstation rivals that assured the continuation of open architecture and publication of application programming interfaces as well as the maintenance of efficient interoperability of Alias's major software packages with rival workstations. Silicon Graphics also agreed to construct an institutional firewall to block the transfer of workstation rivals' proprietary information from its applications software working group to its systems group.

Despite the Horizontal Merger Guidelines' explicit limitation to goods markets, each of the three cases brought by federal enforcement agencies has proceeded from concerns about effects on competition in innovation and technology markets. Each has been permitted to proceed, but under consent decrees that required the new firms to license or otherwise make available to competitors or customers intellectual property for the purpose of maintaining pre-existing levels of competition.

Appendix A: an overview of the *Microsoft* antitrust cases

Antitrust litigation against Microsoft in the United States began with an extensive but inconsequential FTC investigation in 1990, continued with monopolisation cases filed by the Justice Department in 1994 and 1998, and persists in private suits as well as ongoing proceedings stemming from the remedies granted in the 1998 case.

The 1994 case was settled by consent decree. In 1997, the Justice Department filed a civil contempt action, alleging that Microsoft's bundling of Internet Explorer with Windows 95 violated the consent decree. The District Court agreed, granting a preliminary injunction.

Shortly before the District of Columbia Court of Appeals would reverse the finding of contempt and dissolve the injunction, the Justice Department filed its second *Microsoft* case, joined by twenty states and the District of Columbia. After a 76-day bench trial, the District Court issued 412 findings of fact and concluded that Microsoft had violated Sherman Act sections 1 and 2 by engaging in a predatory course of conduct to maintain the applications barrier to entering the market for Intel-compatible operating systems for personal computers, the market dominated by its Windows software. As well, the court held that Microsoft attempted to monopolise the market for web browser software but did not engage in unlawful exclusive dealing.

The remedy phase proceeded rather quickly, with the District Court judge rejecting Microsoft's request for further evidentiary hearings and adopting plaintiffs' proposed remedies. Most notably, the court ordered that Microsoft be divided into two separate firms, one the Windows operating system company and the other an applications software enterprise. The remedy was stayed pending appeal of the liability case. On appeal, the D.C. Circuit left unchanged the findings of fact, affirmed in part and reversed in part the conclusions of law, and vacated the decree for remedy. In short, only the holding of monopolisation was affirmed and the case was remanded for remedies consistent with the circuit court's determinations.

After extensive hearings before a newly assigned judge, the Justice Department and Microsoft agreed to a settlement, which eleven states immediately joined. Adopting the settlement, the new remedial decree retains district court oversight for five years and includes only behavioural constraints. In particular, Microsoft is required to disclose the information necessary to foster interoperation between Windows and third-party software products, including server operating systems. The decree limits Microsoft's ability to enter into agreements that exclude competitors from the market place. Moreover, the decree explicitly prohibits Microsoft from retaliating or threatening to retaliate against licensees for supporting competing products. In this regard, the decree pays special attention to the competitive importance of 'Non-Microsoft Middleware', which would include products such as Sun Microsystem's Java technology. Original equipment manufacturers are permitted flexibility in configuring icons, shortcuts, and menu items on desktop screens, including automatic launching of innovative software programmes, so long as the programmes do not 'drastically alter the Windows user interface'. As a general matter, Microsoft must license Windows under the same terms to all PC makers, although quantity discounts are permitted. Pricing terms must be published on a website. Finally, Microsoft must appoint an internal compliance officer to assure that Microsoft officers and managers read the settlement. A committee was appointed by plaintiffs to supervise compliance with the decree.

It should be noted that the court issued an extensive opinion accompanying the remedial decree that approved the settlement. The opinion characterised the settlement as a consent decree and declared that 'Nothing in this Final Judgment is intended to confer upon any other persons any rights or remedies of any nature whatsoever hereunder or by reason of this Final Judgment.' Much criticized, this language negated Sherman Act section 5(a), which gives prima facie effect in follow-on private cases to findings of antitrust liability in fully litigated government actions.

The opinion approving the settlement under the Tunney Act is reported at *United States* v. *Microsoft Corp.*, 231 F. Supp. 2d 144 (D.D.C. 2002). The opinion with regard to the remedies sought by the non-settling states is reported at *New York* v. *Microsoft Corp.*, 224 F. Supp. 2d 76 (D.D.C. 2002). Final Judgment available at http://www.usdoj.gov/art/cases/f200400/200457.htm (12 November 2002). For a discussion and bibliography, see Peritz, *Competition Policy in America* at pp. 305–30 (*Afterword*).

According to the *New York Times*, two recent court-ordered status reports 'suggest that the November 2002 consent decree … has neither fostered significant competition nor changed Microsoft's anticompetitive behaviour': *New York Times* at C2 (17 January 2002). In addition to six substantive reports of recent violations, Microsoft's licensing programme has resulted in only three new licensees since the preceding status report, filed with the court six months earlier. The preceding report complained that the licence contained anti-competitive terms, including the requirement that a company sign a non-disclosure agreement even before reading the licence terms, a stipulation deterring use and development of free software like Linux, and a provision prohibiting licensees from suing Microsoft. Linux, of course, is a significant competitor in the market for network server operating systems. Separately, Microsoft agreed with the Justice Department to offer a software update to Windows XP so that it would no longer force users searching for music online to use Internet Explorer. The Commonwealth of Massachusetts filed a separate report, stating the intention to investigate allegations that Microsoft is 'engaged in a campaign against various Internet search engines similar to the campaign it previously waged against Netscape's navigator browser': Steve Lohr, 'Microsoft Eases Licensing Under Pressure from US', *New York Times* at C3 (4 July 2003).

By mid-January 2004, all state plaintiffs except Massachusetts had agreed to join the settlement. West Virginia, for example, joined as part of settling for $21 million in an associated suit accusing Microsoft of overcharging consumers in that state for Windows. California earlier joined as part of a similar $1.1 billion settlement. In all, Microsoft established a reserve of $1.55 billion to cover state settlements: Laurie J. Flynn, 'Microsoft Settles 6 More Suits', *New York Times* at C6 (29 October 2003); a press release describing Massachusetts' position to appeal the Final Judgment is available at http://www.ago.state.ma.us/press_rel/microsoft2.asp?head1=Press+Releases§ion=5.

There have been a number of private lawsuits. In 2000, Microsoft paid Caldera $155 million in settlement of an antitrust suit claiming predatory use of Windows 3.1 to monopolise the DOS platform. In 2003, Microsoft paid $23.3 million to settle an antitrust lawsuit with Be Inc., a software company no longer in business. Microsoft recently agreed to pay $750 million to AOL Time Warner, the current owner of Netscape software, to settle its suit. The agreement included a long-term licence allowing AOL to use Microsoft's Windows Media Player for distributing and playing digital media: 'Caldera, Microsoft Settle Suit,' retrieved from http://wire.ap.org/APnews/center–story.html (January 10, 2000); 'Microsoft Settles Antitrust Suit with Be Inc.', *New York Times* at C5 (8 September 2003)(AP wire); Steve Lohr, 'Digital Media Becomes Focus as Microsoft and AOL Settle', *New York Times* at C1 (2 June 2003).

Windows Media Player is in a competitive battle with Real Networks' Real One Player, with each having in excess of 300 million registered users. In December 2003, Real Networks filed a $1 billion antitrust suit claiming that Microsoft is using its monopoly power to restrain competition and limit consumer choice in digital media markets by bundling Windows Media

Player with Windows. While bundling has been a successful marketing strategy for Microsoft since Windows first arrived as a middleware interface for DOS, it should be noted that in the Justice Department's second *Microsoft* suit, the court rejected Microsoft's claim that web browsers were integral components of PC operating systems. It will be even more difficult to persuade a federal court that a media player is integral to an operating system: John Markoff, 'Real Networks Accuse Microsoft of Restricting Competition', *New York Times* at C1 (19 December 2003).

Finally, Sun Microsystems filed suit for antitrust violations and copyright infringement seeking at least $1 billion in damages as well as injunctive relief. The Fourth Circuit Court of Appeals recently dissolved a district court injunction ordering Microsoft to distribute the Java software but upheld a second preliminary injunction that prohibits Microsoft from distributing its own version of Java technology because it likely violated Sun's copyright. Microsoft had customised Java to run more efficiently with Windows, with the result that Java would not run at all on other platforms: Steve Lohr, 'Court Lifts Order that Required Windows to Include Java', *New York Times* at C3 (27 June 2003); Amy Harmon, 'Microsoft Loses a Round to Rival Sun', *New York Times* at C1 (24 December 2002).

Notes

1. The chapter does not address state antitrust laws for two reasons. First, they are largely similar to federal antitrust, although their enforcement policies occasionally differ. Second, their impact is relatively slight in comparison to the three bodies of law discussed. Nonetheless, when applicable, they must be taken into account.
2. Exclusive possession or use seems more often an artefact of property law than an attribute of tangible property. Tractors and plots of land are often used or held in common, even if the criterion is simultaneous use or possession. Indeed, property law recognises such states of property rights, which were explained perhaps most clearly by Hohfeld, who made the fundamental point that property rights can be best understood as relations between persons rather than relations between a person and a thing. Wesley Hohfeld, 'Some Fundamental Legal Conceptions as Applied in Judicial Reasoning' (1923) 23 *Yale Law Journal* 16.
3. Harold Demsetz, 'Toward a Theory of Property Rights' (1967) 57 *American Economic Review* 347. But there is considerable debate among historians regarding the causative link between public property and wasteful overuse. See, e.g. Daniel N. McCloskey, 'The Prudent Peasant: New Findings on Open Fields' (1991) 51 *Journal of Economic History* 343; James Boyle, 'The Second Enclosure Movement and the Construction of the Public Domain' (2003) 66 *Law & Contemporary Problems* 33; Duncan Kennedy and Frank Michelman, 'Are Property and Contract Efficient' (1980) 8 *Hofstra Law Review* 711.

4. Jane Radin, 'Property and Personhood' (1982) 34 *Stanford Law Review* 957; Immanuel Kant, 'Of the Injustice of Counterfeiting Books' (W. Richardson trans., 1798) in 1 *Essay and Treatises on Moral, Political, and Various Philosophical Subjects* 225.

5. U.S. Constitution, Art. I, sec. 8, cl. 8.

6. *Fox Film Corp.* v. *Doyal*, 286 U.S. 123, 127 (1932). *Bonito Boats Inc.* v. *Thunder Craft Boats Inc.*, 489 U.S. 141, 150–1 (1988) (describing patent system as 'carefully crafted bargain for encouraging the creation and disclosure' of inventions 'in return for the exclusive right to practice the invention').

7. *White v. Samsung Electronics America Inc.*, 989 F.2d at 1512–3 (9th Cir. 1993) (Kozinski, J., dissenting).

8. *The Economist* has defined 'public goods' as things that can be consumed by everybody in a society, or nobody at all. They have three characteristics: (1) non-rival – one person consuming them does not stop another person consuming them; (2) non-excludable – if one person can consume them, it is impossible to stop another person consuming them; (3) non-rejectable – people cannot choose not to consume them even if they want to. Examples include clean air, a national defence system and the judiciary. The combination of non-rivalry and non-excludability means that it can be hard to get people to pay to consume them. Thus public goods are regarded as an example of market failure (available at http://www.economist.com).

9. Compare Kenneth Arrow, 'Economic Welfare and the Allocation of Resources to Invention,' in R. Nelson (ed.), *The Rate and Direction of Inventive Activities* (1962) with Edward Kitch, 'The Nature and Function of the Patent System' (1977) 20 *Journal of Law & Economics* 265; Louis Kaplow, 'The Patent–Antitrust Intersection: An Appraisal' (1983) 97 *Harvard Law Review* 1813; see, generally, M. Richard, 'Brunell, Appropriability in Antitrust: How Much is Enough?' (2001) 69 *Antitrust Law Journal* 1.

10. See L. Ray Patterson and Craig Joyce, 'Copyright in 1791' (2003) 52 *Emory Law Journal* 910, 938 n. 79. The authors also discuss the broader eighteenth-century notion of science as well as the debate over the relationship between the constitutional language of progress and information dissemination.

11. 35 U.S.C. §§ 101, 154, 271.

12. See Edward C. Walterscheid, 'The Early Evolution of the United States Patent Law: Antecedents' (1994) 76 *Journal of the Patent and Trademark Office Society* 697 (Part I); *Journal of the Patent and Trademark Office Society* at 849 (Part II); (1995) 77 *Journal of the Patent and Trademark Office Society* at 771 and 847 (Part III); (1996) 78 *Journal of the Patent and Trademark Office Society* at 77 (Part IV).

13. The report discusses utility patents but not design and plant patents.

14. 35 U.S.C. §§ 2, 6, 131–46. Of course, there is the additional step of filing a writ of certiorari to seek Supreme Court review.

15. 447 U.S. 303 (1980).

16. Yet the opinion was carefully written 'not to suggest that § 101 has no limits . . . *The laws of nature, physical phenomena, and abstract ideas have been held not patentable.*' There is respected precedent for the proposition that naturally occurring products, when extracted or purified to 'create a new thing commercially and therapeutically', is patentable subject matter. See *Parke-Davis & Co.* v. *J.K. Mulford Co.*, 189 Fed. 95 (S.D.N.Y. 1911) (L. Hand, J.).

17. *Rubber-Tip Pencil Co.* v. *Howard*, 87 U.S. 498, 507 (1874).

18. 409 U.S. 63, 67, 64, 72 (1972). Note that software applications take the form of 'process' rather than 'product' claims. As stated in the Patent Act § 101, product inventions involve tangible things – 'machines, manufactures or compositions of matter'. Process claims refer to a series of steps – methods or techniques used to produce a particular result.

19. 450 U.S. 175 (1981).

20. Ibid; also *In re Abele*, 684 F.2d 902 (C.C.P.A. 1982).

21. 149 F.3d 1368 (Fed. Cir. 1998) (also rejecting 'business method' exception); *AT&T* v. *Excel Communications*, 172 F.3d 1352 (Fed. Cir. 1999).

22. See also *In re Lowry*, 32 F.3d 1579 (Fed. Cir. 1994) (rejecting application of 'printed matter' exclusion to encoded computer instructions); *In re Beauregard*, 53 F.3d 1583 (Fed. Cir. 1995) (referring to PTO Bd. of Appeals' rejection of same).

23. 15 F.Cas. 1018, 1019 (C.C.D. Mass. 1817).

24. *Brenner* v. *Manson*, 383 U.S. 519 (1966).

25. 51 F.3d 1560 (1995).

26. R. Schechter and J. Thomas, *Intellectual Property* (St Paul: West Publ. Co., 2003) p. 323.

27. Ibid.

28. 35 U.S.C. § 102(b) '. . . the invention was patented or described in a printed publication in this or a foreign country or in public use or on sale in this country, more than one year prior to the date of application'. See also ibid. § 102(c), (d). Note that the inventor's own actions can create a statutory bar. One common example is prior publication in a scholarly journal.

29. *General Electric* v. *United States*, 654 F.2d 55, 61 (Ct. Cl. 1981)(en banc) [citations omitted]. Note that the standard is more lenient than the rule in trade secret law, which defines 'secret' as not 'generally known or readily ascertainable' in a particular industry.

30. *In re Hall*, 781 F.2d 897 (Fed. Cir. 1986).

31. *Pfaff* v. *Wells Electronics Inc.*, 119 S.Ct. 304 (1998).

32. *Evans Cooling Systems Inc.* v. *General Motors*, 125 F.3d 1448 (Fed. Cir. 1997).

33. *Metalizing Engineering Co.* v. *Kenyon Bearing & Auto Parts*, 153 F.2d 516, 520 (2d Cir.), cert. denied, 328 U.S. 840 (1946).

34. 97 U.S. 126 (1877).

35. *Lough* v. *Brunswick*, 86 Fed.3d 1113 (Fed. Cir. 1996); *In re Smith*, 714 F.2d 1127 (Fed. Cir. 1983).

36. 218 F.2d 72 (5th Cir. 1955), cert. denied, 349 U.S. 916 (1955).

37. Julie E. Cohen, 'Reverse Engineering and the Rise of Electronic Vigilantism' (1995) 68 *Southern California Law Review* 1091, 1178.
38. See, e.g., *Fonar v. General. Elec. Co.*, 107 F.3d 1543 (Fed. Cir. 1997).
39. The body of prior art is not identical for § 102 and § 103 purposes. See R. Schechter and J. Thomas, above note 26, at 371–3.
40. *Rockwell International Corp. v. United States*, 147 F.3d 1358 (Fed. Cir. 1998).
41. Ibid.
42. *Graham v. John Deere Co.*, 383 U.S. 1 (1966); *In re Baxter Travenol Labs.*, 952 F.2d 388 (Fed. Cir. 1991).
43. 111 F.3d 887 (Fed. Cir. 1997).
44. See, e.g., Cohen, 'Reverse Engineering' 1178; Richard H. Stern, 'Tales from the Algorithm War' (1991) 18 *American Intellectual Property Law Association Quarterly Journal* 371.
45. 425 U.S. 219 (1976).
46. See, e.g., John H. Barton, 'Non-Obviousness' (2003) 43 *IDEA* 475, 490–6.
47. Section 112 also requires the description to specify the 'best mode' for production and use considered by the inventor.
48. See, e.g., *Fiers v. Revel*, 984 F.2d 1164, 1170–1 (Fed. Cir. 1993) (rejecting patent claim for DNQ sequence coding for human beta-interferon).
49. 159 U.S. 465 (1895).
50. *Lockwood v. American Airlines, Inc.*, 107 F.3d 1565 (Fed. Cir. 1997).
51. The Software Patent Institute is compiling a data base of software techniques to supplement the 'prior art' source materials currently available. For a somewhat dated bibliography of such sources, see Gregory A. Stobbs, *Software Patents* 109–47 (1995).
52. See, e.g., *Pennwalt Corp. v. Durand-Wayland Inc.*, 833 F.2d 931 (Fed. Cir. 1987) (en banc), cert. denied, 485 U.S. 961 (1988).
53. *Graver Tank & Manufacturing Co. v. Linde Air Products Co.*, 339 U.S. 605 (1950).
54. 27 U.S.P.Q.2d 1280 (E.D.Pa. 1993).
55. 893 F.Supp. 1440 (D.Idaho 1994).
56. *Weiner v. NEC Electronics Inc.*, 102 F.3d 534 (Fed. Cir. 1996).
57. 149 F.3d 1335 (Fed. Cir. 1998).
58. 717 F.2d 1351 (Fed Cir. 1983).
59. 102 F.3d 1214 (Fed. Cir. 1996).
60. *Texas Instruments Inc. v. U.S. International Trade Communication*, 805 F.2d 1558 (Fed. Cir. 1986).
61. *Boyden Power-Brake Co. v. Westinghouse*, 170 U.S. 537, 569 (1898).
62. For an economic theorem supporting the view that competition policy should prevail at the margin, see Ian Ayres and Paul Klemperer, 'Limiting Patentees' Market Power Without Reducing Innovation Incentives: The Perverse Benefits of Uncertainty and Non-injunctive Remedies' (1999) 97 *Michigan Law Review* 985.

63. Patent Act § 271 (a)(direct infringement), (b)(active inducement), (c)(contributory infringement).

64. 274 F.Supp. 2d. 972 (N.D. Ill. 2003).

65. See, e.g., *Hewlett-Packard Co.* v. *Bausch & Lomb Inc.*, 909 F.2d 1464 (Fed. Cir. 1990).

66. *Aro Manufacturing Co.* v. *Convertible Top Replacement Co.*, 377 U.S. 476, 488 (1964). See also *Sony Corp.* v. *Universal City Studies, Inc.*, 464 U.S. 417 (1984) (contributory copyright infringement). In 1996 Congress recognised the potential impact on medical treatment and amended the statute to exempt doctors who performed medical procedures from liability. 35 U.S.C. § 287 (c)(1).

67. *Imagexpo LLC.* v. *Microsoft Corp.*, 2003 WL 22216400 (E.D.Va., 23 September 2003).

68. In addition to the three defences discussed, there are six that are only mentioned here: the shop rights of an employer, the right to repair the patented product, the inequitable conduct of the patent holder, the rights of a prior user under 35 U.S.C. § 273, and the equitable doctrines of estoppel and laches. Of the six, the most frequently asserted is the defence of inequitable conduct, which relates to abuse of the patent prosecution process. Courts have found inequitable conduct when the patent holder has intentionally misrepresented or failed to disclose material information to the PTO. See *Molins PLC* v. *Textron Inc.*, 48 F.3d 1172 (Fed. Cir. 1995); *Kingsdown Medical Consultants Ltd* v. *Hollister Inc.*, 863 F.2d 1435 (Fed. Cir. 1991). The chapter will discuss abuse of the patenting process in the antitrust section on monopolisation.

69. 243 U.S. 502 (1917).

70. Ibid.

71. 314 U.S. 488 (1942).

72. Ibid. Also *B.B. Chem. Co.* v. *Ellis*, 314 U.S. 495 (1942). Successful assertion of a misuse defence in a patent or copyright infringement case results in the owner's incapacity to enforce the grant – the practical equivalent to a compulsory royalty-free license for all the world – until the misuse ends and its effects are abrogated.

73. *Rohm & Haas Co.* v. *Dawson Chemical Co.*, 599 F.2d 685 (5th Cir. 1979).

74. See, e.g., *Intel Corp.* v. *ULSI System Tech.*, 995 F.2d 1566 (Fed. Cir. 1993), cert. denied, 510 U.S. 1092 (1994).

75. 976 F.2d 700 (Fed. Cir. 1992).

76. 124 F.3d 1419, 1426–7 (Fed. Cir. 1997).

77. *B. Braun Medical Inc.* v. *Abbott Labs. Inc.*, 124 F.3d 1419, 1426–7 (Fed. Cir. 1997); see also, *Monsanto Co.* v. *McFarling*, 302 F.3d 1291 (Fed. Cir. 2002).

78. 29 F. Cas. 1120, 1121 (C.C.D. Mass. 1813).

79. *Whittemore* v. *Cutter*, 29 F. Cas. 1120, 1121 (C.C.D. Mass. 1813).

80. 733 F.2d 858 (Fed. Cir. 1984).

81. *Roche Products Inc.*, v. *Bolar Pharmaceutical Co.*, 733 F.2d 858 (Fed. Cir. 1984), cert. denied, 469 U.S. 856 (1984). 35 U.S.C. § 271(e)(1). Patent holders were permitted to extend their patents in these circumstances to compensate for the testing exemption.

82. *Madey* v. *Duke University*, 307 F.3d 1351, 1362 (Fed. Cir. 2002).

83. For an extended argument consistent with this view, see Maureen A. O'Rourke, 'Toward a Doctrine of Fair Use in Patent Law' (2000)100 *Columbia Law Review* 1177.

84. Patterson and Joyce, 'Copyright in 1791' 938 n.79 discuss parallels between the Copyright Act and the English Statute of Anne, which limited the power of the sovereign to grant perpetual publishing monopolies.

85. Unpublished works enjoyed perpetual protection under state common laws until largely pre-empted by section 301 of the Copyright Act of 1976.

86. It should be noted that the Copyright Office had been accepting registration for computer programs prior to 1980, although registration alone does not make a work copyrightable.

87. 17 U.S.C. § 102.

88. H.R. Rep. No. 94–1476, 94th Congress, 2d Session 51 (1976).

89. *Alfred Bell & Co.* v. *Catalda Fine Arts Inc.*, 191 F.2d 99, 103 (2d Cir. 1951).

90. 499 U.S. 340 (1991).

91. *Feist Publications* v. *Rural Telephone Service*, 499 U.S. 340 (1991). There is controversy in the United States about the relationship between copyright and contract law. Some have argued that copyright pre-empts contracts that seek to extend protection beyond copyright while others claim that contract should be seen as a state law supplement to federal protection.

92. Protection of most unfixed expression is left to state law. 17 U.S.C. § 301(b)(1).

93. These are discussed later in the report. But see 17 U.S.C. § 117, which allows the owner of a copy of a computer programme to make copies in certain circumstances. The Copyright Act sometimes imposes additional requirements and offers options such as notice, publication, and registration. Furthermore, questions of ownership sometimes arise, especially when the protected work is produced by an employee. None of these issues are discussed in this chapter.

94. 17 U.S.C. § 106 (granting 'rights to do and to authorise' listed uses). There are also public performance and display rights not discussed herein. Ibid. at §§ 106 (4) & (5). Authors retain an inalienable power of reverter that permits them to terminate transfers during statutorily defined five-year periods midway through the copyright term. Ibid. at §§ 203(a)(3) & 304(c).

95. 17 U.S.C. § 501 (a) (direct and contributory infringement), subject to defences enumerated in ibid. at §§ 107–18.

96. 537 S.Ct. 186 (2003).

97. *Eldred* v. *Ashcroft*, 537 S.Ct. 186 (2003) (finding constitutional the 1998 Sonny Bono Copyright Term Extension Act). The Court also rejected further arguments regarding the limits of congressional power, arguments based on the Copyright Clause and the First Amendment.

98. Unless otherwise protected. Yet, there is no clear line between 'expression and what is expressed'. As Judge Learned Hand observed, 'Nobody has ever been

able to fix that boundary, and nobody ever can.' *Nichols* v. *Universal Pictures Corp.*, 45 F.2d 119 (2d Cir. 1930).

99. *Steinberg* v. *Columbia Pictures Ind. Inc.*, 663 F.Supp. 796 (S.D.N.Y. 1987) (citations omitted).

100. 17 U.S.C. § 117.

101. When they do not have alternative ways to write the software, then the expression merges into the idea and takes the programme outside copyright protection. Cf. *Morrissey* v. *Procter & Gamble Co.*, 379 F.2d 675 (1st Cir. 1967) (holding writer's expression unprotectable when only few ways to express idea).

102. 982 F.2d 693 (2d Cir. 1992).

103. *Computer Associates International* v. *Altai*, 982 F.2d 693 (2d Cir. 1992). *Scènes à faire* are discussed in text accompanying note 106 below.

104. *Arnstein* v. *Porter*, 154 F.2d 464 (2d Cir. 1946).

105. On the issue of copying, courts have viewed the question of similarity in technical terms that call for expert testimony to 'aid the trier of the facts' and, thus, involve 'objective criteria'. On the issue of unlawful appropriation, 'the test is the response of the ordinary lay' person and, hence, 'subjective'. Ibid.

106. *Gates Rubber Co.* v. *Bando Chemical Industries Ltd.*, 9 F.3d 823 (10th Cir.1993) (meaning, by *scènes à faire*, those expressions of an idea that are standard, stock, or common to a particular topic, or that necessarily follow from a common theme or setting). See also, *Apple Computer Inc.* v. *Microsoft Corp.*, 759 F.Supp. 1444 (N.D.Cal. 1991) (Microsoft arguing that visual displays are common and ordinary expressions of unprotectable ideas and are not susceptible to copyright protection under the *scènes à faire* doctrine of copyright law). *Cf. Liberty American Ins. Group Inc.* v. *WestPoint Underwriters LLC.*, 199 F.Supp.2d 1271 (M.D.Fla. 2001).

     Other limitations on the right to copy include limited exemptions for libraries, broadcasters, and consumers, as well as mandatory licensing to record musical compositions upon payment of a statutory royalty. Ibid. at §§ 108, 112 & 118(d), 1008, 115 (respectively).

107. *Gates Rubber Co.* v. *Bando Chemical Industries Ltd*, 9 F.3d at n.14.

108. 977 F.2d 1510, 1524–6 (9th Cir. 1992)(fair use case in which court determined that APIs not protectable); *Sony Computer Entmt. Inc.* v. *Connectix Corp.*, 203 F.3d 596, 603–04 (9th Cir. 2000) (same); *Atari Games Corp.* v. *Nintendo of America Inc.*, 975 F.2d 832, 843 (Fed. Cir. 1992) (same); but see *MAI Systems Corp.* v. *Peak Computer Inc.*, 991 F.2d (9th Cir. 1993) (finding infringement by intermediate copying in other circumstances). Congress responded in a limited way by amending section 117 to expressly permit the owner or lessee of a machine to make or permit the making of a copy when starting a machine in the course of repair or maintenance, 17 U.S.C. § 117(c) & (d). Though seemingly trivial, the change opens the repair and maintenance markets to competitors without software copyright licences.

109. 239 F.3d 1004 (9th Cir. 2001); but see *Metro-Goldwyn-Mayer Studios Inc.* v. *Grokster Ltd*, 259 F.Supp.2d 1029 (C.D.Cal. 2003) (granting defendants' motion for summary judgment and holding that: (1) distributors were not liable for contributory infringement absent showing that they had any material involvement in users' conduct, and (2) distributors were not liable for vicarious infringement absent showing that they had any right or ability to supervise users' conduct).

110. See Copyright Act §§ 106A–122.

111. We return to the subject of compulsory licensing in the antitrust section, below. Another limitation on the distribution right reflects the pale American version of moral rights, granting authors the right, for example, 'to prevent the use of his of her name as the author of the work of visual art in the event of a distortion, mutilation, or other modification of the work which would be prejudicial to his or her honour or reputation'. See § 106A of the Act.

112. 210 U.S. 339 (1908).

113. 118 S.Ct.1125 (1998). See also §§ 115(a)(2) & 203.

114. Scholars have suggested that Congress contemplated that parties might attempt to contract out of a first sale right. 'Congress was explicit in the context of section 109(a) that it intended for vendors who "contract around" the first sale doctrine to be limited to contract remedies. The approach of shrinkwrap licenses – to attempt to extend vendor rights by contract while retaining the panoply of copyright remedies – was explicitly disavowed by the Committee Note.' Mark A. Lemley, 'Intellectual Property and Shrinkwrap Licenses' (1995) 68 *Southern California Law Review* 1239, 1283 (citing H.R. Rep. 94–1476 (1976) (providing that the parties may contract around the first sale doctrine in 17 U.S.C. 109(a), but limiting the copyright owner to contract rather than copyright remedies if they do so). *Softman Products Co. LLC* v. *Adobe Systems Inc.*, 171 F.Supp.2d 1075, at n.19 (C.D.Cal., 2001). The exhaustion doctrine applies to patents as well. See, e.g., *Monsanto Co.* v. *McFarling*, 302 F.3d 1291 (Fed. Cir. 2002).

115. 125 F.3d 580 (7th Cir. 1997).

116. The Court also held that the 'first sale' doctrine did not permit the defendant to make derivative works based on the copyrighted materials.

117. 125 F.3d 580 (7th Cir. 1997).

118. See, e.g., *Lee* v. *A.R.T. Inc.*, 125 F.3d 580 (7th Cir. 1997); M. Nimmer and D. Nimmer, *Nimmer on Copyright*, vol. 1 § 3.03 (2000).

119. Often licensing agreements provide for the treatment of derivative works. For example, the much-litigated agreement between Sun Microsystems and Microsoft to license Java included a provision permitting Microsoft to create and distribute derivative works so long as they met certain defined standards.

120. 704 F.2d 1009 (7th Cir. 1983), cert. denied, 464 U.S. 923 (1983).

121. 2d 965 (9th Cir. 1992), cert. denied, 507 U.S. 985.

122. *Lewis Galoob Toys Inc.* v. *Nintendo of America Inc.* 964 F.2d 965 (9th Cir. 1992), cert. denied, 507 U.S. 985 (1993). See generally, *ITOFCA Inc.* v. *MegaTrans*

Logistics Inc., F.3d 928 (7th Cir. 2003) (modifications to computer programme were derivative work); *Alcatel USA Inc.* v. *DGI Technologies Inc.*, 166 F.3d 772, 787 n.55 (5th Cir. 1999) ('infringing work [derivative work] must incorporate a sufficient portion of the pre-existing work').

123. These defences include First Amendment speech, inequitable conduct, independent creation, and immoral or obscene work. Note that the 'first sale' doctrine is a limit on the distribution right.

124. 17 U.S.C. §107. The factors are purpose and character of use, nature of copyrighted work, amount and substantiality of portion copied, and effect of use on value of copyrighted work. The section also offers an illustrative list of fair uses including news reporting, teaching and research.

125. *Harper & Row Publishers Inc.*, v. *Nation Enterprises*, 471 U.S. 539 (1985) (Ford memoirs); *Suntrust Bank* v. *Houghton Mifflin Co.*, 268 F.3d 1257 (11th Cir. 2001) (*Gone with the Wind* retelling).

126. 464 U.S. 417 (1984).

127. Ibid. Analogizing to patent cases, the Court 'recognised the critical importance of not allowing the [IPR holder] to extend his monopoly beyond the limits of his specific grant', noting that a successful infringement claim and injunction in those circumstances would likely lead to 'a continuing royalty pursuant to a judicially created compulsory licence'.

128. Typically, networks are also systems and systems are also networks.

129. Above, note 19. See Sony *Computer Ent. Inc.* v. *Connectix Corp.*, 203 F.3d 596 (9th Cir. 2000); *Atari Games Corp.* v. *Nintendo of America Inc.*, 975 F.2d 832 (Fed. Cir. 1992); see also *Lotus Dev. Corp.* v. *Borland International Inc.*, 49 F.3d 907 1st Cir. 1995, affirmed by an equally divided Court, 516 U.S. 233 (1996) (holding Lotus menu tree unprotectable as a 'method of operation' under § 102(b)).

130. *Lasercomb Am. Inc.* v. *Reynolds*, 911 F2d 970, 976 (1990).

131. Ibid.; also *A&M Records Inc.* v. *Napster* Inc., 239 F.3d 1004, 1097 n.8 (2001) (suggesting that a unilateral refusal to license a copyrighted work could be misuse); *Alcatel USA Inc.* v. *DGI Technologies Inc.*, 166 F.3d 772, 793 (5th Cir. 1999); *Practical Management Information Co.* v. *American Medical Assosciation*, 121 F.3d 516, 521 (9th Cir. 1997) (holding exclusive supply provision misuse). *Cf. United States* v. *Loew's Inc.*, 371 U.S. 38, 44–50 (1962) (alluding to misuse defence); *United States* v. *Paramount Pictures*, 334 U.S. 131, 157–9 (1948) (same).

132. Antitrust courts apply the rule of reason as a fact-intensive inquiry into purpose, power and anticompetitive effects to determine the legality of most strategic market conduct. The chapter takes up these matters in the section on antitrust.

133. See also *Alcatel USA* v. *DGI Technologies Inc.*, 166 F.3d 772 (5th Cir. 1999) (enjoining enforcement of software copyright licence on account of misuse in form of provision prohibiting installation of related expansion cards manufactured by competitors).

134. Lanham Act, 15 U.S.C. §§ 1051–125; Economic Espionage Act, 18 U.S.C. §§ 1831–9.

135. State statutes are listed in Restatement (Third) of Unfair Competition at pp. 437–8 (1994).

136. 416 U.S. 470 (1974).

137. *Kewanee Oil Co. v. Bicron Corp.*, 416 U.S. 470 (1974).

138. 244 U.S. 100, 102 (1917).

139. *E. I. DuPont & Co. v. Masland*, 244 U.S. 100, 102 (1917).

140. *Rockwell Graphic Systems Inc. v. DEV Industries Inc.*, 925 F.2d 174 (7th Cir. 1991).

141. *Bonito Boats Inc. v. Thunder Craft Boats Inc.*, 489 U.S. 141 (1989).

142. Schechter & Thomas, above, note 26 at 536.

143. Although these thorny questions are usually left entirely to the courts, Congress did amend the Copyright Act to address the relationship between federal and state copyright. 17 U.S.C. § 301.

144. Above, note 137.

145. Josh Lerner, 'The Importance of Trade Secrecy: Evidence from Civil Litigation' (Dec. 1994) *Harvard Business School Working Paper* No. 95–043.

146. *Metallurgical Industries Inc. v. Fourtek*, 790 F.2d 1195 (5th Cir. 1986).

147. Douglass North, 'Structure and Performance: The Task of Economic History' (1978) 16 *Journal of Economic Literature* 963 (arguing that market participants must be persuaded of system's fairness and legitimacy).

148. 925 F.2d 174 (7th Cir. 1991).

149. Some courts have required more 'meaningful security provisions'. See, e.g., *Electro-Craft Corp. v. Controlled Motion Inc.*, 332 N.W.2d 890 (Minn. 1983).

150. *Young Dental Manufacturing Co. v. Q3 Special Prods. Inc.*, 891 F.Supp. 1345 (E.D.Mo. 1995) (no); *Management Science of America v. Cyborg Sys. Inc.*, 1977–1 Trade Cas. (CCH) ¶ 61, 472 (N.D.Ill. 1977) (yes).

151. 825 F.Supp. 340, 349 (D.Mass. 1993).

152. Object code is produced by a language compiler from the source code written by a programmer in a source language such as FORTAN, BASIC, COBOL, or C. The object code is then typically linked, assembled or otherwise massaged to constitute the machine code that is used by the particular computer.

153. There was no evidence of reverse engineering, which is not misappropriation. The topic is discussed in the next section on misappropriation.

154. Courts have disagreed about the status of combining publicly known software utility programmes into a suite. *Cash Management Serv. v. Digital Transactions Inc.*, 920 F.2d 171 (2d Cir. 1990) (yes); *Comprehensive Tech. Inc. v. Software Artisans Inc.*, 3 F.3d 730 (4th Cir. 1993) (no). But so long as the combination is ascertainable by inspecting a legitimately obtained copy of the suite itself, there appears to be no secret.

155. *Rivendell Forest Prods. v. Georgia-Pacific Corp.*, 28 F.3d 1042 (10th Cir. 1994), reversing 824 F.Supp. 961 (D.Colo. 1993).

156. *Cataphore Corp.* v. *Hudson*, 444 F.2d 1313, 1315 (5th Cir. 1971).

157. *SI Handling Sys. Inc.* v. *Heisley*, 753 F.2d 1244, 1256 (3d Cir. 1985).

158. Schechter & Thomas above, note 26 at 533.

159. See, e.g., Restatement of Torts Section 757 (1939).

160. 506 F.2d 471 (9th Cir. 1974).

161. See, e.g., *Engelhard Ind. Inc.* v. *Research Instrumental Corp.*, 324 F.2d 347 (9th Cir. 1963).

162. 178 F.Supp. 655 (S.D.N.Y. 1959).

163. *Warner-Lambert Pharmaceutical Co.* v. *John J. Reynolds Inc.*, 178 F.Supp. 655 (S.D.N.Y. 1959).

164. See, e.g., *Gary Van Zeeland Talent Inc.* v. *Sandas*, 267 N.W.2d 242 (Wisc. 1978); Restatement (Third) of Unfair Competition Section 39, Comment d (1994).

165. See, e.g., *Meehan* v. *PPG Indus.*, 802 F.2d 881, 886 (7th Cir. 1986); *Boggild* v. *Kenner Prods.*, 776 F.2d 1315, 1320 (6th Cir. 1985).

166. *E. I. duPont de Nemours & Co.* v. *Rolfe Christopher*, 431 F.2d 1012 (5th Cir. 1970).

167. *Pioneer Hi-Bred International* v. *Holden Foundation Seeds Inc.*, 35 F.3d 1226 (8th Cir. 1994).

168. The Restatement of Torts, section 757(1) includes discovery by independent invention, observation of the item in public use or on public display, and obtaining it from published literature, as well as reverse engineering.

169. See, e.g., *Kewanee Oil Co.* v. *Bicron Corp.*, 416 U.S. 470 (1974).

170. 209 F.2d 493, 495 (2d Cir. 1953).

171. *Smith* v. *Dravo Corp.*, 203 F.2d 360 (7th Cir. 1953).

172. Ibid.

173. *SI Handling Sys.* v. *Heisley*, 753 F.2d 1244, 1267–8 (3d Cir. 1985).

174. See, e.g., *Blue Ridge Anesthesia & Critical Care Inc.* v. *Gidick*, 389 S.E.2d 467, 469 (Va. 1990).

175. Unless otherwise indicated, this chapter will use 'trademark' to refer collectively to trademarks, service marks, and trade names, certification marks and collective marks.

176. 248 U.S. 90, 97 (1918).

177. Ibid. The Lanham Act, in a clear departure from the common law, permits registration of trademarks if the application shows a 'bona fide intention . . . to use' the mark in commerce: 15 U.S.C. §1051(1)(b).

178. *Reddy Communications* v. *Environment Action Foundation*, 477 F.Supp. 936 (D.D.C. 1979).

179. The Trademark Cases, 100 U.S. 82, 94 (1879).

180. Trademark protection as an incentive to invest in product quality is an indirect, uncertain and thus questionable proxy for encouraging innovation. Indeed, product quality seems to be a limited concern in trademark policy. For example, one prominent decision upheld the assignment of a trademark

even though the quality of the underlying product clearly suffered in the hands of the new owner. *Bambu Sales Inc.* v. *Sultana Crackers Inc.*, 683 F.Supp. 899 (E.D.N.Y. 1988). The holding is telling because the court permitted the assignment despite the traditional prohibition of 'assignments in gross'. Under that doctrine, trademarks can only be assigned together with the goods to which they are affixed because of concerns that sale of the mark alone would risk lower quality goods, thereby confusing or misleading consumers. The Court betrayed no such concern.

181. See, e.g., Richard Schmalensee, 'Advertising and Market Structure' in (Joseph Stiglitz and G. Frank Matthewson (eds.), *New Developments in the Analysis of Market Structure* 373 (1991); Edward Chamberlin, *The Theory of Monopolistic Competition* (1932); Rudolph J.R. Peritz, 'Innovation Economics and U.S. Antitrust Law' in A. Cucinotta, R. Pardolesi, R. Van den Bergh (eds.), *Post-Chicago Developments in Antitrust Law* (London: Elgar Press, 2002); Mark A. Lemley, 'The Modern Lanham Act and the Death of Common Sense' (1999) 108 *Yale Law Journal* 1687; Paul Milgrom and John Roberts, 'Price and Advertising Signals of Product Quality' (1986) 94 *Journal of Political Economy* 796; J. Thomas McCarthy, *Trademarks and Unfair Competition* §2.10–11(4th edn, 2001). Compare Lee Bentham, 'The Effect of Advertising on the Price of Eyeglasses' (1972) 15 *Journal of Law & Economics* 337 (advertising correlates with lower prices) with John A. Rizzo, 'Advertising and Competition in the Ethical Pharmaceutical Industry' (1999) 42 *Journal of Law & Economics* 89 (1999) (drug advertising reduces consumer sensitivity to price).

182. Schechter and Thomas, above note 26, at 550.

183. The examining attorney evaluates the application and, if there are no objections, the proposed mark is published in the PTO *Gazette* to allow for objections. If no opposition is filed within 30 days, a registration certificate is issued. The certificate is effective for ten years, can be used as prima facie evidence of ownership in litigation, and is renewable. Registration of trade names (company names) is not permitted, unless the name also identifies a particular good and thus qualifies as a trade mark as well.

184. 760 F.2d 1383 (3d Cir. 1985).

185. 979 F.2d 499 (7th Cir. 1992).

186. 497 F.2d 433 (2d Cir. 1974).

187. 1999 WL 988533 (S.D.N.Y. 1999).

188. *Franklin Knitting Mills* v. *Fashionit Sweater Mills*, 297 F. 247, 248 (S.D.N.Y. 1923).

189. 698 F.2d 786 (5th Cir. 1983).

190. Ibid.

191. Available at http://www.net2.com/lindows/, accessed on November 9, 2003 (documents in .pdf format).

192. *Blau Plumbing Inc.* v. *S.O.S. Fix-It Inc.*, 781 F.2d 604, 609 (7th Cir. 1986).

193. 43 U.S.P.Q.2d 1778 (N.D.Cal. 1997).
194. The settlement is reported in Matt Richtel, 'Microsoft to Pay $20 Million to Settle Lawsuit Over Java' in *New York Times* at Section C, page 4 (24 January 2001).
195. 505 U.S. 763 (1993).
196. See e.g., *Accuimage Diagnostics Corp* v. *Terarecon Inc.*, 260 F.Supp.2d 941 (N.D.Cal. 2003); *Computer Access Technology Corp.* v. *Catalyst Enterprises Inc.*, 2001 WL 34118030 (N.D.Cal. 2001); *CIC Corp. Inc.* v. *AIMTech Corp.*, 32 F.Supp.2d 425 (S.D.Tex. 1998).
197. See, e.g., *Apple Computer* v. *Microsoft Corp.*, 35 F.3d 1435 (9th Cir. 1994).
198. *Bonito Boats Inc.* v. *Thunder Craft Boats Inc.*, 489 U.S. 141 (1989).
199. 532 U.S. 23 (2001).
200. 376 U.S. 225 (1964).
201. *American Safety Table Co.* v. *Schreiber*, 269 F.2d 255, 272 (2nd Cir. 1959).
202. *AMF Inc.* v. *Sleekcraft Boats*, 599 F.2d 341 (9th Cir. 1979).
203. See, e.g., *In re E.I. DuPont DeNemours & Co.*, 476 F.2d 1357 (1973).
204. See, e.g., *Computer Access Technology Corp.* v. *Catalyst Enterprises Inc.*, 273 F.Supp.2d 1063 (N.D.Cal. 2003); *Brookfield Communications Inc.* v. *West Coast Entertainment Corp.*, 174 F.3d 1036 (9th Cir.1999).
205. See, e.g., *Interstellar Starship Services Ltd.* v. *Epix Inc.*, 304 F.3d 936 (9th Cir. 2002).
206. Schechter and Thomas, note 26 above, at 696.
207. Lanham Act section 43(c)(1); Restatement (Third) of Unfair Competition §25 comment e.
208. One example of a dilution claim against direct competitors, a questionable development, is *E. P. Lehmann Co.* v. *Polk's Modelcraft Hobbies Inc.*, 770 F.Supp. 202 (S.D.N.Y. 1991) (interpreting New York dilution statute). The development is questionable because it permits a claim even if the competitor's use of a similar mark does not cause consumer confusion. Thus, the property right extends to a rival mark that is not similar enough to cause confusion but somehow similar enough to dilute the mark's value.
209. *Hormel Foods Corp.* v. *Jim Henson Prods.*, 73 F.3d 497 (2nd Cir. 1996).
210. See, e.g., *Deere & Co.* v. *MTD Products Inc.*, 41 F.3d 39, 43 (2nd Cir. 1994); *New York Stock Exchange Inc.* v. *New York, New York Hotel, LLC*, 69 F.Supp.2d 479, 491 (S.D.N.Y.1999).
211. *Eastman Photo. Mats Co.* v. *Kodak Cycle Co.*, 15 [British] R.P.C. 105 (1898).
212. *Illinois High School Association* v. *GTE Vantage Inc.*, 99 F.3d 244 (7th Cir. 1996).
213. 141 F.3d 1316 (9th Cir. 1998).
214. Ibid; *Planned Parenthood Fed.* v. *Bucci*, 42 U.S.P.Q.2d 1430 (S.D.N.Y. 1997).
215. 15 U.S.C. §§1052, 1064, 1091 (1998). Where there is a configuration whose elements include a trademarked component, such as a personal computer or laptop with an Intel or Cyrix processor, the producer of the more complex

product – Compaq or Sony, for example – is permitted to identify the component by its trademarked name. See, e.g., *Warner-Lambert Co.* v. *Northside Devel. Corp.*, 86 F.3d 3 (2nd Cir. 1996).

216. *The New Kids on the Block* v. *News America Pub. Inc.*, 971 F.2d 302 (9th Cir. 1992).

217. *L. L. Bean Inc.* v. *Drake Pub. Inc.*, 811 F.2d 26 (1st Cir. 1987).

218. *Harley-Davidson Inc.* v. *Grottanelli*, 164 F.3d 806 (2nd Cir. 1999).

219. The part ends with a few words about remedies, jurisdiction and reach.

220. See generally, Rudolph J. R. Peritz, *Competition Policy in America: History, Rhetoric, Law* (New York: Oxford Univ. Press, rev. edn, 2001).

221. Scholars who adhere to the strict 'Chicago School' creed of Robert Bork believe that antitrust should be concerned with the broader category of social welfare and thus be indifferent to transfers of wealth between consumers and producers. However, the dominant view still holds that antitrust policy should not be indifferent to wealth transfers that result from unreasonable exercises of market power. Compare Robert Lande, 'Wealth Transfers as the Original and Primary Concern of Antitrust' (1982) 34 *Hastings Law Journal* 67 with Robert Bork, *Antitrust Paradox* (New York: Basic Books, 1978) p. 427. For criticism of Bork's historical analysis, see Rudolph J. R. Peritz, 'The "Rule of Reason" in Antitrust Law: Property Logic in Restraint of Competition' (1989) 40 *Hastings Law Journal* 285.

222. *Aluminium Co. of America* v. *U.S.*, 148 F.2d 416 (2nd Cir. 1945).

223. *Trans-Mo. Frt. Assn.* v. *U.S.*, 166 U.S. 290 (1897). Even when a federal judge mentioned market share, as Judge William Howard Taft did in his discussion of direct and ancillary restraints, the analysis remained common law: *U.S.* v. *Addyston Pipe & Steel Co.*, 85 F. 271 (6th Cir. 1898), modified and affirmed, 175 U.S. 211 (1899).

224. *Socony-Vacuum Oil Co. Inc.* v. *U.S.*, 310 U.S. 150 (1940).

225. Consumer welfare is the technical term that reflects the deadweight welfare loss associated with a shift from competition to monopoly. In particular, it is defined as the loss suffered by consumers who would pay a competitive price but who have switched to a second-best substitute because of the monopoly price. Monopolists are also worse off to the extent of consumers lost to substitutes. Hence, the loss is deadweight. It should be noted that this notion has nothing to do with Ralph Nader's consumerism or other consumer movements in the United States.

226. Donald F. Turner, 'The Definition of Agreement under the Sherman Act' (1962) 75 *Harvard Law Review* 655; for a short-hand rendition of the Posner–Turner debate, see Posner and Easterbrook, *Antitrust* (2nd edn 1981), p. 336–40.

227. *U.S.* v. *Airline Tariff Pub. Co.*, 836 F.Supp. 9 (D.D.C. 1993) (consent decree).

228. Joseph A. Schumpeter, *Capitalism, Socialism and Democracy* (1942). For discussion of the development of innovation economics, see generally,

Rudolph J. R. Peritz, '*Dynamic Efficiency*' in *Post-Chicago Developments in Antitrust Law* 108 (London: Elgar Press, 2002) (Cucinotta, A., Pardolesi R. & Van den Bergh, R., eds.) (European Association of Law and Economics).

229. Adam M. Brandenburger and Barry J. Nalebuff, *Co-opetition* (1996). See, generally, Rudolph J. R. Peritz, 'Toward a Dynamic Antitrust Analysis of Strategic Market Behaviour' (2003) 47 *New York Law School Law Review* 101.

230. Moreover, the Federal Trade Commission and Department of Justice, Antitrust Division, have issued a series of joint guidelines and have become increasingly more active in enforcing the statutes.

231. See generally, Peritz, *Competition Policy in America*, Chapter 1, above, note 220.

232. Also prohibited were price discrimination and interlocking directorates. Neither will be discussed in the report.

233. Doctrinal differences that once separated the two statutes have disappeared almost entirely. There has been a jurisprudential convergence of tying and exclusive dealing doctrines under Clayton Act section 3 and Sherman Act section 1, although the Clayton Act applies only to goods and other commodities. If there is a difference between Sherman Act and Clayton Act jurisprudence, it is in the extent of injury to competition. The Sherman Act prohibits unreasonable restraints of competition, while the Clayton Act was intended to stop the threat of such harm in its incipiency. But in practice the differences if any have not been great. Cf. *Brooke Group Ltd* v. *Brown & Williamson Tobacco Corp.*, 509 U.S. 209 (1993).

234. *National Society of Professional Engineers* v. *U.S.*, 435 U.S. 679, 692 (1978).

235. *FTC* v. *Superior Court Trial Lawyers Association*, 493 U.S. 411, 432–6 (1990). See also, DOJ/FTC, Antitrust Guidelines for Collaborations among Competitors § 1.2, 4 Trade Reg. Rep. (CCH) ¶ 13, 161 (Apr. 2000) (available at http://www.ftc.gov/os/2000/04/ftcdojguidelines/pdf).

236. *North Pacific Railway* v. *United States*, 356 U.S. 1, 5 (1958).

237. *California Dental Association* v. *FTC*, 526 U.S. 756 (1999).

238. Ibid.

239. 85 F. 271 (6th Cir. 1898), modified and affirmed, 175 U.S. 211 (1899).

240. 273 U.S. 392 (1927).

241. *United States* v. *Socony-Vacuum Oil Co.*, 310 U.S. 150 (1940).

242. 441 U.S. 1, 19–20 (1979).

243. 457 U.S. 332, 351 (1982).

244. Ibid.

245. 468 U.S. 85 (1984).

246. If, on the other hand, there is proof that trading partners are forced to accept the terms, then the Court need go no further to conclude that the restraint is illegal.

247. *NCAA* v. *Board of Regents of University of Oklahoma*, 468 U.S. 85 (1984).

248. 526 U.S. 756 (1999).

249. *California Dental Association* v. *FTC*, 526 U.S. 756 (1999), reversing 128 F.3d 720 (9th Cir. 1997).

250. Ibid. at 770.

251. Ibid. at 776.

252. Ibid. at 769.

253. Ibid. at 776 et seq.

254. With direct evidence of forcing, proof of market power is not necessary. But even in those instances, the plaintiff's prima facie case includes proof of a tie, which calls for evidence that the two elements of the tie are separate products. That element of the case requires evidence of separate demand functions for the two elements, proof of which must begin with market definition. It should be noted that direct proof of anticompetitive effects is acceptable in any rule of reason case.

255. See 15 U.S.C. §§ 4, 16, 23, 25 (2000) for DOJ powers. See 15 U.S.C. §§ 45, 46 (2000) for FTC powers.

256. 28 C.F.R. §50.6 (1998).

257. The FTC went beyond its usual practice of seeking only cease-and-desist orders in its investigation of a conspiracy among pharmaceutical manufacturers. As part of its request for equitable relief under FTC Act section 13(b), the FTC sought 'disgorgement of ill-gotten profits'. In July 2000, the FTC announced that Mylan Laboratories agreed to pay almost $150 million to settle the price-fixing case. Section 13(b) requires a serious violation of the antitrust laws, a substantial injury, and an ability to identify and return a substantial amount of the funds to injured consumers. Richard Parker, *Report from the Bureau of Competition*, 7 April 2000 (Director, Bureau of Competition, FTC), available at http://www.ftc.gov/speeches/other/rparkerspingaba2000.htm; 'Generic-Drug Maker Agrees to Settlement in Price-Fixing Case', *New York Times*, 13 July 2000, at A1.

258. FTC Act §6, 15 U.S.C. §46(a).

259. 16 C.F.R. §1.1–1.4 (1998).

260. The National Association of Attorneys General was created to limit duplicative investigative and discovery efforts among the states. The association focuses most of its efforts on Clayton Act section 7 violations through its Voluntary Pre-Merger Disclosure Compact and 1993 Horizontal Merger Guidelines. See NAAG, Voluntary Pre-Merger Disclosure Compact, 4 Trade Reg. Rep. (CCH) ¶ 13, 410 (revised 1994); NAAG, 1993 Horizontal Merger Guidelines, 4 Trade Reg. Rep. (CCH) ¶ 13, 406.

261. The Supreme Court has created a state action doctrine based on the language of the Sherman Act, which 'makes no mention of the state as such, and gives no hint that it was intended to restrain state action or official action directed by the state'. Thus established in *Parker* v. *Brown*, 317 U.S. 341 (1943), the doctrine can shield state and local governments as well as private parties from antitrust liability. *California Retail Liquor Dealers Association* v. *Midcal*

Aluminium Inc., 445 U.S. 97 (1980), remains the leading case because its clarity has survived the wavering doctrine that followed it. The *Midcal* test for state action immunity has two elements: first, the restraint under scrutiny must be 'clearly articulated and affirmatively expressed as state policy'; second, the policy must be 'actively supervised by the state itself'. Two principles remain clear. First, conduct by state officials that facially violates federal antitrust law is exempt if compelled or specifically authorised by a clear state statute. Second, conduct by private parties is also exempt if it is compelled by state law and is actively supervised by the state. The consequence is antitrust immunity for state regulation, whether anticompetitive or hyper-competitive. That said, the case law since *Parker* has raised questions about the rigour and shape of the *Midcal* test as applied to municipalities and private actors. Regarding private actors, compare *Southern Motor Carriers Rate Conference* v. *United States*, 471 U.S. 48 (1985)(policy authorised but not compelled; minimal supervision) with *FTC* v. *Ticor Insurance Co.*, 504 U.S. 621 (1992) (actual supervision inadequate). Regarding municipalities, see *Town of Hallie* v. *City of Eau Claire*, 471 U.S. 34 (1985) (policy authorised; no state supervision necessary).

262. See Protocol for Coordination in Merger Investigations between the Federal Enforcement Agencies and State Attorneys General (available at http://www.usdoj.gov/atr/public/guidelines/1773.htm).

263. The guidelines are available at the agency web sites. See http:// www.usdoj.gov/atr/public/guidelines.

264. Horizontal Merger Guidelines (8 April 1997) (http://www.usdoj.gov/atr/public/guidelines/hmg.pdf).

265. The HHI arrives at its results by adding the numerical squares of the market share for each firm in the industry, first pre-merger and then post-merger.

266. Non-Horizontal Merger Guidelines, available at http://www.usdoj.gov/atr/public/guidelines/2614.htm.

267. Horizontal Merger Guidelines at § 4.0.

268. *In re American Stores Co.*, 111 F.T.C. 80 (1988).

269. National Association of Attorneys General, 1993 Horizontal Merger Guidelines, 4 Trade Reg. Rep. (CCH) ¶ 13, 406.

270. National Association of Attorneys General, Voluntary Pre-Merger Disclosure Compact, 4 Trade Reg. Rep. (CCH) ¶ 13, 410.

271. DOJ/FTC, Antitrust Guidelines for Collaborations among Competitors, 4 Trade Reg. Rep. (CCH) ¶ 13, 161 (Apr. 2000) (available at http://www.ftc.gov/os/2000/04/ftcdojguidelines/pdf).

272. Ibid. at Preamble. The guidelines also set forth criteria for distinguishing between competitor collaboration and mergers: Ibid. at §1.3.

273. Ibid. at §3.3.

274. Ibid. at §2.1.

275. Ibid. at § 4.2.

276. Ibid. at § 4.3.
277. 15 U.S.C. §§ 1, 2 (2000); 15 U.S.C. § 45(a)(1) (2000).
278. 401 U.S. 321 (1971).
279. *Hartford Fire Insurance Co.* v. *California*, 509 U.S. 764 (1993).
280. DOJ/FTC, Antitrust Enforcement Guidelines for International Operations (1995).
281. DOJ/FTC, Antitrust Guidelines for the Licensing of Intellectual Property § 2.1. See also DOJ/FTC, Horizontal Merger Guidelines § 1.4 (April 8, 1997). The international operations guidelines at §4 set forth the applicability of the merger guidelines and Clayton Act §7A to foreign firms.
282. Even on its own terms, however, the static 'fixed sum' theory is limited by rigid and counterfactual assumptions of perfect monopoly in the tying product market and perfect competition in the tied product market. Those conditions simply do not apply to real markets. Nonetheless, price theorists argue that tying makes economic sense only as a strategy to price discriminate. Under conditions of perfect competition in the second product market and perfect (and costless) information about intensity of demand in the monopolised product market, price discrimination yields competitive levels of output and eliminates the deadweight welfare loss of single price monopoly. But under less than perfect conditions, the results vary. Under all conditions, the analysis ignores market imperfections and wealth transfers.
283. Louis Kaplow, 'Extension of Monopoly Power through Leverage', (1985) 85 *Columbia Law Review* 515, 523–4. See Robert Bork, *The Antitrust Paradox* 373–4.
284. Antitrust and intellectual property analyses should not be understood as categorically limited, respectively, to ex post and ex ante incentives for at least three reasons. First, identifying the life cycle of innovation and thus drawing the line between ex ante and ex post circumstances is not an easy task. Second, intellectual property doctrines sometimes extend forward into clearly ex post territory, just as antitrust doctrines sometimes reach back into clearly ex ante circumstances. Examples include antitrust limits on licensing and the intellectual property defence of copyright fair use. Finally, because ex ante incentives to innovate are reasonable expectations of future benefits, the incentives can be understood as largely artefacts of the legal regimes that define those benefits. At the very least, this circularity means that expectations at the time of invention are defined by the legal regime then in place, including antitrust law. At most, the circularity suggests some sort of reliance interest in the legal regime in place at the time of the invention. These issues are complex and call for closer analysis of the legitimacy and the impact of regime changes. But the ex ante and ex post framework is robust enough for purposes of this chapter.
285. 377 U.S. 13, 24 (1964).
286. *SCM Corp.* v. *Xerox Corp.*, 645 F.2d 1195, 1206 (2d Cir. 1981); *Data General Corp.* v. *Grumman Systems Support Corp.*, 36 F.3d 1147 (1st Cir. 1994).

287. Available at http://www.ftc.gov/opa/2003/10/cpreport.htm.
288. 785 (S.D.N.Y. 1990).
289. 1994 WL 750645, 1994–2 Trade Cases ¶70, 842 (D. Ariz. 1994).
290. Gordon Doerfer, 'The Limits on Trade Secret Law Imposed by Federal Patent and Antitrust Supremacy' (1967) 80 *Harvard Law Review* 1432, 1462.
291. *Dr. Miles Medical Co.* v. *John D. Park & Sons Co.*, 220 U.S. 373 (1911).
292. 372 U.S. 253 (U.S. 1963). For a recent claim that the tort of business disparagement can be monopolising conduct under Sherman Act section 2, see *Aldridge* v. *Microsoft Corp.*, 995 F.Supp. 728 (S.D.Tex. 1998) (holding, in part, that claim failed because of failure to prove injury and that essential facility doctrine applied to Windows 95 but not to portions at issue).
293. *Borden Inc.* v. *FTC* (the *ReaLemon* case), 674 F.2d 498 (6th Cir. 1982), cert. denied, judgment vacated, 461 U.S. 940 (1983).
294. Department of Justice and Federal Trade Commission, Antitrust Guidelines For the Licensing of Intellectual Property (1995) (available at http://www.ftc.gov/atr/public/guidelines) (accessed 18 November 2003).
295. Guidelines at §2.0(a). Critics include James Langenfeld, 'Intellectual Property and Antitrust' (2001) 52 *Case Western Reserve Law Review* 91, 93–4; Richard Gilbert and Willard Tom, 'Is Innovation King at the Antitrust Agencies' *Competition Policy Ctr. Working Paper No. CPC-01-020* (3 May 2001), http://repositories.cdlib.org/ibr/cpc/CPC01-020.
296. Guidelines at §2.0(b). This view, though correct, goes against presumptions of market power adopted in Supreme Court opinions. See, e.g., *Jefferson Parish Hospital* v. *Hyde*, 466 U.S. 2 (1984) (tying case). It is not clear whether the current court would still presume that patents or copyrights by their nature produce market power.
297. Ibid. at §3.2. The agencies begin by looking at goods markets. However, when rights to intellectual property are marketed separately from the products in which they are used, they may rely on technology markets. Ibid. at §3.2.2. The agencies will evaluate innovation markets when a licensing arrangement has competitive effects on innovation that cannot be adequately addressed through the analysis of goods or technology markets. For example, the arrangement may affect the development of goods that do not yet exist: Ibid. at §3.2.3.
298. Ibid. at §2.0.
299. Ibid. at §4.1.
300. Ibid. at §4.3.
301. Antitrust remedies have on occasion included compulsory licenses or compulsory terms. Most of those occasions have followed court determinations that the defendant's business or property amounts to an 'essential facility'. The recent *Microsoft* case concluded with remedies that included some compulsory licence provisions. *New York* v. *Microsoft*, 231 F. Supp.2d 203 (D.D.C. 2002) (remedy). It should be recalled that successful assertion of the misuse

defence in a patent or copyright infringement case results in the owner's incapacity to enforce the grant – the practical equivalent to a compulsory royalty-free
license for all the world – until the misuse ends and its effects are abrogated.

302. *Walker Process Equip.* v. *Food Mach. & Chem. Corp.*, 382 U.S. 172 (1965).

303. *Nobelpharma AB* v. *Implant Innovations Inc.*, 141 F.3d 1059 (1998).

304. Ibid., see, also, *Handgards Inc.* v. *Ethicon Inc.*, 743 F.2d 1282 (9th Cir. 1984)
(finding suit by firm with dominant position to enforce patent known to be
invalid Sherman Act section 2 violation). *Walker Process* cases raise a second
antitrust issue simply because potential liability stems from the conduct of
filing suit, which is understood in the United States as a form of petitioning
government and thus a constitutionally protected right. As a general matter,
antitrust liability cannot attach to conduct that involves petitioning the
courts, regulatory agencies or legislature. *Eastern RR. Pres. Conf.* v. *Noerr
Motor Freight Co.*, 365 U.S. 127 (1961); *United Mine Workers* v. *Pennington*,
381 U.S. 657 (1965). But not all petitioning conduct is constitutionally
protected. In the context of an antitrust suit, the courts have articulated a
'sham' exception to the constitutional protection of petitioning government.
Although the most recent Supreme Court case has raised as many answers as it
resolved, it is clear that a suit to enforce an intellectual property right is not
a 'sham' unless it is 'objectively baseless'. *Professional Real Est. Investors* v.
Columbia Pictures, 508 U.S. 49 (1993).

305. 185 F.Supp.2d 363 (S.D.N.Y. 2002).

306. FTC Docket No. C-4076 (2003)(decision and order) (available at http://
www.ftc.gov/os/2003/04/bristolmyerssquibbdo.pdf).

307. 508 U.S. 49 (1993).

308. See *Pilkington plc*, 1994 WL 750645, 1994–2 Trade Cases ¶ 70, 842 (D. Ariz.
1994); but see *Christianson* v. *Colt Indus. Operating Corp.*, 870 F.2d 1292 (7th
Cir. 1989) (permitting trade secret to extend beyond patent term so long as
Patent Act §112 did not require disclosure of those secrets in application
specifications).

309. 312 U.S. 457 (1941).

310. *Broadcast Music Inc.* v. *CBS Inc.*, 441 U.S. 1 (1979).

311. See, for example, *C-O-Two Fire Equip. Co.* v. *U.S.*, 197 F.2d 489 (9th Cir.),
cert. denied, 344 U.S. 892 (1952) (finding that an agreement to standardise
fire extinguishers facilitated collusion). Standardisation programmes with
exclusionary features – e.g., 'you cannot sell this product unless you follow
these standards' – are normally addressed under the law of boycotts and
Sherman Act section 1. For a useful discussion, see Horizontal Restraints –
Industry Standard Setting. Commission Member's Views, 1994 Trade
Regulation Reports (CCH) ¶ 50,132 (Remarks by FTC member Deborah K.
Owen, discussing dangers in setting industry standards). Cf. FTC Staff Report,
*Anticipating the 21st Century: Competition Policy in the New High-Tech, Global
Marketplace* (May 1996) (available at 1996 WL 293773).

312. See, e.g., Rudolph J. R. Peritz, 'Antitrust Policy and Aggressive Business Strategy: A Historical Perspective on Understanding Commercial Purposes and Effects, in Workshop and Conference on Marketing' *Competitive Conduct and Anti-trust Policy* (2002) 21 *Journal of Public Policy & Marketing* 237. The market structure equilibrium depends on numerous factors including the extent of interoperability and the relative attractiveness of incompatible alternatives.

313. For a brief introduction, see Lawrence Lessig, *The Future of Ideas* 26–44 (2001).

314. But see allegations of antitrust violations involving Windows 3.1 in Caldera's lawsuit against Microsoft, discussed in Rudolf J. R. Peritz, *Competition Policy*, note 220 above, at p. 394 n. 32.

315. *Berkey Photo Inc.* v. *Eastman Kodak Co.*, 603 F.2d 263 (2d. Cir 1979), cert. denied, 444 U.S. 1093 (1980).

316. *In re Intel Corp.*, 1999 FTC. LEXIS 145 (3 August 1999) (complaint, Dkt. No. 9288); FTC Decision and Order available at http://www.ftc.gov/os/1999/08/intel.do.htm.

317. *United States* v. *Microsoft Corp.*, 84 F.Supp.2d 9 (D.D.C. 1999) (Finding of Fact 116).

318. For a summary of the Microsoft antitrust cases, see Appendix A to this chapter.

319. *Addamax* v. *Open Software Foundation*, 888 F. Supp. 274, 278, 284–4 (D. Mass. 1995).

320. The Open Software Foundation was registered under the National Cooperative Research Act of 1984 (NCRA), 15 U.S.C. §4301. The NCRA, as amended in 1993, is intended to encourage cooperative research and offers limited antitrust protection to research joint ventures which have filed the required notifications with the FTC and Department of Justice: §4301(a)(6). In any subsequent antitrust litigation brought against the joint venture, the statute provides for rule of reason treatment and, for those that have registered, limits liability to actual damages: §4304–5. Finally, a prevailing defendant is entitled to collect attorneys' fees.

321. *Addamax* v. *Open Software Foundation*, 888 F. Supp. 274, 278, 284 (D. Mass. 1995).

322. 486 U.S. 492 (1988).

323. 121 F.T.C. 616 (Federal Trade Commission 1996).

324. 2002 FTC LEXIS 31 (FTC Dkt. No. 9302, June 18, 2002) (complaint); complaint counsel's proposed findings of fact available at http://www.ftc.gov/os/adjpro/d9302/030909ccpropfofconcloflaw.pdf.

325. *Rambus* v. *Infineon Techs.*, 155 F.Supp.2d 668 (E.D.Va. 2001).

326. *Rambus* v. *Infineon Techs.*, 318 F.3d 1081 (Fed. Cir. 2003).

327. 410 U.S. 366 (1973).

328. *AT & T Corp.* v. *Iowa Utilities Bd.* 525 U.S. 366, 428 (1999) (Breyer, J., concurring in part and dissenting in part) (observing that Court never explicitly adopted essential facilities doctrine).

329. *United States* v. *Terminal RR Assn*, 212 U.S. 1 (1912); *Lorain Journal Co.* v. *United States*, 342 U.S. 143 (1951); *Otter Tail Power Co.* v. *United States*, 410 U.S. 366 (1973); *TV Signal Co. of Aberdeen* v. *AT&T*, 617 F.2d 1302, 1309 n.7 (8th Cir. 1980).

330. 3 F.Supp.2d 1255 (N.D.Ala. 1998), reversed, 195 F.3d 1346 (Fed. Cir. 1999).

331. Ibid.

332. 708 F.2d 1081, 1132–33 (7th Cir.1983); see also, *Alaska Airlines Inc.* v. *United Airlines, Inc.*, 948 F.2d 536, 542 (9th Cir.1991) ('Stated most generally, the essential facilities doctrine imposes liability when one firm, which controls an essential facility, denies a second firm reasonable access to a product or service that the second firm must obtain in order to compete with the first.').

333. Courts have disagreed over the essential facility doctrine's application to Microsoft Windows. Compare *Aldridge* v. *Microsoft Corp.*, 995 F.Supp. 728 (S.D.Tex. 1998) (does apply to some portions) with *In re Microsoft Corp. Antitrust Litigation*, 274 F.Supp.2d 743 (D.Md. 2003) (does not apply).

334. The narrow circumstances include: the Copyright Act requires owners to grant performance licences for musical compositions that have been publicly performed; the Telecommunications Act of 1996 requires cable companies to carry local broadcast stations under certain circumstances; the Nuclear Regulatory Act has some mandatory licensing provisions; research and development projects done with federal government funding are not permitted to seek intellectual property protection in certain circumstances; physicians are immune from patent claims of contributory infringement while in the course of performing surgeries; finally, the conduct of patent or copyright misuse can grant what amounts to a universal, compulsory, royalty-free licence during the term of misuse.

335. *Data General Corp.* v. *Grumman Systems Support Corp.*, 36 F.3d 1147 (1st Cir. 1994). 35 U.S.C. §271(d) (1988).

336. *United States* v. *Microsoft Corp.*, 147 F.3d 935 (D.D.C. 1998).

337. However, if termed a group boycott of the sort seen in *FOGA* or *Allied Tube*, the refusal is illegal per se.

338. *Eastman Kodak Co.* v. *Image Tech. Serv. Inc.*, 504 U.S. 451, 482–3 (1992) (citations omitted); *Data General Corp.* v. *Grumman Systems Support Corp.*, 36 F.3d 1147 (1st Cir. 1994). It should be noted that *Kodak* was an antitrust case that did not involve intellectual property issues.

339. *Image Tech. Serv.* v. *Eastman Kodak*, 125 F.3d 1195, 1218 (9th Cir. 1007). The owner of any property right has a presumptive right to refuse to deal. The decision most often cited as authority is *United States* v. *Colgate & Co.*, 250 U.S. 300 (1919), which is technically incorrect because the case was litigated under Sherman Act section 1 and dismissed on that section's issue of agreement. The question of refusals to deal under Sherman Act section 2 was explicitly reserved. Nonetheless, the principle that contracting is voluntary lies at the heart of American political economy. The fundamental freedom of

contract has consistently been viewed as the presumed general rule that must be overcome by proof of some special circumstance. At common law, special circumstances carrying a duty to deal were limited to innkeepers and common carriers.

340. *In re Independent Service Organisations Antitrust Litigation*, 203 F.3d 1322 (Fed. Cir. 2000); see also *Intergraph Corp.* v. *Intel Corp.*, 52 U.S.P.Q. 2d 1641 (Fed. Cir. 1999). Cf. *Advanced Micro Devices Inc.* v. *Intel Corp.*, 885 P.2d 994 (Cal.1994) (upholding arbitrator's award of permanent, non-exclusive, and royalty-free licence to defendant's intellectual property embodied in the microchip plaintiff developed through reverse engineering, and also award of two-year extension of certain patent and copyright licenses, insofar as they related to defendant's new microprocessor, that originated in a prior and extended agreement).

341. *Simpson* v. *Union Oil Co.*, 377 U.S. 13, 24 (1964).

342. 157 F.3d 1340 (Fed. Cir. 1998).

343. Ibid. But the plaintiff's case is not easy. Compare *Telex Corp.* v. *IBM Corp.*, 510 F.2d 894 (10th Cir. 1975) (no antitrust violation found) with *United States* v. *Microsoft*, n. 336 above (antitrust violation found).

344. 540 U.S. 398, 124 S.Ct. 872 (2004).

345. 472 U.S. 585 (1985).

346. *Licensing Guidelines* §2.3.

347. Ibid. at §3.1.

348. 498 U.S. 46 (1990).

349. 396 F.2d 710 (9th Cir. 1968).

350. That view is also reflected in *A&E Plastik Pak Co.* v. *Monsanto Co.*, 396 F.2d 710 (9th Cir. 1968).

351. *United States* v. *Imperial Chemical Industries*, 100 F.Supp. 504 (S.D.N.Y.1951); *United States* v. *Timken Roller Bearing Co.*, 83 F.Supp. 284 (N.D.Ohio 1949), affirmed, 341 U.S. 593 (1951); *United States* v. *General Electric Co.*, 82 F.Supp. 753 (D.N.J.1949).

352. *Eastman Kodak Co.* v. *Image Tech. Serv.*, 504 U.S. 451 (1992).

353. *Jefferson Parish Hosp. Dist. No. 2* v. *Hyde*, 466 U.S. 2 (1984). While concurring in the disposition of the case, four Justices joined in a separate opinion that left the Supreme Court deeply divided on the very question of per se treatment for tying agreements. In short, they called for a rejection of per se treatment. Nonetheless, the majority decision has stood for almost 20 years. For a more recent rendition of the per se test, see *Datagate, Inc.* v. *Hewlett-Packard Co.*, 60 F.3d 1421, 1423–24 (9th Cir. 1995).

354. *United States* v. *Microsoft Corp.*, 253 F.3d 34, 85–6 (D.C. Cir. 2001).

355. For a discussion of these issues, see Rudolph J. R. Peritz, 'Theory and Fact in Antitrust Doctrine: Summary Judgment Standards, Single-Brand Aftermarkets, and the Clash of Microeconomic Models' (2000) 45 *Antitrust Bulletin* 887.

356. *United States* v. *Microsoft Corp.*, 147 F.3d 935, 950 (D.C.Cir. 1998).

357. Ibid. at 952–3.

358. *United States* v. *Microsoft Corp.*, 253 F.3d 34, 84–5 (D.C.Cir. 2001).

359. Since this chapter was completed, the Supreme Court has declared that market power will no longer be inferred from the existence of a patent: *Illinois Tool Works Inc.* v. *Independent Ink Inc.*, 126 S. Ct. 1281 (2006).

360. *Zenith Radio* v. *Hazeltine Research Inc.*, 395 U.S. 100 (1969).

361. *Automatic Radio Manufacturing Co.* v. *Hazeltine Research*, 339 U.S. 827 (1950); *MCA Television Ltd.* v. *Public Interest Corp.*, 171 F.3d 1265 (11th Cir. 1999).

362. *International Salt Co.* v. *United States*, 332 U.S. 392 (1947).

363. *Tricom Inc.* v. *Electronic Data Sys.*, 902 F.Supp. 741 (E.D.Mich. 1995).

364. *U.S.* v. *Jerrold Electronics Corp.*, 187 F.Supp. 545 (E.D.Pa. 1960), affirmed, 365 U.S. 567 (1961).

365. Exclusive selling arrangements and tying demands made of sellers are certainly possible but will not be discussed.

366. Exclusive dealing provisions may restrain the licensor from developing the licensed or competing technology.

367. See, e.g., *Tampa Elec. Co.* v. *Nashville Coal Co.*, 365 U.S. 320 (1961).

368. 466 U.S. at 32, et seq.

369. 127 F.3d 1157 (9th Cir. 1997).

370. 100 F.T.C. 68 (1982).

371. See, e.g., *Ryko Manufacturing Co.* v. *Eden Services*, 823 F.2d 1215, 1234 (8th Cir. 1987).

372. *United States* v. *Microsoft Corp.*, 84 F.Supp.2d 9, 52 (D.D.C.1999) (Findings of Fact).

373. *United States* v. *Microsoft Corp.*, 253 F.3d 34, 70–1 (D.C.C. 2001).

374. 148 F. 2d 416 (2d. Cir. 1945).

375. 379 U.S. 29, 32 (1964).

376. *Scheiber* v. *Dolby Labs. Inc.*, 293 F.3d 1014, 1017 (7th Cir. 2002).

377. *Zenith Radio Corp.* v. *Hazeltine Research Inc.*, 395 U.S. 100 (1969).

378. *United States* v. *Microsoft*, 159 F.R.D. 318 (D.D.C.), reversed on other grounds, 56 F.3d 1448 (D.C.Cir. 1995).

379. *Dr. Miles Medical Co.* v. *John D. Park & Sons Co.*, 220 U.S. 373 (1911). The Supreme Court has put maximum price fixing into the rule of reason category after concluding that the practice does not always produce only anticompetitive effects: *State Oil Co.* v. *Khan*, 522 U.S. 3 (1997).

380. See, e.g., *United States* v. *Univis Lens Co.*, 316 U.S. 241 (1942) (patents); *Bobbs-Merrill Co.* v. *Straus*, 210 U.S. 339 (1908) (copyrights).

381. *United States* v. *General Electric Co.*, 272 U.S. 476 (1926).

382. *Continental TV Inc.* v. *G. T. E. Sylvania Inc.*, 433 U.S. 36 (1977).

383. 584 U.S. 717 (1988).

384. 377 U.S. 13 (1964).

385. *United States* v. *U.S. Gypsum Co.*, 333 U.S. 364 (1948).

386. *United States* v. *Line Material Co.*, 333 U.S. 287 (1948).

387. See also *United States* v. *New Wrinkle Inc.*, 342 U.S. 371 (1952) (per se illegal).

388. See, e.g. *Atari Games Corp.* v. *Nintendo of America*, 897 F.2d 1572 (Fed. Cir. 1990) (patented products); regarding patented processes and unpatented products, compare *American Equip. Co.* v. *Tuthill Bldg. Mat. Co.*, 69 F.2d 406 (7th Cir. 1934) with *Q-Tips Inc.* v. *Johnson & Johnson*, 109 F.Supp. 657 (C.N.J. 1951), modified, 207 F.2d 509 (3rd Cir. 1953).

389. 1997 WL 269491 (D.Mont. 1997).

390. 35 U.S.C. §261; See, e.g., *Atari Games Corp.* v. *Nintendo of America*, 897 F.2d 1572 (Fed. Cir. 1990).

391. See, e.g., *Palmer* v. *BRG*, 498 U.S. 46 (1990); *A. & E. Plastik Pak* v. *Monsanto Company*, 316 F.2d 710 (9th Cir. 1968); *International Wood Processors* v. *Power Dry Inc.*, 792 F.2d 416 (4th Cir. 1986).

392. *General Talking Pictures Corp.* v. *Western Elect. Co.*, 304 U.S.175 (1938).

393. *Automatic Radio Manufacturing Co.* v. *Hazeltine Res.*, 339 U.S. 827 (1950); *United States* v. *Westinghouse Elec. Corp.*, 471 F.Supp. 532, 541 (N.D.Cal. 1978), affirmed 648 F.2d 642 (9th Cir. 1981).

394. *Virginia Panel Corp.* v. *MAC Panel Co.*, 1996 WL 335381, reversed on other grounds, 133 F.3d 860 (Fed. Cir. 1997).

395. See, e.g., *United States* v. *Ciba-Geigy Corp.*, 508 F.Supp. 1118 (D.N.J. 1976) (field of use).

396. Licensing Guidelines §5.5.

397. Joel Klein, 'Cross-Licensing and Anti-trust Law' (2 May 1997) speech given at the American Intellectual Property Law Association, available at www.usdoj. gov/atr/public/speeches/1123.htm.

398. *Standard Oil Co.* v. *U.S.*, 283 U.S. 163 (1931); see also *Clorox Co.* v. *Sterling Winthrop*, 932 F.Supp. 469 (E.D.N.Y. 1996) (approving settlement of trademark dispute that included provision limiting product markets each could enter because competition under other marks not prohibited).

399. 705 F.2d 1030 (9th Cir. 1983).

400. See, e.g., *U.S.* v. *Penn-Olin Chemical Co.*, 246 F.Supp. 917 (D.Del. 1965) (applying no individual entrant test), affirmed by an equally divided court, 389 U.S. 308 (1967), on remand from 378 U.S. 158 (1964) (applying individual entrant test).

401. MPEG-2 Business Review Letter (26 June 1997) available at http://www. usdoj.gov/atr/public/busreview/1170.htm; DVD Business Review Letter No. 1 (26 December 1998) available at http://www.usdoj.gov/atr/public/bus review/2121.htm; DVD Business Review Letter No. 2 (10 June 1999) available at http://www.usdoj.gov/atr/public/busreview/2485.htm; 3G Business Review Letter (November 12, 1999) available at http://www.usdoj.gov/atr/public/ busreview/200455.htm. The FTC challenged a patent pool allegedly arranged to unblock patents for laser eye surgery machinery. The case was settled with a

consent decree prohibiting a price fixing provision and requiring the firms to cross-license their patents on a royalty-free non-exclusive basis. *In re Summit Technology & VISX Inc.*, 1999 FTC LEXIS 23, 113 (1999).

402. Steven C. Carlson, 'Patent Pools and the Antitrust Dilemma' (1999) 16 *Yale Journal on Regulation* 359, 372.

403. 339 U.S. 827, 834 (1950).

404. Concerted acquisitions of intellectual property are subject to review under Sherman Act section 1, as are restraints on distribution, both price and non-price. The issues have already been discussed in preceding sections. Moreover, preceding sections have discussed some aspects of unilateral acquisition – for example, enforcement of invalid patents and exclusive dealing.

405. *Kobe Inc.* v. *Dempsey Pump Co.*, 198 F.2d 416 (10th Cir. 1952).

406. *United States* v. *United Shoe Mach. Corp.*, 110 F.Supp. 295, 333 (D.Mass. 1953), affirmed per curiam, 347 U.S. 521 (1954).

407. 442 F.2d 1 (7th Cir. 1971).

408. 329 U.S. 637 (1947).

409. But see *SCM Corp.* v. *Xerox Corp.*, 645 F.2d 1195 (2d. 1981).

410. Licensing Guidelines §4.1.2.

411. In the Matter of *Biovail Corp.*, 2002 FTC LEXIS 56 (4 October 2002) (consent order Dkt. No. C-4060), available at http://www.ftc.gov/opa/2002/04/biovailtiazac.htm.

412. *Biovail Corp. International* v. *Andrex Pharmaceuticals Inc.*, 458 F.Supp.2d 1318 (S.D.Fla 2000).

413. Licensing Guidelines §5.6.

414. See, e.g., *Hartford-Empire* v. *United States*, 323 U.S. 386 (1945) (findings that invention of glass-making machinery had been discouraged, that competition in manufacture and sale or licensing of such machinery had been suppressed, and that system of restricted licensing had been employed to suppress com-petition in manufacture of unpatented glassware and to maintain prices of the manufactured product), supplemented, 324 U.S. 579 (1945).

415. *United States* v. *Borland International Inc.*, 1992 WL 101767 (N.D. Cal. 1992) (consent decree).

416. 645 F.2d 1195 (2nd Cir. 1981). Cross-licensing among competitors has also been challenged under the merger provision. See, e.g. *Automated Bldg. Components Inc.* v. *Trueline Truss Co.*, 318 F.Supp. 1252 (D.Ore. 1970); *United States* v. *Lever Bros. Co.*, 216 F.Supp. 887 (S.D.N.Y. 1963).

417. *Ciba-Geigy, Ltd*, 123 F.T.C. 842 (Mar.24, 1997) (consent order Dkt. No. C3725). The two companies also competed head to head in several product categories.

418. See John Wilke, 'U.S. Forces New Drug Giant to Share Genetic Research', *Wall Street Journal* B4 (18 December 1996).

419. *In re Silicon Graphics Inc.*, 120 F.T.C 928 (consent order Nov. 14, 1995) (Dkt. No. C-3626).

4

The interface between competition law and intellectual property in Japan

CHRISTOPHER HEATH

I. General introduction

A. Purpose and outline of intellectual property laws

1. Industrial property and economic development

When Japan was forced to open up to the West in the 1860s, it became apparent that the medieval state of Japan's technology was no match for the West. In 1868, Emperor Meiji decreed that 'knowledge shall be brought from all over the world', so as to attain the goals of a rich country, a strong army and an increase in industrial productivity. While most civil and criminal law in Japan was subsequently enacted in order to repeal the so-called unequal treaties and thus put Japan on an equal footing with other major powers, industrial property laws were enacted out of self-interest: it was perceived from early on that industrial property laws were the motor of industrial development, as was clearly stated by the first President of the Japanese Patent Office, Korekiyo Takahashi, when visiting the US Patent Office: 'We have looked about us to see what nations are the greatest, so that we can be like them. We said, "What is it that makes the United States such a great nation?" and we investigated and we found it was patents, and so we will have patents.'

Practically all industrial property laws date back to the nineteenth century: the Trade Mark Act of 1884, the Patent Act of 1871/1885, the Design Act of 1888, and, modelled after the German Utility Model Act, the Japanese Utility Model Act 1905. In order to attract foreign technology, Japan acceded to the Paris Convention as of 1900. Judging by the application figures, the system proved a success. Already in 1885, 425 patents were applied for, in 1899 the figure had climbed to 1,915. Utility models were particularly successful in Japan, with application figures that well into the 1980s exceeded those of patents, almost exclusively due to domestic applications.

2. Purpose of industrial property laws

The Japanese Patent Act was deemed necessary for economic development.[1] In a country where the perception of individual rights was weak at best, the recognition that patents and copyrights should be granted as an equitable reward for inventors was clearly absent. Considerations about the individual rights of inventors are also absent in the purpose of the current Patent Act of 1959 that in section 1 states: 'The purpose of this Act shall be to encourage inventions by promoting their protection and utilisation so as to contribute to the development of industry.'

The industrial approach taken by the Patent Act also becomes apparent in the frequent changes made in accordance with a changing industrial environment. Already the first Patent Act of 1885 was frequently overhauled. In the last decade, the Patent Act has been changed no less than ten times, coupled with the enactment of the 'Industrial Property Basic Act' in 2002.[2]

It should be added that the Trade Mark Act takes a different approach and was enacted in order to avoid confusion in trade.[3] Trade mark law thus has stronger links to consumer protection, which is also apparent from the purpose of the Act: 'The purpose of this Act shall be to ensure the maintenance of the business reputation of trade marks by protecting trade marks, and thereby to contribute to the development of industry and to protect the interests of consumers.'

The Copyright Act aims at enhancing the general level of creativity. Also here, individual rights of authors are protected, but in the wider context of their contribution towards overall intellectual development.

To sum up, intellectual property rights in Japan have always been regarded as a motor of industrial development and have been enacted and interpreted primarily for the purpose of general industrial or intellectual development rather than the protection of individual rights.

True to its original purpose, intellectual property laws have remained fairly 'lean' in subsequent amendments and interpretations by the court. As will be demonstrated in section III of this chapter (Competition policy in IP legislation) and section IV (Competition policy through the interpretation of intellectual property rights), neither the legislature nor the courts have ever given in to right owner pressure groups in the development of IP laws. Rather, intellectual property has always been interpreted in the wider context of competition policy and domestic development. This has often been regarded as a discrimination of foreign right owners. It is true that Japan has never granted broader intellectual property rights to foreigners than was strictly necessary under international agreements. However, Japanese lawmakers and the courts have acted equally lean towards domestic right owners to the point of favouring the right of imitation over innovation (see III.B below, Protection of investment by prohibiting slavish imitation).

B. Purpose and outline of the Antimonopoly Act

1. History

The Antimonopoly Act of 1947 (AMA) in almost every aspect is the opposite of the above-mentioned Patent Act. Japan had supported a policy of heavy concentration of industry since the mid-1930s and actively supported cartel-like structures in order to render its industry capable of military confrontation.[4] The policy of economic democratisation that was practised by the US Occupation in Japan was deemed a punishment detrimental to Japan's economic interests. The Antimonopoly Act of 1947, practically written by US specialists, was perceived in Japan to be against her interest in quick economic recovery.[5]

2. Purpose and Outline of the Antimonopoly Act

Section 1 AMA reads as follows:

> This Act, by prohibiting private monopolisation, unreasonable restraint of trade and unfair business practices, by preventing excessive concentration of economic power and by eliminating unreasonable restraint of production, sale, price, technology and the like, as well as other undue restrictions of business activities through mergers, agreements or otherwise, aims at promoting free and fair competition, stimulating the creative initiative of entrepreneurs, encouraging business activities of enterprises, increasing the level of employment and a general income level, and thereby at promoting the democratic and wholesome development of the national economy as well as safeguarding the interests of consumers in general.

Both the industrial property laws and the AMA aim at economic and industrial development. Yet, as its purpose makes clear, the AMA has broader macro-economic goals in mind and does not only aim at the individual protection of entrepreneurs, but also those of consumers and the economy in general. This difference is also emphasised by the enforcement methods stipulated in intellectual property laws on the one side and antitrust law on the other.

While the purpose of intellectual property laws is reached by the enforcement of private rights through civil lawsuits, the AMA is upheld and interpreted by the Fair Trade Commission (FTC) that according to the courts enjoys a monopoly over such enforcement activities:

> A procedure under the Antimonopoly Act basically aims at a prevention of unlawful practices and thus serves the protection of public interests. Yet, it is not the purpose to protect individual interests affected by such behaviour ... Even if section 45 AMA stipulates that possible cases of infringement can be notified to the Fair Trade Commission by anyone, this can not be understood as an individual right that the FTC indeed has to take the requested measures.[6]

An aggrieved individual cannot challenge any decision taken by the FTC. Only persons 'affected' by a decision are allowed to raise a legal challenge.

> Such right of appeal requires a legal interest, in other words, the fact that personally or legally protected interests are affected, or the concern of an unavoidable damage to occur . . . An interpretation of this provision for the individual consumer . . . must mean that the latter's interests are protected under these provisions as part of the interests of the public at large, yet abstractly and generally. In other words, the interests protected according to the purpose of the law are effectively protected in the abstract or de facto, yet not in a manner that the protection of the individual could be the object of an individual right to be protected under the law.[7]

Thus, the enforcement of contraventions against the AMA is the exclusive domain of the FTC. Only in 2001 did an amendment to the AMA give individual consumers and entrepreneurs a right to request cessation of acts contrary to the AMA through the civil courts (now section 24).

As mentioned above, the AMA basically prohibits acts of private monopolisation, acts of undue restraint of trade (that is, cartels), and unfair business practices. Private monopolisation aims at obtaining even greater market power by excluding or controlling the business activity of other entrepreneurs. Unreasonable restraints of trade refer to joint activities of several entrepreneurs who mutually agree on business activities to the detriment of others. And finally, unfair business practices refer to vertical restrictions,[8] often in the framework of contracts, which may impede competition. Examples of such acts are the unjust discrimination against other entrepreneurs, tie-in sales, dealing at unjust prices, unjustly inducing or coercing customers of a competitor to deal with oneself, dealing with another party on terms that will restrict the business activities of said party, abuse of a bargaining position in dealing with another party, and unjustly interfering with another entrepreneur's business activities. In short, both horizontal and vertical restraints are prohibited by the AMA.

For the sake of completeness, it should be mentioned that Japan also has an Unfair Competition Prevention Act (UCPA) that aims at the protection of individual entrepreneurs and that in part also covers activities considered to be undue vertical restraints under the AMA.[9] Where appropriate, reference is made to the UCPA in the following.

II. Antitrust law and policy related to intellectual property rights

A. The exemption provision of section 21 AMA

1. The provision

Section 21 in its present wording could already be found in the original AMA of 1947 and was not affected by any of the subsequent amendments made in 1953, 1977, or 1992. The provision reads as follows:

Section 21 (intellectual property rights)

The provisions of this act shall not apply to acts that qualify as the exercise of rights under the Copyright Act, the Patent Act, the Utility Model Act, the Design Act, or the Trade Mark Act.

Section 21 was renumbered in 2000 in an amendment to the AMA, and literature prior to 2000 refers to the section as section 23. The wording, however, remained completely unchanged.

2. The position of the legislature and the Fair Trade Commission

2.1 Legislature In 1947, the legislature apparently wanted to exclude patent rights from the scope of the AMA regardless of whether such technical monopoly developed into an act of private monopolisation against the public interest. Correctly, the patent monopoly was distinguished from the monopolies under the AMA. Based on this assumption, section 21 then should clarify that even if an entrepreneur on the basis of a patent right could broaden its enterprise and therefore exclude or dominate other enterprises, section 3 AMA (private monopolisation) would not apply.[10] No mention was thus made of acts that would constitute undue restraint of trade or unfair business practices: exercise of the patent right still could fall foul of these.

2.2 The Fair Trade Commission It took the FTC a long time to explicitly state its opinion on the relationship between section 23 and the application of the AMA. One would have expected such a statement in the first guidelines on patent and know-how licensing agreements of 1968. However, as will be explained below, these guidelines were based on section 6 AMA, the prohibition of unfair business practices in international agreements. The guidelines were less concerned with intellectual property rights as such than with restrictions imposed on the (presumably weaker) Japanese licensee. Only the 1999 guidelines make explicit mention of the relationship between intellectual property rights, the AMA and section 21 (then 23):

(i) Section 23 of the Antimonopoly Act provides: 'The provisions of this Act shall not apply to such acts recognizable as the exercise of rights under the Copyright Act, the Patent Act, the Utility Model Act, the Design Act, or the Trademark Act.

With respect to restrictions in patent licensing agreements, there are some acts that are considered to be an exercise of rights under the Patent Act, etc., such as restrictions on territory, duration or field of use of the license. However, those acts also can often restrict the business activities of the other parties or other firms. So, it is first necessary to evaluate such acts in light of the provisions of section 23 of the Antimonopoly Act.

It is also necessary to evaluate as well other acts that are considered to be an exercise of rights under the Patent Act, etc., such as decisions to license or not to license a patent, or filing a suit demanding a suspension of violation of the licensor's rights.

(ii) Section 23 is viewed as having been enacted for the purpose of confirming that (1) 'acts recognizable as the exercise of rights' under the Patent Act, etc., are not subject to the Antimonopoly Act and shall not constitute a violation of the Antimonopoly Act; but that (2), on the other hand, even if acts are considered to be the 'exercise of rights' under the Patent Act, etc., if the said acts are considered to deviate from or run counter to the purposes of the IPR system to, among other things, encourage innovation, the said acts will no longer be deemed 'acts recognizable as the exercise of rights' and the Antimonopoly Act shall be applicable to them.

For instance, even if an act is, on its face, considered to be an exercise of rights under the Patent Act, etc., if the said act is conducted under the pretext of exercising rights but in reality is considered to be employed as part of a series of acts that constitute an unreasonable restraint of trade or private monopolization, the said act is considered to deviate from or to run counter to the purposes of the IPR system to, among other things, encourage innovation and, for this reason, the said act is no longer deemed an 'act recognizable as the exercise of rights' under the Patent Act, etc., and is subject to the Antimonopoly Act.

Furthermore, in addition to the above-mentioned situation, even if an act on its face appears to be an exercise of rights under the Patent Act, etc., if the said act, after evaluating its purpose and particular circumstances and the extent of its impact on competition in a market, is considered to deviate from or to run counter to the purposes of the IPR system, it is possible that the Antimonopoly Act will also apply to such act, since it would no longer be deemed an 'act recognizable as the exercise of rights' under the Patent Act, etc.

(iii) If, after evaluating the act in light of the provisions of section 23 of the Antimonopoly Act, the Antimonopoly Act is deemed applicable, the act will then, in accordance with the views in Part 3 or Part 4, be evaluated to determine whether it falls under unreasonable restraints of trade, private monopolization or unfair trade practices, etc.

(iv) In addition, when making a determination regarding the exercise of rights under the Patent Act, etc., it is also necessary to take into account whether the rights have been exhausted. In other words, the patent holder, in its exploitation of the patented invention, not only has exclusive possession of the rights to manufacture and use the patented invention, but also to sell patented products. When parties who have not been granted a license individually from the patent holder sell the patented products, the said act would also appear to be an act that infringes upon the patent rights in form. However, when the patented products are distributed lawfully according to the wishes of the patent holder, as far as the said patented products are concerned, in the domestic context, this is interpreted to mean that the patent rights have already achieved their objective and that the patent rights for the products have been exhausted. Consequently, restrictions on the sale of patented products that were once lawfully distributed according to the wishes of the patent rights holder are handled in the same manner as restrictions on the sale of products in general under the Antimonopoly Act.

(v) In addition, like other property rights or goods with value as property, know-how is subject to the Antimonopoly Act. However, because know-how is intellectual property with a confidential nature, it is necessary to take account of this nature when problems under the Antimonopoly Act concerning conduct regarding use, profit and sale of know-how itself or particular conduct based on know-how are considered.

Moreover, compared with patents, know-how is characterised by an uncertain technological scope, weak exclusivity protection and uncertainty as to the duration of protection. Therefore, in determining the effect on competition in a market for know-how licensing agreements, it is necessary to take into account these specific characteristics of know-how.[11]

Subsequently, the FTC issued a decision that concerned restrictions on the sale and distribution of software. The copyright owner and defendant Sony Computer Entertainment had requested retailers and wholesalers to strictly comply with the policy of no discount, no second-hand sales and no under-the-counter sales of PlayStation software. The case as such is further explained in section D below, (Patent pools and cross-licensing schemes). In its decision, the FTC held that:

> Sec. 21 Antimonopoly Act is deemed to have been enacted for the purpose of confirming that even if acts are considered to be the 'exercise of rights' under the Copyright Act, if those acts are considered to deviate from or run counter to the purposes of the IP protection system considering their effect on orderly competition, those acts will no longer be regarded as acts considered the exercise of rights, and the Antimonopoly Act shall apply to them . . . In this case, the act of prohibiting the sale of second-hand goods was carried out in connection with the act of fixing the retail price, and worked as an additional fortification thereof. However, the act of fixing retail prices including the act of prohibiting the sale of second-hand articles is detrimental to fair competition. Therefore, even if, as argued by the defendant, the PlayStation software is considered a cinematographic work which is given additional distribution rights, and if the act of prohibiting the sale of second-hand articles is within the scope of such distribution rights, such act would still deviate from or run counter to the purpose of the IP protection system.[12]

The current FTC stance thus goes beyond what was originally intended by the legislature. The FTC does not regard attempts of private monopolisation as exempt from the application of the AMA, and regards the imposition of permissible clauses as a contravention if used for purposes that are prohibited by the AMA. The decision is in contrast to previous ones that required a higher level of proof regarding failed attempts of retail price maintenance,[13] and may have been caused by parallel court decisions that refused to afford distribution rights to computer software (see section IV.B below, Decisions in connection with licensing or transfer agreements).

Also another aspect is remarkable: the FTC not only takes a pro-competitive stance when interpreting the limits of intellectual property rights, but also regards a transgression of such rights as an offence against the AMA. This is particularly so in the case of attempts to prevent parallel imports, as is further elaborated under section V below (The special case of exhaustion). Potential licensors thus have to tread very carefully, as restrictions outside the scope of intellectual property rights will fall foul of the AMA, as will restrictions permissible under intellectual property rights, but with intentions contrary to the AMA.

2.3 Academic views on section 21 (formerly 23) A number of academics specialised both in intellectual property and in antitrust have published their opinions on the interpretation of section 23/21 AMA.

One of the earliest views was taken by Toyosaki.[14] Toyosaki takes the view that section 23 is meant to ensure that the specific contents granted under an intellectual property law can indeed be realised; he specifically denies that there is any contradiction between patent law and antitrust law. Toyosaki then mentions that only certain conditions in licensing agreements can be considered part of the patent right. This is not the case particularly when the licensor tries to impose clauses on retail price maintenance.

The next academic article on the problem was published 20 years later by another intellectual property specialist, Monya.[15] Monya sees it as an issue of friction that the AMA may prohibit monopolies, while the Patent Act may cause them. However, both laws aim at the development of domestic industry. In that respect, market monopolies cannot be justified by a patent right, as they often lead to an inhibition of competition in research. The purpose of the patent monopoly is not the protection of a strong position in commerce, but rather the possibility of obtaining a just reward. This should also determine the scope of section 23.

Kawaguchi[16] takes the view that section 23 should be deleted. Rather, a comparative analysis on the respective scopes of protection of both patent law and anti-monopoly law should decide on the scope for the application of sections 3 (undue restraints of trade) and 19 (unfair business practices) of the AMA.

Also Shôda[17] takes the view that section 23 is a self-explanatory provision that stipulates, first, that exclusive rights related to real property are not contrary to the competitive order, and, second, that a contract whose object is the intellectual property right as such (for example licensing) is recognised as part of the exclusive right. Shôda then takes the view that the exercise of intellectual property rights in toto should be made subject to the provision of the AMA. Where a single patent right would become a market monopoly, the provisions on monopolistic positions (section 8(4) AMA) could apply. Acts of private monopolisation could be the strategic purpose or non-use of rights in order to curb the competitive freedom of other entrepreneurs. The same could hold true for the termination of licensing agreements or the refusal to license. This could be likened to a refusal to deal as stipulated under the AMA.

Negishi[18] regards intellectual property rights as 'competition laws in the broader sense'. In his view, both the AMA and intellectual property laws complement each other. Intellectual property rights would stimulate dynamic competition, while the AMA provided methods to curb restrictions resulting from the unfair use of intellectual property rights. Both the AMA and intellectual property rights should be interpreted as preventing acts of unfair copying, free-riding on the achievements of others, and the undue exploitation of achievements without due cause. Particularly the latter aspect could explain why the AMA prohibited the use of intellectual property rights in order to achieve restrictions that could not be justified by the scope of the right as such. The exercise of intellectual property rights for purposes other than prevention of copying and piggy-backing constitute an abuse of such rights and are subject to the AMA.

Nakayama[19] regards the stated purpose of the Patent Act as well as the Antimonopoly Act as basically identical despite different wording. He sees both laws as supporting each other in order to achieve a wholesome development of industry. Nakayama thus regards section 23 as having only declaratory character.

The most detailed analysis was undertaken by Hienuki.[20] Hienuki takes the view that intellectual property laws on the one side and the AMA on the other share no common purpose, yet complement each other in the development of the economy. In fact, the so-called monopoly granted under patent law was a right to prevent or eliminate patent infringements, which could be likened to a form of competition by way of undue copies. Section 23 AMA was a provision that confirmed that the prevention of patent infringement by way of competition through undue copying would not amount to a contravention against the free and fair competition and thus would not contravene the purpose of protection of the AMA. On the other hand, the AMA would apply once the exercise of the patent right had effects that limited competition, and where such limitation of competition was primarily done for the purpose or with the effect of suppressing normal competition. Hienuki's point of reference is section 100 of the Patent Act and the right to request injunctive relief and damages against acts considered infringing. Acts undertaken by the patentee with such purpose in mind are consistent with free and fair competition, as the AMA only protects competition based on achievements rather than on imitation. Hienuki explains his view in relation to private monopolisation, undue restraints of trade and unfair business practices, according to which acts of private monopolisation may be the aggressive and active investment policy of the market leader, the strategic purchase of patents by a market leader or the aggressive exercise of patent rights by way of warning letters and unjustified threats. Particularly interesting are Hienuki's views on cases of patent pools, cross-licensing agreements and patents in co-ownership where several patentees practise a joint licensing policy. The discrimination of one member in a group should be considered an act of domination by the majority of members and thus a case of private mono-polisation. The exclusion of an outside entrepreneur from membership in a patent pool or cross-agreement without just cause should also be considered an act of private monopolisation. To what extent an act would contravene section 23 AMA would not depend on the formal or literal meaning of the patent right, but rather would be judged according to the contents of the act and its effects on the real market.

Finally, Shibuya[21] mentions three new aspects. First, that a refusal to license should not be considered a case of private monopolisation, because the Patent Act already offers the possibility of granting compulsory licences, a provision tailor-made for prevention of the non-use of patents and thus taking preced-ence over remedies under the AMA. Furthermore, Shibuya considers the use and exercise of homemade inventions as exempt from section 23, yet not the use and exercise of patent rights purchased from third parties. The use of homemade inventions and patent rights could be likened to a natural mono-poly, the use of purchased ones could be likened to attempts of private mono-polisation. Finally, Shibuya mentions section 6 of the old Unfair Competition Prevention Act of 1934 that exempted acts under intellectual property rights from the application of the law. Shibuya notes that this provision was basically identical to section 23 and might have served as a reference. The old provision in the UCPA could only be invoked against charges of causing confusion in trade, yet not in connection with licensing agreements.[22]

It is interesting to note that despite differences in the details, both intel-lectual property as well as antitrust specialists are of the unanimous opinion that section 23 does not justify restrictive clauses in licensing agreements. The application of the AMA to restrictive clauses in licensing agreements has consequently been the primary focus of the FTC's practice.

B. Guidelines of the Fair Trade Commission on licensing agreements

1. General remarks

As a country of sparse natural resources and enormous industrial backward-ness (in 1868), Japan was keen to import foreign technology in order to make optimum use of it. In order to do so, joining the Paris Convention for Protection of Industrial Property in 1900 was viewed as instrumental. At the same time, mechanisms had to be developed, allowing for a control of contractual provisions that subjected the use of foreign technology in overly restrictive terms. The FTC, set up by the US Occupation under the AMA of 14 April 1947, seemed ideally suited for this task after a relaxation of foreign exchange controls in the mid-1960s no longer necessitated permission of international agreements by the Bank of Japan.

The FTC published its first guideline on antitrust rules for patent and know-how licensing agreements on 24 May 1968.

These guidelines, very short and heavily biased towards a protection of the (presumably) Japanese licensee, were substituted by new ones as of 15 February 1989. These guidelines introduced a distinction between clauses that were always lawful (white clauses), clauses that in certain circumstances would constitute unfair trade practices (grey clauses), and those that were always deemed unlawful (black clauses). Also for the first time, the guidelines clearly distinguished between patent and know-how agreements, and provided for an informal clearing procedure before the agreement was concluded. The 1989 guidelines were subsequently complemented by the 1991 Guidelines on the Distribution System, the 1993 Guidelines on Joint Research and Development, and were finally repealed by the new Guidelines of 1998 on Patent and Know-How Licensing Agreements (see the following section, Doctrinal approach on restrictions on patent and know-how licensing agreements).

The strictest interpretation of the guidelines can be detected between 1975 and 1980, and the most frequently cited clauses were those for grant-back and non-use of competing products.[23]

Licensing agreements that involved intellectual property rights had to be notified to the FTC under a guideline issued in 1971. The duty of notification concerned only international agreements, was limited in 1992, and completely abolished in 1997.

2. Doctrinal approach on restrictions on patent and know-how licensing agreements

The underlying considerations of the FTC when issuing the Guidelines of 1968, 1989 and 1999 were basically the following:

(i) Cases where the licensor imposed sanctions on the licensee for contractual clauses that were unenforceable;

(ii) Restrictions on the licensee's research capacity; and

(iii) Use of the leverage of the IP right in order to impose other restrictions that are deemed anti-competitive.

Apart from these three types, the FTC has also pursued anti-competitive behaviour on a horizontal level and attempts to stymie otherwise permissible parallel imports (see p. 267 below).

Cases of (i) can best be exemplified by the FTC's *Nihon Record II* decision.[24] Here, certain manufacturers of audio discs had tried to prevent shops from renting out these discs to customers. Since the Copyright Act at that time did not provide for any specific rights of rental and lending, the obligation was unenforceable, as the rights over these audio discs were exhausted by the first sale. It was anticompetitive to try to enforce the restriction by way of a boycott against these shops.

Case (ii) concerns limits imposed on the licensee in further developing the licensed technology, or unilateral grant-back clauses, without due remuneration.[25]

Case (iii) concerns other restrictions imposed on the licensee, for example tie-in sales[26] or resale price maintenance schemes.[27]

3. FTC Guidelines for Patent and Know-how Licensing Agreements

3.1 General remarks The above three considerations could be called the basis for the promulgation of the Guidelines for Patent and Know-how Licensing Agreements. Considerable differences between these Guidelines can be explained by two factors: first, the first Guidelines of 1968 assumed that the licensee, in principle, was in a weaker bargaining position. Furthermore, the Guidelines of 1968, and to some extent those of 1989, did not sufficiently take into account the agreement as a whole and rather focused on individual clauses. This was of particular relevance when determining the lawfulness of grant-back clauses.

The yardstick for the evaluation of vertical restraints is section 2(9) of the Antimonopoly Act ('unfair trade practices') and the more specific FTC Guidelines on Unfair Trade Practices of 1982.[28] These Guidelines mention 16 cases of unfair trade practices, of which the following should be mentioned: concerted refusal to deal; discrimination; tie-in sales; trading on exclusive terms; resale price maintenance; dealing on restrictive terms; abuse of a dominant bargaining position, and interference with a competitor's business transactions. In connection with licensing agreements, particular attention focused on clauses that were deemed to be a dealing on restrictive terms, or an abuse of a dominant bargaining position.

The 1999 Guidelines[29] take a more balanced view and have considerably reduced those clauses regarded as unlawful per se. For the first time, the guidelines include horizontal restrictions and interpret the above-mentioned section 23 of the Antimonopoly Act.

The following vertical restraints are deemed unlawful:

(i) Abuse of a bargaining position by imposing an obligation to pay royalties after expiration of the patent right; licensing more than one patent as a package if unnecessary for the technology involved; requiring the licensee to assign rights over improvement inventions without compensation or granting exclusive licenses for improvement inventions without corresponding obligations of the licensor.

(ii) Prohibiting the licensee from challenging the patented technology,[30] from manufacturing competing products or employing competing technology after the expiration of the licensing agreement, or other restrictions, to the extent that they have a measurable impact on the market, for example preventing the licensee from asserting his own IP rights against the licensor or restricting the licensee in sales activities of the patented products.

Retail price maintenance schemes are a violation per se.

3.2 Details   The 1999 Guidelines consist of four parts. The first contains a preface and a number of introductory remarks and definitions. The second concerns the above-mentioned FTC view on the relationship between section 23/21 AMA and patent licensing agreements. The third part is completely new and contains the FTC's viewpoint on patent licensing agreements and undue restraints of trade or private monopolisation. These aspects are considered in further detail below (see p. 267). Finally, the fourth part contains the relationship between patent licensing agreements and unfair business practices. Only the last part corresponds to the contents of the previous Guidelines of 1968 and 1989. The Guidelines distinguish between four kinds of vertical restraints: restraints concerning the scope of the licence; restraints concerning ancillary restrictions, obligations, etc.; restraints and obligations in connection with the manufacture of patented products, etc.; and finally, restraints and obligations in connection with the sale of patented products. The previous two Guidelines followed a different structure and distinguished between white, grey, and black clauses. These are now listed within the different categories.

Black clauses, that is, prohibitions per se, concern only retail price maintenance and the restriction of retail prices. Other restrictions, previously labelled as black, have moved into the grey area. This is particularly true for limitations on research and development activities, and obligations for the transfer or exclusive licensing of improvement inventions. In these cases, reasonable grounds for the restriction may render it lawful. In the case of transfer or exclusive licensing, reasonable grounds can be the joint ownership of improvement inventions, appropriate payments made in consideration of the transfer, or an obligation only for those countries where the licensee does not plan to engage in business activities. Other grey clauses are: limitation on the manufacture and use of competing products, limitations on the sales of competing products, the limitation on the sales territory, the calculation of the licensing fee according to the number of products sold (that is, unrelated to use of the patented technology), the obligation to license several patents unless necessary for the use of the technology, obligations not to challenge the patented technology, obligations against the licensee not to invoke the licensee's own patent rights against the licensor, unilateral rights of termination, agreements on maximum production figures, limitations on the sources for obtaining raw materials, parts, etc., obligations with respect to quality of the patented products, limitations on sales numbers, restrictions on customers, restrictions on the sale of competing products, and finally, obligations to use a certain trade mark, etc. These grey clauses are generally measured against the General Guidelines of 1982, in particular, undue restrictions of contractual freedom or tie-in sales. Some of the clauses are more grey than others. Particularly the obligations to pay licensing fees after the expiration of the patent right, limitations in research and development activities, unilateral obligations to transfer improvement inventions, and restrictions in the manufacture, use and sale of competing products are prohibited unless the licensor can show particularly good reasons for such clauses. For the other grey clauses, all circumstances of the case will be considered.

However, all clauses limiting the licensee will be judged against the prohibition of an abuse of a dominant bargaining position: where the licensor is found to be in a dominant bargaining position, any restricting clause may be deemed unlawful unless there are justifying reasons. Abuse of a bargaining position may occur when the licensee requires the licence for the continuation of his business and is thus forced to give in to the licensor's demands even when detrimental to the licensee's business. Additional factors would be the market position of licensor and licensee, the difference in size between licensor and licensee, the licensee's competitive position with respect to his customers, but not the value of the patent at issue.

In addition, the Guidelines list 15 white clauses that are not deemed anticompetitive:

(i) the division of a licence in manufacture, use, sale, etc.;
(ii) temporary limitations of the licence;
(iii) territorial restrictions;
(iv) restrictions in the field of technology;
(v) payment of the licensing fee according to the number of manufactured products where this simplifies the calculation;
(vi) obligations of payment after the expiration of the patent where these are deferred payments;
(vii) the obligation to license several patents where this is necessary to guarantee the functioning of the technology in the agreement;
(viii) the licensor's right to terminate the agreement once the licensee challenges the validity of the patent;

(ix) obligations to license back improvement inventions on a non-exclusive basis;
(x) obligations of information regarding improvements and experience with the licensed technology;
(xi) best efforts clauses;
(xii) obligations to manufacture a minimum number of products;
(xiii) obligations to purchase basic materials, spare parts, etc., in order to guarantee the effectiveness of the licensed technology or to maintain trust in the trade mark;
(xiv) obligations to maintain certain qualities in order to guarantee the efficacy of the licensed technology; and
(xv) obligations for minimum sales targets.

Finally, it should be noted that the lawfulness of territorial restrictions is now explicitly measured against the exhaustion rules. Since the latter assume an exhaustion of rights after the first sale, territorial restrictions that relate to exhausted goods can no longer be deemed unproblematic as such.

C. Guidelines of the Fair Trade Commission in research and development

The Guidelines of the FTC on joint research and development of 20 April 1993[31] apply to joint research and development projects where several enterprises are involved. Reference points for determining unlawfulness are the number of enterprises involved and their market share, the kind of research (basic research, applied research or development research), the necessity of joint conduct and the object and duration of the research. In more detail, the Guidelines distinguish between acts that

(i) concern the implementation of the project;
(ii) concern the technology developed by the project; and
(iii) relate to the products developed by such technology.

At all three stages, the Guidelines list white, grey, and black clauses.
  At the stage of implementation of the project, the following clauses are deemed grey:

(i) limitations in the use of technologies, unless such technologies are protected by know-how;
(ii) prohibition of the use of competing or similar technologies by one of the parties involved, unless for implementing the project.

The following clauses are listed as black:

(i) limitations in the research and development in fields other than those concerning the project;

(ii) limitations in the research and development within the field of the project after its termination;

(iii) limitations concerning the application of already existing technologies vis-à-vis one of the parties, or restrictions in the grant of licences for such technologies to third parties;

(iv) limitations in the production or sale of competing products with the exception of those that have been developed under the project.

Regarding the technology developed by the project, the following clauses are deemed black (there are no grey clauses listed in this field):

(i) limitations in the research and development in using the developed technology;

(ii) obligations for the transfer or use of improvement inventions related to the developed technology on an exclusive basis.

Regarding the use of products manufactured under the jointly developed technology, the following acts are considered grey:

(i) restrictions on the sale or territory for the manufactured product;

(ii) restrictions on customers;

(iii) restrictions on suppliers of raw materials for the manufactured product;

(iv) obligation to meet certain quality standards.

The only black clause listed is one on retail price maintenance regarding the products sold.

Although the Guidelines concern an extremely important field, to the author's knowledge no relevant FTC decisions have been handed down. It is also interesting to note that the Guidelines on patent licensing have received far more academic attention than the Guidelines on research and development.

D. Patent pools and cross-licensing schemes

While the FTC has been very active in pursuing vertical restraints in technology transfer agreements, horizontal restraints ('undue restraint of trade' under section 3 AMA)[32] or attempts of private monopolisation (also, section 3 AMA)[33] were rarely subject to the FTC's scrutiny. Private monopolisation concerns unlawful means aiming at excluding others in order to maintain or increase market domination; undue restraints of trade refers to a decrease in competition by mutual agreements.

In its Guideline on Joint Research and Development of 20 April 1993 the FTC addressed the problem of undue restraints of trade in the course of technical cooperation agreements. It particularly identified restrictions regarding research activities, either outside the field of common research or beyond the contractual period of time, as unlawful. The same applies to restraints in research and development for jointly developed technology, restraints in the grant-back for improvement inventions and restraints in the sale of the developed products in terms of territory, suppliers, or retail price maintenance.

Restrictions in joint venture agreements may be objectionable when limiting competition between the partners setting up the joint venture. In one instructive case, a foreign and a domestic undertaking founded a joint venture meant to produce 'power shovels' with technology obtained from the foreign partner. The domestic enterprise agreed not to compete with the products developed by the joint venture and not to export certain products to a number of Asian markets. The FTC qualified this as an abuse of a superior bargaining position (unfair trade practice),[34] yet one might well argue that since the restrictions were not imposed on the recipient of the licensed technology, it should have been classified as a case of undue restraint of trade between two potential competitors.[35]

In the 1999 Guidelines for Patent and Know-how Licensing Agreements, the FTC for the first time offered a systematic approach on how to deal with private monopolisation and undue restraints of trade in connection with intellectual property rights.

Acts of prohibited private monopolisation are:

(i)   Forming patent pools or cross-licensing agreements and refusing to grant licences without justifiable reasons to new entrants or existing undertakings, or taking other means that have the effect of impeding the market entry of other undertakings;
(ii) Acquiring patents and behaving as described in (i) above; and
(iii) Using licensing terms aimed at the exclusion of outsiders.

The above shall apply in cases where withholding the licence makes it difficult for an undertaking to conduct business activities in a particular field of trade. In other words, the patent as a commercial monopoly must have become a market monopoly. This is more difficult if it is only one patent, and easier if a cluster of patents is involved. And it would constitute an abuse if a licence was withheld under conditions where the patent is deemed an essential facility for market entry.

Undue restraints of trade in connection with intellectual property rights can occur if several enterprises in a cross-licensing or patent pool agreement impose a mutual restriction on the sales price, manufacturing volume, sales volume, sales outlets, sales territories, or other aspects of the patented products. It would be immaterial if these restrictions were directly agreed upon, agreed through a trade association (this would make section 8 AMA applicable), or if made in the course of founding a joint venture.

Particular attention is given to the frequent Japanese practice of cross-licensing, of granting several non-exclusive licences, and of patent pools. In the case of cross-licences, any additional restrictions in the cross-licensing agreement on sales prices, quantities of production or sale, and territorial restrictions would be interpreted as undue restraints of trade if this had an effect on the market. The same would be assumed for limitations on research and development. In the case of licensing the patent to several licensees, the agreement on mutual restrictions on sales prices, quantity of production, etc., would be considered as an undue restraint of trade. Patent pools per se are not regarded as restricting competition, as they may have a pro-competitive effect. However, where the members of the patent pool agree on mutual restrictions of sales prices, quantities of production, research and development, this may amount to an undue restraint of trade.

Where cross-licensing agreements, open licensing schemes or patent pools are used in a manner contrary to the purposes of the system to stimulate innovation, this may also become a prohibited act of private monopolisation. The FTC would regard it as an act of private monopolisation where a cross-licensing scheme is set up for the purpose of accumulating all future improvement inventions made by members and where the scheme is meant to deny licensing the jointly held patents to new market entrants without justifiable reason.[36] Also the strategic accumulation of patents in order to prevent others from entering the market could be regarded as an act of private monopolisation. Restrictive clauses in licensing agreements concluded by a licensor holding a patent that has become a market standard would also be regarded as an act of private monopolisation.

Particularly with respect to the FTC's opinions on undue restraints of trade and private monopolisation in connection with patents, it has to be stressed that these views have never been tested in court. The FTC's views come close to the obligations of a market dominating patentee or patent pool to license on non-discriminatory terms. This view, it has to be stressed, is not universally accepted. However, the FTC has not rendered any decisions that would clearly spell out such thinking.

E. Decisions of the Fair Trade Commission related to IP rights

1. Overview

Due to its limited personnel, the FTC rarely renders more than ten formal decisions per year. It heavily relies on informal enforcement requesting the entrepreneur concerned to modify the infringing practice. Exceptions to this rule have always been international licensing agreements that could be examined fairly easily due to the notification requirement, and that usually entailed a formal measure by the FTC, presumably also because compliance with informal measures by foreign companies could not be as easily assumed as compliance by Japanese ones.

Between 1969 and 1996, the clause most frequently found in contravention of the FTC's Guidelines was a limitation imposed on the licensee in further developing the licensed technology, or unilateral grant-back clauses without due remuneration. There are a total of almost 2,000 cases in this respect.

Apart from that, the FTC would only take up those cases on a formal level that are of interest in further developing the law, or in clarifying a field that might be of future importance.

2. Clauses meant to limit the free distribution of (exhausted) products

2.1 Nihon Record II[37]   Here, certain manufacturers of audio discs had tried to prevent shops from renting out these discs to customers. Since the Copyright Act originally did not provide for any specific rights of rental and lending, the obligation as such would have been unenforceable, as the rights over these discs were exhausted by the first sale. The obligation thus clearly went beyond what the intellectual property right could grant to the owner, and it would have been anticompetitive to impose such a limitation on a commercial basis. Conversely, it was anticompetitive to try to enforce the restriction by way of a boycott against those shops renting these discs to customers.

2.2 Sony Computer Entertainment[38]   Here, the Sony Computer Entertainment company requested retailers and wholesalers to strictly comply with a policy of no discount, no second-hand sales and no under-the-counter sales. It would supply PlayStation products only to dealers complying with this request. According to the FTC, 'prohibiting the sale of second-hand products contributed to an effective implementation of the act of constraining the retail price of new PlayStation software, and can be regarded as a reinforcement thereof. Consequently, in this respect, the prohibition of the sale of second-hand products encompasses the act of constraining the retail price and overall is deemed detrimental to fair competition.' It has already been mentioned that at that time it was not entirely clear if game software should be regarded as film works (see p. 279 below, Retail of software video games), with the owner enjoying the additional rights of rental and lending, thus permitting restrictions on further levels of distribution. Regardless thereof, the FTC found that even additional rights of rental and lending could not justify an act prohibited per se, that is, retail price maintenance. The opinion is interesting insofar as the FTC did not look at the rights formally allocated to the copyright owner, but to the objective behind the exercise of such rights.

3. Post-contractual limitations

It has been mentioned above that obligations of the licensee to pay licensing fees after the intellectual property right has expired or restrictions of the licensee on the further development of the licensed technology would almost always fall foul of antitrust rules. The case of *Asahi Electrics*[39] concerned a licensing agreement over know-how transferred to a Taiwanese licensee. While the licensing agreement contained no specific post-contractual secrecy agreement, the licensee was not allowed to export products making use of the licensed technology into Japan even after the expiration of the contract. No time limit was contained in the clause. Another know-how licensing agreement was concluded between Oxylon Chemical and the same Taiwanese licensee, Chôshun Petrochemicals. The contract contained a comparable clause.

Bar any secrecy agreement after the expiration of the contract, the licensee was otherwise free to use the know-how as he saw fit. Under these circumstances, the contract is rather one of the sale of know-how than of licensing. In the case of a true licensing agreement, the licensee could be obliged to stop using the licensed know-how after the expiration of the contract, unless that know-how had become publicly known. The contractual clause limiting the export sales thus went beyond what could be requested under a contract for sale of an intellectual property right. The FTC held that the clause in question was an undue limitation of the licensee's business and thus unenforceable. Since the sale of the know-how made the Taiwanese enterprise an actual competitor, the contract could also be interpreted as an international cartel with the purpose of separating markets. Due to its effect on the Japanese market, the cartel could be prosecuted by the Japanese authorities.[40] A similar example of undue restraint of trade between two potential competitors has already been mentioned in the *Komatsu/Bicycrus* case (see p. 265, Patent pools and cross-licensing schemes).

4. Restrictions in cross-licensing schemes

In *Fujizawa Pharmacy*,[41] the latter company had been the licensee of a French patent since 1965. In 1970, three other enterprises also began to manufacture and sell the patented technology that related to the pharmaceutical. Fujizawa raised an infringement suit based on the French patent that had also been granted in Japan. After negotiations, three potential infringers and the licensee reached an agreement whereby the licensee would not object to the manufacture and sale of the patented product by the three potential infringers, while the latter would not challenge the patent's validity and would pay a royalty of 7 per cent to the licensee. In addition, all four enterprises would join forces in order to prevent the market entry of other competitors. The patent rights were to be held jointly by the three potential infringers, the licensee and the licensor, and patent infringement suits should be conducted jointly. No party would grant further licences to third parties or transfer any rights. The scheme was modestly successful, yet held to be anticompetitive and an undue restraint of trade. The first part of this agreement (according to this author) should not have been regarded as anticompetitive: It is common currency to conclude settlement agreements in order to avoid lengthy litigation. It is also common for patent infringement suits to be settled on the basis of an agreement stipulating that the potential infringer pay a certain licensing fee and in turn do not challenge the patent. The lawfulness of this behaviour has now explicitly been confirmed in the 1999 Guidelines. However, the further agreement to pool resources in order to exclude further competitors goes beyond the scope of section 100 of the Patent Act (prevention of infringements). The mutual dependence on each other (use of the patented technology by the potential infringers, obligation not to challenge the granted patent) makes all five players potential competitors rather than dependent licensees. For that reason, it would be correct to regard this case as one of undue restraint of trade.[42]

5. Patent pools

In 1997, the FTC for the first time had an opportunity to rule on an unreasonable restraint of trade by way of a patent pool.[43] The case concerned ten undertakings engaged in the production and development of pachinko slot machines, with an aggregate market share of 90 per cent and a turnover of around 4 million Euros per year. Over the years, the ten enterprises held all relevant patents for manufacturing pachinko machines and had set up a trade association for the slot machine industry in Japan responsible for the management of licences for such patent rights. Licences were not granted to outsiders. Licensing agreements with members contained a clause whereby the licence could be terminated in case one of the members was bought by an outsider. When the majority of shares of one of the members in 1985 was purchased by an outsider, the association promptly refused an extension of the licence. In 1995, the association refused the grant of the licence on behalf of an ex-member who had formed a joint venture with an outsider for the joint production of pachinko machines. The FTC found both activities unlawful: Both the clauses regarding a termination in the case of a takeover were deemed impermissible, as well as the refusal to grant a licence because it would lead to use of the technology by an outsider not bound by the association's restrictive terms.

F. FTC's studies on intellectual property and competition policy

1. In general

It is common for the FTC to set up so-called 'study groups' prior to the enactment of new guidelines or prior to taking a legal stance towards certain behaviour. This procedure is also common in other fields of law and has two advantages. First, the Japanese administration has no specific think tanks that could conduct in-house studies on a certain complicated legal or political issue. It is thus advisable to ask for outside assistance. Second, the enactment of guidelines falls within the inherent jurisdiction of the FTC under section 2(9) AMA, yet their content is open to challenges before the courts. The views of the study groups and final reports are regularly published, and guidelines are enacted where there is a certain consensus within the study group regarding a specific topic. The study groups themselves are normally convened from the private sector: the Federation of Japanese Industry, academia, and practising attorneys.

The enactment of the Patent Licensing Guidelines of 1968 and 1989 was of course preceded by the convening of study groups. However, only in the last decade has the topic of intellectual property and antitrust been of primary interest within the larger framework of Japanese politics. The Japanese Government set up the Strategic Council on Intellectual Property in March 2002 and an intellectual property policy outline was published in July of that year. The outline also addressed the issue of intellectual property and antitrust:

> Although a strengthening of intellectual property is inevitable in the information age, and as a nation we should make efforts towards this goal, the strengthening of rights also brings with it adverse effects such as obstacles to the principle of competition due to monopolies and the abuse of dominant position ... Such adverse effects resulting from efforts to strengthen intellectual property rights must be eliminated. Competition laws such as the Antimonopoly Act focus on the elimination of obstacles of competition and must be strengthened. In the United States, the antitrust law is also strictly applied to intellectual property monopolies. This engenders competition and leads to the development of new industries. Japan, too, must find a balance and take the appropriate responses.

As a response to this study paper, the Basic Intellectual Property Act was enacted in March 2003 and in section 10 states that 'when promoting measures concerning the protection and use of intellectual property, it is necessary to keep in mind its fair use and the interests of the public, and consideration must be given to promoting fair and free competition'.

The following reports have been published by study groups in the last couple of years:

2. Report of the study group on technical standards and competition policy, July 2001

The study group dealt with de facto and de jure standards. De facto standards are those that emerge from one superior or dominant technology and are usually owned by one company only. This company should then not be permitted to unlawfully broaden its de facto monopoly, for example by tie-in sales of the dominant with related products.[44] In the case of de jure standards, that is standards agreed on by a standard-setting organisation or several companies, it would not be permissible to curtail the development in competing technologies by the companies participating in the forum, or to deny outside companies access to R&D results. Denying licences to outsiders for patents that have become standards is viewed as problematic, yet no firm stance has been taken.

3. Study group on software and the Antimonopoly Act, March 2002

The study group dealt in particular with software licensing agreements and the dominant marketing positions of platform software providers. Its recommendations found it impermissible for a provider of platform software to engage in discriminatory treatment of manufacturers of hardware or of software applications to which technical information is provided, to impose refusals to deal or not permit hardware manufacturers or software application providers to deal with alternative suppliers or customers, or to oblige a transfer of rights and know-how relating to proprietary technology that these hardware manufacturers or software application providers have developed themselves. Such type of unilateral grant-back clauses should not be permissible.

4. Study group on patents and competition policy for new technical fields, June 2002

This study group dealt primarily with patents in new fields such as business software and biotechnology. It first pointed out that patents in the field of business models are a new phenomenon and have not been granted in the past. For that reason, there is no prior art that can be properly relied upon, making it very likely that patents with a broad and unclear scope will be granted, and that a good many patents may be prone to invalidation. In other words, the problem with these patents is the fact that the examination procedure as a filter for unpatentable subject matter to be weeded out will not function. Regarding biotechnology-related patents, these are often positioned at the most extreme stage in the R&D process that infer broad rights for which there are no substitutes. There may also be patents on fundamental and universal research tools whose use is difficult to circumvent. The report points out that improper licensing agreements or the refusal to license such patents may seriously hamper the incentives for R&D. Here, a strict application of the AMA is recommended.

5. Study group on digital content and competition policy, March 2003

The study group report focused on the very specific topic of the legal relationship between TV production companies and TV stations and the division of copyrights between the two. Here, TV stations, often in a dominant bargaining position, request transfer of copyright from the TV production companies without good cause. Further issues addressed by the study group were the dissemination of content over a network, the management of copyright to content, and the technical means that the legal system has for protecting content. No recommendations were made with respect to these points, however.

III. Competition policy in IP legislation

Traditionally, intellectual property owners in Japan have not been in a particularly favourable position vis-à-vis infringers. In particular, the enforcement system in the civil courts proved clumsy and not particularly adapted to the enforcement of IP rights.[45] Apart from this problem, intellectual property rights were interpreted by the courts rather narrowly and, more often than not, imitation was given preference over innovation. Only in a very few cases could the legislature or the courts be convinced that the ultimate goal of intellectual property laws to stimulate innovation and creation required additional rights. In the sections covering the purpose and outline of intellectual property laws (p. 250) and antitrust law and policy related to intellectual property rights (p. 253) two examples are given for copyright and unfair competition prevention law. On the other hand, the section dealing with the Guidelines of the Fair Trade Commission in Research and Development (p. 264) shows how Japanese lawmakers from the very start (1885) thought it necessary to install safeguards against overly broad monopolisation and in favour of further research and development for protected inventions. Legislative attempts to balance intellectual property and competition have been less consistent than the corresponding attempts of the FTC (see section II above) and the courts (see section IV below, Competition policy through the interpretation of intellectual property rights). The need for such a balance, however, has been reiterated by section 10 of the Basic Intellectual Property Act 2002, that specifically mentions the need to curb abuses of intellectual property rights.

A. Copyrights, rental and lending of phonograms

The case of additional rental and lending rights for phonograms is instructive because it led to the introduction of such a right in the TRIPS Agreement.

In the 1980s, an increasing number of phonogram rental shops opened in Japan, and by the mid-1980s their number was estimated at around 1,900. Japanese copyright law did not provide for any rights of rental and lending after the first sale of a phonogram. What made matters worse was the fact that next door to many rental shops the same shop owners often offered customers the possibility of copying the rented phonograms on tape. It was thus quite clear that these activities dented the profits of phonogram producers, although their claim that the customers, for the most part penniless students, would otherwise have purchased originals was looked on with scepticism in Japan.[46] Attempts by the phonogram industry to instigate a boycott of these rental shops was regarded as a violation of the AMA by the FTC (see section II.A above). However, successful lobbying by the copyright industry culminated in the enactment of a provisional act on the right of copyright owners and others to control the rental of commercial phonograms on 2 December 1983. Subsequent legislation (Law No. 46/1984) came into force on 1 January 1985 and led to the new provisions contained in sections 26(2), 95(2) and 97(2) of the Japanese Copyright Act. The main feature of the newly introduced provisions was an exclusive right over rental and lending to copyright owners, phonogram producers and performing artists for a period of between one month and one year, and for the rest of the protection period, a right of equitable remuneration. The exact duration was to be determined by a governmental circular. True to Japanese fashion, the phonogram industry and the rental shops representatives reached an agreement whereby the rental of new phonograms would be permitted two months after the first date of marketing, but limited to 20 per cent of the total repertoire of a phonogram producer. The picture was further complicated by foreign phonograms that in principle would only become protectable after Japan joined the Rome Convention in 1989. But even upon accession, there was no obligation to grant further rights of rental and lending, as such rights were not stipulated in the agreement. Still, due to US pressure, comparable rights over rental and lending were eventually granted to foreign phonogram producers as of 14 December 1994 (Law No. 112). In contrast to domestic phonogram producers, foreign producers were unwilling to engage in any informal negotiations on the exact protection period and insisted on the maximum provided by law, that is, an exclusive right to prohibit rental and lending for the first year after commercial marketing.

Legislation in this case was based on the assumption that phonogram producers would not be given their fair share if uncontrolled rental and lending were to continue. Similar arguments are voiced today in connection with Internet copying services such as Napster, Gnutella, etc. The argument rests on the assumption that those who rent or copy would otherwise purchase an original, which is not particularly convincing given the limited purchasing power of the potential buyers.

B. Protection of investment by prohibiting slavish imitation

It has been mentioned that the UCPA in Japan is a more flexible instrument in the area of protection against denigration or passing-off than legislation in common law countries. In particular, the UCPA has been used to plug uncomfortable gaps in intellectual property legislation where widespread copying would lead to an undue abuse of financial and creative efforts by imitators. This was exactly the purpose of section 2(3) of the Japanese Unfair Competition Prevention Act, newly introduced in 1994. The provision prohibits 'the act of transferring or dealing in (including the display for such purpose), or exporting or importing products that imitate the configuration of another party's products (excluding such configurations as are commonly used for such or similar goods, or that fulfil an identical or similar function or effect), provided that no more than three years from the date of first commercial distribution have elapsed'.

The Drafting Committee explained the reasoning behind this new provision as follows:

> Introducing a new product contributes to society in that it enhances progress. Prohibiting the imitation of newly released products is problematic insofar as a general prohibition would distort free competition and obstruct progress. On the other hand, making an identical copy would deprive the first person to put such goods on the market of the incentive for development and would therefore not be fair. Thus, when considering to what extent imitation should be made illegal, a balance has to be struck between society's need for progress and the need of people marketing products for incentives. The requirements of economic development and social benefit should both be taken into account. The object of intellectual property laws is the protection of creative efforts by way of granting a specific right. Hitherto this has been thought as the limit of the extent to which imitation should be prohibited. However, the object of the Unfair Competition Act is to prevent certain unfair acts, against which civil remedies (injunction, damages) can be granted in order to maintain the system of fair competition. Especially in view of recent developments in copying and reproductive technologies, the increasingly shorter life cycle of products and the way in which retail structures have developed, it has become increasingly easy to deprive persons of the benefits of their financial and manpower investment by developing imitative products. While the costs and risks of marketing copied products have decreased greatly, so has the benefit to the person who first puts goods on the market. So much so, that the competitive relationship between the person who copies and the person who has developed the products has become unfair, and the incentive to develop original products and put them on the market has been reduced. In this situation, the possibility that the system of fair competition will collapse cannot be ruled out. Therefore it is necessary to recognise that direct imitations of another's goods down to the millimetre represent an act of unfair competition. In this way it will be possible to protect another's financial and human investment in the development of goods if there is also a possibility of choice in order to make them differently, regardless of the fact that protection under industrial property laws may be available or not (so-called 'dead copy').[47]

To be sure, there would not have been any rush to legislate but for the Tokyo High Court's decision of 17 December 1991, which ruled the identical copying of another person's design an infringement of commercial interests under the general tort clause of the Civil Code (section 709): 'If an enterprise is responsible for the production and sale of goods whose value is enhanced by their original design, it must be regarded as an infringement of business interests if a third party sells identical goods of virtually the same design in the same geographical area at a lower price. According to the principles of free and fair competition, such an action has to be regarded as unlawful, as the protected business interests of a third party are infringed by unlawful means.'[48]

The Tokyo High Court's decision fell short of granting an adequate remedy, as section 709 of the Civil Code is generally considered a remedy against financial loss only. Thus, only the damage claim was upheld, while the claim for injunctive relief was dismissed. The inclusion of a provision against identical copies in the Unfair Competition Act remedied this shortcoming. In addition, ministerial guidance in matters of unfair competition might have suffered significantly if the courts had gone on to deliver judgments in an area unregulated by special provisions. It can thus be considered as in the interests of the Ministry of Trade and Industry that a special provision against certain forms of copying was included in the law, although this provision does not exclude the application of the Civil Code in cases outside the scope of the Unfair Competition Act.[49]

The provision is an interesting attempt to balance rights of imitation and protection of innovation in a competition-friendly manner. Other countries have tried to do the same, by, for example providing for the protection of unregistered designs. It is clear that although anti-competitive, acts of imitation outside the scope of intellectual property law cannot be prohibited by the AMA either. For that reason, it was necessary to enact specific legislation.

C. Compulsory licences for dependent inventions

The current section 72 of the Patent Act states the obvious: that the grant of a dependent patent does not allow the patentee to use the invention unless consent has been obtained by the owner of the prior right. The provision is self-evident, as the patent as such does not give a right to use, but rather a right to exclude others. Section 92 of the Patent Act allows the patentee of the dependent patent to request a non-exclusive licence from the owner of the basic patent. To this end, the owner of the dependent patent has to engage in consultations, and if these bear no result, the Patent Office may ultimately decide. As mentioned above, such provision was already contained in the first Japanese Patent Act of 1885 and was regarded as an important tool for achieving the Patent Act's goal of promoting innovation and enhancing the level of technology. The Patent Act does not stop here, however. It gives the owner of the basic patent a form of counterclaim to also request a non-exclusive licence from the owner of the improvement patent. This remedy was also already contained in previous laws. The system had been abolished with the new Patent Act of 1959, but was reintroduced when Japan for the first time allowed patents for pharmaceutical substances in 1975.

The system described above may serve an important goal, yet is of no practical relevance. There has not been a single case reported where consultations for the grant of a licence were requested.[50] But just as in the case of compulsory licences in general, the value of this provision can be seen more as a threat rather than in terms of the actual use that has been made of it.

IV. Competition policy through the interpretation of intellectual property rights

While the foregoing section III has dealt with attempts by the legislature to properly limit the scope of intellectual property rights, this section deals with the interpretation of intellectual property rights by the courts. Some of these cases appear quite distant from parallel efforts of the FTC to properly interpret the AMA with respect to intellectual property rights, yet others neatly complement the FTC's case law as set out in section II.E, FTC's studies on intellectual property and competition policy. This is particularly true for those cases that involve the interpretation of intellectual property rights in licensing agreements. What follows therefore distinguishes between the interpretation of intellectual property rights unrelated to licensing agreements and decisions in connection with issues of technology transfer.

A. Interpretation of intellectual property rights unrelated to technology transfer agreements

1. Clinical trials and generic drugs[51]

According to section 69(1) of the Japanese Patent Act, the effects of the patent right shall not extend to the working of the patent right for the purposes of experiment or research. It is self-evident that such an exception is necessary, for example, for verifying that the patented invention actually works. It is less clear to what extent experiments conducted for the purpose of obtaining approval from the health authorities also qualify as 'experiment or research'. The question is of enormous economic significance. If generic drug makers were permitted to conduct clinical trials with the aim of obtaining marketing approval already during the life span of a patent, marketing generic drugs could immediately start upon expiration of a patent. If, on the other hand, experiments were only possible after the expiration of a patent, the patentee could enjoy an effective monopoly for another couple of years. On average, the period required for clinical trials of pharmaceuticals is an astonishing 7.7 years.[52] The Supreme Court ultimately upheld an interpretation that allowed such clinical trials already during the life span of a patent.[53] The Supreme Court particularly relied on the fact that a patent monopoly under no circumstances could be extended over more than 20 years. In particular, the Supreme Court gave the following reasons:

(i) By granting an exclusive use of a certain invention for a limited period of time in exchange for a disclosure of the invention, the patent system promotes inventive activity. Yet at the same time, the patent system provides the general public with the opportunity of using these publicly disclosed technologies, thereby contributing to the overall development of industry. It is one of the basic principles of the patent system to allow anyone to exploit freely a new technology after the expiry of the patent term, thereby generating a benefit to society.

(ii) For reasons of safety in the production of pharmaceuticals, the Pharmaceuticals Act requires their prior approval by the Ministry of Health and Welfare. The corresponding application must be accompanied by various data obtained from clinical trials, which have to be conducted over a certain period of time, even if the approval relates to a generic product. It is necessary to manufacture and use pharmaceuticals within the scope of the patent right in order to conduct such clinical trials. It stands to reason that if such clinical trials would not qualify as 'experiments' under section 69(1) of the Patent Act, they could not be conducted as long as the patent remained in force. As a result, third parties would not be in a position to exploit freely the patented invention for a certain period of time even after the patent had expired. This, in turn, would contradict the basic principles of the patent system.

(iii) However, patent law would not allow third parties to manufacture and use components of patented pharmaceuticals during the lifespan of a patent beyond what would be required under the Pharmaceuticals Act in order to obtain government approval. Limiting the exemption in this way, the patent owner would still be able to reap the commercial benefit of exclusively exploiting his invention for the lifespan of the patent right. Extending such protection to cover also clinical trials conducted by generic drug makers carried out for the purpose of obtaining government approval would effectively prolong the lifespan of the patent, a benefit that cannot be said to be intended by the Patent Act.

Thus, the Court's attempt to balance intellectual property rights and aspects of free competition becomes quite apparent in this decision.

2. Cases related to parallel imports in order to stimulate domestic competition

This is further explained under section V (p. 284 below) in relation to patents, trade marks and copyrights.

3. The retail of software video games

In Japan there is, of course, an enormous economic potential for rental or retail sales of computer software for games. However, the copyright owners of such games opposed attempts to set up such an industry, relying on the rights of rental and lending accorded to film works under section 26(1) of the Copyright Act, and even applying for these rights after their works were first put on the market. The courts ultimately denied that the additional rights of rental and lending should apply to computer game software, as the rights mentioned in section 26 were introduced in order to stimulate the production of film works meant to be shown in movie theatres. Without such additional rights, the economic risks of film production would not correspond to the expected rewards, thus stymieing creative production in this field. These considerations, however, could not apply to video software. The Supreme Court[54] further mentions the following issues:

> In the course of enacting the present Copyright Act, section 26 (1) on the distribution right was introduced in order to meet the obligations imposed by the Berne Convention for the Protection of Literary and Artistic Works (revised in Brussels on 26 June 1948) which provides for such a distribution right with regard to cinematographic works. That such a distribution right was only provided for cinematographic works is due to the huge investment into a film production and the necessity of an effective capital return by controlling the film circulation; when the Copyright Act was enacted, the above-mentioned distribution system was customary, which was mainly based on the rental of a number of copies, and because the act of showing the film without the consent of the copyright owner was hard to control, it was necessary to control the previous act of distribution, including ownership transfer and rental. Starting from this situation, section 26 of the Copyright Act is interpreted in that the right to transfer or to rent (Copyright Act, sections 26 and 2 (1) (xix)) a cinematographic work or its reproductions within the above-mentioned distribution system for the purpose of public display does not exhaust upon first sale. Section 26, however, provides for no further rule which would give a definite answer to the question whether the distribution right exhausts or not, so that this question must be understood as left open to interpretation.
>
> Consequently, with regard to the assignment of ownership in reproductions of cinematographic works intended for use on home TV game devices and not for public showing, and from the viewpoint of securing a smooth market circulation of goods ... the right in the public transfer of these works is exhausted. Once legally assigned, it has achieved the purpose of its

grant, so that the copyright has no more effect on the act of subsequent
public distribution of computer game reproductions.

Thus, the case is another example where the courts have narrowed the scope
of an intellectual property right (or differently worded, broadened the scope
of an exception) based on considerations of competition policy and the
underlying goal of intellectual property laws in general.

4. Unjustified threats for alleged infringement of intellectual property rights

Two different types of undue exercise of intellectual property rights should
be distinguished, although academic writings sometimes seem to mix them
up:[55] first, the act of denigration that requires an alleged infringement to be
circulated to third parties; and second, the undue exercise of an intellectual
property right as such (for example by court action) as an act of unduly
interfering with a competitor's business. The first is discussed under 4.1, the
second under 4.2.

4.1 Acts of denigration   Undue exercise of an intellectual property right
by way of denigration requires infringement not only to be claimed against
the alleged infringer, but in particular to be communicated to third parties. If
the infringement has not been positively established by a court, the allegation
of infringement is no more than an assumption. Such an assumption can be
very damaging to the business reputation of the alleged infringer, as trading
partners may stop commercial dealings with the alleged infringer, not least
for fear of being held liable for contributory infringement. Cases brought
against such cases of denigration seem to have started in the mid-1970s,[56] and
have been used ever since.[57]

   In the cases concerned, the defendants were quite candid in their allegations. Either, the alleged infringement was communicated to the plaintiff's
trading partner, or else widely published in newspapers.

   Since these acts went far beyond the first step of ascertaining the infringement against the alleged infringer, the courts in the past practically imposed a
no-fault liability for such acts: 'Unless there are specific facts [to establish
infringement], the defendant in stating that there is infringement is assumed
to have acted negligently.'[58] Perhaps in view of some academic critics,[59] a
2002 High Court decision has introduced a rule of reason for determining the
unlawfulness of such warning letters to third parties:

> When a patentee warns to customers of a competitor by stating that the
> competitor's product infringes patentee's patent, and when (i) the invalid-
> ation judgment of the patent is finalized, or (ii) the judgment that declares
> non infringement is finalized afterwards, such warning by the patentee is
> a prima facie unfair competition act as 'the spreading of untrue facts'.

However, in certain case, such warning are regarded as the legal exercise of patentee's patent right and it is a legitimate conduct ... It must thus be determined whether the warning letter directed at customers of the competitor was part of the exercise of the patent right or rather beyond what was necessary according to common sense. Whether such letter was part of the exercise of the patent right or only formally complied with such exercise should also be determined by looking at the synthesis of the negotiation process with the competitor until the warning, the timing and the distribution of the warning letter, the number and range of customers the letter was distributed to, the size and type of business concerned, the relationship and the style of dealing with the competitor, the allegedly infringing products, the way a patent infringement can be dealt with at the level of customers supplied with the allegedly infringing goods, the reaction to the distribution of the warning letter, the conduct of the patentee and the customers after the distribution, and other circumstances.[60]

The court's reasoning is difficult to apply in practice and – to this author – is not particularly convincing. After all, a registered right under no circumstances carries the irrebuttable presumption of validity. For one thing, alleging unlawful behaviour without a ruling by the courts should be entirely at the risk of the defendant. And second, in the Japanese environment which treasures long-term economic relationships and responds very sensitively towards allegations of unlawful behaviour, spreading word of an infringement either by directly addressing the plaintiff's trading partners or by publication in newspapers is extremely effective, but for this very reason also extremely dangerous. Imposing a no-fault liability thus seems justifiable.[61]

If the court finds the allegations either true,[62] or for other reasons not damaging to the plaintiff's business,[63] the claim is dismissed. In all other cases, the court would grant injunctive relief and damages for loss of reputation, and sometimes require an apology.[64]

The claim is time-barred after three years from the date the misleading information was first disseminated, even though it may only be established later that no infringement had occurred.[65] As a result, the alleged infringer will have to raise the claim for denigration as a counterclaim in the infringement suit in order to avoid such time-bar.

4.2 Other cases of improper exercise of an intellectual property right To be actionable under the Unfair Competition Prevention Act, false allegations imply a communication to third parties. The mere threat of suing, or the actual suit brought against the alleged infringer, may be harassing or vituperative, yet does not qualify as an act of denigration. In the absence of a remedy of this kind, the plaintiff has an actionable cause only under section 709 of the Civil Code, which provides neither for injunctive relief, nor for a presumption of damages such as can be found under intellectual property laws and the

Unfair Competition Prevention Act. For these reasons, there is a notable lack of court decisions on the subject.

In the well-known *Parker* decision,[66] the plaintiff and parallel importer of genuine goods tried to enjoin the defendant (and sole import distributor) from preventing the importation of genuine goods, as the latter was able to do under the rules of the Customs Office at that time. While the Court held that the plaintiff's imports and sales did not infringe upon the defendant's trade mark licence, it refused to grant injunctive relief on the basis that this was 'available only in special cases such as when there is direct interference with business activity coupled with unethical intent; then, there is a right to have this infringement stopped based upon the right to unhindered business activity'.[67] The Court also refused to accept that the (unwarranted) request of the defendant to the Customs Office to have the allegedly infringing goods seized at the border could qualify as the dissemination of false allegations.[68]

As yet, the FTC has not explicitly dealt with the improper exercise of intellectual property rights by way of denigration as an antitrust offence. Remedies under antitrust law should be considered where the Unfair Competition Prevention Act does not grant sufficient remedies, however.

B. Decisions in connection with licensing or transfer agreements

1. Non-competition clauses and scope of patent rights

In the *Drilling Device* case,[69] the licensor had obliged the licensee to produce and sell the licensed technology only according to the contractual terms. The licensed technology referred to a patent application whose scope after the conclusion of the agreement was substantively narrowed. Thereupon, without the licensor's consent, the licensee produced technology that would have fallen into the scope of the initial patent application, yet not into the scope of the patent ultimately granted. The Supreme Court held that under these circumstances, the contract should be interpreted as referring to the narrower scope of the actually granted patent only, rather than the scope of the patent application. One could also have argued differently: it is a clear policy both of patent law and antitrust law to allow third parties to manufacture technology that is not otherwise protected by individual rights. Preventing the licensee from the use of 'free' technology would thus run counter both to antitrust laws and the intention of the Patent Act. At any rate, the result is consistent with the underlying purpose of antitrust law.

2. Restrictions on export

In another decision the courts again interpreted a contractual obligation to be binding only within the scope of the underlying intellectual property right. Here the licensor had imposed an export ban on the licensee who was thereby not permitted to export the patented technology to other countries. The Court[70] held this clause not binding, as the object of the licensing agreement was a domestic patent only, and such right was unaffected by the export of the patented technology.[71] The same interpretation would have been more difficult to reach under antitrust considerations, as the AMA only applies to acts that have an effect on the Japanese market, which may well not be the case for export limitations.

3. Implied guarantees as to the working of the licensed technology

The anti-trust laws particularly of developing countries often contain provisions that oblige the licensor to furnish only such technology that is state of the art and that actually works. Examples of such provisions are to be found in China and Vietnam. While Japan's first Guidelines on Patent and Know-how Licensing Agreements of 1968 also aimed at the protection of the licensee, this protection has never actually encompassed determining the state of the art or workability of such patented technology.[72] This is correct: to the extent the technology is actually patentable, that patented technology can be the object of a licensing agreement; to the extent the licensed technology is not patentable, the licensee or any third party may well request revocation of the patent, exonerating the licensee from further obligations of payment. In the case of know-how, this equation does not function in the same way. A technology that cannot be successfully applied is not considered commercially valuable information which can be the object of know-how protection. The courts have thus made it the obligation of the licensor to see that the know-how licensed under the agreement can actually fulfil its purpose.[73]

4. Licences for certain acts of use

Also in accordance with the FTC's viewpoint on restrictions in licensing agreements, the courts have held that it is permissible for a licensor to limit the licensee to acts of sale and exclude acts of production, in other words, to split licences according to the acts of possible use that exist under an IP right.[74]

5. Obligations to use the licensed technology

In respect of use obligations, in contrast to the above decisions, the courts have not interpreted intellectual property rights in a particularly competition-friendly way. Obligations of use are common for patents and trade marks. Non-use can result in a request of a compulsory licence, or the possibility that the right is actually invalidated. For that reason, the use requirement has always been considered as an important counter-balance to the monopoly granted under an intellectual property right. Against the background of an industrial policy that encourages the actual use of inventions, one would assume that the courts have interpreted licensing agreements in a way that implied an obligation to use. However, this is not the case. Even where an exclusive licence has been granted, there seems to be no obligation to actually work the patent in the absence of any clear wording in the contract to this effect.[75] In practice, even a 'best efforts' clause is difficult to enforce, as it does not imply an actual duty to produce or sell, thus requiring the licensor to prove the licensee's bad faith, which is well-nigh impossible.[76]

Yet, with the exception of the use requirement, the courts have interpreted intellectual property rights in a competition-friendly fashion and thus considerably strengthened the point of view taken by the FTC under the AMA. Japan is thus a good example where the competition authorities and the courts have successfully complemented each other in defining the interface between antitrust and intellectual property laws.

V. The special case of exhaustion

A. Introduction

While legislation is mostly silent on the issue, decisions on the parallel importation of both patents and trade marks date back to the 1960s. The majority of decisions, however, were rendered in the 1990s or later and not only concern issues of parallel importation as such, but also the limits of domestic exhaustion in general. Also the FTC has taken an active stance in promoting parallel imports in order to weed out inefficiencies in Japan's notoriously complicated distribution system. In a nutshell, the approach of Japanese authorities towards parallel importation and exhaustion rules has been comprehensive, fairly consistent and generally pro-parallel imports.

B. Patents

1. Legislation

No legislation in the patent field has been enacted for the primary purpose of dealing with parallel imports. Section 68 of the Patent Act gives the patentee the exclusive right to commercially work the patented invention. Sections 2(3)(i) and (iii) of the Patent Act define 'working' as including the act of importation. The Act is silent on both domestic and international exhaustion, however.

2. Court decisions

2.1 Domestic exhaustion
2.1.1 General principle
The principle of domestic exhaustion has been defined by the Supreme Court as follows:

> According to section 68 of the Japanese Patent Act, a patentee shall have the exclusive right to work the patented invention commercially. In the case of

a product invention, 'working' means the acts of manufacturing, using, assigning, leasing, importing, or offering for assignment or lease of the product (s. 2(3)(i) Patent Act). Any person who has purchased products covered by a patented invention, either from the patentee or from a licensee with consent of the patentee, commits an act of use by re-selling these goods to a third party. Equally, such a third party who has obtained the patented products in such a way is, at least formally, working the patented invention when further leasing it, and would thus be liable for patent infringement. However, if patented products are sold domestically, either by the patentee or with his consent, the patent is deemed exhausted because it has fulfilled its purpose. The patent does not give rights to subsequent use of the patented product by acts of transfer or lease. First, patent law has to be understood as balancing the interests of invention protection, and the public benefit of society at large. Next, if a tangible object is transferred, the rights are obtained by the transferee, and the transferee obtains those rights that were originally vested in the transferor. Also insofar as patented products are distributed on the market, the transferee obtains an object from the patentee whose exercise of the right suggests that the right in further acts of re-sale has been transferred as well. If with respect to any acts of marketing patented products, the patentee's consent were necessary each time a transfer occurs, the free movement of goods would be seriously impeded, the smooth distribution of patented products would be hampered and, as a result, the interests of the patentee himself would suffer. This would run counter to the purpose of the Patent Act 'to encourage inventions by promoting their protection and utilisation so as to contribute to the development of industry' (s. 1 Patent Act). Finally, by making the invention available to the public, the patentee will have the opportunity to obtain the reward from selling the product or granting a licence for the use of the patent and thereby obtain a licensing fee. In order to protect the financial interests of the patentee who has made his invention public, it would not seem necessary to give the patentee or the licensee rights beyond the first act of marketing, as the patentee would then obtain an unnecessary double reward in the course of further distribution.[77]

Here, the Supreme Court follows a double line of reasoning. For one, the Court finds it reasonable that where property is transferred, also the intellectual property rights vested in such property should be transferred to the purchaser as well. This would come close to the common law doctrine of implied licence. However, the Court also bases its reasoning on the remuneration doctrine. The patentee should receive one reward for each patented item (usually by the act of first sale), and thereby exhaust patent rights for this specific article. Both grounds are very different. The first is based on considerations of contract law, the second on public policy. The difference becomes clear once the patentee withholds title. In such case, property does not change hands, and according to the first theory, neither would the intellectual property rights. Resale of the patented article by the purchaser in the second case might be a contractual violation, but not a patent infringement. The question is important as there are cases where one doctrine would lead to exhaustion, the other to infringement, as is subsequently shown.

2.1.2 Subsequent application of the exhaustion doctrine

A very good example of how the above principle is applied is provided by the *Acycrobil* decision.[78] Here, the defendant had obtained marketing approval for a generic drug containing the same active formula as the one described in the plaintiff's (Glaxo Wellcome) patent. Marketing approval would expire unless the products were actually brought on the market within six months from the date of marketing approval. The defendant thus purchased the plaintiff's pharmaceuticals containing the active ingredient, distilled the latter and used this basic patented substance for producing the generic drug. As the patentee had received the economic benefits deriving from the patent by the act of first marketing, he could no longer control further acts of commercial exploitation by the purchaser. The action was thus dismissed. The court applied the remuneration doctrine in this case and cited the Supreme Court's decision in this respect.

The outcome of the second case was more doubtful in light of the two above-mentioned theories. In the *Tissue Paper* case,[79] the plaintiff and patentee had supplied hospitals with tissue paper in patented dispensers. The patentee claimed that he had retained title in the dispensers and under such retention obliged hospitals to have the dispensers refilled with tissue paper only through the patentee. The defendant was a company that had refilled the dispensers with tissue. According to the first instance decision,[80] the plaintiff had validly retained title and refilling by third parties thus amounted to an infringement. The High Court found that the retention of title was invalid (as not clearly expressed) and refilling was permissible under the exhaustion doctrine, as the paper as such was not patented.

It is easy to see that the Court was uncomfortable with this sort of tie-in construction. Yet its legal reasoning is not convincing: a retention of title is nothing other than a failure to transfer property. Even if the retention of title was ambiguous or ambiguously expressed, the question must have been to what extent the plaintiff wanted to pass title. If this was not so, property was not transferred even though the purchaser was not aware of this, or may even have had a claim for such transfer to be made. In other words: unless the proprietor wanted to pass title, property did not pass. And in such event, the patented dispensers would still be the property of the patentee. The Osaka District Court's reasoning would be correct if the implied licence doctrine was applied: where property as such does not pass, there is no assumption that the intellectual property rights would, and the goods could therefore not be deemed exhausted. Their refill by a third party would amount to a commercial use. If exhaustion, on the other hand, is regarded as a public policy instrument (remuneration doctrine), the Osaka High Court may have reached the correct result: the hospital might have committed a breach of contract, yet in refilling the dispensers third parties merely used an item already exhausted. The result in this case does not depend on the question of whether property was transferred or not. Additional questions would be to what extent the hospital could be sued for breach of contract or to what extent the patentee tried to abuse his patent monopoly by imposing additional and unwanted services. Since the hospital was not sued for breach of contract these questions did not require an answer.

2.1.3 Acts of repair[81]

Even when applying the above principles, deciding cases between permissible repair and impermissible reconstruction is not easy.

The first case concerned a patented device for crushing stones. While the device as such was made to last for about two or three years, the life of the battering plate was about one week. Substitution of such plate by a third party was nonetheless deemed infringing.[82]

The case that attracted far more publicity concerned the refill of disposable cameras. The plaintiff Fuji held several utility models and designs related to 'units of film and camera', which in essence described the function of such disposable cameras. The defendant had recycled these cameras by inserting a new film and a new battery. In view of its patent, the plaintiff held this an infringing act. The Tokyo District Court agreed.[83] The District Court tried to draw the line between repair and reconstruction by arguing that the defendant's acts commenced at the very stage where the patented product's useful life had come to an end, and that invoking the patent right here would not amount to a double remuneration of the patentee. It further argued that the defendant was replacing an important part of the principle item essential to the invention. After the defendant's action, one could no longer speak of the same product.

It is interesting to note that the Federal Circuit[84] and the New Jersey District Court[85] reached the opposite conclusion. According to the US courts, the defendant's acts served the function of preserving the useful life of the cameras and could thus qualify as a permissible repair.

First of all, it is useful to clarify that the patentee's intention of how the patented item should be used has no influence on the breadth of the patent right. Thus, the reuse of disposable items as such cannot amount to infringement. Next, one should also note that the defendant did not replace patented items, but rather unpatented ones (the film and the battery). It is therefore not very convincing for the Japanese court to argue that a principal element of the patented item has been replaced.

In a case that received widespread publicity, the newly established Intellectual Property High Court had to decide on the refill of patented toner cartridges. The court developed a two-step test in order to distinguish repair from reconstruction:

> A patent right is not exhausted and the patentee can enforce its right in the following situations:
>
> – *Scenario 1:*   When a patented product is re-used or recycled after the patented product has fulfilled its original service life and thus fulfilled its function, or
> – *Scenario 2:*   When a third party adds or exchanges part or all of the substantial element of the patented invention of the patented products.
>
> Scenario 1 depends on whether or not the patented products have fulfilled their function (determination is made based on the patented products). Scenario 2 depends on whether or not the addition or exchange has been made to part or all of the substantial element of the patented invention (determination is made based on the patented invention).[86]

In the case at issue, the Court found the refill infringing, although no patented part of the cartridge was exchanged.

2.2 International exhaustion
2.2.1
The first decision on the international exhaustion of patent rights was rendered by the Osaka District Court in 1969.[87] The case dealt with the import of a secondhand machine from Australia via Hong Kong by the defendant. The plaintiff, a US company that owned a patent for the machine in Japan and Australia, successfully objected to such importation. The Osaka District Court held that the patentee enjoyed the unrestricted right of use within Japan. The Court discussed the problem of market separation, but felt bound by 'the basic principles of patent law' to protect national patent rights against free competition. For 25 years, this decision was regarded as the precedent on how the parallel importation of patented products should be dealt with.

In the *BBS* case, the Tokyo District Court at first instance basically decided along the same lines.[88] Already at that stage, some criticism was voiced by academic writers.[89] Still, it came as a considerable surprise when the Tokyo High Court overturned this decision on the grounds of the remuneration doctrine:[90]

> In the following, it shall be examined whether the importation and sale of products manufactured according to the above patent and manufactured and marketed by the patentee or with his consent, and subsequently commercially imported by third parties to Japan (so-called parallel importation of original goods) amounts to an infringement of the Japanese patent, which is held by the Japanese patentee for an identical invention. The question thus lies in determining whether the effect of a Japanese patent with respect to certain patented products, their lawful marketing

abroad by the same patentee should be taken into account or not. It has already been mentioned above that when determining the effects of a patent in Japan, taking circumstances abroad into consideration in no way contravenes the principles of independence of patent rights or territoriality. Even in section 29(1)(iii) of the Patent Act, events that have occurred abroad are considered as one of the legal obstacles to obtaining a patent right, i.e. the fact that an invention for which a patent has been applied has already been published abroad. Thus, also in the above-mentioned case, one should examine whether there are significant reasons that should be considered in order to balance the interests of the patentee with those of the general public in economic development. Viewed from this angle, it makes no legal difference whether the patentee markets his products abroad and is able to freely determine the prices for such patented products as a compensation for the publication of his invention, or if this occurs domestically with the consequence of exhaustion. Thus, the possibility of the patentee obtaining a reward for the publication of his invention is limited to one time. Taking into account the above doctrine of national exhaustion in correspondence with the economic development, it makes no material difference if the first commercial sale occurs domestically or abroad. The fact that borders are crossed are no reasonable grounds for giving the patentee another opportunity to economically profit from the publication of his invention. This is the more so against the background of international trade that has made Japan's economy and trade considerably international and will do so even more in the future.

The decision stirred a lot of controversy and was criticised by a number of eminent academics.[91] The former Managing Director of the Max Planck Institute, Friedrich-Karl Beier, even supplied an expert opinion to the court arguing that international exhaustion contravened the principle of independence of patent rights as laid down in Article 4bis (1) Paris Convention.[92] On the other hand, support was voiced for the decision as a prevention of parallel imports under patent law could hardly be justified for legal reasons.[93] The Supreme Court took slightly over two years to reach a decision. It rejected the High Court's theory of double remuneration at least in the international context as these 'considerations are not applicable if the owner of a Japanese patent markets the patented products abroad. For one thing, in the country where the products have been marketed, the patentee may not even hold a parallel patent that corresponds to the one in Japan. But even so, the domestic patent right and the parallel patent right in the country of marketing have to be regarded as separate rights. It cannot be argued that although selling the product under a parallel patent would give a double reward, it may qualify as an act of use of the domestic patent right.'[94]

Rather, the Supreme Court came out with the following solution:

> Yet some thought should be given to the relationship between the free movement of goods in international trade and the interests of the patentee.

In our present day society, international trade and economy affect us very broadly and permit conditions of rapid development. Even in the case that goods are purchased abroad, imported into Japan and put into circulation in the domestic market, there is the need to create conditions for the free distribution of goods, including their importation. Even if economic transactions have been made abroad, as a general principle, the transferee obtains not only the object as such, but also the rights vested therein. In other words, the transferor transfers his rights. To enable such transactions and to set the conditions for international trade in modern day society, it is assumed that the patentee who has transferred the ownership of patented goods abroad has also endowed the transferee or any subsequent purchaser with the right to undertake further transactions with third parties, including the importation to Japan, use in Japan, and transfer of ownership on our domestic market.

Opposed to the above concept, a domestic patentee who markets patented products abroad and wishes to exclude their sale and use by subsequent purchasers, has to make clear his intention of such a restriction when dealing with the transferee, and has to clarify such restriction on the patented goods for the benefit of subsequent purchasers. In the absence thereof, such acts cannot be understood as a use of the patent in Japan. That is to say:

(i) According to the above, if the patented products were marketed abroad, then it can be naturally expected that such goods may be imported into Japan if the patentee puts such goods into circulation abroad without any reservations at the time of transfer. The transferee or any other subsequent purchaser is understood to have purchased the product without any restrictions that might apply to such products in Japan.

(ii) On the other hand, if the patentee reserves his rights at the date of transfer with respect to the use in Japan when selling the patented products abroad, at the time of transfer the patentee has agreed with the transferee that sale or use of the patented product should not be allowed in Japan. If clearly indicated on the products, such a restriction is also valid against subsequent purchasers of the patented product along the distribution chain even with a number of intermediaries. Here it is understood that the above products have been sold under certain restrictive conditions, and any purchaser is free if he wants to obtain products bearing such a limitation or not.

(iii) In the case where the marketing activities abroad have been undertaken by an affiliated company, a subsidiary or a person with the same standing as the patentee, the case should be treated as if the patentee himself had marketed the patented products.

(iv) In view of the fact that the transferee's right of further distribution of the patented products should be maintained, it appears correct to attach no importance to the existence of a parallel patent in the country of marketing.[95]

2.2.2 Evaluation

It is worth mentioning that the above Supreme Court decision does *not* endorse the principle of international exhaustion as was advocated by the Tokyo High Court and as would be applied to provide an in-built limit to the patent right. Rather, the Supreme Court states that there is an assumption of exhaustion of rights unless the contrary was clearly indicated on the goods at the time of transfer. One can of course speculate why the Supreme Court would have applied a doctrine that has its roots in common law and is basically the one applied by the English courts in comparable cases.[96] One explanation might be that the Supreme Court wanted to open up the Japanese market to parallel imports, yet felt that doing so under the High Court's theory would render it subject to too much criticism as that solution, while advocated by academics, had not found favour with any courts abroad. In choosing the implied licence doctrine, the Court in effect allowed parallel imports without completely depriving the patentee of the right to stop them.

No subsequent cases have been reported, which may also be due to a change in the relevant customs provisions that would allow patentees to oppose parallel importation only when the goods are clearly marked to this extent.

C. Trade marks

1. Legislation

Section 25 of the Japanese Trade Mark Act gives the owner the exclusive right to use the registered trade mark with respect to the designated goods or designated services. 'Use' is defined in section 2(3) as the acts of applying the mark on goods or packaging, displaying trademarked goods, advertising, etc. Acts of infringement under section 37 are, inter alia, use of a trade mark similar to the registered mark in respect of the designated goods/services or similar ones. Also the act of importation is mentioned.

There is thus no provision explicitly dealing with parallel imports.

2. Court decisions

2.1 Function of trade mark Trade mark law is meant to guarantee the source of origin and the quality of goods as well as to protect the goodwill of the trade mark owner:

> It is the purpose of the law to protect the special functions of a mark: as a designation of the source of goods, as a guarantee of the quality of goods, and as a symbol of the goodwill of the trade mark owner as acquired by use of the mark for his goods. At the same time, a certain trading pattern is sought to be maintained so that customers can ascertain the identity of goods based on their source and so that they do not make wrong choices in

purchasing but rather obtain the desired goods having proper quality; thus the interests of consumers are safeguarded. As stated above, these functions are the subject of protection, and this protection is not only for the benefit of the trade mark owner but also for the benefit of the public at large. It can be said, therefore, that trade mark law as compared with other areas of industrial property protection is characterised by its very strong and common interest aspects. The scope of protection is also limited by public policy considerations within the framework of the principle of registration, even though basically a trade mark can be characterised as a private property right.[97]

On this basis, the courts have consistently held that only acts that cause confusion as to the origin are deemed trade mark infringements. Thus, the courts have held that it is not a case of trade mark use where the mark is not associated by the general public with an indication of origin, for example in cases of title in a CD,[98] or an eye-catcher.[99]

Further, the trade mark owner commits an abuse of rights when invoking the mark contrary to its function, especially where the public associates the trade mark with a different origin than the registered trade mark owner.[100]

2.2 Parallel imports[101]
2.2.1 The first cases
In the 1960s, the parallel importation of trademarked goods was held infringing in a number of cases. These cases are only of historical interest, however, and have been largely forgotten.[102]

2.2.2 The *Parker* decision
In *Parker*,[103] the defendant company Shriro was the sole import distributor of Parker fountain pens in Japan. The plaintiff's company NMC had obtained original Parker pens from Hong Kong and tried to import them to Japan, whereupon the defendant asked the customs office to confiscate the shipment. The plaintiff argued that the import could not be considered illegal; although the importation constituted a formal infringement under the Trade Mark Act, trade marks were not meant to protect legal monopolies for trade mark owners, but, as stated in the Trade Mark Act preface, 'to ensure the maintenance of the business reputation of persons using trade marks by protecting trade marks, and thereby to contribute to the development of industry and to protect the interests of consumers'. Applying this standard, the parallel importation was thus allowed, as the business reputation of the trade mark owner did not suffer from the importation of genuine goods and consumers were not misled:

> If the trade mark is registered for the same person domestically and in
> a foreign country, there are many European precedents holding that

exhaustion of foreign trade mark rights as a result of lawful marketing of goods by the foreign trade mark owner in the foreign country has effect also for domestic trade mark rights, and that this does not conflict with the principle of independence of the mark pursuant to the Paris Convention ... Both the Parker goods sought to be imported and sold by plaintiff and the Parker imported and sold by defendant are identical and indistinguishable as to their quality. Therefore, there is not likelihood of confusion as to the source or quality of goods when goods with the Parker trade mark are imported and sold by plaintiff; the functions of the trade mark are not impaired thereby. If the expectations of consumers concerning goods with the Parker mark are not adversely affected, then there is no impairment of consumer protection, and, further, the business standing of *The Parker Pen Company* as owner of the trade mark and its interests regarding marketing of goods are not jeopardised. When a world-famous trade mark such as the present one is involved, consumers will generally not be interested in whether the mark is registered domestically or in a foreign country; they buy goods with the mark, and also consider the statement of the place of production important ... Still to be examined is whether or not plaintiff's imports and sales interfere with fair competition. Defendant began to import Parker goods on a large scale around 1964, while the goodwill of Parker goods had existed in Japan long before this time ... With this course of events, it cannot be assumed that plaintiff [that is, the parallel importer] is taking advantage of defendant's advertising imports in order to engage in unfair competition in importing and marketing Parker goods; neither is the manner of importing to be considered as unfair.[104]

Prior to this decision, the soil had already been tilled by the Japanese academic S. Kuwata, who had translated the German Federal Supreme Court's *Maja*[105] decision that had allowed parallel imports for the same reasons. The case on behalf of the parallel importer was successfully argued in court by Dr. Shoen Ono, one of the foremost Japanese experts on trade marks and unfair competition law. The action succeeded because the goods were genuine, the Japanese trade mark owner and its foreign licensor could be regarded as the same entity and the general consumer did not associate the trade mark 'Parker' with Shriro and thus the latter had established no goodwill of its own.

2.2.3 Subsequent decisions
In the three cases that followed, the parallel importers could not meet the legal requirements set out by *Parker*; either the source of origin and the standard of quality was different,[106] or the close legal and/or economic connection between the Japanese and the foreign trade mark owner had ceased to exist[107] or never existed at all.[108]

The following two cases, however, broadened the scope of legitimate parallel importation. In *Lacoste*,[109] the plaintiff La Chemise Lacoste owned the trade mark 'Lacoste' in various countries, including Japan. The trade mark was licensed to the co-plaintiff, a Japanese company which produced and sold Lacoste goods in Japan. The defendants had obtained Lacoste goods from a US company in which La Chemise Lacoste held a 47 per cent interest. Although the quality of the goods imported by the defendants differed to some degree from that of those manufactured by the co-plaintiff in Japan, the Tokyo District Court dismissed the action for damages and held that even though the trade mark was owned by different entities in the US and Japan, the source of origin as well as the source of goodwill these goods enjoyed with the general consumer could be identified as 'Lacoste' and were thus identical. In the following case, it was ironically the very BBS company that enjoyed the benefits of parallel importation. The plaintiff in this case was an import distributor of German car parts who sought relief against the defendant importing original BBS parts whose serial numbers had been deleted. The trade mark registration was effected without consent of the BBS company, yet with the prospect of establishing a commercial relationship with the foreign trade mark owner later. The Court[110] examined (a) the relationship between the foreign and the domestic owner of the trade mark, and (b) the similarity of the parallel imports to those being domestically distributed. On the first issue, the Court found that though at the time of registration of the domestic trade mark there was no relationship between the Japanese entity and the German BBS company, the registration had been made with this prospect in mind, and that at the time of importation of the goods, a relationship had been established. On the second issue, the Court found that the goods were of the same origin and of similar quality despite the serial numbers being erased. Accordingly, the Court dismissed the action and allowed the parallel importation.

2.2.4 Alteration of goods

The *Lacoste* decision had found slight alterations of quality to be immaterial for the lawfulness of parallel importation. The case was again discussed much later in the *Fred Perry* decisions. Here the licensee was given the right to produce goods marked 'Fred Perry' in Singapore, Indonesia and Malaysia. In breach of the licensing agreements, the licensee also subcontracted production to China. Some of these Chinese goods then were imported to Japan, where the trade mark owner objected to their distribution. While it was clear that the parallel importation of genuine goods was not infringing, the issue was whether these goods could be deemed 'genuine'. The question was affirmed by the Tokyo District Court[111] and Tokyo High Court.[112] The Tokyo courts found that even though there was a breach of the licensing agreement, this did not make the goods infringing. After all, the goods were indistinguishable from those manufactured in Singapore and Malaysia, and the only thing that a third party could reasonably ascertain was the fact that there was a licensing agreement at all. To the extent that the goods could be attributed to the licensee, third parties should not be burdened with the risk that they had purchased pirated goods. In other words, the Tokyo courts stressed the importance of protecting third parties. However, the courts also stressed that the function of the trade mark in such case was not impeded:

> Even though the licensee committed a breach of the licensing agreement with his act, save in the event that the licensing agreement is terminated, this does not alter the fact that the goods have been produced and sold by someone who has obtained consent of the trade mark owner. The origin of the goods thus has to be attributed to the trade mark owner, and the function of indicating an origin is thus not impeded ... The existence of a breach of contract has no influence on the question to what extent the parallel importation of original goods is deemed lawful when judging trade mark infringement. Whether the goods were produced in the location as agreed upon or not is a matter that does not transcend the internal relationship between the trade mark owner and the licensee. In relation to third parties, the goods have to be attributed to the origin of the trade mark owner and the function of origin is thereby not impeded. Even though the trade mark owner may attach high importance to the location of production, the trade mark owner [in cases of breach] may do nothing other than take appropriate remedies to stop such breach of contract (for example by inspecting the goods or installing control mechanisms). This does not disadvantage the trade mark owner who can terminate the agreement upon breach of contract. If, on the other hand, these goods would not be deemed original, this would seriously harm the free distribution of goods and damage the interests of traders and consumers, thereby being contrary to the purposes of trade mark law.[113]

This result of course posed alarming prospects to licensors, who treasured the convenience of having their goods produced cheaply elsewhere, yet were unable or unwilling to monitor what their licensees were doing in late night shifts or in other countries. It thus came as a relief when the Osaka courts came to a different conclusion.[114] The Osaka courts found that the function of origin vis-à-vis third parties was only maintained where the goods were actually produced within what had been agreed upon in the licensing contract. This position was ultimately shared by the Supreme Court which held that such goods were infringing:

> In the case at bar, the source function of the trade mark is harmed by the importation of the disputed goods: Ocea, the licensee of the mark that is identical with the registered trade mark in Singapore and three other states, had the goods manufactured in a factory in China, which is not included in the licensed territory, and thus manufactured and marked the goods in breach of a provision of the agreement that relates to the scope of the licence. Restrictions in the licensing agreement that relate to the country of

origin and issues of subcontracting are also of great importance for controlling the quality of the goods and insuring the quality function by the
holder of the trade mark. The disputed goods, having been manufactured
and marked in breach of such restrictions, may harm the quality function
of the trade mark, since they could be out of the trade mark owner's quality
control and thus be different in quality as guaranteed by the latter for all
goods to which the registered trade mark is attached and that are put onto
the market by the defendant.[115]

Thus, the Supreme Court is not concerned with differences in quality as such,
but stresses that the lack of the possibility of supervision by the licensor
impedes the function of origin.

Interestingly enough, both sides base their arguments on the public interest: the Supreme Court with the public interest in the proper function of the
trade mark, the Tokyo courts with the consideration that trade would be
seriously impeded if there was no certainty whether the goods were original
or counterfeit. The second consideration is one of the theories in which
exhaustion is rooted: Josef Kohler argued that without the exhaustion principle, trade would be seriously hampered. The Tokyo courts have qualified
this approach by indicating that the public can be expected to take reasonable
care at least insofar as ensuring that a licensing agreement exists. The consideration of the Supreme Court would be convincing if the law established
the duty of the licensor to properly supervise the licensee as some trade
mark laws do. The Japanese Trade Mark Act, however, does not. Under
section 53(1), invalidation of a trade mark can be requested 'where the
owner of a right of exclusive or non-exclusive use uses the registered trade
mark or a similar trade mark in respect of the designated goods or designated
services or goods or services similar thereto in a way which may be misleading
as to the quality of goods or services or which may cause confusion with the
goods or services connected with any other person's business'. However, 'this
provision shall not apply where the owner of the trade mark right was both
unaware of the fact and had taken appropriate care'. According to the
Supreme Court, quality would extend to the possibility of supervision.
This, however, is apparently not how this provision should be interpreted,
as otherwise the Supreme Court would introduce an absolute duty of supervision that is not foreseen in the law. Rather, the provision seems to indicate
that the material quality of the goods must be different from what the
consumer expects, i.e. there must be a discrepancy between goods (previously
or currently) produced by the licensor and those produced by the licensee.
The trade mark can be invalidated only in those cases where the licensor
did not take appropriate care. In other words, the Supreme Court's reasoning would be convincing where the law stipulates the licensor's duty of
supervision, as otherwise the production and sale of unsupervised goods
by the licensee would trigger sanctions under trade mark law, for example

invalidation of the mark. Japanese trade mark law, however, does not stipulate such duty of the licensor. Rather, the licensor's duty is restricted to
preventing misconceptions in trade that stem from the expectation of the
public in a certain quality. Further, sanctions are limited to cases where the
licensor was aware of that fact or did not take appropriate care with respect to
this issue. Thus, lack of supervision, for example regarding the place of
production or the production numbers as such, is not a reason for invalid-
ating the mark. This being so, it would rather tip the balance towards an
interpretation of the 'public interest' that favours unimpeded trade rather
than interests that trade mark law regards as those of the licensor. In other
words, the licensor cannot have the cake of not having to supervise the
licensee and eat it by invoking the public interest when the licensee fails to
perform according to the contract. Where the law frees the licensor from
having to supervise the licensee, it is clear that such supervision is no longer
regarded as in the public interest, and the licensee's transgressions should
accordingly be qualified as a private interest between two parties, unless, of
course, under Japanese law such transgressions lead to misconceptions in
quality.

2.2.5 Repackaging

The first case of repackaging that came before the Japanese courts was decided
by the Osaka District Court and concerned the repackaging of US-made
garden fertilizer:[116]

> For the designated goods, the trade mark owner has the exclusive right of
> use over the registered mark (right of exclusive use), and has the right to
> prohibit third parties from using an indication similar to the registered
> mark (right of exclusion). The law thus protects against the use by third
> parties and since the use of the registered mark is reserved for the right
> owner, the mark can fulfil its function as an indication of origin or
> protection of quality to the extent that it can distinguish the trademarked
> goods from those of others. If it was possible for persons other than the
> trade mark owner to use the registered mark, especially those not having
> the trust of the trade mark owner, the result would be that faith in that trade
> mark would drop, and there would be the danger that the trade mark
> owner's goodwill would suffer harm, a result that the trade mark's function
> clearly does not have in mind. Therefore, the question to what extent the
> [repackaged] trademarked goods are original or not is not at issue, nor is
> the question whether the repackaging of trademarked goods carries the
> danger that the quality might be changed. Rather, taking the goods that
> have been put into circulation and distributed by the trade mark owner,
> and subsequently without his consent splitting them into smaller units and
> reaffixing a trade mark that is identical or similar to the registered one, and
> then putting these goods into further circulation ... affects the trade mark
> owner's exclusive right to use the registered trade mark for the designated

goods ... and can damage the trade mark owner's interests by impeding
faith in the quality of the goods.

In the subsequent *Viagra* case,[117] the Tokyo District Court confirmed this
approach. In this case, an importer had repackaged Viagra tablets into boxes
of a different size in order to cater to the needs of individual customers. The
defendant had promoted his activities through the Internet and other advertising media to the extent that it would import Viagra tablets on behalf of
individual customers. Upon receiving such orders, it would import Viagra
tablets with either 50 or 100 mgs of active ingredient and in package sizes of
10 or 30 tablets. It repackaged these into small units of 3, 6, or 15. The first
question in the case was to whom the active importation could be attributed,
the importation company or the individual customer. The Court found that
the company did not import as an agent of the customers, and was therefore
responsible for the act of importation. Further, the Court confirmed that
repackaging was a trade mark infringement, yet refused to extend the injunction to the act of importation as such.

D. Copyrights

1. Legislation

In contrast to patents and trade marks, the Copyright Act has a provision
which touches upon exhaustion, in section 26bis (2) of the Act:

(1) The author shall have the exclusive right to offer his work ... to the public
by transfer of ownership of the original or copies of the work ...
(2) The provision of the preceding paragraph shall not apply in the case of
transfer of ownership of the original or copies of a work under the
following conditions:
  (i) The original or copies of a work, the ownership of which has been
  transferred to the public by a person so authorised under the preceding paragraph, or with his consent; ...
  (iv) The original or copies of a work, the ownership of which has been
  transferred abroad, without prejudice to the right equivalent to that
  mentioned in the preceding paragraph or by a person who has the
  right equivalent to that mentioned in that paragraph or with the
  authorisation of such person.

The provision is somewhat clumsily worded, yet seems to indicate that acts of
first sale, be it domestically (alternative (i)), or abroad (alternative (iv))
trigger exhaustion. Exhaustion does not apply to the additional rights mentioned in section 26bis (1), that is, copies of cinematographic works specifically covered by section 26. The above interpretation is also given by
academic writers.[118] The revision was introduced in 1999.

2. Court decisions

2.1 Questions of domestic exhaustion   That the domestic first sale of ordinary copyrighted items exhausts further rights of distribution has never been questioned. What was extremely contentious, however, was the extent of section 26(1) of the Copyright Act that grants additional rights of rental and lending to film works, and according to the courts has the following function:

> According to the current Copyright Act, section 26(1), the copyright owner holds the exclusive rights of rental and lending. Together with the corresponding provision of the Berne Convention (Brussels revision) on the distribution right for cinematographic works, the following should apply: if the maker/author produces the film with the intention of presentation in a cinema and an indeterminate number of copies are made thereafter, the maker/author in order to secure his rental/lending rights in the film will make his consent to further distribution or assignment subject to payment to those cinemas to whom he has rented out the film for presentation. This shall serve the protection of the maker/author of a cinematographic work. Pursuant to section 2(1)(xx) of the Copyright Act, this right is independent of 'whether the transfer and lending of copies of a work to the public is made' with or without payment, and in the case of a cinematographic work or a work reproduced therein, it includes the transfer and lending of copies of such work for the purpose of making the cinematographic work available to the public. According to section 26(1) of the Copyright Act, the presentation in cinemas is only a special, but not the only, expression of the author's exclusive rights. To this extent it is obvious that the sale of videotapes meant for public presentation also falls under the rental/lending right in section 26(1) of the Copyright Act.[119]

In other words, film works enjoy inexhaustible rights over the subsequent distribution of works. The decision already indicates that this would apply only to films produced 'with the intention of presentation in a cinema', and not to other works that might also fall under the definition of cinematographic works, for example video games.[120]

The scope of works with 'inexhaustible' rights is thus limited to film works and other works that enjoy in particular rights of lending, for example phonograms, sections 95ter and 97ter Copyright Act (exclusive right of rental and lending for the first 12 months, thereafter upon equitable remuneration).

2.2 International exhaustion   There has been no copyright case directly related to international exhaustion of ordinary copyrighted works. The only precedent concerned the importation of video cassettes of a Walt Disney film. The Court prohibited further distribution, though not based on international exhaustion rules, but rather on the specific provisions of section 26(1) of the Copyright Act that would apply equivalently to domestic films:

> It was established above that Disney owns a rental/lending right in Japan in the cinematographic work and its copy. Through the unauthorised sale of the videotapes, the plaintiff infringed the copyright (rental/lending right) of the copyright owner in the film, Disney. As stated above, the copies were produced and distributed in the US with the consent of the copyright owner, the US Walt Disney company. The plaintiff purchased the copies from a US company and imported them. Therefore, the videotapes are parallel imported goods. According to the opinion of the plaintiff, Disney received reasonable compensation already through the sale of the video-tapes so that the further distribution of the videotapes purchased in the US within the country cannot constitute an impairment of the copyright owner in any way and thereby no infringement of the rental/lending right can be construed. If, within the country, consent of the copyright owner to the distribution of copies of a cinematographic work in the form of videotapes (as is the case with regard to parallel imported goods) does not exist, the lack of an infringement of the distribution right cannot be based on law or on relevant court decisions. As far as the Copyright Act gives the copyright owner certain exclusive rights under the provisions of sections 21–28, only the author or the party to whom he has assigned the rights or the exercise thereof is entitled to exercise such rights. This contains an unambiguous presumption in favour of protection of the author's rights. To this extent, the copyright owner currently decides for each country when a cinematographic presentation shall take place and when he, or third parties with his consent, put videotapes on the market to secure an adequate return in investment on the production of the film. If, for example in a country after the launch of the film, videotapes of that film are sold and these are parallel imported in great amounts into another country while the film is still being shown in cinemas, this means a substantial loss of interest in the presentation in cinemas, and in the end may lead to enormous damage incurred by the person who, without authorisation, undertakes the sale of the videotapes of the film financed by the copyright owner. Allowing the copyright owner in a film, i.e. a motion picture company, to decide on the time of the presentation, as well as on the sale of videotapes separately for each country, for Japan is an obligation under the Berne Convention with regard to cinematographic works. This obligation was met by the enactment of section 26 of the Copyright Act that regulates the exercise of the rental/lending right, and to that extent is also determined to serve the purpose of copyright as such, namely protection of the author. The videotapes in question were pro-duced and distributed in the US with the consent of the copyright owner. There, Article 109a of the Copyright Act and the first sale doctrine are applicable according to US copyright law. This means that after the first international release, a limitation of distribution or dissemination is not permissible. There is no sufficient evidence to assume that this consent also

includes the distribution in Japan, however. For this reason, infringement of the domestic distribution right by the parallel importation of the video-tapes cannot be ruled out just because of the consent to distribution on the US market. The above understanding leads to a limitation of the market for parallel imports and thereby to a limitation of price competition for videotapes of the film. The possibility of deciding on the time of distribution of videotapes in Japan regardless of other countries may also limit the conditions for a direct distribution of videotapes for the film here. That this right, which serves the protection of the author, disregards public use of cultural property or does not contribute to cultural development is an opinion that cannot be agreed to.[121]

In other words, the court bases its reasoning on the specific provision of section 26 and the domestic (inexhaustible) right of further distribution, not the importation as such.

E. Antitrust law

The Japanese FTC has always taken a very active stand in the promotion of parallel imports in accordance with the limits of intellectual property rights. The FTC issued its first guideline on parallel imports in 1987 and slightly revised its position in the 1991 guidelines concerning distribution systems and business practices.[122] According to the FTC, parallel imports facilitate the entry of foreign goods into the domestic market and thus confront the licensed distributors with competitive pressure in setting prices. Under the FTC guidelines, the sole import distributor is considered to have engaged in unfair trade practices under section 19 AMA and the general designation of unfair trade practices[123] when he:

(i) prevents parallel importers from purchasing genuine products in overseas markets;
(ii) obstructs retailers in the handling of parallel imports;
(iii) induces wholesalers not to sell to retailers handling parallel imports;
(iv) prejudices the marketing of parallel imports by alleging that they are counterfeit;
(v) corners parallel imports;
(vi) refuses to undertake repairs, etc., on parallel imports; or
(vii) obstructs the advertising of parallel imports.

Even before the publication of the above guidelines and in line with the decisions that held the parallel importation of trademarked, copyrighted and patented products as lawful, the FTC issued a number of warnings to entrepreneurs who tried to obstruct parallel imports.[124] The FTC also views refusal to guarantee maintenance and supply spare parts for parallel imported goods as an improper obstruction.[125]

F. Customs regulations

1. Trade marks

In response to the *Parker* case that allowed the parallel importation of trade-marked goods, the Ministry of Finance issued an order[126] covering the importation of trademarked goods which provides:

> This paragraph applies when a petitioner asks the Customs Office to prevent importation of goods bearing a mark identical to the petitioner's registered trade mark. If such goods are imported by a person other than the petitioner but are considered to be genuine goods legitimately distributed with such mark attached, they shall be treated as not infringing the petitioner's trade mark. The permission to make parallel imports of genuine goods extends to those goods which are legitimately trademarked and distributed by a person who is the trade mark holder in Japan or who has a special relationship with the latter so that both persons can be regarded as one person. But if the source or quality indicated or guaranteed by the trade mark attached to the goods thus distributed differs from the source or quality indicated or guaranteed by the trade mark under petition and the trade mark as used by the parallel importer is considered to be separately used under circumstances similar to those of the petitioner's trade mark, then in such cases those genuine goods should be excluded from Japan.

2. Patent rights

In response to the *BBS Car Wheels* decision, the Ministry of Finance amended the relevant directive on parallel importation[127] in the following manner:
Procedure upon the parallel importation of patented products:

(i) Patented products that have been brought into commerce abroad by the patentee or a related party (in the following: patentee) and have been imported into Japan by a third party that is not the patentee, infringe the domestic patent right upon importation only in the following cases:
- To the extent that the importer has obtained the goods and prior to such acquisition or distribution the importation to Japan has been mutually excluded between patentee and acquirer;
- To the extent that the importer has acquired the goods from a third party or otherwise and the patentee and acquirer prior to the acquisition or distribution have mutually excluded the importation to Japan, and this is clearly indicated on the patented goods.

(ii) Documents for proving that prior to the acquisition or distribution such importation has been mutually excluded can be, for example, the text of the contract or other documents.

(iii) In the following cases, a clear indication on the goods bearing such notification at the time of distribution is considered the following: on the goods themselves or their packaging, a seal is imprinted or branded, or a tag is attached, and these indications without difficulty draw the attention already prior to the acquisition to the fact that importation into Japan with the purpose of sale or distribution is excluded. In such circumstances, the indication made at the time of distribution is considered made at the time of importation.

These provisions also apply to the importation of goods protected by utility models or designs.

However, there seem to be no specific customs' rules on the parallel importation of copyrighted works.

Notes

1. G. Rahn, 'The Role of Industrial Property on Economic Development: The Japanese Experience' (1983) 14 *IIC* 449.
2. I. Nakayama and T. Takenaka, 'Overhauling Japan's Intellectual Property System for the 21st Century: Intellectual Property Basic Law and Its Implementation Through the Strategic Program', 35 *IIC* 877 (2004).
3. C. Heath, *The System of Unfair Competition Prevention in Japan* (Kluwer Law International, 2001) 56.
4. A detailed account of pre-war and post-war competition policy in Japan is given by E. Hadley, *Antitrust in Japan* (Princeton, 1970).
5. An interesting overview in this respect is provided by H. Iyori, 'A Comparative Analysis on Japanese Competition Law: An Attempt to Identify German and American Influences', in *Die Japanisierung des westlichen Rechts* (Tübingen, 1990) 227–54. See also, Y. Kanazawa, *Keizaihô no shiteki kôsatsu* (Historical Overview of Japanese Economic Laws) (Tokyo, 1985).
6. Supreme Court, 16 November 1972, 26-2 Minshû 1573 in *re Ebisu shokuhin kigyo kumiai*.
7. Supreme Court, 1 March 1978, 360 *Hanrei Times* 132, 134, *Orange Juice*.
8. Tokyo High Court, 9 March 1953, 6 Minshû 435, *Asahi*.
9. C. Heath, *The System of Unfair Competition Prevention in Japan*, 191–3.
10. R. Ishii, *Dokusen kinshihô* (Antimonopoly Law) (Tokyo, 2nd edn 1948) 278–80.
11. *Guidelines for Patent and Know-how Licensing Agreements*, FTC, July 1999, accessible at the FTC's homepage at www.jftc.go.jp, both in Japanese and in English.
12. FTC, decision of 1 August 2001, 612 *Kôsei Torihiki* 64 (2001) with comment by Suwazono, *Sony Computer Entertainment*.
13. Namely in cases where Shiseido and Kao, producers of cosmetics, insisted on sales by personal consultation, which inevitably led to high prices in the retail and outlet stages of distribution. Although it was fairly obvious that the scheme was meant to keep prices artificially high, the Courts denied this: Supreme Court, 18 December 1998, 1664 *Hanrei Jihô* 3, *Shiseido* and 1664 *Hanrei Jihô* 14, *Kao*.

14. K. Toyosaki, *Kôgyô shoyûkenhô* (Industrial Property Law) (Tokyo, 1956) 273 et seq.

15. N. Monya, *Tokkyo ken, know-how to dokusen kinshi seisaku* (Patent Law, Know-how and Anti-trust Policy), in *Dokusen kinshihô Course II* (Course on the Antitrust Law II) (Tokyo, 1976) 293 et seq.

16. H. Kawaguchi, *Tokkyo ken no kôshi to dokusen kinshihô no kankei* (The Exercise of Patent Rights, etc., and its Relation to the Antimonopoly Act, 21 *Keizaihô* 23 et seq. (1978)).

17. A. Shôda, *Zentei dokusen kinshihô I* (Commentary on the Antimonopoly Act, Vol. 1) (Tokyo, 1981) 223 et seq.; also idem, *Patentlizenzverträge im japanischen Antimonopolgesetz*, 1997 *GRUR Int.* 206 et seq.

18. A. Negishi, 'Chiteki zaisan kenhô to dokusen kinshihô' (Intellectual Property Rights and the Antimonopoly Act), 15 *Nihon Kôgyô Shoyûken Gakukai Nempô* 65 (1991).

19. N. Nakayama, *Kôgyô shoyûkenhô I* (Industrial Property Rights, Vol. I), (Tokyo, 1994) 38 et seq.

20. T. Hienuki, *Chiteki zaisan to dokusen kinshihô* (Intellectual Property and the Antimonopoly Act) (Tokyo, 1994).

21. T. Shibuya, *Tokkyo hô to dokusen kinshihô* (Patent Law and Antimonopoly Law), N. Kokusaika, 'Jidai no dokusen kinshihô no kadai' (The Task of the Antimonopoly Act in an Era of Internationalisation), *Writings in Honour of Akira Shôda* (Tokyo, 1993) 578 et seq.

22. K. Toyosaki, 'Unfair Competition in Japan' (1971) 2 *IIC* 372, 378.

23. Iyori and Uesugi, *The Antimonopoly Laws and Policies of Japan* (New York, 1994), 305–6. Complete statistics between 1969 and 1996 by Iyori and Uesugi, *Chiteki shoyûken to dokusen kinshihô* (Intellectual Property and Antitrust), 25–6 (Japanese only).

24. FTC, 15 December 1983, 389 *Kôsei Torihiki* 34, *Nihon Record II*.

25. Between 1969 and 1996, the FTC found a contravention against this prohibition in no less than 1,986 contracts: Iyori and Uesugi, *Chiteki shoyûken to dokusen kinshihô* (note 23 above), 25–6.

26. FTC, 14 December 1998, (1999) 30 *IIC* 478, *Microsoft*: 'The licensing of a computer program to manufacturers of personal computers with the obligation to license also other programs of the same software maker with a significant market share constitutes an unfair trade practice and is unlawful.' The case concerned the bundling of the programs 'Word' and 'Excel'.

27. FTC, 13 September 1965, 13 KTIS 72, *Yakult*: resale price maintenance scheme for imported patented products.

28. FTC Notification No. 15/1982, accessible at the FTC's homepage under www.jftc.go.jp (English text).

29. Accessible at the FTC's homepage under www.jftc.go.jp (English text).

30. Permissible, though, when agreed in a court settlement of an infringement action: FTC, 23 April 1982, 381 *Kôsei Torihiki* 21, *Fujisawa*.

31. Reprinted in English on the FTC's homepage, www.jftc.go.jp.
32. FTC, 23 April 1982, 381 Kôsei Torihiki 21, *Fujisawa*: the parties to a lawsuit used a settlement to agree on a licensing agreement that obliged the licensee not to sell below a certain price. The FTC viewed this as an unlawful restraint of trade, which it is not: it is rather a vertical restriction between licensor and licensee, and thus an unfair trade practice (resale price restriction): Iyori and Uesugi, *Chiteki shoyûken to dokusen kinshihô* (note 23 above), 40. FTC, 10 September 1993, 40 *KTIS* 3, *Fukuoka Sewage System*: concerned a joint activity of seven sewage companies, one the patentee, the others licensees, to agree on certain margins for bid-rigging schemes.
33. FTC, 19 September 1951, 3 KTIS 166, *Toho Subaru*: one market-dominating cinema tried to bully others out of the market by using its distribution rights for film works.
34. FTC, 26 October 1981, 28 KTIS 79, *Komatsu/Bicycrus*.
35. Considered by Iyori and Uesugi, *Chiteki shoyûken to dokusen kinshihô* (note 23 above), 39.
36. The example given in the Guidelines shows that the FTC does not regard the grant of a compulsory licence in such cases as a factor that would eliminate an antitrust violation or that should be given precedence over any measures taken under the AMA.
37. FTC, 15 December 1983, 389 *Kôsei Torihiki* 34, *Nihon Record II*.
38. See note 12 above.
39. FTC, 20 September 1995, 42 *KTIS* (official compilations on FTC decisions) 163, *Asahi Electrics*.
40. K. Eguchi, *Know-how licence keiyaku ni tomonau seigen jôkô no kôsei kyôsô sogaisei* (The Prevention of Fair Competition through Contracts in Know-how Licensing Agreements) (1996) 1089 *Jurist* 324.
41. FTC, 23 April 1982, 381 Kôsei Torihiki 27 (1982), *Fujizawa Pharmacy*.
42. T. Shibuya, 'Case comment in Dokkinhô shinketsu, hanrei hyakusen' (One hundred Decisions on Antitrust Law) *Jurist Special Issue* 141, 5th edn March 1997, 197.
43. FTC, 20 June 1997, 4 *Zeitschrift für Japanisches Recht* 148, *Pachinko Slot Machine*.
44. The case the study group had in mind was FTC, 14 December 1998, (1999) 30 *IIC* 478 1999, *In re Microsoft*. The case concerned the tie-in sale of the program 'Excel' together with the program 'Word'.
45. An overview is provided by C. Heath, 'The Enforcement of Patent Rights in Japan' (2000) in C. Heath and L. Petit (eds.), *Patent Enforcement Worldwide* (2005) 23 *IIC Studies*, 323–56.
46. S. Matsuoka, 'Copyright and Neighboring Rights Protection in the Japanese Record Rental Industry, Copyright' (1989) *Monthly Review of the World Intellectual Property Organization* 152.
47. Sangyo kôzô shingikai chiteki zaisan seisaku bukai hôkoku, January 1993, 15.

48. Decision of the Tokyo High Court, 17 December 1991, *Decorative Veneer* (1994) 25 *IIC* 805.

49. For slavish imitations outside the scope of the UCPA's provision confirmed by Osaka District Court, 29 June 1995, 242 *Hanketsu Sokuhô* 5 (1995), *Decorative Columns*.

50. As is reported by N. Nakayama, *Shûkai tokkyo hô* (The Patent Act Annotated) (Tokyo, 3rd edn 2000) 897.

51. Supreme Court, 16 April 1999 (1999) 30 *IIC* 448; Tokyo High Court, 31 March 1998 (1999) 30 *IIC* 454.

52. Figures for 1994/1995 reported by *The Economist*, 1 February 1997, 93.

53. Supreme Court, 16 April 1999, 30 *IIC* 448, *Clinical Trials III*.

54. Supreme Court, 25 April 2002, 1785 *Hanrei Jihô* 3 (2002).

55. For example, K. Shimamura, (1996) 49/5 *Patent* 67.

56. K. Dohi, 5 *Kôgyô Shoyûken Hôgakukai Nempô* 60 (1982): Tokyo District Court, 17 March 1972, 278 *Hanrei Times* 374 (1972); Osaka District Court, 10 September 1974, 6-2 *Mutaishû* 217 (1974); Tokyo District Court, 6 October 1975, 338 *Hanrei Times* 324 (1976), *Digital Watch*; Osaka District Court, 21 January 1976, 361 *Hanrei Times* 331 (1978); Osaka District Court, 15 December 1977, 386 *Hanrei Times* 138 (1979); Osaka District Court, 19 December 1978, 10-2 *Mutaishû* 617 (1978); Osaka District Court, 28 February 1979, 398 *Hanrei Times* 157 (1979); Tokyo District Court, 4 June 1979, 396 *Hanrei Times* 135 (1979); Osaka District Court, 29 June 1979, *Tokkyo Kanri Bessatsu* 554 (1979); Osaka District Court, 12 September 1979, *Tokkyo Kanri Bessatsu* 586 (1979); Tokyo District Court, 30 January 1980, *Tokkyo Kanri Bessatsu* 6 (1980).

57. More recent cases include: Nagoya District Court, 27 February 1984, 16-1 *Mutaishû* 91 (1984), *Walking Beam*; Nagoya District Court, 31 August 1984, 16-2 *Mutaishû* 568 (1984), *Magnetic Recorder*; Tokyo District Court, 19 December 1990, *266 Tokkyo To Kigyô* 46, *University Entrance Exam*; Nagoya District Court, 8 October 1992 (1993/10) *Patents & Licensing* 25, *Fungus Growing Device*; Tokyo High Court, 26 May 1993, 46/10 *Patent* 142 (1993), *Cap Transport Device*; Osaka High Court, 23 February 1993 (1993/10) *Patents & Licensing* 25, 1994/1 *AIPPI Journal* (Engl.ed.) 23, *Fish Processing Device*; Osaka District Court, 22 July 1993, 47/1 *Patent* 95 (1994), *Rice Seedling Mat*; Osaka District Court, 27 October 1994, 234 *Hanketsu Sokuhô* 11 (1994), *Swinging Doors*; Tokyo District Court, 26 December 1994, 236 *Hanketsu Sokuhô* 8 (1995), *Design*; Osaka District Court, 31 August 1995, 244 *Hanketsu Sokuhô* 4 (1995).

58. Osaka District Court, 29 June 1979, *Tokkyo Kanri Bessatsu* 554 (1979).

59. K. Dohi, 5 *Kôgyô Shoyûken Hôgakukai Nempô* 59 (1982).

60. Tokyo High Court, 29 August 2002, *Hanrei Jihô* 128, *Metal Powder II*.

61. It is sometimes very difficult to distinguish between alleging infringement and merely asking for further and better particulars, as a German decision shows (German Federal Supreme Court, 10 July 1997, I ZR 42/95, unreported): here, the defendants had not openly accused the plaintiff of infringing their

copyrights, but (very firmly) asked for further and fuller particulars of the plaintiff's allegedly better rights in the matter. This request was communicated not only to the plaintiff, but also to the plaintiff's licensee who subsequently terminated the contract. According to the German Federal Supreme Court, the request for further and fuller particulars did not constitute a denigration, but rather an exchange of information in order to protect the defendants' interests in the matter.

62. Tokyo District Court, 1 July 1995, (1996), 27 *IIC* 570 *Beauty and the Beast*: instead of suing against the parallel importation of video cassettes, the defendant had informed cinemas that the plaintiff was offering infringing copies. When he was sued for denigration, the Court found that distinct from normal copyrighted works, cinematographic works were granted additional distribution rights and thus the supply of copies without consent was indeed infringing.

63. Osaka District Court, 31 August 1995, 244 *Hanketsu Sokuhô* 4 (1995), *Teddy Bears*: a fairly difficult case involving two manufacturers of teddy bears who had accused each other of passing-off and other groundless allegations.

64. Damages were refused in cases where the defendant's allegations were not taken seriously: Osaka District Court, 27 February 1992 (1993/4) *Patents & Licensing* 19; damages for loss of reputation were granted, but no public apology was required by Tokyo High Court, 19 July 1995, 243 *Hanketsu Sokuhô* 8 (1995); while lost sales are most difficult to prove and only rarely accepted as a basis for damages (Osaka High Court, 23 February 1993 (1993/10) *Patents & Licensing* 25: 14 million yen, loss of reputation seems to be calculated at between 2 million and 3 million yen: Osaka High Court, 23 February 1993 (1993/10) *Patents & Licensing* 25: 3 million yen; Osaka District Court, 22 July 1993, 47/1 *Patent* 95 (1994): 2 million yen including the attorneys' fees.

65. Tokyo District Court, 13 May 1994, 236 *Hanketsu Sokuhô* 199 (1994); Tokyo District Court, 18 March 1996, 251 *Hanketsu Sokuhô* 10 (1996).

66. Osaka District Court, 27 February 1970 (1971) 2 *IIC* 325, *Parker*.

67. Osaka District Court, 27 February 1970 (1971) 2 *IIC* 325, 329.

68. While this is certainly correct, it is not quite in line with the above cases of Osaka District Court, 22 July 1993 (1994/1) *Patent* 95, *Rice Seedling Mat*. The Court regarded the request for an interim injunction (granted, but later overturned) as dissemination of false allegations. However, courts do not qualify as third parties (neither do the customs officers), and in the particular circumstances, the Court should have examined the question of negligence; at least on an interim basis, the Court was persuaded to find for the patentee.

69. Supreme Court, 19 November 1993, 1492 *Hanrei Jihô* 134, *Drilling Device*.

70. Tokyo District Court, 16 May 1963, 239 *Hanrei Jihô* 34 and 145 *Hanrei Times* 165.

71. The issue would be more problematic now that a specific right of exportation has been stipulated in the Patent Act in the wake of the TRIPS Agreement. Yet,

one could still argue that the right of exportation just as any other rights of use would be exhausted for specific goods once these are first marketed.

72. Tokyo District Court, 27 August 1998, 989 *Hanrei Times* 249.
73. Kobe District Court, 25 September 1985, 565 *Hanrei Times* 52, *Mangala*.
74. Osaka District Court, 28 June 1985, reprinted in *Hanrei licence hô* (Writings in Honour of Kazunori Yamagami) (Tokyo, 2000) 259.
75. Tokyo High Court, 16 September 1991 (1993) 24 *IIC* 391, *Liquid Fuel Component*. The first instance court had held the reverse, however.
76. District Court, 30 March 1979, 'Writings in Honour of Kazunori Yamagami, 407.
77. Supreme Court, 1 July 1997 (1998) 29 *IIC* 331, 333, *BBS Wheels III*.
78. Tokyo District Court, 18 January 2001, confirmed by Tokyo High Court, 29 November 2001 (2002) 15 *Law & Technology* 83, *Acycrobil*.
79. Osaka High Court, 1 December 2000 (unreported), Case wa 11089/1998 – *Tissue Paper*.
80. Osaka District Court, 3 February 2000.
81. K. Tamai, *Nihon kokunai ni okeru tokkyohô no shomô* (Domestic Exhaustion of Patent Rights), in Makino and Iimura, *Chiteki zaisan kankei sosho hô* (Claims Related to IP Enforcement) (Tokyo 2001) 233–56.
82. Osaka District Court, 24 April 1989, 21-1 *Mutaishû* 279.
83. Interim injunction of 6 June 2000, 1712 *Hanrei Jihô* 175, decision in the main action: Tokyo District Court, 31 August 2000, unreported, *Fuji Camera*.
84. *Jazz Photo Corporation* v. *U.S. International Trade Commission*, 264 F.3d 1094 (2001).
85. New Jersey District Court, *Fuji Photo Film* v. *Jazz Photo Corporation*, (2003) 1614 *Patent, Trademark and Copyright Journal* 447.
86. Decision of the IP High Court, Special Division (Grand Panel), 31 January 2006, Case No. Hei 17 (Ne) 10021 37 *IIC* (forthcoming). A critical comment is provided by C. Heath and M. Môri, 'Ending is Better than Mending', 37 *IIC* (forthcoming).
87. Osaka District Court, 9 June 1969, 1 *Mutaishû* 160, *Brunswick*.
88. Tokyo District Court, 22 July 1994, 1501 *Hanrei Jihô* 70, *BBS Car Wheels I*.
89. Especially T. Shibuya, *Tokkyohin no heikô yunyû ni tsuite* (The Importation of Patented Products) *Tokyo News*, 9 November 1994, 1, and 15 November 1994, 2.
90. Tokyo High Court, 23 March 1995, 1524 *Hanrei Jihô* 3.
91. For example S. Ono, *Heikô tokkyo to yunyu* (Parallel Patents and Importation), in *Chiteki zaisan to kyôsô hô no riron* (Writings in Honour of F.K. Beier) (Tokyo, 1996) 459; N. Koizumi, 563 *NBL* 13; 567 *NBL* 31.
92. F.K. Beier, 'Zur Zulässigkeit von Parallelimporten patentierter Erzeugnisse' (1996) *GRUR Int.* 1.
93. Yoshifuji, *Tokkyo hô gaisetsu* (Outline of Patent Law) (Tokyo, 10th edn 1994) 349; N. Nakayama, *Shûkai tokkyohô* (Patent Law Annotated) (2nd edn 1989) 631.
94. Supreme Court, 1 July 1997 (1998) 29 *IIC* 334, *BBS Wheels III*.
95. Supreme Court, 1 July 1997 (1998) 29 *IIC* 334, 337, *BBS Wheels III*.

96. *Merck* v. *Primecrown*, 13 July 1995, English High Court (1995) *Fleet Street Reports* 909.

97. Osaka District Court, 27 February 1970 (1971) 2 *IIC* 325, 326, *Parker*.

98. Tokyo District Court, 22 February 1995 (1995) *GRUR Int.* 607, *Under the Sun*: here, the plaintiff had registered the trade mark 'Under the Sun' for, inter alia, phonograms. The defendant had produced an album and called it *Under the Sun*. The Court held that the public would not regard the album title as the origin of the product and therefore dismissed the case.

99. Osaka District Court, 24 February 1976, 8-1 *Mutaishû* 102, *Popeye T-shirts II*. Here, a third party had registered the trade mark 'Popeye Plus Device' for, inter alia, clothing. The T-shirts were imported by a US company related to the copyright owner of the Popeye drawings. In the front, the T-shirts displayed a Popeye drawing and the word 'Popeye'. The Court held that the public would regard such drawing and script as an eye-catcher rather than an indication of origin. For the general public, the origin of clothing was normally displayed on little tags inside, rather than displayed on the outside in such a prominent fashion.

100. Kobe District Court, 21 December 1982, 14-3 Mutaishû 813, *Dorothee Bis*: here, the plaintiff was a retailer of original French Dorothee Bis goods and unbeknownst to the French company had registered the Dorothee Bis mark in Japan. After the contract was terminated, the defendant imported original Dorothee Bis goods to Japan, an act objected to by the plaintiff. The Court dismissed the action, reasoning that the trade mark here could not serve as an indication of origin, as the general public perceived Dorothee Bis goods as coming from the French company rather than the Japanese trade mark owner. One could say that this was a case of reverse parallel importation, further explained below for the 'BBS' trade mark case.

101. C. Heath, 'From *Parker* to *BBS* – The Treatment of Parallel Imports in Japan' (1993) 24 *IIC* 179.

102. Tokyo District Court, 29 February 1964, 3 *Kokusai Torihiki Hanreishû* 37, *Aspirin*; Tokyo District Court, 1 June 1964, 3 *Kokusai Torihiki Hanreishû* 45, *Parker I*; Tokyo District Court, 29 May 1965, 178 *Hanrei Times* 199, *Nescafe*.

103. Osaka District Court, 27 February 1970, 2 *IIC* 325, *Parker*.

104. Osaka District Court, 27 February 1970, 2 *IIC* 325, 328, *Parker*.

105. German Federal Supreme Court, (1964) *GRUR Int.* 202, *Maja*.

106. Fukui District Court, 29 March 1974, Case 40/1972, *Ramie*.

107. Tokyo District Court, 31 August 1973, 301 *Hanrei Times* 267, *Mercury*.

108. Tokyo District Court, 31 May 1978, 10-1 *Mutaishû* 216, upheld by Tokyo High Court, 22 December 1981, 13-2 *Mutaishû* 969, *Technos*.

109. Tokyo District Court, 7 December 1984, 1141 *Hanrei Jihô* 143, *Lacoste*.

110. Nagoya District Court, 25 March 1988, 1277 *Hanrei Jihô* 146, *BBS Trade Marks*.

111. Tokyo District Court, 28 January 1999, 1670 *Hanrei Jihô* 75, *Fred Perry Tokyo I*.

112. Tokyo High Court, 19 April 2000, *Fred Perry Tokyo II*.

113. Tokyo District Court, 28 January 1999, 1670 *Hanrei Jihô* 75, *Fred Perry Tokyo I*.
114. Osaka District Court, 21 December 2000, 1063 *Hanrei Times* 248; Osaka High Court, 29 March 2002, 16 *Law & Technology* 84, *Fred Perry Osaka*.
115. Supreme Court, 27 February 2003, 35 *IIC* 216 (2004), *Fred Perry III*. The author has provided a more detailed comment on this decision: C. Heath, 'Fred Perry – A Case of Identity' in D. Beier, L. Brüning-Petit, C. Heath (eds.), *Festschrift für Jochen Pagenberg* (Cologne, 2006), pp. 135–50.
116. Osaka District Court, 24 February 1994, 1522 *Hanrei Jihô* 139, *Mag Amp*.
117. Tokyo District Court, 26 March 2002, 16 *Law & Technology* 95, *Viagra*. The case applied the principles of the above-mentioned *Parker* decision in finding that the act of repackaging was incompatible with the functions of the trade mark. However, the claim based on trade mark law was dismissed, because the Court could not find any damage caused to the trade mark owner by such repackaging, and in this respect, the plaintiff only prevailed on the basis of unfair competition prevention law. This, of course, raises the question as to what extent repackaging can be effectively prevented in cases where the trade mark in question is not well-known and the unfair competition prevention law would not apply.
118. M. Kato, *Chôsakuken chikujô kôgi* (Copyright Act Annotated) (Tokyo, 2000) 117. Ministry of Culture (ed.), *Chôsakukenhô, fusei kyôsô boshi hô gaisetsu* (Explanation on the Copyright and Unfair Competition Prevention Acts) (Tokyo 1999) 194.
119. Tokyo District Court, 1 July 1995 (1996) 27 *IIC* 570, 571 *Beauty and the Beast*.
120. This view has ultimately been confirmed by the Supreme Court, 6 May 2002, 16 *Law & Technology* 89, *Video Games*, after the Tokyo and Osaka High Courts arrived at the same result, yet with different reasoning: Tokyo High Court, 27 March 2001, and Osaka High Court, 29 March 2001, reprinted in *CASRIP Newsletter* Summer 2001.
121. Tokyo District Court, 1 July 1995 (1996) 27 *IIC* 570–2, *Beauty and the Beast*.
122. 'Guideline on Unreasonable Obstruction of Parallel Importing Under the Antimonopoly Act', 17 April 1987 as amended by 'Antimonopoly Guidelines Concerning Distribution Systems and Business Practices', 11 July 1991, Part III, Chapter 3, 'Unreasonable Obstruction of Parallel Imports: reprinted in Iyori and Uesugi', *The Antimonopoly Laws and Policies of Japan* (New York, 1994) 493.
123. FTC Notification No. 15/1982, accessible at the FTC's homepage at www.jftc.go.jp.
124. FTC, formal decision (recommendation) 18 April 1978 against *Old Bar*, the sole import distributor of Old Bar Scottish Whisky, 330 *Kôsei Torihiki* 36 (1978) and 331 *Kôsei Torihiki* 45 (1978); FTC, formal decision (recommendation), 5 September 1990, 37 KTIS 29, against attempts to prevent parallel importation of French handbags; FTC, informal warning, 25 February 1991 against Canon, the sole import distributor of Apple computers in Japan

(Yomiuri Shinbun, 26 February 1991); FTC, formal decision (recommendation), 6 June 1991 against Arms-Shop Ginza, the sole import distributor of German Feinberg airguns, 489 *Kôsei Torihiki* 66–67 (1991); FTC, formal decision (recommendation), 28 September 1993, 40 KTIS 123: attempts to prevent parallel imports of blood analysis spectrometres; FTC, formal decision (recommendation), 29 February 1996 against Hoshi Shôji, *KTIS* 42, 195 and 560 *Kôsei Torihiki* 25 (1997); FTC, formal decision (recommendation), 8 May 1996, 552 *Kôsei Torihiki* 52 (1996): attempted obstruction of imported Steinway pianos; FTC, formal decision (recommendation), 25 April 1997, 1132 *Jurist* 150 and 562 *Kôsei Torihiki* 74 (1997) against Häagen Dazs trying to prevent parallel importation of ice cream: comments on these two cases by Ishimoto and Komuro, in 562 *Kôsei Torihiki* 74 (1997); FTC, formal decision (recommendation), 28 November 1997, 1148 *Jurist* 342 against Hobby Japan; FTC, formal decision (recommendation), 24 July 1998, 579 *Kôsei Torihiki* 71 (1999), against preventing parallel imports of water filters; FTC, formal decision (recommendation), 28 July 1998, 1163 *Jurist* 144, against Nike that restricted the supply of shoes to shoe stores if parallel imports were discovered in the shop. Iyori and Uesugi, *Chiteki shoyûken to dokusen kinshihô* (Intellectual Property and Antitrust), *NBL Bessatsu* No. 52 (Tokyo, 1998) 25–6 list a total of 97 unlawful attempts of trying to prevent parallel imports where the FTC took formal or informal measures.

125. See the FTC's precedents for consultations on unfair trade practices, published in 26 *FTC/Japan View* 37 (1996).

126. Kurakan 1443 of 25 August 1972, modifying Directive No. 522.

127. Kurakan 257 of 26 March 1998.

PART II

Intellectual property rights and competition law in smaller and medium sized open economies

Intellectual property rights and competition in Australia

FRANCES HANKS

I. Provisions in intellectual property statutes

A. Introduction

Intellectual property rights, like all property, are a right to exclude. At a general level, competition concerns lie at the heart of the definition of any intellectual property right – the circumstances in which the law grants the right, the period for which the right endures, and the general scope of the right.

This chapter takes that generic trade-off for granted. It looks at the provisions in the various Australian intellectual property statutes that seem facially to reflect a specific concern that the scope of a property right or the way in which the right is exercised should be limited in the interests of competition. These include provisions for compulsory licensing, provisions that narrow the property right to excise a use or dealing so that it is not an infringement of the right (including parallel importation provisions), and provisions that affect the terms on which a right owner can license.

Australian IP law is in the process of change. A few years ago, the government commissioned an ad hoc committee, the Intellectual Property and Competition Review Committee (IPCRC), to review IP laws from the standpoint of competition. The Committee's report[1] recommended some changes to the IP statutes. The Australian government has accepted some but not all of the Committee's recommendations. This account of Australian IP law includes a projection of where the law is headed.

B. Compulsory licensing

The *Patents Act*, the *Copyright Act* and the *Designs Act* all make provision for compulsory licensing. They differ on the circumstances in which a licence may be compelled.

1. Patents

For patents, section 133 of the *Patents Act 1990* provides that an order compelling licensing may be awarded if the Federal Court is satisfied that:

(a) the reasonable requirements of the public in respect to the invention have not been satisfied, and

(b) the patentee has given no satisfactory reason for failing to exploit the patent.

Whether the 'reasonable requirements of the public' have been satisfied depends on whether Australian industry is unfairly prejudiced, or demand in Australia for the patented product is not 'reasonably met', because of the patentee's failure to manufacture the product to an adequate extent and supply it on reasonable terms,[2] or to grant licences on reasonable terms.[3] A further basis is that the patent is not being worked in Australia.[4]

There appear to be no cases in which section 133 has led to a court-granted licence.[5] Rather the role of the section appears to have been to strengthen the bargaining position of potential licensees in their negotiations with foreign rights owners.[6]

The IPCRC recommended that the current criteria be replaced with a competition-based test. It recommended amendment so that an order requiring a compulsory licence be made, if and only if the following conditions are met:

(a) access to the patented invention is required for competition in the (relevant) market;

(b) there is a public interest in enhanced competition in that market;

(c) reasonable requirements for such access have not been met;

(d) the order will have the effect of allowing these reasonable requirements to be better met; and

(e) the order will not compromise the legitimate interests of the patent owner, including that owner's right to share in the return society obtains from the owner's invention, and to benefit from any successive invention, made within the patent term, that relies on the patent.[7]

The Committee did not purport to have drafted the amendment that it had in mind. It went on to explain that it expected 'required for competition in the (relevant) market' would amount to there being no other option for competition in that market; and that the enhancement of competition that would be secured by the grant would have to be 'material and substantial'.

The government has announced that it proposes to enact a compulsory licensing provision along the lines proposed by the IPCRC, but not *instead* of the current provision. The new competition-based ground for granting a licence is to be a *complement* to the current provision.

2. Copyright

There are many circumstances in which the Australian *Copyright Act 1968* converts a right owner's right to a right to reasonable remuneration, leaving the owner with no power to exclude the would-be user. Nor to bargain advantageous terms. In the case of many of these provisions it is clear that the policy behind the incursion into the copyright owner's rights has nothing to do with competition policy. For instance, different social policies lie behind the Act's mandates that educational institutions and those that serve persons with a disability should be entitled to use copyright material.[8]

Part VI of the Act, which provides for licensing schemes for rights to perform in public or to broadcast literary, dramatic or musical works, is a response to the market power of copyright collecting societies.[9] The Copyright Tribunal, whose president must be a judge, is arbiter on the terms of those licences. On its face, the Act applies to individual authors, not just collectives,[10] and it applies even if they have never granted a licence.[11] However the thrust of the legislation remains to control the market power of collectives of IP owners. This has been its use. The process is premised on the assumption that the collectives might have market power. The response is to limit the extent to which that power can be exploited in dealings with users.

Different is section 47D, inserted in the Act in 1999 and applying only to computer programs. It permits the owner of a copy of a computer program to reproduce that program to the extent that is necessary for it to make a new program that interoperates with the original program. This provision does not talk in the language of compulsory licence. Nor does it condition its sanction of the reproduction on the payment of any remuneration. In effect it is the same as a compulsory licence at no fee. The provision can be seen as pro-competitive in two ways. First, it fosters competition in products downstream from the original program. Second, where the original program has market power protected by network effects, that other programs can interoperate with the popular program increases the prospect of the popular program itself being challenged by a later better program.

3. Designs

Section 28 of the *Designs Act 1906* is like a stripped down version of section 133 of the *Patents Act*. It simply permits the court to grant a licence of a registered design if the design is not applied within Australia 'to such an extent as is reasonable in the circumstances of the case'.[12]

C. Parallel importation

The legislation on patents, registered designs and copyright all include in the property right the right to import goods that embody the IP.[13] Trade marks are different. The courts have ruled that a trade mark is merely a badge of origin and so the owner of the mark has no power to exclude from Australia goods to which that mark was properly applied overseas.[14]

Copyright is in a process of change. The provision that makes it an infringement to import for sale goods that could not legally have been made in Australia without the licence of the copyright owner has been qualified in respect of books,[15] and no longer applies to packaging and labelling,[16] sound recordings,[17] computer software products[18] and electronic forms of books, periodicals and sheet music.[19] The IPCR Committee recommended complete repeal of the parallel importation provisions for copyright.[20] The government has not accepted this recommendation in its entirety. It is adopting an industry by industry approach.

D. Restrictions in patent licences

Section 144 of the Patents Act renders void some conditions in contracts related to the sale, lease or licence of a patented invention. The conditions to which the provision applies are those which in essence tie other goods and services to the acquisition of rights to the patented invention.

The details of the section and its jurisprudence do not warrant discussion. The provision has its genesis in a perception of a competition problem in respect of patents long before there was a generic competition law. The IPCRC has recommended its repeal because the conduct it addresses is better dealt with under competition law[21] and the government has accepted the recommendation.

II. Framework of competition law

A. Scheme of the Australian Trade Practices Act

The general scheme of the *Trade Practices Act* 1974 is that it prohibits conduct that is shown to be likely to lessen competition – anti-competitive agreements (s. 45), anti-competitive mergers and acquisitions (s. 50) and misuse of market power (s. 46). Section 47, which prohibits some forms of vertical conduct when it is anticompetitive, covers ground that would otherwise have been covered by section 45 (when the other party has agreed to restrictive conditions) or perhaps s. 46 (when there has been refusal to license). There are also some per se prohibitions – prohibitions of conduct without the need to establish any likely effect on competition. These include price fixing between competitors, collective boycott (both in s. 45), and resale price maintenance (s. 48 – defined in such a way that in respect of a licence of intellectual property, the prohibition applies only to stipulations of minimum prices charged on a sub-licence).[22]

The sanctions for contravention of the Act include large fines and liability in damages to any private litigant who is made worse off by the contravening conduct.

Unlike the law in the USA, the *Trade Practices Act* provides for administrative exemption ('authorisation') of conduct that, although it may lessen competition, would be likely to result in a net public benefit (ss. 88 and 90). This is similar to the exemption process under Article 81(3) of the European Community Treaty but there are differences between the Australian and European systems. A difference of substance is that unlike Article 81(3), the Australian test for authorisation is not constrained by requirements that consumers are allowed a fair share in the resulting benefit or that competition not be eliminated. In Australia the chief public benefit that might justify anticompetitive conduct is simply the achievement of efficiency which encompasses allocative, productive and dynamic dimensions.[23] A difference in process that is of particular relevance to intellectual property is that under the Australian law authorisation is granted only on a case-by-case basis in response to an application by a party. There are no Australian equivalents of the European Technology Transfer Regulation.

B. *Provisions specific to intellectual property*

There are two provisions in the Australian *Trade Practices Act* that are specific to intellectual property. They beat in different directions.

Section 51(1)(a)

Section 51(1)(a) directs courts applying the competition provisions to disregard anything specifically authorised by another Act of the Australian Commonwealth *except* an Act relating to patents, trade marks, design or copyrights. In other words, that an IP statute specifically gives the right owner the sole right to exploit the right or states that the right may be licensed in a part of Australia does not give the right owner a defence to proceedings under the *Trade Practices Act* for its refusal to license or its creation of geographic territories for its licensees. There is nothing sacrosanct about the ordinary incidents of IP just because those incidents are set out in statutes. The Act applies in full force to the exploitation of intellectual property rights.

Section 51(3)

Section 51(3) qualifies the stance that IP is to be treated in the same way as other property. It provides:

> A contravention of a provision of this Part other than section 46, 46A or 48 shall not be taken to have been committed by reason of:

(a) the imposing of, or giving effect to, a condition of:
  (i) a licence granted by the proprietor, licensee or owner of a patent, of a registered design, of a copyright or of EL rights within the meaning of the Circuit Layouts Act 1989, or by a person who has applied for a patent or for the registration of a design; or
  (ii) an assignment of a patent, of a registered design, of a copyright or of such EL rights, or of the right to apply for a patent or for the registration of a design;
  to the extent that the condition relates to:
  (iii) the invention to which the patent or application for a patent relates or articles made by the use of that invention;
  (iv) goods in respect of which the design is, or is proposed to be, registered and to which it is applied;
  (v) the work or other subject matter in which the copyright subsists; or
  (vi) the eligible layout in which the EL rights subsist;
(b) the inclusion in a contract, arrangement or understanding authorizing the use of a certification trade mark of a provision in accordance with rules applicable under Part XI of the Trade Marks Act 1955, or the giving effect to such a provision; or
(c) the inclusion in a contract, arrangement or understanding between:
  (i) the registered proprietor of a trade mark other than a certification trade mark; and
  (ii) a person registered as a registered user of that trade mark under Part IX of the Trade Marks Act 1955 or a person authorized by the contract to use the trade mark subject to his or her becoming registered as such a registered user;
  of a provision to the extent that it relates to the kinds, qualities or standards of goods bearing the mark that may be produced or supplied, or the giving effect to the provision to that extent.

So under section 51(3), for conditions that 'relate to' the relevant intellectual property, rights owners and their licensees can go about their business without worrying about sections 45 and 47. They do not have to be concerned about the operation of the per se provisions in section 45. Nor do they have to give a thought to whether the condition might today (or some time in the future) be found to lessen competition and so contravene sections 45 or 47.

There are a number of features of section 51(3) which limit its operation. These limitations will now be discussed. Following this the meaning of 'relates to' will be examined.

Limitations of section 51(3)

First, the exception does not apply to the prohibitions of misuse of market power (s. 46) and resale price maintenance (s. 48).

Second, it applies only to statutory intellectual property, not to 'know how' and confidential information. And the exception for trade marks does not apply to matters other than those relating to quality control.

Third, applying only to *conditions in assignments or licences*, section 51(3), does not exempt:

(i) Assignments in themselves. An acquisition of IP remains exposed to the substantial lessening of competition test in section 50 which prohibits the acquisition of assets where the likely effect is to lessen competition.

(ii) Refusals to license or assign. Even if the refusal is for the reason that the potential licensee or assignee would not agree to a condition that would be exempted as 'related to' the IP, a refusal to license does not come within the exemption.

(iii) Underlying agreements, as for instance agreements between competitors that all will accept a particular IP licence and so become subject to its restrictive terms.

Fourth, the exemption does not extend to licenses and assignments of *future intellectual property*, although it does extend to patent and design applications. Where a research centre (such as a university) agrees to provide, in exchange for research funding, an exclusive licence to the investor over any patentable innovations that may be developed as a result of the research, section 51(3) offers no protection to the agreement. In each licence granted by the research centre, the condition of exclusivity may 'relate to' its patent, and so be exempted, but the agreement that imposes the obligation to grant the exclusive licence is not.

Fifth, applying only to conditions in assignments or licences of *intellectual property*, the exemption does not protect conditions in contracts of supply of goods which, though the goods embody intellectual property, do not themselves entail a licence of intellectual property. Each transaction has to be analysed in the light of the scope of the intellectual property right. Patents and copyright differ.

In respect of a patent, the owner's exclusive right to exploit includes the right to use the patented process and to make, hire, sell, use or import products made by the process.[24] This is comprehensive. Without some licence of the patent rights the purchaser of patented goods can do nothing fruitful with the goods. Patent law copes with the width of the patent grant by implying into a sale by the patentee a licence to the purchaser to deal with the goods in any way she thinks fit, subject to any express restriction stipulated by the patentee.[25] For the purposes of section 51(3), any restriction on what the purchaser may do with the goods can be seen as a condition in the licence to exercise the patent rights in respect of those goods.

Copyright is not so simple. Copyright does not give its right owners the same blanket control over downstream activities as patentees have. For instance, the purchaser of a book does not need the licence of the copyright owner to read it, nor to sell or hire it out. Purchasers of goods that embody copyright do not always need, and so do not routinely acquire, a licence of any copyright. Where there is no licence of copyright section 51(3) cannot operate to protect any restriction imposed by the copyright owner as a condition of the sale. That copyright is a complex patchwork of rights means that in some circumstances the supply of a particular good embodying copyright will entail a licence, and so a 'home' for the purposes of section 51(3) of a condition imposed by the supplier, and in other circumstances it will not. For instance, section 31(1)(c) of the *Copyright Act* makes it an infringement of copyright in a literary work in a sound recording to enter into an arrangement for commercial hire of the recording. So a buyer from the copyright owner who is known to be buying for the purpose of hiring out the recording will acquire a licence to do that, and any restrictions accepted by the buyer are candidates for the protection of section 51(3). Restrictions imposed on a reseller of sound recording are outside the safe haven of section 51(3) because the resale of recordings does not infringe copyright and so no licence of copyright is needed to give business efficacy to the contract of sale to a reseller.

'Relates to'

The use of the expression 'relates to' creates some uncertainty in the application of section 51(3). Some licence terms seem on their face to relate to the subject matter of the licence. For example, a condition which defines the qualities of the licensed product would seem clearly to relate to that product. Other conditions seem clearly not to relate to the licensed IP, for example a condition which precludes the licensee from dealing in products that compete with the licensed product. Such a condition seems to relate to the excluded product rather than the licensed IP. More difficult is whether a price restraint or a territorial restraint relates to the licensed product. Those restraints certainly relate to the price at which or territory in which a product is to be sold, but is that the same thing as relating to the product?

To date there has been only one decision – *Transfield* v. *Arlo*[26] – and in that decision only one judgment (of Mason J) that has considered the meaning of the 'relates to' test. Talking in terms of a patent, Mason J said:

> In bridging the different policies of the *Patents Act* and the *Trade Practices Act*, section 51(3) recognises that a patentee is justly entitled to impose conditions on the granting of a licence or assignment of a patent in order to protect the patentee's legal monopoly … Section 51(3) determines the scope of the restrictions the patentee may properly impose on the use of the patent. Conditions which seek to gain advantages collateral to the patent are not covered by section 51(3).[27]

Under Mason's 'collateral advantage' test it is clear that any condition which operates simply to carve up the relevant IP into geographic territories or fields of use would relate to the IP, and so be exempted by section 51(3). Division of the property does not extend the scope of the monopoly right. In this respect, Mason's test seems to draw the line between the legitimate exploitation of intellectual property and matters of possible interest to competition law at the same point as the US Antitrust Guidelines which make it clear that the enforcement agencies will not use competition law to require the owner of intellectual property to create competition in its own technology.[28]

It is not so clear whether a licensee seeks an advantage that is collateral to the IP when it stipulates the minimum price at which products that embody the IP may be sold. Guidelines issued by the Australian regulator state that a price stipulation is likely to relate to the licensed product because an important aspect of the exclusive rights granted to the IP owner is the ability to derive a profit from the price at which the product is sold.[29] However, the courts could take a different view. Whilst accepting that the basis of IP monopoly rights is to give the creator a reward for his endeavours, it can be argued that this does not justify the receipt of a royalty in addition to freedom from competition.

If the view adopted in the Australian guidelines is correct, Australian competition law treats price restrictions much more generously than does the law in the USA[30] or the European Union.[31] For patents, because section 51(3) expressly exempts conditions to the extent that they relate to the patented invention *or articles made by use of the invention*, it is not possible to confine the exemption to patented articles as has been done in the USA.[32] Nor is there any basis in the subsection for distinguishing between a single licence and multiple licences.[33] Further, although section 51(3) does not provide protection for conduct that constitutes resale price maintenance prohibited by section 48, the definition of resale price maintenance (in ss. 96 and 96A) is technical and has a narrow application to IP. It captures the supply of *goods* on condition that the goods not be resold below a specified price. It captures the supply of a *licence* on condition that the licensee will not grant a sub-licence at a price below a specified price.[34] However it does not straddle goods and services so as to capture the grant of a licence of IP on condition that goods made pursuant to the licence will be not be supplied below some price.

A condition that requires a licensee to acquire other goods or services from the licensor would seem to be a classic instance of seeking to gain an advantage that is collateral to the licensed IP. The 'bundling' of other products seems to leverage the power of the licensed IP beyond the scope of the property right. In respect of tying and bundling conditions the Australian guidelines baldly state that these conditions are outside the protection of section 51(3) because they do not 'relate to' the licensed product.[35] But this conclusion is too sweeping.

Sometimes tying is simply a device for solving problems that arise in the licensing situation. A tie of materials to be used as inputs in the manufacture of a patented product might be explained as a means of maintaining quality in the licensed product, so that the licensor's reputation is not damaged by the licensee. A tie of consumables to be used in conjunction with the licensed product might be a metering device designed to overcome the problem that the licensee does not know how much value to place on the licensed product. Or, the other side of the same coin, the tie of consumables might be the licensee's way of extracting the full market value of its product by charging its various licensees according to the intensity of their use.

When tying is used to protect the value of the IP or to get in the revenue that measures its value the tying condition would survive Mason's collateral advantage test. So section 51(3) would shield tying in these circumstances from the full force of the competition provisions in the *Trade Practices Act*.

Evaluation of the 'relates to' test in section 51(3)

On a literal construction of the phrase, whether a condition 'relates to' the subject matter of an IP licence is a question whose answering entails meta-physical distinctions. Whether a condition relates to the IP or, instead, to something else – place, price or, in the case of tying conditions, the tied product – can be answered either way.

It is only with Mason J's gloss that the 'relates to' test acquires the discipline of a principle. Conditions that serve only to carve up the IP relate to the subject matter of the licence because they do not seek to gain an advantage that goes beyond the monopoly right granted by the IP.

The discussion above of tying conditions shows that Mason J's 'collateral advantage' gloss on the 'relates to' test sometimes involves more than a classification of terms. Identical terms might assume a different character in different settings. In these cases an examination of the ends to be served by the condition is a necessary part of determining whether its imposition is to gain an advantage collateral to the licensed IP. To this extent, licensors who seek the comfort of a certain answer to the question whether a particular kind of term is exempted by section 51(3) will not find it in Mason's test.

III. Proposals for change to section 51(3)

There have been two reviews of section 51(3) in the past few years. Both have recommended change.

A. National Competition Council (1999)

The National Competition Council (NCC) was asked in 1998 to report to the government on the competition effects of the exemption in section 51(3) of the *Trade Practices Act*. Its report[36] recommended that section 51(3) be retained but amended to remove from exemption the conduct the NCC considered most likely to have an anticompetitive effect.

First, the NCC noted that section 51(3) does not distinguish between horizontal and vertical relationships. A condition in a license to an existing competitor of the licensor is protected in the same way as a condition in a licence to a person who would not be able to compete with the licensor in the absence of the licence. It recommended that the subsection be amended so as not to apply to horizontal agreements.[37]

Second, the NCC could see few justifications for price and quantity restrictions. It recommended that section 51(3) be amended to remove these restrictions from its purview.[38]

B. *Intellectual Property and Competition Review Committee (2000)*

The government did not respond to the NCC's recommendations. Rather, as it was commissioning an ad hoc committee to review the whole of intellectual property law from the perspective of competition principles, it fed the NCC's recommendations into that committee's deliberations.

The Intellectual Property and Competition Review Committee (IPCRC) did not form its own view on the application of the 'relates to' test, either at large or in the light of Mason's 'collateral advantage' test. It sought advice from the Australian Government Solicitor. The advice it got was not helpful. It was a survey of the views of others.[39] The IPCRC noted that on some views section 51(3) had a very narrow operation and on others a very broad operation.[40]

The IPCRC saw the recommendations of the NCC as too sweeping, saying that the vast majority of intellectual property licences could fall within the categories of horizontal arrangements, and price and quantity restrictions. The adoption of the NCC's proposal, it said, would amount to the repeal of the section.[41]

The IPCRC thought that some version of section 51(3) should be retained. First it looked to features of intellectual property that make it particularly dependent on contracts, licences and assignments to achieve an efficient use of the property.[42] The initial owners of IP rights are often not best placed to exploit the rights. In many areas of technology, the commercialisation of IP rights involves combining technological inputs owned by multiple rights owners. That knowledge is non-rivalrous means that the benefits of immediate allocative efficiencies that might come from inventing around the knowledge might be swamped by the productive inefficiency the duplication of outlays entails.

The Committee was concerned particularly that the per se provisions of the Act could be invoked to wreak havoc on dealings in IP, and that the Act's procedure for authorisation is too burdensome. It also saw no policy rationale for the uneven coverage of the section – that the provisions dealing with resale price maintenance and misuse of market power are excluded. It recommended that section 51(3) be replaced by a provision that ensures that:

> [A] contravention of Part IV of the [Trade Practices Act] ... shall not be taken to have been committed by reason of imposing conditions in a licence, or inclusion of conditions in a contract, arrangement or understanding, that relates to the subject matter of that intellectual property statute, *so long as those conditions do not result, or are not likely to result in a substantial lessening of competition.*
>
> *The term 'substantial lessening of competition' is to be interpreted in a manner consistent with the case law under the TPA more generally.* [emphasis added][43]

The recommendation went on to explain that the intended change was to apply not just to conditions imposed in a licence or contract that was actually made, but also to a refusal by the owner of the right to enter into a licence or contract.

The proposed change substitutes the 'substantial lessening of competition' test for the current *exemption* in section 51(3). It is clear that such a change will not work to achieve the policy objectives that underlie the IPCRC's recommendations.

In its review of section 51(3) the IPCRC expressed a view on the policy that underlies intellectual property.

> The Committee recognises that the IP legislation confers upon the intellectual property right owner a series of exclusive privileges designed to promote innovation. Given that these rights are conferred by legislation, they should be able to be effectively exercised even when this involves (as it generally must) the exclusion of others. However those rights should not be capable of being used to *go beyond* the market power those rights directly confer ... The system of IP rights acts to provide those who invest in creative effort a claim on the differential efficiency associated with their investment – that is, of the social gain consequent upon that investment's outcomes. [emphasis in the original][44]

By this view, intellectual property policy favours the creator of successful intellectual property being able to capture the whole of the value society places on the property. Every owner should be entitled to exploit its property for what it is worth. That would include licensing of the property on terms that assist in extracting the value that each of its various users place on the property. That the 'substantial lessening of competition' test in Part IV of the *Trade Practices Act* does not operate in this way is demonstrated in the next section.

It is just possible that the IPCRC did not intend to endorse a policy that an intellectual property owner should be able to secure a reward measured by whatever the market will pay. The IPCRC refers constantly to efficiency. It talks of 'the cost of impeding efficient licensing',[45] and that it is 'essential that firms have the scope to enter into efficient contracts that involve intellectual property rights'.[46] Perhaps the Committee assumed that whether a contract is efficient is a matter the court can take into account when applying the competition test. This is discussed in Section 2 below.

1. Effect of IPCRC recommendation – the lessening of competition test

It is apparent that the IPCRC did not understand the significance of replacing the current exemption of conditions that relate to the intellectual property with exposure to the competition test under Part IV of the *Trade Practices Act.*

The IPCRC seems to have thought that the test of substantially lessening competition is satisfied only where a right owner deals with its property on terms that increase its own market power. Neither the provisions of the Act nor the jurisprudence of the lessening of competition support that view. The mere transfer of market power from an upstream owner of intellectual property to a downstream licensee substantially lessens competition in the sense in which that phrase is used in the *Trade Practices Act.*

Both sections 45 and 47 specify two markets in which the court is directed to look for a lessening of competition.[47] One of those markets is the market in which the supplier/licensor competes with its own competitors. This is the market that the IPCRC assumes matters. The other market in sections 45 and 47 is the market in which the licensees compete (or might have competed but for the provision in the contract that prevents them). In terms of the relevant provisions in the Act there can be a lessening of competition when all that has happened is that a licensor prevents its licensees from competing with one another in the on-supply of the licensor's own product.

The cases bear out this reading. In *Mark Lyons* v. *Bursill Sportsgear,*[48] Bursill was found to have lessened competition (in contravention of s. 47) by refusing supply of its product (ski-boots) to Mark Lyons because Mark Lyons carried out hit-and-run sales at low prices in the territories of other retailers of Bursill's product. The trial court's analysis is not beyond criticism. But one of the criticisms would not be that the Court looked at the effect of Bursill's exclusive distribution arrangements in the retail market (a market in which Mark Lyons operated, but Bursill did not). Section 47 directs the court to register as a lessening of competition a reduction of competition in the downstream market.

Stirling Harbour Services v. *Bunbury Port Authority*[49] is another case on point. Bunbury Port Authority (BPA) had the right to determine who could supply towage services to ships in its port. BPA called for tenders, offering the successful tenderer an exclusive licence for five years. Stirling Harbour, the incumbent towage provider, argued that the grant of an *exclusive* licence would lessen competition and breach section 45 or section 47 of the Act. The Court found otherwise. Satisfied that only one towage provider could survive in the port, and that whoever that provider happened to be was unlikely to be open to challenge by a new entrant, the Court found that the tender process with its promise of formal exclusivity would not lessen competition. For present purposes, the significant aspect of this case is that the lessening of competition was asserted, and analysed by the Court, in the context of the market for towage services within BPA's port – not the market in which the BPA competes for business with other ports. It is clear that BPA's unilateral decision to grant exclusivity in a downstream market to which BPA happened to be the gateway could 'lessen competition' within the *Trade Practices Act*.

The *Mark Lyons* and *Stirling Harbour* cases are not controversial decisions in Australian competition law. They are mainstream. They reflect the language of the Act, and there are no contrary authorities. An owner of intellectual property that is powerful in its market lessens competition merely by preventing competition between its licensees. A condition that serves only to carve up the intellectual property may nonetheless 'lessen competition'.

A partial concession is in order. To date cases on the application of the competition test to vertical restrains have focused on the effect of the *restraint*. This focus is not inevitable.

The competition test requires a comparison of the likely state of competition with the challenged conduct and the likely state of competition without that conduct.[50] It may be that in the absence of a particular restrictive condition there would have been no licence. Perhaps the right owner would have chosen to exploit the property itself rather than grant licences without the condition. Perhaps no licensees acceptable to the right owner would take a licence in the absence of the condition. Where the facts support a conclusion that in the absence of the condition there would have been no licence, the analysis of the future state of competition in the downstream market without the condition is the same as the analysis of the future without the licence.

However the 'no licence' alternative is often not available on the facts. Not all rights owners are in a position to exploit their property on their own. Sometimes licensees take a licence on second-best terms in preference to no licence at all. If a restrictive condition serves only to improve the terms of a licence that would have been granted and accepted without that condition then the competition test in the Australian Act will contrast the future with and without that restriction. The IPCRC recognised that licensing was often the only way to exploit IP.[51] It did not understand that when licensing is going to happen anyway, the focus of the competition test is on the restrictive conditions in the licence.

2. Efficiencies and the competition test

On the way to its recommendation in respect of section 51(3), the IPCRC often mentioned the need for competition law not to impede efficient licensing practices. Its recommendation that all conditions in dealings in intellectual property be subject to the competition test suggests that the Committee thought that the competition test distinguishes between efficient and inefficient transactions. It does not. That a licensing practice is efficient has nothing to do with the competition test.

Under the scheme of the *Trade Practices Act*, the competition test is a market power test. In respect of a condition in a licence, the issue is whether the condition enhances the market power of the licensor or confers market power on the licensee.

That conduct is efficient is not a matter for the court under the competition test. It is a matter to be taken into account in the administrative authorisation process. Part VII permits the Australian Competition and Consumer Commission (and, on appeal, the Australian Competition Tribunal) to grant exemption from the competition provisions of the Act[52] when it is satisfied that the conduct would result in a benefit to the public and that benefit would outweigh the detriment to the public constituted by any lessening of competition.[53]

The Tribunal has made clear that the chief public benefit that might justify anticompetitive conduct is the achievement of efficiency.[54] Conditions in licences of intellectual property might improve allocative efficiency (by price discrimination that gives low-value users access), or technical efficiency (by preventing free riding), or dynamic efficiency (by preserving incentives for innovators). But none of these efficiency explanations finds a place in the competition test. There is not a case in the court that trades off lessened rivalry for increased efficiency under the competition test.[55] For better or for worse, the *Trade Practices Act* sends competition issues down a different decision-making track from efficiency issues.

C. Government's response to IPCRC recommendation

The government has accepted the gist of the IPCRC's recommendation, but not its entirety.[56] In line with the recommendation, it proposes to replace section 51(3) with a provision that substitutes a substantial lessening of competition test for the current total exemption from sections 45, 47 and 50.

The government did not adopt the recommendation that the substantial lessening of competition test should apply across all the provisions of Part IV of the Act. It proposes that the prohibitions of misuse of market power (s. 46) and resale price maintenance (s. 48) should continue to apply in full force to intellectual property, just as they do now under section 51(3). The exclusion of resale price maintenance is of limited effect because (as explained at p. 323 above) resale price maintenance has a narrow application to licences and assignments of intellectual property.

The continued exclusion of section 46 from the protection of section 51(3) will also have little effect. The earlier discussion shows that the imposers of licence conditions that relate to the IP have nothing to gain from section 46 being made subject to an added test of 'substantial lessening of competition'. In respect of conditions that give licensees exclusivity in some territory or field of use, if the IP rights confer market power, the licensor will fall foul of the competition test by subdividing its right. However the IPCRC proposed that the competition test should apply also to refusals to deal. It is possible that a right owner which refuses to licence, perhaps because it chooses to self exploit, might contravene section 46 even though its refusal is not likely to result in a substantial lessening of competition in any market. If so, the government's decision to leave section 46 outside the protection of section 51(3) will matter. The application of section 46 to refusals to licence is discussed at p. 331 below.

At the time of writing, the government has not issued a draft of its proposed new section 51(3).

IV. Application of competition law to intellectual property

A. Preliminary observations

In Australian competition law there have been few cases about intellectual property. Why that is so is not clear. It may be that the exemption in section 51(3) has forestalled litigation over conditions in licences. It is also a reflection of the fact that much significant IP tends to be significant globally, and so the state of competition in Australia often turns on conduct that happens outside its jurisdiction, beyond reach of the domestic competition law. Microsoft's conduct in the mid-1990s, designed to suppress the Internet browser and middleware program that threatened the dominance of its disk operating system, was a problem for Australia, but it was a problem whose resolution depended on the US regulator seeking remedies under US competition law.

Given there are few decisions in the courts, this part of the chapter is a mixture. It looks beyond court decisions to the work of the Australian Competition Tribunal in authorisation proceedings and to the stance adopted by the Australian regulator, the Competition and Consumer Commission, in proceedings that have been settled before trial. It also draws on court decisions on the application of competition law to cases that did not involve intellectual property – applying the principles established in those cases to property that is intellectual.

B. Proceedings for infringement

The only provision of the *Trade Practices Act* that might be contravened by a right owner which brings proceedings to stop infringement of its IP right is the prohibition against misuse of market power (s. 46).

Section 46(1) prohibits a firm with substantial market power from taking advantage of that power for the purpose of (a) damaging one of its competitors, (b) preventing a person from entering a market, or (c) deterring someone from engaging in competitive conduct in a market.

Market power has been explained as 'the ability of a firm to raise prices above the supply cost without rivals taking away customers in due time, supply cost being the minimum cost an efficient firm would incur in producing the product'.[57] Another formulation goes: 'A firm possesses market power when it can behave persistently in a manner different from the behaviour that a competitive market would enforce on a firm facing otherwise similar cost and demand conditions.'[58]

The Australian High Court has explained 'take advantage' of market power as meaning to 'use' that power. A firm uses its market power when it acts in a way which it could not afford, in a commercial sense, if it were operating in a competitive market.[59] Another way of formulating the concept is to ask whether the firm has a legitimate business reason for the conduct that would have seen it pursue that same conduct if it lacked market power.[60]

Even where an IP right confers substantial power in a market, and a purpose of the proceedings is to stop an infringer from competing with the right owner, the bringing of the proceedings does not contravene the section because it is not a taking advantage of the market power. No one in a competitive market stands by and lets someone steal its assets.[61] This analysis assumes that the proceedings are brought in good faith. The position would be different if the litigator lacked an honest belief that its legal rights were being infringed. There is no Australian case on this point, but in a competitive market no rational commercial actor invests resources merely to stop entry by yet another competitor.

C. Refusal to license

There is no Australian decision that addresses whether competition law might require the owner of IP to grant a licence on some sort of commercial terms to an existing competitor or a would-be competitor of the right owner. A refusal to license is open to challenge only as a misuse of market power (s. 46). If the IP confers market power, the anticompetitor purpose element of section 46 will be readily established, and so the only live issue is whether a refusal to license can be a taking advantage of that market power.

Property rights are not sacrosanct under the *Trade Practices Act*. In *Queensland Wire Industries* v. *BHP*[62] the High Court held that a unilateral refusal to deal can be (and in that case was) a taking advantage of market power in contravention of section 46. That case was about tangible property – a steel product.

It is not open to Australian courts to reach an accommodation between intellectual property and the *Trade Practices Act* by holding, as the US court did in *SCM Corp*. v. *Xerox Corp*,[63] in respect of patents, that competition law cannot be used to require a patent holder to forfeit its basic right to exclude others from exploiting the patent. Section 51(1)(a)[64] of the *Trade Practices Act* rules out an approach that gives the rights set out in intellectual property statutes precedence over competition law.

Nor does it appear that the interface can be managed by means of a rebuttable presumption as adopted in respect to copyright in the US case *Data General Corp*. v. *Grumman Systems Support Corp*.[65] That case took into account the need to preserve the economic incentives fuelled by copyright and held that an author's desire to exclude others from use of its copyrighted work is a presumptively valid business justification. The test of 'take advantage' in section 46, as presently expounded, does not invite the importation of the policies that underlie intellectual property. It mandates an inquiry that is factual, albeit based on a hypothetical state of affairs – whether this right owner would have been likely to grant a licence if it lacked substantial market power.

Without the assistance of legal rules and presumptions it might seem that a right owner's choice to exclude others from its property will routinely be found to be a taking advantage of its market power. However, there are many competitive industries in which granting access to one's property is not the common practice. An IP right owner may be able to sever the connection between its market power and its refusal to licence by pointing to its own practice of not licensing others of its products in which it is not dominant.[66] Or by pointing to the practice of other market participants. It may be able to articulate the business reasons that would lead it to self-exploit regardless of its power. Maybe self-exploitation is the simplest way of ensuring that it gets in all the revenue from the product. Maybe the success and reputation of the intellectual property depends on services to be delivered on distribution, services which the owner believes it is best placed to provide, or which it would not entrust to others who do not share its interest in the property's overall success. The possible explanations are legion. They will succeed, by displacing the market power explanation, if the court is satisfied they are real.

Outside the courts, some influential bodies looking at the application of competition principles to IP favour access to IP whenever access will generate competition in a market downstream from the property.

First, the Australian Competition and Consumer Commission apparently sees its role as facilitating access to 'essential' information, and twice has extracted undertakings to grant access to IP as a condition of abandoning suit under section 46.[67]

Second, the IPCRC's recommended change to the *Patents Act* (see p. 325 above) treats compulsory licensing as a normal response whenever access to a patented invention is necessary for competition in some market. It recognises the interests of the patentee by requiring that 'any order will not compromise the legitimate interest of the patent owner', and then immediately redefines the legitimate interest of a patent owner by saying that it includes 'the right to share in the benefit society obtains from the invention'. The right to *share* in the benefit of an invention is quite different from the right *to* that benefit. The IPCRC's treatment of the public interest confirms that it is not much concerned with preserving incentives for innovative activity. It stipulates that a compulsory licence should only be granted if there is a public interest in enhanced competition in the market opened up by access to the patent. That is an easy test to pass – assuming the patent; use by others is likely to increase competition in the market in which the patent is applied. There is no mention of the public interest in preserving incentives for innovative activity.

D. Pricing

High fees

Simple monopoly pricing does not contravene the *Trade Practices Act*.[68] Charging a monopoly price *may* be a taking advantage of market power.[69] But if so, it is not a misuse of power caught by section 46 because it is not done for any of the proscribed purposes set out in section 46(1). It is no part of the monopolist's purpose to damage its competitors, to deter anyone from entering a market, or to deter anyone from engaging in competitive activity. Its only purpose is to maximise its revenue.

However a price that is set so high that no rational licensee can afford to take a license is effectively a refusal to deal. If the potential licensee would have taken business from the licensor, the purpose element of section 46 can readily be spelled out. If the owner of the IP has substantial market power, the setting of the price may be a taking advantage of that power. *Queensland Wire Industries v. BHP* concerned a constructive refusal to deal. BHP did not refuse outright to supply its product to Queensland Wire. It asked a 'high' price that the High Court saw as not a serious offer. The judgments are not explicit about what made the price unrealistic, but they seem to have in mind a price squeeze – that the price at which BHP offered to supply its raw product was too close to the price at which BHP supplied its finished product to permit a buyer of the raw product to compete in the market for the finished product.[70]

A more sophisticated explanation of the price that constitutes a use of market power is to be found in the decision of the Privy Council in *Telecom Corporation of New Zealand Ltd* v *Clear Communications Ltd.*[71] The Privy Council was applying section 36 of the New Zealand *Commerce Act* which is modelled on section 46 of the Australian Act. As in *Queensland Wire*, the issue was whether the price at which a monopolist offered to supply a competitor was a use of market power. The Privy Council ruled that a monopolist was entitled to charge its competitors a price that compensated the monopolist for revenue foregone because those competitors would be serving its former customers.[72] Supply at this price would not be a use of market power even if the price included a component of monopoly rent.

Discriminatory pricing

Australian competition law does include a provision directed at discriminatory pricing.

Where a right owner simply charges users different prices according to the value each puts on the property, the only provision that might apply is section 46. The analysis is the same as for simple monopoly pricing.

Even if a strategy of price discrimination would not have been sustainable if the right owner faced competition (and so is a taking advantage of market power), the right-owner does not breach section 46 because it does not do that pricing for one of the purposes in section 46(1). It does not set different prices in order to damage the higher payer, or to prevent the lower payer from entering the higher payer's market, or to prevent anyone from engaging in competitive conduct in the market. Its only purpose is to maximise revenue.

For many products simple price discrimination does not work. It needs to be reinforced by some mechanism that prevents those who buy cheaply from on-supplying to those who are ready to pay more. When effective separation of those who would pay more from those who would pay less requires licensing on terms that prevent arbitrage between groups of users, the terms that secure that separation are subject to a different analysis. The application of the Act to licensing on terms that divide the downstream market is discussed below in section H.

E. Acquisition

Section 50 of the *Trade Practices Act* prohibits the acquisition of shares or assets from another entity where the effect is likely to be a substantial lessening of competition. So the acquisition of any IP (an asset) is exposed to the competition test, just like a merger through acquisition of shares. Authorisation is available in case of an acquisition that is in the net public benefit regardless of its effect on competition.

Section 50 is cast in language that makes it difficult to apply to 'creeping' acquisitions – the acquisition of a number of assets over time. If no single one of these acquisitions can be said to lessen competition substantially, there is no contravention.[73] A firm that adopts the practice of buying up each new piece of intellectual property in its field may escape section 50 regardless of the effect on competition of the combined acquisitions. It may be that the pattern of acquisitions spells out a misuse of market power under section 46. But proceedings under section 46 face the difficulty of establishing that the firm is taking advantage of its market power – that in the absence of its market power the firm would not have acquired some or all of the IP. Unless there is evidence from within the firm to the effect that its policy is to buy in IP regardless of the use the firm might make of it, it is not likely that a case under s. 46 will be made out.

F. Collective licensing

Collective licensing of intellectual property will almost always infringe the *Trade Practices Act* and so require authorisation.

Even if the collectivity does not have market power, and its arrangement for joint selling does not have the purpose or likely effect of substantially lessening competition in the market (s. 45(2)(a)(ii)), it is likely to fall foul of one or both of the per se provisions in section 45. One is price fixing between competitors (deemed by s. 45A to lessen competition substantially). The other is what the Act calls an 'exclusionary provision', prohibited by section 45(2)(a)(i) and defined in section 4D. If competitors agree to restrict the persons to whom they will supply, perhaps only to supply their product to the collective licensing agent, their agreement is an exclusionary provision.

Agreements between competitors for collective licensing of IP do not qualify for exemption under section 51(3). They are not conditions in a licence of the IP. It would be an extraordinary hole in competition law if these agreements were exempt. It seems to be the intent of the IPCRC that its proposed amendment to section 51(3) would remove all dealings in IP from the per se provisions of the Act. This would leave collective licensing subject only to the competition test. That seems appropriate, but the reality is that most collective licensing does evince a purpose and/or likely effect of lessening competition in the market in which the IP is supplied. So it remains dependent on authorisation.

The decision of the Australian Competition Tribunal in *Re Applications by Australasian Performing Right Association Limited* (APRA)[74] suggests that authorisation of the best-justified collective schemes will come at the cost of considerable regulation. On the one hand, the Tribunal accepted that the collective administration of performing rights operated in the public interest, so that the arrangements that made up APRA's operating system should be authorised.[75] On the other hand, and rather inconsistently, the Tribunal identified the regulation of APRA's operations 'to ensure that it does not take advantage of its monopoly position' as a 'key issue'.[76] It took it on itself to add another layer of regulation. It noted that the scheme set up in the *Copyright Act*[77] acts as a constraint against APRA's ability 'to give less and charge more' in respect of large users, but is too complex and expensive for small users.[78] It required APRA, as a condition of authorisation, to put in place an informal dispute mechanism process that would do for small users what the Copyright Tribunal does for large users.

G. Joint research and development

Unlike the USA[79] and EU,[80] Australian competition law makes no special provision for joint research and development. Apart from the application of section 51(3), agreements between competitors to combine efforts in order to make a new product are exposed to the full force of the *Trade Practices Act*. This includes the per se prohibition against exclusionary provisions in section 45(2)(a)(i).

Section 51(3) has little application to collective activity in pursuit of a new product. It exempts conditions in cross-licences to the extent that those conditions relate to the IP that is licensed. According to the Australian regulator's guidelines, it even exempts conditions in those licences that stipulate the price of products made by a party as a result of the cross-licensing.[81] But it does not exempt the underlying agreement to cross-license. If the sharing of the cross-licensed IP in itself lessens competition that would otherwise exist between the parties the arrangement will contravene section 45.

Importantly, section 51(3) does not exempt restrictions in agreements for R&D joint ventures. Common requirements designed to make the joint project work may contravene the law, not only if they turn out to lessen competition substantially, but also sometimes per se as an exclusionary provision.[82] Conditions that preclude the parties from innovating outside the joint venture in competition with it, however necessary to ensure dedication of all to the joint venture, will commonly be illegal per se. So too may be conditions that confine the benefit of the joint venture to its parties, agreements not to share the fruits of the joint venture with cherry-picking outsiders.

In sum, many agreements for joint R&D risk contravening competition law unless they have been sanctioned under the authorisation process. Even agreements that do not harm competition are likely to contain conditions that are illegal unless authorised. This is an unsatisfactory state of affairs because authorisation takes time and costs money.

The Australian law would be aligned with the US law on joint R&D, and similar in effect to the EU Regulation, if joint R&D were excused from per se liability and so subject only to the competition test. There are two current proposals that move in that direction.

First, the Dawson Committee[83] has proposed that the Act should be amended so that it is a defence in proceedings based on the prohibition of an exclusionary provision to prove that the provision did not have the purpose, effect or likely effect of lessening competition.[84] This is a proposal for a narrowing of the reach of a per se prohibition that is considered too wide in general, not just for its impact on joint R&D in IP.

Second, the IPCRC's recommendation in respect of section 51(3)[85] is based on the view that IP should be spared from the per se prohibitions in the Act, and subject always to a competition test. However the IPCRC confined its discussion and its recommendation to dealings (and refusals to deal) in IP. Its report has nothing to say on, and makes no recommendation about, collaborative arrangements for research directed towards the generation of new IP.

H. Conditions in licences

1. General

This part of the chapter divides conditions in licences of IP into three groups: first, conditions that serve to carve up the property into territories – spatial or field of use; second, restrictions on price; third, restrictions that tie another product to the licensed IP. There are other restrictions common in the licensing of IP – grant-back clauses, no-challenge clauses etc. They are not dealt with here because Australian competition law has nothing useful to say.

2. Restrictions that carve up the property and/or give the licensee exclusivity

As was explained at p. 322 above, conditions that merely carve up intellectual property among various customer groups are classic cases of conditions that 'relate to' the IP within section 51(3) of the Australian Trade Practices Act. These conditions do not seek to gain an advantage that goes beyond the rights conferred by the IP. As such, they are exempted from the general provisions that catch anticompetitive agreements. They contravene the Act only if their imposition constitutes a misuse of market power under section 46.

Assuming market power, there are two issues in the application of section 46 to market division. One is whether the segmentation evinces one of the purposes in the section. The other is whether the market division is a taking advantage of that power.

First, if a firm has market power, the *effect* of its division of its property will be to lessen competition.[86] But section 46 requires purpose. It is not sufficient that the effect of the division will be to prevent its licensees from competing in each other's markets. Purpose involves an intention to achieve a result.[87] The undeniable purpose of subdividing one's property into different exclusive zones is to prevent outsiders from exploiting the *property* within these zones. That is not a section 46 purpose. The section 46 purposes are concerned with *markets* – an intention to prevent entry into a market in which the property is exploited, or to deter a person from engaging in competitive conduct in a market.

However, past Australian cases on distribution arrangements have tended to lose sight of the distinction between the property and the market. Having defined the market and found the property powerful in its market, the courts have readily found that the purpose to exclude from the property entailed a section 46 purpose.[88] In *Melway Publishing* v. *Robert Hicks*, the High Court cautioned against too simplistic an assumption that the adoption by a manufacturer, whether with or without market power, of a system of distribution that involves vertical restraints manifests an anticompetitive purpose of the kind referred to in section 46.[89] It remains to be seen how the courts respond to this caution.

The 'take advantage' question asks whether the firm would have adopted a different model of distribution if it lacked substantial market power. Without market power, would it have granted unrestricted licences rather than a set of exclusive licences? If exclusive distribution downstream is adopted as a means to prevent free riding on services that the licensor looks to licensees to provide, it is not an exercise of market power. Without market power the licensor would adopt the same strategy.

A more difficult case for the 'take advantage' element of section 46 is market division as a means of discriminating between high value users and low value users. On the one hand it is clear that market power is not a necessary condition for price discrimination. In an industry with significant common costs (such as IP industries) differential pricing has been said to be not only explicable,[90] but even inevitable (whenever producers are able to separate customers).[91] The literature that talks of the ordinariness of price discrimination in competitive markets is talking of firms that collect different contributions to their *costs* from all available sources. There is no monopoly profit available. When a solidly entrenched monopolist sets out to maximise its revenue by dividing its market it is using market segmentation to maximise its *profits*: to extract a monopoly rent. If charging a monopoly price is a taking advantage of market power (an issue not clearly decided in Australian law) then using market segmentation as a means of extracting that rent will also be a taking advantage of that power.

Under the IPCRC's recommended change to s. 51(3), as was pointed out at pp. 327, licensing that carves up IP will fall foul of the competition test in the Act whenever the IP is powerful in its market.

3. Pricing restrictions

The Australian guidelines say that a price restriction in a licence is likely to be protected by section 51(3).[92] That would make price restrictions exempt from the general prohibition of anticompetitive agreements, which includes the per se prohibition of price fixing between competitors (section 45). On that assessment, price fixing in a licence of IP is always legal except for the very limited circumstances in which vertical price fixing is resale price maintenance within section 48[93] or when the setting price of on-supply can be said to be a misuse of market power caught by section 46.

If the guidelines are wrong, and price of downstream supply does not 'relate to' the IP for the purposes of section 51(3), the application of the law to restrictions on price expands past resale price maintenance and misuse of market power. If the licensor and the licensee will compete in the downstream market in which the licence fixes prices, the restriction is deemed to lessen competition and so contravenes the Act.[94] If the restriction is purely vertical, but falls outside the definition of resale price maintenance – perhaps the price to be charged for goods made by the use of a patent, or a minimum admission price in a licence to exhibit a film – its legality turns on the effect of the restriction on competition in (presumably) the market in which the licensee competes.[95]

One thing that can be said in favour of the IPCR's recommendation for a competition standard for all dealings in IP is that it would leave no dealings outside the law. If licences that impose price restrictions on products to be supplied in competition with the licensor are now beyond the law, that is something to be rectified. That is especially so if (as the Australian guidelines say) the exemption that applies to a single licence should also apply to each licence in a cross-licensing arrangement.

4. Tying and bundling

At first glance, a condition that a licensee of IP take other property along with the licensed IP might seem to relate to the *tied* property and not to the licensed IP, and so to be outside the exemption from sections 45 and 47 given by section 51(3). That is the view expressed in the Australian guidelines.[96] As was pointed out at p. 322 above, the picture is more complex when the 'relates to' connection is given flesh by Mason J in *Transfield* v. *Arlo*. There are circumstances in which bundling has nothing to do with gaining an advantage that is collateral to the IP.

As competition law catches tying conduct only when it substantially lessens competition,[97] it might seem to make little difference whether the conduct is exempt. But it can make a difference. One window of difference could be when a dominant licensor insists that licensees get their raw materials or consumables from the licensor for reasons that make lots of sense to any licensor of a product like the licensor's. This condition may lessen competition in the market for raw materials or consumables, but on Mason's view of the 'relates to' test in section 51(3) it would be exempt from the competition test in section 47.

There have been two decisions in Australia that look at tying conduct in the context of intellectual property.

The Australian Competition Tribunal looked at tying in the context of APRA's system for the administration of performance rights.[98] It was APRA's practice to offer only a blanket licence that gave access to the whole of its repertoire. Users argued as an anticompetitive detriment of the blanket licence, that it requires users to pay for music that they do not want. The Tribunal dismissed this criticism as arising from a misunderstanding of the blanket licence.[99] There was no logic in thinking that a licence that allowed licensees to use everything in APRA's repertoire was bought at a higher price than would obtain under a system in which licensees could select item by item. In any industry, this would be a sound conclusion. A monopolist cannot use tying to extract a premium that goes beyond the value the buyers place on the product they want to buy.

In principle, an anticompetitive detriment of APRA's blanket licences might have been that they raised barriers to entry to competition that could undermine APRA's market power. As the Tribunal saw the blanket licence as essential for efficient licensing, it was not going to require changes that would threaten the blanket licence. It did, however, tinker around the edges of the system to permit the emergence of new competition. Individual members were to be allowed to take a licence-back from APRA of any composition so that they could license others. But the licence-back was to be non-exclusive, so that there would be no hole in the repertoire to which APRA could grant a blanket licence.[100]

Universal Music Australia Pty Ltd v. *ACCC*[101] was about tying conduct intended to exclude new competition. As constructed under Australian domestic competition law the case concerned the refusal of the appellant (the Australian subsidiary of a global parent) to supply CDs to Australian retailers who bought CDs in the appellant's catalogue from (cheaper) sources outside Australia.[102] 'If you want any CDs from me, you must not get any that I can supply from anyone else.' There were findings that most record stores could not afford to source all their business offshore because some titles were available only from the Australian distributor and supply from overseas was not quick.

The Full Federal Court upheld the finding that Universal Australia had acted for the purpose of substantially lessening competition in the market for sound recordings in Australia. The Court's reasoning went that although Universal had only 20 per cent of the overall market, its was a market in which products were so highly differentiated that stopping competition from imports in this sector of the market could lessen competition substantially. Further, the introduction of price competition in Universal titles would have flown through to competition between record companies and so affected the whole market.[103] While the result in *Universal* is controversial because of Universal's relatively small market share, the case is an instance of the application of competition law to tying conduct that raises barriers to entry.

V. Two lessons from Australian competition law

A. A statutory exemption for some dealings in intellectual property is not useful

Building the rules for managing the interface between intellectual property and competition law into the competition law itself seems attractive. Law offers more comfort than guidelines on prosecutorial policy. The regulator might change its mind. Private litigants do not share the regulator's perspective.

Some would say that section 51(3) of the Australian Trade Practices Act has been a success. Their measure of success is that there have been few competition law cases involving dealings in intellectual property.

Against that, more than 30 years after the introduction of the Act with section 51(3) in place, there is little consensus on the operation of the section. It is tempting to say that section 51(3) is poorly drafted, and could be cured with a bit of attention. That does not seem to be the case. Two proposals for amendment have not succeeded in delivering a coherent alternative.[104]

Australian experience would suggest that the hunt for a simple test of generic application to intellectual property is likely to be unproductive.

B. The utility of guidelines depends on why? who? how?

If there is one thing that Australian competition lawyers have learned from the 1991 guidelines issued by the Australian regulator it is that the value of guidelines depends on their pedigree and their focus.

The Australian guidelines are a classic in how not to achieve anything. They were compromised from the outset. The regulator, lacking the expertise to produce the guidelines, contracted the task out to private lawyers. A consultative process thereafter saw more IP lawyers argue over the terms of the draft. The result was a mishmash that serves no purpose. The guidelines are neither (a) a coherent, let alone expert, statement of the law, nor (b) a statement of policy that the regulator has felt bound by.

In Australia we risk more of the same. The IPCRC accompanied its proposal for the change to section 51(3) with a recommendation of guidelines that are to do everything, and so nothing.

The ACCC should be required by the legislation to issue guidelines as to the manner in which it will implement any enforcement activities related to these provisions. Those guidelines should provide sufficient direction to owners of intellectual property rights to clarify the types of behaviour likely to result in a substantial lessening of competition ...

The ACCC should be required to consult widely with intellectual property owners, users, facilitators and the public generally in preparing these guidelines.

The recommendation starts off with a role for the guidelines (the ACCC's enforcement policy). It then clouds that role – the guidelines are to go beyond enforcement policy and be a general treatise on the application of the Act to dealings in IP (which IPCRC takes as *types* of behaviour that are likely to lessen competition rather than the market circumstances in which many forms of behaviour will be found to lessen competition). The requirement that there be wide consultation in the preparation of the guidelines is a politic way of hosing down anxiety at the proposed change. Unless the ACCC has the expertise to remain in control of the process, the consultation process risks disembodied guidelines that will not fulfil their first purpose of being a guide to the regulator's enforcement policy.

The guidelines issued by the US Department of Justice and the Federal Trade Commission[105] strike a fine note. Their role is clear – to announce the agencies' prosecutorial policy. The gravitas is clear – the agencies own these guidelines so they will not change policy tomorrow.

Guidelines are useful only if they come with a ring of authority and they are specific about their role. Guidelines that are all things to all men are guides to nothing.

Notes

1. Intellectual Property and Competition Review Committee, *Review of Intellectual Property Legislation under the Competition Principles Agreement* (Canberra: IP Australia, 2000).
2. *Patents Act* s. 135(1)(a)(i).
3. *Patents Act* s. 135(1)(a)(iv).
4. *Patents Act* s. 135(1)(c). Cf. the UK Patents Act which permits grant of a licence on the ground that the patent is not being worked in the UK only if the proprietor is not domiciled in a country which is a member of the World Trade Organisation.
5. In *Fastening Supplies Pty Ltd* v. *Olin Mathieson Chemical Corporation* (1969) 119 CLR 572 the Court found that the reasonable requirements of the Australian public had not been satisfied in respect of an invention but did not grant a licence because the patent holder's Australian licensee gave reason for the delay and by the time of the hearing was making the product available. *Amrad*

Operations Pty Ltd v. *Genelabs Technologies Inc.* [1999] FCA 633 was an application to serve process outside the jurisdiction based on a prima facie case under s. 135(1)(c).

6. Intellectual Property and Competition Review Committee, *Review of Intellectual Property under the Competition Principles Agreement* (2000), 162.

7. Ibid. 163.

8. *Copyright Act* Parts VA and VB.

9. The *Copyright Act 1968* basically implemented the report of the Copyright Law Review Committee 1959 (Spicer Committee) which in turn was based on the 1951 report of the Gregory Committee in the UK.

10. *Copyright Act* s. 136(1): 'licence' means a licence granted by or on behalf of the owner of the copyright.

11. *Copyright Act* s. 157(3).

12. *Designs Bill 2002* clause 90 proposes to retain provision for compulsory licensing.

13. *Patents Act* s. 13 and definition of 'exploit' in Schedule 1; *Designs Act* s. 30(1); *Copyright Act* s. 37.

14. *R & A Bailey & Co Ltd* v. *Boccaccio Pty Ltd* (1986) 77 ALR 177.

15. *Copyright Act* s. 44A.

16. *Copyright Act* s. 44C.

17. *Copyright Act* s. 44D.

18. *Copyright Act* s. 44E.

19. *Copyright Act* s. 44F.

20. Intellectual Property and Competition Review Committee, *Review of Intellectual Property under the Competition Principles Agreement* (2000), 73.

21. Ibid. 162.

22. *Trade Practices Act* s. 96A prohibits vertical price maintenance in the re-supply of services. S.4C(f) defines re-supply of services to include 'a supply of the original services to another person in an altered form or condition' and 'a supply to another person of services that are substantially similar to the original services, and could not have been supplied if the original services had not been acquired by the person who acquired them from the original supplier'.

    There is a fourth per se offence – third-line forcing, prohibited by subsections 47(6) and (7). It is not discussed here both because it is peculiar to Australian law and the government proposes its repeal.

23. See the Trade Practices Tribunal in *Re 7-Eleven Stores Pty Ltd* (1994) Australian Trade Practices Reports 41-357 at 42, 677.

24. *Patents Act*, s. 13 and definition of 'exploit' in Schedule 1.

25. *Betts* v. *Willmott* (1871) LR 6 Ch App 239, 245.

26. (1980) 144 CLR 83.

27. Ibid. 102–3.

28. US Department of Justice and Federal Trade Commission, *Antitrust Guidelines for the Licensing of Intellectual Property* (1995), 8.

29. Trade Practices Commission, *Application of the Trade Practices Act to Intellectual Property* (1991), 24. The guidelines are available on the Commission's website at: http://www.accc.gov.au/fs-pubs.htm.

30. *United States* v. *General Electric Co.*, 272 U.S. 476 (1926) (holding that an owner of a product patent may condition a licence to manufacture the product on the fixing of the first sale price of the patented product) has been qualified in later decisions.

31. Article 3 (1) of EC Regulation 240/96 (a price restriction in a patent and know-how licensing agreement is not exempted from Article 81).

32. *Cummer-Graham Co* v. *Straight Side Basket Corp.*, 142 F.2d 646 (5th Cir. 1944).

33. Cf. in USA *Newburgh Moire Co.* v. *Superior Moire Co.*, 237 F.2d 283 (3rd Cir. 1956) (grant of multiple licences each containing a price restriction does not come within the *General Electric* doctrine).

34. See *Trade Practices Act 1974* s. 96A and definition of re-supply in respect of services at s. 4C(f).

35. Trade Practices Commission, *Application of the Trade Practices Act to Intellectual Property* (1991), 29 at paras 5.61 (full or third line forcing) and 5.66 (leveraging).

36. National Competition Council, *Review of Sections 51(2) and 51(3) of the Trade Practices Act 1974: Final Report* (March 1999).

37. Ibid. 243 (recommendation) and 202–4 (discussion).

38. Ibid. 243 (recommendation) and 212 (discussion).

39. Australian Government Solicitor 'Memorandum of Advice', January 2000. The advice is available at: http://www.ipcr.gov.au/interim/advice.pdf.

40. Intellectual Property and Competition Review Committee, *Review of Intellectual Property under the Competition Principles Agreement* (2000), 207 (apparently talking of the scope of protection in copyright 'works').

41. Ibid. 213.

42. Ibid. 210–11.

43. Ibid. 215.

44. Ibid. 211.

45. Ibid.

46. Ibid.

47. See s. 45(3) and s. 47(13(b).

48. (1987) Australian Trade Practices Reports 40-809.

49. (2000) Australian Trade Practices Reports 41-752.

50. *Stirling Harbour Services Pty Ltd* v. *Bunbury Port Authority* (2000) Australian Trade Practices Reports 41-783 at [12] and [86].

51. See text referred to in note 42 above.

52. Authorisation is not directly available for s. 46. But s. 46(6) exempts from s. 46 conduct that has been authorised under other sections. Conditions in licences may contravene s. 45 or s. 47, and so may be authorised.

53. *Trade Practices Act* s. 90(6). There are various formulations of the public benefit test in s. 90, but the Tribunal has said that the inquiry is the same under all formulations.

54. The Tribunal has described 'public benefit' as 'anything of value to the community generally, any contribution to the aims pursued by society, including as one of the principal elements . . . the achievement of efficiency. . . . [C]ommonly efficiency is said to encompass allocative efficiency, production efficiency, and dynamic efficiency': *Re 7-Eleven Stores Pty Ltd* (1994) Australian Trade Practices Reports 41-357 at 42, 677.

55. In the context of a merger, the prospect of increased economies of scale from the merger has been seen in the court as a negative factor – likely to strengthen the acquirer's market power – and so a reason to condemn the merger: *Trade Practices Commission* v. *Arnotts Ltd* (1990) Australian Trade Practices Reports 41-062 at 51, 885; *QIW Retailers Ltd* v. *Davids Holdings Pty Ltd* (1993) Australian Trade Practices Reports 41-226 at 41, 145; *Davids Holdings Pty Ltd* v. *Attorney-General* (1994) Australian Trade Practices Reports 41-304 per Drummond J at 42,098.

56. The government's response to IPCRC Report is available at: http://www. ipaustralia.gov.au/pdfs/general/response1.PDF. The proposal on s. 51(3) is number 26.

57. *Queensland Wire Industries* v. *BHP* (1989) Australian Trade Practices Reports 40-925 at 50,008 (Mason CJ and Wilson J).

58. Ibid. at 50,015 (Dawson J).

59. Ibid. at 50,011 (Mason CJ and Wilson J), at 50,014 (Dean J), at 50,016-7 (Dawson J), at 50,025 (Toohey J).

60. *Melway Publishing* v. *Robert Hicks* (1999) Australian Trade Practices Reports 41-693 at 42,693-4 (Heerey J).

61. *Warman International Ltd* v. *Envirotech Australia Pty Ltd* (1986) 67 Australian Law Reports 253 (proceedings for infringement of copyright did not contravene s. 46 because to exercise in good faith an extraneous legal right is to take advantage of that right, not of market power). The reasoning in the judgment, turning on the distinction between the legal right that is the source of the market power and market power itself, does not survive the High Court's decision in *Queensland Wire Industries* v. *BHP* (1989) Australian Trade Practices Reports 40-925. However the outcome would be the same applying the High Court's test of 'take advantage'.

62. (1989) Australian Trade Practices Reports 40-925.

63. 645 F.2d 1195 (2d Cir. 1981) 1204.

64. See p. 319 above.

65. 36 F.3d 1147 (1st Cir. 1994).

66. In *Queensland Wire Industries* v. *BHP* a factor in the court's conclusion that BHP's refusal to supply the rolled steel product relevant to the case was taking

advantage of its market power was that BHP supplied all other products of its rolling mill.

67. Undertaking from Telstra to give access to its subscriber database to firms that wish to produce directories that compete with Telstra: ACCC media release 'Telephone Directory Data Now Accessible to All', 19 February 1997. See also ACCC media release 'Weather Court Case Settled', 21 May 1997. The media releases invoke s. 46, but do not attempt to explain why in each case the refusal was a taking advantage of market power.

68. *Pont Data Australia Pty Ltd* v. *ASX Operations Pty Ltd* (1991) Australian Trade Practices Reports 41-109 at 41,145.

69. If the question is framed 'Could the supplier charge so much money without market power?', any price above the price that would be set in a competitive market is a taking advantage of market power.

70. (1989) Australian Trade Practices Reports 40-925 at 50,006 (Mason CJ and Wilson J), 50-012 (Deane J) and 50,017-8 (Toohey J).

71. (1994) 5 New Zealand Business Law Cases 103, 522.

72. Ibid. at 103, 567-103, 571. This pricing formula became known in the course of the proceedings as the Baumol–Willig rule after the economists who proposed it.

73. The ACCC's Merger Guidelines (June 1999) at para. 5.99 suggest that analysis under s. 50 can take into account 'a pattern of creeping acquisitions which have a significant cumulative effect on competition'. The guidelines are available at: http://www.accc.gov.au/merger/fr_mergers.html. The guidelines do not attempt to reconcile this view with the language of s. 50. Since these guidelines the ACCC has sought changes to s. 50 to cover creeping acquisitions.

74. (1999) Australian Trade Practices Reports 40-701.

75. Ibid. at 360.

76. Ibid. at 293. The Tribunal's decision to require APRA to amend its scheme to improve outcomes for users has been criticised as not consistent with the statutory test for authorisation: J. Gans, F. Hanks and P. Williams, 'The Treatment of Natural Monopolies under the Australian Trade Practices Act: Four Recent Decisions' (2001) 29 *Australian Business Law Review* 492, at 504–6.

77. See p. 317 above.

78. (1999) Australian Trade Practices Reports 40-701 at 312-15.

79. National Co-operative Research Act 1984 (US).

80. Regulation No. 2659/2000 on the application of Article 81(3) to research and development agreements (EC).

81. See discussion of 'relates to' at p. 322 above.

82. Section 4D defines an exclusionary provision. All that is necessary is that (a) the provision is in an agreement between persons who are competitive with one another (or would have been in competition but for the provision), and (b) the provision has the purpose of preventing or restricting a party to the agreement dealing with particular persons or class of persons.

83. *Review of the Competition Provisions of the Trade Practices Act* (January, 2003). The report is available at http://tpareview.treasury.gov.au/content/report.asp.
84. Ibid. 131.
85. See p. 325 above.
86. See p. 330 above.
87. *Melway Publishing* v. *Robert Hicks* (2001) Australian Trade Practices Reports 41-805 at 42, 755 (High Court).
88. See *Mark Lyons* v. *Bursill Sportgear* (1987) Australian Trade Practices Reports 40-809 at 48, 802; *Robert Hicks* v. *Melway Publishing* (1999) ATPR 41-668 at 42,524 (trial court).
89. (2001) Australian Trade Practices Reports 41-805 at 42, 756.
90. OECD, *Joint Group on Trade and Competition, Synthesis Report on Parallel Imports* (2002), 45.
91. Levine, M. E., 'Price Discrimination Without Market Power' (2002) 19 *Yale Journal on Regulation* 1.
92. Trade Practices Commission, *Application of the Trade Practices Act to Intellectual Property* (1991), 24. See discussion of 'relates to' at p. 322 above.
93. See text of the law at note 22 above and discussion of 'relates to' at p. 322 above.
94. S. 45A (1) and s. 45(2).
95. The terms on which the licensor has contracted with other licensees figure in the assessment of substantial lessening of competition in respect of any single licence: s. 45(4).
96. Trade Practices Commission, *Application of the Trade Practices Act to Intellectual Property* (1991), 29.
97. S. 47(2) and (10). There is a per se prohibition of 'third line forcing' in ss. 47(6) and (7), but it is ignored in this treatment because it is to be repealed and has no overseas equivalents.
98. *Re Applications by Australasian Performing Right Association Limited* (1999) Australian Trade Practices Reports 40-701.
99. Ibid. at 333, 196–209.
100. Ibid. at 347–58.
101. [2003] FCAFC 193 (22 August 2003).
102. From the perspective of the corporate group the conduct was global market division for the purpose of price discrimination. But the global strategy of Universal Australia's parent was not part of the analysis in the proceedings in Australia.
103. Ibid. at 269.
104. Even the IPCRC, which said that the problem with the current s. 51(3) is that it could mean anything, stuck with the phrase 'relate to' in the change it proposed.
105. US Department of Justice and Federal Trade Commission, *Antitrust Guidelines for the Licensing of Intellectual Property* (1995).

6

Irish competition law and IP rights

IMELDA MAHER

I. The competition law regime

A. Introduction

Irish competition law has undergone rapid transformation in the last fifteen years. This transformation has been parallel to an unprecedented period of growth with GDP rising by 9.6 per cent between 1994 and 2000.[1] A small, open economy located within the EU, Ireland has been described as an outpost of the US economy at the periphery of Europe[2] with US firms accounting for more than 80 per cent of foreign direct investment in the late 1990s.[3] A number of factors contributed to this growth, one of which was the creation of the single European market. The promise of increased competition from imports and the opportunities for export provided by an integrated European market were the main impetus for reform of the competition regime[4] with the Competition Act 1991 replacing a 'control of abuse' system[5] with a prohibition system modelled on EC competition rules (specifically, Articles 81 and 82). The Act combined substantive rules similar to those of the EC regime with weak enforcement mechanisms including an emphasis on private actions. It was subject to two major waves of reform. First, in the Competition (Amendment) Act 1996 stronger enforcement mechanisms were introduced including criminal sanctions for breaches of the main statutory prohibitions.[6] Second, a wide interpretation had been given to the Act by the Competition Authority to include mergers even though they were subject to separate mergers legislation that required notification and ministerial approval in the light of a public interest test.[7] This problem of dual regulation was addressed in the Competition Act 2002 where mergers were removed almost entirely from ministerial control and a single substantial lessening of competition test was introduced.[8] The 2002 Act also anticipated the modernisation of the EC competition rules[9] by removing the notification system and giving the Competition Authority the power to implement the EC rules.[10]

The 1991 Act was passed at a time when certain sectors of the economy were dominated by state-owned monopolies, notably in energy, communications and transport. While it contained no explicit rules relating to state-owned enterprises, the Act could not override pre-existing legislation conferring such monopoly status; hence it had no special provisions akin to those found in Article 86 EC which applies the competition rules to such enterprises while providing a limited safe haven for those firms carrying out services of general economic interest. A wave of liberalising legislation in the 1990s extended the scope of the competition law regime to sectors previously dominated by state-owned monopolies.[11] This liberalisation programme has been driven by obligations under EC law and in general reform has been limited strictly to what those rules require.[12] Thus the extension of competition into sectors previously controlled by state-owned enterprises is top-down in nature unlike the adoption of competition legislation, which was a bottom-up response to the single market.

This chapter provides an introduction to the Irish competition regime before turning to its specific application to intellectual property rights. One of the reasons for adopting this approach is that one of the main characteristics of Irish competition and intellectual property law is the limited amount of law in the area.

B. The constitutional context

The Irish competition rules are subject to the Irish constitution that makes limited reference to competition where it sets out directive principles on social policy. These non-binding guidelines for the Oireachtas (the Irish legislature) call on the state to develop policies that will advance the common good. In particular, Article 45.2 warns that competition should not be allowed to operate so freely as to allow for the concentration of ownership or control of essential commodities in the hands of a few individuals to the common detriment. Similarly, the state is to ensure that private enterprise is conducted in a manner that is reasonably efficient in the production and distribution of goods and shall protect the public against unjust exploitation.[13] The inclusion of references to competition in this part of the constitution is of some, but not of much, significance. Nonetheless the competition regime has to be located within its constitutional context.

An unusual and flawed application of the constitutional property provisions in the context of competition law arose in the *HB* case,[14] one of several cases between the two multinationals, Mars and Unilever (parent of the Irish subsidiary HB), over the provision and/or use of ice-cream refrigerators in retail outlets.[15] The case was argued on the basis of EC law and concerned the market exclusion effect of the exclusive use provisions in contracts between Unilever and retailers, under which Unilever provided fridges to retail outlets free of charge. The Irish High Court while expressly recognising the supremacy of EC competition law relied on Article 295 that states that the EC Treaty does not prejudice national property ownership systems. Side-stepping a Commission decision[16] that a similar set of agreements were not protected by Article 295, Keane J held there was a serious case to be tried on the issue of wrongful interference with HB's property rights in its freezers. It is difficult to see how constitutional property rights were under threat here, as HB did not, in the end, have to transfer ownership of the freezers or to conclude contracts with anyone it had not selected in order to remove the anticompetitive effect of the exclusivity clause. It could – as the Court of First Instance suggested – impose a rental fee for use of the freezers.[17] The Court of First Instance thus agreed with the Commission and rejected the argument based on Article 295. HB was not denied its property rights in the freezers nor was it prevented from commercial exploitation of those rights. However any such exploitation could not constitute an abuse of dominance under Article 82 by causing market foreclosure as it had done in this instance.

C. EC competition law[18] and Irish competition law

Formally, the EC competition rules are contained in the EC Treaty and hence have a quasi-constitutional status. Articles 81 and 82 have direct effect under EC law. This means that individuals can rely on them before national courts. Thus these rules do not require implementing measures in order to be invoked before the courts and they apply wherever there is an effect on inter-state trade – a somewhat vague but widely drawn test. Member States are obliged to abstain from doing anything that would hamper the effectiveness of the EC rules.[19] Thus the Irish rules are not a result of EC legal obligations but are subject to the duty of loyalty in Article 10 and, more specifically, the rules governing the relationship between national and EC competition law now contained in Article 3 of Regulation 1/2003. This provision requires national courts and competition authorities to apply the EC rules where there is an effect on inter-state trade but also allows the application of equivalent national competition rules save that stricter national rules pertaining to restrictive agreements cannot be applied.

By voluntarily adopting national law based on the EC rules, Ireland was at the forefront of a trend in competition law seen across Europe,[20] one which in turn provided the context within which decentralised enforcement of EC competition law could be introduced conferring additional powers on national competition agencies, extending the scope of EC law, and reducing the risk of double jeopardy. The Irish government chose to adopt the EC model as one that was familiar and ready-made.[21] The Irish Act is freestanding formally but substantively is nested within the EC regime with the courts (and the Competition Authority) adopting a principle of consistency tempered by practicability.[22] Thus the two regimes are broadly similar with the new powers of the Authority to apply Articles 81 and 82 and its participation in the European Competition Network (of competition authorities) likely to reinforce consistency in interpretation.[23] Nonetheless differences remain.

From a policy perspective, the Irish and EC competition regimes differ, as there is no market integration agenda at the national level – an agenda that has had a profound impact on EC competition law. As the internal market has become more of a reality, the integration imperative has been weakened leading to a shift in emphasis at the EC level notably in relation to vertical restraints that are now tolerated to a much greater degree.[24] In Ireland, the policy underlying the law is one of promotion of competition[25] although the Supreme Court has indicated that regard also has to be had to the requirements of the common good[26] – adding a constitutional 'flavour' to the regime.

Institutionally, the two regimes also differ. Unlike the EC Commission, the Irish Competition Authority cannot itself impose fines. Article 38.1 of the constitution states that '[N]o person shall be tried on any criminal charge save in due course of law'. Fines are deemed to be a criminal sanction and hence can only be imposed by the courts.[27] While the Competition Authority cannot fine, both civil and criminal sanctions – including imprisonment – are available for breach of the competition rules – it thus has a wider arsenal of sanctions available than the Commission.[28] Formally, the Irish rules do not enjoy the quasi-constitutional status of Articles 81 and 82 but are statute-based and hence do not trump existing law.[29] There are also textual differences between the two regimes. For example the definition of 'undertaking' differs with Irish law requiring an undertaking to be 'engaged for gain' – a requirement not found under EC Law. Both the High Court and Supreme Court considered this difference in one of the first cases under the 1991 Act.[30] The High Court interpreted 'gain' as meaning profit but this was overruled on appeal with the Court taking a purposive approach extending the remit of the Act to include, in that case, a non-profit statutory body which charged for its services. Despite two reforms of the Act, the reference to 'engaged for gain' remains in the statutory definition of an 'undertaking'.

Despite these differences, EC competition rules exert a powerful influence on Irish law.[31] Shanley J, speaking of the 1991 Act, provided a clear statement of the relationship between the two regimes that still holds good today:

> The 1991 Act is an autonomous Act of the Oireachtas and not one implementing a directive of the European Union. It has its own machinery for implementing its rule on competition which is quite different to those of the Treaty. In applying the jurisprudence of the European Court of Justice, the Court of First Instance and the Commission, to sections 4 and 5 of the 1991 Act, there is no doubt that decisions of those bodies should have very strong persuasive force – however, it should be borne in mind that such decisions are based upon competition rules which are, textually and contextually, different from the 1991 rule and which often are decisions

influenced or affected either by policy considerations, objectives or Articles
of the Treaty which do not necessarily underpin the 1991 Act.[32]

A difference between these two regimes is inevitable given differing policy
concerns, market environment and the constitutional and institutional contexts. What is important is that the Authority and courts seek to maintain the
integrity of these two largely complimentary regimes so as to ensure consistency of the law both within and between the two regimes. This task will
become easier over time due to modernisation of the EC regime with its
emphasis on decentralised enforcement by national competition authorities
including the Irish authority.[33]

D. The competition rules

1. The prohibitions

The Irish regime is closely modelled on Articles 81 and 82 EC. Thus section 4 of
the Competion Act 1991 prohibits agreements, decisions by associations of
undertakings or concerted practices which have as their object or effect the
prevention, restriction or distortion of competition in trade in any goods or
services in the state or in any part of the state. Such agreements are void.
Exemptions are possible for agreements, decisions or concerted practices which
contribute to improving the production or distribution of goods or to promoting technical or economic progress while allowing consumers a fair share of the
resulting benefit, and which do not impose restrictions which are not indispensable nor eliminate competition. Under section 5, abuse of dominance by
one or more undertakings is prohibited. The prohibitions apply to all sectors of
the economy. Thus there is no equivalent to Article 86(2) that provides limited
exemptions for publicly owned companies or those awarded special rights.
However, the competition rules do not override other legislation conferring
special rights and hence the exercise of those rights may fall outside those
rules[34] (although there has been extensive liberalisation and the scope of any
special rights is subject to the EC competition regime where there is an effect on
inter-state trade). The prohibitions apply to undertakings engaged for gain,
which the courts have defined functionally by distinguishing commercial
activities from the exercise of administrative, regulatory, or industrial relations
functions, even where there is a charge involved. For example, a minister may
constitute an undertaking but is not engaged for gain when she imposes a
charge for the provision of a licence.[35] Thus, it is possible for a body to be an
undertaking within the Act for some purposes but not for others.[36] This is
echoed in the interpretation of the reference to restriction on competition in
trade or services and dominance in trade or services where a broad interpretation has been given, so trade is not limited to carrying on business for profit
but includes charging for services.[37]

The aim of the prohibitions is to protect competition and not competitors, thus evidence of impact on a competitor is not in itself enough to bring an arrangement or conduct within the Act.[38] In determining the object of an agreement the courts have regard not to the subjective intentions of the parties but to the objective situation.[39] Only if there is no such object is regard had to the effect of the agreement by looking to the whole economic context in which the arrangement operates.[40] Section 4(1) does not apply (i) if the restriction on competition can be objectively justified, e.g. to ensure food traceability;[41] (ii) if the effect on competition is not appreciable e.g. price discrimination of less than 1p per unit;[42] and (iii) if the restrictive clauses in an agreement are ancillary and necessary such that the agreement would not have come into existence without them, e.g. non-compete clauses in sale of business agreements which are of limited duration.[43] The legislation only applies to the state. This means that it does not apply to agreements that affect competition in markets outside the state;[44] or to restrictions that extend to a geographic area beyond the state.[45] Similarly, dominance must be in all or part of the state under section 5(1). For both provisions, the Commission decisions and European courts case law are treated as highly persuasive, especially given the limited amount of litigation on competition law in Ireland.

2. Mergers

The merger regime in Ireland is less closely modelled on the EC merger regulation substantively, although procedurally the two systems are very similar. The 2002 Act introduced a new competition regime for mergers both substantively and procedurally removing almost entirely any ministerial input,[46] enhancing the role of the Competition Authority, and emphasising competition as the relevant benchmark.[47] It also removed the controversial dual regulation that previously arose under section 4 of the Competition Act and the 1978 Mergers, Takeovers and Monopolies (Control) Act.[48] The statutory test for evaluating the effect on competition for mergers is now the substantial lessening of competition with any statutory reference to the common good removed.[49] This differs from the EU merger regulation where the test used to assess mergers is whether they create a significant impediment on effective competition, in particular as a result of the creation or strengthening of a dominant position.[50] A merger or acquisition arises where: previously independent undertakings merge; undertaking(s) acquire direct or indirect control of the whole or part of other undertaking(s); as a result of the acquisition of assets, one undertaking substantially replaces another in business (or part thereof).[51] In addition, a joint venture is a merger where it is created to perform on an indefinite basis all the functions of an autonomous economic entity.[52] Regard is had to all circumstances when establishing if there has been acquisition of control[53] with the test a functional one of decisive influence.[54] A merger is notified to the Authority[55] when it has been agreed or will occur, if a public bid is made and accepted and if it falls above three thresholds:

- a worldwide turnover of each of two or more of the undertakings involved is not less than 40 million euros;
- and each of two or more of the undertakings involved carries on business in any part of the island of Ireland (this includes Northern Ireland which is part of the United Kingdom but shares a common border);
- and the turnover in the state of any one of the undertakings involved is not less than 40 million euros.[56]

Failure to meet notification requirements can lead to prosecution and fining of the person in control of the undertaking.[57] A merger cannot be given effect pending a determination by the Authority within the time limits set down in the Act.[58] Like the EC Commission, the Authority considers the merger within an initial one-month period and then, if further consideration is warranted, completes its investigation within four months.[59] In making its determination, the Authority can consider submissions made by the under-takings involved or by any individual or other undertaking[60] and can enter into discussions with them with a view to identifying measures that would ameliorate any effects of the merger on competition.[61] This approach gives the Authority considerable bargaining power and flexibility in achieving a negotiated outcome where the merger can be approved on the basis of the parties' proposals. There is an appeal from a determination of the Authority to the High Court which the Court must hear within two months[62] and from there to the Supreme Court.[63] Compliance with a determination can be secured by the Authority or any other person through the civil courts.[64] In addition, criminal sanctions including fines and/or imprisonment can be imposed on any person who contravenes a determination or commitment or anyone who aids and abets them.[65]

3. Institutions

The Minister for Enterprise Trade and Employment is ultimately responsible for competition policy although the 2002 Act reduced her role and cor-respondingly strengthened the role of the Authority. The Minister necessarily retains the power to enact secondary legislation[66] and the Authority is accountable to her through planning and reporting mechanisms notably the production of three-year plans and annual programmes of activities as well as annual accounts.[67] The Authority's annual report also goes to both the Minister and Oireachtas.[68] Finally, any cooperation agreement entered into with other regulators must be given to the Minister within six months[69] and her consent is required for exchange of information agreements entered into with foreign competition agencies.[70] The Minister has a number of powers in relation to the members of the Authority. She appoints the Authority[71] and its staff.[72] She can remove a member but this power is constrained by the requirement that she lay before both Houses of the Oireachtas a reasoned statement explaining the removal.[73] She fixes the terms and conditions of employment of the members and their staff.[74] She can reduce the number of members required for the Authority to be quorate.[75] She can sanction borrowing and the acquisition, holding or disposing of land or other property by it.[76] Perhaps most significantly, she controls the budget of the Authority with resourcing decisions taking in consultation with the Minister for Finance.[77] In relation to mergers, as well as retaining special powers in relation to media mergers, the Minister can annually review the size of the thresholds[78] and has power to bring a class of merger within the Act even outside the thresholds.[79]

The Competition Authority has a chairperson and not less than two or more than five members appointed for not more than five years.[80] The chairperson is responsible for the management and control of the Authority.[81] The Authority has an advocacy role under which it can carry out studies on its own initiative or at the behest of the Minister;[82] advise government of the implications for competition policy of any legislation being proposed; advise public authorities on competition matters; and identify and comment on any constraints imposed by enactment or administrative practice on the operation of competition in the economy. It also provides guidance to those subject to the law through publishing notices offering practical guidance on competition issues.[83]

The Authority enjoys extensive powers of investigation. It can carry out an investigation either on its own initiative or on foot of a complaint.[84] Investigations are backed up by criminal sanctions (fines and imprisonment), and civil actions and are assisted by the appointment of authorised officers who can, on production of a court warrant, exercise entry and search powers.[85] In summary proceedings the Authority can bring the action to the courts itself but where proceeding on indictment, it must refer the matter to the public prosecutor, the Director of Public Prosecutions.[86] The fact that enforcement of the competition rules has to be mediated through the courts means that the Authority has less control over enforcement. This can be seen in a positive and negative light. On the one hand, it becomes more difficult for the Authority to develop an enforcement strategy when it is dependent on the DPP to bring a case. Second, the imposition of fines by the EC Commission (and indeed other competition agencies) is controversial with concerns about the impartiality of the agency when making its decision where it has also investigated the matter.[87] This implies that effective enforcement of the rules may be compromised where it is mediated through the general courts but due process is preserved. The emphasis at the outset was on private enforcement of the competition rules and initially there was no means for the

Authority to enforce the rules through the courts. This proved ineffectual and was changed by the 1996 Act although few cases are pursued in the courts.[88] In the meanwhile, there are few cases concerning private enforcement[89] with the adage 'do business first and sue later' all the more appropriate in the very small Irish economy. The Competition Authority also suffered crippling resource problems with it describing itself as 'barely operational' in its 2000 Annual Report[90] although this seems to have improved in more recent years. In short, while the statutory regime has improved with each revision, resources have lagged behind creating the impression of some ambivalence in government towards competition policy.

Unlike the EC regime where all competition appeals go to the Court of First Instance, there is no designated court to deal with competition matters in Ireland, although recently a number of High Court judges have been given responsibility for hearing competition cases that come before that court.[91] This means that major cases will be brought before judges with some specialism but lower courts also have jurisdiction to hear competition cases (depending on the damages being sought), and there is no specialism at those levels.

Finally, sectoral regulators also have a role to play in monitoring and promoting competition within those sectors for which they are responsible although they do not have a role under the Competition Act. The Commission for Electricity Regulation (and the relevant Minister) has the duty to promote competition within the electricity sector – although this is one of many others including e.g. protection of the environment.[92] The Director of Communications Regulation also includes clauses equivalent to section 5 in licences issued. The Authority and statutory bodies with competition powers have entered into agreements to facilitate cooperation, avoid duplication and ensure consistency. The agreements will allow for the exchange of information, sharing of activities and consultation. This should avoid problems of dual regulation although there are no legal sanctions to ensure compliance with the agreement.[93] The Director of Consumer Affairs was responsible for the enforcement of the anachronistic fair trade measure – the Groceries Order[94] – and the Prices Acts.[95]

II. Intellectual property law and competition law

A. The constitutional and EC context

While the constitutional provisions offering protection to property rights have generated case law, these provisions have had little impact in practice on intellectual property rights. Article 40.3.2 requires the state to protect, inter alia, the property rights of every citizen and Article 43 explicitly allowing for the regulation and delimitation of the exercise of property rights by the state.[96] The state thus has a constitutional role to play in reconciling private property rights with the exigencies of the common good, the exercise of such rights being subject to principles of social justice. The constitutional guarantee – with the two constitutional provisions mutually reinforcing each other[97] – extends to intangible property rights including intellectual property[98] and can be invoked by legal, as well as natural, persons.[99] Hogan and Whyte identify a two-step test for deciding whether a limitation on property rights offends against the constitutional guarantee of private property.[100] First, whether the objective that gave rise to the restriction was justified in terms of social justice and the exigencies of the common good and, second, are the means for securing that objective compatible with the Constitution? In practice they note that in those relatively small number of cases where a restriction on a property right is unconstitutional it tends to be the means that are the problem rather than the objective with the courts in recent years using a proportionality test to assess those means. The Authority in its application of the competition rules to intellectual property rights has not discussed these constitutional provisions and the issue has not arisen before the Irish courts.

Irish intellectual property law – contained in statutes dating from the 1960s – was reformed in the 1990s mainly due to the need to incorporate EC directives into domestic law. The main legislation is the Trade Marks Act 1996, the Patents Act 1992, the Copyright and Related Rights Act 2000 and the Industrial Designs Act 2001.

B. Authority decisions

The Irish courts have not considered the relationship between IPR and Irish competition law although one of the most famous cases concerning the interface of IPR and EC competition law arose out of a dispute in Ireland. In *Magill*, television companies sought to rely on their (Irish) copyright in television listings to justify a refusal to supply to a magazine owner wanting to introduce a weekly listings magazine – a new product that did not previously exist on the Irish market. This was the first case where the European court controversially introduced mandatory licensing of copyright.[101]

The Authority has generally seen IPRs in a positive light. It expressly takes the view that there should be no presumption of dominance where there are IPRs.[102] In most instances it is of the view that there are substitutable processes that allow for competition and the incentives for competitors to innovate are high provided barriers to entry are not themselves too high. Thus even if there is market power it will be short-lived in these circumstances.[103] It sees the dynamic gains from innovation as outweighing any static losses conferred e.g. by patent rights.[104] It applies an economic analysis in its decisions, offering an analysis of the risks associated with R&D noting that only a small proportion of R&D projects are successful. It repeatedly notes the public good nature of innovation which is very costly to achieve but can often be disseminated almost without cost. Thus it allowed a Telco R&D joint venture established to take advantage of EC Commission R&D schemes.[105] In general, it sees R&D joint ventures between non-competitors as not falling within the competition prohibitions as there is little risk of collusion and it achieves the societal (and individual) objective of efficient R&D – which in turn is an engine of growth for the economy.[106] It is in language such as this we see the extent to which the Authority does not engage in a literal interpretation of the competition legislation[107] but instead relies more and more on an explicit economic analysis.

There are about 50 Authority decisions concerning IPRs. Few are likely in the future given the abolition of the notification system but these decisions are likely to continue to be influential as they set out the Authority's view of the relationship between IP and competition law and what sorts of clauses are acceptable in licensing and other agreements concerning IPRs. Most decisions concern scrutiny of particular clauses in the licensing agreements which might constitute entry barriers, e.g. non-compete clauses,[108] non-disclosure,[109] exclusivity, no-challenge clauses,[110] and quality maintenance clauses,[111] with the Authority time and again commencing its analysis by noting that the dynamic gains of innovation outweigh static loss. It notes there can be a tension between IP law and competition law but adopts an economic perspective which generally sees it giving a benign interpretation to the licensing agreements it has assessed.

1. Exclusivity

The Authority certified a number of exclusive licensing agreements indicating that they fell outside the section 4(1) prohibition on anti-competitive arrangements. Exclusivity can lead to market foreclosure thus raising competition concerns but where there is effective competition in the market already and the licence allows a new player onto the Irish market, then section 4(1) is not breached. Thus an exclusive trademark and know-how licensing agreement between a British and Irish manufacturer of animal feedstuffs fell outside the section. The exclusivity of the agreement, the requirements to manufacture according to the specifications of the licensor and to maintain quality standards were deemed unproblematic from a competition perspective.[112] An exclusive patent licensing agreement[113] also allowing a new market entrant in a highly competitive market was certified. Under the licence between an American patent holder and an Irish producer of a hypertension drug the licensee was free to produce other products and to introduce generics on expiry of the patent and there was no restriction on inter-brand competition.[114]

The Authority did not certify an exclusive distribution agreement between two actual or potential competitors in the *Smith & Nephew* decision. Such horizontal distribution agreements would normally fall foul of the competition rules[115] but in this decision an exemption was granted partly because of the unusual IPR. The distribution agreement was part of a wider deal where S&N was selling its trademark for the Nivea brand in Ireland and the UK to Beiersdorf who owned the rights elsewhere. The split in ownership dated back to sequestration at the end of World War II. The agreements had already been subject to a comfort letter from the Commission. The consolidation package removed the possibility of restricting parallel imports – a clear benefit to competition – and also allowed S&N which is a relatively small player in a market dominated by multinationals – to improve R&D. Strict reporting requirements were imposed on the parties to remove the risk of price collusion.[116] The decision follows and relies on the ECJ judgment in *Hag II* that also concerned the consequences of sequestration of IPRs.[117]

2. Software licensing

The Authority sees computer software development as a form of R&D with licensing to third parties being socially beneficial and the market one with low entry barriers; thus conflict between the competition rules and such licences are unlikely.[118] A non-exclusive licence for the production, development and use of software was certified[119] with the Authority accepting the importance of the protection of source codes for computer programs and hence allowing a three-year post-term non-compete clause (usually only two years is allowed where there is no know-how involved).[120] It also accepted the provision of end-users lists to the licensor because ownership in the programs remains with the licensor as well as a licensing back arrangement of any improvements made by the licensee.

3. Mergers and sale of business

The merger notice indicates that where there are any concerns on the part of the Authority in relation to the competitive effect of a merger then it is for the parties to show that there is sufficient risk of new market entrants to ameliorate that concern. The Authority provides a non-exhaustive list of factors that would imply high barriers to entry, including the question of whether the market incumbents have exclusive access to superior technology and/or the ownership of intellectual property rights.[121] Where there is the sale of a business, the Authority is concerned to ensure that the vendor can re-enter the market after the expiry of a legitimate non-compete clause. This does not preclude restrictions, unlimited in time, on the use of company trade names as this does not preclude re-entry.[122] Similarly, restrictions on disclosure of confidential information (including know-how) are also acceptable – provided they are not used to prevent re-entry by the vendor.[123] Indefinite restrictions on disclosure of confidential information – which the Authority sees as akin to know-how – are also allowed on termination of principal/agent agreements given the proximity of the relationship between the parties during the agreement, the need to protect the information and the fact that the former agent cannot be prevented from disclosing it should it otherwise enter the public domain.[124]

4. Vertical agreements

The extent to which vertical agreements fall outside or are exempt from the section 4 (1) prohibition is set down in a notice[125] and declaration.[126] The declaration is akin to the EC block exemption regulation (BER) on vertical restraints and the Authority advises business to read the declaration in the light of the BER. There is not – and never has been – an equivalent to the Technology Transfer Regulation in Irish law.[127] Vertical agreements for the sale or production of goods or services are deemed to meet the conditions for exemption in section 4(5). Competing undertakings that enter into vertical agreements fall outside the declaration save where they operate at different levels of the supply chain in relation to the goods or services subject to the agreement and the buyer does not produce competing goods or services.[128] The exemption can only apply where the supplier's market share is less than 30 per cent of the market on which it sells the goods or services. Where the agreement relates to exclusive supply, then it is the buyer that cannot hold more than a 30 per cent relevant market share.[129]

Vertical agreements, even if they contain provisions assigning or licensing IPRs,[130] are still exempt subject to three conditions. First, the IPRs must not constitute the primary object of the agreements and, second, the IP provisions must be directly related to the use, sale or resale of goods or services by the buyer or its customers.[131] Finally, the provisions must not contain restrictions of competition that have the same object or effect as vertical restraints not covered by the declaration. These restraints are dealt with in Articles 4 and 5 of the declaration. Agreements not covered by the declaration are those which have as their object a ban on resale price maintenance; restrictions on the sort of customer or the territory where the buyer can sell; or restrictions on sale of components by the supplier to end-users or others not entrusted to carry out the repair or service by the buyer. In selective distribution agreements, restrictions on sales to end users and restrictions on cross-supplies fall outside the scope of the declaration[132] as do any restriction on the sale of competing brands.[133] Non-compete clauses of 5 years or indefinite duration fall outside the declaration.[134] Post-termination restrictions on manufacture, purchase or sale by the buyer also fall outside the declaration save where: first, the restriction is limited to goods or services that compete with the contract goods or services; second, is limited to the premises and land the buyer operates from during the contract; third, is indispensable to protect know-how[135] transferred by the supplier; and finally, the post-term non-compete clause is limited to one year. The restriction can however be unlimited in time in relation to disclosure of know-how where the know-how has not entered the public domain.[136]

The notice provides a safe harbour for non-exclusive distribution agreements and genuine agency agreements irrespective of market share. Other vertical agreements – exclusive purchasing, exclusive distribution, franchises and selective distribution all fall outside section 4(1) where the combined market share of the undertakings to the agreement is less than 15 per cent in the relevant market. If the parties' market share is between 15 and 30 per cent then they can avail of the declaration for exemption. In all instances, the agreements cannot contain the blacklisted clauses that are the same in both the notice and declaration and mirror those found in the EC block exemption, thus ensuring consistency between the two regimes.

Exclusive purchasing agreements for motor fuels and liquefied petroleum gas are excluded from the declaration.[137] The early exemption for solus agreements – exclusive purchasing agreements between oil producers and petrol stations – remains in force.[138] The agreements – which contain ancillary provisions protecting the trademarks of the oil producers – are deemed exempt with the IP provisions not raising any concerns on the part of the Authority. The cylinder gas market was investigated by the Authority that expressed concern about the reduction in competition following the expiry in 1999 of a category licence that had limited the duration of exclusive distribution contracts and replaced it with a declaration.[139]

5. Collecting societies[140]

Collecting societies provide a one-stop-shop for composers and performers and those wishing to reproduce their works – especially music. Because of the difficulties for individual composers, musicians and music publishers to collect royalties every time their music is played publicly, they become members of the society that then collects royalties and negotiates terms and conditions for reproduction of their works. The network effects of the agreements pose a problem for competition while the efficiency and convenience of the societies also have considerable benefits.[141] Collecting societies was the one area of IP law where there were several Competition Authority decisions.[142] These took place in the context of the emergence of effective collecting societies in Ireland[143] and a long running dispute over payment for the playing in public of recordings between collecting societies and trade associations representing hotels and nightclubs.[144] In general, the Authority's approach has been that once the membership rules allow members a certain amount of freedom to ensure some competition they have been deemed to either fall outside section 4(1) entirely or to be exempt. This is despite the important network effects in particular of the membership rules.

The Authority initially refused a certificate or licence for the standard contract of assignment of copyright from the composer/publisher to a collecting society for performing rights (the Performing Rights Society).[145] The agreements fell within section 4(1) for a number of reasons. The society was an economic entity separate from its members, thus there was an agreement between undertakings. The agreement locked in its members. The scope of the assignment made it difficult if not impossible for members to administer part of their copyright themselves (which super-bands might want to do). Termination was difficult and could only occur every three years. Price competition between members was removed through the uniform rates for royalties. Because almost all active composers and performers in the UK and Ireland were members of the society it was in effect an exclusive collective copyright enforcement system that restricted the ability of users to secure material from anywhere else. The agreement was not exempt, because even though it improved the provision of services and allowed consumers a fair share of the resulting benefit by reducing transaction costs and ensuring a greater variety of music, the exclusivity of the agreements and their price controls eliminated competition while terms relating to duration and exclusivity were not indispensable for the benefits of collective licensing.

After the Irish Music Rights Organisation (IMRO) separated from the Performing Rights Society (PRS) in January 1995,[146] it notified and secured a licence for its standard agreements for assignment of copyright by members.[147] PRS was entitled to appoint three directors of IMRO but when the Authority expressed concern about a potential competitor having such a power IMRO changed its memorandum to remove it. Section 4(1) was breached by the agreements for the same reasons as given in Decision No. 326. However, the agreements were exempt this time round because they had been changed to include a grant-back clause allowing a grant-back to a member of a non-exclusive licence to allow them to exercise all or part of their performing rights and restrictions on termination and the dividing up of rights were annual rather than once every three years. The existence of the grant-back arrangement meant that copyright holders could provide some price competition and, in any event, the Authority noted that there was some degree of non-price competition.[148]

A number of agreements between collecting societies and users were held to fall outside the section 4(1) prohibition. Thus a non-exclusive licence between IMRO and independent radio stations was certified.[149] It was in effect a blanket licence to play all copyright music, given the reciprocal arrangements IMRO had with overseas collecting societies. IMRO did not have an absolute monopoly as copyright users could negotiate directly with individual copyright holders and with overseas collecting societies, as their arrangement with IMRO was non-exclusive. In practice however the blanket licence saved on transaction costs, which for small radio stations could prove prohibitive. The agreement ensured such small operators could continue to broadcast and hence facilitated competition in the independent radio sector.

Synchronisation licences were also held to fall outside section 4(1). These licences are granted by a collecting society to television or radio production companies where they are supplying an end product – making use of commercially exploited music performed by recognised artists for television and radio broadcast.[150] The copyright owners had the right to refuse the use of their music or to set the royalty rate. Thus there was no price-fixing and nothing in the agreement that restricted competition. The agreements with radio stations allowing them to use members' music e.g. for advertising, were also outside section 4(1). The only controversial requirement – allowing MCPSI, the collecting society, to enter the radio premises to ensure compliance with the licence – was deemed no more than was necessary.

In other decisions exemptions were granted usually for a period of 15 years. The question of renewal was unlikely to arise given the move away from notification in the 2002 Act. An exemption was granted to IMRO and television companies for their non-exclusive licensing agreements allowing retransmission of UK television terrestrial services by cable operators and Multipoint Multiwave Distribution System operators for a four-year period.[151] A certificate was not possible because of the cartel effect of the agreements with actual or potential competitors joining together. The collective licensing agreements infringed section 4(1) per se because they removed price competition. The Authority noted that retransmission would be extremely difficult without a blanket licence as consent by both broadcasters and copyright holders is required. A licence was issued as the agreement benefited consumers, improved services and did not contain any unnecessary terms. It did not eliminate competition because new broadcasters could be added to the agreement and consumer satellite dishes also provided some competition.[152]

The Authority received submissions from the Association of Independent Radio Stations (AIRS) arguing that IMRO could charge excessive royalties because of its monopoly position and that its agreements should not be certified or exempted. The Authority noted that the pricing system was not discriminatory but did not express an opinion as to its fairness as that did not impinge on competition. AIRS also alleged abuse of dominance but this argument was not relevant to a notification under section 4.[153] In a later decision where similar objections were raised, the Authority noted that section 5 does not prevent monopoly – simply its abuse. Within the context of section 4, the Authority did not believe it could require there to be more than one collecting society in the state. There were no impediments in its view to the creation of other such societies.[154]

Membership and user agreements involving the Mechanical Copyright Protection Society (a collecting society for mechanical copyright which is the restriction on reproducing the work in material form) (MCPS) were granted an exemption in 1999.[155] This is unusual as agreements that allow for horizontal price fixing would rarely qualify but the Authority recognised the very unusual nature of this particular market. MCPS had argued that the agreement with members was an agency agreement and thus outside the scope of section 4(1). The Authority disagreed because of the autonomy MCPS had in making commercial decisions; thus it was instead an agreement between an association of undertakings and its members. The fact that MCPS membership had to be exclusive brought the membership rules within section 4(1) as it constituted a barrier to market entry. There was also scope for horizontal price fixing between members. The one-year membership rule was deemed reasonable and other agents could be appointed outside the UK – which included Ireland and hence introduced an element of flexibility for members. The agreements with users also led to price fixing as between members. However, the agreements were all licensed. The collecting society promotes the production and distribution of a service. Composers can focus on their creative work while users save on costs by dealing with a single intermediary. Even the fact that the MCPS had 95 per cent of the market did not preclude exemption. In practice, an alternative collecting society is unlikely to emerge because of the network effects involved – composers and users have incentives to use a single society.[156] The exclusive nature of the membership agreement was mitigated by the fact that members could choose to exercise their own rights while retaining their membership. Thus the agreement did not impose any indispensable terms nor afford the possibility of eliminating competition contrary to section 4(2). Users also benefited from the membership arrangement in that they could be confident that MCPS had the authority to act for the composer thus improving the distribution of copyright material. In fact, the Authority saw the intermediary role of the collecting society as indispensable since it allowed for the legal use of copyright material in a safe and uncomplicated manner. The horizontal price fixing was indispensable as it was not feasible to revert to a composer on each occasion to fix a royalty rate; thus users and ultimately consumers received a fair share of the resulting benefit. The lowering of transaction costs by the existence of the collecting society was deemed a benefit for users and composers. Overall the arrangements were pro-competitive as they facilitated the distribution of intellectual property to end-users. The Authority put some weight on the fact that the 1963 Copyright Act had recognised the existence of collecting societies and noted that where there are any disputes from licensing schemes these can be dealt with by the Controller of Industrial and Commercial Property.

An exemption was also granted to MCPS for its side agreements with members who control copyright in certain production music[157] and recordings. Under the agreements the members appointed MCPS as exclusive agent to manage and administer the members' Sound Recording Rights that subsist in Production Recordings.[158] The agreements fell within section 4(1) because of their exclusivity – no other supplier of the rights was available to users. Royalty rates were also uniform thus eliminating price competition between members. However, the agreements were exempt under section 4(2). The Authority repeated what it had said in Decision 569 as to the benefits collecting societies bring to the distribution of copyright material in the state which carry through both to the users and ultimate consumers. The prohibition in the agreement preventing members from issuing licences themselves was deemed indispensable because it improved production and distribution of the copyright material – the quick, easy and reliable system would be undermined if members could grant licences themselves directly for some of their works but not others.

A licence was granted to Phonographic Performance (Ireland) Limited (PPI) – the collecting society whose members were record companies who assigned their copyright in performing rights to it – in relation to its member-ship and user agreements.[159] The membership agreement fell within section 4(1) due to its exclusivity – users could not purchase the global perform-ing rights from anyone other than PPI. Price competition was restricted due to uniform royalty rates. The agreements with radio stations also had uniform royalty rates thus constituting horizontal price-fixing. The Authority grant-ing a licence again relied on Decision 569 and repeated its position as to the benefits to competition of the role of collecting societies. In relation to assign-ment, it referred to its approach to IMRO noting that the assignment of copyright was in principle licensable (although no member had ever requested it or indeed made any representation about it to the Authority), and while the PPI assignment did vary a little from those of the IMRO agreements that had been exempted, the differences were not such as to lead to a different outcome. Should PPI refuse a request for a licence from one of its members then the Authority indicated that this would constitute a material change of circum-stances in relation to the exemption.

There have been few controversies as between Irish competition law and intellectual property law with the Competition Authority emphasising the importance of IPRs for innovation. Exemptions or exclusions are generally granted provided entry barriers are not too high. There is likely to be even less activity by the Authority after the 2002 Act now that the notification system has been abolished.

III. Conclusion

Irish competition law has succeeded in accomodating IPRs relatively uncon-troversially. The context is one of low activity but for the series of decisions relating to collecting societies and even then, after one decision pointing out which clauses were unacceptable, agreements have been either exempted or deemed to fall outside section 4(1) entirely. Section 5 has not given rise to any litigation which is partly a product of the reticence to resort to litigation on competition matters. The picture is one of Irish competition law broadly shadowing EC competition law in this field as in others.[160]

Notes

1. J. Haughton, 'The Historical Background' in J. W. O'Hagan (ed.), *The Economy of Ireland: Policy and Performance of a European Region* (Gill & Macmillan, 8th edn, 2000) at 39.
2. Ibid. at 44.
3. M. O'Sullivan, 'Industrial Development: A New Beginning?' in O'Hagan (ed.), *The Economy of Ireland: Policy and Performance of a European Region* at 264.
4. National Economic and Social Council, *Ireland in the European Community: Performance, Prospects and Strategy*, Report no. 88 (1989) 446 et seq.; I. Maher, 'The Implementation of EC Competition Law in Ireland: The Transition to a new Statutory Regime' (1993–1995) 28–30 *Irish Jurist* 21 at 27.
5. For a discussion of the previous regime, see D. S. J. Grehan, 'EEC and Irish Competition Policy and Law' (1983) 47 *RabelsZ* 22; I. Maher, 'Ireland' in P. Behrens (ed.), *EEC Competition Law in National Courts* vol. II (Baden-Baden: Nomos, 1994) 251–5.
6. See I. Maher, 'Country Analysis – Ireland' in G. Dannecker and O. Jansen (eds.), *The Transnational Application and Enforcement of Law in the European Legal Sphere* (The Hague: Kluwer, 2004).
7. Mergers, Takeovers and Monopolies (Control) Act 1978 as amended.
8. See generally A. W. J. McCarthy & V. J. G. Power, *Irish Competition Law: The Competition Act 2002* (Dublin: Butterworths, 2003) chs. 9 and 10.
9. Regulation 1/2003 on the implementation of the rules on competition laid down in Articles 81 and 82 EC OJ L 1/1 (4.1.2003).
10. See generally, M. C. Lucey, *Competition Act 2002, Irish Current Law Statutes Annotated* (Dublin: Round Hall, 2002).
11. See e.g. the Telecommunications (Miscellaneous Provisions) Act 1996; European Communities (Postal Services) Regulation 2000 SI 320/2000; Electricity Regulation Act 1999; Aviation Regulation Act 2001. See P. Massey and D. Daly, *Competition and Regulation in Ireland: The Law and Economics* Part IV (Oak Tree Press, 2003).
12. J. Fingleton and O. Hogan, 'Competition and Regulatory Policy' in O'Hagan (ed.), *The Economy of Ireland: Policy and Performance of a European Region* at 137.
13. Article 45.3.
14. *Mars* v. *HB* [1993] ILRM 145, [1992] 3 CMLR 830; see I. Maher, *Competition Law: Alignment and Reform* (Dublin: Round Hall Sweet & Maxwell, 1999).
15. See S. O'Keeffe, 'First Among Equals: the Commission and the National Courts as Enforcers of EC Competition Law' (2001) *European Law Review* 26.

16. Commission Decision, *Scholler & Langnese-Iglo GmbH* [1993] OJ L 183/1 & 19.
17. The European Court of First Instance upheld a decision of the Commission that the exclusivity clauses were indeed anticompetitive because of the combination of HB's dominance in the market and the exclusivity clauses: see T-65/98 *Van Den Bergh Foods* v. *EC Commission* [2003] ECR II-1583.
18. See S. Anderman in this volume for a discussion of the EC competition rules and intellectual property rights. This chapter focuses on the interface of the Irish rules with the EC rules.
19. Article 10 (the duty of loyalty, previously Article 5); see generally 66/86 *Ahmed Saeed* [1989] ECR 803, [1990] 4 CMLR 102. More recently see C-198/01 *Fiammiferi Consorzio Industrie Fiammiferi (CIF)* v. *Autorita Garante della Concorrenza e del Mercato* [2003] 5 CMLR 16 discussed by J. Temple Lang, 'National Measures Restricting Competition and National Authorities under Article 10 EC' (2004) 29(3) *European Law Review* 397–406. Article 3 Regulation 1/2003 of 16 December 2002 [2003] OJ L1/1 now governs the relationship between national competition laws and Articles 81 and 82 EC.
20. See generally, M. Drahos, *Convergence of Competition Laws and Policies in the European Community* (The Hague: Kluwer, 2001); I. Maher, 'Alignment of Competition Laws in the EC' (1996) *Yearbook of European Law* 223.
21. Minister D. O'Malley TD, 129 Seanad Debates cols. 1449–50.
22. See for example *Donovan* v. *Electricity Supply Board* [1994] IR 305, [1994] 2 ILRM 325.
23. Recital 15 and Ch. IV Regulation 1/2003 of 16 December 2002 [2003] OJ L1/1; Commission Notice on Cooperation within the Network of Competition Authorities [2004] OJ C 101/43; s. 46 Competition Act 2002.
24. Regulation 2790/99 on the application of Article 81(3) to Categories of Vertical Agreements and Concerted Practices [1999] OJ L 336/21.
25. 407 Dáil Debates Col. 1489.
26. *Cronin* v. *The Competition Authority and others* [1998] 2 ILRM 51.
27. Art. 38.1: J. MacMenamin, 'Crimes Created by 1991 and 1996 Acts will be hard to Prosecute' (1995–6) 5(2) *Competition* 29 at 29.
28. Ss. 6,7, and 8 Competition Act 2002.
29. See *Callinan* v. *VHI Board* (unreported, 22 April 1993) High Court Keane J; Competition Authority, Decision no. 16, Association of Optometrists, Ireland, 29 April 1993. The Authority however has been given an explicit advisory role in the 2002 Act to advise government as to the implications for competition of proposed legislation (including statutory instruments): see s. 30(1)(c).
30. *Deane* v. *Voluntary Health Insurance Board* [1992] 2 IR 319.
31. The High Court referred to the persuasive value of EC Commission decisions and European Court judgments in *Donovan* v. *Electricity Supply Board* [1994] 2 IR 305, [1994] 2 ILRM 325. See generally, I. Maher, *Competition Law: Alignment and Reform*, 103 et seq. and V. Power, *Competition Law and Practice* (Dublin: Butterworths, 2001) 181 et seq.

32. *Bleming* v. *David Patton Ltd* (unreported, 15 January 1997) High Court Shanley J.

33. Ss. 6 and 7 2002 Act. See also Maher, 'Country Analysis – Ireland' in Dannecker and Jansen (eds.), *The Transnational Application and Enforcement of Law in the European Legal Sphere.*

34. *Callinan and others* v. *VHI Board* (unreported, 22 April 1993) High Court Keane J.

35. *Carrigaline Community Television Broadcasting Co. Ltd* v. *Minister for Transport and others* [1997] 1 ILRM 241 at 290. See also *Greally* v. *Minister for Education* [1995] 1 ILRM 481. This was a preliminary ruling on a point of law (whether or not a trade union and the Minister for Education were undertakings within the Competition Act), so its precedental value is limited.

36. Ibid. at 484.

37. *Callinan and others* v. *Voluntary Health Insurance Board* (unreported, 22 April 1993) High Court, Keane J.

38. *Chanelle Veterinary Ltd* v. *Pfizer (Ireland) Ltd (No. 2)* [1998] ILRM 161.

39. Ibid. Cf. *Donovan* v. *Electricity Supply Board* [1994] 2 IR 305; [1994] 2 ILRM 325.

40. *Bleming* v. *David Patton Ltd* (unreported, 15 January 1997) High Court, Shanley J.

41. Ibid.

42. Ibid.

43. See e.g. Decision No. 12 Scully Tyrell/Edberg (29 January 1993).

44. Decision No. 31, Energy Control Systems Ltd/Erinova Ltd (9 September 1993).

45. Decision No. 142, PJD Investment Co/Fitzwilton plc and others (27 October 1993).

46. Even in the sensitive area of media mergers where the minister does retain a role, he can only require the full investigation of a merger which the Authority initially allowed and review a determination to allow a merger according to special criteria contained in s. 23(1). The minister's decision cannot be appealed but must be laid before the Oireachtas and can be annulled within 21 days in which case the decision of the Authority stands: see s. 25. Media mergers are defined in s. 23(1). The rules concerning media mergers will not be discussed, but see McCarthy and Power, *Irish Competition Law: The Competition Act, 2002* ch. 10.

47. See the Competition Authority Notices: N/03/001 Notice in respect of the Review of Non-Notifiable Mergers and Acquisitions; N/02/004 Notice in respect of Guidelines for Merger Analysis; N/02/003 Notice with respect to Certain Terms used in s. 18(1) Competition Act 2002.

48. Ss. 4(8) and 5(3). See chs. 6 and 7 Report of the Competition and Mergers Review Group PN 8487 (May 4 2000) and Competition and Mergers Review Group, Proposals for Discussion in Relation to Mergers (July 1998).

49. S. 8(2) Mergers, Takeovers and Monopolies (Control) Act 1978. See generally, I. Maher, *Competition Law: Alignment and Reform*, ch. 5.

50. Article 2(3) Regulation 139/2004 [2004] OJ L 42/1.
51. S. 16(1).
52. S. 16(4). A merger or acquisition does not occur where a receiver or liquidator is appointed; the undertakings involved are directly or indirectly under the control of the same undertaking; control arises as a result of inheritance or there is the temporary holding of securities in anticipation of disposal: see s. 16(6)–(9).
53. S. 16(5).
54. S.16(2) and (3).
55. S. 18(1) although notification by the EC Commission under the Merger Regulation is also adequate: see s. 18(13).
56. S. 18(1)(a). Even if a merger does not fall within the thresholds, the parties may still notify the Authority. The minister also has power to specify a class of mergers to be within the Act irrespective of these thresholds where the common good requires it: see s. 18(5). The amount of the thresholds can be reviewed annually by the minister: see s. 27.
57. S. 18(9) – (11). On summary conviction the fine is up to €3000; on indictment up to €250,000.
58. S. 19(4) and (5). The parties have 16 months to give effect to the merger where the Authority has acted within the initial one-month period but failed then to act within the 4-month period.
59. Ss. 21 and 22. How time limits are to be defined is set out in s. 19(6). On procedure see Competition Authority, *Revised Procedures of the Competition Authority for the Review of Mergers and Acquisitions* (February 2006).
60. S. 20(1)(a)(ii). The notice must be published within 7 days of receipt unless it would not be in the public interest to do so. 'Public interest' is not defined in the Act.
61. S. 20(1)(b) and (3).
62. S. 24.
63. S. 24(9).
64. S. 26(2).
65. S. 26(4) and (5). Where the offence is committed by a body corporate, officers of the company who can be shown to have consented, connived or were negligent can also be prosecuted: see s. 26(6).
66. S. 52. All regulations are subject to parliamentary scrutiny but of a limited kind. They are laid before both Houses of the Oireachtas and are only annulled if a resolution annulling them is passed by either House within 21 days. Specific powers in the Act include the amendment of the list of statutory bodies in Schedule 1 (see s. 34(11)) and the designation of persons who may disclose information relating to offences under the Act (see s. 47).
67. S. 33. The Minister sets down the form and manner of these and the annual report. For accounts see s. 41.
68. S. 42.

69. S. 34(6). Agreements have been entered into with the Commission for Aviation Regulation, the Commission for Energy Regulation, the Broadcasting Commission of Ireland; the Commission for Communications Regulation and the Director of Consumer Affairs: see www.tca.ie and McCarthy & Power, *Irish Competition Law: The Competition Act, 2002* 39–42.

70. S. 46(2).

71. S. 35. Initial appointment is via open competition and the Civil Service Commission advises the Minister as to who to appoint but not re-appointment or the appointment of temporary staff (due to temporary incapacity of a permanent member), or part-time staff: see subsections (3) and (4).

72. S. 39 and schedule 2(2) in relation to transfer of staff from the Ministry.

73. S. 35(12) and (13).

74. S. 35(6) and (8), (9), s. 39 and s. 44 in relation to superannuation of members and staff of the Authority.

75. S. 37(1).

76. S. 29(2).

77. Ss. 43 and 53.

78. S. 27.

79. S. 18(5) – the 'exigencies of the common good' must warrant it.

80. S. 35(1)(a). S. 37(1) sets the quorum at three members unless the Minister otherwise allows.

81. S. 38(1).

82. Ss. 30(1)(a) and 31(2).

83. S. 30(1)(d). This it has done in relation to vertical agreements: see below.

84. S. 30(1)(b).

85. S. 45.

86. Immunity from prosecution can be granted by the DPP under the Cartel Immunity Program: Competition Authority Annual Report, Annex 5. See also I. Maher, 'Country Analysis – Ireland' p. 601.

87. See e.g. K. Lenaerts and J. Vanhamme, 'Procedural Rights of Private Parties in the Community Administrative Process' (1997) 34 *Common Market Law Review* 531; W. P. J. Wils, 'The Combination of the Investigative and Prosecutorial Function and the Adjudicative Function in EC Antitrust Enforcement: A Legal and Economic Analysis' (2004) 27 *World Competition* 201.

88. See the Annual Reports of the Competition Authority available at www.tca.ie..

89. See generally, J. Meade, Study on the conditions of claims for damages in case of infringement of EC competition rules: Ireland, a report for the EC Commission conducted by Ashurts (2004), http://europa.eu.int/comm/competition/ antitrust/others/private_enforcement/national_reports/ireland_ en.pdf.

90. At p. 1. See also Massey and Daly, *Competition and Regulation in Ireland: The Law and Economics* at 43.

91. J. Meade, note 89 above at p. 4.

92. S. 9(4) Electricity Regulation Act 1999.

93. S. 34.
94. Restrictive Practices (Groceries) Order, 1987, SI 142/1987, repeated by Competition (Amendment) Act 2006.
95. See Director of Consumer Affairs, Annual Report 2001.
96. See generally, G. W. Hogan, G. F. Whyte and J. M. Kelly, *The Irish Constitution* (Dublin: Butterworths, 4th edn 2003) ch. 7.7.
97. Ibid. at 1993.
98. See e.g. *Phonographic Performance (Ireland) Ltd* v. *Cody* [1998] 4 IR 504, [1994] 2 ILRM 241.
99. *Iarnród Éireann* v. *Ireland* [1996] 3 IR 321, [1995] 2 ILRM 500.
100. Hogan, Whyte and Kelly, *The Irish Constitution* at 1994.
101. C-241, 242/91P *R. T. E.* v. *Commission* [1995] ECR I-743, [1995] 4 CMLR 718.
102. *Dalgety Agriculture Ltd/Spillers Ltd/Thomas Hill & Company Ltd* [1998] IECA 502 (16 June 1998).
103. *Celtic International Insurance Company Ltd/Stellar International Ltd/Dotinga Investments B. V.* [1998] IECA 519 (17 July 1998) at para. 19.
104. See e.g. *Dalgety Agriculture Ltd/Spillers Ltd/Thomas Hill & Company Ltd* [1998] IECA 502 (16 June 1998).
105. *Bord Telecom Eireann/L M Ericsson Holdings Ltd* [1998] IECA 506 (16 June 1998).
106. Even where the joint venture is between direct competitors it may be certified/exempted. In *Moulinex S. A./Glen Dimplex/Irish Sugar plc* [1999] IECA 556 (27 May 1999) a clause prohibiting the sharing of intellectual property saved a joint venture between three companies, two of which were direct competitors. The ring-fencing of the IPRs meant that the new company could not be used as a vehicle to share IP in a cartel-like manner.
107. *Dalgety Agriculture Ltd/Spillers Ltd/Thomas Hill & Company Ltd* [1998] IECA 502 (16 June 1998).
108. *Unisolutions/Dascom/Manix* [1998] IECA 533 (19 November 1998).
109. *Computa Tune Services Franchise* [1995] IECA 447 (15 December 1995). A non-disclosure clause in a franchise agreement was prohibited as it applied even where the know-how had come into the public domain; cf. *Odenberg Engineering/Inspectron* [1998] IECA 534 (19 November, 1998).
110. For example in a non-exclusive trademark licensing agreement; see *Ir.Distillers/Celtic Glass/Celtic Glass/Celtic Glass/L.Derg Hand/Lledo plc/Tobler Such.* [1994] IECA 284 (7 February 1994).
111. Ibid. The licence could be terminated if the licensor thought the products did not meet the requisite standard.
112. *Dalgety Agriculture Ltd/Spillers Ltd/E. Morrin & Sons Ltd* [1998] IECA 505 (16 June 1998).
113. *E. R. Squibb & Clonmel Healthcare* [1999] IECA 540 (24 March 1999).
114. An agreement for the purchase of technology and the exclusive manufacture and distribution of bacterial products was also certified with minimal

discussion by the Authority in *Green Science & Micro-Bac International* [1999] IECA 547 (16 April 1999).

115. See Article 2(4) Regulation 2790/1999 on vertical agreements [1999] OJ L 336/ 21, [2000] 4 CMLR 398.

116. *Smith & Nephew Ltd/Beiersdorf UK Ltd* [2001] IECA 589 (25 June 2001).

117. C-10/89 *CNL-SUCAL v. Hag* [1990] ECR I-3711, [1990] 3 CMLR 571.

118. *Celtic International Insurance Company Ltd/Stellar International Ltd/Dotinga Investments B. V.* [1998] IECA 519 (17 July 1998).

119. *Unisolutions/Dascom/Manix* [1998] IECA 533 (19 November 1998).

120. *Statoil Ire. Ltd/Baldoyle Oil Co. Ltd* Asset Purchase Agreement [1998] IECA 493 (30 January 1998).

121. Competition Authority, Notice in respect of guidelines for merger analysis, Decision No. N/02/004, 16 December 2002 para. 5.7.

122. *Spring Grove/Conkenner* [1993] IECA 148 (18 November 1993).

123. *Barlo Group/Kingspan Group* [1994] IECA 302 (25 March 1994).

124. *Cerestar UK Ltd/Betco Marketing Ltd* [1994] IECA 374 (21 November 1994).

125. Competition Authority, Notice in Respect of Vertical Agreements and Concerted Practices, Decision No. N/03/002 (5 December 2003).

126. Declaration in Respect of Vertical Agreements and Concerted Practices No. D.03/001 (5 December 2003).

127. Regulation 772/2004 [2004] OJ L 123/11; Guidelines on the application of Article 81 to technology transfer agreements [2004] OJ C 101/2.

128. Art. 2(3).

129. Art. 3.

130. Intellectual property rights include industrial property rights, copyright and neighbouring rights.

131. Art. 2(2).

132. Under Art. 5; in general vertical agreements with 5-year or indefinite non-compete clauses or restrictions on manufacture or sale after the agreement are outside the declaration.

133. Article 5(c).

134. Where the supplier owns the premises, then the non-compete clause can last as long as the occupancy of the buyer (Art. 5(a)).

135. 'Know-how' is defined as a package of non-patented practical information, resulting from experience and testing by the supplier, which is secret, substantial and identified. 'Secret' means that the know-how as a body or in the precise configuration and assembly of its components is not generally known or easily accessible. 'Substantial' means that the know-how includes information which is indispensable to the buyer for the use, sale or resale of the contract goods or services. 'Identified' means that the know-how must be described in a sufficiently comprehensive matter so as to make it possible to verify that it fulfils the criteria of secrecy and substantiality: see Art. 1(h) of the declaration and 2(k) of the notice. This is the same definition as that in

Article 1(f) of the EC Vertical Agreements block exemption see Regulation 2790/1999 [1999] OJ L 336/21, [2000] 4 CMLR 398.

136. Art. 5(b).

137. Art. 6.

138. Motor Fuels Category Licence [1993] IECA 25 (1 July 1993). See also Competition Authority Decision, Agreement between Statoil Ireland Ltd. And Motor Fuel Retailers Allegedly Fixing the Retail Price of Motor Fuels in Letterkenny, E/03/002 (4 November 2003).

139. Competition Authority, Declaration No. D/05/001 in respect of Exclusive Purchasing Agreements for Cylinder Liquefied Petroleum Gas.

140. EC Commission, Communication to the Council, European Parliament and ECOSOC on the Management of Copyright and Related Rights in the Internal Market COM(2004) 261 final.

141. See Commission, Green Paper on Copyright and Related Rights in the Information Society COM(95) 382 final (19 July 1995).

142. See I. Maher, *Competition Law: Alignment and Reform*, pp. 420–5; R. Clark and S. Smyth, *Intellectual Property Law in Ireland* (Dublin: Tottel, 2nd edn 2005) pp. 313–18.

143. See the submission of IMRO in *MCPS/MCPSI/Various Agreements* [1999] IECA 569 (8 October 1999).

144. See *Carrickdale Hotel Ltd.* v. *The Controller of Industrial and Commercial Property and Phonographic Performance (Ireland) Ltd* [2004] IEHC 86 (12 May 2004).

145. Decision No. 326, *PRS/Creators/Publishers* (18 May 1994).

146. Decision No. 5, *PRS and IMRO Transfer of Function Agreement* (30 June 1992). The assignment of musical works by the British parent collecting society (PRS) to its Irish subsidiary (IMRO) did not fall within the competition rules as they fell within the single economic unit doctrine.

147. Decision No. 445, *IMRO/Writers/Publishers (No-corporate)/Publishers (Limited company)* (15 December 1995).

148. The Vintners Federation of Ireland initiated proceedings (later settled) to challenge this decision: see Clark and Smyth, *Intellectual Property Law in Ireland*, at p. 315.

149. *IMRO Ltd/Independent Radio Stations* [1995] IECA 449 (18 December 1995).

150. *MCPSI/Synchronisation Licence; MCPSI/Radio Station Licence Agreement* [1999] IECA 570 (8 October 1999).

151. Decision No. 383 *IMRO/UK Television Companies and other Copyright Holders/Cable Relay and MMDS Operators* (16 December 1994). See also *IMRO/TV Companies* [1994] IECA 384 (16 December 1994).

152. The EC Commission had issued a comfort letter for the agreements stating that there was a prima facie justification for an exemption under Article 81(3): see ibid. at para. 13.

153. See also Decision No. 456, *IMRO Ltd/RTE* (21 December 1995).

154. Decision No. 457, *IMRO Ltd/Public Performance Users* (21 December 1995).

155. *MCPS/MCPSI/Various Agreements* [1999] IECA 569 (8 October 1999).

156. Although IMRO had made representations in the case indicating that it was thinking of entering the market and noting that the administration of performing and reproduction rights was carried out by a single organisation in most European states.

157. 'Production Music is music specifically written for inclusion in audio and audio-visual productions, and is normally used by *facility houses* and *production companies*. It is available on various high quality carriers, usually compact discs, for convenient and cost-effective synchronisation, or "dubbing", into such productions. The "product" involved here, therefore, is a musical work which is exploited by means of dubbing from a Library Sound Recording . . .' Competition Authority, *MCPSI/Production (Library) Music Side Agreement* [1999] IECA 573 (15 November 1999), para. 4.1.

158. *MCPSI/Production (Library) Music Side Agreement* [1999] IECA 573 (15 November 1999).

159. *Phonographic Performance (Ireland) Ltd/Various Agreements* [2000] IECA 580 (28 January 2000).

160. But for the substantial lessening of competition test in mergers which is the same as that found under the UK Enterprise Act 2002.

7

The interface between intellectual property law and competition law in Singapore

BURTON ONG

I. Overview: IP and competition laws within the Singapore legal framework

As a former British colony, Singapore's legal framework has been modelled closely after the common law and statutory instruments of the United Kingdom. The three primary intellectual property statutes in Singapore – concerned with copyright, patents and trade marks – bear a close resemblance to the corresponding UK statutes and their predecessors. Similarly, Singapore's recently-introduced competition law regime is based substantially on equivalent legislation from the UK which was, in turn, a codification of the European Community's competition law framework.

Despite the strong influence of UK laws on the domestic legislative framework which Singapore has enacted, a number of substantive modifications have been made by the legislature to further specific policy objectives which reflect domestic commercial and socio-economic conditions. Singapore has a small domestic market of less than 4 million consumers, but a relatively large, open and export-oriented economy. This chapter will highlight and discuss the various features of the Singapore legal framework which mediate between the frequently opposing goals of intellectual property law and competition law. Both these areas of law have evolved through, and continue to exist in, a state of flux as a result of Singapore's commitment to implement various international conventions and, more recently, to achieve compliance with its obligations under various free-trade agreements. Readers should therefore expect subsequent additions or changes to these two areas of law to continue beyond the publication date of this work. This chapter will therefore focus primarily on the broader themes connected to the interface between intellectual property rights and competition policy which emerge from an examination of the current features of Singapore's legislative framework.

A brief summary of the legislative history behind the relevant statutory instruments that will be discussed in greater detail below might be useful in contextualising the origins of the principal legal provisions which impact upon the relationship between the law of intellectual property and competition law in Singapore.

The *Copyright Act 1987*,[1] which replaced the Imperial Copyright Act 1911, has been amended substantially over the last two decades to accommodate new technologies and the new media in which works are produced, stored and transmitted, particularly as a result of Singapore's accession to the Berne Convention,[2] the WIPO Copyright Treaty,[3] and the WIPO Performances and Phonograms Treaty.[4] The *Patents Act 1994*,[5] which repealed the Registration of United Kingdom Patents Act 1937, inherited many features from the UK Patents Act 1977 and has been amended to reflect Singapore's accession to the Patent Cooperation Treaty,[6] the Budapest Treaty[7] and the Paris Convention.[8] The *Trade Marks Act 1998*,[9] which was based largely on the UK Trade Marks Act 1994 and which replaced the legislative antecedents modelled after the UK Trade Marks Act 1938, has been amended after Singapore joined the Nice Agreement[10] and the Madrid Protocol[11] and when it implemented the WIPO Joint Recommendations for the Protection of Well-Known Marks.[12] These three major pieces of Singapore legislation which comprise the foundations of domestic intellectual property law have also been significantly amended over the years to achieve compliance with Singapore's obligations under the TRIPS Agreement[13] and the various free-trade agreements which Singapore has entered into with its major trading partners.[14]

In contrast with the relatively more developed intellectual property system, the competition law regime is an extremely recent addition to the Singapore legal landscape. The recently enacted *Competition Act 2004*[15] was implemented in 2005 and its substantive prohibitions – against anticompetitive agreements and conduct which abuses use of a dominant position – have only just come into force.[16] Unlike many developed market economies, Singapore has hitherto operated without any comprehensive law to address instances of anticompetitive behaviour: there were previously no legal means of dealing with cartel behaviour, exclusionary conduct by a dominant firm, or mergers which had an adverse impact on the competitive structure of a market. Apart from a residual common law action against excessive restraints of trade[17] that were contrary to public policy, the Singapore legal system had no experience in administering its own domestic competition law.

Singapore's relative unfamiliarity with competition law places it in a good position to learn from the experiences of other jurisdictions which have had more time to develop policy frameworks to implement these laws. Starting with a fresh slate of sorts, the Competition Commission of Singapore is able to draw upon the policies and practices formulated by established competition regulators towards the treatment of intellectual property rights. The basic objectives of the Commission in this respect are no different from those which inform its more experienced counterparts. The ultimate goal is to adopt a competition policy which strikes an optimal balance between, on the one hand, the incentives for innovation generated by the availability of intellectual property rights against, on the other hand, the exclusionary effects which these limited legal monopolies have on competition and further innovation by third parties. In deciding when and how to limit a right holder's freedom to exercise his proprietary entitlements, the Commission is also tasked with the difficult role of ensuring that the intellectual property rights in question are not used as a vehicle for anticompetitive behaviour in commercial transactions. The Commission must also be concerned with preventing the right holder from exploiting the intellectual property system as a means of acquiring a species of market power which can then be abused to the detriment of its competitors and customers.

It should always be borne in mind that the occasionally paradoxical relationship between intellectual property law and competition law makes the role of any competition regulator very challenging – especially where the regulator lacks sufficient expertise in the administration of intellectual property rights. At one level, grants of intellectual property are fundamentally contradictory to the basic impulses of competition law: exclusive proprietary rights are created and recognised by the law to protect the investment and creative efforts of the individual, demarcating a sphere of activity over which he has a legal monopoly. Empowering the intellectual property right owner with a legal means to prevent his competitors from encroaching upon this zone of exclusivity immediately creates an obstacle to competition. In extreme cases, where the intellectual property subsists over an industry standard or over a basic 'platform' technology, the adverse consequences to competition are more pronounced: the law of intellectual property becomes used as an instrument to raise barriers to market entry and to restrict later market entrants from making subsequent technological advances. On the other hand, the incentives created by the lure of a potential grant of intellectual property might actually spur competitors to direct their efforts towards the generation of new technologies and other innovations which make their products and services superior substitutes to what is currently available. This would encourage a desirable mode of competition – by innovation, rather than just by imitation – which is entirely consistent with the core objectives of competition law.

II. Exogenous vs. endogenous limits placed on the exercise of intellectual property rights

Even though Singapore has not had very much formal experience with competition law and its regulatory mechanisms, it should be recognised that the pro-competition policy objectives which underlie competition law can also be found within the law of intellectual property itself. While competition law may be used as an instrument to address conduct involving the exercise of intellectual property rights which curtail competitive market processes, similar pro-competitive outcomes may also be facilitated from within the law of intellectual property through its internal checks and balances which circumscribe the extent of the right holder's ability to exercise his proprietary interests.

The interface between competition law and intellectual property therefore converges at two fronts. The more visible interface takes place when competition law intervenes to deprive an owner of the full extent of the rights conferred upon him by the law of intellectual property. The less apparent, but equally significant, interface takes place within the law of intellectual property itself: where the legal anatomy of the qualifying criteria for acquiring these proprietary rights, the nature and scope of these rights, and the defences available to third parties may have been shaped by policies that recognise the importance of ensuring that competition can still take place despite the grant of intellectual property.

The latter interface is what I shall refer to as the 'internal interface' within the various major intellectual property systems which reflect pro-competition policies at two levels: the first promotes competition between distinct goods and services offered by rival firms ('inter-brand' competition), while the other promotes competition between goods and services that are the subject of, or connected with, the same set of intellectual property rights ('intra-brand' competition).

From the first aspect, competition is fostered between products or services that are protected by intellectual property rights and their substitutes. The legal standards and prerequisites that have to be met by a party seeking to secure intellectual property rights give third parties some leeway to come up with their own competing products and services which may or may not qualify for independent intellectual property protection. For example, by confining copyright protection to particular expressions of ideas, rather than ideas themselves, a competitor is free to offer a competing work based on the same ideas if he does not copy from the expression used by the author of the earlier work. Likewise, a patentee can only secure a patent over an invention rather than the raw ideas, scientific principles or discoveries which underpin the invention – his competitors being free to develop variants and alternatives which 'invent around' the claims and specifications of the patented invention. Similarly, the law of trade marks places limits on the words and signs that a trader can lay exclusive claim to in the interests of ensuring that his competitors are not unduly deprived of access to the vocabulary necessary for them to describe their substitute products or services to consumers in the marketplace. In other words, the internal rules of the law of intellectual property recognise the value of competition between suppliers of goods and services and strive to confine the exclusive rights enjoyed by the intellectual property owner to subject matter within reasonable limits, seeking at the same time to make it possible for his rivals to offer consumers competing alternative products and services.

From the second aspect, competition is also promoted between identical products and services that are protected by intellectual property rights. Specific provisions are built into the law of intellectual property to limit the ability of right owners to exploit their intellectual property in ways which are detrimental to the public interest in having competition. Most notably, subject to specific criteria being met, the copyright law, patent law and trade mark law in Singapore permit parallel imports of genuine goods without the consent of the intellectual property owner. This encourages price competition between goods released into the Singapore market with lower priced genuine goods that are released in foreign markets.[18] In a similar vein, the law of patents facilitates the release of generic versions of patented pharmaceuticals immediately after the expiry of the patent term to facilitate competition between 'branded' and 'generic' pharmaceuticals.[19] The availability of compulsory licences under the various intellectual property regimes also enables third parties to gain access to protected subject matter and, in limited cases, offer consumers an alternative avenue for goods or services which are identical to those supplied by the intellectual property owner.[20] In all these instances, competition is fostered within a single-product market where the law of intellectual property enables third parties to make perfect substitutes (which were made by the IP holder himself or with his consent) for the IP-protected product available to the market.

Both these aspects of the 'internal interface' will be explored further in the sections below which discuss the major species of intellectual property that are statutorily protected in Singapore. The 'external interface' between competition law and intellectual property law, where exogenous means are employed to limit the IP holder's ability to exercise his exclusive rights when his private interests are outweighed by the wider public interest in promoting competition, will then be examined in the last section which will look at the new competition framework which Singapore has recently adopted.

III. Copyright law in Singapore

The *Copyright Act 1987* articulates basic copyright principles which are broadly similar to those found in most other developed copyright systems. Copyright subsists in original literary, dramatic, musical or artistic works, which are the intellectual products of authorial expression rather than the ideas which are communicated through those modes of expression.[21] Copyright in a work is infringed only through acts of copying[22] and not by independent creation. Copyright endures for the duration of the author's life plus 70 years after his or her death.[23]

The availability of copyright protection to qualifying works nurtures a particular mode of competition in the market. Where a firm offers copyright-protected products for sale in the market, his competitors are able to offer substitute products which employ the same ideas so long as they do not replicate a substantial part of the expression used by the copyright holder. Competition is therefore permitted to take place so long as it is not pre-mised on slavish imitation. However, competition-related problems emerge from the law of copyright because of the wide range of subject matter which is entitled to copyright protection. Compilations of data, from tele-phone directories to television listings, software, as well as data organisa-tional structures, can qualify as copyrightable subject matter – raising concerns for the competition regulator where the protected subject matter is an industry standard or some 'essential facility' indispensable for market entry and the copyright owner refuses to grant the requisite licences to new entrants.[24]

A. Copyright law – the fair dealing defence

One important competition-facilitating internal mechanism found within Singapore's copyright law is the general 'fair dealing' defence against copy-right infringement. Significant legislative changes have been made to broaden the scope of the defence in the last decade, particularly in the context of those who made copies of works for private study or research, in response to judicial applications of earlier versions of the relevant stat-utory provisions. In Aztech Systems v. Creative Technology,[25] a rival com-puter soundcard manufacturer made unauthorised copies of Creative's copyright-protected software in the course of manufacturing products which were technologically compatible with Creative's products. The Singapore courts were tasked with considering whether the defence of 'fair dealing' for the 'purpose of research or private study'[26] was available to Creative's rival. At the time, the statutory definition of 'research' in section 35(5) of the Copyright Act was limited to research carried out for non-commercial purposes. The question for judicial interpretation was whether the definition of 'private study' was similarly limited.[27] Section 35(2)(a) provided that one of the factors to be taken into account when determining if a dealing was a 'fair' dealing was 'the purpose and character of the dealing, including whether such dealing is of commercial nature or is for non-profit educational purposes'.[28] In the High Court of Singapore, Judicial Commissioner Lim Teong Qwee held that the 'private study' pur-pose was established because 'a study is private if the study and the infor-mation and knowledge acquired through it are kept or removed from public knowledge or observation and that this is so even if the purpose may be of a commercial nature'.[29]

Furthermore, the Judicial Commissioner held that the copyist's dealing was a 'fair dealing' because the public interest in promoting competition was a factor which the court could consider when evaluating the availability of the defence to an act of copyright infringement:

> The factors mentioned in s. 35(2) are not intended to be exhaustive. The expression used is 'the matters . . . shall *include*'. I think there is the matter of public interest to be considered and it is in consonance with the purpose of the Act. Aztech copied the program in TEST-SBC in order to develop and market a Sound Blaster compatible sound card. This may open the market to more than just Creative and those licensed by it. It may also place more sound cards on the market and to that extent Creative's immediate profitability may be affected but there is no evidence that the market is so limited that it cannot support the potential increase in the supply. *Competition* is not necessarily a bad thing and there may be longer term benefits even for Creative. The very popular game application X-Wing may be run on more than just a Sound Blaster sound card. There may be other such applications as well. Software developers will be freed from the restrictions inherent in the want of compatibility in sound cards. With compatible sound cards in the market an application written to run with a Sound Blaster sound card may be run with others which are compatible. This is likely to be good for the industry. The end user will have a choice of sound cards. There is a benefit to the industry in the development and marketing of sound cards and of applications software. There is a benefit to the large and growing number of end users. I think that on *balance the public interest is served by the copying complained of.*[30]

Even though the High Court's decision to allow the defence of fair dealing for private study or research to succeed was ultimately overturned by the Court of Appeal, this was a landmark case in 1995 which set in motion subsequent legislative amendments which made it easier for competitors to invoke the defence against copyright holders. In 1998, the *Copyright Act* was amended by the deletion of section 35(5) so as 'to make available the defence under section 35 to persons undertaking research, whether or not commercial, so long as their dealing with the work is fair'.[31] This amendment has been interpreted to mean that 'private study' for commercial purposes should also qualify for the defence so long as the dealing is fair.[32] The commercial purpose behind the copying was only one factor to be taken into account in the overall assessment of whether the dealing was a 'fair dealing'. In 2005, the defence was expanded further to make any 'fair dealing' a defence to copyright infringement: the purposes of 'research and study' are but one example of purposes which might constitute a 'fair dealing' of a copyright protected work.[33] The general 'fair dealing' defence, in its present form, gives competitors greater leeway to legitimise their actions when making unauthorised use of a copyright holder's work in the course of developing product substitutes for the Singapore market.

B. Copyright law – defences for copyright infringement of artistic works

Other specific defences have also been incorporated into Singapore's *Copyright Act* to address the competition-related problems associated with undue terms of protection for industrial design drawings as copyright-protected artistic works. With the recent extension of the statutory term of protection under the *Copyright Act* to the duration of the author's lifespan plus 70 years,[34] copyright owners of technical drawings currently enjoy exclusive rights against copying for an extremely long period of time. Copyright protection enables the copyright owner to prevent others from making three-dimensional objects which are reproductions of two-dimensional artistic works,[35] thereby giving the copyright owner a de facto legal monopoly over products which embody the features recorded in the two-dimensional artistic work. Given that copyright could be used to prevent the copyright owner's competitors from utilising the copyright subject matter to supply substitute products to the market, a situation which would have seriously adverse repercussions on competition in these markets, appropriate defences were therefore necessary to curtail, or eliminate, the availability of copyright protection in cases involving industrial artefacts and utilitarian objects.[36]

These defences allow the competitors of the copyright owner to reproduce the copyright-protected designs recorded in the design drawings by making these acts of copying non-infringing if the relevant statutory criteria are met. The defences can be divided into two categories of designs: the first relates to designs which have been registered under the *Registered Designs Act 2000*,[37] or unregistered designs which are registrable under that Act, while the second category encompasses all designs, whether registrable or unregistrable under the Act.

Within the first category of industrial designs, where a design has been registered under the *Registered Designs Act*, section 74(1) of the *Copyright Act* renders it no infringement of copyright in the design drawings (as an artistic work) to perform any act which falls within the scope of the exclusive rights conferred by the *Registered Designs Act*. This removes the overlap between the exclusive rights enjoyed by the copyright owner concurrently under the *Copyright Act* and the *Registered Designs Act*, permitting him to sue only in respect of the intellectual property rights created in his favour by the latter statutory regime. At the same time, the section 74(1) defence also disables the copyright owner from reasserting his copyright (which lasts for a much longer duration than his Registered Design rights) in the design after his Registered Design rights have expired. This effectively limits the period of exclusivity of use for registered designs to a maximum of 15 years, as provided for under the *Registered Designs Act*, after which it becomes available for competitors to incorporate into their own products.

Where the design in question satisfies the qualifying criteria for registration under the *Registered Designs Act* but was not, in fact, registered under that Act, section 74(3) provides a similar defence to an action for copyright infringement brought by the copyright owner against third parties who have copied the design features embodied in the artistic work. The section 74(3) defence is only available if the copyright owner has consented to the industrial application of his design onto articles which have been commercially exploited in the market place.[38] The underlying purpose of this statutory provision is to compel the copyright owner to seek the registration of his design under the *Registered Designs Act*, if his design meets the registrability criteria set out in the Act, and to avail himself of the exclusive rights provided to proprietors of registered designs under that Act, if he wishes to commercially exploit his design in this way. In other words, a copyright owner who chooses to mass produce products or articles which incorporate the (registrable, but unregistered) design features of his artistic work stands to lose the statutory protection afforded to him under the *Copyright Act*, so that the design becomes available to his competitors for their own use.

The section 74 defences are therefore targeted at facilitating competition in the area of industrial designs by limiting intellectual property protection to the much shorter term of protection provided for under the registered designs system. This ensures that aesthetically pleasing designs are not locked away from a copyright owner's competitors for decades under the copyright system, thereby shortening the timeframe within which a competitor may supply the market with substitute products bearing identical design features.

In the second category of industrial designs, another defence to copyright infringement is set out in section 70 of the *Copyright Act*. Section 70(1) provides that 'the making of any useful article[39] in 3 dimensions...does not infringe the copyright in an artistic work if, when the useful article or reproduction is made, the artistic work has been industrially applied[40] in Singapore or in any other country at any time before the useful article...is made'. This defence operates is very much the same way as the section 74 defences, except that its reach is much wider: even unregistrable designs – those which would not have fallen within the scope of section 74 of the *Copyright Act* because they did not meet the statutory qualifying criteria – are denied copyright protection so long as these designs have been industrially applied to mass-produced products for commercial purposes. This means that purely functional designs, which are excluded from registration under the *Registered Designs Act* under a 'functionality' bar,[41] may be deprived of copyright protection under section 70 of the *Copyright Act* if their respective copyright owners have made use of them in the relevant manner.

The section 70 defence directly addresses a familiar issue squarely within the interface between competition law and intellectual property law – the competition-related problems arising from IP owners (who supply complex articles to the market) asserting copyright in their design drawings to prevent their rivals from making 'spare parts' for sale to the former's consumers, thereby using their intellectual property rights as a means of foreclosing competition in a downstream after-market. The English House of Lords has grappled with this issue in the well-known case of *British Leyland* v. *Armstrong*,[42] in which the common law concept of 'non-derogation from grant' was applied as a defence to copyright infringement, a decision which appears to have been endorsed by the Singapore courts as well.[43] However, with the availability of the section 70 defence, there appears to be no real need to strain the Singapore copyright system with land law doctrinal devices if a case should arise where a copyright owner seeks to rely on his copyright in a design drawing of a functional component product to stop a rival from supplying the after-market with competing substitute products. Competition between rival suppliers in any market for functional utilitarian articles is facilitated by denying copyright owners the right to bring copyright infringement actions in respect of their design drawings for these articles.

C. Copyright law – parallel imports

Copyright holders who market their copyrighted works in Singapore are exposed to potential competition from parallel imports of articles embodying the same protected subject matter.[44] Singapore copyright law takes a very liberal approach towards parallel imports of copyright-protected works and substantial amendments were made to the copyright legislation in 1994 to broaden the scope of previous law on parallel imports.[45] Sections 32 and 104 of the *Copyright Act* make it an infringement for a person to import copyright-protected articles for commercial purposes without the Singapore copyright owner's authorisation 'where he knows, or ought reasonably to know, that the making of the article was carried out without the consent of the owner of the copyright'.[46] Sections 33 and 105 make it an infringement for a person to sell or otherwise commercially exploit imported articles in the same circumstances. The scope of the parallel importer's freedom to import foreign-made articles is therefore dependent on whom 'the owner of the copyright' refers to in those sections and the character of the 'consent' he must have given.

Section 25(3) of the Act explains that:

> Where reference is made . . . to an imported article the making of which was carried out without the *consent* of the owner of the copyright, the reference to the owner of the copyright shall be as a reference to –
>
> (a) the *person entitled to the copyright* in respect of its application to the making of that description in *the country where the article was made*; or

(b) if there is no person entitled to copyright in respect of its application to the making of an article of that description in the country where the article was made, the *person entitled to the copyright* in respect of that application *in Singapore.*

Section 25(4) of the Act goes on to clarify that:

> The making of the article shall be deemed to have been carried out with the *consent* of the owner referred to in subsection (3) if, after *disregarding all conditions as to sale, distribution or other dealings* in the article after its making, the article was made with his licence (other than a compulsory licence).

The net effect of these statutory provisions is to make it permissible for persons to import copyright-protected articles into Singapore which have been lawfully made abroad with the consent of the copyright holder, or anyone authorised by him, in the country where the article was made. In other words, as long as the copyright was not violated in the country where the article was manufactured, the article will not be treated as an infringing article if it is brought into Singapore, even if the copyright holder in Singapore (who may be unconnected to the copyright holder in the country of manufacture) is not the importer. This approach eliminates the problem arising from situations where the copyright owner has licensed his copyright to different and independent entities in different territorial jurisdictions. Furthermore, this generous attitude towards parallel imports is bolstered by the breadth of the definition given to the 'consent' which has to be given by the copyright holder in the place where the article is made: any conditions placed on the manufacturer of those goods on where the goods can be sold and so forth are disregarded. Even if the licence given by the copyright holder to manufacture the goods came with restrictions on exporting the finished articles to Singapore, these articles are still treated as legitimate copies of the copyrighted product if they are imported into Singapore and the importer will not be exposed to liability for copyright infringement. If, on the other hand, where the imported articles were made under a compulsory licence in the country of manufacture, these articles will probably be considered as having been made without the requisite 'consent' of the relevant copyright holder.

The liberal approach towards parallel imports extends to accessories which accompany parallel imports. Under sections 40A and 116A of the Act, no copyright infringement arises from the importation or use of accessory articles which accompany non-infringing imported articles. In these circumstances, copyright holders cannot assert their copyright in instruction booklets, packaging, labels, pamphlets, brochures, warranties, manuals or other works ancillary to the main product as a means of keeping parallel imports of the main product from entering the Singapore market.

D. Copyright law – compulsory licences

Compulsory licences of works protected by copyright are available under Singapore copyright law where there are matters of public interest requiring derogation from the copyright owner's exclusive rights. The specific circumstances in which these licences are automatically available are prescribed in detail by the *Copyright Act*, but there are no statutory provisions which explicitly cover situations involving anticompetitive behaviour by the copyright owner. These statutory licences are available, for example, to educational institutions and institutions assisting handicapped students as part of a wider legislative effort to balance the rights of copyright owners with the interests of users and the public at large.[47] Special statutory licences are also available to enable sound recording manufacturers to record musical works for commercial retail purposes.[48] Royalty payments under these licences are regulated under the Act, with a specialist Copyright Tribunal to mediate disputes involving the licensing schemes of collecting societies and other bodies which represent copyright owners.[49]

IV. Patent law in Singapore

The *Patents Act 1994* sets out a legislative framework for patent grants with substantive similarities to the UK patent law regime. Patentable inventions have to meet the requirements of novelty, inventive step and industrial application.[50] An invention cannot arise from raw ideas, discoveries or scientific principles – it must have been developed into technological applications with a practical utility in any area of industry. Unlike copyright protection, patents have to comply with a comprehensive set of registration formalities through which adequate disclosures have to be made about how the invention works. These are the claims and specifications which the patentee must articulate in his patent application so that a hypothetical person skilled in the relevant area of technology would understand how to perform the invention.[51] The quid pro quo for these disclosures is the grant by the state to the patentee of a 20-year patent monopoly over the invention.[52] Unlike copyright protection, patent protection enables the patentee to prevent third parties from both copying and independently creating the invention. Given the more comprehensive exclusive rights[53] enjoyed by the patentee, coupled with the patentee's potential ability to carve out a wide scope of protected subject matter through the claims and specifications he has to submit in his application to the Patent Office, patents are generally considered the strongest species of intellectual property available today. As such, the potential for market foreclosure and other competition-related problems arising from the exploitation of patent rights is a serious issue for the law of patents. These concerns about the potentially adverse effects patents might have on competition are reflected throughout the internal structure of Singapore patent law – perhaps more evidently than in the other domestic intellectual property statutes – with specific provisions enacted to address the various instances where patents may be abused by their owners.

It should be reiterated that the grant of the patent monopoly does not, of itself, confer on the patent holder the necessary market power which puts him in a dominant position.[54] Substitutes for many patented products will very often be available, and many patented technologies may face competition from alternative technologies which achieve similar results through different means. Competition law concerns really emerge in situations where there are no real substitutes for the patented subject matter, such that the patentee is in a position to exploit his legal monopoly in a way which is detrimental to competition in an adjacent, ancillary or downstream market. Where patents are acquired over the primary tools or building blocks which comprise the foundations of a new area of technology, the patentee's ability to control research and development in this technological field by excluding the participation of later market entrants also gives rise to competition-related concerns as well.

A. Patent law – claims, specifications and infringement by variants

One of the central features of the internal interface between patent law and competition law is the way in which the patentee's exclusive rights over the invention are circumscribed by the language he has used in his patent claims and specifications. By requiring patentee to define the scope of his claimed invention with some degree of precision, patent law attempts to communicate to his competitors the boundaries of the patent monopoly he receives, thereby making it easier for these competitors to 'invent around' the patent and avoid infringement if they should want to develop a competing product.

The 'purposive approach' taken in Singapore towards interpreting the patentee's claims and specifications, when determining whether a competitor's product variant has infringed his patent or not, is modelled after the well known *Catnic*[55] and *Improver*[56] decisions of the UK courts. The trilogy of questions articulated by Hoffmann J (as he then was) was accepted by the Singapore Court of Appeal[57] as an appropriate framework for determining whether a variant of the invention which did not fall within the literal wording used in the claims and specifications nevertheless amounted to an infringement of the patent:

(i) Does the variant have a material effect upon the way the invention works? (If the answer to question (i) is negative, then question (ii) arises)

(ii) Would this (the fact that the variant had no material effect) have been obvious at the date of publication to the reader skilled in the art? (If the answer to question (i) is affirmative, then question (iii) arises)

(iii) Would the skilled reader nevertheless have understood from the language of the claim that the patentee had intended strict compliance with the primary meaning of the language used to describe the invention?[58]

Section 113(1) of the *Patents Act* sets out the scope of the invention over which the patentee can assert his legal monopoly:

> For the purposes of this Act, an invention for a patent . . . shall, unless the context otherwise requires, be taken to be that specified in a claim of the specification of the . . . patent . . . as interpreted by the description and any drawings contained in that specification, and the extent of the protection conferred by a patent shall be determined accordingly.

This statutory provision is *in pari materia* to section 125(1) of the UK Patents Act which, in turn, is based on Article 69 of the European Patent Convention (EPC). The Protocol on the interpretation of Article 69 of the EPC, while not binding on Singapore courts, is nevertheless a persuasive indicator of how the Singapore courts interpret the language used by patentees in the claims and specifications of their patents:[59]

> Article 69 should not be interpreted in the sense that the extent of the protection conferred by a European patent is to be understood as that defined by the strict, literal meaning of the wording used in the claims, the description and drawings being employed only for the purpose of resolving an ambiguity found in the claims. Neither should it be interpreted in the sense that the claims serve only as a guideline and that the actual protection conferred may extend to what, from a consideration of the description and drawings by a person skilled in the art, the patentee has contemplated. On the contrary, it is to be interpreted as defining a position which combines a fair protection for the patentee with a *reasonable degree of certainty for third parties*.[60]

Third parties who wish to develop competing technologies as substitutes for the patented subject matter should be able to discern the boundaries of the patentee's invention from the language used in the patent claims and specifications. The many cases involving alleged infringement of a claimed invention by a variant product or process illustrate the importance of giving third parties sufficient certainty in the interpretation of patent claims and specifications so that they may conduct themselves with some measure of confidence and security. The effort made by the law of patents to navigate between the demands of the patent holder for as broad a scope of protection as possible, and the interests of third parties who may seek to compete legitimately with them, reflects a conscious policy to achieve a fair balance which gives third parties the opportunity to compete with the patent holder by 'inventing around' what has been disclosed in the latter's patent claims and specifications.

B. Patent law – parallel imports

The position on parallel imports under Singapore patent law is similar to the liberal approach taken under the law of copyright: a broad defence to patent infringement is available to those who make unauthorised imports of patented products or products obtained from patented processes where the imported products were lawfully produced in their country of origin.[61] Section 66(2)(g) provides that this shall not be an act of infringement if:

> subject to subsection (2A), it consists of the import, use or disposal of, or the offer to dispose of, any patented product or any product obtained by means of a patented process or to which a patented process has been applied, which is produced by or with the *consent (conditional or otherwise)* of the proprietor of the patent or any person licensed by him, and for this purpose 'patent' includes a patent granted in any country outside Singapore in respect of the same or substantially the same invention as that for which a patent is granted under this Act and 'patented product', 'patented process' and 'licensed' shall be construed accordingly.[62]

Parallel importers who compete with the Singapore patent holder are therefore permitted to import patent-protected products into Singapore without infringing the Singapore patent holder's patent so long as the patent holder in the country of manufacture has consented to the manufacture of those products. The words in parentheses – 'conditional or otherwise' – make it clear that even if the consent given was conditioned on contractual restrictions which prevented the product manufacturer from exporting the products to Singapore, the Singapore courts will treat these products as legitimate parallel imports.

The breadth of the defence was reined in by legislative amendments in 2004 which introduced section 66(2A): in response to pressure from the United States,[63] the section 66(2)(g) defence is not available to patented pharmaceutical products when the product has not previously been sold or distributed in Singapore with the consent of the Singapore patent proprietor or his licensee,[64] where the import of the products would result in their being distributed in breach of a contract between the Singapore patent proprietor and a foreign licensed distributor, and where the importer has actual or constructive knowledge of these matters.

C. Patent law – pharmaceutical products

While the above statutory provision may dampen competition between parallel imports and non-parallel imports of patented pharmaceutical products to some extent, other legislative amendments were simultaneously introduced in 2004 which have a pro-competitive effect on the market for certain patented pharmaceutical products in statutorily specified circumstances.

Parallel imports of patented pharmaceutical products are permitted under section 66(2)(i) if they are made 'for use by or on a specific patient in Singapore' where the products are 'required for use by or on that patient', 'the relevant authority has granted approval specifically for the import of that product for use by or on that patient' and 'that product was produced by or with the consent (conditional or otherwise) of the proprietor of the patent or any person licensed by him'.[65]

This so-called 'specific patient' defence to patent infringement allows parallel imports of patented pharmaceutical products to be made to meet the healthcare needs of individual consumers who can then take advantage of the lower-priced drugs that are available abroad. The secondary, and perhaps unintended, effect of this defence is the imposition of additional competitive pressures on firms which supply the same patented pharmaceutical products in Singapore. These imported pharmaceutical products may be brought into Singapore as non-infringing articles even if exporting them from their country of origin resulted in a breach of the licence conditions under which they were manufactured.

The other recently introduced statutory defence to patent infringement permits third parties to engage in any activity (which would otherwise infringe upon the patentee's exclusive rights) 'in relation to the subject matter of the patent to support any application for marketing approval for a pharmaceutical product'. Section 66(2)(h) protects third parties from patent infringement liability provided that 'any thing produced to support the application is not (i) made, used or sold in Singapore, or (ii) exported outside Singapore, other than for purposes related to meeting the requirements for marketing approval for that pharmaceutical product'. Otherwise known as the 'Bolar'[66] defence, this provision is based on an equivalent feature of US patent law which enables third parties to manufacture generic versions of patented drugs so that they may obtain the necessary regulatory approvals without having to wait for the relevant patents to expire. By permitting these drug manufacturers to secure the approval of the requisite authorities just before the end of the patent's lifespan, generic versions of these drugs can be made available to the market immediately once the drug is patent-free. This facilitates immediate competition between 'branded' drugs manufactured by patent holders and generic versions of these drugs to take place after the 20-year period of exclusivity ends, rather than giving the former a post-patent window period in which they are the sole suppliers of the drug while generic drug manufacturers are held back by the marketing approval process.

D. Patent law – preventing abuse of the patent monopoly

Given that patent grants confer a near-absolute legal monopoly in favour of patent holders, there is a real concern that these exclusive rights may be abused through ancillary contractual restraints imposed upon third parties in transactions involving patented inventions. The *Patents Act* specifically addresses a number of anticompetitive restraints which patent holders might include in their agreements with their licensees and other contracting parties. Section 51(1) of the Act renders the following contractual terms void:

> Subject to this section, any *condition or term of a contract* for the supply of a patented product or of a *licence* to work a patented invention, or of a contract relating to any such supply or licence, shall be void in so far as it purports –
>
> (a) in the case of a *contract for supply*, to require the person supplied to acquire from the supplier, or his nominee, or prohibit him from acquiring from any specified person, or from acquiring except from the supplier or his nominee, *anything other than the patented product*;
> (b) in the case of a *licence* to work a patented invention, to require the licensee to acquire from the licensor or his nominee, or prohibit him from acquiring from any specified person, or from acquiring except from the licensor or his nominee, *anything other than the product which is the patented invention* or (if it is a process) other than any product obtained directly by means of the process or to which the process has been applied; or
> (c) in either case, to *prohibit* the person supplied or the licensee from *using articles* (whether patented products or not) which *are not supplied by*, or any *patented process* which *does not belong to, the supplier or licensor*, or his nominee, or to restrict the right of the person supplied or the licensee to use any such articles or process.[67]

These prohibitions in the *Patents Act* are directed against 'tie-in' clauses – contractual restraints which tie the supply or licence of the patented subject matter to other goods or services.[68] These tying clauses are classic examples of anticompetitive behaviour by firms occupying a dominant position in the market for the tying product: the competition-related concern here is the patent holder's ability, because of the legal monopoly he enjoys, to leverage on the market power he wields in relation to the patented subject matter (the tying product or process) and use the tying arrangement to gain a commercial advantage in an adjacent market (the tied product or service). Competition law has traditionally recognised such behaviour as possessing a dominant position in one market but abusing that dominance in another market – leveraging on the market power enjoyed in the market for the tying product into the market for the tied product.[69] Similar concerns are shared by the law of patents and section 51(1) is directed at curtailing the patent holder's freedom to exploit his patent monopoly by 'over-reaching' beyond the patented subject matter over which he has been granted exclusive proprietary rights.

Apart from nullifying the legal validity of 'tie-in' clauses, the *Patents Act* also penalises the patent holder who utilises such contractual restraints by creating a special defence for third parties in patent infringement proceedings.

The patent holder's ability to enforce his exclusive rights is therefore sterilised until he terminates those contracts or licences containing the offending clauses. Section 51(2) of the Act provides the following disincentive to the patent holder:

> In proceedings against any person for infringement of a patent, it shall be a *defence* to prove that at the time of the infringement *there was in force a contract relating to the patent* made by or with the consent of the plaintiff or a *licence under the patent* granted by him or with his consent and containing in either case a *condition or term void* by virtue of this section.[70]

Section 51(5) goes on to make it clear that the prohibitions set out in section 51(1) do not extend to an exclusive sales arrangement, which 'prohibits any person from selling goods other than those supplied by a specific person', or contracts which give a party the exclusive right to 'supply such new parts of the patented product as may be required to keep it in repair'.

In addition, the *Patents Act* also prevents the patent holder from abusing his patent by entering into contracts or granting licences in relation to patented inventions which extend beyond the duration of the patent monopoly. Section 52(1) of the Act[71] creates a statutory right to terminate such contracts or licences after the relevant patents 'have ceased to be in force'. Notwithstanding anything in the licence or contract, these legal agreements may be determined from this time onwards 'to the extent (and only to the extent) that the contract or licence relates to the product or invention, by either party giving 3 months' notice in writing to the other party'.[72] This provision is directed towards dismantling 'tie-up' clauses, by which the patent holder seeks to contractually bind third parties on terms favourable to him even beyond the expiry or invalidation of the patent. This is consistent with a sound pro-competition policy which strictly limits the duration of benefits which patent holders can extract from their legal monopolies to what they are entitled to under the law of patents. Any attempt to use private contractual or licensing agreements to extend this time-frame is defeated by these provisions in the Act.

E. Patent law – compulsory licences

Recent amendments to the *Patents Act* in 2004 pursuant to Singapore's obligations under the US–Singapore FTA[73] clearly highlight the internal interface between patent law and competition law in the area of compulsory licences. Section 55(1) of the Act provides that the courts may grant a compulsory licence on one ground only: 'that the grant of the licence is necessary to remedy an anticompetitive practice'.

Without prejudicing the generality of what can constitute an 'anticompetitive practice', section 55(2) describes the following specific circumstances in which a court may find it necessary to grant a compulsory licence to remedy an anticompetitive practice:

(a) there is a market for the patented invention in Singapore;
(b) that market –
   (i) is not being supplied; or
   (ii) is not being supplied on reasonable terms; and
(c) the court is of the view that the proprietor has no valid reason for failing
   to supply that market with the patented invention, whether directly or
   through a licensee, on reasonable terms.

Any compulsory licence granted by the court, on the application of any
interested person, will be made upon such terms as the court thinks fit. The
compulsory licence granted under these statutory provisions is not exclusive
and cannot be assigned otherwise than in connection with the goodwill of the
business in which the patented invention is used. The licence may be terminated by the court if it is satisfied that the ground upon which the licence was
granted has ceased to exist and is unlikely to recur. Compulsory licences
granted under the Act will require the licensee to pay remuneration to the
patentee as mutually agreed between them or as determined by the court.[74] In
exercising its discretion under the Act to grant compulsory licences, the
powers of the court are to be 'exercised with a view to securing that the
inventor or other person beneficially entitled to a patent shall receive reasonable remuneration having regard to the economic value of the licence'.[75]

Even though compulsory licences under section 55 of the *Patents Act* have
been available in Singapore for many years prior to the recent amendments
which have been made to it in 2004, the Singapore courts have not had the
opportunity to apply this provision as yet. It remains to be seen if the courts
will have a chance to interpret the scope of the new statutory language and, in
particular, demarcate the parameters of what might constitute an 'anticompetitive practice'. It is interesting to note that the legislature chose to vest
the function of determining when a compulsory licence is an appropriate
remedy to the court – rather than the competition regulator, the Competition
Commission of Singapore – and to internalise compulsory licensing as one of
the features of the patent law system rather than delegating this remedial
device to those responsible for administering the competition law regime.[76] It
is likely that there will be some congruence between patent law and competition law on the sorts of conduct of a patent holder which amounts to an
'anticompetitive practice' – refusals to supply, refusals to licence, and so forth – a
matter which will be addressed below when the 'external' interface between
intellectual property law and competition law is discussed.

V. Trade mark law in Singapore

The *Trade Marks Act 1998* promulgates the legal framework which supports
the registered trade mark system in Singapore, setting out the legal standards

for acquiring intellectual property rights in signs which are used in indicators of origin for goods or services. Modelled broadly after the UK Trade Marks Act 1994 but with modifications made to take into account the European Community-centred features of the latter, the Singapore Act has undergone a number of legislative amendments in recent years to strengthen the exclusive rights enjoyed by trade mark proprietors. The most significant of these changes include broadening the scope of the Act to allow for the registration of non-visual trade marks,[77] the enhanced levels of protection conferred on 'well-known' trade marks[78] and enhancing the range and gravity of the remedial relief which trade mark proprietors may seek against third parties in infringement proceedings.[79]

Registered trade marks have to be signs which are capable of graphical representation and can serve the function of distinguishing the goods or services of their proprietor from those supplied by third parties. To qualify for registration under the Act, the trade mark must either have an inherently distinctive character or have acquired a de facto distinctiveness from its use in the market-place. Generally speaking, trade marks which are descriptive of the goods or services for which they are registered, including laudatory words and other signs, are less likely to qualify for registration.[80] Before a new trade mark can be registered in Singapore, the Registrar of Trade Marks must be satisfied that it does not conflict with an existing registered trade mark that is identical or similar to it.[81]

Each registration lasts for ten years, but may be renewed indefinitely for subsequent ten-year periods.[82] The proprietor of a registered trade mark enjoys exclusive rights over the use of the trade mark on goods and services as an indicator of origin. The scope of his exclusive rights depend on the categories of goods or services for which the trade mark has been registered and the degree of similarity between the registered trade mark and the mark used by the third party: where an identical mark is used on identical goods or services by the third party, the proprietor's intellectual property rights are infringed in most cases. Where the third party makes use of an identical mark on similar goods or services, or a similar mark on identical or similar goods or services, the proprietor's rights are infringed only if the latter can establish a likelihood of confusion by the public from such use.[83] Where the third party uses an identical or similar mark on dissimilar goods or services, the proprietor's rights are only infringed if his trade mark has acquired the status of a 'well-known' trade mark in the public mind. 'Well-known' trade marks enjoy protection from unauthorised uses of identical or similar signs which cause public confusion, as well as additional protection from certain forms of dilution (tarnishment and blurring) and misappropriation.[84]

Unlike copyrighted works or patented inventions, the species of intellectual property arising from the trade mark system is not directly embodied within the goods or services supplied by the trade mark proprietor. The trade mark is merely an ancillary device that is affixed onto these goods or services to indicate their trade origins. The competition-related issues arising from trade mark law are thus distinguishable from those encountered where copyright and patent law are concerned. The acquisition of a registered trade mark by a proprietor does not prevent his rivals from offering exactly the same type of goods or services as those for which the trade mark has been registered: the existence of the registered trade mark just means that his rivals are not allowed to supply substitute goods or services using an identical or similar mark.

Given the trade mark proprietor's exclusive rights over the use of the trade mark in relation to those goods or services for which his trade mark has been registered, competition-related issues arise when the registered trade mark is secured over words or other signs which deprive his rivals of the commercial vocabulary necessary to compete effectively with the trade mark proprietor. Competition-related issues also arise where the trade mark proprietor's control over the use of the trade mark in the market place may enable him to shut out competitors in an after-market that is downstream from, or adjacent to, the market for the primary goods or services supplied by the proprietor. An appropriate balance also needs to be reached to enable the trade mark proprietor's competitors to use the protected trade mark in certain instances of commercial speech – as a means of indicating product substitutability, for example – which are supportive of the competitive process. As with copyright and patents, the treatment of parallel imports under the law of trade marks involves a policy choice as to how far 'intra-brand' competition should be facilitated within Singapore.

A. Trade mark law – registration criteria and protectable subject matter

The statutory requirements prescribed by the *Trade Marks Act*, which have to be satisfied before a trade mark qualifies for registration, ensure that would-be trade mark proprietors do not secure exclusive rights over ordinary signs which other traders might have a legitimate interest in using themselves. A trade mark cannot, for example, be registered in respect of a word or picture which exactly describes the product or service on which the trade mark is used: the word 'soap' cannot be registered as a trade mark for soaps, neither can a photograph or drawing of a bar of soap. Such signs are viewed by the law as incapable of performing the basic functions of a trade mark – to indicate the origin of the goods or services on which the mark is applied and to distinguish them from the goods or services of another trader. Giving any single soap manufacturer a legal monopoly over the use of the word 'soap' or a picture of a soap bar would deprive his competitors of a basic tool of communication in the market-place. If no one but the trade mark proprietor could use these signs on soaps and soap-based products, then other soap manufacturers would not be able to use the mark on their goods and would find it impossible to inform customers that they supply products which are substitutes for the trade mark proprietor's products. The competitive process would grind to a halt if one soap-selling trader in the market for soap products had the exclusive right to use the word 'soap' on his goods.

Other restrictions on the types of marks that qualify for protection under the Act reflect similar concerns about the impact which registered trade marks may have in depriving the trade mark proprietor's competitors of access to words or other signs which the latter should be able to use freely. For example, by requiring would-be trade mark proprietors to show that their trade marks are 'not devoid of any distinctive character',[85] the law of trade marks makes it difficult for ordinary words, symbols or other such signs to qualify as registered trade marks. In cases involving trade mark applicants seeking to obtain protection for word marks, the legal standard of 'distinctiveness' is satisfied in most cases involving invented words, uncommon words, or words not typically associated with the goods or services to which they are applied. On the other hand, laudatory words or words commonly associated with the goods or services on which they are applied will probably not satisfy this standard of 'distinctiveness' unless it can be shown that such words are de facto distinctive[86] of the goods or services of the trade mark applicant – typically where these words have been used in the market for some time and the public have come to associate them with a particular source of goods or services. In this way, the 'distinctiveness' criterion serves as an important safeguard which is mindful of the legitimate interests of third parties who compete in the same markets as the trade mark applicant. The ability of third parties to compete with the trade mark applicant would be severely limited if the latter could secure for itself exclusive rights over the use of common laudatory words and other advertising devices which are relevant to the categories of goods or services for which the trade mark is registered. Third parties supplying the goods or services which fall within the same categories for which trade mark protection has been secured could not, for example, use these words in their efforts to market or promote their goods or services. Distortions in the competitive process would therefore result if such restraints were imposed on the commercial vocabulary of the trade mark proprietor's competitors.

Apart from word marks and picture marks, three-dimensional shapes are also registrable as trade marks under the *Trade Marks Act* if they are not caught by any of the statutory bars found in section 7(3) of the Act:

> A sign shall not be registered as a trade mark if it consists exclusively of –
>
> (a) the shape which results from the nature of the goods themselves;
> (b) the shape of the goods which is necessary to obtain a technical result; or
> (c) the shape which gives substantial value to the goods.[87]

These provisions prevent would-be trade mark proprietors from registering the natural shapes of goods as trade marks for that category of goods. Shapes which are valuable because they contribute to the functionality of the goods on which they are applied, or because they make the goods more aesthetically pleasing to the customer's eye, are also excluded from registration.[88] These are shapes which do not operate primarily as badges of origin for the goods on which they are applied. Given the potentially perpetual monopoly which trade mark proprietors enjoy if their registrations are renewed every ten years, these statutory provisions ensure that the trade mark system is not used to lock away these shapes which could be more appropriately protected by way of patents or registered designs. Once again, the law of trade marks takes into account the interests of the trade mark proprietor's competitors who would be severely disadvantaged if they were deprived of access to these shapes when designing and developing their own products. Similar concerns have also been voiced by the UK courts in the context of applicants seeking to register colours as trade marks.[89]

B. Trade mark law – defences to infringement

The internal interface between trade mark law and competition law is also apparent in the nature and range of defences available to third parties who may wish to use the registered trade mark for their own purposes. These statutory provisions identify situations where traders other than the trade mark proprietor may have legitimate reasons for making use of the trade mark in their own commercial pursuits. Pro-competition policies have left their mark on some of these defences. For example, where a trade mark is used by another trader to indicate the substitutability of his goods for the trade mark proprietor's goods, the former is permitted to make reference to the trade mark to communicate information about the similarities or compatibility between these goods, thus demonstrating a legislative commitment towards facilitating the competitive process.[90]

The positive impact of these statutory defences to trade mark infringement on competition between the trade mark proprietor and his competitors arises in two ways. Firstly, it fosters competition in the market for the principal goods or services offered by the trade mark proprietor because competitors are able to use the trade mark to indicate that they are offering viable alternatives to the former's goods or services. Secondly, the availability of these defences in the law of trade marks also enables competition to take place in adjacent or ancillary after-markets, particularly where references to a registered trade mark are essential to communicate the connection between the goods or services being offered and the trade marked goods or services supplied by the trade mark proprietor.

Section 28(1) of the Act provides that:

> ... a person does not infringe a registered trade mark when –
>
> (a) he uses –
>   (i) his name or the name of his place of business; or
>   (ii) the name of his predecessor in business or the name of his pre-
>   decessor's place of business;
> (b) he *uses a sign to indicate* –
>   (i) the *kind, quality*, quantity, intended purpose, value, geographical
>   origin, or other *characteristic of goods or services*; or
>   (ii) the time of production of goods or of the rendering of services; or
> (c) he uses the trade mark to indicate the *intended purpose* of goods (in
>   particular as *accessories or spare parts*) or services,
>
> and such use is in accordance with honest practices in industrial and
> commercial matters.[91]

In the same vein, section 28(4) of the Act provides that:

> ... a person who uses a registered trade mark does not infringe the trade
> mark if such use –
>
> (a) constitutes fair use in *comparative commercial advertising* or *promotion*;
> (b) is for a non-commercial purpose; or
> (c) is for the purpose of news reporting or news commentary.[92]

Taken together, these provisions from the *Trade Marks Act* permit the trade
mark proprietor's competitors to use the trade mark – not on their own
goods or services, such as to pass off their own goods or services as the goods
or services of the trade mark proprietor – but to facilitate the competitive
process between them. In essence, these third parties will avoid trade mark
infringement liability if the trade mark is used descriptively in relation to
goods or services. Unauthorised use of the trade mark would be lawful if it is
employed to identify the trade mark proprietor's goods in the following
commercial circumstances: the third party could be in the business of repair-
ing these goods, or making complementary goods such as spare parts and
accessories, and needs to identify these goods using the registered trade mark
in order for consumers to be aware of the relationship between these goods
and his own goods or services. Giving third parties the right to use the trade
mark in this way, where consumers are not misled into thinking that the third
party's goods originate from the trade mark proprietor or vice versa, prevents
trade mark proprietors from exercising their legal monopoly in a way which
restricts competition in a closely connected downstream market.

Allowing third parties to use registered trade marks in fairly executed
comparative advertising campaigns also promotes competition between the
trade mark proprietor's goods or services and those supplied by his rivals.
Comparative advertising allows traders an effective means of communicating

the relative merits of their products against the characteristics of the products supplied by the trade mark proprietor. This fosters a commercial climate in which the consuming public are well-informed of what is available in the market, thereby creating market conditions which are conducive to the vigorous competitive processes which competition law looks favourably upon.

C. Trade mark law – parallel imports

Competition between legitimate parallel imports of trade marked goods and goods placed on the domestic market by the trade mark proprietor is facilitated through the legislative enactment of a defence which embodies a doctrine of international trade mark exhaustion. The trade mark proprietor's intellectual property rights are exhausted once goods bearing the trade mark are put onto the market in any country by him or with his consent. Section 29 of the Act provides that:

> (1) . . . a registered trade mark is not infringed by the use of the trade mark in relation to goods which have been *put on the market,* whether *in Singapore or outside Singapore,* under that trade mark by the proprietor of the registered trade mark or with his *express or implied consent (conditional or otherwise).*[93]

The approach taken towards parallel imports of trade marked goods in Singapore is more generous compared to the position in the United Kingdom, largely because the latter's status as a member of the European Community has required it to adopt a Community-wide exhaustion principle. Singapore's statutory position on parallel imports makes it clear that any form of consent from the proprietor – whether expressly or impliedly given, whether qualified with conditions or not – in relation to goods he has put on the market is sufficient to exhaust his rights in the trade mark. In contrast, the equivalent statutory provision on parallel imports in the UK Trade Marks Act 1994 is not entirely clear on how the issue of the proprietor's 'consent' should be dealt with in the absence of sufficiently detailed legislative language.[94]

However, the scope of this statutory provision which permits parallel imports of trade marked goods is narrower than the positions taken in relation to copyright and patent protected parallel imports under the Copyright and Patent statutes in Singapore.[95] The 'proprietor of the registered trade mark', whose consent must be established, referred to in this provision is limited to the registered proprietor in Singapore.[96] The territorial nature of registered trade marks means that different entities can register the same trade mark in different territories. Goods which were legitimately made and put in the market under the trade mark in a foreign territory may be genuine goods in that territory, but may infringe the registered trade mark proprietor's legal monopoly in Singapore if those goods are brought into Singapore. Such imported goods are not genuine goods in Singapore because they are not the goods of the Singapore trade mark proprietor. They will therefore not be treated as parallel imports in relation to which the trade mark proprietor's exclusive rights have been exhausted under section 29(1) of the Act. Where the trade mark is applied to goods manufactured abroad by an entity related to the Singapore trade mark proprietor, it is possible for trade mark exhaustion to take place if the relationship between them is such that the Singapore trade mark proprietor has implicitly consented to the use of the trade mark on those foreign-made goods.[97]

Singapore trade mark proprietors are therefore unable to divide their domestic markets from their foreign markets by placing export restrictions on the goods they have made available for sale abroad. The *Trade Marks Act* permits third parties to bring in these goods as parallel imports without infringing the Singapore trade mark, thereby potentially exposing the trade mark proprietor to competition from his own goods which were originally released in a foreign territory. Such an approach is consonant with the pro-competition policies which underlie competition law as it discourages market discrimination and segmentation along national boundaries.

VI. Competition law in Singapore

The discussion thus far has surveyed the major limitations imposed by the various intellectual property regimes in Singapore on the recognition, creation and enforcement of an IP owner's exclusive rights in his copyright, patent or trade mark. These limitations emanate from within copyright law, patent law and trade mark law – making them endogenous features of the law of intellectual property which have been influenced by a range of pro-competition policies consistent with the basic objectives of competition law.

We now turn our attention to the 'external interface' between intellectual property and competition law, where the balancing exercise involving the private proprietary rights of IP owners and public policy in favour of greater competition in the market takes place exogenously from the law of intellectual property. Given that the *Competition Act 2004* has only just taken root in Singapore, no specific cases have emerged to illustrate its interaction with the various species of intellectual property rights. However, the discussion below will seek to set out the structural features of Singapore competition legislation and, by extrapolating from the similarities and differences between those features and the legislative frameworks of more mature jurisdictions, predict the likely impact this area of the law will have on IP owners in Singapore.

The 'external interface' revolves around the application of competition law principles to curtail the IP owner's freedom to exercise the exclusive proprietary rights conferred upon him by the law of intellectual property. The IP owner's ability to determine how he wishes to exploit his IP (if at all), with which parties, and on what terms, may be qualified by the operation of competition law when his conduct attracts anti-competitive repercussions that go against the public interest. For example, transactions involving the licensing of his intellectual property, or any other IP-related dealings, might be subject to competition law prohibitions against agreements which are anticompetitive in character or which give rise to anticompetitive consequences. Such exogenous derogations from the legal monopoly which IP owners receive from the law of intellectual property would probably not occur in too many cases, given that those who administer Singapore's competition law framework have emphasised that the incentive-reward functions of the law of intellectual property should not be unnecessarily disrupted by the legal uncertainty that would result. This is reflected in one of the earliest public statements made by the then-proponents of Singapore's new competition law, where the interface between competition law and intellectual property was described in the following manner:

TREATMENT OF IP UNDER COMPETITION LAW IP laws and competition law are not necessarily inconsistent; rather they can work together to help develop Singapore into a knowledge economy. Competition law, by helping to promote efficient markets, ensures that undertakings innovate to the extent dictated by consumers and other market pressures. The rewards to innovation provided by IPR should thus be maintained. The specific rights provided by IP laws, and the business advantages these confer, would thus not in any way be circumscribed by competition law.

However, IPR is a reward to innovation for specific invention or creation, and should not become a tool for engaging in anticompetitive activities. Where the exercise of the IPR is anticompetitive, it would be subject to competition law.

In considering whether a business activity involving the exercise of IPR would have any competition concerns, the Competition Commission would adopt an 'economics-based cost-benefit analysis' or 'rule of reason' approach. This means that the *Competition Commission would take a holistic view and look at the overall net welfare effects of the activity to decide whether a particular use of an IPR reduces welfare in Singapore.*

To help provide further clarity, the Competition Commission will develop guidelines after the enactment of the competition law on how it would view IPR-related business activities.[98]

The architects of Singapore's competition law framework have also explicitly acknowledged that Singapore's intellectual property law may convey some degree of market power to IP developers, and that there is a need for competition law to address those situations where 'undertakings abuse their IPR for unfair commercial advantage that is detrimental to overall market efficiency'.[99]

The challenge ahead for the Competition Commission of Singapore (CCS) is to fit IP-related instances of commercial conduct which raise competition-related concerns within the general competition law framework, while administering block exemption schemes for those transactions which are recognised to be pro-competitive on the whole. One of the more contentious issues here is the extent to which IP-related transactions or commercial conduct should be differentiated from similar situations involving non-IP proprietary interests when brought under the scrutiny of competition law, bearing in mind the special policy considerations which underlie the various intellectual property systems and the internal checks and balances that exist within each of them.

Two key statutory prohibitions found within Singapore's *Competition Act 2004* will have a direct impact on the extent to which IP owners are able to fully exercise the legal monopolies conferred upon them by the various intellectual property statutes. The first is the section 34 prohibition against anticompetitive agreements which prevent, restrict or distort competition; this will impose limitations on the types of licensing arrangements IP owners can enter into. The second is the section 47 prohibition against conduct which abuses a dominant position; this may also impose specific demands on a dominant IP-owning firm's IP-related dealings. Before analysing these two statutory prohibitions specifically, a brief introduction to the relevant guidelines issued by the Competition Commission of Singapore on the treatment of intellectual property rights under the *Competition Act* is appropriate.

A. The CCS Guideline on the Treatment of Intellectual Property Rights

Guidelines issued by the CCS are policy statements which reflect the Singapore competition regulator's analytical approach towards the interpretation and application of the statutory prohibitions found in the *Competition Act 2004*. The contents of the CCS Guideline on the Treatment of Intellectual Property Rights[100] have no legal force on their own, are non-exhaustive in character, and may be revised by the CCS should the need arise. The Guideline sets out how the CCS views the interface between IPRs and competition law, indicating some of the factors and circumstances which it may consider when assessing agreements and conduct involving intellectual property. The scope of the Guideline is limited to intellectual property rights granted under the *Patents Act, Copyright Act, Plant Varieties Protection Act, Layout-Designs of Integrated Circuits Act*, and the *Registered Designs Act*, as well as trade secrets.[101]

The Guideline contains a collage of policy elements drawn from the United States Antitrust Guidelines for the Licensing of Intellectual Property[102] and the European Commission's Technology Transfer Block Exemption Regulations.[103] The following basic policies underpin the approach of the CCS towards evaluating intellectual property-related agreements and conduct under the *Competition Act 2004*:[104]

- For competition law purposes, the CCS regards IPRs as being essentially comparable to any other form of private property and therefore subject to the same fundamental analytical principles, even though intellectual property has distinguishing characteristics which should be taken into account in the competition analysis – they are costly to develop but often easy to copy, non-rivalrous in the way they are used, and susceptible to free riding.

- The various species of intellectual property have individual characteristics which distinguish them from each other, but the general analytical principles applied to all IPR-related situations are the same.

- The possession of an IPR does not necessarily create market power in itself, as the 'legal' monopoly enjoyed is not the same as the 'economic' monopoly required for market power to subsist – the latter only arises when there are insufficient actual or potential close substitutes from alternatives supplied by the intellectual property owner's competitors.

- When analysing the competitive effects of IP-related agreements and conduct, the CCS will normally investigate the relevant product markets (goods or services which integrate the relevant IPRs), though in some cases it may have to consider the competitive effects on the relevant technology markets (comprising substitutable technologies which are available to IP licensees) or innovation markets (comprising the research and development efforts of undertakings directed towards a particular new or improved product or process, and their close substitutes).[105]

- IP licensing arrangements are viewed as pro-competitive 'in the vast majority of cases' because they lead to the more efficient exploitation of the IP (by integrating the IP with other complementary factors of production supplied by other undertakings), promote innovation by giving incentives to IP owners, and reduce transaction costs in some circumstances (such as technology 'packages' and 'pooling' arrangements involving multiple IP owners).

B. Anticompetitive agreements under the Competition Act

The IP owner may exploit his intellectual property on his own by utilising the protected subject matter on those goods or services which he puts onto the market. However, in many cases, the IP owner chooses to collaborate with third parties in the exploitation of their intellectual property – especially where he lacks the necessary resources or expertise to realise the full commercial potential of his legal monopoly. Competition law becomes concerned when private agreements are made between the IP owner and his collaborators – licensees, suppliers, manufacturers, distributors and so forth – to the extent that there may be aspects of these agreements which have further objectives that are detrimental to the competitive process in some way. These competition-related concerns are magnified when the IP owner enters into a collaborative arrangement with his competitors because any contractual restraints arising from an agreement between these parties may have a direct impact on their freedom to compete against each other.

Section 34(1) of the *Competition Act 2004* prohibits 'agreements between undertakings, decisions by associations of undertakings or concerted practices which have as their object or effect the prevention, restriction or distortion of competition within Singapore' unless they are exempted by a block exemption made by the Competition Commission in accordance with sections 36 and 37 of the Act. Vertical agreements are also statutorily excluded from the scope of the section 34 prohibition. Paragraph 8 of the Third Schedule of the Act defines this category of excluded agreements as 'between two or more undertakings each of which operates, for the purposes of the agreement, at a different level of the production or distribution chain, and relating to the conditions under which the parties may purchase, sell or resell certain goods or services'.[106] This special statutory exclusion for vertical agreements is a significant departure from the UK and EC competition framework which inspired Singapore's competition legislation.[107]

The following examples of agreements, decisions or concerted practices which may have the object or effect of preventing, restricting or distorting competition within Singapore are given in the Act. These are agreements which:

(a) directly or indirectly fix purchase or selling prices or any other trading conditions;
(b) limit or control production, markets, technical development or investment;
(c) share markets or sources of supply;
(d) apply dissimilar conditions to equivalent transactions with other trading parties, thereby placing them at a competitive disadvantage; or
(e) make the conclusion of contracts subject to acceptance by the other parties of supplementary obligations which, by their nature or according to commercial usage, have no connection with the subject of such contracts.[108]

Guidance related to the application of the section 34 prohibition against anticompetitive agreements to IP licensing arrangements can be found in two Guidelines issued by the CCS: the first is the CCS Guideline on the Section 34 Prohibition,[109] a statement of the general principles which the CCS will adopt when interpreting the scope of the statutory prohibition. The second is the CCS Guideline on the Treatment of Intellectual Property Rights (the CCS IP Guidelines), already introduced above, which sets out specific issues which need to be considered when analysing competition-related issues in IP-related agreements and conduct. The CCS IP Guidelines set out the following general framework for assessing licensing agreements under the section 34 prohibition:[110]

• Step 1: The nature of the relationship between the parties to the licensing agreement – whether they are competitors or non-competitors[111] – needs to be ascertained. The parties will be treated as being in a competitive relationship if they would have been actual or potential competitors in the absence of the licensing agreement.

- Step 2: The CCS will consider if the restraints in the licensing agreement restrict actual or potential competition that would have existed in their absence, taking into account their impact on inter-technology and intra-technology competition.
- Step 3: The pro-competitive benefits of the licensing agreement will be factored into the CCS analysis and weighed against its negative effects on competition. The licensing agreement will not fall within the scope of the section 34 prohibition if, on balance, it may have a net economic benefit. This would be the case if the agreement 'contributes to improving production or distribution or promoting technical or economic progress and it does not impose on the undertakings concerned the possibility of eliminating competition in respect of a substantial part of the goods or services in question.[112]

In a typical licensing arrangement between an IP-owning licensor and a manufacturer licensee, a number of contractual restraints may run afoul of the section 34 prohibition if they have the object or effect of an *appreciable*[113] negative impact on competition, unless it can be shown that there is a net economic benefit which renders the transaction pro-competitive as a whole.

For example, a price-fixing clause in a licensing arrangement between competitors which required the licensee to sell the IP-protected goods he manufactures at a certain price level would potentially fall within the scope of the example in (a) above.[114] A licensing term which restricted the ability of the licensee to conduct research into and further develop the licensed technology, or which substantially reduced the licensee's incentives to engage in research and development activities – by requiring, for example, the licensee to assign or grantback any further intellectual property developed from his use of the licensed technology – may fall under limb (b) of the examples cited above.[115] Territorial restrictions on the licensee which prevent him from making active or passive sales beyond a defined geographical area may qualify as conduct prohibited under example (c) above, though there are typically pro-competitive justifications for placing such restraints on licensees.[116] Licensing terms which discriminate between the IP-owner's licensees, thereby giving some of them a competitive advantage over others, perhaps pursuant to a group boycott organised by a group of licensees, may be caught by subsection (d) above. Tying clauses which enable the IP owner to leverage upon his legal monopoly into an adjacent or downstream market may also amount to an example of unlawful conduct following the example in (e) above.[117]

However, the apparent anticompetitive character of many of these restraints that are found in IP-licensing arrangements may be tempered by the overall pro-competitive nature of the collaboration between the parties: the licensing agreement may improve the production and distribution of IP-protected goods and services, facilitate technology transfers, or stimulate innovation in related markets. This means that the section 34 statutory prohibition will have to be applied holistically to the licensing arrangement in its entirety before a determination can be made about the legality of any of its restraints.[118] Consideration must be given to the quantitative and qualitative significance of the restraint on competition, and whether or not it is ancillary to a wider collaboration which generates a net economic benefit, when evaluating its compatibility with the policies which underlie competition law. The CCS IP Guidelines establish two 'safety zones' for IP licensing arrangements which 'will generally have no appreciable adverse effect on competition' if the combined market shares of the parties to these agreements fall below the following numerical thresholds:[119]

- Where the licensing agreement is made between competitors, their aggregate market share does not exceed 25 per cent on any of the relevant markets.
- Where the licensing agreement is made between non-competitors, the market share of each of the parties does not exceed 35 per cent of any of the relevant markets.
- Where it may be difficult to classify the status of the parties to the licensing arrangement as competitors or non-competitors, the 25 per cent threshold will be applied.[120]

Even if the market shares of the parties to a licensing arrangement were to exceed these thresholds, the CCS IP Guidelines emphasise that this does not necessarily mean that the effect of the agreement on competition is appreciable.[121] In addition, certain types of IP licensing arrangements may be exempt from scrutiny under the section 34 prohibition because they fall within the scope of the general statutory exclusion for vertical agreements.[122]

The CCS IP Guidelines limit the application of this statutory exclusion to those IP licensing restraints which are ancillary to an agreement whose main object is the purchase and redistribution of products – such as a franchise agreement where the franchisee licences the franchisor's trademark and know-how as part of his agreement to market and resell the franchisor's products.[123] IP licensing arrangements between competitors[124] which do not operate 'at a different level of the production or distribution chain' do not qualify under this statutory exemption because they are not true 'vertical' agreements. Neither do IP licensing agreements between non-competitors which are not directly related to the use, sale or resale of products – such as agreements in which the primary object is the assignment or licensing of intellectual property rights for the manufacture of goods, and pure licensing agreements. These non-qualifying licensing arrangements will have to be assessed for compliance with the section 34 prohibition in accordance with the analytical framework set out in the CCS IP Guidelines outlined above.[125]

Even if some vertical agreements are excluded from the scope of the section 34 prohibition, they are still subject to the section 47 prohibition where one of the licensing parties occupies a position of market dominance and its conduct amounts to an abuse of that dominance. The mode of analysis of such agreements shifts when it is scrutinised under section 47, where no block exemptions are available, and the nature of the inquiry focuses on whether the dominant firm's unilateral conduct in the IP licensing transaction is an acceptable mode of competition for a firm wielding the market power it has in its possession.

C. Abuse of a dominant position under the Competition Act

Under the CCS Guideline on the Section 47 Prohibition, an undertaking which enjoys substantial market power is understood to occupy a dominant position in the market in which it operates.[126] Occupying a position of market dominance requires the undertaking to avoid commercial conduct which distorts competition in the market. This imposes additional restrictions on the freedom of the dominant firm to engage in certain forms of commercial conduct which non-dominant firms are at liberty to practise. Such conduct is viewed by competition law as an 'abuse' of an undertaking's dominant position and is subject to the section 47 prohibition.

Undertakings which have a dominant position on the market are capable of weakening existing competition in the market, or making it more difficult for future competition to take place by raising entry barriers, by making illegitimate use of the market power they wield. The mere possession or acquisition of a dominant position is not unlawful on its own,[127] neither is a firm's maintenance or strengthening of its dominant position by 'conduct arising from efficiencies, such as through successful innovation or economies of scale or scope'.[128] The statutory provision only prohibits conduct which takes advantage of the firm's market power in a way which is detrimental to the competitive process, where the mode of competition does not proceed on a legitimate basis on which consumers stand to benefit – from lower prices, greater product choice, or better quality goods and services, for example. This approach is explicitly recognised in the context of IP-owning dominant undertakings, with the following policy statement put into the CCS Guideline on the Section 47 Prohibition:[129]

> The legitimate exercise of an intellectual property right, even by a dominant undertaking, will not be regarded as an abuse. It is however possible that that the way in which an intellectual property right is exercised may give rise to concerns if it goes beyond the legitimate exploitation of the intellectual property right, for example, if it is used to leverage market power from one market to another.

Section 47(1) of the Act prohibits 'any conduct on the part of one or more undertakings which amounts to the abuse of a dominant position in any market in Singapore'. No exemptions are available for conduct which infringes this provision and 'dominant position' is defined in section 47(3) to mean 'a dominant position within Singapore or elsewhere'.

The following examples of conduct which may constitute an abuse of a dominant position can also be found in the Act:

(a) predatory behaviour towards competitors;
(b) limiting production, markets or technical development to the prejudice of consumers;
(c) applying dissimilar conditions to equivalent transactions with other trading parties, thereby placing them at a competitive disadvantage; or
(d) making the conclusion of contracts subject to acceptance by the other parties of supplementary obligations which, by their nature or according to commercial usage, have no connection with the subject of the contracts.[130]

As far as the IP owner is concerned, the statutory prohibition in section 47 only applies if it qualifies as an undertaking which enjoys a dominant position in a relevant market. This requires an evaluation of the markets in which it operates – both the market for the subject matter of the intellectual property rights (the upstream market for copyrighted works, patented technologies, etc.) and the market for the products or services offered to consumers (the downstream market for goods or services which utilise the intellectual property) – to determine if the IP owner's market share is large enough, in light of the prevailing market conditions and competitive pressures facing the relevant industry, to give it a sufficient degree of market power such that it can be considered a dominant undertaking. It is clear that the legal monopoly which an IP owner enjoys, by merely possessing these intellectual property rights, is not enough for the IP owner to qualify as a dominant undertaking.[131] Further inquiry needs to be made as to the availability of substitutes to the IP-protected subject matter, as well as the alternatives to the goods and services which embody or utilise the intellectual property. This approach towards IPR ownership is clearly reflected in the CCS IP Guidelines:[132]

> Ownership of an IPR will not necessarily create a dominant position. Whether or not an IP owner enjoys dominance in the relevant market will depend on the extent to which there are substitutes for the technology, product, process or work to which the IPR relates.

Where 'persistently high' market shares are held by an IP-owning undertaking as a result of its IPRs impeding market entry in the short term, the CCS IP Guidelines suggest that the Singapore competition regulator may be hesitant to recognise that such an undertaking occupies a position of market dominance because 'any other undertaking may in the long term be able to enter the market with its own innovation'.[133] This complicates the traditional approach of assessing an undertaking's market power with direct reference to its share of the relevant market. To what extent can an IP-owning undertaking argue that, despite having the sizeable market share which has traditionally been used as an indicator of market dominance, it should not be treated as a dominant undertaking (and subjected to the same behavioural restraints) simply because its advantages are time-limited by the finite duration of its IPRs?[134]

Assuming the IP owner does occupy a position of market dominance, regardless of whether this is because of the nature of the intellectual property it owns or some other reason for its commercial success, the sorts of conduct which may violate section 47 of the *Competition Act* would overlap significantly with the anticompetitive conduct discussed earlier in relation to IP licences under the section 34 prohibition.[135] If such restrictive clauses are found in the licence terms imposed by a dominant IP-owning firm on its licensees and an infringement of section 47 is established, the penalty for engaging in such anti-competitive conduct will be levied only against the dominant firm for abusing its position of market dominance, as compared to an infringement of section 34 where the penalty may be shared between all the parties involved in the arrangement. In other cases, the unilateral acquisition of IPRs by a dominant undertaking over a competing technology may also amount to an abuse within the scope of the section 47 prohibition if the object or effect of the conduct was to harm competition.[136]

The CCS IP Guidelines suggest that the real competition-related concerns involving the exercise of an IPR by a dominant undertaking arise primarily in situations where 'the dominant undertaking attempts to extend its market power into a neighbouring or related market, beyond the scope granted by IP law'.[137] This form of 'leveraging' is exemplified in tying arrangements where the dominant undertaking, an IP licensor, imposes a condition on IP licensees that it will only grant licences if the licensee agrees to buy another product not covered by the IPR.[138] As with classic cases of 'product bundling' by a dominant undertaking, a tying arrangement in an IP licence amounts to an abuse of the licensor's dominant position because it is conduct which seeks to extend its market power in the market for the tying product, the IPR, into the market for the tied product.

Similarly, a dominant undertaking which occupies a position of market dominance by virtue of its IPR ownership may, in limited circumstances, also engage in abusive conduct if it refuses to license its intellectual property rights. Such conduct might qualify as an abuse of a dominant position if the refusal 'concerns an IPR which relates to an essential facility, with the effect of (likely) substantial harm to competition', and where the dominant undertaking is not 'able to objectively justify its conduct'.[139] The 'essential facility' doctrine, which was developed in the United States and, to a more limited extent, in the European Community, was traditionally applied to capital-intensive physical infrastructure which competitors in downstream markets needed access to in order to compete in those markets. This doctrine has since been applied to intangible intellectual property, where the IPRs are an indispensable input to actual or potential competitors engaged in downstream business activity.[140]

The IP-owning dominant firm may thus contravene the section 47 prohibition by refusing to license its intellectual property to third parties who have to make use of the protected subject matter to gain entry into a particular downstream market. In these circumstances, the IP owner's exercise of his legal monopoly may cross the line into an abuse of his dominant position in limited cases where the refusal is motivated by a desire to foreclose a downstream market from its competitors, and where access to the intellectual property in question is absolutely essential for competition to take place. It seems, however, that the Competition Commission of Singapore will take a very narrow approach towards the availability of the 'essential facilities' doctrine to cases involving refusals to supply an IP licence:[141]

> A facility will be viewed as essential only if there are no potential substitutes (through duplication or otherwise), and if the facility is indispensable to the exercise of the activity in question. Essential facilities are rare in practice; IPRs by themselves are generally unlikely to create essential facilities.
>
> In determining whether a refusal to supply a licence constitutes an abuse under the section 47 prohibition, the impact on the technology and innovation markets will be considered. Care must be taken not to undermine the incentives for undertakings to make future investments and innovations.

However, if a situation arises where the CCS finds that an IP-related 'bottleneck' has emerged and if anticompetitive consequences are felt in adjacent markets, such that the dominant firm's refusal to licence third parties amounts to an infringement of the section 47 prohibition, the CCS is empowered to remedy the situation by requiring the infringing party 'to enter such legally enforceable agreements as may be specified by the Commission and designed to prevent or lessen the anticompetitive effects which have arisen'.[142] This may include an order for a compulsory licence to be granted, a remedy already specifically provided for under the *Patents Act* where the Singapore courts have been statutorily empowered to award such licences 'to remedy an anticompetitive practice'.[143]

VII. Looking ahead: developing the intellectual property–competition law interface in Singapore

With competition law only at an incipient stage of its development in Singapore's legal landscape, we can expect its external interface with the law of intellectual property to mature gradually and demonstrate increasing legal sophistication in the years to come. The precise contours of this interface will depend largely on the basic competition-related policies which the Competition Commission of Singapore develops in the course of implementing the new legislative framework. Initial indicators suggest that economic analysis will play a significant role in the administration of Singapore's competition law and we can expect this attitude to influence the evaluation by the CCS of IP-related commercial conduct when it has to determine whether or not the statutory prohibitions have been contravened.

One of the primary tensions between the law of intellectual property and the new competition law which may persist into the future is the coexistence of the external interface and the internal interface between these two areas of the law. Given that Singapore's copyright law, patent law and trade mark law have already internalised some of the competition-related concerns in which competition law takes a similar interest, it remains to be seen how ready the Competition Commission of Singapore will be to further curtail an IP owner's legal monopoly through its administration of Singapore's competition framework. Which competition-related problems are best dealt with endogenously, and which problems are more appropriately resolved exogenously?

In the meantime, those aspects of the different species of intellectual property which contribute to the internal interface between competition law and Intellectual Property Law will remain the most visible indications of Singapore's attempts to balance the private interests of IP owners with the public interest in competition. Some of these statutory provisions reflect Singapore's domestic interest in maintaining an open trading economy with a high dependence on imported goods: this comes across in the liberal approach which has been taken towards parallel imports of IP-protected goods and points clearly to the public interest taking precedence in this arena. The recent amendments to Singapore's intellectual property statutes indicate conscious parliamentary efforts to strengthen the position of IP owners as part of the country's efforts to evolve into a knowledge-based economy. These legal developments should, eventually, be met with corresponding counter-balancing efforts, whether by the local courts or the competition regulator, that address the competition-related issues that will inevitably arise in future from the acquisition, ownership and exploitation of intellectual property in Singapore.

Notes

1. Chapter 63, most recently amended in 2005.
2. On 21 December 1998, Singapore joined the WIPO-administered Berne Convention for the Protection of Literary and Artistic Works of 1886 which secures reciprocal protection of works made by authors from member states.
3. On 17 April 2005, Singapore joined the WIPO Copyright Treaty (WCT) of 1996 which strengthens the rights of copyright owners in the response to new

technological developments in the realm of information and communication technologies.

4. On 17 April 2005, Singapore joined the WIPO Performances and Phonograms Treaty of 1996 which protects the interests of performers and phonogram producers in performances and recordings of performances.

5. Chapter 221, most recently amended in 2004.

6. On 23 February 1995, Singapore joined the WIPO-administered Patent Cooperation Treaty of 1970 which enables patent applicants to make single international patent applications for multiple PCT-contracting states through the Singapore receiving office.

7. On 23 February 1995, Singapore joined the WIPO-administered Budapest Treaty on the International Recognition of the Deposit of Micro-organisms for the Purposes of Patent Procedure of 1977 which enables patent applicants to deposit samples of micro-organisms with any of the designated International Depository Authorities as part of their patent applications.

8. On 23 February 1995, Singapore joined the WIPO-administered Paris Convention for the Protection of Industrial Property of 1883 which enables patent applicants who apply for protection in any Convention country within 12 months of their initial application in Singapore to enjoy the earlier priority date.

9. Chapter 332, most recently amended in 2004.

10. On 18 March 1999, Singapore joined the WIPO-administered Nice Agreement Concerning the International Classification of Goods and Services for the Purposes of the Registration of Marks of 1957 which sets up a system of classifying goods (34 categories) and services (11 categories) to facilitate the protection of registered trade marks.

11. On 31 October 2000, Singapore joined the WIPO-administered Madrid Protocol of 1989 (for the Madrid Agreement Concerning the International Registration of Marks of 1891) which enables trade mark proprietors to obtain trade mark protection in multiple member states through an international application and registration system.

12. The Joint Recommendation Concerning Provisions on the Protection of Well-Known Marks was adopted by WIPO and the Assembly of the Paris Union for the Protection of Industrial Property on 29 September 1999. Singapore undertook to comply with these recommendations as part of its obligations under the US–Singapore Free Trade Agreement.

13. Joining the World Trade Organisation in 1 January 1995 required a major overhaul of Singapore's domestic Intellectual Property regime to achieve compliance with the Agreement on Trade Related Aspects of Intellectual Property Rights of 1994 (TRIPS).

14. The principal Free Trade Agreements (FTAs) which required Singapore to strengthen its domestic intellectual property regime are those which were entered into with the European Free Trade Area (EFTA) (signed on 26 June 2002: see Article 54 and Annex XII of the Agreement) and the United States

of America (signed on 6 May 2003 and passed by the US Senate on 1 August 2003: see Chapter 16 of the FTA). The text of these agreements is available online at http://app.fta.gov.sg/asp/fta/us.asp.

15. Act 46 of 2004. Modelled closely after the UK Competition Act 1998, the newly erected regulatory regime adopted by Singapore incorporates legislative language derived from Articles 81 and 82 of the European Community's Competition Law framework.

16. The *Competition Act 2004* came into force on 1 January 2005 pursuant to Singapore's obligations under the US–Singapore FTA (see Chapter 12 of the Agreement). At the time of writing, the newly established Competition Commission of Singapore was in the process of issuing guidelines to facilitate the implementation of the substantive provisions of the Act, with the prohibition against agreements which prevent, restrict or distort competition (s. 34) and conduct which abuses a position of market dominance (s. 47) taking effect only from 1 January 2006 onwards. The merger regulation provisions are expected to come into force at least 12 months from this date.

17. See *National Aerated Water Co. Pte Ltd* v. *Monarch Co. Inc.* [2000] 2 SLR 24 (involving a contractual restraint on the seller of a beverage business from engaging in any trade involving beverages sold under a similar sounding name). The common law requires contractual restraints of trade, especially those arising from post-employment contractual obligations and post-sale of business contractual obligations, to be evaluated using a test of reasonableness.

18. See discussion below accompanying notes 46, 62 and 93 for the approaches taken under the different statutory regimes towards the treatment of parallel imports of copyright-protected, patent-protected and trade marked goods.

19. See discussion below accompanying note 66.

20. See discussion below accompanying notes 73 to 75.

21. See ss. 26–7, note 1 above. The idea–expression dichotomy, while not explicitly spelt out in the Copyright statute, has nevertheless been accepted by the Singapore courts as a fundamental principle of Singapore copyright law. See *Robert John Powers* v. *Tessensohn* [1993] 3 SLR 724.

22. S. 26(1)(a)(i), note 1 above, articulates the copyright holder's central exclusive right to 'reproduce the work in a material form'.

23. See s. 28(2), note 1 above. This was extended from life plus 50 years in accordance with Singapore's obligations under the US–Singapore FTA: see Article 16.4, para. 4(a), of the FTA.

24. See Chapter 2, at pages 56–71 for a discussion of these issues which have been addressed by the European Court of Justice in the *Magill* case and *IMS* v. *NDC*. See discussion below at text accompanying notes 139 to 141.

25. [1996] 1 SLR 683 (Singapore High Court). The decision of the Court of Appeal is reported in *Creative Technology* v. *Aztech Systems* [1997] 1 SLR 621.

26. At that time, the Singapore *Copyright Act* did not have a specific defence permitting reverse engineering of computer programs to enable third parties

to develop compatible software programs, unlike in the United Kingdom which had a decompilation provision in s. 50B of its Copyright, Designs and Patents Act 1988. Recent amendments made to the Singapore *Copyright Act* in 2004 have addressed this problem and s. 39A makes it lawful to decompile a computer program if 'it is necessary to decompile the computer program to achieve the objective of obtaining the information necessary to create an independent computer program which can be operated with the computer program decompiled or with another computer program', provided that this information is not used for any other purpose.

27. S. 35(5), as it then read, provided that '. . . "research" shall not include industrial research carried out by bodies corporate (not being bodies corporate owned or controlled by the Government), companies, associations or bodies of persons carrying on any business'.

28. The other relevant factors in s. 35(2) – which are non-exhaustive – to be considered when assessing the fairness of a dealing are the nature of the work, the amount and substantiality of the part copied, the effect of the dealing upon the value of the work, and – most recently added – the possibility of obtaining the work within a reasonable time at an ordinary commercial price. These factors were largely inspired by the factors found in the US Copyright Statute relating to the 'Fair Use' defence. See 17 U.S.C. 107.

29. See note 25 above at para. 51. This interpretation of 'private study' was over-turned on appeal and the copyist was not allowed to raise this defence. The Court of Appeal, at paras. 70 to 77 of its judgment (cited above at note 25), held that it was wrong to extend the concept of 'private study' to include 'private study for commercial purposes' because this would render otiose the specific exclusion of commercial research under s. 35(5) 'in that all commercial research will almost inevitably be private study as well'. In the Court of Appeal's opinion, the legislative intention behind these provisions in the *Copyright Act*, as they had been initially drafted, was tolerably clear: the fair dealing defence was not meant to be invoked by commercial organisations engaging in research-related activities.

30. See note 25 above at paragraph 57 (emphasis added).

31. See the explanatory statement to the Copyright (Amendment) Bill 1998, which introduced these changes to the *Copyright Act 1987* on 16 April 1998.

32. See G. Wei, The Law of Copyright in Singapore (Singapore: SNP Editions Pte Ltd, 2000) at §9.40.

33. See s. 35(1) and 35(1A) of the Act, note 1 above. The other classic examples which may constitute a fair dealing that are identified in *Copyright Act* are fair dealings 'for the purpose of criticism or review' or 'for the purpose of reporting current events'.

34. The extension of the statutory term of protection took effect on 1 July 2004 pursuant to the *Intellectual Property (Miscellaneous Amendments) Act 2004*

(Act No. 21 of 2004), adding 20 years to the length of the copyright owner's legal monopoly. See note 23 above.

35. See s. 15(3) of the *Copyright Act.*

36. The copyright system was originally developed for the protection of intellectual creations associated with human creative expression – literary (novels, poems, etc.), dramatic (plays, scripts, etc.), artistic (paintings, drawings, sculpture, etc.) and musical works – works of 'authorship' rather than mundane technical or commercial chattels. However, with the expansion of the scope of copyright protection to include the copyright owner's exclusive right to three-dimensional reproductions of two-dimensional artistic works, the copyright system came to be used as an instrument to prevent competition from competitors who copied the copyright owner's products (thereby copying the latter's design drawings indirectly). This led to the introduction of special statutory safeguards to ensure that such copyright owners do not enjoy unduly long periods of protection, or that certain acts of copying by competitors do not amount to an infringement of their copyright in the artistic work, such that alternative suppliers may utilise the same designs to make substitute products available to the market.

37. Chapter 266, most recently amended in 2004. The *Registered Designs Act* offers intellectual property protection, upon the registration of a design to be applied to specified articles in accordance with the statutory framework, for the aesthetic appearance of novel designs for a period of up to 15 years.

38. See s. 74(2) of the *Copyright Act*, which sets out the qualifying circumstances in which the design is used by the copyright owner in products manufactured on a commercial scale. Regulation 12 of the *Copyright Regulations* (Chapter 63, Regulation 4) further provides that, for the purposes of s. 74 of the *Copyright Act*, 'a design shall be deemed to be applied industrially' if it is applied 'to more than 50 articles' or 'to one or more articles (other than hand-made articles) manufactured in lengths or pieces'.

39. 'Useful article' is defined in s. 70(4) of the *Copyright Act* to mean 'an article having an intrinsic utilitarian function that is not merely to portray the appearance of the article or to convey information'.

40. See s. 70(2) of the *Copyright Act.*

41. See s. 2(1) for the definition of a registrable 'design' under the *Registered Designs Act*, note 37 above.

42. [1986] 1 All ER 850, which was subsequently narrowed by the Privy Council (on appeal from Hong Kong) in *Canon Kabushiki Kaisha* v. *Green Cartridge Co.* [1997] 3 WLR 13.

43. See the Singapore Court of Appeal's decision in *Creative Technology* v. *Aztech*, referred to above at note 25 and accompanying text, at para. 85.

44. No equivalent provisions are found in the UK Copyright, Designs and Patents Act 1988 which has a European Community-centred approach towards parallel

imports. See s. 18 of that Act which sets out the exclusive right to 'issue to the public copies of the work' enjoyed by copyright holders, encompassing acts of 'putting into circulation in the EEA copies not previously put into circulation in the EEA by or with the consent of the copyright owner'.

45. See G. Wei, note 32 above, at §8.199 to §8.211, for an explanation of the legislative changes which statutorily overruled the Singapore High Court's decision in *Public Prosecutor* v. *Teo Ai Nee* [1995] 2 SLR 69.

46. In a straightforward case, the parallel imports would be goods available abroad through the distributor of the Singapore-based copyright holder who supplies the Singapore market. In such a scenario, the Singapore copyright holder could not claim that these articles were made without his consent. See *Remus Innovation Forschungs- und Abgasanlagen-Produktionsgesellschaft GmbH* v *Hong Boon Siong* [1995] 2 SLR 148.

47. See ss. 51, 52, 54 and 54A of the *Copyright Act*.

48. See ss. 55–62 of the *Copyright Act*.

49. See ss. 156A–65 of the *Copyright Act*.

50. See s. 13 of the *Patents Act*.

51. See s. 25(4) and s. 25(5) of the *Patents Act*.

52. See s. 36 of the *Patents Act*. S. 36A was introduced in 2004 to provide for extensions of the patent term by up to 5 years where the patent applicant experiences unreasonable delays in obtaining his patent, or, in the case of pharmaceutical patents, where his opportunity to exploit his patent was unreasonably delayed by the process of obtaining the necessary marketing approval from the relevant authorities for the pharmaceutical product.

53. See s. 66 of the *Patents Act*.

54. See note 73 below. Under footnote 16–12 of the US–Singapore FTA, which circumscribes the situations in which compulsory patent licences can be issued, 'the Parties recognise that an intellectual property right does not necessarily confer market power upon its owner'.

55. *Catnic Components* v. *Hill & Smith Ltd* [1982] RPC 183.

56. *Improver Corporation* v. *Remington Consumer Pte Ltd* [1990] FSR 181.

57. *Genelabs Diagnostics* v. *Institut Pasteur* [2001] 1 SLR 121.

58. See *Improver* case at p. 189. The variant would only infringe the patent if the answer to the third question was in the negative.

59. Article 69 of the EPC was also referred to by the Singapore High Court in *V-Pile Technology (Luxembourg) SA and Others* v. *Peck Brothers Construction Pte Ltd* [2000] 3 SLR 358 at paras. 63 and 91.

60. Emphasis added. A recent amendment to the Protocol on Article 69 makes a further statement that: 'For the purpose of determining the extent of protection conferred by a European patent, due account shall be taken of any element which is equivalent to an element specified in the claims.'

61. No equivalent provision exists in the UK Patents Act 1977. See s. 60(5) of that Act for a list of the defences to patent infringement in the UK.

62. Emphasis added. S. 66(2A) was added in 2004 to comply with the legislative amendments sought by the United States under the US–Singapore FTA.

63. See Article 16.7.2 of the US–Singapore FTA which states that: 'Each party shall provide a cause of action to prevent or redress the procurement of a patented pharmaceutical product, without the authorization of the patent owner, by a party who knows or has reason to know that such product is or has been distributed in breach of a contract between the right holder and a licensee, regardless of whether such breach occurs in or outside its territory. Each Party shall provide that in such a cause of action, notice shall constitute constructive knowledge.' This is qualified by the following footnote: 'A Party may limit such cause of action to cases where the product has been sold or distributed only outside the Party's territory before its procurement inside the Party's territory.'

64. The explanation given by the Senior Minister of State for Law, Associate Professor Ho Peng Kee, in the Patents (Amendment) Bill 2004 for this provision is illuminating: '. . . a patent owner will have a right to bring an action to stop a parallel importer from importing the patent owner's patented pharmaceutical product, if the product has not been sold or distributed in Singapore. However, once the owner brings in the patented product, the right to bring an action ceases, and he will be subject to the same competitive pressures from parallel imports. This is a delicate balance we have sought to preserve between the interests of the patent owner and the interests of users of pharmaceutical products. Essentially, the patent owner has a "first mover" advantage in the Singapore market, but once he is in, will have to compete with the parallel importers.'

65. The definition of 'patent' and the other key terms in this statutory provision is the same as that provided for in s. 66(2)(g). See text accompanying note 62 above.

66. In *Roche Product Inc.* v. *Bolar Pharmaceutical Co.* 733 F.2d 858 (Fed. Cir. 1984), 469 U.S. 856 (1984), the US Federal Courts held that the 'experimental use' defence to patent infringement (similar to the one found in s. 66(2)(b) of the Singapore *Patents Act*) did not extend to clinical trials of a patented drug for the purposes of marketing approval. This decision was subsequently superceded by the US Legislature by an amendment to the US Patents Act via the Drug Price Competition and Patent Term Act 1984. 35 U.S.C. 271(e)(1) which provides that: 'It shall not be an act of infringement to make, use, offer to sell, or sell within the United States or import into the United States a patented invention other than a new animal drug or veterinary biological product . . . solely for uses reasonably related to the development and submission of information under a Federal law which regulates the manufacture, use, or sale of drugs or veterinary biological products.'

67. Emphasis added. These three categories of anticompetitive contractual restraints are void unless both the conditions set out in s. 55(3) of the Act are met. The supplier or licensor must have been willing, at the time the contract was made

or when the licence was granted, to enter into the transaction 'on reasonable terms' and 'without any such condition or term as is mentioned in' s. 55(1). Furthermore, the party supplied or the licensee must be entitled under the contract or licence to 'relieve himself of his liability to observe the condition or term on giving to the other party 3 months' notice in writing' after compensating the supplier or licensor.

68. The English antecedent to this provision was found in s. 38 of the UK Patents and Designs Act 1907 which was repealed by the UK Patents Act 1949. See *Tool Metal* v. *Tungsten Electric Co. Ltd* (1955) 72 RPC 209.

69. The leading cases from the European Courts under Article 82(d) EC are *Hilti* v. *Commission* [1991] ECR II-1439, [1992] 4 CMLR 16 (Case T-30/89) and *Tetra Pak International SA* v. *Commission* [1996] ECR I-5951, [1997] 4 CMLR 662 (Case C-333/94). Tying clauses of this variety are viewed as anticompetitive because they allow a dominant firm to abuse its dominance in a market in which it does not occupy a position of dominance. The tying clauses have the effect of foreclosing the market for the tied product to the detriment of competitors in that market. Also, in the context of technology licensing and bundling, see the European Commission's Guidelines on Technology Transfer Agreements [2004] OJ C101/2 at para. 191.

70. Emphasis added. The contractual or licensing conditions or terms referred to are those found in s. 51(1) of the Act, see note 67 above. Note that the defendant in the patent infringement proceedings need not be a party to the contract or the licence in which the offending tying clauses are located.

71. The English antecedent to this provision was found in s. 58 of the UK Patents Act 1949, which was repealed by the UK Patents Act 1977. See *Hansen* v. *Magnovox Electronics* [1977] RPC 301.

72. S. 52(3) of the Act also permits a court to vary the terms or conditions of a contract or licence, 'having regard to all the circumstances of the case' as 'it thinks just as between the parties', if the consequence of the relevant patents ceasing to be in force would make it 'unjust to require the applicant to continue to comply with all the terms and conditions of the contract or licence'.

73. See Article 16.7(6) of the FTA, which states that 'neither party shall permit the use of the subject matter of a patent without the authorisation of the right holder except in the following circumstances: (a) to remedy a practice determined after judicial or administrative process to be anticompetitive under the competition laws of the Party; and (b) [public non-commercial uses, national emergencies, and other circumstances of extreme urgency]'. The parties to the FTA also agreed to abide by the 12 conditions set out in the provisions of Article 31 of the TRIPS Agreement.

74. See s. 55(3), (4), (5) and (6) of the *Patents Act*.

75. See s. 55(10) of the *Patents Act*.

76. In contrast, the compulsory licensing framework under the UK Patents Act 1977 is a lot broader, and more complex as a result, in that it permits

compulsory licences to be sought on competition-related grounds (upon a report by the UK Competition Commission and an application from the appropriate minister) and non-competition-related grounds (for which any person may apply though the grounds on which the licence is available will vary depending on whether the patent proprietor is a WTO proprietor or not). Decisions relating to the grant of compulsory licences in the UK are administered by the comptroller of the UK Patent Office. See ss. 48, 48A, 48B, 49, 50, 50A and 51 of the UK Patents Act 1977.

77. See s. 2(1) of the *Trade Marks Act*, where the definition of a 'trade mark' was amended to remove a requirement that it had to be a 'visually perceptible' sign. In theory, sounds, smells, tastes and textures are capable of being registered as trade marks under the Act, from 2004 onwards, provided they meet the other registration criteria.

78. See ss. 8(3A) and 55 of the *Trade Marks Act*. These changes were made pursuant to Singapore's obligations under its FTAs with its trading partners in the developed world. See Article 6 of Annex XII of the EFTA–Singapore FTA, as well as Articles 16.1(2)(b) and 16.2(4) of the US–Singapore FTA.

79. See s. 31 of the *Trade Marks Act*, which includes a newly introduced remedy of 'statutory damages' which dramatically increases the quantum of damages available to the trade mark proprietor. In awarding these damages, s. 31(6) requires the Court to have regard to factors which include 'the flagrancy of the infringement of the registered trademark' and 'the need to deter other similar instances of infringement'.

80. See ss. 2(1), 7(1) and 7(2) of the *Trade Marks Act*.

81. See s. 8 of the *Trade Marks Act*.

82. See s. 18 of the *Trade Marks Act*.

83. See ss. 27(1) and 27(2) of the *Trade Marks Act*.

84. See ss. 27(3) and 55 of the *Trade Marks Act*.

85. See s. 7(1)(b) of the *Trade Marks Act*.

86. See s. 7(2) of the *Trade Marks Act*.

87. The legislative antecedent to these provisions can be found in s. 3(2) of the UK Trade Marks Act 1994, which in turn was based upon the criteria set out in Article 3(1)(e) of the European Community's Trade Mark Directive 89/104/EEC.

88. See the leading decisions of the UK courts and ECJ which interpret these statutory bars: *Philips Electronics NV* v. *Remington Consumer Products* [1998] RPC 283 (UK High Court), [1999] RPC 809 (Court of Appeal), [2003] RPC 2 (ECJ).

89. See *Smith Kline & French Laboratories Ltd's Cimetidine Trade Mark* [1991] RPC 17, where the UK High Court affirmed the UK Trade Mark Registry's decision to reject an application to register a pale shade of green as a trade mark for SKF's cimetidine drug (which was also marketed under the TAGAMET trade mark). Peter Gibson J held, at p. 34, that 'in considering whether the claimed

trade mark is inherently adapted to distinguish, the court takes into account the likelihood that other traders may, without improper motive, desire to use the trade mark in relation to their own goods. On grounds of public policy a trader will not be allowed to obtain, by a trade mark registration, a monopoly in what other traders may legitimately wish to use.' It was held that the pale green colour had a very small inherent distinctiveness and lacked the capacity to function as a trade mark on its own as the drug was frequently identified using its colour in conjunction with the TAGAMET word mark. Two legitimate reasons were given, at p. 36, for why other traders might want to use the colour pale green for their (generic) versions of cimetidine tablets: firstly, the colour was functional insofar as it might have a 'therapeutic effect' for patients with gastro-intestinal disorders; secondly, patients would have become accustomed to the drug having a particular appearance such that, if any other get-up were used on the drug, they might query the pharmacist or doctor dispensing them the medication and may accuse them of having made a mistake, 'and that can cause the patients anxiety'. The court decided that a single colour for a medicinal tablet was not distinctive in law: 'Given the evident utility of the use of colour for tablets, whether for distinguishing one drug from another ... it would seem to me wrong in principle that a pharmaceutical company should be allowed to appropriate to itself a single colour as a registrable trade mark for its tablets. If that were permitted then the choice of colours available to manufacturers would rapidly diminish.'

90. A rival of the trade mark proprietor may also wish to use the registered trade mark in comparative advertising to *distance* himself from the trade mark proprietor, thereby reminding consumers that the former is not connected to, and should not be confused with, the latter. Such unauthorised use of the trade mark is entirely consistent with the *raison d'être* of registered trade marks – as indicators of trade origin which distinguish the goods and services of one trader from those of his rivals. This was the purpose of the unauthorised trade mark use in *Bee Cheng Hiang Hup Chong Foodstuff Pte Ltd* v. *Fragrance Foodstuff Pte Ltd* [2003] 1 SLR 305, which was settled before a number of important issues could be dealt with by the Singapore High Court, including an unresolved concurrent allegation of copyright infringement over the use of the logo which comprised the registered trade mark.

91. Emphasis added. This provision was based substantially on s. 11.(2) of the UK Trade Marks Act 1994 which, in turn, incorporated the requirements of Article 6(1) of the European Community's Trade Mark Directive 89/104/EEC.

92. Emphasis added. This provision was introduced in recent amendments made to the Singapore *Trade Marks Act* in 2004 pursuant to its obligations under the US–Singapore FTA. The legislative antecedent to this provision can be found in a similar provision of the US Lanham Act 1946: see 15 U.S.C. 1125(c)(4).

93. Emphasis added. This provision is a modified version of s. 12(1) of the UK Trade Marks Act 1994, which reflects an exhaustion principle limited to goods

which have been put on the market only within the European Economic Area 'by the proprietor or with his consent'. The proviso to s. 29(1) of the Singapore *Trade Marks Act* was recently amended in 2004 to prevent trade mark exhaustion from occurring where 'the condition of the goods has been changed or impaired after they have been put on the market' and where 'the use of the registered trade mark in relation to those goods has caused dilution in an unfair manner of the distinctive character of the registered trade mark'.

94. For a good comparison of the Singapore and English positions on parallel imports, and the trade-offs arising from Singapore's decision to clarify the law in this area, see Ng-Loy Wee Loon, 'Exhaustion of Rights in Trade Mark Law: The English and Singapore Models Compared' (2000) 22(7) E.I.P.R. 320.

95. See text accompanying notes 44 to 46, and 61 to 64.

96. See *Pan-West (Pte) Ltd* v. *Grand Bigwin Pte Ltd* [2003] SGHC 250 at paragraph 14, and §2(5) of the Singapore *Trade Marks Act*.

97. This was the reasoning used in the well-known UK case involving parallel imports of 'Revlon Flex' shampoo from the United States – *Revlon Inc.* v. *Cripps & Lee Ltd* [1980] FSR 85 – which was implicitly endorsed by the Singapore High Court in the *Pan-West* v. *Grand Bigwin* case. See also *Hup Huat Food Industries (S) Pte Ltd* v *Liang Chiang Heng* [2003] SGHC 244, a case involving related companies in Singapore and Malaysia, each holding registered trade marks for the same confectionery brand in their respective territories, with a dispute arising from the importation of products bearing the trade mark from Malaysia into Singapore.

98. Emphasis added. See the 'Competition Bill Consultation Paper', issued 12 April 2004, by Singapore's Ministry of Trade and Industry (available online at http://www.ccs.gov.sg/archival-First.html), Annex C (The Relationship between Competition Law and Intellectual Property Rights) at paras. 7 to 10.

99. Ibid. paras. 4 and 5.

100. The CCS Guideline on the Treatment of Intellectual Property Rights is available online at the CCS website at http://www.ccs.gov.sg/Doc/FinalisedGuidelinesDec05/GuidelineRevised_IPRs_Dec05.pdf.

101. The CCS has indicated that the Guideline is only intended to deal with the competition-related issues concerned with technology transfer and innovation aspects of IPRs. This Guideline is not intended to regulate the product differentiation functions performed by trade marks and geographical indications. The intellectual property rights statutorily granted under the *Trade Marks Act* (Chapter 332) and the *Geographical Indications Act* (Chapter 117B) are therefore not within the scope of this Guideline. See paragraph 1.2 of the Guideline and para. 3 of the explanatory policy paper which accompanied it.

102. Issued by the US Department of Justice and the Federal Trade Commission on 6 April 1995.

103. Commission Regulation No. 772/2004 on the application of Article 81(3) of the Treaty to categories of technology transfer agreements (L 123/11), issued

by the European Commission on 27 April 2004. This was accompanied by a Commission Notice (Guidelines on the application of Article 81 of the EC Treaty to technology transfer agreements) at 2004/C 101/02.

104. See Section 2 (The Interface between IPRs & Competition Law) of the CCS Guideline on the Treatment of Intellectual Property Rights.

105. See paras. 2.8, 2.9 and 2.10 of the Guideline, which are condensed versions of paragraphs 3.2.1, 3.2.2 and 3.2.3 of the US Antitrust Guidelines.

106. See para. 8 of the Third Schedule of the *Competition Act 2004*. S. 35 of the Act provides that the s. 34 prohibition does not apply to subject matter specified in the Third Schedule. Paragraph 8(1) of the Third Schedule provides that 'the section 34 prohibition shall not apply to any vertical agreement, other than such vertical agreement as the Minister may by order specify'.

107. The following policy justification was offered for this deliberately crafted feature of Singapore's competition legislation:

> Vertical agreements are agreements between undertakings along the same value chain, for example, between manufacturer and distributor. In general, vertical agreements should be allowed as firms in such agreements have a mutual interest in ensuring that as many goods and services are sold to consumers as possible. Relative to horizontal agreements, *most vertical agreements have pro-competitive effects*. Therefore, vertical agreements will in the first instance be excluded from the scope of competition law (para. 8, Third Schedule). However, there may be cases of vertical agreements where the potential anticompetitive effects outweigh the pro-competitive effects. In such cases, the Minister may issue an order to declare that the competition law will apply to a certain type of vertical agreement (i.e. such types of agreement will now be subject to the law).

Emphasis added. See the 'Competition Bill Consultation Paper', referred to above at note 98, Annex A (Prohibited Activities) at paras. 3 and 4.

108. See s. 34(2) of the *Competition Act*. These examples were replicated from s. 2(2) of the UK Competition Act 1998 which, in turn, incorporated the language used in Article 81(1) of the EC Treaty.

109. The Guideline is available online at http://www.ccs.gov.sg/Firstset_Revised Guidelines.htm. The CCS will only consider an agreement as falling within the scope of the s. 34 prohibition if it has as its object, or effect, the *appreciable* prevention, restriction or distortion of competition.

110. See paragraph 3.2 of the CCS IP Guidelines.

111. The status of the parties will be reviewed only at the time the licensing agreement is entered into, and will not be reconsidered even if they become competitors subsequently, unless the agreement is subsequently amended materially. A licensing agreement is between 'competitors' if they are parties that, in the absence of the agreement, would have been *actual or potential competitors* on a relevant market. Conversely, a licensing agreement is between

'non-competitors' if they would not have been actual or potential competitors in the absence of the agreement. See paras. 3.2 and 3.5 of the CCS IP Guidelines which was inspired by paragraph 31 of European Commission's Notice on the Technology Transfer Block Exemption Regulations. This reflects the position taken in Article 4(3) of European Commission's Regulation 772/2004, the Transfer Technology Block Exemption Regulations, where the status of the parties is determined ex ante, at the time the agreement is entered into, and will not change for the purposes of applying the block exemption even if subsequently the licensee were to develop or exploit a competing technology, or the licensor were to enter the product market in which the licensee was active, unless the licensing agreement was amended 'in any material respect'.

112. A block exemption order excluding the application of the s. 34 prohibition, issued by the Minister under the Third Schedule of the *Competition Act 2004*, operates by virtue of s. 35 of the *Competition Act 2004* to automatically legitimise IP licensing agreements which meet these criteria.

113. See paras. 2.19 to 2.23 of the CCS Guideline on the Section 34 Prohibition. The CCS will only consider an agreement as falling within the scope of the s. 34 prohibition if it has its object, or effect, the *appreciable* prevention, restriction or distortion of competition.

114. According to the CCS IP Guidelines, licensing agreements between competitors 'involving price-fixing, market-sharing or output limitations will always have an appreciable effect on competition' and it is not necessary to apply the 'appreciable adverse effect on competition' test that requires consideration of the pro-competitive aspects of the agreement. See para. 3.15 of the *CCS IP Guidelines*.

115. Grantback arrangements are specifically dealt with in para. 3.23 of the *CCS IP Guidelines*. The CCS takes the view that grantback provisions 'can increase a licensor's incentives to license, and promote the dissemination of licensees' improvements to the licensed technology'. It also notes that 'there are often pro-competitive reasons for including grantback provisions, and these generally do not pose competition concerns, especially where they are non-exclusive in nature'.

116. Territorial restrictions (on the geographical territories in which the licensed IP may be exploited) and field-of-use restrictions (on the types of products or services to which the licensed IP may be applied) that are imposed on licensees may serve pro-competitive objectives. The curtailment of intra-technology or inter-brand competition might be necessary to promote inter-technology or inter-brand competition. Such restraints may increase the licensor's incentives to licence its IP for use in areas which do not compete with its core markets, or may increase the licensee's incentives to invest in fully exploiting the licensed technology without having to deal with free-riding competitor licensees. See para. 3.24 of the CCS IP Guidelines, which characterise such restraints as 'simply a sub-division of the licensor's original right granted by

IP law'. The CCS takes the view that 'these licensing restraints are generally no more restrictive of competition than if the original IP owner had exercised the rights itself'.

117. Specific statutory provisions can also be found in the Singapore *Patents Act* which deal with competition-related concerns arising from product-tying. See s. 51 of the *Patents Act*, and the text accompanying note 67 above. In addition, under para. 4.9 the CCS IP Guidelines, tying arrangements involving intellectual property rights are potentially anticompetitive conduct if the licensor enjoys market power in the tying product (the intellectual property right) such that the tie constitutes an abuse of his dominant position – this would fall within the scope of the s. 47 prohibition. See text accompanying notes 137 and 138 below.

118. Unlike the UK or EC competition law framework, where individual exemptions are available under Article 81(3) EC for conduct which infringes the basic prohibition in Article 81(1) EC, any 'balancing' exercise between the anticompetitive and pro-competitive aspects of a contractual restraint have to be carried out simultaneously when s. 34(1) of the Singapore *Competition Act* is applied because the Singapore legislative framework does not provide for individual exemptions. The criteria used for individual exemptions in the EC and UK can be found in s. 41 of the Act, but they are relevant only to the formulation of the block exemptions which the Competition Commission of Singapore is entitled to issue.

119. See para. 3.14 of the CCS IP Guidelines.

120. These market share thresholds are slightly higher than those used in the general Guidelines on the s. 34 prohibition. See para. 2.19 of the CCS Guideline on the Section 34 Prohibition which indicates that an agreement will generally not have an appreciable adverse effect on competition if the aggregate market share of the parties is less than 20 per cent (where the parties are competing undertakings) or where the individual market shares of each party are less than 25 per cent (where the parties are non-competing undertakings). Similarly, the market share thresholds in the CCS IP Guidelines are higher than the 20 per cent figure found in paragraph 4.3 of the 1995 US Antitrust Guidelines.

121. See para. 3.16 of the CCS IP Guidelines.

122. See note 106 above.

123. In a standard franchising agreement, the IP-owning franchisor–licensor is in a vertical relationship with the franchisee–licensee which qualifies for the statutory exclusion for vertical agreements because it is an agreement 'between 2 or more undertakings each of which operates, for the purposes of the agreement, at a *different level of the production or distribution chain*, and *relating to the conditions* under which the parties may *purchase, sell or resell certain goods or services*'. See note 106 above.

124. In some IP licensing arrangements, the IP may be licensed to a licensee who manufactures products which incorporate the IP, when the licensor himself is already exploiting the IP himself by manufacturing his own products, making the licensor an actual or potential competitor of the licensee – perhaps as part of a risk-diversification strategy, to cope with growing market demand, or to supply a new geographical market. Other IP licensing arrangements may also involve parties in a horizontal relationship with each other: for example, a cross-licensing or patent-pooling agreement may involve IP owners who are actual or potential competitors in the relevant product or technology markets.

125. See paras. 3.10, 3.11 and 3.12 of the CCS IP Guidelines.

126. 'Market power' is understood as 'the ability to profitably sustain prices above competitive levels or to restrict output or quality below competitive levels' and it arises 'where an undertaking does not face sufficiently strong competitive pressure'. This is the explanation given to the concept of 'dominance' in the CCS Guideline on the Section 47 Prohibition, at para. 3.3.

127. Ibid. para. 2.1.

128. Ibid. para. 4.1.

129. A crucial distinction is drawn between the mere *exercise* of an IP owner's exclusive rights, and unlawful *abuse* of those rights. See ibid. para. 4.3.

130. See s. 47(2) of the *Competition Act*. The language used in examples (b), (c) and (d) originated from s. 18(2) of the UK Competition Act 1998 which, in turn, was based on Article 82 of the EC Treaty. The language used in example (a), however, was a deliberate departure from the corresponding language used in the UK statute and the EC Treaty, which describes the abuse as 'directly or indirectly imposing unfair purchase or selling prices or other unfair trading conditions'. The objective here was to limit the notion of abusive conduct to situations involving below-cost pricing or other modes of predatory behaviour by the dominant firm, and not to permit an interpretation which made excessive pricing by the dominant firm an infringement of this statutory prohibition. The European Court of Justice has, for example, accepted that excessive pricing of goods supplied by a dominant firm can amount to an abuse of dominance if the price bears 'no reasonable relation to the economic value of the product supplied'. See *Case 27/76 United Brands* v. *Commission [1978] 1 CMLR 429* at para. 250. Excessive pricing has also been addressed as a relevant issue in relation to the prices charged by IP owners for their IP-protected products: see *Case 24/67 Parke, Davis & Co.* v. *Probel* [1968] CMLR 47 and Case 53/87, *CICCRA* v. *Renault* [1990] 4 CMLR 265.

131. See note 54 above and accompanying text.

132. See para. 4.2 of the *CCS IP Guidelines*.

133. Ibid. para. 4.3. The view taken here by the CCS is that 'in markets where undertakings regularly improve the quality of their products, a persistently high market share may indicate no more than persistently successful innovation'.

134. This raises a slew of further questions involving complex policy choices: should unilateral anticompetitive behaviour have to be tolerated in the 'short term' (the statutory term of protection for IPRs – which ranges from 15 years for registered design rights, to 20 years for patents, and the author's life plus 70 years for copyright) on the understanding that others will have the opportunity to challenge the IP-owning undertaking down the road when the latter's IPRs expire? Doesn't this approach abdicate the role which competition law can, and should, play as a counterbalance to intellectual property rights for the duration of their subsistence? Should such undertakings be relieved of the statutory restraints of the s. 47 prohibition simply because they have achieved, maintained, and possibly enhanced their market shares through their intellectual property ownership?

135. See text accompanying notes 108 to 117 above.

136. See para. 4.11 of the *CCS IP Guidelines*.

137. Ibid. para. 4.4.

138. Ibid. para. 4.9. The use of tying arrangements as an example of abusive conduct by a dominant undertaking is tempered somewhat by statements which suggest that 'the conduct of the dominant undertaking may be an objectively justified and proportionate response, if it can show that such provisions are necessary for a satisfactory exploitation of the IPR, such as for ensuring that the licensee conforms to quality standards or for technical interoperability'.

139. See para. 4.6 of the *CCS IP Guidelines*.

140. See the discussion in this volume at Chapter 2, at pages 56–71, on the application of the 'essential facilities' doctrine to cases involving refusals to grant intellectual property licences, and the 'exceptional circumstances' test espoused by the competition law jurisprudence of the European Community.

141. See paras. 4.7 and 4.8 of the *CCS IP Guidelines*.

142. See s. 69(2)(d)(i) of the *Competition Act*.

143. See text accompanying notes 73 to 76 above.

PART III

Issues related to the interface between intellectual property rights and competition law

8

Parallel imports

MIRANDA FORSYTH AND WARWICK A. ROTHNIE

A recent Japanese High Court decision provides a useful example of parallel importing. In *BBS Kraftfahrzeugtechnik AG* v. *Racimex Japan Corp. and Jap Auto Products Co.*,[1] BBS was the holder of both Japanese and German patent rights to an invention entitled 'A Wheel of an Automotive'. BBS sold and licensed aluminium wheels made under their patents in both countries. As the products sold in Germany were considerably cheaper than in Japan, a middleman, Jap Auto, bought the wheels in Germany, imported them into Japan and sold them to Racimex, a Japanese wheel distributor.

Such importation is known as 'parallel importation' because the goods are imported outside the distribution channels that have been contractually negotiated by the intellectual property owner. As the intellectual property owner has no contractual connection with the parallel importer, the imported goods are sometimes referred to as 'grey market goods'.

Parallel importing therefore occurs when goods that are manufactured legally in Country A are imported into Country B without the consent of the intellectual property owner in Country B. Strictly speaking, the same person would own the intellectual property right in both Country A and Country B, but the terminology is commonly extended to cases where the owners are different (especially where they are members of the same corporate group). In *BBS* the parallel import market existed because of international price differences that were taken advantage of by a middle man. In other situations, the market for parallel imports may exist because the product, or the particular version imported, is not available on the local market.

If parallel imports can be prevented, consumers in Country A may be deprived of the benefits of the lower prices for the product actually imported and consumers generally in the market for similar products may be deprived of the benefits of price competition. Where the imports arise because of availability issues, consumers may be denied access to the product at all or their access may be delayed. On the other hand, the intellectual property owner may face disruption of its marketing arrangements if parallel imports are allowed. This in turn may just mean that the owner's profits are lower. But, it may also mean that consumers' access to the product and future developments is reduced as incentives to make the product, or to develop 'local' versions, or otherwise to invest in market-making activities are reduced or impaired.

The question of whether the actions of companies such as Jap Auto and Racimex Japan should be allowed or not has been referred to as being 'one of the most iridescent and enigmatic phenomena of international trade'.[2] From an intellectual property perspective, the answer to whether or not such behaviour is legal depends on what sort of policy the country of importation has adopted in relation to exhaustion of intellectual property rights.

Exhaustion of intellectual property rights means that once a product embodying the intellectual property right has been put on the market, then the ability to control commercial exploitation of the product through the intellectual property right is used up and can no longer be exercised. Consequently, unless otherwise specified by law, subsequent acts of resale, rental, lending and, possibly, other forms of commercial use by third parties can no longer be controlled or opposed by the intellectual property owner. Sometimes this limitation is also called the 'first sale doctrine', as the rights of commercial exploitation for a given product end with the product's first sale.

There are three broad approaches to exhaustion that are currently used by countries throughout the world: national exhaustion, international exhaustion and regional exhaustion.

The concept of national exhaustion means that the intellectual property rights in a product are only exhausted if the product is put on the domestic market. This is the most protective type of exhaustion and allows the intellectual property owner (or his authorised licensee) to oppose the importation of original goods marketed abroad based on the right of importation. At the other end of the spectrum, the doctrine of international exhaustion means that intellectual property rights throughout the world are exhausted once the product has been marketed by the intellectual property owner, or with his consent, in *any* part of the world. This means the intellectual property owner cannot oppose the importation of original goods marketed abroad, although of course he can still continue to oppose the importation of pirated copies. The European Union has adopted a doctrine of exhaustion falling somewhere in between these two extremes, namely regional exhaustion. This means that the first sale of the protected product by the intellectual property owner, or with his consent, not only domestically but within the whole European Economic Area (EEA), exhausts any intellectual property rights over these products, and consequently parallel imports within the region can no longer be opposed based on the intellectual property right.

If the doctrine of national or regional exhaustion were applied to the BBS example above, Jap Auto and Racimex Japan would have infringed the Japanese intellectual property owner's rights. However, if the doctrine of international exhaustion were applied their actions would not have been illegal.

Many countries have adopted different approaches to exhaustion for different types of intellectual property rights. Thus, for example, there may be one rule for trade marks and a different approach for patents or copyright within a given country.

Further, even in countries which have adopted a rule of exhaustion for a particular kind of intellectual property right, there will be questions about what kind of act or acts trigger the exhaustion rule and, when triggered, what acts comprised in the 'bundle' of intellectual property rights are 'exhausted'. Thus, for example, the owner of a copyright generally has the exclusive right to make copies of the copyright material, to sell or distribute the copies, to broadcast or communicate the copyright material and to perform it in public. When the owner of copyright sells a copy of the protected material embodied in a book, or music CD or DVD, the owner usually loses the power under copyright to control further sale of the copy by the purchaser. In this respect, the copyright owner's right is said to be exhausted by the first act of selling the particular copy. The copyright owner does not usually lose, however, the power to control the making of further copies or the rights to broadcast or perform in public the particular copy. If (as is increasingly the case) copyright includes a rental right, that aspect of the right likewise is usually not exhausted by sale.[3]

International treaty obligations over parallel imports

Historically, each country has been able to set its own policy on parallel imports. There are no international treaties which clearly mandate a particular exhaustion doctrine.[4] For example, the Agreement on Trade Related Aspects of Intellectual Property (TRIPS) does not specify one approach or another, merely providing in article 6 that '... nothing in this Agreement shall be used to address the issue of the exhaustion of intellectual property rights'.

This neutrality is due to the failure to find international agreement on the issue during the TRIPs negotiation.[5] There is still debate about whether TRIPS should be amended to achieve a consistent global approach, be it national or international exhaustion. A similar debate has arisen in relation to other new intellectual property treaties, such as the WIPO Performances and Phonograms Treaty and the WIPO Copyright Treaty, which are also neutral on the issue.

Given the lack of international obligations, the decision by each country about which doctrine of exhaustion to adopt will depend on many factors unique to each country. The first part of this chapter examines some of the arguments for and against parallel imports, highlighting the relevant factors to be taken into account. The second part of the chapter then discusses how parallel imports are currently treated in Singapore, the USA, the EEA, Malaysia, Japan, Hong Kong, South Korea, Australia and New Zealand (NZ). It should be observed that the international situation is far from fixed, with several ongoing debates around the world concerning issues related to parallel imports. The final section of the chapter deals briefly with the question of parallel importation of digital works.

A. *What are the arguments for and against allowing parallel imports?*

The question of whether or not parallel imports should be allowed is a hotly contested issue in many countries in the world. Detailed discussion of these issues depends on an analysis of a range of economic, political and social factors in each country, which is beyond the scope of this chapter.[6]

Rather, this chapter considers generally the competing interests of various groups who are affected by the decision over whether or not to allow parallel imports. There are basically two different categories of interest group: intellectual property owners and their authorised manufacturers and distributors on the one hand, and consumers on the other. However, it must be stressed that the various considerations will depend heavily on the prevailing economic and political imperatives of the country under consideration, and these in turn will vary from industry to industry.

Different considerations may apply to different types of intellectual property rights. This is partly due to the fact that different intellectual property rights are supported by different justifications. For example, the justification in common law countries for copyright and patents is to provide an incentive for appropriate forms of investment in creative endeavour.[7] The justification for trade marks, on the other hand, is usually more concerned with preventing consumer confusion over the source of a product than purely economic considerations.[8] Thus, for example, it might be legitimate to question whether in fact the prohibition of parallel imports acts as a stimulant to create for the purposes of copyright, but not for trade mark.

1. Intellectual property owners and local distributors

The position of intellectual property owners and their associated distributors and licensees (collectively referred to as 'intellectual property owners') on the issue of parallel importing is clear: it should be prohibited. For example, the International Trade Mark Association's position is that international exhaustion should not apply to parallel imports in the absence of clear proof that the trade mark owner expressly consented to such imports, and that the burden of proof should be on the party seeking to prove such consent.[9]

There are a number of different arguments that intellectual property owners put forward to justify their position.

The first is that it is suggested allowing parallel importation will reduce the incentive to invest in innovation. Creating incentives to innovate is the key rationale for the existence of copyright and patent (at least). If parallel importing undermines the returns that innovators can earn on their invest-ment, then the amount of future investment in innovation could fall. Parallel imports create a risk to intellectual property owners' return because they restrict their ability to engage in territorial price discrimination. In addition, they may be forced to buy back old stock from authorised distributors because parallel importers create an oversupply in the market.

In considering the weight that should be given to this argument, an important consideration is whether or not the country in question forms a large part of the international market. If the country only forms a small part of the international market, then the allowing of parallel imports may be unlikely to have a very significant affect on overall incentives to innovate, but it is often argued that parallel imports in such situations will undermine incentives to engage in market making activities (of the kind discussed below) in the 'open' market. It is also important to consider the various factors that lead to the price discrimination in the first place. It may be solely due to a manufacturer trying to take advantage of a willingness of consumers in a country to pay higher prices, or it may be due to other factors beyond the manufacturer's control. In the latter instance, there is a concern that parallel imports may make it difficult for industries whose expenditure level depends on national factors (salaries, production and research costs) to develop.

Second, intellectual property owners are concerned that parallel importers will 'free ride' by selling identical goods to those sold by full-service dealers, without incurring the expenses of promoting and servicing the product. There are two different types of free riding: advertising free riding, where the parallel importer takes advantage of the advertising and marketing work done by the authorised sellers; and point-of-sale free riding, where the importer fails to provide ancillary services desired by consumers. Examples of such ancillary services are product instruction, provision of warranty and repair services, and the maintenance of an inventory of spare parts.

A third concern is that parallel importers may sell goods without taking proper care to ensure their quality, for example by compromising on storage and transportation to keep the prices lower. This may generate consumer dissatisfaction with the trade mark, which will lead to negative consumer attitudes to the authorised seller's goods as well. Consequently, this may undermine the intellectual property owners' investment in building and protecting the reputation of their product by careful shipping, storage, inventory control, and quality management. If parallel imports be allowed, therefore, intellectual property owners argue that the incentives to invest in market making activities of these kinds will be undermined. Proponents of parallel importing argue, however, that the price the licensee/distributor negotiates with the intellectual property owner should be discounted to reflect matters such as the risk of parallel imports and any need for the licensee/distributor to invest in market-making activities.[10]

Fourthly, manufacturer–distributor relations may also be strained by the appearance of parallel imports. Distributors may feel frustrated by having them in their markets and look to the manufacturer to reduce or eliminate this unforeseen competition. Parallel imports may have financial consequences for licensed distributors, as they may not derive sufficient revenue from the sale of official goods.

A fifth reason is that intellectual property owners also argue that parallel importation restrictions help to prevent the importation of pirated and/or counterfeit goods. This is because parallel importation restrictions have the effect of channelling imported goods through recognised distribution arrangements, thereby assisting the work of customs agencies in policing the entry of goods into a country and in ascertaining their authenticity. There are, however, some who argue that in fact this piracy argument is a 'scare tactic' and not justified by an analysis of the evidence.[11] The Australian Intellectual Property and Competition Review Committee's Report on the *Review of Intellectual Property Legislation under the Competition Principles Agreement* (IPCRC Report) states that 'while piracy and other forms of infringement are a serious concern, removing restrictions on parallel imports is not likely to materially aggravate the situation'.[12]

Many of these arguments are hotly contested by consumer groups and academics on a variety of different levels. Generally, they argue that banning parallel imports is an inappropriate tool to prevent the undesired conduct specified above, and that there are many other regulatory options, which unlike such a ban, do not have the negative effect of raising prices for consumers, that could be used instead.

From a more legalistic analysis, it can be argued that the purpose of the intellectual property right is to confer on the intellectual property owner the power to control the number of 'articles' embodying the intellectual property in the jurisdiction. At its most basic, the intellectual property right gives the intellectual property owner some power to regulate the price charged for the embodiment by limiting how many embodiments are available in the market. The two main ways that that number could be affected are by manufacture or by importation. On this approach, allowing parallel imports undermines the fundamental premise of the grant of the intellectual property right. On the other hand, it can be argued that this kind of justification is less applicable to trade mark rights – at least to the extent that they are justified only as indicators of source or origin. Unlike patents, copyright has less clearly granted control over importation. Historically, countries deriving their copyright law from UK models have not given the copyright owner absolute control over imports: at least since the Imperial Copyright Act 1911, it has been qualified by a knowledge requirement.[13] Critics of this view argue that it fails to take into account the realities of globalisation and the breaking down of purely national markets by technologies such as the Internet.

2. Consumers

Those in favour of parallel importation argue that international price discrimination restricts competition to the disadvantage of consumers in countries having higher prices. They say that parallel imports foster competition and efficiency, benefiting consumers.

Even the European Commission has concluded that banning parallel importation may lead to higher prices for consumers in at least some cases, stating '[i]t may be true that some branded goods are more expensive than they would be if a system of international exhaustion prevailed within the EU'.[14]

Further, consumer advocates argue that consumers may get access to a greater range of goods if retailers or parallel importers bring a wider variety of products into the country, and may also get better service. This latter benefit may be achieved because domestic suppliers must enhance the service they provide to remain competitive. A study by the NZ Institute of Economic Research on the impact of removing the restrictions on parallel imports on books in NZ found that it was precisely by offering a wide range of services that NZ publishers had remained the preferred supplier for booksellers and other retailers in NZ.[15]

Parallel importation restrictions enable manufacturers and distributors to erect 'vertical restraints' in the market through exclusive distribution agreements. In the last thirty years there has been a shift in thinking about the economic desirability of vertical restraints; from initially viewing them as anticompetitive, to a general view that they may be pro-competitive. Frankel and McLay state:

> Those who believe that vertical restraints tend to be pro-competitive focus on the incentives underpinning why manufacturers agree to exclusivity clauses. The argument runs that a manufacturer wishes to optimise both the amount of product sold to consumers, and the proportion it receives of the same amount paid for each unit sold. Competition amongst retailers assists such a result. Competition forces the retail price to fall as close as possible to the price at which the manufacturer sells goods to the retailers. A vertical restraint that prevents such competition would normally, under this analysis, be against the interests of the manufacturer.[16]

The insight has been the recognition of an apparent contradiction between the manufacturer's best interests and the manufacturer adopting a vertical restraint. Assuming that manufacturers and intellectual property owners will act rationally, economists have argued that exclusivity agreements might be explained on the basis that certain goods require distributors or retailers to make significant investments in pre- or post-sale service or other market making activities, which they may be unprepared to do if they can be undercut.[17] If that be the explanation, the contradiction between conduct and interest is apparent rather than real.

The contradiction would be real rather than apparent, however, where the distributor/licensee had market power and so could act unconstrained by the manufacturer's interests.

This view has not been universally accepted.[18]

Some have argued, moreover, that intellectual property is not an appropriate tool through which vertical restraints may be enforced and it may be preferable to leave manufacturers to regulate their distribution networks through contract rather than restrictions on parallel imports.[19] A different view of this is taken by Barfield and Groombridge who argue that there are four strong reasons why national governments and international agreements such as TRIPS should codify the legality of restrictions on parallel imports rather than rely on private contractual enforcement of vertical restraints:

1. legal structures of some developing countries make it difficult/impossible to enforce contracts privately;
2. there are difficulties in tracing the source of parallel imports and hence the party in breach of the contract;
3. globalisation is not a reality at the present; and
4. the ineffectiveness of contractual remedies.[20]

The Australian Competition and Consumer Affairs Commission (ACCC) argues that the existence of parallel importation restrictions may impact detrimentally on competition in Australia:

> Parallel import restrictions grant a 'monopoly' or exclusive right to import to IP owners. By preventing international arbitrage, these import monopolies may be used to support international price discrimination by firms with market power (either unilateral or coordinated market power). Indeed, the very existence of these exclusive rights tends to create a climate conducive to coordination rather than competition, since IP owners know they are not constrained by import competition.[21]

Against this view, it has been argued that parallel imports cause at least two certain and real detriments to the economy, while the economic benefits are at best uncertain.[22] The first, certain detriment identified is the impact of free riding on authorised manufacture and distribution channels; the second is the disruption of sales volume predictions resulting in production inefficiencies. The uncertainty about the benefits from parallel importing arises from a number of factors. First, price discrimination is not necessarily bad: for price discrimination to result in anticompetitive effects the intellectual property owner must have market power and consumers be restrained in their ability to switch to substitute products. Secondly, any welfare gains to consumers resulting from parallel imports causing lower prices must entail welfare losses to producers. Assuming that welfare transfers between producers and consumers are welfare neutral, therefore, it is argued that there will be fairly certain gains for the domestic economy only where intellectual property rights are mostly foreign owned.

Over a powerful dissent, however, the Australian IPCRC Report concluded:

> The Committee believes that the restrictions are likely to confer on the owners of copyrighted material the power to charge higher prices to Australian consumers than would otherwise be the case.[23]

The IPCRC had been appointed to investigate the relationship of intellectual property and competition policy as part of the national competition principles review which required all Australian governments to review their legislation, identify any restrictions on competitive market operations and retain only those which could be justified in the public interest. In considering whether or not copyright owners' power to block parallel imports was justifiable on competition grounds, the IPCRC considered that the onus of proving the justification fell on those seeking to continue the power to block parallel imports.[24] It considered that where the intellectual property owner did not have market power, any restrictions on parallel importing would be ineffective and, accordingly, there was no public policy case for perpetuating such restrictions.[25] On the other hand, the IPCRC concluded that there were clearly cases where copyright owners did have market power, especially as copyright industries were relatively concentrated and becoming increasingly so.[26] It noted that Australia is a net importer of copyright material;[27] and that it is a relatively small market with high per capita incomes and a high degree of willingness to purchase material covered by copyright.[28] Consequently, Australian consumers were price inelastic for copyright materials. The logical proposition was that a supplier of such material, with some degree of market power, and the ability to price-discriminate internationally, would be likely to set higher prices in Australia than elsewhere.[29] Accordingly, the IPCRC concluded that it would be in the public interest for Australia to repeal the provisions of the Copyright Act that restrict parallel importation.[30]

A further argument against national exhaustion specific to trade marks is more theoretical. It is based on the view that the function of a trade mark is to act as a badge of origin. Parallel imports are goods which legitimately bear the mark of the trade mark proprietor and as such do not deceive the consumer as to their origin. The trade mark proprietor's monopoly therefore cannot be justified to the extent it permits him to prevent future dealings in such goods.[31] Against this view, however, it has been argued that parallel importing may create confusion for consumers, as a trade mark stands as a badge of quality as well as origin.[32]

B. How are parallel imports treated in different jurisdictions?

Part two of this chapter discusses the way in which parallel imports are treated in Singapore, the USA, the EEA, Malaysia, Japan, Hong Kong, South Korea, Australia and NZ. Where appropriate, different intellectual property rights are examined separately, as often the treatment of parallel imports is not consistent across different intellectual property rights. Recent changes and directions for future reform are also highlighted, together with outstanding issues, where these are relevant. The conclusion discusses some of the general trends that can be observed in the international treatment of parallel imports.

1. Singapore

The state of the law relating to parallel imports in Singapore is one of the clearest of all the jurisdictions discussed in this chapter. With very few exceptions, parallel importing of goods is allowed and the doctrine of international exhaustion applied.

1.1 Copyright   Singapore's Copyright Act[33] is modelled to a large extent on the Australian Copyright Act of 1968. When the Copyright Bill 1986 was originally presented to Parliament, it therefore contained the (then) strict Australian provisions on parallel imports, determining the question of liability by considering whether the imported articles would have infringed copyright if made by the actual importer in the country of importation.[34] However, as a result of subsequent legislative debate, the provisions were modified to treat parallel imports more favourably. As a result, section 7 of the Copyright Act provides that '... an infringing copy ... means ... an article the making of which constituted an infringement of the copyright in the [work] ... or, in the case of an article imported without the licence of the owner of the copyright, the making of which was carried out without the consent of the owner of the copyright'.[35]

As noted by Wei, writing soon after the introduction of the new Act, the provisions are 'essentially in favour of parallel imports'.[36] However, he warned that '[j]ust how generous these provisions are will depend ultimately on how the courts approach the question of consent and the identity of the copyright owner problem'.[37]

The issue of parallel importing of copyrighted goods was first dealt with in dicta by Chan J in *Television Broadcasts Ltd & Ors* v. *Golden Line Video & Marketing Ltd*[38] who stated that 'it would appear that, in the area of copyright protection, our legislation has adopted a mercantile policy of allowing in Singapore a free market where copyright articles, whether parallel imports or made under licence in Singapore, may be sold or dealt with in competition with one another'.[39]

This interpretation of the Copyright Act as being consistent with the policy of allowing parallel imports was followed at first instance in the case of *Public Prosecutor* v. *Teoh Ai Nee*, where the District Court held that the 'owner of the copyright' referred to in section 7 should be read to mean the owner of the copyright in the country in which the article was manufactured, rather than the owner of the copyright in Singapore.[40] This decision was overturned on appeal by the High Court[41] which held that the owner of the copyright in the section refers to the owner of the copyright in Singapore, thus placing a substantial limitation on the situations in which parallel imports would be legal. In his decision, Yong Pung How CJ stated that the copyright in articles which are in some way connected to the Singapore copyright holder, by virtue of being manufactured by or with the consent of the Singapore copyright holder, will be exhausted when placed on the international market. However, Singapore copyright owners would be able to repel imports into Singapore of articles placed on the international market by the owner of copyright in the place of manufacture who is unconnected with the Singapore owner.[42]

Shortly after this decision, Parliament passed the Copyright (Amendment) Act 1994[43] which amended the Copyright Act.[44] One of the major amendments made was to clarify the position on parallel imports through a clear definition of the 'owner' mentioned in the definition of 'infringing copy'. Taking a stance that 'was obviously slanted towards parallel imports',[45] Parliament amended section 25 by adding a new subsection (3). The subsection reads:

> Where reference is made in this Act to an imported article the making of which was carried out without the consent of the owner of the copyright, the reference to the owner of the copyright shall be read as a reference to –
>
> a) the person entitled to the copyright in respect of its application to the making of an article of that description in the country where the article was made; or
> b) if there is no person entitled to the copyright in respect of its application to the making of an article of that description in the country where the article was made, the person entitled to the copyright in respect of that application in Singapore.[46]

These new provisions were considered by the High Court in *Highway Video Pte Ltd* v. *Public Prosecutor (Lim Tai Wah) and Other Appeals.*[47] Yong Pung How CJ stated:

> [I]t is clear that Parliament has clearly chosen a course of action favouring parallel imports save for situations where an article is not protected by the copyright laws of the country in which it is manufactured ... Now that Parliament has taken a firm stance favouring parallel imports, contrary to the law existing at the time of *PP v Teoh Ai Nee*, the full effect of this choice has to be applied. Based on section 136 read with sections 7(1) and 25(3) of the Copyright Act, in order for persons accused of possessing infringing articles to be convicted under section 136, the prosecution has to prove, inter alia, that the imported article which is alleged to be an infringing article was not imported with the consent of the Singapore copyright owner *and* manufactured without the consent of the copyright owner in the country of manufacture, i.e. it is not a legitimate parallel import. Moreover, the prosecution will have the burden of proving this beyond reasonable doubt. The principles of evidence and criminal procedure apply in the full rigour that they do when other offences are concerned, and when

only circumstantial evidence is adduced; the totality of such evidence must lead the court to the irresistible conclusion that the elements of the offence are made out before an accused person can be convicted.[48]

1.2 Trade mark   Singapore also applies a doctrine of international exhaustion to the importation of trade marked goods. Section 29 of the Trade Marks Act 1998 provides that a registered trade mark is not infringed by the use of the trade mark in relation to goods which have been put on the market, whether in Singapore or outside Singapore, under that trade mark by the proprietor of the registered trade mark or with his express or implied consent (conditional or otherwise). There is only one exception to this, namely that it will not apply where the condition of the goods has been changed or impaired after they have been put on the market, and the use of the registered trade mark in relation to those goods is detrimental to the distinctive character or repute of the registered trade mark.[49]

Unlike some other jurisdictions, the Trade Marks Act thus specifies that the doctrine of exhaustion is international, that consent may be implied, and clearly defines the circumstances in which the proprietor can object to further commercialisation of his goods. Wee Loon Ng-Loy argues that although this clarity is a cause for some celebration, it may also mean that it is unable to help a consumer who becomes the victim of deception. He argues that in three situations – (1) where consent to the use of the mark on the goods is subject to restrictions; (2) where the packaging of the goods is tampered with after the goods have been placed on the market; and (3) where goods of different quality are put on the market under the same mark – the approach in Singapore may give rise to the occasional injustice.[50] In relation to (1) he argues that when determining whether the proprietor has given consent under section 29, an express restriction which imposes some condition on the use of the goods should be disregarded.[51] In relation to (2) he argues that tampering with the packaging of the goods which changes only the 'mental condition of the goods', such as the removal of the outer packaging of goods which does not have any adverse effect on the condition of the goods themselves, would be tolerated under the Singapore Act.[52] In relation to (3) he argues that section 29 'caters only for the situation where the condition of goods has been changed after they have been put on the market, and no other' and therefore cannot assist a proprietor confronted with such a situation.[53] In conclusion, he notes:

> If the Singapore Act cannot protect a trade mark proprietor and the consumer against the most basic form of unfair trading practices, that is, those which lead to confusion in the market, perhaps the clarity in the Singapore model of exhaustion has been achieved at too high a price.[54]

The legality of parallel importing in the context of passing off was discussed by the High Court in the recent case of *Remus Innovation* v. *Hong Boon*

Siong,[55] where it held that the 'sale of parallel imports was a perfectly lawful business'. The Court stated that:

> Apart from contract or misrepresentation there is nothing to prevent a person from acquiring goods from a manufacturer or his buyer and selling them in competition with him, even in a country into which the manufacturer, or his agent, has been the sole importer and distributor.[56]

1.3 Patent The doctrine of international exhaustion also applies to patented goods. Section 66(2) of the Patents Act (Chapter 221) provides that:

> An act which, apart from this subsection, would constitute an infringement of a patent for an invention shall not do so if –
> (g) it consists of the import, use, disposal or offer to dispose of, of any patented product, or of any product obtained by means of a patented process or to which a patented process has been applied, which is produced by or with the consent (conditional or otherwise) of the proprietor of the patent or any person licensed by him, and for this purpose 'patent' includes a patent granted in any country outside Singapore in respect of the same or substantially the same invention as that for which a patent is granted under this Act and 'patented product', 'patented process' and 'licensed' shall be construed accordingly.[57]

An outstanding question in relation to both trade mark and patent law is whether 'the proprietor of the patent (or trade mark)' means only the Singapore owner or the owner of the patent (or trade mark) in the relevant place or may also embrace the owner in the place of exportation. As discussed above, uncertainty over this question in relation to copyright resulted in the amendment of the Copyright Act to explicitly state that the relevant owner is the owner of the copyright where the goods were made. However, under traditional rules of interpretation, the patent referred to under section 66 would be limited to patents owned elsewhere by the Singapore owner.

2. United States of America

The law in the United States with regard to parallel imports is not uniform with regard to different types of intellectual property rights, and moreover is far from clear. The general approach is to prohibit parallel imports and to adopt a national exhaustion doctrine.

2.1 Copyright The question of whether or not parallel importing of copyrighted goods is permitted is a matter of some debate. Two relevant sections of the US copyright laws apparently contradict each other. The 'first sale' doctrine in section 109(a) of the US Copyright Act[58] states that a copyright holder cannot control the future sale or distribution of a lawfully made copy once ownership is passed on. However, section 602(a) of the same Act states that the importation of a copyright good without the authorisation of the copyrighted owner is an infringement of the exclusive distribution right provided by the laws.[59] The lower courts have reached disparate conclusions on which provision should prevail.

The US Supreme Court in *Quality King Distributors Inc.* v. *L'Anza Research International*[60] held that the rights under section 602 to prevent importation yield to the 'first sale doctrine' under section 109(a). That is, the parallel imports in that case could not be blocked. The case concerned, however, goods which had been placed on the market in the United States first and then exported, so called 'round trip' goods. Whether the first sale doctrine would apply to goods which had been placed on the market for the first time outside the United States still seems to be an open question. Prior to the Supreme Court's ruling, the Ninth Circuit had held in *Parfums Givenchy Inc.* v. *Drug Emporium Inc.*[61] that 'sales abroad of foreign manufactured United States copyrighted materials do not terminate the United States copyright holder's exclusive distribution rights in the United States under sections 106 and 602(a)'.[62] A recent District Court decision summarised the existing state of the law by concluding that 'Section 109 and the first sale doctrine do not, necessarily, provide a defence to a Section 602(a) claim where the allegedly infringing copies were manufactured and sold abroad.'[63] It therefore appears that parallel importing of goods that have been manufactured in the United States is allowed, while there is no exhaustion for goods manufactured abroad which have not yet been placed on the US market.[64] Indeed, the National Association of College Stores has recently written to the main educational publishers protesting about the higher prices that students in the United States are paying for text books compared to the prices for corresponding texts in the United Kingdom.[65]

2.2 Trade mark   The parallel importation of trade marked goods into the United States is governed by two pieces of legislation at federal level. Under the Lanham Act cases involving parallel imports (in the United States, 'grey market goods') have arisen under the general provision for infringement of registered trade marks, section 32.[66] Section 43, applying to both registered and unregistered trade marks, provides a prohibition on making false advertisements or representations, including about origin, in connection with goods.[67] Further, section 42 of the Lanham Act provides inter alia that 'no article of imported merchandise which shall copy or simulate the name of any domestic manufacture ... shall be admitted to entry at any customhouse of the United States'.[68] Similarly to section 42 of the Lanham Act, section 526(a) of the Tariff Act (1930) prohibits the importation of merchandise bearing a registered trade mark owned by a US trade mark holder unless the US trade mark holder has consented in writing.[69] Cases alleging infringement of these provisions have also arisen within the jurisdiction of the International Trade Commission conferred by section 337 of the Tariff Act.

The Supreme Court's decision in *A. Bourjois & Co.* v. *Katzel*[70] recognised the territorial boundaries of trade marks, stressing that the reputation and goodwill of the holder of the corresponding US mark warrants protection against unauthorised importation of goods bearing the same mark, although the mark was validly affixed in the foreign country. In that case, however, the owner of the trade mark in the foreign country had assigned the US trade mark to the US owner for valuable consideration.

Since the *Bourjois* decision, the regional circuits and the Federal Circuit have drawn a variety of distinctions in dealing with parallel imports, primarily in consideration of two issues. The first is whether the foreign source of the trade marked goods and the US trade mark holder are related commercial entities. In cases where the parties are related companies, the courts have been inclined to reason that there is no need to protect the domestic company's investment in goodwill based on the quality of the trade marked goods because where the companies are commonly controlled there is a reasonable assurance of similar quality.[71]

In *K Mart Corp.* v. *Cartier*[72] the Supreme Court was called upon to decide whether regulations enacted by the Customs Service were consistent with section 526 of the Tariff Act. The regulations permitted the entry of goods manufactured abroad in two situations – first where the 'same person' held the US trademark or was 'subject to common control' with the US trademark holder; and secondly where the foreign manufacturer had received the US trademark owner's authorisation to use its trademark. The Supreme Court upheld (by a 5–4 majority) the regulations as far as the first circumstance – where there is 'common control' – was concerned, but (by a different 5–4 majority) rejected the second exception. The Court declared that '[u]nder no reasonable construction of the statutory language can goods made in a foreign country by an independent foreign manufacturer be removed from the purview of the statute'.[73]

Even where the parallel imports may pass the customs barrier under section 526 of the Tariff Act, the goods may still be subject to infringement actions under the Lanham Act and presumably before the International Trade Commission.[74]

The second issue the courts have focused on is whether or not there are material differences between the domestic goods and the imported goods bearing the same mark. In cases where there are material differences, the courts have generally excluded such goods, even when the holders of the domestic and foreign trademarks are related companies, on the grounds of both safeguarding the goodwill of the domestic enterprise and protecting consumers from confusion or deception as to the quality and nature of the product bearing the mark.[75] Differences that have been held to be 'material' include the fact that the 'adoption papers' and 'birth certificate' of imported cabbage patch dolls were in Spanish rather than English;[76] the fact that

Hungarian Herend porcelain tableware and figurines were painted with different animals or different patterns and colours to those on the authorised imports;[77] and the difference of one and a half calories between imported and local TicTac mints.[78]

Thus the most fundamental questions in determining the legality of parallel imports are the relationship between the domestic enterprise and the foreign importer, and whether or not the two products are materially different.[79]

2.3 Patent The Patent Code grants the patentee the right to exclude others from making, using or selling the patented invention within the United States, or importing into the United States the patented invention, during the term of the patent.[80] A US patent is a territorial right, conferring exclusive rights within the United States. Accordingly, infringement of a US patent requires the doing of an act comprised in the patent monopoly *within* the United States.

Prior to 1989 it was not an infringement of a US patent to import into the United States a product made abroad according to a process which was patented in the United States. However, as of 23 February 1989 the Process Patents Amendment Act of 1988 came into force, conferring on US patentees of processes power to sue for importation of products made abroad according to the patent.[81]

In one of the earliest cases, *Boesch* v. *Graff*,[82] the Supreme Court held that the sale or use in the United States of a patented product purchased abroad, even from an authorised seller of the product in the foreign country, constitutes patent infringement.[83] The patentee in *Boesch* owned both US and German patents for lamp burners. The defendant acquired the burners in Germany from an individual who was not licensed by the patentee to make or sell the product in either country, but was permitted to make or sell the burners under German law.[84] The Supreme Court found the defendant's sale of the product in the United States to be infringement.[85]

This decision left open the question of whether a foreign sale by the holder of both United States and foreign patents (or its licensee with a licence to sell in both countries) 'exhausts' the patentee's rights 'under the United States patent'. Subsequently, lower courts have ruled that, on the one hand, the unrestricted foreign sale of a patented article constituted exhaustion where the sale was by the patentee or licensee which also had rights to sell in the United States. On the other hand, the parallel imports could be blocked if the sale abroad was by a licensee with no authority to sell the product in the United States or there was an exclusive licensee in the United States which had not made the sale abroad.[86]

The Federal Circuit appears recently to have adopted a more stringent approach to exhaustion, limiting it to products which have been sold in the United States by, or with the consent of, the patentee. In *Jazz Photo Corp* v.

ITC[87] the Federal Circuit held that in order for a sale to be 'under the United States Patent' such that the patentee's rights are exhausted, the sale must be 'in the United States'. According to the Court:

> United States patent rights are not exhausted by products of foreign provenance. To invoke the protection of the [exhaustion by first sale] doctrine, the authorised first sale must have occurred under the United States patent [citing *Boesch*] . . . Our decision applies only to [products] for which the United States patent right has been exhausted by first sale in *the United States*.[88]

3. European Economic Area and European Union

The EEA was constituted in 1994–5 to establish free trading obligations between the European Community (EC) and certain former European Free Trade Area States, namely Iceland, Liechtenstein and Norway. The principles of freedom of movement and competition rules now apply equally to EEA relations as to EC relations, although in rather complex ways.[89] Therefore, unless specified otherwise, the discussion below applies to all countries in the EEA.

Perhaps unsurprisingly, the issue of parallel imports in the European Union has been very controversial, being described as 'of great political moment, yet . . . wracked with conflicting policy demands'.[90]

The EEA was formed with the goal of a single market with a free flow of goods unrestricted by national laws. Accordingly, with regard to goods placed on the market within the EEA, the EU has adopted a regional approach to parallel importing of goods, holding that a first sale within the EEA by or with the consent of the right holder generally exhausts intellectual property rights within the EEA.[91] This applies whether or not the goods are protected by trade mark,[92] patent,[93] copyright[94] or registered design.[95] If the goods have been placed on the market outside the EEA, however, there is no exhaustion.[96] This arrangement has sometimes been referred to as 'fortress Europe'. For example, if a product protected by an intellectual property right such as a patent is first sold in Spain, it can be resold in France without the patentee's consent. However, if the same product is first sold in India, it cannot be imported into Spain or France without the patentee's consent.

These straightforward rules have been qualified in relation to trade marks. Article 13 of the Community Trade Mark Regulations provides:

1. A Community trade mark shall not entitle the proprietor to prohibit its use in relation to goods which have been put on the market in the Community under that trade mark by the proprietor or with his consent.
2. Paragraph 1 shall not apply where there exist legitimate reasons for the proprietor to oppose further commercialisation of the goods, especially where the condition of the goods is changed or impaired after they have been put on the market.[97]

The European Court of Justice (ECJ) has found that legitimate reasons to oppose parallel imports will exist when the trade mark function is unavoidably compromised, notably where there has been relabelling or repackaging of goods by the parallel importer which fails to meet the limits the Court has defined.[98]

Repackaging is where the trade mark owner uses the same mark in the relevant Member States, but for some reason the packaging is different. For example, in *Hoffman-La Roche* v. *Centrafarm*[99] the practice in Germany was to supply certain drugs in packages of 20 to 50, while in the United Kingdom sales were in lots of 100 or 250. A parallel importer marketed in Germany the drugs which had been purchased in Great Britain in the original packages and then put into new packages of 1000 tablets, with the trade mark of Hoffmann-La Roche affixed to the box, together with a notice that the product had been marketed by Centrafarm. The ECJ found that regard must be had to the essential function of the trade mark, namely to guarantee the identity of the origin of the trade-marked product to the consumer or ultimate user, by enabling him without any possibility of confusion to distinguish that product from products which have another origin, while also taking care not to let intellectual property owners use trade marks as a disguised restriction on trade. Consequently, the ECJ held that:

a) the proprietor of a trade mark right which is protected in two Member States at the same time is justified pursuant to the first sentence of Article 36 of the EEC Treaty in preventing a product to which the trade mark has lawfully been applied in one of those states from being marketed in the other Member State after it has been repacked in new packaging to which the trade mark has been affixed by a third party.
b) however, such prevention of marketing constitutes a disguised restriction on trade between Member States within the meaning of the second sentence of Article 36 where:
   • it is established that the use of the trade mark right by the proprietor, having regard to the marketing system which he has adopted, will contribute to the artificial partitioning of the markets between Member States;
   • it is shown that the repackaging cannot adversely affect the original condition of the product;
   • the proprietor of the mark receives prior notice of the marketing of the repackaged product; and
   • it is stated on the new packaging by whom the product has been repackaged.[100]

Re-branding or re-affixing cases arise where the trade mark owner uses different marks in different Member States and the parallel importer affixes the mark used in the country of importation. In *Bristol-Myers Squibb* v. *Paranova* the European Court held that the same principles apply to these types of conduct as to repackaging. The general position is that trade mark rights cannot be enforced to prevent parallel imports from elsewhere in the EEA where the importer has repackaged the goods fairly.[101] The Court reiterated its comments in *Hoffman-La Roche* and added additional instances of permitted conduct. The rationale relied upon by the ECJ to prohibit parallel imports in such cases is to ensure that the source/origin function of the trade mark is preserved and the consumer is not misled into believing that the goods come unaltered from the originating enterprise.

The exhaustion of rights conferred by copyright is limited in some respects. Importantly, the sale of an article embodying copyright material (such as a computer program or a book) does not exhaust the rental rights conferred by the copyright.[102] As discussed below, the European Commission contends that these provisions mean that there is no exhaustion of rights in digital downloads.

In relation to the issue of consent, it is clear from the ECJ's recent ruling in *Zino Davidoff SA* v. *A & G Imports Ltd*[103] that for goods placed on the market outside the EEA, consent will not be implied from a sale and the absence of restrictions.[104]

3.1 Reform As a consequence of claims that trade marks holders are using the Community exhaustion regime to charge higher prices in the EU than elsewhere, the European Parliament charged the European Commission with investigating cases of trade mark abuse, and in May 2003 the Commission produced the EC Report.[105] The Commission concluded:

> It may be true that some branded goods are more expensive than they would be if a system of international exhaustion prevailed within the EU, although the NERA study [a study by National Economic Research Associates published in 1999 at the request of the Commission] suggests that such an effect is in general rather minor. However, such a pricing situation cannot be considered to constitute an abuse of dominant position in the sense of Article 82 EC . . .
>
> It follows that the Commission, as a result of the investigations carried out in the preparation of this report, has not found any deficiencies in current legal provision relating to possible abuses of trade marks within the EU.[106]

Importantly, the Committee noted that abuse of a dominant position by a trade mark owner can be regulated by the competition law provisions in the European Community Treaty. Strothers has commented on this report as follows:

> By focussing so much on competition issues, and to a lesser extent on free movement issues, the Commission has avoided most of the demands made by Parliament and, more fundamentally, has not dealt with many of the issues which are behind the unhappiness with the current provisions. While

this may satisfy the Commission, those in the European Parliament and the Member States who desire change remain free to cast themselves as fighting for the consumer in doing so. Indeed, in some ways their hands have been strengthened as, on the basis of the Commission's paper, it seems that the competition provisions of the EC Treaty are unlikely to limit the ability of trade mark holders to charge higher prices in the EU or indeed to prevent supply of certain products to the EU.[107]

The findings of this report, together with the recent rulings of the ECJ discussed above, suggest that there is no current move in the EU towards an adoption of a doctrine of international exhaustion of rights.

4. Malaysia

As a result of recent legislative changes and clarifications, parallel importing of copyrighted and patented goods is generally permitted in Malaysia.

4.1 Copyright   Malaysia's copyright law is contained in the Copyright Act 1987. Under the Act as it originally stood, parallel importation was an infringing act. However, the Act was amended by the Copyright (Amendment) Act 1990 which removed the restrictions on parallel imports. Section 36(2) now reads:

> Copyright is infringed by any person who, without the consent or licence of the owner of the copyright, imports an article into Malaysia for the purpose of [lists the exclusive rights] where he knows or ought reasonably to know that the making of the article was carried out without the consent or licence of the owner of the copyright.

Tee notes that two major changes have been made. First, unlike the former section 36(2), the prohibition extends only to infringing articles and does not include articles manufactured lawfully with the consent or licence of the owner of the copyright. Second, the onus is on the plaintiff and not the importer to prove the lack of knowledge or reasonable grounds. Thus, as Tee observes, parallel importing is permissible in Malaysia with effect from 1 October 1990.[108]

4.2 Patent   Parallel importation of patented goods is generally allowed in Malaysia.[109] The issue was first discussed by the landmark case of *Smith Kline & French Laboratories Ltd* v. *Salim (M) Sdn. Bhd.*[110] where the High Court moved towards a doctrine of international exhaustion. V. C. George J held:

> ... where the plaintiffs by themselves or by their associated company sell their patented product in, say, the United Kingdom, without giving effective notice of any restrictions in respect of the resale and the produce is purchased by a Malaysian merchant by way of import, that the plaintiffs or some associated company of the plaintiffs happen to have patent rights

in West Malaysia that gives them exclusive rights to import the product into West Malaysia will be of no avail to them vis-à-vis such an innocent importer of the product.[111]

Smith Kline was decided under the old Registration of United Kingdoms Patent Act 1951. However, the doctrine of international exhaustion is more clearly provided in section 37(2)(1) of the new Patents Act (1983), which states that rights under the patent shall not extend in respect of products which have been put on the market by the owner or an authorised person. Azmi states that to add further clarification to the position of parallel imports in Malaysia, a new section 58A was inserted into the parent Act via the 2000 amendment. The new section 58A provides that:

> It shall not be an act of infringement to import, offer for sale, sell, or use any patented product or any product obtained directly by means of the patented process which is produced by, or with the consent, conditional or otherwise, of the owner of the patent or his licensee.[112]

As in Singapore, there may be an issue about whether the consent must be the consent of the owner of the Malaysian rights or may include the owner in the place of exportation.

5. Japan

Japan has recently adopted a doctrine of international exhaustion for patented goods, in line with its long standing doctrine of exhaustion for trade marked goods.

5.1 Trade mark   Japan considers trade mark rights to be exhausted on an international basis such that a first sale of a product bearing a trade mark exhausts trade mark rights with respect to that item throughout the remainder of the world. The leading decision on parallel imports of trade marked goods is the *Parker* case[113] where the Court held that although parallel imports may constitute a literal infringement of the trade mark law, parallel imports do not affect the function of a trade mark under Japanese law, namely, to guarantee the source and quality of the goods; they do not harm the business reputation of the trade mark owner and they do not generally mislead consumers.[114]

5.2 Patent   In 1998 the Supreme Court of Japan adopted a doctrine of international exhaustion of patent rights in relation to parallel imports of patented products into Japan, overturning the previous doctrine of national exhaustion. The Court held in the case of *BBS Kraftfahrzeugtechnik AG v. Racimex Japan Corp.* that the patentee was not permitted to enforce his patent right in Japan against third parties or subsequent purchasers except where the patentee has agreed with the (first) purchaser to exclude Japan from the territories for sale or use and has explicitly indicated the same on the patented product.[115] The Court arrived at its decision by stressing the importance of unimpeded international trade. Tessensohn and Yamamoto observe that this decision marks the 'end of the generation-old Japanese legal proposition . . . that prohibited parallel imports of patented products into Japan. The non-infringing position of parallel imports is now final and conclusive'.[116]

The principle adopted is not a true exhaustion doctrine, however, as the Supreme Court accepted that intellectual property owners could prohibit parallel imports by proposing a method for contracts and notices to preclude international exhaustion. The Court explained that the patent owner should be allowed to agree with the assignee at the time of making an assignment to exclude Japan from the authorised region of sale or use of the patented product. Moreover, a clear notice of this agreement could be placed onto the patented product enabling subsequent purchasers of the product to recognise the restriction on the product.

6. Hong Kong

6.1 Copyright   The Hong Kong Copyright Ordinance 1997[117] prohibits parallel importation. Parallel importing of an article incorporating a copyright work is a criminal offence during the 18 months starting from the work's first publication anywhere in the world.[118]

On 20 November 2003 the Copyright (Amendment) Ordinance 2003 came into force, which removes the restriction on parallel imports from articles which contain a computer program. However, if the principal attraction of a computer software product is musical sound or visual recordings, movies, television dramas, e-books, or a combination of them, the restriction will continue to apply.[119] The Hong Kong Intellectual Property Department notes that this liberalisation is due to the fact that:

> The public had generally expressed the view that the restrictions on parallel importation of computer software should be removed. They believe that allowing parallel importation of computer software would increase competition and availability of products in the market, resulting in more choice and lower prices for consumers.[120]

6.2 Trade mark   The new Hong Kong Trade Mark Ordinance[121] came into effect on 4 April 2003. The Ordinance permits parallel imports. Section 20 states:

1. Notwithstanding section 18 (infringement of registered trade mark), a registered trade mark is not infringed by the use of the trade mark in relation to goods which have been put on the market anywhere in the world under that trade mark by the owner or with his consent (whether express or implied or conditional or unconditional).

2. Subsection (1) does not apply where the condition of the goods has been changed or impaired after they have been put on the market, and the use of the registered trade mark in relation to those goods is detrimental to the distinctive character or repute of the trade mark.

7. South Korea

7.1 Trade marks   In June 2002 the Korean Trade Commission ruled against two parallel importers of computer games and granted a request for an injunction made by the only authorised South Korean distributor of the games. The Korean Trade Commission stated that, because the distributor held the exclusive claim to the trade mark for these products in South Korea, the two parallel importers must cease selling those products there. Prior to this decision, parallel importing had never been restricted or banned.[122]

In light of this decision, the Korean Trade Commission established the country's first official guideline on regulating parallel imports. According to the Commission, the primary importer will have an exclusive local franchise to import its product provided that some or all of the following criteria are met:

(1) the primary importer has registered its claims locally to the intellectual property rights affiliated with the imported product;
(2) the importer is not associated with the manufacturer other than by licence agreement;
(3) the importer has the licence to produce the import in its location;
(4) the importer's product quality is equal to or better than parallel imports; and
(5) the importer has a large customer base.[123]

7.2 Patent   The South Korean Patent Act provides that importation of patented products into South Korea shall constitute a patent infringement. Accordingly, even though the patented products have been put on the market in another country by a patent owner or with his consent, it is construed that the patent owner can use his rights against parallel imports from that country.[124]

8. Australia

The Australian position on parallel importation has been the subject of much ongoing debate. It varies according to different types of intellectual property right and, occasionally, different types of product.

8.1 Copyright   The Australian copyright system is based on national exhaustion. Generally it is an infringement of copyright to import an article into Australia for commercial purposes without the copyright owner's consent, where the importer knew, or should have known, that if the article had been made by the importer in Australia it would have infringed copyright.[125]

Recently, however, the general prohibition on parallel imports has been relaxed for certain categories of subject matter, and separate regimes have been introduced to govern books,[126] sound recordings,[127] computer programs[128] and articles embodying electronic literary or music items.[129] The Act has also been amended so that copyright in labels, packaging and other accessories materials cannot be used to prevent parallel imports.[130]

There are convoluted differences between the various regimes partly arising from the subject matter and partly arising from historical factors. In broad terms, parallel imports of sound recordings, computer programs and products bearing labels, packaging or accessories are permitted where the imported article was made by or with the consent of the copyright owner in the place of manufacture, provided that the place of manufacture is a member of the Berne Convention or the WTO.

For books, parallel importation is legal if the book was first published on or after 23 December 1991 and the place of first publication was not Australia. In determining whether or not first publication took place in Australia, publication in Australia within 30 days of first publication elsewhere will suffice. Even if the book was first published in Australia, parallel imports will still be possible in a number of situations.

First, a reseller may import a single copy for the purpose of supplying it to someone who has placed a written order, or verifiable telephone order, with the reseller. Secondly, a reseller may import multiple copies if it has placed an order for a version of a book with the copyright owner (or local representative) and either the copyright owner has not responded within 7 days confirming that it will supply the order or the copyright owner does not in fact fulfil the order within 90 days. This provision seems to be responsible for paperback versions of books being available in Australia much earlier than the traditional 12 months after release of the hardback version. In addition, it is common to find multiple paperback versions on the shelves of bookshops of differing quality and pricing. Thirdly, a reseller may import two or more copies to supply orders placed with the reseller by a library that is not conducted for profit.

While the regimes have their differences, the rationale (apart from the labels, packaging and accessories provisions) is the same. It is clearly explained in the Explanatory Memorandum to the Copyright Amendment (Parallel Importation) Act as follows:

> Studies over the last decade, in relation to books, sound recordings and computer software have clearly demonstrated that this power to control the distribution of imported copyright subject matter has enabled copyright owners to exercise market control. It has resulted, over time, in higher prices being charged to Australian consumers. The studies also show some inefficiencies resulting from this legal environment as it impedes competition or the threat of competition.[131]

The rationale for allowing parallel imports related to labels, packaging and other accessories is simply that it is not thought appropriate that copyright in such ancillary material be used to restrict what would otherwise be legitimate importation.

8.2 Trade mark   Australia has adopted a principle of international exhaustion with respect to trade marks, whereby placing the goods onto the market by or with the consent of the trade mark owner exhausts the owner's ability to control subsequent dealings with the goods or services.[132] It would appear that the consent must be the consent of the owner of the Australian trade mark so parallel imports will not be possible if the foreign trade mark is owned by someone other than the Australian owner.[133] The Copyright Act was recently amended, however, so that an assignment of a registered trade mark could not be used to defeat parallel imports which would be permissible under the parallel importation provisions of the Copyright Act.[134]

The current Australian provisions are not limited to situations where the imported goods are the same quality as the official goods.[135] If the parallel imports are of inferior quality, therefore, any restriction on parallel importation would need to be found in passing off or under provisions of the trade practices legislation to similar effect.[136]

8.3 Patent   The Australian doctrine of patent exhaustion depends on the circumstances surrounding the first foreign sale. If the goods are first put into circulation without any restriction outside Australia by the Australian patentee or a licensee which also has rights to sell in Australia, then there will be no infringement because consent to parallel importing will be implied.[137] As it is implied, however, the presumption of consent can be defeated if the patentee expressly imposes a term prohibiting importation into Australia.[138] The patentee will be able to block parallel imports if they are put on the market in the foreign country by a licensee which does not have authority to sell in Australia.[139]

9. New Zealand

In NZ, as in Australia, different exhaustion regimes are adopted depending on the type of intellectual property involved. Thus for copyright there is the doctrine of international exhaustion, while for patent there is the doctrine of national exhaustion, and for trade marks the position is unclear.

9.1 Copyright   The NZ position on parallel importing changed dramatically in 1998 when the doctrine was changed from one of national exhaustion to one of international exhaustion. The position now is that goods are allowed to be imported provided they do not constitute an infringing copy in the country in which they were made.[140]

9.2 Trade mark   The law relating to parallel importation of registered trade marks is conflicted and unclear.[141] There is no statutory provision directly regulating the importation of goods bearing registered trade marks.

9.3 Patent   There is a prohibition on parallel importing of all goods subject to NZ patents. However, courts have sometimes been prepared to accept that there might be an implied licence to import goods into a particular jurisdiction that goes with the sale of the original patented object. Frankel and McLay observe:

> In comparison to copyright and trade marks there is a dearth of recent cases on the parallel importation of patents. It is unclear what New Zealand Courts would make of the implied licence doctrine in light of the increasingly diverse range of views on the rights of intellectual property owners.[142]

C. Parallel importation of digital works

Increasingly across the globe, more and more works are being made available digitally and therefore in intangible, rather than tangible, form. However, as discussed above, the laws relating to parallel importation have focused on the 'first sale' of a tangible embodiment of the intellectual property right. There is therefore a need to consider how these principles should apply to digital work. As with so many other issues concerning the 'grey market', the principles concerning exhaustion of digital works are unclear and controversial. The problems in this area have been exacerbated by the fact that the European Union and the USA appear to have taken divergent approaches to the issue.

The European Commission has expressly excluded digital copies from the scope of the exhaustion principle.[143] Consequently, the intellectual property owners of the software or other works are free to impose additional restrictions on the use and transfer of products embodying their intellectual property rights. The rationale for this exclusion has been suggested as being that the Commission considers online delivery to be equivalent to an online broadcast which is a service intended just to be viewed online.[144]

In contrast, the US has adopted a 'limited' first sale doctrine for digital works. Tai observes that while there is no consensus as to whether an extensive 'digital first sale doctrine' should apply, consensus does exist for the case where files are downloaded with the consent of the copyright owner and a lawfully made copy or phonorecord is created on the PC hard drive or tangible portable medium. In such a case, the limited digital exhaustion principle means that that copy could not be transmitted to a third party without destroying the original copy.[145]

Tai notes that due to the Berne Convention, the difference of approach between the USA and the EU means that American companies can prohibit the further assignment and delivery of digital works in Europe, while European companies cannot prohibit the same actions in the United States.[146] There are a number of arguments in favour and against the positions that both the US and the EU have taken.[147] The arguments in favour of the EU approach centre around concerns over piracy and the difficulty of proving title to a digital copy. On the other hand, the US limited exhaustion right is considered to more accurately replicate the position in the 'real' world. Tai argues:

> It is fair that the customer is not allowed to distribute the work to others in so far as he intends to keep his own copy. Not so in the case where the customer transfers a copy to a single other party and deletes his own copy, or in the case where he transfers the material object (disk) containing the digital copy. Digital exhaustion should apply to these cases. The ratio is that the rightholder has already paid for the single use of his product: it should not matter subsequently which specific individual is the user or on which machine it is used.[148]

Conclusion

The issue of parallel imports involves consideration of a plethora of economic, legal and political issues. It is no wonder that it remains one of the 'flashpoints' for international controversy.

The first obvious point is the increasing attention that the issues are being given. Initially, the question over how to treat parallel imports was mainly a consideration for Western countries, such as the USA and countries in the EU. However, in recent years parallel imports have become an increasingly pressing issue also for countries such as Singapore, Japan, South Korea and Hong Kong.

There is debate about whether or not the increasing trend towards globalisation will make parallel importing more or less of a problem. Skoko argues that:

> The impacts of globalisation on parallel importation are twofold. First, as trade barriers between nations decrease, it will become more difficult to implement price discrimination policies based on country boundaries. Implicitly, parallel traders are therefore likely to gradually disappear, as there will be fewer opportunities for arbitrage. The issue of parallel importation may therefore become less significant as globalisation continues.[149]

However, for countries such as China, it is globalisation that has created the problem of parallel imports as previously the price of products in China was lower than in international markets due to the import quota and high customs duties. The rapid development of the economy and the lowering of tariffs following China's accession to the WTO have resulted in the emergence of parallel imports into China.[150]

The second trend is that of flux. Almost every jurisdiction discussed above is in a state of change with regard to their laws regulating parallel imports. Some of these changes are due to judicial initiatives, such as the rather surprising adoption of the doctrine of international exhaustion by Japan in the *Aluminium Wheels* case, and some are due to deliberate government policy, such as the reforms to the Copyright Acts in Australia and New Zealand. Almost always, such changes reflect current economic and political imperatives, rather than purely legal issues.

Prior to the Federal Circuit's decision in *Jazz Photo*, the field of most uniformity was patents. For patents, most countries allowed parallel importation if the product protected by the patent had been put on the foreign market by a person with authority to sell also in the country of importation. If not, parallel imports infringed. This was not a true doctrine of exhaustion however, as in most countries the patentee could usually prohibit parallel importation by imposing appropriate notices.

The United States (at least since the *Jazz Photo* decision) and the EU (by analogy to the ECJ's ruling on trade marks in cases like *Zino Davidoff*) and (perhaps surprisingly) South Korea have moved strongly against the legality of parallel imports.

The position of trade marks has been less clearly uniform. Arguably the most common approach has been to treat the right as exhausted where the same person owns the trade mark rights in both jurisdictions. This has often extended to situations where the ownership is separated between members of the same corporate group.

Many jurisdictions that have adopted this approach have also had to deal with quality differences and in particular what quality differences, if any, defeat the exhaustion rule. Similar issues have arisen where the goods have been repackaged or relabelled or otherwise interfered with by the importer. These cases raise the question of the scope of trade mark protection and, in so doing, necessitate a consideration of the rationale for trade mark protection. On the one hand it could be argued that a trade mark only has a source function, and therefore as long as the parallel imports come from an authorised source that function is not compromised (this appears to be the approach taken by Australia). That approach may lead, however, to deception of consumers in cases like *Colgate Palmolive* v. *Markwell*. On the other hand, if the trade mark is also perceived as being a guarantee of quality then complaints raised by intellectual property owners about lower quality parallel imports are accepted as validly based in trade mark law (this appears to be the approach taken in the USA).

The approach in copyright has been less clearly uniform probably because consideration of importation and distribution rights, while often part of particular countries' domestic copyright laws, have only recently become the subject of consideration in international treaties. The issue has been further complicated as some very significant copyright subject matter, particularly recorded music, has often been the subject of statutory licences permitting third party use once the music has been published.

In all jurisdictions where parallel imports have been allowed, the issue of consent has generated considerable debate, both in respect of whether the consent justifying parallel imports must be the local owner's or that of the owner in the place of sale and whether or not consent of another member of the same corporate group or even a licensee or assignee will suffice. This issue required legislative intervention in Singapore and in Australia. Another aspect of the debate has been whether the consent can be implied and what circumstances give rise to a sufficient implication.

A result of the controversy created by the question of parallel imports has been the production of a number of governmental reports on the desirability of allowing parallel imports. Interestingly, all of the reports have acknowledged that prohibiting parallel imports will result in higher prices, at least for some products. This price differential has led to strong charges that blocking parallel imports is anticompetitive. The proponents of parallel importing have also sought to rebut claims that such charges are better dealt with under antitrust laws by pointing to the cost, complexity, uncertainty and delays attendant upon such actions.

Notwithstanding the price differentials where they exist, the factors affecting the decision a country takes with regard to its treatment of parallel imports are numerous, although it is clear that a significant factor is whether the country is a net exporter or a net importer of intellectual property. Thus countries such as Australia and New Zealand, which are net intellectual property importers, are loosening their restrictions, while the USA is maintaining its tight restrictions. Increasingly, however, countries that are net exporters of intellectual property have sought to use multilateral and bilateral trade negotiations as avenues to protect their own interests. The US Supreme Court rejected the relevance of such developments, however, to the interpretation of its own laws.[151] As well as adopting different policies towards different types of intellectual property rights, some jurisdictions have also tailored their parallel importing laws for different types of products. For example, while both Hong Kong and Australia generally adopt a national exhaustion approach for copyrighted products, both have modified this for computer software.

In conclusion, it appears the only certainty with regard to the future of parallel imports is that they will continue to be a difficult and contentious issue on both the domestic and the world stage.

Notes

1. Unreported, H-7 (o) No. 1988 (1 July 1997) Supreme Court of Japan. Discussed in Tessensohn and Yamamoto 'The Big Aluminium Wheel Dust Up – International Exhaustion of Rights in Japan' (1998) 20(6) *European Intellectual Property Review* 228.

2. C. Heath, *Parallel Imports and International Trade*, document ATRIP/GVA/99/6 presented at the Annual Meeting of the International Association for the Advancement of Teaching and Research in Intellectual Property (ATRIP) at the headquarters of WIPO in Geneva (7–9 July 1999).

3. See e.g. TRIPS Agreement, Article 11; WIPO Copyright Treaty 1996, Article 7 and the more explicit WIPO Performances and Phonograms Treaty 1996, Article 9.

4. There is a body of thought that the Berne Convention protects rights on a territorial basis: see D. Gervais, *The TRIPS Agreement: Drafting History and Analysis* (Thomson Sweet & Maxwell, 2nd edn 2003) 2.69–2.70.

5. Ibid.

6. A more in depth discussion of the relevant issues can be found in the reports prepared by various commissions to advise the Australian and New Zealand Governments and the European Union on issues surrounding parallel importation. See New Zealand Institute of Economic Research (Inc.), *Parallel Importing: A Theoretical and Empirical Investigation Report to Ministry of Commerce* (February 1998) available at http://www.med.govt.nz/buslt/int_prop/parallel/parallel-04.html#P670_70977 (NZ Report); Intellectual Property and Competition Review Committee, *Review of Intellectual Property Legislation under the Competition Principles Agreement* (2000), available at www.ipcr.gov.au (IPCR Report); Commission of the European Communities, *Possible Abuses of Trade Mark Rights within the EU in the Context of Community Exhaustion*, (Brussels, 21 May 2003 SEC (2003)) 575 available at http://europa.eu.int/comm/internal_market/en/indprop/tm/docs/sec-2003-575/sec-2003-575_en.pdf (EC Report). See also W. Rothnie, *Parallel Imports* (Sweet & Maxwell, 1993) and F. M. Abbott, 'First Report (final) to the Committee on International Trade Law of the International Law Association on the subject of Parallel Importation' (1998) 1(4) *Journal of International Economic Law* 607. This chapter does not deal with parallel importation of products protected by registered designs, however some of the issues involved in the parallel importation of designs are discussed in: Australian Law Reform Commission, Report 74 *Designs* (1995) at Chapter 15, available at http://www.austlii.edu.au/au/other/alrc/publications/reports/74/ALRC74.html.

7. 6 IPCR Report, at 48. Countries from a civil law tradition, with their emphasis on the primacy of moral rights, may place a stronger emphasis on natural rights as the justification at least of copyright.

8. Economists do argue that the incentive theory also applies to trade marks: legal protection of trade marks provides an incentive for brand owners to invest in the

quality and reputation of the goods or services provided under the brand: see e.g. W. Landes and R. Posner 'Trademark Law: An Economic Perspective' (1987) 30 *Journal of Law and Economics* 265; N. Economides 'Economics of Trademarks' 78 *Trade Mark Reporter* 523 (1988); National Economic Research Associates, *The Economic Consequences of the Choice of Regime of Exhaustion in the Field of Trade Marks* (8 February 1999), available at http://europa.eu.int/comm/internal_ market/en/indprop/tm/summary.pdf at 3.

9. International Trade Mark Association website, available at http://www.inta.org/parallel.

10. An example of this would appear to be *Quality Distributors Inc.* v. *L'Anza* 118 S Ct 1125 (1998), discussed below where the price L'Anza charged its overseas distributors was some 45 per cent less than the price it charged its US distributors because it did not undertake the market making activities overseas which it did in the USA. The price difference may well have been a factor, however, in making parallel importing into the USA attractive.

11. See IPCR Report, at 58.

12. Ibid. at 71.

13. See e.g. Imperial Copyright Act 1911 section 2(2)(d); Copyright Act 1956 (UK) section 5(2). The Copyright Act of 1976 s. 602(a), 17 U.S.C. §602(a), does not impose such a requirement.

14. EC Report, at 17. As noted below, however, the European Commission considered that the general competition rules should be sufficient to constrain such effects.

15. NZ Report.

16. Frankel and McLay, *Intellectual Property in New Zealand* (2002) 74. See also N. Gallini and A. Hollis, 'A Contractual Approach to the Grey Market' (1999) 19 *International Review of Law & Economics* 1.

17. Frankel and McLay, *Intellectual Property in New Zealand* 74.

18. See e.g. S. Corones, 'Parallel Importing Computer Software: Consumer Welfare Considerations' (1992) 3 *Australian Intellectual Property Journal* 188 at 192–3. The European Commission would appear to have departed significantly from this position, see e.g. in the distribution context, Commission Regulation (EC) No. 2790/1999 of 22 December 1999 on the application of Article 81(3) of the Treaty to categories of vertical agreements and concerted practices, *Official Journal* L 336, 29/12/1999 P. 0021 – 0025 and Communication from the Commission on the application of the Community competition rules to vertical restraints: Follow Up to the Green Paper on Vertical Restraints available at http://europa.eu.int/comm/competition/antitrust/com1998544_en.pdf, but note Article 4(b).

19. Frankel and McLay, *Intellectual Property in New Zealand* at 75.

20. Barfield and Groombridge, 'The Economic Case for Copyright Owner Control over Parallel Imports' (October 1998) 6 (1) *The Journal of World Intellectual Property* 32, in IPCR Report, above note 6 at 51.

21. Ibid. at 49.
22. See J. S. Chard and C. Mellor, 'Intellectual Property Rights and Parallel Imports' (1989) 12(1) *World Economy* 69 esp. 76–80; discussed in Rothnie, above note 6 at 571–8 and the more recent consideration in an EU context by National Economic Research Associates, *The Economic Consequences of the Choice of Regime of Exhaustion in the Field of Trade Marks* (8 February 1999) available at http://europa.eu.int/comm/internal_market/en/indprop/tm/summary.pdf.
23. IPCR Report, above note 6 at 62.
24. Ibid. at 61.
25. Ibid. at 62.
26. Ibid. at 63.
27. Ibid. at 65.
28. Ibid. at 62.
29. Ibid. at 73.
30. Ibid. at 60.
31. See N. Goss, 'Trade Mark Exhaustion: The UK Perspective' (2001) 23(5) *European Intellectual Property Review* 224, 228.
32. See e.g. *Colgate-Palmolive Limited* v. *Markwell Finance Limited* [1989] RPC 497 (CA).
33. Chapter 63.
34. G. Wei, 'Parallel Imports and the Law of Copyright in Singapore' (1992) 14(4) *European Intellectual Property Review* 139, 143.
35. Cited in *Highway Video Pte Ltd* v. *Public Prosecutor (Lim Tai Wah) And Other Appeals* [2002] 1 SLR 129 at 141.
36. Wei, 'Parallel Imports and the Law of Copyright in Singapore' at 140.
37. Ibid. at 143.
38. [1989] 1 MLJ 201; [1988] 1 SLR 930.
39. [1988] 1 SLR 930, 937.
40. Discussed in *Public Prosecutor* v. *Teoh Ai Nee* [1994] 1 SLR 452.
41. [1994] 1 SLR 452.
42. Ibid. at 460.
43. (No. 14 of 1994).
44. The amendments came into force on 1 October 1994.
45. *Highway Video Pte* v. *Public Prosecutor* (Lim Tai Wah) [2002] 1 SLR 129 at 143.
46. Ibid.
47. [2002] 1 SLR 129.
48. Ibid. at 143.
49. W. L. Ng-Loy, 'Exhaustion of Rights in Trade Mark Law: The English and Singapore Models Compared' (2000) 22(7) *European Intellectual Property Review* 320.
50. Ibid. at 327.
51. Ibid. at 323.

52. Ibid. at 326.

53. Ibid.

54. Ibid.

55. [1999] 1 SLR 179.

56. Ibid. at 185. See also *Imperial Tobacco* v. *Bonnan* (1924) 41 R.P.C. 441 (Privy Council), where it was held that it was not passing off to import genuine 'Gold Flake' cigarettes into India as the public regarded the goods as coming from the foreign producer and not the local distributor. See also *Colgate Palmolive* v. *Markwell* [1988] R.P.C. 283 (CA) where it was held that there was passing off because the use of the trade mark misrepresented to consumers that the imported toothpaste was of the same quality as the domestic product.

57. See s. 66 Patent Act.

58. 17 U.S.C. s. 109(a).

59. 17 U.S.C. s. 602(a).

60. 523 U.S. 135; 118 S. Ct. 1125 (1998).

61. 38 F.3d 477 (9th Cir. 1994).

62. Ibid. at 482.

63. *Ligo Corp* v. *Topix Inc.*, (unreported) S.D.N.Y. 2003 (31 January 2003).

64. Paul Goldstein, *International Copyright*, (New York: Oxford University Press, 2001), 308; Nimmer and Nimmer, *Nimmer on Copyright*, §8.12[B][6][c], 8-178.3 (Matthew Bender, Release 57-4/02). Nimmer's analysis identifies passages in the leading opinion in *Quality King* which appear to favour parallel importing and other passages which appear to favour banning parallel importing.

65. T. Lewin, 'Students find $100 Textbooks cost $50, Purchased Overseas,' *New York Times*, 21 October 2003, available at http://www.nytimes.com/2003/10/21/education/21BOOK.html.

66. 15 U.S.C. s. 1114(1).

67. 15 U.S.C. s. 1125.

68. 15 U.S.C. s. 1124.

69. 19 U.S.C. s. 1526. See also s. 337(a)(1)(c) which prohibits the importation into the United States, the sale for importation, or the sale within the United States after importation by the owner, importer, or consignee, of articles that infringe a valid and enforceable United States trademark registered under the Trademark Act of 1946 (19 U.S.C. s. 1337).

70. 260 U.S. 689, 43 S.Ct 244, 67 L.Ed. 464 (1923).

71. See for example *NEC Electronics* v. *CAL Circuit Abco*, 810 F.2d 1506, 1 U.S.P.Q.2d 2056 (9th Cir. 1987); *Weil Ceramics & Glass Inc.* v. *Dash*, 878 F.2d 659, 11 U.S.P.Q.2d 1001 (3d Cir. 1989); *Sebastian Int'l Inc.* v. *Longs Drug Stores* Corp., 53 F.3d 1073, 34 U.S.P.Q.2d 1720 (9th Cir. 1995); *Matrix Essentials* v. *Emporium Drug Mart*, 988 F.2d 587, 26 U.S.P.Q.2d 1532 (5th Cir. 1993); *R. J. Reynolds Tobacco Co.* v. *Premium Tobacco Stores Inc.*, 1999 WL 495145, 21 ITRD 2031, 52 U.S.P.Q.2d 1052.

72. 108 S.Ct. 1811.

73. Ibid. at 1819.

74. For Lanham Act proceedings, see e.g. *Lever Bros Co* v. *United States* 877 F 2d 101 (D.C. Cir. 1989).

75. See for example *Societe Des Produits Nestle* v. *Casa Helvetia Inc.*, 982 F.2d 633, 25 U.S.P.Q.2d 1256 (1st Cir. 1992) and *Lever Brothers Co.* v. *United States*, 981 F.2d 1330, 25 U.S.P.Q.2d 1579 (D.C.Cir. 1993).

76. *Original Appalachian Artworks Inc* v. *Granada Electronics Inc.*, 816 F. 2d 68 (2nd Cir 1987).

77. *Martin's Herend Imports Inc* v. *Diamond & Gem Trading USA Co.*, 112 F.3d 1296.

78. *Ferrero USA Inc.* v. *Ozak Trading Inc.*, 19 U.S.P.Q. 2d 1468 C.A.3. For further examples, see T. McCarthy, *McCarthy on Trademarks and Unfair Competition* (4th edn) at 29.51.2.

79. See *Gamut Trading Company* v. *United States International Trade Commission* 200 F. 3d 775. For a detailed discussion of the US case law, see Rothnie, above note 6 at 97–101.

80. 35 U.S.C. s. 271(a) (2003).

81. Rothnie, above note 6 at 143.

82. 133 U.S. 697.

83. See 133 U.S. at 702–3, 10 S.Ct. 378.

84. Ibid. at 379–80, 10 S.Ct. 378.

85. Ibid. at 380, 10 S.Ct. 378. For a similar result under early European Court of Justice decisions, see C-19/84 *Pharmon* v. *Hoechst* [1985] ECR 2281.

86. See *Dickerson* v. *Matheson*, 57 F. 524 (2d Cir. 1893); *Curtiss Aeroplane & Motor Corp.* v. *United Aircraft Engineering Corp.*, 266 F. 71, 78 (2d Cir. 1920); *Sanofi, SA* v. *MedTech Veterinarian Products Inc.*, 565 F.Supp. 931 (D.N.J. 1983). See also *Dickerson* v. *Tinling*, 84 F. 192 (8th Cir. 1897) (dictum); *Kabushiki Kaisha Hattori Seiko* v. *Refac Tech. Devel. Corp.*, 690 F.Supp. 1339, 1342 (S.D.N.Y. 1988) (dictum); *PCI Parfums et Consmetiques Int'l* v. *Perfumania Inc.*, No. 93 Civ. 9009 (KMW), 35 U.S.P.Q.2d 1159, 1160, 1995 WL 121298, at 1 (S.D.N.Y. 1995).

87. *Jazz Photo Corp.* v. *ITC*, 264 F.3d 1094. But see Donald S. Chisum, *Chisum on Patents*, §16.03[2][a][iv] and §16.05[3][a][ii] Lexis Nexis, 2003 Cumulative Supplement (Rel 89-v5). See also F. M. Abbott, 'Jazz Photo Summary' at http://lists.essential.org/pipermail/ip-health/2002-June/003089.html.

88. Ibid. at 1106. Jazz sought a stay of the Federal Circuit's ruling, rehearing *en banc*, and certiorari to the Supreme Court on the exhaustion issue. In its various petitions, Jazz argued that the Federal Circuit improperly changed the law and that foreign exhaustion should remain viable if the patented article is sold by the holder of a licence in both the United States and the foreign country. Jazz's petitions were denied.

89. Cornish and Llewelyn, *Intellectual Property: Patents, Copyright, Trade Marks and Allied Rights* (Sweet & Maxwell, 2003) 41.
90. Ibid. at 48.
91. See Articles 30, 36, and 222 of the European Economic Community Treaty; see also Cornish and Llewellyn, *Intellectual Property* at 48.
92. See article 7 of the Trade Mark Directive, Directive 89/104/EEC.
93. Joined cases C267/95 and C268/95 *Merck* v. *Primecrown* and *Beecham* v. *Europhram* [1997] 1 C.M.L.R. 83; Community Patent Convention Articles 28 and 76 (not yet in force).
94. Software Dir. 91/250, Article 4(c); Rental Lending and Related Rights Dir. 92/100, Article 9(2) and note Article 1(4); Cornish and Llewellyn, *Intellectual Property* at 435–6.
95. *Keurkoop* v. *Nancy Kean Gifts* [1982] ECR 2853.
96. *Silhouette International* v. *Hartlauer* [1999] F.S.R. 729; *Sebago Inc* v. *GB Unic SA* (C173/98) [2000] R.P.C. 63; cf. *Zino Davidoff SA* v. *A&G; Imports Ltd* [1999] R.P.C. 631. For a detailed commentary on this case, see T. Heide, 'Trade marks and Competition Law After Davidoff' (2003) 25(4) *European Intellectual Property Review* 163–8 and see Cornish and Llewellyn, *Intellectual Property* at 48–50. The ECJ has recently confirmed that the marketing of copyright material outside the EEA by or with the consent of the copyright owner does *not* exhaust the distribution right provided by Article 4(2) of Directive 2001/29 on the harmonisation of certain aspects of copyright and related rights in the information society: Case C-479/04, *Laserksiken ApS* v. *Kulturministiriet* (Grand Chamber 12 September 2006).
97. See also Article 7 of the Trade Mark Directive, Directive 89/104/EEC.
98. See Cornish and Llewellyn, *Intellectual Property* at 731, 746–7.
99. [1978] E.C.R. 1139. Note that the ECJ refused to upset this decision in *Bristol-Myers Squibb* v. *Paranova* [1996] F.S.R. 225.
100. Ibid. at 14.
101. *Bristol-Myers Squibb* v. *Paranova* [1996] F.S.R. 225. Discussed in Cornish and Llewellyn, *Intellectual Property* at 746–7.
102. Computer Software Directive, Article 4(c) Directive 91/250 of 14 May 1991, [1991] O.J. L122/42. The Database Directive, Directive 96/9 of 11 March 1996, [1996] O.J. L77/20, Recitals 33 and 34 and Articles 5(c) and 7.2(b) and Copyright Directive, Directive 2001/29 of 22 May 2001, [2001] O.J. L167/1, Recitals 28 and 4.
103. (C414/99) [2002] Ch. 109 (ECJ).
104. For a detailed commentary on this case, see Heide, 'Trade marks and Competition Law After Davidoff'.
105. See EC Report note 6 above.
106. Ibid. at 17–18.
107. C. Strothers, 'Political Exhaustion: The European Commission's Working Paper on Possible Abuses of Trade Mark Rights within the EU in the Context of

Community Exhaustion' (2003) 25(1) *European Intellectual Property Review* 457, 461.

108. K. Tee, 'The 1990 Amendments to the Malaysian Copyright Act 1987' (1991) 13(4) *European Intellectual Property Reivew* 132, 136.

109. I. Azmi, 'Pharmaceutical Patents in Malaysia' [2002] 2 *Malayan Law Journal Articles* 1 at 22.

110. (1989) 15 IPR 677; [1989] FSR 407 (HC, Kuala Lumpur) discussed in Rothnie, above note 6 at 139–142.

111. Ibid. at 140.

112. Discussed in Azmi, *Pharmaceutical Patents in Malaysia* at 23.

113. *Parker* case, Osaka District Court, decision of 27 February 1971, 2–1 Mutaishu 71.

114. For further discussion of this case and other Japanese parallel importing decisions, see C. Heath, 'From *Parker* to *BBS* – The Treatment of Parallel Imports in Japan' (1993) 24 *International Review of Industrial Property and Copyright* (IIC) 179–89.

115. Unreported, H-7 (o) No. 1988 dated 1 July 1997 Supreme Court of Japan.

116. Tessensohn and Yamamoto, 'The Big Aluminium Wheel Dust Up – International Exhaustion of Rights in Japan' 228, 231.

117. Chapter 528.

118. Hong Kong Intellectual Property Department website, available at http://www.info.gov.hk/ipd/eng/faq/copyrights/cpr_general.htm.

119. Hong Kong Intellectual Property Department website, available at http://www.info.gov.hk/ipd/eng/faq/copyrights/cpr_amend.htm.

120. Ibid.

121. Chapter 559.

122. Josephberg, Lange et al., 'Korean Trade Commission Rules against Parallel Imports' (2003) 15(2) *Intellectual Property & Technology Law Journal*, 21(2).

123. Ibid.

124. D. Choi, *Report on International Exhaustion for Industrial Property Rights for the International Association for the Protection of Intellectual Property*, available at http://www.aippi.org/reports/q156/gr-q156-Rep.%20of%20Korea-e.htm.

125. Ss. 37 and 102 Copyright Act 1968.

126. Copyright Act 1968 sections 44A and 112A introduced by the Copyright Amendment Act 1991.

127. Copyright Act 1968 sections 44D and 112D introduced by the Copyright Amendment Act (No. 2) 1998 and extended by Copyright Amendment (Parallel Importation) Act 2003.

128. Copyright Act 1968 section 44E introduced by the Copyright Amendment (Parallel Importation) Act 2003.

129. Copyright Act 1968 sections 44F and 112DA introduced by the Copyright Amendment (Parallel Importation) Act 2003.

130. Copyright Act 1968 ss. 44C and 112C introduced by the Copyright Amendment Act (No 1) 1998 and extended by the Copyright Amendment (Parallel Importation) Act 2003.
131. Explanatory Memorandum to the Copyright Amendment (Parallel Importation) Bill 2001.
132. Trade Marks Act 1995 (Cth) s. 123(1).
133. The question was not resolved in *Transport Tyres* v. *Montana Tyres, Rims & Tubes Ltd* (1999) 43 IPR 481 (Full FC) as the imports took place before the rights were assigned to the local distributor.
134. Copyright Act 1968 (Cth) s. 198A.
135. Unlike the situation under the Trade Marks Act 1994 s. 132(b), which never came into operation.
136. For example, Trade Practices Act 1974 (Cth) s. 52 (prohibiting misleading or deceptive conduct in trade or commerce).
137. *Betts* v. *Wilmott* (1879) LR 6 Ch App 239.
138. *National Phonograph Co of Australia Ltd* v. *Menck* [1911] AC 336; 12 CLR 15 (JC).
139. *Société Anonyme des Manufactures de Glaces* v. *Tilghman* (1883) 25 Ch D 1 (CA).
140. Copyright Act (1994) ss. 35 and 12(3).
141. See Frankel and McLay, above note 16 at 85.
142. Ibid. at 79.
143. Report on the implementation of the Software Directive, COM(2000) 1999, 10 April 2000, 17.
144. E. Tai, 'Exhaustion and Online Delivery of Digital Works' (2003) 25(5) *European Intellectual Property Review* 207, 208.
145. Ibid.
146. Ibid.
147. Ibid., where the arguments are summarised by Tai.
148. Ibid. at 209a.
149. H. Skoko, 'Theory and Practice of Parallel Imports' available at http://athene.mit.csu.edu.au/~hskoko/parallel%20imports/pimppaper.pdf.
150. See X. Yuan, 'Research on Trade Mark Parallel Imports in China' (2003) 25(5) *European Intellectual Property Review* 224.
151. See *Nimmer on Copyright* note 64 above.

Technology transfer

ROHAN KARIYAWASAM

I. Introduction

The institution that most changes our lives we least understand, or more correctly, seek most elaborately to misunderstand. That is the modern corporation.

John Kenneth Galbraith, *The Age of Uncertainty* (1977)

There is no doubt that since World War II, licences and other forms of technology transfer agreements have fulfilled technological needs that could not be met by local technical and scientific capabilities. Currently, the Asia–Pacific region, including Singapore, is one of the most important acquirers of foreign technologies through contractual channels in the developed world. The aim of this chapter is to look at the competition implications faced by producers in developing and newly developed economies in licensing-in technology or through some form of foreign direct investment (FDI) from the developed world or other parts of the global economy with the aim of stimulating domestic production or with the aim of using as inputs into local manufacturing process, and creating new outputs for export. FDI is moving into services, but its relationship with technology transfer, particularly in developing countries, has always been complex.[1] As a recent United Nations Conference on Trade and Development (UNCTAD) report stressed: 'As commercial enterprises, transnational companies (TNCs)[2] in principle do not have an interest in transferring knowledge to and supporting innovation in foreign affiliates beyond what is needed for the production process or product in question. Developing countries therefore cannot expect that, by simply opening their doors to FDI, TNCs will transform their technological base.'[3]

This chapter will discuss FDI and technology transfer, but its main thrust will be to consider the available regulatory mechanisms that can increase the bargaining power of local producers when negotiating for technology transfer as well as discussing in outline some provisions on technology transfer that can be found in international investment agreements/bilateral trade agreements, and in World Trade Organisation (WTO) covered agreements, particularly the Agreement on Trade Related Aspects of Intellectual Property ('TRIPS Agreement'). The concept underlying the thematic discussion is that the market for technology is imperfect, and that the small medium size enterprises (SMEs) in developing countries are in a disadvantageous position vis-à-vis suppliers often located in the developed world, although this position is fast changing as regards some countries, such as Singapore, China (including Hong Kong), and India, as described in the recent UNCTAD World Investment Report 2004.[4] However, the position for many developing and least developing countries (DCs and LDCs) remains the same.

Much discussion on technology transfer has tended to focus on the transfer process itself, but not so much on the host policy environment to facilitate absorption and spillover of technology,[5] once transferred. For such countries, how then can the technology transfer package be drafted to improve the recipients' position and therefore the conditions under which technology is to be transferred? What relevance do movements, such as the free and open-source software (FOSS) movement, have for developing countries as regards technology transfer? What relevance does the recent (Geneva 2003) and upcoming talks (Tunis 2005) at the World Summit on the Information Society (WSIS) have for technology transfer to developing countries? This chapter discusses these issues and concludes with a number of forward-looking recommendations.

II. The position of developing countries

'Technology transfer has been, and will continue to be, one of the main mechanisms through which developing countries may advance in their industrialisation processes.'[6] Correa's point is well understood and documented in various forms in a large body of existing literature on technology transfer and developing countries.[7] In many ways, technology encapsulates both theoretical and empirical techniques. Although technology can be envisaged as a material good in the form of machines and products in tangible form, the concept also covers intangibles in the form of services and know-how. More than anything in the conventional package associated with technology transfer,[8] it is the intangible component often referred to as 'know-how' that is crucial for the creation of a technological base. However, what does technology transfer actually mean in a strict legal sense?

The UNCTAD draft International Code on the Transfer of Technology in its definition of 'technology transfer', describes technology as 'systematic knowledge for the manufacture of a product, for the application of a process or for the rendering of a service, which does not extend to the transactions involving the mere sale or mere lease of goods'.[9] The definition therefore excludes goods for hire or sale, but seems to refer specifically to the knowledge that goes into the creation and provision of a product or service (and not the finished product or service).[10] The United Nations' own definition of the different components that constitute technology transfer can be summarised as four key aspects to technology transfer: 'technoware', or the physical objects or equipment; 'humanware', which includes skills and human aspects of technology management and learning; 'infoware', including designs and blueprints which constitute the document-embodied knowledge on information and technology; and 'orgaware', which covers production arrangement linkages within which the technology is operated.[11] The UN definition may appear imprecise for the purposes of defining technology transfer within legal documentation, but it nevertheless gives a good snapshot as to what technology transfer should encapsulate.[12] Developing countries are also concerned that too narrow a definition of technology transfer would exclude the relevant factors and processes that hinder their access to technology and that any definition should be 'inclusive and *inter alia* comprise the processes and factors relating to the access and use of technology'.[13] For example, access to information communications technology will be crucial in implementing the goals set out in the Declaration and Action Plan agreed at the WSIS in Geneva 2003, discussed later in this chapter at section IV.[14]

The way in which developing countries acquire technology transfer can also be summarised in three main categories: (1) acquisition of skills and know-how; (2) access to document-embodied knowledge and licensing; and (3) acquisition by importation and business partnerships.[15] The bulk of this chapter is devoted to discussing the third of these categories, although (1) and (2) are covered in brief initially.

A. Acquisition of skills and know-how

The UNCTAD World Investment Report 2004 has highlighted the shift in FDI towards the services sector.[16] Trade in services, particularly through commercial presence, can serve as a means of affecting technology transfer, for example in creating a subsidiary or joint venture in the host country to provide a service either in relation to own production or to introduce a new service or compete with existing services in the local market, and/or linked to a licensing contract.[17] Multinational corporations (MNCs) in the services sector can bring both hard technology (plant, equipment, industrial processes), and soft technology (knowledge information, expertise, skills in organisation, management, and marketing).[18] MNCs which also outsource/offshore (discussed below) part of their production to DCs or LDCs will want to ensure the quality of the outputs provided by subcontractors and may transfer part of their knowledge and methods together with specifications, designs, and drawing, although this will depend on the likelihood of enforcing confidentiality provisions, and also to the effective enforcement of intellectual property rights (IPRs) in the host country.[19] IPR protection is important: in a recent World Bank report, Smarzynska argues that empirical analysis confirms the hypothesis that weak protection of IPRs has a significant impact on the composition of FDI inflows for two reasons: (a) it deters foreign investors in five technology-intensive sectors: drugs, cosmetics and health care products, chemicals, machinery and equipment, and electrical equipment; and (b) it encourages foreign investors to set up distribution facilities rather than engage in local production.[20]

Offshoring of services can either be internally through the establishment of foreign affiliates (sometimes called 'captive offshoring'); or by outsourcing to a third party service provider ('offshore outsourcing'). For reasons mentioned above, MNCs will often prefer the captive approach so as to maintain control and confidentiality. The effect of this on technology transfer is uncertain. UNCTAD states that although some evidence exists that services FDI does provide transfer of skills, expertise, and knowledge, it does acknowledge that data on the overall extent of such transfers are scarce.[21] Nevertheless, developing countries stand to gain from the international outsourcing market. In 2001, Ireland, India, Canada, and Israel in that order, accounted for 70 per cent of the total market for offshored services, mostly in software development and other IT-enabled services.[22] Furthermore, the share of developing countries in offshored projects is increasing: Between 2002 and 2003, the total number of offshored projects in developing countries rose from 39 to 52 per cent. South and Southeast Asian developing countries have taken the lion's share of service offshoring projects, particularly in the area of IT.[23]

Although we see growth of selected offshored services to a small group of DCs, particularly in IT services, there is a danger that this trend could be jeopardised if for any reason developed countries were at some stage to introduce tariff peaks on imports of technology-related products. Tariff peaks apply mainly to goods and not services, and the application of tariff peaks to electronic products is uncertain. In future years, much will depend on whether electronic products (electronic intangibles) are classed as services under the General Agreement on Trade in Services (GATS) or as goods under the General Agreement on Tariffs and Trade (GATT).[24] In recent years, this issue has been a bone of contention between the US, which would prefer a GATT classification, and the European Communities, which would prefer a classification under the GATS.[25] If electronic products were to be classed as goods, then the very success that certain developing countries such as India, Singapore, Taiwan, China (including the Special Economic Zone of Hong Kong) have had in exporting such goods could be endangered by the imposition of tariff peaks on certain product lines classed as 'sensitive' by importing countries, particularly the Quad countries of Canada, the EU, Japan, and the US. This danger is not illusory as the Quad has a history of applying tariff

peaks to products that are of export interest to developing countries, particularly in the area of agricultural staple food products: such as sugar, cereals
and fish; tobacco and certain alcoholic beverages; fruits and vegetables; food
industry products with a high sugar content; clothing and footwear.[26] At one
stage, around 1,077 tariff lines out of a total of 5,032 at the 6 digit level of the
Harmonized System faced a Most-Favoured-Nation (MFN) tariff of more
than 15 per cent in at least one member of the Quad. Tariff rates could be as
high as 343 per cent in Canada, 252 in the EU, 171 in Japan and 121 in the
United States.[27] Tariff peaks already create strong disincentives for DCs and
LDCs in moving towards processing raw materials and agricultural commodities and higher value added manufacturing products. They reduce the gains
from trade, hinder efforts to technologically upgrade, and restrict a country's
financial capacity to import technology.[28] If applied to electronic products,
say as an indirect consequence of the WTO membership at some future stage
agreeing to classify electronic products as goods rather than services,[29] then
the gains already made by certain DCs in the IT sector could in time be
severely curtailed.[30]

B. Access to document-embodied knowledge

One of the main problems that DCs and LDCs have is in easily identifying the
particular innovations they need amongst the myriad information sources
that are available, and particularly with information available on the Internet.
For example in the area of patents, with countries that have a patent system in
place, information on technology will generally be available from the patent
database (if available), which will hold details of a description of the patent,
a list of claims, the drawings, and an abstract of the names and contact details
of the rights holders. So for firms wishing to acquire the technology covered
by the patent, the firm can contact the patent holder with a view to seeking
a licence, or may try to imitate the patent if the innovation has already entered
the public domain. Article 7 of the TRIPS Agreement calls for the protection
and enforcement of intellectual property rights, but it also addresses 'the
promotion of technological innovation and the transfer and dissemination of
technology, to the mutual advantage of producers and users of technological
knowledge'. In an ideal world, an effective patent system will allow for the
dissemination of technology as set out in Article 7. However, disclosure of
patent information alone does not permit developing countries with weak
technological capabilities to innovate around existing patents.[31]

Furthermore in negotiating the licence(s) for the technology transfer
package, developing country producers will often be at a disadvantage in
terms of bargaining position. Local producers will want to negotiate licence
clauses that are not restrictive and that allow the licensee some flexibility.
MNCs however may try to abuse their position of market influence or

dominance in negotiating technology transfer clauses that are unfair. Articles 8.2 and 40 of the TRIPS Agreement attempt to redress this imbalance, provided such provisions have been enacted into local law. For example, Article 8.2 of the TRIPS Agreement allows for measures to prevent the abuse of intellectual property rights by right holders or their resorting to practices which unreasonably restrain trade or adversely affect the international transfer of technology. Similarly, Article 40 of the TRIPS Agreement allows for members to adopt appropriate measures into national law to prevent or control such abusive practices, which may include, for example, exclusive grantback conditions, conditions preventing challenges to validity, and coercive package licensing.[32]

C. Acquisition by importation and business partnerships

Although licensing, as introduced above, is an important element of technology transfer, the importation of machines and intermediate goods is also one of the primary sources of technology transfer by DCs and LDCs. Innovation is appropriated through imports allowing firms to bypass the need for long-term investment in research or equipment-testing capabilities. However, there are dangers in this approach, for example when used machinery and equipment is not formally exported by manufacturers and therefore not accompanied with the relevant know-how or unpatented information required to operate the machine, or where the imported technology is just not 'up for the job'. Mytelka cites the example of DCs and LDCs attempting to diversify exports by developing their fishing industries, and importing used refrigerator trucks whose compressors no longer work, to transport fish. Clearly this has important implications for sanitary and phytosanitary standards.[33] Notwithstanding the provisions of Article 10 of the WTO Agreement on the Application of Sanitary and Phytosanitary Measures, which provides special and differential treatment to DCs and LDCs (particularly longer time frames for compliance with sanitary and phytosanitary standards on products of interest to DCs so as to maintain opportunities for their exports), DCs without access to the appropriate technology will fall foul of Article 5 of the same agreement, which lays out for WTO members provisions for the assessment of risk and determination of the appropriate level of sanitary or phytosanitary protection.

WTO provisions also allow DCs and LDCs to seek reductions in tariffs and the removal of unjustified non-tariff barriers, to obtain access to technological goods by DC and LDC producers, in particular, the acquisition of environmentally sound technologies (ESTs) and pollution control and measurement equipment. For example paragraph 31(iii) of the Doha Ministerial Declaration deals with the elimination of/reduction of tariff and non-tariff barriers to environmental goods and services.[34] The transfer of environmentally sound technologies is addressed in Chapter 34 of Agenda 21,[35] the Action Plan of the World Summit on Sustainable Development, to which all WTO members have committed themselves, as well as in several multilateral environmental agreements, where members have adopted obligations to phase out the use of certain substances or technologies.[36] However, although Chapter 34 of Agenda 21 recognises the need for favourable access and transfer of ESTs to DCs and LDCs, little has been done to implement them.[37] The TRIPS Agreement has reinforced the power of private parties to control the use and eventual transfer of ESTs, allowing for private parties to retain their technologies under patent or protection of 'undisclosed information', or set high royalties for access.[38] Correa cites the example of access by the Indian government to chlorofluorocarbons (CFCs) technology. The Indian government tried to access HFC 134 A, recognised as the best replacement for certain CFCs, but because the technology was covered by patents and trade secrets, the companies that possessed them were unwilling to transfer the technology without majority control over the ownership of the Indian company that would take receipt.[39]

Besides importation, business partnerships are also a major source of technology transfer including FDI, Build Operate Transfer (BOT) agreements, subcontracting, licensing and franchising. There has been much discussion of FDI in recent years. For example, the UNCTAD World Investment Report 2004 focuses on the shift to services in world trade and the role that FDI will play in that shift. According to the 2004 report, although global inflows of FDI declined in 2003 for the third year in a row, the prospects for FDI look to improve, particularly in Asia, and to developing countries, which experienced a growth of 9 per cent in 2003 rising to $172 billion overall.[40] In terms of law, there were 244 changes in laws and regulations affecting FDI in 2003, 220 of which further liberalisation.[41] FDI is discussed in more detail in the next section.

1. FDI

FDI can be defined as the act of establishing or acquiring a foreign subsidiary (foreign affiliate) over which the investing firm (parent) has substantial management control.[42] Firms that engage in FDI operate in more than one country and are MNCs. Although the UNCTAD 2004 report paints a favourable picture as regards FDI in-flow into developing countries, only a select group of DCs are actually receiving this investment: The majority lose out. In the last ten years, although global FDI figures have increased by almost a factor of five, only 0.5 per cent of global FDI flows have been invested in 49 LDCs.[43] In terms of global R&D expenditure, the share of developing countries is estimated to have fallen from nearly 6 per cent in 1980 to nearly 4 per cent in the early 1990s,[44] notwithstanding substantial increases in R&D expenditure in Korea and Chinese Taipei.[45] United Nations Industrial

Development Organisation's (UNIDO) World Industrial Development Report (UNIDO 2002/2003), also highlights that upper-middle-income DCs accounted for almost 90 per cent of total enterprise financed R&D expenditures by developing countries in 1998: Korea accounted for 53 per cent, Chinese Taipei 14 per cent, Brazil 12 per cent, and China 6 per cent.[46] In the lowest ranked 30 developing countries, no such expenditure was registered.[47] Furthermore, R&D expenditure by foreign affiliates in developing countries is focused on countries such as Brazil, Mexico, Chinese Taipei, and Singapore.[48] It is anticipated that the decentralisation of R&D activity by MNCs will likely continue to be focused on a small number of DCs. For example in 2003, the top ten recipients for FDI in Asia were headed by China, Hong Kong (China), Singapore, India and the Republic of Korea, in that order.[49]

1.1 FDI-internalised/externalised transfers When examining MNC involvement in technology transfer in DCs and LDCs, there is also a need to distinguish between internalised and externalised transfers.[50] An internalised transfer takes place between a parent and its subsidiary, whereby the parent has a controlling share of the subsidiary in terms of share ownership. By contrast, an external transfer takes place between legal entities where the relationship is dictated by contract including joint venture, licensing, technical cooperation agreements etc. In choosing between internalised and externalised transfers, the MNC will often balance issues that apply to rent-extracting potential and the transaction costs of the transfer with host country characteristics and regulatory policies.[51] Internalised modes of transfer of technology tend to dominate with relatively novel technologies that are subject to quick change, such as information communications technologies (ICTs), whereas externalised modes of transfer are preferred in the case of more mature, standardised technologies.[52] The absorption factor of a host country to absorb the transfer of technology is also a determining issue in choosing between an external and internal transfer. So where there is a limitation on technological capability, an internalised transfer will often be preferred. Also host country regulatory policies, particularly the IPR regime, will have a direct bearing on mode of transfer. Thus, while Singapore has traditionally been mentioned as an example of an 'internalisation-oriented' approach that tends to rely on the acquisition of foreign technology through FDI, Korea's approach has been through licensing and the import of capital goods in order to facilitate the development of domestic technological capability and to minimise foreign ownership of domestic assets.[53] Likewise, Japan is often cited as an example of a country that has been able to restrict foreign investment but still obtain the technology required for industrialisation through a predetermined policy of licensing.[54] Japan was able to 'unbundle' the technology transfer package, extracting the rights that were most suitable.[55]

Singapore's fast developing regulatory regime and the soon to be introduced amendments to IPR, competition, and copyright legislation could
continue to encourage more internal transfers into Singaporean foreign
affiliates, as MNCs use Singapore as a hub for the re-export of technology
into the Asia–Pacific region. For example, the UNCTAD World Investment
Report 2004, lists Singapore as top of the table in terms of FDI outflow as a
percentage of gross-fixed capital formation.[56] This perhaps continues a general trend which shows that internalised transfers of technology by MNCs
have recently gained in significance relative to externalised transfers.[57] Since
the mid-1980s royalties and technology fees received by MNCs in the US,
Germany and the UK from their foreign affiliates represent an increasing
share of the total technology payments received by MNCs.[58] In a recent study,
Borga and Zeile find that during the period 1996–9, exports of intermediate
inputs by US parents to their foreign affiliates increased forty-fold, and the
share of intra-firm exports of intermediate products in US total merchandise exports increased from 8.5 to 14.7 per cent during the same period.[59]
Similarly, FDI in China rose tenfold between 1990 and 1995, and Malaysia,
Indonesia and Thailand have also received rising inward FDI flows.[60] In the
1990s, Thailand's investment abroad rose sharply and Singapore became a
significant supplier of FDI itself.

The internalisation approach through FDI, may however, be limiting in
terms of diffusion of know-how into the local domestic market. In a recent
WTO paper, the WTO Working Group on Trade and Investment (WGTI)
argue that 'while FDI may be efficient in respect of the transfer of operational
technology, its contribution to a process of deepening of local innovative
capabilities tends to be limited'.[61] Maskus also makes the point that if the
links to other economic sectors are weak, FDI may operate in enclaves with
limited spillovers[62] into technologies adopted and wages earned by local firms
and workers.[63] In an enclave situation where neither products nor technologies
have much in common with local firms, there may be little scope for learning
and spillovers may not materialise.[64] From this perspective, the disadvantage
of internalised transfers of technology resides in the fact that the transfer of
operational 'know-how' often is not accompanied by a transfer of 'know-why'
and that the transferred technology may be suited to a country's static endowments but not to its dynamic endowments.[65] The WGTI goes on to argue that
externalised transfer of technology may provide for greater scope in upgrading
local technological capability on condition that the local market is able to
absorb such know-how, for example in having the requisite domestic skills
and a competitive environment that facilitates technological learning.[66]
Furthermore, local markets that have the technological capability of using
foreign technology but find that they are unable to 'unbundle' the package of
assets transferred by way of internal transfer, will incur greater costs in acquiring technology than by way of externalised transfer.[67]

By contrast, Moran argues that FDI involving internalised transfers is the best way forward. He argues that 'domestic content, joint venture, and technology-sharing requirements create inefficiencies that slow growth, and generate, in many cases, a negative net contribution to host country welfare (especially if they are backed by trade protection or other kinds of market exclusivity)'.[68] MNCs often prefer FDI by way of direct investment and internal transfers to licensing. The preference for FDI is increased when the newest and most profitable technologies (or closest to the MNC's actual line of business) are to be exploited.

1.2 FDI-horizontal/vertical   Two types of FDI generally apply, horizontal and vertical. Horizontal FDI involves the subsidiary producing products or services similar to those produced at home by the parent, whereas vertical FDI involves the subsidiary producing inputs or assembling from components.[69] For example, the construction of vertically integrated networks, sometimes known as 'production fragmentation', 'delocalisation', or 'outsourcing' is the most significant recent trend in vertical FDI.

If the technology is transferred by way of FDI (whether horizontal or vertical), it is unlikely to be licensed to domestic competitors in the host market, which will often mean that the only way that local competitors will be able to gain access to the technology (particularly IT) will be in reverse engineering (and this will depend on the skills available: with software, decompilation and disassembly, the technical procedures for reverse engineering, is a timely and expensive business)[70] or by hiring MNC employees with specialist skills or by some other form of spillover (see p. 477 below). In high technology markets where database and object/source code acts as the technological platform, a provision for reverse engineering built into the regulatory framework is crucial for both competition and innovation. Although such a provision has been the subject of heated debate, several jurisdictions allow for it: in the US for example, in *NEC Corp.* v. *Intel Corp.*, the court did not condemn the disassembling of an Intel microcode for the purpose of researching and developing a competitive microcode program.[71] The European Council Directive 91/250 on the Legal Protection of Computer Programs allows for reverse engineering if it is intended to achieve 'interoperability' with the evaluated program.[72] The US Digital Millennium Copyright Act (DMCA) allows for a similar provision.[73] In Asia, at the time of writing, the government of Singapore has just completed a public consultation on a new Copyright (Amendment) Bill 2004,[74] which, if introduced in full, will adopt new measures on anti-circumvention that will attract both civil and criminal liability if breached. The Bill also provides for new exceptions relating to decompilation, restricted for purposes of research into interoperability, observing, studying and the testing of computer programs.[75]

In the field of high technology, communications or similar network-based industries characterised by vertical integration, industry characteristics that

will signal high barriers to entry, high concentration, and possible inefficiency that follows from low levels of local competition will include scale
economies, high initial capital requirements, intensive advertising, and
advanced technology, the kind of market characteristics that suit MNCs. By
contrast, entry by domestic firms in potential host countries into markets
characterised by such indicators is likely to be difficult. The entry of MNCs by
way of FDI (internalised transfers through foreign affiliates) into local markets characterised in this way (for example monopolistic or oligopolistic
markets) can result in two outcomes: (a) either increase the level of competition forcing local firms to become more efficient, or (b) force the least
efficient firms out of business. The fear is that MNCs could outcompete all
local firms and establish positions of market influence or dominance greater
than the historical position of the local firms, and go on to repatriate profits
and avoid taxation through transfer pricing.[76] As Gurak argues, 'foreign
investors enjoy monopolistic/oligopolistic advantages in the host country
over the quantity/quality of production, distribution, source of inputs and
finance, prices, quantity/type of exports, and the method of production.
These monopolistic/oligopolistic advantages may cause serious adverse
effects on the economy of recipient countries, such as imbalance of payments,
"non-transfer" of technology, deterioration of income distribution or the
introduction of inappropriate (luxury) products.'[77]

Lall[78] argues that MNCs could escalate the natural concentration process
in DCs, or that the weakness of local competitors will allow MNCs to achieve
a higher degree of market dominance than in developed countries. MNCs
may buy out local firms or force them out of business, thus increasing the
barriers to entry to markets. In a WTO paper, the WGTI refers to Lall's study
of the effect of Multinational Enterprises (MNEs)[79] on concentrations in 46
Malaysian industries. In its paper, the WGTI cites Lall's conclusions that the
presence of foreign firms on balance increases concentration, and that this
was brought about by 'the MNEs' impact on general industry characteristics –
such as higher initial capital requirements, capital intensity, and advertising
intensity – and by some apparently independent effect of foreign presence,
perhaps related to "predatory" conduct, changes in technology and marketing practices, or gains of policy concessions from the government'.[80] In effect
FDI has the tendency to increase concentration in most host countries with
the added risk that MNCs could crowd out local firms more in developing
countries than developed because of their technological advantages.[81] The
UNCTAD World Investment Report 2004 also raises the issue of local firms
being crowded out by MNCs.[82]

In Europe, the European Commission (EC) together with the European
Court of Justice (ECJ) has developed a body of jurisprudence that deals with
the effect of concentrations, whether concentrative joint ventures or by way
of merger.[83] The EC has also recently introduced the revised Technology

Transfer Block Exemption (TTBE) and Guidelines to assist with its interpretation.[84] In the US, there is the Sherman and Clayton Acts. Both the US antitrust acts and the European TTBE are discussed elsewhere in this book and the author will not dwell on them here. At the multilateral level, Articles 31 and 40 TRIPS Agreement also deal with the issue of unfair competition.[85]

On the point of transfer pricing, Gurak goes on to argue that a transfer pricing mechanism can sometimes be used as a clandestine transfer of company revenues (invisible profits) from the subsidiary to the parent firm.[86] Often a transfer pricing mechanism accompanied by restrictive clauses in the technology transfer agreement obliges the foreign affiliate (subsidiary) to '(1) buy the necessary capital goods and other inputs of production from the sources, and at the prices, determined by the technology supplier (over-pricing); and/or (2) to sell the subsidiary's output to customers, and at prices, determined by the technology supplier (under-pricing)'.[87] The MNC will favour such an approach for a number of reasons including avoiding any double taxation provisions or host country taxation provisions that may exist, maximising profits in predetermined profit centres, for example where the MNC has set up a profit centre located within its regional headquarters, and overcoming host country controls and regulations on remittances (such as payment of royalties).

2. Spillover

As mentioned above, the actual diffusion of technology into the local market is as important as the technology transfer itself. Diffusion will take place by way of various types of knowledge spillover on other firms in the local market. There is also the related issue of absorption. It is one thing to create policy incentives to encourage MNCs in generating spillover, but quite another for developing country producers to use bare, documented technological information, which is dependent on the absorption capacity of the producers. DCs and LDCs with limited absorption ability are much more likely to place greater reliance on unpatented know-how to assure effective transfer. Welch in citing studies by F. Contractor indicates that: 'less developed countries place greater emphasis on organisational and production management assistance in licensing arrangements than do advanced countries'.[88] Some commentators argue that spillover effects are far more important for diffusion than the formal transfer of the technology itself.[89] Spillover has been defined in various ways by economists and lawyers alike,[90] but in the context of the WTO, spillovers generally occur 'when the entry or presence of MNC affiliates leads to productivity or efficiency benefits for the host country's local firms, and the MNCs are able to internalise the full value of these benefits'.[91]

Spillover in the host country is achieved in various ways including: (a) demonstration effects; (b) the establishment of vertical linkages between foreign investors and customers and suppliers which can transfer knowledge about quality standards, process improvements or techniques of management; (c) the movement of labour which enables employees to transfer the experience they have acquired in a foreign firm to a local firm; and (d) the impact of FDI on competition.[92] FDI is dealt with under the WTO Agreement on Trade Related Investment Measures (TRIMS), although in its current form, the TRIMS offers little attention to the quality of the FDI or its relevance to technology transfer.[93]

Mytelka is sceptical as to the benefits of FDI in generating spillover.[94] Her organisation, the United Nations University/Institute for New Technologies is conducting a number of studies on spillover in the developing world.[95] Mytelka argues that studies of technology spillover in selected developing countries show very mixed results and that the actual measurement of spillover is problematical in itself. She argues that: 'many studies of technology spillover measure this as increases in productivity that is in output per person/hour worked. But increased productivity may merely reflect a situation in which smaller local firms are driven out of the market by larger foreign firms in industries where scale economies are important. Unless we know more about the ability of smaller local firms to acquire the financing needed for expansion, we cannot attribute the change in productivity to a technology spillover but merely to the replacement of existing capacity by more capital-intensive foreign firms. Productivity increases, moreover, are not necessarily accompanied by growing competitiveness as measured by market shares in the domestic or export markets. Measuring technology spillover is thus a problem.'[96]

III. Unbundling the IPR package

The development of an IPR framework within a host country can be linked to the way in which FDI evolves within that country. For example, as vertical FDI begins to diminish, horizontal FDI takes its place. One can think of the process as a form of a cycle. By the time that horizontal FDI takes root, the host economy is often in a position to be an attractive market for the production of high quality, differentiated consumer and capital goods, due fundamentally to the achievement of higher income levels. Singapore for example has been able to achieve the transition from vertical FDI to horizontal FDI in a single generation.

With the uptake of horizontal FDI, IPRs take on increased relevance as the host country has a greater interest in developing a stronger IPR regime to deal with an expanded ability to develop new products and technologies. As mentioned earlier, the IPR package will consist of a number of intellectual property rights including licences for patents and trademarks, supply of industrial technology, technical-industrial corporation, specialised technical services, and marketing rights. The mix of the various subsidiary rights included in a technology transfer package will, however, vary from country-to-country and project-to-project. For illustrative purposes, in a study of Finnish industrial companies licensing to independent foreign licensees, the proportionate inclusion (in percentages) of the different IPRs licensed broke down as follows: (a) technical know-how (96.1); (b) patents (48); (c) trademarks (36.4); (d) marketing know-how (24.7); (e) management know-how (11.7); and (f) designs (5.2).[97]

Maskus has looked at a range of studies on the effect of IPRs on technology transfer.[98] He concluded that: 'Studies based on game theory demonstrate that, while the mode of technology transfer is affected by the level of IPRs protection, the quality of the transferred technology rises with stronger IPRs. Another theoretical study shows that technology transfer expands with stronger patents where there is competition between foreign and domestic innovators.' He also argues that where local imitation requires knowledge that is available only through the licensed use of technology, the foreign licensors often make only lower-quality technologies available. As we have seen earlier in this chapter, this is perhaps one reason why MNCs prefer an internalised approach of technology transfer through a foreign affiliate. However, strengthening the IPR regime can also have negative knock-on effects for developing nations. For example, a more effective patent system can slow technology diffusion by limiting the use of key technologies through restrictive licensing arrangements.

Developing countries who have acceded to the WTO, and have therefore accepted the TRIPS in full, will have to adopt a certain level of minimum standards in patent (and other IPR rights) protection and enforcement as set out in section 5 of the TRIPS Agreement (patents). For example, the minimum duration for a patent as set out in Article 33 of the TRIPS Agreement is a period of twenty years from the filing date. Some developing countries have argued that this term of protection is not particularly conducive for easy or quick transfer of technology.[99] In these countries, imitation will become harder as foreign patents are enforced, which will likely slow innovation, although the flip-side is that as licensees, developing country producers could also benefit from a strong patent system in that it would provide a degree of protection in the licensee's market as well as forestalling competition to some extent. A strong patent could also provide a degree of technological credibility to an inexperienced licensee.

However, MNCs can also take advantage of a stronger IPR regime to exploit their market positions by way of their IPR asset base. For example, in exploiting stronger IPRs MNCs can engage in abusive practices such as setting restrictive licensing conditions, requiring technology grantbacks, engaging in tied sales, tying-up technology fields through cross-licensing arrangements, establishing vertical controls through distribution outlets that prevent product competition, and engaging in price discrimination as well as predation against local firms.[100] Even where technology has been licensed, MNCs can impose restrictions in the licence on the export of products which are manufactured utilising the technology transferred.[101] To counterbalance such effects, developing countries need to adopt effective laws dealing with abuse of market power or anticompetitive agreements, balancing the IPR rights holders' interests with that of encouraging competition. This is no easy matter. The ECJ for example in deciding cases such as *Magill*[102] and *IMS*[103] has shown just how complex achieving the balance between effective IPR protection and competition can be. Anderman, when discussing the competition/IP interface, argues that 'many, if not most, legal systems today monitor the exercise of IPRs within the framework of their competition policies. Even though the exercise of IPRs is already extensively regulated by IPR legislation, an extra tier of regulation is added by competition law to ensure that the grant of exclusivity by IPR legislation is not misused by being incorporated into cartels and market sharing arrangements or monopolistic practices which deny access to markets.'[104]

Besides the use of competition law, developing country states can directly intervene to help redress the imbalance between the MNC and developing country producers. For example, governments could impose local content requirements (LCRs) to promote the objectives of technology transfer and also the establishment of local suppliers: as Balasubramanyam and Elliott argue 'such backward linkages between foreign firms and locally owned firms constitute one of the major benefits to host countries from FDI'.[105] The objective of putting in place LCRs would be to promote the transfer of know-how from MNCs to local firms.[106] In Latin America, the emergence of technology transfer regulations entailed a substantial change in contractual patterns for the acquisition of foreign technology, and in the transfer pricing policies conducted by MNCs.[107] Governments decided that technology transfer was not a matter for private negotiation, but that state intervention was allowed on grounds of 'public order' and 'national interest'.[108] Governments had the right to both examine technology transfer contracts and refuse their terms, demanding changes that had not been sought by the parties to the contract themselves. Correa cites a number of the objectives sought by governments in these regimes including: '(a) the improvement of the commercial conditions of agreements, particularly as to prices to be charged by the supplier; (b) the elimination of restrictive practices; and (c) the unpacking of different components included in technology transfer'.[109] Other objectives were the avoidance of importation of technology that was available locally, conditions for diffusion of technology into the local market, and the control of intra-firm operations of MNCs.

Regulatory authorities also looked quite closely at price. In fact, the reduction of prices charged for foreign technologies was one of the primary objectives for state intervention. Issues examined included: (a) the item-isation of the price, for example the identification of the price to be charged for each item included in the agreement; (b) the limitation on the use of certain forms of remuneration; and (c) the determination of the amount to be remitted (setting maximum royalty rates acceptable to the type of technology or the industrial activity of the recipient party).[110] Some countries, such as Brazil, prohibited royalty payments between parent and subsidiaries in respect of licences on patents and trademarks. The Andean Group adopted a similar approach on grounds that any transfer of technology to developing countries had no marginal cost, and therefore any price obtained from it would be a monopoly rent.[111] It is difficult to see how this could be justified, given that to create an internal accounting system in its own right between parent and subsidiary to account for royalty receipts on transfers would in itself incur a measure of transfer costs. Welch cites a study of the cost of technology transfer by US MNCs, including both transmission and absorp-tion costs, highlighting that transfer costs were on average 19 per cent of total project costs, ranging from 2 to 59 per cent.[112] This is contrary to the expectation that the marginal cost of transferring technology, once devel-oped, will be low.

Other restrictions commonly seen in technology transfer agreements include restrictions on the use of IPRs after expiry of such rights and restrictions on the use of non-patented technology after expiry of the tech-nology transfer agreement. The result of the former restriction is that it has the effect of excluding the licensee from the market with the consequent loss of any investments made by the licensee in exercising the patent, or the restriction will result in the licensee having to renegotiate a new agreement from a much weakened bargaining position. The result of the restriction on the use of non-patented technology could potentially be very wide. Often it is the unpatented know-how that is crucial in technology transfer to making the technology work. The knowledge embodied in the patent itself is often insufficient. As Welch argues: 'The pre-eminence of unpatented know-how demonstrates that the clearly specified technical information for public registration does not fulfill the demand of effective technology transfer in most situations. The technological know-how which is considered of greater importance is of a more intangible, company-specific nature, and requires person-to-person interaction for the transfer to be realised.'[113]

However, many developing countries keen to attract FDI are reluctant to impose onerous regimes that might deter investors.[114] There might be lessons from Latin America's experience in allowing state intervention in negotiating technology transfer agreements. For example, the UNCTAD World Investment Report 2004 indicates that Latin America in comparison to a number of regions (particularly Asia) has suffered a decline in FDI.[115] It is difficult to prove whether this may or may not be down to state intervention, as the parameters for FDI are often quite complex, sometimes involving a web of interlinking investment/bilateral trade treaties and obligations through multilateral treaties, such as the GATS (discussed at section V of this chapter). However, state intervention could be a factor in reduced FDI flow.

Perhaps, one can conclude that as a matter of general commercial practice, direct state intervention in contracts between private parties is not the best solution. In any case, such supervision requires a high level of human resource within the national regulatory authority that is both well-informed and well-resourced, and the majority of DCs and LDCs do not have such an advantage. A better approach might be in adopting flexible ex post measures (competition policy) that can correct market failure (anticompetitive agreements that have material effect on the relevant market or abuse of a dominant position), but can also reserve for the regulator certain ex ante (or sector-specific) measures for situations where competition law is difficult to apply, for example in tariff setting for technology transfer inputs or tax provisions effecting economic development zones.[116]

An example of a combined ex ante/ex post approach is found in the European Commission's new regulatory framework for electronic networks and services, where the EC combines the competition powers of the National Regulatory Authority in monitoring markets for effective competition (where no undertaking with significant market power[117] exists in a relevant market) with ex ante powers to impose conditions whether or not effective competition exists (for example in mandating access to a network facility or granting access to a software interface). The EC's new TTBE,[118] discussed in detail elsewhere in this book, is also a very good example of a combined flexible approach using both ex ante and ex post provisions and is more directly related to the issue of technology transfer, for example in setting market thresholds for licences negotiated between undertakings,[119] and distinguishing further licences between competitors, and between non-competitors. The TTBE provides a measure of legal certainty in that so long as undertakings do not exceed the market share thresholds set out in the TTBE, the technology transfer agreement will automatically be block-exempted from the application of Article 81(1) of the Treaty of Rome relating to anticompetitive agreements between undertakings, provided that the agreement contains no hardcore restrictions.[120]

IV. Technology transfer at the multilateral level

In the first phase of the WSIS held in Geneva in 2003, one of the principle aims of which is to reduce the digital divide between the developed and developing worlds, various member states of the United Nations,[121] including the European Communities, the US, Japan, and many other developed and developing nations committed to a Declaration of Principles which contained three main articles on technology transfer:[122]

33. To achieve a sustainable development of the Information Society, national capability in ICT research and development should be enhanced. Furthermore, partnerships, in particular between and among developed and developing countries, including countries with economies in transition, in research and development, technology transfer, manufacturing and utilization of ICT products and services are crucial for promoting capacity building and global participation in the Information Society. The manufacture of ICTs presents a significant opportunity for creation of wealth.

40. A dynamic and enabling international environment, supportive of foreign direct investment, transfer of technology, and international cooperation, particularly in the areas of finance, debt and trade, as well as full and effective participation of developing countries in global decision-making, are vital complements to national development efforts related to ICTs. Improving global affordable connectivity would contribute significantly to the effectiveness of these development efforts.

63. We resolve to assist developing countries, LDCs and countries with economies in transition through the mobilization from all sources of financing, the provision of financial and technical assistance and by creating an environment conducive to technology transfer, consistent with the purposes of this Declaration and the Plan of Action.

The second phase of the WSIS took place in Tunisia in 2005. One of the main objectives of the WSIS is to achieve by 2015, the following targets as set out in Article 6 of the WSIS Action Plan:[123]

(a) to connect villages with ICTs and establish community access points;
(b) to connect universities, colleges, secondary schools and primary schools with ICTs;
(c) to connect scientific and research centres with ICTs;
(d) to connect public libraries, cultural centres, museums, post offices and archives with ICTs;
(e) to connect health centres and hospitals with ICTs;
(f) to connect all local and central government departments and establish websites and email addresses;
(g) to adapt all primary and secondary school curricula to meet the challenges of the Information Society, taking into account national circumstances;
(h) to ensure that all of the world's population have access to television and radio services;
(i) to encourage the development of content and to put in place technical conditions in order to facilitate the presence and use of all world languages on the Internet;
(j) to ensure that more than half the world's inhabitants have access to ICTs within their reach.

How will these targets be achieved without adequate access to technology? Clearly to achieve the targets, DCs and LDCs will require not only access to the technology of ICTs, but also the ability to innovate around these technologies as well. To achieve these goals, LDCs and DCs will require access to information technology products, semiconductor technology, and software.

The WTO has worked hard to reduce both tariff and non-tariff barriers on the importation of IT products. In December 1996, the Ministerial Declaration on Trade in Information Technology Products (ITA) was concluded by 29 participants at the Singapore Ministerial Conference. The ITA provided for participants to completely eliminate duties on IT products covered by the agreement by 1 January 2000. Developing country participants were granted extended periods for some products. At the time of writing, there were 63 participants in the ITA, including a number of developing countries.[124]

Many DCs and LDCs however still face the problem of innovating around the technology that they are importing, particularly in the area of semiconductor technology. Both the Washington Treaty on Intellectual Property in Respect of Integrated Circuits (1989), and the EU Directive 87/54/EEC on the Legal Protection of Topographies of Semiconductor Products (1986), create rights in the topological design of semiconductors.[125] The protection offered by US and EU law together with provisions set out in the TRIPS Agreement,[126] will make it increasingly difficult for developing countries to get access to semiconductor technology despite the provisions of the ITA. Furthermore, the TRIPS sets out at Article 38 that in respect of an integrated circuit incorporating an unlawfully reproduced layout-design or any article incorporating such an integrated circuit, the importer be required to pay a royalty as would be found in a typical freely negotiated licence agreement had the technology been properly licensed. Such provisions put potentially onerous burdens on developing country producers to have the requisite knowledge that chip technology is non-infringing, and to compensate design title-holders in the event that it is. Furthermore, although the sui generis regime on integrated circuit designs allows for reverse engineering of protected layout designs, very few countries have the resources and skills necessary to undertake it.[127] Also, given that less than a handful of companies in the world control substantial patent pools (blocks of patents) in relation to semiconductor technology, DCs and LDCs have even less chance of gaining access to the technology for the purposes of innovation. This is particularly the case where leading developed country manufacturers are also involved in the setting of standards in relation to chip design.[128]

If the goals of the WSIS are to be met, DCs and LDCs will need to take a greater role in participating in the technical standard-setting activities of the developed countries, particularly in relation to information technology. Countries such as Singapore, Korea, Taiwan, and increasingly China and India, should be in a position to take a greater role.[129]

The WTO's Technical Barriers to Trade Agreement sets out provisions at Article 11 to help LDCs gain technical assistance with standards,[130] but many developing countries complain that such assistance has not been forthcoming.[131] As such, some developing countries are calling on the WTO to implement an 'early warning system' with regard to standards, and a mechanism to facilitate adjustment by developing countries to meet new standards.[132] Clearly the WTO Secretariat needs to meet this challenge if DCs and LDCs are to increase their contribution to world trade. The solution is essentially a political one which requires the WTO to enforce existing special and differential treatment provisions,[133] for example, Article 66.2 of the TRIPS Agreement, which calls for developed country members to 'provide incentives to enterprises and institutions in their territories for the purpose of promoting and encouraging technology transfer to least-developed country Members in order to enable them to create a sound and viable technological base'. Paragraph 11.2 of the Doha Decision on Implementation-Related Issues and Concerns ('Implementing Decision') reaffirms that the provisions of Article 66.2 are mandatory, and that the TRIPS Council 'puts in place a mechanism for ensuring the monitoring and full implementation of the obligations in question'.[134] On 19 February 2003, the TRIPS Council made a decision on implementing Article 66.2 in compliance with paragraph 11.2 of the Implementing Decision, requiring developed country members to submit annual reports on actions taken or planned in pursuance of their commitments under Article 66.2.[135]

With the failure of the discussions at Doha, there should perhaps be further movement here. For example, in a Decision ('General Cancun Decision') adopted by the WTO's General Council in August 2004, the Council has instructed the Committee on Trade and Development to 'expeditiously complete the review of all the outstanding Agreement-specific proposals (on special and differential treatment) and report to the General Council, with clear recommendations for a decision, by July 2005'.[136] We will, however, have to wait and see to determine whether the review will have any meaningful outcome for DCs and LDCs.[137]

In an ideal world, an effective IPR regime should not block innovation or effective competition. As mentioned earlier, Article 7 of the TRIPS Agreement sets out the objective that the protection and enforcement of intellectual property rights should contribute to the promotion of technological innovation and to the transfer and dissemination of technology. Furthermore, the TRIPS Agreement also contains a number of provisions that deal with anticompetitive conduct, including Articles 8 and 40. Article 8.2 allows for members to adopt 'appropriate measures' to prevent the abuse of intellectual property rights by right holders or the resort to practices which 'unreasonably restrain trade or adversely affect the international transfer of technology'. For example, in the WTO Working Group on the Interaction of Trade and Competition Policy, the view was expressed that 'one of the effects of international cartels could be to restrict the transfer of technology, particularly to developing countries'.[138] Again under Article 40.2 of the TRIPS Agreement, members may adopt appropriate measures to prevent or control anticompetitive practices, which may include for example 'exclusive grantback conditions, conditions preventing challenges to validity and coercive package licensing'. Finally, in terms of gaining access to technology, DCs and LDCs could make use of the compulsory licensing provisions of the TRIPS Agreement. Article 31 of the Agreement sets out the conditions for compulsory licensing.[139] Correa, argues that 'the conditions that govern the granting of compulsory licences will determine the extent of the system's effectiveness in promoting local innovation and the transfer of technology', and that 'the existence of a statutory provision itself may persuade rights holders of the need to act reasonably in cases of requests for voluntary licences, while strengthening the bargaining position of potential licensees'.[140]

However, in order to implement such measures, LDCs and DCs are left with the task of putting in place effective legislation on competition, which requires both trained personnel and resources.[141]

V. International investment agreements and technology transfer

At the bilateral level, the number of bilateral investment treaties (BITs) covering FDI in services reached 2,265 by the end of 2003, involving 175 countries.[142] Earlier in this chapter, the point was made that if the links to other economic sectors are weak, FDI may operate in enclaves with limited spillover into technologies adopted and wages earned by local firms and workers.[143] One way of addressing this weakness of FDI is perhaps something that can be addressed in an International Investment Agreement (IIA) or BIT, where FDI is included in the services chapter of the treaty.[144] This is already happening to some extent. For example, the latest report on investment from UNCTAD lists the move of FDI into the services market.[145] The reasons why such agreements are negotiated include, for the LDCs and DCs, increased options for attracting foreign investment for development on the one hand, and on the other, increased certainty for foreign investors that their investments will be secure as well as increasing market access and obtaining better conditions for national treatment for MNCs (than perhaps provided by DCs' or LDCs' special commitments under the GATS).

However, a number of BITs contain prohibitions on certain performance requirements with regard to technology transfer. Restrictions on performance requirements are not necessarily advantageous for DCs and LDCs. This is particularly the case with the North American Free Trade Agreement (NAFTA), which, in the performance requirements sections, prohibits the imposition or enforcement by a party of requirements 'to transfer technology, a production process or other proprietary knowledge to a person in its territory' in connection with the admission or treatment of an investment of an investor of any party or non-party (unless required to do so by a competition authority).[146] Similar technology transfer performance requirements can be found in other free trade agreements.[147] The bilateral investment treaties of the US also often include a prohibition of mandatory requirements 'to carry out a particular type, level or percentage of research and development' in the territory of a party.[148] Although performance requirements restricted only to control the competitive conditions of a market may be good for the general economic development of the host DC or LDC, more extensive requirements as to the generation, transfer and diffusion of technology, which go beyond competition-related issues, could also be prohibited under performance requirement restrictions.[149] Therefore DCs and LDCs interested in including development-oriented clauses in the IIA which touch on local personnel training requirements or the regulation of royalty payments by the developing country licensee would be restricted from doing so by the restrictions on performance in the IIA.[150] However, as the UNCTAD World Investment Report 2004 points out, 'IIAs covering services FDI are proliferating at the bilateral, regional, and multilateral levels. The resulting network of international rules on FDI in services is multifaceted, multilayered and constantly evolving, with obligations differing in geographical scope and substantive coverage. These rules are increasingly setting the parameters for national policies in the services sector.'[151] Clearly DCs and LDCs, entering into such agreements to attract FDI are increasingly going to face the difficult challenge of striking a balance between using IIAs to attract FDI on the one hand, and maintaining sufficient flexibility to pursue national development plans in the services sector on the other.[152]

VI. Recommendations going forward

The failure of the WTO Ministerial Conference held in Cancun in September 2003 meant that no decision was taken on any of the issues under negotiation or consideration in the Doha Work Programme, including deliberations of the Working Group on Technology Transfer, which was set up by ministers at Doha to examine 'the relationship between trade and transfer of technology, and any possible recommendations on steps that might be taken within the mandate of the WTO to increase flows of technology to developing countries'.[153]

The Doha Ministerial Declaration introduced for the first time in the WTO a binding mandate for WTO members to examine the relationship between trade and technology transfer.[154] As this chapter has discussed, there are a number of provisions within the WTO covered agreements that can be enforced to ensure that the international process of technology transfer can be better achieved, for example Articles 7, 31, 40, 65 and 66 of the TRIPS Agreement. However as Roffe and Tesfachew have argued, there has perhaps been too much concentration of analysis on the imperfections of the international technology transfer process and not enough on the domestic absorptive and adaptation capacity of the host country.[155] If DCs and LDCs are to truly benefit from technology transfer, more attention has to be paid to improving host country legislation on technology transfer in terms of making it more effective in attracting foreign investment, creating spillover, and also in dealing with potential abuses of market power by MNCs. As mentioned earlier, this is no easy task given that many DCs and LDCs do not have adequate resources to put such competition legislation into effect, even if the know-how were available.

What would be the objective of introducing better provisions on competition into host country legislation? Abbott argues that the 'promotion of technology transfer through competition policy involves assuring that technical information appropriately enters the public domain (i.e. private appropriation of technology should not impose unreasonable social welfare costs), preventing and correcting market-related abuses, and assuring that granting of patents and other IPRs are accomplished in a measured way'.[156] Simply copying the patent systems of the US and EU may not be the best step forward. Abbott cites a recent Federal Trade Commission (FTC) study of competition and patents in the United States that focuses on the anticompetitive risks of overprotection, including through the grant of patents of suspect quality.[157] He argues that the thrust of the FTC Report is that 'the competition enforcement proceedings are a costly and inefficient mechanism for addressing the adverse impact of patent overprotection, as compared with reducing the grant of low quality patents and facilitating early challenges. Promoting greater vigilance over the granting of patents is characterized as "competition" policy.'[158]

As mentioned above, DCs and LDCs often do not have the resources to put in place the legislation and infrastructure required for effective competition authorities in the absence of funding, for example through the World Bank or WTO. Although external consultants can be funded to draft the necessary competition legislation, recruiting local skilled personnel to enforce the new legislation is another matter. Perhaps what is required is a mix of both sector-specific (ex ante) measures that sets out basic rules on technology transfer in advance, for example in the setting of price controls and compulsory licensing by government, as well as general competition-type (ex post) provisions which deal with issues of discrimination, transparency, and unfair competition.

For example, and as mentioned earlier, the European Commission has recently adopted a revised TTBE Regulation[159] as well as a series of new directives that adopt a mix of ex ante and ex post provisions for regulating electronic networks and services.[160] Article 12 of the Access & Interconnection Directive[161] is a very good example of where the EC uses a combined ex ante and ex post approach in dealing with anticompetitive practices with regard to the granting of access to an electronic network or software protocol or interface:

> A national regulatory authority [NRA] may, in accordance with the pro-
> visions of Article 8, impose obligations on operators to meet reasonable
> requests for access to, and use of, specific network elements and associated
> facilities, inter alia in situations where the national regulatory authority
> considers that denial of access or unreasonable terms and conditions
> having a similar effect would hinder the emergence of a sustainable com-
> petitive market at the retail level, or would not be in the end-user's interest.

By doing this, the EC gives a great deal of discretion for NRAs to act and impose access conditions in agreements between operators so as to create effective competition: NRAs can impose access conditions even in the absence of any one operator having dominance in a particular market.[162] In this instance, there may be no need for the NRA to conduct an extensive demand and supply-side substitutability test as regards the imposition of access obligations. In other words, access is seen as an area where immediate remedies may be required without the need for expensive and time-consuming market analysis.

However there are dangers of the enforcement by DCs and LDCs of measures of this type. Enforcement of host country competition provisions on MNCs for example could result in threats of trade and/or financial retaliation by developed country governments. To avoid the risk of this kind of retaliation, DCs and LDCs could make better use of regional trade or economic area agreements, where a common set of rules (both ex ante and ex post) for technology transfer could be adopted and integrated into the framework of the regional agreement.[163] For example, to help maintain a level of consistency of regulatory treatment amongst European NRAs, the EC has included harmonisation-type clauses at Articles 6 and 7 of the Framework Directive, which require NRAs to consult with the EC in introducing measures which would have a significant effect on the European internal market.[164] In a similar way, by harmonising competition provisions within the framework of a regional trade agreement, DCs and LDCs could have a better chance of enforcing such provisions against MNCs at a national level. Furthermore the competition schedule/chapter/section of a regional trade agreement could provide for the creation of a regional competition advisory body that could supply resources and skills to member governments, which all parties to the regional agreement could help fund, minimising the expense for a country in creating its own extensive infrastructure. Given the proliferation of regional trade agreements in recent years, consensus between regional trade partners with similar trade interests may be easier to achieve than creating a competition agreement or compact at the level of the WTO. As Balasubramanyam and Elliott argue: 'The WTO is often dismissed as an inappropriate forum, simply because its mandate is restricted to trade and not investment, and whilst the organisation can parley with the governments of member countries on trade issues, it cannot negotiate with MNEs which are privately owned.'[165]

What type of provisions could be included in a competition chapter? A starting point could be greater cooperation between competition authorities in developing and developed countries, licensing rules to reduce the transaction costs of enforcement, and punitive damages (e.g. triple damages) as a warning to prospective violators.[166] To this list can be added best practice recommendations from both the OECD's MNC Guidelines as well as sections from the UNCTAD's draft Transfer of Technology Code, discussed earlier. Regional measures might go hand-in-hand with changes in WTO procedure. For example, Abbot argues that the 'WTO Dispute Resolution Understanding might be expanded to include remedial measures directed at patent holders that initiate threats of trade sanctions by home government as "abuse of dominant position" including, in egregious cases, recommendation of patent forfeiture', as well as the desirability of increasing technology and information in the public domain.[167] Although Balasubramanyam and Eliott generally conclude that the WTO might be an appropriate body to take responsibility for a future multilateral competition policy,[168] they also argue that the WTO's Dispute Settlement Body is primarily interested in resolving disputes between competition authorities as opposed to disputes between individual firms.[169]

The point made by Abbott on increasing access to information in the public domain has also been gaining considerable ground in academic thinking in recent years. Perhaps one of the most influential advocates of the public domain has been Lawrence Lessig of Stanford University. Lessig together with colleagues from Harvard's Berkman Center for Internet & Society have pioneered the concept of the Creative Commons, which seeks to use copyleft licensing to encourage rights holders to place their work in the public domain.[170] Clearly as more innovators in the developed world seek to use copyleft licensing and vehicles such as the Creative Commons, more producers in the LDCs and DCs stand to gain, subject of course to their continued use of the copyleft mantra in terms of derivative works produced. A very good example of this is the FOSS movement and GNU/Linux. FOSS is software that has made its source code public and allows users to change the source code and redistribute the derivative software. GNU/Linux is an operating system developed, originally as a UNIX-like kernel by Linus Torvalds, on the open-source model and which has now become a serious competitor to proprietary Microsoft products. Allowing access to the source code allows for broad collaborative development in software production, better porting between different applications and programs produced by independent developers, and the customisation of software to meet local needs.[171] As a recent UNCTAD report states: 'Its technological opposite, closed-source or proprietary software . . . requires a significant upfront investment in licence fees for installation and upgrades: it is not always adaptable to local concerns; and its exclusive or even dominant use may not adequately support the local development of the expert knowledge and skills needed to fully embrace the information economy.'[172]

The UNCTAD report argues that a business or government using FOSS could avoid becoming locked into using software manufactured by a controlling monopolist,[173] and that 'freeing the source code makes software non-excludable as well, and as a result software acquires the characteristics of a public good'.[174] For developing countries,[175] however, freeing up the software would be of no use without the corresponding hardware and networks through which the software will flow: This is particularly important given that with the advent of digital networks, intelligence is moving closer to the terminal, resulting in cheaper transmission costs, and greater positive network externalities for those countries that have the resources to upgrade their legacy networks. There is no reason, however, why such digital networks that are proliferating in the developed world should expand geographically into the developing world, unless we have enlightened policy that will allow for it. This is one reason why the talks in Tunis in 2005, as part of the second phase of the WSIS, must succeed.[176]

Maskus argues for the need to take the commons to the multilateral level. He argues for a 'Multilateral Agreement on Access to Basic Science and Technology. An agreement at the WTO would be negotiated in which all signatories would place into the public domain, or find other means of sharing at modest cost, the results of publicly funded research. The idea is to preserve and enhance the global commons in science and technology, while setting out a public mechanism for increasing the international flow of technical information, especially to developing countries, without unduly restricting private rights in commercial technologies. The agreement could cover "input liberalisation", which would permit researchers from other countries to participate in, or compete with, local research teams for grants and subsidies. This could be combined with increased opportunities for temporary migration of scientific personnel and additional student visas.'[177]

The idea of getting consensus at the WTO between developed and developing members post-Doha on such a treaty would seem to be quite unlikely in the short term.[178] However given that Lessig has been successful in launching the Creative Commons in both the USA and the UK, and that the idea is soon set to take off in many other countries as well, Maskus may not be so far out of the ball-park as one might imagine. Perhaps again, there is a need to focus first at the regional level: in Africa, a number of regions have already collaborated on FOSS, launching the Free and Open Source Software Foundation for Africa (FOSSFA), which seeks to promote the use of FOSS throughout the region.[179] 'FOSSFA anticipates that FOSS will provide opportunities to develop local programmes built by Africans for use in Africa.'[180] Perhaps it is only through regional organisations, such as FOSSFA, that funds can be mobilised and channelled and links made with educational institutions, whereby educators can be trained to help young people across the region to 'learn, use, maintain, and modify software'.[181]

As Theodore Roosevelt once said: 'Great corporations exist only because they are created and safeguarded by our institutions; and it is our right and our duty to see that they work in harmony with these institutions ... The first requisite is knowledge, full and complete; knowledge which may be made public to the world.'[182] His words have as much relevance now as they did in 1901.

Notes

1. For example, the OECD-sponsored Multilateral Agreement on Investment, which at its heart placed significance on protection of foreign investment and market access as incentives to stimulate the free flow of FDI into developing countries (by removing all impediments to FDI), was rejected by many developing countries. For a further discussion, see V. N. Balasubramanyam and C. Elliott, 'Competition Policy and the WTO' in Homi Katrak and Roger Strange (eds.), The WTO and Developing Countries (Palgrave Macmillan, 2004).
2. In this chapter, TNCs will also be referred to throughout as Multinational Corporations (MNCs).
3. UNCTAD Transfer of Technology, UNCTAD/ITE/IIT/28 (2001) p. 92.
4. UNCTAD World Investment Report, section B ch. 1 (2004).
5. Discussed in this chapter at p. 477.
6. C. M. Correa, Intellectual Property Rights, the WTO and Developing Countries (Zed Books, 2000) 31.
7. See, for example, the extensive literature survey compiled by Kamal Saggi, Trade, Foreign Direct Investment, and International Technology Transfer: A Survey (World Bank, 2000).
8. For example, licences for patents and trademarks, supply of industrial technology, technical-industrial cooperation, specialised technical services, and marketing rights etc.
9. The draft Transfer of Technology Code was abandoned due to disagreement between developing and developed nations as to the emphasis placed on various clauses within the code. Developing countries were looking for clauses that would deal effectively with economic regulation and development, whereas developed countries were more interested in clauses that would promote effective competition. See UNCTAD, ch. 1, para 1.2 (1985).
10. UNCTAD Transfer of Technology Report, UNCTAD/ITE/IIT/28 (2001) p. 6.
11. UN ESCAP, 1989. Cited by Ajay Mathur, Preety M. Bhandari and Sharmila B. Srikanth in 'Effective Technology Transfer: Issues and Options' in Tim Forsyth (ed.), Positive Measures for Technology Transfer under the Climate Change Convention (The Royal Institute of International Affairs, 1997).
12. The draft Transfer of Technology Code provides a more detailed list of the elements of technology transfer: '(a) The assignment, sale and licensing of all

forms of industrial property, except for trade marks, service marks and trade names when they are not part of transfer of technology transactions; (b) The provision of know-how and technical expertise in the form of feasibility studies, plans, diagrams, models, instructions, guides, formulae, basic or detailed engineering designs, specifications and equipment for training, services personnel training; (c) The provision of technological knowledge necessary for the installation, operation and functioning of plant and equipment, and turnkey projects; (d) The provision of technological knowledge necessary to acquire, install and use machinery, equipment, intermediate goods and/or raw materials which have been acquired by purchase, lease or other means; (e) The provision of technological contents of industrial and technical co-operation arrangements', UNCTAD 1996a, Vol. I p. 183.

13. WT/WGTTT/5 para. 19.
14. 'Technology transfer at the multilateral level'.
15. IP/IC/W/398.
16. UNCTAD World Investment Report 2004 p. xx.
17. IP/IC/W/398 para. 30.
18. UNCTAD World Investment Report 2004 p. xxiii.
19. IP/C/W/398 para. 35.
20. K. Beata Smarzynska, *Composition of Foreign Direct Investment and Protection of Intellectual Property Rights: Evidence from Transition Economies* (The World Bank, 2002) p. 2.
21. UNCTAD World Investment Report 2004 p. xxiii.
22. Ibid. p. xxvii.
23. Ibid. p. xxvii.
24. In looking at the classification issue, a certain category of electronic intangibles could fall to be classified under either the GATS or the GATT. This includes a narrow range of media products that can be imported under both HS classifications (the classification system for trade in goods under the GATT), and/or downloaded over the Internet (and hence classified as a service under the GATS system of classification W/120). The WTO has estimated such trade in intangibles to amount to approximately 1 per cent of total merchandise trade and 1 per cent of total duties collected worldwide. This would not include the vast majority of services, all media/information products that never did cross borders in physical formats, being clearly under the GATS (most media/entertainment forms that have traditionally been regarded as services: broadcast TV programming, radio programming), such trade amounting to approximately 99 per cent of trading merchandise, and more than 99 per cent of duties collected worldwide. See presentation by Lee Tuthill, WTO Trade in Services Division, 'WTO implications of classification issues' at: http://www.wto.org/english/tratop_e/devel_e/sem05_e/presentation_tuthill.ppt. (Date accessed October 2004).
25. WT/GC/W/497.

26. B. Hoekman, F. Ng and M. Olarreaga, *Tariff Peaks in the Quad and Least Developed Country Exports* (The World Bank, February 2001).

27. Ibid. p. 1.

28. WT/WGTTT/M/1 para. 41.

29. Or potentially as a long-shot, the WTO's Dispute Resolution Body (DSB) ruling on the point, although it could be argued that the DSB should be used to interpret the WTO members' collective intent rather than forcing governments to legislate because they could not agree on a common approach. For a more detailed discussion, see Drake and Nicolaidis, 'Global Electronic Commerce and GATS: the Millennium Round and Beyond' in P. Sauve and R. Stern (eds.), *GATS 2000 New Directions in Trade in Services* (Brookings Institute Press, 2000) ch. 14 p. 410.

30. Presently WTO members have agreed a moratorium on the use of customs duties for electronic transmissions. The moratorium was still in place at the last meeting of the General Council of the WTO in 2003. This moratorium is not legally binding and it remains free for WTO members to agree to impose customs duties on electronic intangibles at some point in the future, WT/GC/W/509.

31. One solution to the problem would be to require MNCs, as part of an FDI or licensing strategy, to locate the production of goods and services that embody patents in the local market and put in place the necessary training and partnership programmes that will increase the chance that spillover (discussed later) and diffusion will take place. Many DCs and LDCs are not in a position to achieve this and would require both technical and financial assistance from UNCTAD World Association of Investment Promotion Agencies, and the World Bank. See the excellent speech by Lynn Mytelka, Director INTECH to the first session of the WTO Working Group on Trade and Transfer of Technology (April 2002) WT/WGTTT/M/1 para. 55(a).

32. Specific issues in relation to technology transfer licensing are discussed in more detail in this chapter at p. 480.

33. UNCTAD World Investment Report 2004 para. 43.

34. WT/MIN(01)/DEC/1 (November 2001).

35. Chapter 34 WT/MIN(01)/DEC/1 (20 November 2001) contains detailed provisions on actions to be undertaken to support and promote the access to and use of EST, including on concessional and preferential terms.

36. WT/WGTTT/W/5 p. 10.

37. 'Agenda 21 a Programme of Action for Sustainable Development', was approved by the United Nations Conference on Environment and Development, also known as the 'Earth Summit', held in Rio de Janeiro, 1992.

38. C. M. Correa, *Intellectual Property Rights* p. 33.

39. Ibid.

40. UNCTAD World Investment Report 2004.

41. Ibid. overview section.

42. K. Maskus, 'The Role of Intellectual Property Rights in Encouraging Foreign Direct Investment and Technology Transfer' (1998) 9 *Duke Journal of Comparative and International Law* 7.

43. IP/C/W/398 at p. 4.

44. According to the UNIDO World Industrial Development Report 2002/2003 (p. 36), the share of developing countries in world R&D expenditure financed by productive enterprises was 5 per cent in 1998.

45. N. Kumar, *Technology Generation and Technology Transfers in the World Economy: Recent Trends and Implications for Developing Countries*, Discussion Papers 2, United Nations University, Institute for New Technologies (1997), pp. 10–11.

46. China became the world's largest FDI recipient in 2003, overtaking the USA, traditionally the largest recipient. In 2003, FDI flows to Southeast Asia rose by 27 per cent to $19 billion (UNCTAD World Investment Report 2004, p. xix).

47. Note 11 above p. 6.

48. UNCTAD World Investment Report 1999 p. 218.

49. Ibid. p. 50.

50. E. K. Y. Chen 'Introduction: Transnational Corporations and Technology Transfer to Developing Countries' in *The United Nations Library on Transactional Corporations* (London: Routledge, 1994) Vol. 18 p. 10.

51. Ibid. p. 11.

52. UNCTAD World Investment Report 1999 p. 204.

53. UNIDO World Industrial Development Report 2002/2003 p. 139. Further discussion of technology transfer policies in Southeast Asia can be found in L. Westphal, 'Technology Strategies for Economic Development' in *Economics of Innovation and New Technology* Vol. 11, No. 4–5 (August–October 2002) pp. 275–320.

54. S. L. Welch, 'The Technology Transfer Process in Foreign Licensing Arrangements' in *The Economics of Communication and Information* (1996) ch. 17 p. 156.

55. Unbundling is discussed in more detail later in this chapter.

56. See table 1.10 UNCTAD World Investment Report 2004 p. 19.

57. C. M. Correa, 'Emerging Trends: New Patterns of Technology Transfer' in S. Patel, P. Roffe and A. Yusuf (eds.), *The International Transfer of Technology: The Origins and Aftermath of the United Nations Negotiations on a Draft Code of Conduct* (The Hague: Kluwer Law International, 2000) pp. 268–70.

58. N. Kumar, *Technology Generation and Technology Transfers*, pp. 26–7.

59. M. Borga and W. J. Zeile, 'International Fragmentation of Production and the Intrafirm Trade of US Multinational Companies', presented at National Bureau of Economic Research/Conference on Research on Income and Wealth Workshop on 'Firm-level Data, Trade and Foreign Direct Investment', Cambridge Mass., 7–8 August 2003.

60. IP/C/W/398 p. 4.

61. WT/WGTI/W/65.

62. This concept is discussed in more detail later in this chapter at p. xxx.
63. IP/C/W/398 p. 20.
64. WT/WGTI/W/65 para. 64.
65. WT/WGTI/W/136 para. 20.
66. Ibid.
67. Ibid.
68. H. T. Moran, *Parental Supervision: The New Paradigm for Foreign Direct Investment and Development*, No. 64 Policy Analyses in International Economics, Institute for International Economics (August 2001) p. 63.
69. For a more thorough analysis of vertical and horizontal FDI, see Smarzynska, *Composition of Foreign Direct Investment and Protection of Intellectual Property Rights*, p. 20.
70. Correa, *Intellectual Property Rights*, p. 154. He makes the point that rather than reverse engineering large and complex programs, which is time intensive and costly, a better approach might be to gain access to the *user interface* (the 'look and feel') of existing applications. In this way, competitors could develop alternative applications using the same command-type sets of existing applications. However, in the US case of *Lotus* v. *Paperback* (28 June 1990 740 F.Supp. 37) Justice Keeton, in the District Court of Massachusetts, recognised Lotus' rights to the protection of menu command structures.
71. *NEC, Corporation* v. *Intel Corporation* 67.434 ND. Cal. (6 February 1989).
72. Article 6, EC 91/250.
73. A decompilation provision is provided by s.1201(f) of the DMCA 1998. The provision allows a person to circumvent access control measures around a copyrighted work, if the motive is to assist in the production of a separate program meant to be interoperable with the copyrighted work, or other programs that depend on the copyrighted work.
74. Introduction to the Copyright (Amendment) Bill 2004 at: http://www.newiplaws. org.sg/pdf/Intro_Copyright.pdf (date accessed October 2004).
75. Ibid. p. 11: Defined in the public consultation document as 'The act of translating machine-readable computer language into a humanly-readable form'.
76. WT/WGTI/W/65, paras. 15 and 16.
77. G. Hasan, 'Hidden Costs of Technology Transfer' *YK-Economic Review* (June 2003) 10.
78. S. Lall, 'Transnationals, Domestic Enterprises and Industrial Structure in LDCs: A Survey' *Oxford Economic Papers* Vol. 30 pp. 217–48.
79. Also in this chapter referred to as MNCs.
80. WT/WGTI/W/65 para. 49.
81. Ibid.
82. In the banking and retail sectors for example, the UNCTAD report highlights how local firms have been crowded out of host country markets. In banking this has been due mainly to local banks' lack of geographical diversication and experience, limited financing capacity, and higher costs of new product

implementation. In retailing, the problems have been due to new ways of doing business, new pricing structures, improved information management processes and new marketing and merchandising methods. UNCTAD World Investment Report 2004 p. xxiii.

83. Articles 81, 82 Treaty of Rome, the new EC Merger Regulation (EC) No. 139/2004. See also Commission Regulation (EC) No.802/2004 April 2004 implementing the new Merger Regulation and annexes (Form CO, Short Form CO and Form RS) and the jurisprudence of the EU Court of First Instance, and the ECJ.

84. Commission Regulation 772/2004 (April 2004) and Commission Notice 2004/C 101/02 (April 2004) respectively.

85. Discussed in more detail later in this chapter at p. 486.

86. Hasan, 'Hidden Costs of Technology Transfer', p. 22.

87. Ibid., p. 13.

88. S. L. Welch, 'The Technology Transfer Process in Foreign Licensing Arrangements' in *The Economics of Communication and Information* 1996 ch. 17 p. 159, citing F. Contractor, 'The Composition of Licensing Fees and Arrangements as a Function of Economic Development of Technology Recipient Nations' *Journal Of International Business Studies*, 1980.

89. WT/WGTI/W/65 para. 10.

90. See, for example, V. Ramachandran, 'Technology Transfer, Firm Ownership and Investment in Human Capital' (1993) 75 *Review of Economics and Statistics* 664–70.

91. WT/WGTI/W/65 para. 11.

92. WT/WGTI/W/136 para. 23.

93. Furthermore, the TRIMS does not apply to services (Article 1 TRIMS), although it can apply to measures regulating services FDI, for example when performance requirements applied to service investors affect trade in goods (see the Annexe to the TRIMS).

94. L. Mytelka, Director INTECH, speech to the first session of the WTO Working Group on Trade and Transfer of Technology, April 2002, WT/WGTTT/M/1 para. 51.

95. See, for example, the INTECH website at: http://www.intech.unu.edu/research/index.htm (date accessed October 2004).

96. Ibid. para. 51 and UNCTAD World Investment Report, Section B ch. 7 (2004).

97. N. Oravainen, *International Licensing and Know-how Agreements of Finnish Companies* (1979) Helsinki School of Economics, FIBO publication No. 13 p. 35.

98. IP/C/W/398 p. 14.

99. WT/WGTTT/W/6, p. 2 (para ii).

100. Ibid. p. 20.

101. WT/WGTTT/W/6 p. 3.

102. *Magill*, a case involving limiting the extent of IPR (copyright protection in television broadcast listings) to prevent abuse of a dominant position and

leveraging of market power under Article 82 EC Treaty (then Article 86) Joined cases C-241/91 and C-242/91P [1995] ECR I-743.

103. *IMS*, Case C-418/01 April 2004. The case hinges on the controversial issue of when an intellectual property owner's refusal to license the use of its copyright (in this instance relating to a brick structure used to supply regional sales data for pharmaceutical products in an EC Member State) to a third party competitor constitutes an abuse of a dominant position (refusal to supply) under Article 82 EC Treaty.

104. S. Anderman, *EC Competition Law and Intellectual Property Rights: The Regulation of Innovation* (Oxford: Clarendon Press, 1998) p. 5.

105. N. V. Balasubramanyam and C. Elliott, 'Competition Policy and the WTO' in H. Katrak and R. Strange (eds.) *The WTO and Developing Countries* (Palgrave Macmillan, 2004) ch. 13 p. 306.

106. Ibid. p. 308.

107. C. Correa, *Transfer of Technology in Latin America: A Decade of Control*, (1998) p. 391.

108. Ibid.

109. Ibid. p. 392.

110. Ibid. p. 396.

111. Ibid. p. 397.

112. S. L. Welch, 'The Technology Transfer Process in Foreign Licensing Arrangements' in *The Economics of Communication and Information* (1996) ch. 17 p. 160.

113. Ibid. p. 158.

114. See, for example, section V of this chapter.

115. UNCTAD World Investment Report 2004 p. xvii.

116. Discussed further at section VI.

117. Defined at Article 14(2) Framework Directive 2002/21/EC: 'An undertaking shall be deemed to have significant market power if, either individually or jointly with others, it enjoys a position equivalent to dominance, that is to say a position of economic strength affording it the power to behave to an appreciable extent independently of competitors, customers and ultimately consumers.'

118. EC 772/2004 (April 2004).

119. Ibid. Article 3.

120. Ibid. Recital 13 and Article 4.

121. The Declaration also refers to other important development goals including the development goals of the *Millennium Declaration*, namely the eradication of extreme poverty and hunger; achievement of universal primary education; promotion of gender equality and empowerment of women; reduction of child mortality; improvement of maternal health; to combat HIV/AIDS, malaria and other diseases; ensuring environmental sustainability; and the development of global partnerships for the attainment of a more peaceful,

just and prosperous world. The Declaration also refers to the sustainable development goals contained in the Johannesburg Declaration and Plan of Implementation and the Monterrey Consensus. See the WSIS, Document WSIS-03/GENEVA/DOC/4-E (December 2003) Article 1.

122. Ibid.

123. WSIS, Document WSIS-03/GENEVA/DOC/5-E (December 2003).

124. For a complete list of countries who are signatories to the ITA see the WTO's website at: http://www.wto.org/english/tratop_e/inftec_e/itapart_e.htm (date accessed 15 October 2004).

125. See Article 6(1) US Washington Integrated Circuits Treaty, and Article 3(7) EU Directive 87/54. See also the European Council Decision of 19 December 1994 on the extension of the legal protection of topographies of semiconductor products to persons from certain territories (94/828/EC), which extended the provisions of the earlier EU Directive 87/54, by extending protection to qualifying nationals of additional countries not covered by the earlier directive, and to comply with the TRIPS Agreement.

126. Article 36 TRIPS Agreement sets out the scope of protection with regards to integrated circuits: 'Members shall consider unlawful the following acts if performed without the authorization of the right holder: importing, selling, or otherwise distributing for commercial purposes a protected layout-design, an integrated circuit in which a protected layout-design is incorporated, or an article incorporating such an integrated circuit only in so far as it continues to contain an unlawfully reproduced layout-design.'

127. Correa, *Intellectual Property Rights* p. 157.

128. See, for example, the cases of *Rambus* v. *Infineon Technologies AG*, No. Civ. A. 3:00cv524 (2001) and *Dell Computer* 121 FTC 616 (1996). Both cases involved anticompetitive conduct by chip manufacturers who had previously been involved in chip standard-setting processes, and who allegedly used patents to block innovation.

129. For example in the area of software development, there should be no reason why software innovations should not come increasingly from developing countries, particularly with the take-up of the FOSS, discussed in more detail in the final section of this chapter: Recommendations going forward.

130. For example, Article 11.2 says that: 'Members shall, if requested, advise other Members, especially the developing country Members, and shall grant them technical assistance on mutually agreed terms and conditions regarding the establishment of national standardizing bodies, and participation in the international standardizing bodies, and shall encourage their national standardising bodies to do likewise.'

131. WT/WGTTT/W/6 p. 3.

132. Ibid. para. (v) p. 3.

133. Virtually all WTO agreements have special provisions with respect to developing country members, known as Special and Differential Treatment terms.

See the WTO report, Implementation of Special and Differential Treatment Provisions in WTO Agreements and Decisions, WT/COMTD/W/77.

134. WT/MIN(01)/17 Article 11.2. Around 100 implementation issues were raised in the lead-up to the Doha Ministerial Conference. The implementation decision, combined with paragraph 12 of the main Doha Declaration, provided a two-track solution for agreeing some of the implementation issues prior to the Doha Round. According to the WTO, more than 40 items under 12 headings were settled at or before the Doha conference. See the WTO website at: http://www.wto.org/english/tratop_e/dda_e/dda_e.htm#implementation (date accessed October 2004).

135. IP/C/28.

136. Clause 1(d) WT/L/579.

137. In October 2004, the WTO Committee on Trade and Development did produce a report listing all the special and differential treatment provisions to be found in the WTO covered agreements for LDCs. See WT/COMTD/W/135, October 2004. The report simply lists the provisions, but makes no recommendations going forward.

138. WT/WGTTT/5 para. 15.

139. Selected conditions include: authorisation to be based on individual merits, requirements for the rights holder to be already approached with a reasonable offer of licensing (unless a national emergency applies), in the case of semi-conductor technology use restricted only for public non-commercial use or to remedy a practice determined after judicial or administrative process to be anticompetitive, non-exclusive, predominantly for the domestic market, provisions for economic remuneration, possibility of revocation of the licence.

140. Correa, *Intellectual Property Rights*, p. 244. See also recent developments in the area of compulsory licences with regard to public health. Given the proliferation of HIV/AIDS in the developing world, international institutions, such as the WTO have come under increased pressure to recognise the difficulties that WTO members with insufficient or no manufacturing capabilities in the pharmaceutical sector are facing with producing effective drugs for treatment and the need to obtain supplies quickly. As such the WTO has now granted a waiver of condition under Article 31(f) of the TRIPS Agreement on manufacture for domestic markets only, allowing other WTO members to produce drugs cheaply for import by WTO Members who are eligible. See the Decision of the General Council, August 2003, Implementation of Paragraph 6 of the Doha Declaration on the TRIPS Agreement and Public Health (WT/L/540).

141. In the General Cancun Decision the WTO's General Council states at para. 1(d) on development that the: 'Council affirms that such countries, and in particular least-developed countries, should be provided with enhanced trade related technical assistance ('TRTA') and capacity building, to increase their effective participation in the negotiations, to facilitate their

implementation of WTO rules, and to enable them to adjust and diversify their economies. In this context the Council welcomes and further encourages the improved coordination with other agencies, including under the Integrated Framework for TRTA for the LDCs (IF) and the Joint Integrated Technical Assistance Programme ('JITAP').'

142. UNCTAD World Investment Report 2004 p. 221.
143. See p. 478.
144. UNCTAD World Investment Report 2004 p. 221.
145. Ibid.
146. Article 1106(1)(f) NAFTA. See also WT/WGTI/W/136 para. 28.
147. See for example Article G-06 of the Free Trade Agreement between Canada and Chile (1996); Article 15-05 of the Free Trade Agreement between Bolivia and Mexico (1994); Article 9-07 of the Free Trade Agreement between Chile and Mexico (1998); and Article 14-07 of the Free Trade Agreement between Mexico, El Salvador, Guatemala and Honduras (2000). These free trade agreements also include a prohibition of requirements imposed on investments to act as exclusive suppliers of goods or services to a specific region or to the world market (cited from WT/WGTI/W/136).
148. WT/WGTI/W/136 para. 34, which cites article VI(f) of the bilateral investment treaty between the USA and Bolivia (1998) as an example.
149. UNCTAD Transfer of Technology, UNCTAD/ITE/IIT/28 (2001) p. 96.
150. There may be scope however to include performance requirements in the IIA, if the investor is to receive an 'advantage' under the agreement, so long as the contracting state providing the technology has not prohibited performance requirements in any other IIA. Ibid. p. 97. See also the OECD's Guidelines for Multinational Enterprises that look to set requirements on MNCs to cooperate in the technology and science policy of the host country and prevent abusive practices (Sections VIII and IX respectively) at: http://www.oecd.org/dataoecd/56/36/1922428.pdf (date accessed October 2004).
151. UNCTAD World Investment Report 2004 p. 235.
152. The significance of maintaining flexibility for determining national policy has been adopted as a policy objective at the recent UNCTAD XI Conference in Sao Paulo (June 2004) ('the Sao Paulo Consensus') which states at para. 8 that: 'The increasing interdependence of national economies in a globalizing world and the emergence of rule-based regimes for international economic relations have meant that the space for national economic policy, i.e. the scope for domestic polices, especially in the areas of trade, investment and industrial development, is now often framed by international disciplines, commitments and global market considerations. It is for each Government to evaluate the trade-off between the benefits of accepting international rules and commitments and the constraints posed by the loss of policy space. It is particularly important for developing countries, bearing in mind development goals and objectives, that all countries take into account the need for appropriate

balance between national policy space and international disciplines and commitments.' UNCTAD, TDL/L.30 (June 2004).

153. WTO website on Working Group on Trade and Transfer of Technology at www.wto.org. (date accessed October 2004). The first draft of the Cancun Ministerial text (Job(03)/150 of 18 July 2003) simply takes note of the progress made in the WGTTT and agrees that the Group's work 'shall continue to be based on the mandate contained in paragraph 37 of the Doha Declaration'. See Doha Round Briefing Series, International Centre for Trade and Sustainable Development, Vol. 2 No. 11 of 13 (August 2003).

154. Ibid.

155. P. Roffe and T. Tesfachew, 'Revisiting the Technology Transfer Debate: Lessons for the New WTO Working Group', at http://www.ictsd.org. (date accessed, October 2004).

156. F. Abbott, 'The Competition Provisions in the TRIPS Agreement: Implications for Technology Transfer', Joint WIPO-WTO Workshop, Intellectual Property Rights and Transfer of Technology (November 2003) p. 2.

157. US Federal Trade Commission, *To Promote Innovation: The Proper Balance of Competition and Patent Law and Policy* (October 2003).

158. Ibid.

159. Commission Regulation 772/2004 (April 2004).

160. See for example the EC's Framework Directive 2002/21/EC and Access & Interconnection Directive 2002/19/EC as good examples of such combined ex ante/ex post instruments.

161. Directive 2002/19/EC.

162. In the EC's new regulatory framework, dominance is equivalent to Significant Market Power as defined in Article 14 Framework Directive.

163. Utilising for example sections of UNCTAD's draft Code on Transfer of Technology and also provisions on Science and Technology, and Competition from the OECD's Guidelines for MNCs. See also UNCTAD's excellent Compendium of International Arrangements on Transfer of Technology: Selected Instruments, UNCTAD/ITE/IPC/Misc.5 (2001), which contains a detailed analysis of a number of technology transfer clauses used in IIAs/BITs.

164. Directive 2002/21/EC.

165. Balasubramanyam and Elliott, 'Competition Policy and the WTO' p. 306. However, in the chapter the authors generally conclude that the WTO may be an appropriate body to take responsibility for future multilateral competition policy developments, p. 311.

166. Abbott, 'The Competition Provisions in the TRIPS Agreement: Implications for Technology Transfer' p. 4. See also examples of sanctions that can be applied in a personal capacity to directors for companies that infringe the UK's Competition Act 1998.

167. Ibid. footnote 120.

168. Balasubramanyam and Elliott, 'Competition Policy and the WTO', p. 310.

169. The recent WTO DSB case of a dispute on network interconnection payments between Mexico and the United States is a good example of this. See 'Mexico – Measures Affecting Telecommunication Services', *Case DS204* (June 2004).

170. To see the Creative Commons Deed and for more information on copyleft licensing see the Creative Commons website at: http://creativecommons.org/ (date accessed October 2004). The Free Software Foundation has developed a standard copyright agreement, the GNU General Public Licence (GPL) that is often called 'copyleft' which seeks to replace traditional copyright. The GPL attempts to deter programmers from closing the source code of a FOSS computer program to prevent the program from being developed in a proprietary environment. The GPL needs to be distinguished from the licences (based on the Open Source Definition) produced by the Open Source Initiative (OSI), another open-source movement founded in 1998. While the GPL requires any redistribution of GPL software to be released under a GPL licence only (to stop the code being closed-off), licences based on the OSI's Open Source Definition allow redistribution under the same terms, but do not require it. In other words, programmers can take OSI software and go on to release modified software under new terms that include making it proprietary. As such OSI has become very attractive to industry giants such as IBM and Oracle. For a more detailed discussion of Open Source, see the excellent chapter in UNCTAD's E-Commerce and Development Report 2003 (Ch.: 'Free and Open-source Software: Implications for ICT Policy and Development').

171. UNCTAD E-Commerce and Development Report 2003 p. 95.

172. Ibid.

173. Ibid. p. 100.

174. Ibid. p. 106.

175. Developing country public sectors (e.g. in South Africa, India, China) have already to begun to use FOSS and encourage it in the private sector for three basic reasons: (1) a desire for independence from being tied into proprietary products; (2) the need for security, given that to guarantee national security, governments should not have to rely on systems controlled at a distance; and (3) new IPR enforcement on proprietary systems where excessive copyrighting and patent hoarding diverts funds from R&D in the host country to patent acquisition and royalty payments. See E-Commerce and Development Report 2003 p. 113. Singapore, through its Economic Development Board, is providing tax incentives for companies who use GNU/Linux as an operating system as opposed to proprietary applications. Ibid. at p. 116.

176. Discussed earlier in this chapter at p. 483.

177. K. Maskus, *ICTSD–UNCTAD Dialogue, 2nd Bellagio Series on Development and Intellectual Property* (September 2003) p. 14. This proposal was first discussed by J. Barton in 'Preserving the Global Scientific and Technological Commons', Stanford University manuscript (2003).

178. For example at the recent WSIS in December 2003, some of the poorest countries advocated the creation of a Digital Solidarity Fund, envisioned as a UN-administered fund to help technologically disadvantaged countries build telephone lines and other infrastructure in an effort to keep the digital and the wealth gap from widening further. No agreement on the fund could be reached in Geneva, and the idea was postponed to the second phase of talks in Tunis in 2005 where only voluntary agreement was reached.

179. UNCTAD E-Commerce and Development Report 2003 p. 116.

180. Ibid.

181. Ibid. For a detailed case study on the use of ICT in development, see the case study on Jamaica: R. Kariyawasam, *Readiness for the Networked World: Jamaica Assessment* at: http://cyber.law.harvard.edu/home/2002-01 (date accessed October 2004).

182. See quotes from the Stakeholder Alliance at: http://www.stakeholderalliance. org/Buzz.html (date accessed October 2004).

The relationship between intellectual property law and competition law: an economic approach

PIERRE RÉGIBEAU AND KATHARINE ROCKETT

Introduction

The purpose of this chapter is to present an economic analysis of intellectual property right (IPR) law and its relationship with competition policy. The relevant economic literature on this subject is enormous and complex. Here, we will strive for simplicity, trying to extract the main concepts and proposing simple principles that might help to guide the application and design of both intellectual property and antitrust laws. While our analysis does not account for every single aspect of intellectual property law or every single competitive situation, we do believe that the analysis does derive useful general principles.

The overriding thesis of this chapter will be the separation of intellectual property and competition law. This separation will apply to the design of the law: IP law should limit itself to properly *assigning* and *defending* property rights while competition law should be concerned with the *use* of such property rights. More precisely, competition law should be concerned only with the use and abuse of property rights that are sources of monopoly power. This principle of separation also applies to the enforcement of the law. The main theme here is the equality of treatment of various sources of monopoly power, i.e. of the use of various property rights. We will argue that once property rights of various types have been properly assigned, there is no reason for competition policy to further distinguish between the sources of monopoly power. In particular, there is no need to treat monopoly power based on IP as 'special' because of some supposedly unique characteristics such as its importance to innovation or the public good nature of information. This is taken into account already in the special types of property rights that apply to intellectual property.

We develop our main thesis in two parts. Part I of the chapter outlines the economics of property rights in general as well as the economics of intellectual property. In this part of the chapter, we argue that the economics literature broadly supports a design of intellectual property protection that looks similar to the system already in place, taking into account the special features of intellectual property. In Part II of the chapter we use this to make our argument for independence. We summarise our position in a set of principles for competition policy that include restraint, a commitment not to revisit ex post the rights granted by IP law, and a commitment not to make large changes in property right regimes only when very large changes in ex post regulation occur.

This main thesis does not mean that the IP/competition law interface does not have some specificity. We investigate this issue in section C of Part II of the chapter. We find that there are special concerns in the areas of mergers, licensing and cross-licensing, patent pools, grant-backs, various practices that extend the legal patent monopoly beyond the life of the patent, interfaces and interoperability, umbrella branding, and compulsory trademark licensing. Largely, these come from special behaviours that are rarely observed in practice when market power comes from the ownership of other types of exclusive assets.

Part I. Economic analysis of (intellectual) property rights

We first present an overview of the economic analysis of property rights. We ask only later if and how intellectual property rights might be distinct. We find that there are two main differences between intellectual property and 'real' property: intellectual property has strong public good characteristics and tends to generate significant amounts of socially useful information, making diffusion of information an important concern. These differences help one to understand the distinct property regimes that apply to different types of intellectual and 'real' property. In particular, we concentrate on two aspects of property rights: the duration for which they are imparted and the 'scope' of the rights. We follow the economics literature's analysis of the economically optimal duration and scope of rights, finding that the current system does not differ greatly from the system that would be recommended by the existing economics literature. Patents, copyrights and trademarks are considered in turn.

A. Property rights and efficiency

From an economic point of view, property rights are a necessary condition to achieve efficiency. The economic concept of efficiency relies on the notion of opportunity cost. The opportunity cost of using any resource is the return that this resource would have obtained in its best possible alternative use. Hence the opportunity cost of using a piece of land to build new flats might be the net benefits that would have accrued to the community if the land had been developed as a park. It is customary to distinguish between 'static' and 'dynamic' efficiency.

1. Efficiency

Static efficiency is attained when consumers and producers make their decisions, taking into account the true opportunity cost of the resources involved. It is convenient to distinguish between two aspects of static efficiency. Consider first the market for a single product in isolation. Static efficiency requires that the price of the good be equal to the marginal (opportunity) cost of producing it. This ensures that consumers take the appropriate cost of production into account when deciding how much of the product to purchase, so that they purchase neither too little nor too much of the good. If price were above marginal cost – as it would be in the presence of market power – then consumers would purchase too little of the good. The additional satisfaction that consumers would have enjoyed from consuming the units that they would have bought had the price been set at marginal cost is the static social cost of monopoly. It is called the deadweight loss.[1] Once many sectors are considered simultaneously, the fact that the relevant cost of production is the marginal opportunity cost takes its true meaning. As the cost of using a resource is equal to the benefits that it would have generated if it had been employed in another sector, the allocation of resources should be such that their marginal returns are equated across sectors. This aspect of static efficiency is sometimes referred to as allocative efficiency.

There is no universally accepted definition of dynamic efficiency. For our purpose, it suffices to say that it relates to any kind of investment decision. This concept of 'investment' must be understood broadly. While it clearly covers the development of improved machines, products or methods of production (i.e. research and development), it also includes the creation of physical assets (for example new plants, or the clearing of new arable land) as well as their maintenance.

As for static efficiency, let us first consider one investment project in isolation. Dynamic efficiency requires that the project be undertaken if – and only if – its social benefits exceed the opportunity cost of the resources invested. In other words, inefficient investment decisions can occur when the stream of private revenues generated by the investment is not equal to its social benefits. Even in the absence of direct externalities, there is no reason to believe that private investment choices will generally be efficient, as two opposing forces are at play. Consider a firm introducing a new product. On the one hand, it will not usually be able to capture all of the benefits that this new product creates for consumers. This is clearest when the firm charges the same price for each unit of the product, as every consumer purchasing the good enjoys benefits that are at least as high as the price demanded. If consumers differ in their enjoyment of the good but pay the same price, some of them must inevitably obtain benefits that are strictly higher than the price paid. Hence this appropriability effect leads to insufficient investment as the firms cannot capture all of the value that they create. On the other hand, the new product is likely to reduce the sales of older existing products and the profits that other firms obtain from these sales. In other words, the introduction of the new product imposes a loss on other firms that is not properly considered by the innovating firm. This business stealing effect leads to excessive investment.

Once many sectors are considered simultaneously, dynamic efficiency also requires that the allocation of resources between different investment projects be correct. This requires that the (marginal) social rate of return of investment be equalised across sectors. There is unfortunately little hope that such efficiency will always obtain, for two main reasons. Firstly, there are no reasons to believe that the appropriability effect and the business stealing effect discussed above will have the same relative strength across all sectors of activity. This means that, even in the absence of any policy intervention, one would expect over-investment in some sectors and under-investment in others. Secondly, differences in private returns to investment can result from public policy measures. In particular, an uneven application of competition law across sectors or across various sources of monopoly power (for example, intellectual property versus other forms of property rights) would create artificial differences between private returns to various types of investments.

2. Property Rights

From an economic point of view, property rights are assigned for four main reasons.

2.1 To maintain peace and order   Together with other aspects of the legal system, legally enforceable property rights help minimise physical violence – and the associated destruction of economic resources – aimed at securing the control of assets that are sources of economic rewards. This factor clearly applies to all types of property, 'real' or 'intellectual'.

2.2 To assign decision rights   From our discussion of static efficiency, it should be clear that an efficient allocation of resources cannot be obtained unless someone (individual or collectivity) has the right to decide how economic assets are used. However, the consequences of this principle are rather different depending on whether it is applied to 'real' or to 'intellectual' property. This is because most forms of 'real' property are seen as private goods while intellectual property is generally thought to be a public good. Private goods are characterised by rivalry in usage, i.e. they cannot be used by more than one economic agent at the same time: we cannot both eat the same apple. Because of this, it is generally optimal to let a single agent decide how the good ought to be used. Public goods, on the other hand, are such that usage by one agent does not preclude usage by another: Unless the beach is very busy, my view of the sea does not 'crowd out' your view of the sea. As long as there is no rivalry at all in the consumption of a good, it is optimal to let as many agents as possible have access to it. This is the case with knowledge: my using Pythagoras' theorem does not in any respect restrict your own access to it. Hence, once knowledge has been created, the best possible policy is one of free access, making exclusive property rights undesirable. To summarise then, the need to assign decision rights is one of the reasons for allocating property rights on private goods but not on public goods such as most forms of intellectual property.

2.3 To reward investment This factor relates to dynamic efficiency. The idea is simply that no rational economic agent will incur the cost of investing in developing or maintaining property unless she is able to collect some corresponding reward. Hence, if sufficient investment is to be induced, investors must be given property rights over the fruits of their investment so that they can capture a significant proportion of the value that they create. Although this factor applies to all types of property, it is of special importance for assets whose development and/or maintenance require significant effort.

2.4 To favour the diffusion of information Agents investing in assets might try to exploit them 'secretly', expending effort to prevent others from gaining information about the asset. Hence a manufacturing firm might change its production process unbeknownst to the outside world, or a prospector might go to great length to exploit a gold mine without revealing its location. Such secrecy is socially undesirable for two reasons. Firstly, the resources spent on preventing information from leaking out to other agents are diverted from productive uses. Secondly, if information about the asset is useful in the ulterior development of other assets, secrecy reduces the pace of economic development by limiting the information available to other investors.

This second aspect is an issue of dynamic efficiency. Although similar in spirit, it differs from the third factor discussed above, whereby property rights were required to provide a sufficient reward to investors. To see this, consider the case where an invention cannot be reverse-engineered. Property rights are not necessary in order to reward the inventor's investment since the invention can be commercialised successfully without any risk of imitation. On the other hand, the inventor will only reveal information about the innovation if sufficient protection is offered and if this protection is made conditional on the release of information. Without protection the inventor would not only fear direct imitation of her innovation but also the faster emergence of new innovations making her own inventive step obsolete. Without conditionality, the inventor would have no incentive to reveal any information, regardless of the level of protection provided.

This function of property rights is clearly most important for assets that generate large amounts of information that is potentially useful for further investments. As should be obvious from the example above, investments in intellectual assets tend to produce such information abundantly. While one can think of similar examples for some real assets (for example prospecting for gold), this 'information' diffusion factor seems to be more relevant for intellectual property.

Considering these four factors together, we can identify two main differences between intellectual property and 'real' property: intellectual property has strong public good characteristics and tends to generate significant amounts of socially useful information, making diffusion of information an important concern. These differences help understand the distinct property regimes that apply to different types of intellectual and real property. For simplicity, we will concentrate on two aspects of property rights, the 'duration' for which they are imparted and 'scope' of the rights, loosely defined as 'what is actually protected by the rights'.[2]

The scope of property rights on 'real' assets is easily defined. There is usually little room for ambiguity: having rights on my house does not, for example, imply that I can prevent anyone from owning or using a copy of my house on the plot of land next to mine. Rights on 'real' assets are also usually granted without an explicit time limit.[3] Going back to our economic analysis of property rights we can see that this design makes sense: because 'real' property tends to be rival, it is efficient to have exclusive property rights assigned throughout the useful life of the asset (see reason 2 above). Finally, because diffusion of information is a lesser concern, rights on real assets can usually be obtained without having to explicitly divulge information about the asset and/or how it was developed.[4]

As we will discuss at some length in the following sections, the scope of intellectual property is itself a rather complex concept. One should therefore not be surprised that a large chunk of intellectual property law is devoted to its definition and implementation. We also know that, with (some types of) intellectual property, diffusion of information is an important concern. The fact that property rights are often of limited duration should therefore not be surprising.

B. Application to IPRs

In this section we apply our economic analysis of property rights to make two main points. Firstly, we show that the factors identified above can help us to organise an apparently disparate economic literature on IP protection. This is quite useful, as this literature is essential to any economic analysis of the interface between IP law and competition law. Secondly, we argue that there is not much distance between the type of IPR protection that economic analysis would recommend and the actual structure of (most) IPR laws. In particular economic analysis supports the existence of distinct protection regimes for patentable material, copyrightable material and trade marks. In fact, it is when IPR law departs from the traditional assignment of property between these regimes – as in the case of software protection – that it sometimes runs counter to economic analysis.

As we have seen above, the two main factors explaining the need to grant property rights on intellectual assets are the reward effect, which induces investment by ensuring that the inventor can reap significant benefits from her innovation and the information diffusion or disclosure effect, whereby the inventor is 'bribed' into divulging useful information about her innovation. Both effects involve trade-offs between dynamic and static efficiency. The right to exclude others from using an intellectual asset for a given length of time only provides the rights holder with an economic reward or 'bribe' if it provides some monopoly power. The more significant the monopoly power, the larger the reward but also the larger the loss in static efficiency due to the fact that prices rise above opportunity costs. The general principle guiding the design of intellectual property rights should therefore be to find the combinations of duration and scope that ensure a given level of reward to the inventor at the smallest possible cost in terms of induced inefficiencies.

1. Patents

The economics literature on the design of the patent system is very diffused. Different conceptions of how innovation occurs and different aspects of the patent system have led to a wide variety of analyses. Still, these disparate pieces can be fitted broadly into the two effects described above. This section will briefly review some of the more important papers in the literature, attempting to fit the approaches of various authors into our simple framework. While this review is not exhaustive, it should give a feel for how the principles derived from the economic theory of property rights can be applied to design an efficient system of patent protection.

A first strand of the economic literature on patents assumes that there is a single potential innovation for which inventors compete. This set up rules out any role for our disclosure effect since further inventions are not considered. When we only consider the length of the period of protection, the reward effect also takes a very simple form: the longer the length of protection, the greater both the reward and the social cost from the resulting monopoly power. The aim of the earliest contribution to this literature was precisely to generate an optimal patent length, balancing the rewards as inducements to innovation against the deadweight loss generated by a grant of patent monopoly.[5]

This approach was extended to include the determination of both the length and the breadth of patent protection. The issue then is how to structure the reward to innovation, for a given reward size. As the analysis only relates to a single innovation, the appropriate notion of breadth is quite straightforward: the breadth of patent protection is increased by any measure that increases the cost of imitating the protected invention. The first contribution to this line of research was Tandon's analysis of compulsory licensing.[6] In his model, patent holders are obliged to license their intellectual property to all comers at a regulated royalty rate. The lower the royalty, the lower the effective monopoly power of the patent holder and, therefore, the longer the period of protection required to ensure that inventors obtain an adequate reward on their investment. In other words, the regulated royalty rate plays the role of patent breadth. In Tandon's model, a very long patent (infinitely lived, in fact), accompanied by a very low regulated royalty rate on compulsory licences is optimal as this minimises the monopoly distortion per period while maintaining innovation incentives. In fact, Tandon points out that this result favouring length over scope of protection follows from the fact that social welfare is far more sensitive to the royalty rate in his model than to the length of time during which the royalty is paid.

The trade-off involved in Tandon's work is analysed in quite general terms by Gilbert and Shapiro[7] who simply assume that, during the period of protection, greater breadth increases the firm's profit but decreases welfare. They then show that the crucial element is whether greater breadth increases profits more rapidly than the associated welfare deadweight loss. If it does, then a regime with broad protection for a short period of time is optimal. If it does not, then small breadth and long length are called for. While quite general, this principle is not especially useful if one does not know which way the comparison goes. For a relatively general case, where profits and welfare are both concave in output,[8] Gilbert and Shapiro show that the most efficient way to reward innovation is to grant very long patents that are only just broad enough to attain the desired level of reward. They point out, however, that their results favouring long patent lives crucially depend on the assumption that patent breadth only affects price. Hence, the extent of substitution away from the patented product, and the associated deadweight loss, always increase with breadth.[9] Klemperer[10] considers a somewhat different situation, where products are not homogeneous. In his paper, imitators produce 'knock offs' that are of lower quality than the patented product. In this framework, broad patents create a large distortion from monopoly pricing of the patented good but narrow patents result in a suboptimal allocation where most consumers purchase the less desirable 'knock offs'. Klemperer shows that, depending on whether the effect of switching to knock off brands or switching out of the product class entirely dominates, the socially optimal manner of providing the inventor with a given reward can involve either narrow breadth with long length or large breadth with small length. Klemperer's contribution must therefore be seen as showing that

Gilbert and Shapiro's conclusion that narrow patents are optimal is not robust. It only holds when consumers are similar along a particular dimension: they must all face similar costs of substituting to less preferred varieties although they may differ in their costs of substituting out of the patent class. If consumers are similar to each other along other dimensions, this result may be completely overturned. Given that accurate information about the precise form of consumer preferences in each market is unlikely to be available, this portion of the literature does not yield strong policy recommendations toward either extreme in patent protection. The best route might therefore lie somewhere in between, arguing for a finite duration and moderate breadth.

We have assumed so far that, in principle, patents can be granted that confer some degree of monopoly power forever. The starting point of a second, more recent strand of the economics literature is that, in practice, the effective lifetime of the patent may be curtailed by subsequent innovation that supersedes the patented technology. Most of this literature still focuses on what we called the reward effect, but the trade-offs involved are more complex. This reflects the greater complexity of the notion of patent breadth itself. Economists distinguish between lagging breadth and leading breadth.[11] Lagging breadth is the protection granted against imitation while leading breadth refers to protection with respect to further improvements. The distinction between imitation and improvements can be made quite precise: *assuming that the initial innovation is sold at marginal cost,*[12] an imitation does not increase social welfare, while an improvement does. In other words, improvements 'add value' but imitations do not. Notice however, that, to qualify as an improvement a subsequent innovation does not need to be strictly better than the initial invention. It suffices that it be better for at least some users. In economic terms this means that improvements include both 'vertical' and 'horizontal' differentiation. While lagging and leading breadth are economic concepts, they do correspond to distinct aspects of legal doctrine. In legal terms, the strength of lagging breadth is defined by the doctrines of disclosure and enablement, while leading breadth is determined by the interpretations of 'use of a technology', the doctrine of equivalents, and the doctrine of reverse equivalents.

An innovation starts off a research route, after which other innovations build on the first. In this sense, the entire benefit to society that follows from this stream of innovations can be attributed to the first inventor. It follows that a social planner, taking into account this entire stream of benefits, would have full incentives to undertake efforts to initiate entire research paths. Private firms may not, however, as their reward to innovation is limited by time, the 'leading breadth' of the patent (in other words the quality improvements that would actually fall under the original patent), and the transfer of demand to improved products. In order to restore their incentives, then, this literature argues for broad patent protection.

This argument has taken various forms. Green and Scotchmer[13] interpret the novelty requirement as setting the minimum quality improvement that will infringe a patent. O'Donoghue[14] makes this more precise by saying that a patentability requirement, specifying the minimum innovative step that would receive patent protection, is a combination of novelty, non-obviousness, and utility. If an initial innovation is to be improved by another firm, the initial innovator and the improver can increase their joint profits by signing licensing agreements to share industry profits. For example, an agreement can be signed that assures the initial innovator will have sufficient reward to induce him to undertake the initial innovation, and also assures that the improver will have sufficient reward to induce investment in the improvement. Varying the patentability requirement changes the relative bargaining positions of the initial and follow-on innovators in such licensing agreements by changing the rewards to firms if they fail to strike an agreement. As Green and Scotchmer's concern is to transfer more profit to the initial innovator, they argue for a stringent patentability requirement.

In fact, taken literally, Green and Scotchmer's argument implies that all future innovations beyond some 'first' in a research stream should be judged unpatentable and infringing.[15] However, Denicolo[16] points out that the sequential innovation line of reasoning assumes that no patent race occurs to generate innovation. Adding such a race to the model has two effects. First, there may be socially excessive amounts of innovation: because of the business stealing effect discussed above, firms racing for a patent may invest too much compared to what would be socially desirable. Once the possibility of socially excessive innovation is introduced, welfare is not necessarily improved by raising the reward of the first innovator as much as possible. Furthermore, it is possible to show that, when competition for the innovation is explicitly considered, leading breadth might best be relatively narrow for the initial innovation. The reason for this is that too large a breadth on the initial innovation limits the firms' incentives to racing for improvement: if 'winning the race' means paying large royalties to the initial inventor, why bother? In other words, if the improvements are, effectively, reserved for the initial inventor then the lack of competition may result in under-investment in later stages of the inventive process.

It is also useful to understand that most of the papers in this literature assume a specific antitrust regime in the sense that particular licensing arrangements are assumed to be available to firms, or that particular pricing policies are allowed. The optimal patent policy tends to change depending on the antitrust assumptions made. In Gilbert and Shapiro, for example, the breadth of the patent has the effect of raising price, but so would loose competition policy. Hence a more permissive application of competition policy would make it desirable to narrow the breadth of patent protection. In Green and Scotchmer[17] licensing agreements that divide industry profits earned from the stream of innovation are allowed before the improving innovation occurs. In fact, a liberal licensing policy is optimal as it increases the maximum reward that can be transferred to the first innovator. O'Donoghue, Scotchmer and Thisse[18] also suggest that allowing collusive agreements for stimulating the flow of R&D might be beneficial. However, these conclusions are not robust for the reason discussed in the previous paragraph: once competition for the innovations is considered, increasing the reward of the first innovator as much as possible is no longer optimal.

O'Donoghue[19] modifies the approach taken by Scotchmer and co-authors and assumes that the size of the innovative step is a choice variable for the innovating firm. In other words, O'Donoghue focuses not on how patentability affects the *bargaining* power of firms when innovations are improved in given steps, but how a stringent patentability requirement can induce firms to invest in bigger steps and so change the actual type of innovation that occurs. O'Donoghue argues that forcing firms to only patent bigger steps makes innovation more infrequent. As this increases the average incumbency period of an innovator (the effective length of protection), it increases the reward to innovation. This, in turn, stimulates further investment in research.[20] On the other hand, bigger inventive steps also mean that the latest innovation faces less of a competitive constraint from the previous generations of inventions, increasing the static welfare loss. The optimal patent regimes rely on significant – but finite – leading breadth to balance these two effects.

To summarise this second strand of the economics literature, there appears to be little robust argument for either of the extreme policies of very long, narrow patents or very short, wide patents. Some middle ground appears to be the more reasonable path that balances the need to compensate early innovators for the externality they generate in terms of stimulating future innovation, while providing sufficient incentives for researchers to take those follow-on steps in a timely manner. Any more precise recommendations tend not to be general and so are not appropriate to a policy that is not tailored to particular industries.

The streams of literature mentioned above do not generally take into account what we have called the information diffusion effect. Exceptions to this are Scotchmer and Green[21] and Matutes, Régibeau and Rockett.[22] Both of these papers assume some kind of sequential innovation, but the emphasis is different. Scotchmer and Green identify the following trade-off. While a strong novelty requirement confers a large reward to innovation, because it reduces the substitutability between the patentable innovation and other technologies, it also means that relatively minor advances are not patentable. Since the informational spillovers from these minor patents would speed up the development of the field a strong novelty requirement also has a social cost.

Matutes, Régibeau and Rockett[23] focus on the patent protection that a basic innovation should be granted, when that innovation is likely to generate a stream of applications. In their model, the basic innovator may be tempted to 'opt out' of the patent system, at least temporarily, in order to stockpile applications before applying for a patent.[24] This delay in applying for the patent reduces disclosure and so reduces the ability of other firms to benefit by developing applications themselves. The conclusion of the paper is that, by designing patents to grant a 'limited licence to hunt' for applications this wasteful delay can be reduced. Hence, patent protection should be extended to applications beyond the existing demonstrated usefulness of the product or process as specified in the claims in order to induce early disclosure of fundamental innovations, while preserving firms' incentive to innovate. The optimal scope, then, implies that inventors of basic innovations obtain protection on applications that have not yet been fully worked out, requiring a more lenient review of claims than is current practice.

A smaller stream of literature considers whether the patent system might better be redesigned entirely. The more sophisticated and recent of these papers use the tools of mechanism design to completely rework the system of rewarding innovation. Earlier papers adopt a simpler approach. Wright,[25] for example, considers whether a system of prizes in exchange for commissioned work would be more socially optimal. For example, such a system would not necessarily entail the deadweight loss that the patent system's conferral of monopoly generates. Unfortunately, Wright's system places strong informational requirements on governmental authorities so that they can correctly 'pick winners'. If one assumes that firms, or individual inventors, have better information than the government on the relative costs and benefits of innovation then some form of delegation, like patenting, might work better. In the more sophisticated strain, Kremer[26] proposes an auction system to supplement, rather than replace, the existing patent system as a mechanism to stimulate innovation while reducing deadweight loss. He claims that this will solve some of the informational problems of Wright's framework by using the auction mechanism to allow private industry to 'reveal' the true value of the innovation. He acknowledges, however, that collusion amongst the private firms in the auction could result in large compensation being paid to industry for innovations that had very little social value.

In sum, then, the reward function of patents has been investigated in quite a lot more detail than the disclosure function. The literature on optimal patent design has complemented this by investigating not only how protection should be structured to guarantee a given level of reward (whatever that might be), but also whether the patent system is optimal in a broader sense as a way of creating incentives to innovate. The 'bottom line' on this stream of research, however, is that something that looks like the current patent system can be defended as optimal from an economics viewpoint. Within the current patent system, there is a relatively strong argument for broad lagging breadth, as well as for a finite effective patent length guaranteed through a combination of leading breadth and duration of patent protection.

2. Copyrights

Copyright laws are not meant to apply to the same type of material as patent laws. Very roughly, copyright laws seek to encourage and protect creative expression, while patent laws deal with innovation. While sometimes subtle, the difference between the two types of creative activities involved is not purely semantic.

Let us first consider our disclosure/diffusion effect. The 'ideas' or 'knowledge' contained in traditional copyrightable material are automatically revealed through the publication and (possible) sale of the product.[27] While the author can of course keep her work secret, she cannot commercially exploit it without revealing all of its socially useful content. The need to offer protection in order to induce the revelation of all relevant information is therefore smaller than in the case of patentable material. On economics grounds, then, we would expect copyright protection to be 'weaker' than patent protection.

It is sometimes argued that the 'reward' effect is also of little relevance to copyrightable works as they are the result of a 'need to create' that is little influenced by economic incentives. If that were true then, the economic argument for offering any protection at all would be very weak. In fact, the (scarce) empirical evidence available suggests that the production of some types of copyrighted material does respond to economic incentives.[28] Hence, some amount of protection grounded in our 'reward' effect seems justified. But what form should this protection take?

Two characteristics of traditional copyrightable material are relevant. Firstly, the 'sequential' aspect of innovation, which was so important in determining the appropriate patent protection regime, seems less acute. While creative works do sometimes trigger further waves of creation,[29] this process seems somewhat more diffused and harder to define than in the case of patentable innovations. This would make the determination of any significant 'leading breadth' somewhat hazardous. Furthermore, creative work is rarely made obsolete by its progeny: while a 'better mousetrap' makes the original invention useless, another impressionist painting hardly detracts from the value of earlier works from the same school.[30] One would therefore expect copyright law to offer little in terms of 'leading breadth', concentrating instead on lagging breadth, i.e. protection against copying and length.

A second characteristic of importance is that, given the nature of the material it deals with, copyright law is strictly constrained by the desire not to infringe on freedom of expression. In terms of our analysis of property rights, this means that even protection against copying would be of limited scope as greater breadth might have an unacceptable stifling effect on public discourse. In other words, one would expect that protection against copying might not be absolute[31] and that the definition of what constitutes 'copying' would be rather narrow. As there are good reasons to keep both 'leading' and 'lagging' breadth narrow, copyright protection would naturally tend to rely more heavily on the length of the period of protection.[32] Overall then, based on the basic economic principles derived in Part I of this chapter, copyright protection should be quite narrow but long. In that sense, actual copyright protection regimes closely resemble the optimal regime predicted by economic theory.[33]

On the other hand, our analysis also suggests that extending copyright protection to less traditional works might not be appropriate. In particular, using copyright law to protect creations that include inventive steps would not make sense. In the presence of such steps, issues of sequential innovation resurface, calling for a different protection regime. On economic grounds therefore, there is a strong argument for protecting innovative software under patent law rather than under copyright law.

The recent economics literature on copyrights points out two further factors that differentiate copyrights from patents. Both factors refer to the traditional static trade-off between incentives to 'invent' and the welfare loss imputable to monopoly power. On the 'reward' side, several authors have shown that *copying does not necessarily hurt* the producer of copyrighted material. Although the precise mechanism involved varies, the key factor is that copying helps the monopolist commit to pricing strategies that she would like to implement. An example will suffice to illustrate this basic principle.[34] The first example relies on price discrimination. Suppose that the copyrighted good is characterised by network externalities, i.e. the valuation of the good for any given consumer increases with the number of other consumers who also have access to the product (or its copies).[35] To entice consumers to buy, the copyright holder would like to 'promise' to sell enough to create a large network of users. Unfortunately, this promise is not credible as potential buyers know that, once the firm has acquired a basic 'installed base' of consumers, it will find it optimal to increase prices and slow down the growth of the network. In this perspective, weaker copyright protection might help as it guarantees that a large number of copies will in fact be made available: This guarantee increases the willingness to pay by consumers, making them more willing to purchase the product early on and at a higher price. The basic lesson from this strand of the literature is therefore that the reward obtained by the copyright holder does not necessarily increase with the strength of copyright protection. In that sense, it is a further argument for granting weaker protection to copyrighted work than to patentable innovations.

On the other side of the traditional reward/monopoly trade-off, Novos and Waldman[36] have shown that, under some conditions, *an increase in copyright protection can in fact increase static welfare*. In other words, greater protection might increase the copyright holder's reward (subject to the caveat above) without creating a corresponding deadweight loss. In their set-up, the marginal cost of physical production is the same for the original good and each of its illegal copies. However, copying incurs an additional cost that increases with the intensity of copyright protection. Illegal copies are supplied competitively at this augmented marginal cost. The respective market shares of the original product and its copies are such that the marginal customer is indifferent between the two options. This means that this consumer is willing to incur a copying cost equal to the price charged for the original product. Because the copyright holder charges a price in excess of its own marginal cost, this means that the marginal cost incurred by the marginal 'copying' customer is higher than the marginal cost incurred to serve the marginal buyer of the original product. By shifting some consumers from copies to the original, increased copyright protection lowers the cost at which these 'shifted' consumers are served, increasing total welfare.[37] While surprising and interesting, the importance of this result should not be overstated: it depends on specific assumptions about the distribution of imitation costs and there is no evidence as to the likely magnitude of the effect. In particular, we would find it unwise to conclude from Novos and Waldman's analysis that copyright protection can be increased from its current level at no social cost.

3. Trade marks

The economics of trade marks is quite distinct from that of copyrights or patents. Trade marks, roughly speaking, are words, symbols or other signifiers used to distinguish a good or service produced by one firm from those produced by other firms.

The benefits of trade marks are several-fold. First, trade marks reduce consumer search cost by allowing consumers to quickly identify products with desirable attributes. This statement relies on several assumptions about the trade marked goods. First, for the trade mark to have this benefit, it should be the case that the attributes of the product cannot be readily identified by simple inspection of the product. In other words, the trade-marked good should be an experience good in the sense that a consumer must be able to consume it in order to evaluate its true characteristics. Second, the producer of the trademarked good must be able to maintain consistent characteristics in the product, including its quality, over time. Otherwise, past consumption would be no guide to future consumption of the same good. Consumers, in turn, would not be willing to pay more for a trade-marked product because it would not reduce their search cost.

Trade marks also give firms an incentive to improve the quality of their product. Without an exclusive right on an identifying mark, a firm that is producing a lower-quality version of a good might be tempted to free ride on the firms producing high-quality versions by duplicating their trade marks and so misleading consumers into believing that the brands were equivalent. Since this would make it impossible for consumers to distinguish the high quality products, it would lower their willingness to pay for any product in this market. This would, in turn, lower the return to investing in quality and so would lower the incentive to create high quality products. Hence, the average quality of products in markets without trade mark protection would be lower than in markets with trade mark protection.

Clearly, other mechanisms are available to ensure product quality. For example, the legal system allows for damages to be paid to parties that have been subject to deceptive practices. Hence, a firm claiming high quality and, in fact, supplying low quality could be required to compensate its customers. The damage system has disadvantages, however, in the sense that excessive damages can create perverse incentives for customers to induce breach (such as sabotaging a jetliner in order to collect on a particular passenger's death) while inadequate damages might not have the required disciplining function on firms. Reputational costs, imposed through market mechanisms, can work alongside damages to ensure product quality without creating perverse incentives. For example, suppose that a trademarked product proved to have low, rather than high, quality. Consumers would impose a cost on the firm by refusing to purchase. These costs would not go into the pocket of the deceived customers, however, so that they would not have an incentive to induce breach. Furthermore, these reputational costs can be, and in fact have been, measured to be, quite high.[38] This could serve to discipline firms. In fact, De Alessi and Staaf suggest that the reason why damages often are relatively low in deception cases is precisely because the market imposes discipline of its own.

The role of trade marks in ensuring quality can be likened to the reward effect that we have identified in earlier sections: Legal protection of trade marks allows an investment in quality to be rewarded by repeat purchase and other reputation effects (such as word-of-mouth advertising). This reward is associated with some 'monopoly power' over the distinctive trade mark in the sense that others can be excluded from using the same or a confusingly similar trade mark. Still, to the extent that identifying names (and, in particular, fanciful names) are potentially in infinite supply (and at low cost of development) this monopoly power is not associated with a static welfare loss, as it is not associated with exclusion of other identical products from the market. Further, the power to exclude under trade mark protection does not extend to the functionality of the product.[39] Hence, it is not possible to exclude another firm from producing a physically identical product: It is simply impossible to identify it in a way that confuses consumers about its source. This means that there is no static welfare loss associated with monopoly power over a product's function under trade mark law.[40] Notice that the diffusion of information effect is not present in the case of trade marks, as their use discloses all relevant information.

As a result, trade marks have mostly a positive incentive effect, which suggests that they should be legally protected as long as they are used. In fact, when trade marks are allowed to be protected without use, they can be stockpiled. There is some evidence that this stockpiling causes barriers to entry in some markets, as the field of potentially attractive trade marks is reduced.[41] In terms of the scope of protection, the economic benefits of trade marks are present as long as confusion is not present. Hence, the economically appropriate scope is one that permits marks as long as they are not confusingly similar.[42]

Overall, then, the economics of trade mark protection and the intellectual property law of those marks are broadly in line. There are, however, some issues involved in the use of trade marks that need to be discussed. In particular, umbrella branding could raise concerns about extension of monopoly power from one market to another and compulsory licensing of trade marks as a remedy could have welfare-decreasing consequences by reducing the incentive to maintain high quality. These will be discussed later in the paper.

Part II. IPRs and competition policy: an economic perspective

A. Introduction

In this section, we address two sets of issues. We first consider the systemic design of IP and competition law, trying to identify their separate functions and goals and to clarify the nature of their interaction. Our basic message is that, although these two fields of the law have a joint impact on economic incentives and performance, there is little need for explicit coordination. In particular, we argue that the supposed 'conflicts' between IP law and competition law can be resolved by abiding by a few simple rules. The second issue is how, given a systemic design, competition law should be implemented when monopoly power is based on intellectual property rights. We will argue that, as a general rule, the treatment of IP-based monopoly power should not differ from the treatment of monopoly power stemming from any other source. In practice, however, market power rooted in IPRs retains some distinctiveness as some practices (for example cross-licensing) are more likely to emerge. We give some examples of such practices and briefly discuss how they should be treated.

B. The argument for independence

Intellectual property law differs from competition law in both its function and its goals. Broadly speaking, the main function of IP law is to properly assign and defend property rights on assets that might have economic value. The main function of competition law is to regulate the use of (intellectual) property rights *when these rights are sources of market power*. This market power element is important as intellectual property law also regulates the use of the property rights that it assigns but without reference to monopoly power.[43] From an economic perspective, then, the main goal of intellectual property law should be to strike the right balance between the various effects identified in the first part of our paper. On the other hand, the main goal of competition law should be to minimise the adverse consequences of monopoly power.

It is also important to consider the fact that intellectual property law and competition law tend to intervene at different stages of the economic life cycle of an asset. Property rights are generally assigned very soon after the asset has been created, while competition law only intervenes significantly later, once using the asset has become the basis for some market power. An important consequence of this difference in timing is that the information available when property rights are granted is not the same as the information available when competition law cases arise. In particular, competition law authorities are likely to have much better information about the economic importance of a given innovation and about the structure of the market(s) where the innovation is used.

The fact that the two fields of law have distinct functions and objectives does not necessarily mean that they can be designed and implemented separately. In fact, there seems to be an unavoidable source of conflict between the two bodies of law. While IP rights do not necessarily confer significant monopoly power, they can only be effective if they sometimes do. After all, it is the expectation of some monopoly rents that drive both the reward and disclosure effects discussed in Part I of this chapter – Economic analysis of (intellectual) property rights. As competition law effectively constrains an agent's ability to exploit its monopoly power, the two approaches appear to be on a collision course. Moreover, as competition law tends to have access to more detailed information than was available at the time property rights were granted, there is a great temptation to revisit the trade-off between innovation incentives and the inefficiencies resulting from the use of exclusive property rights.

The conflict between IP law and competition law is less 'unavoidable' than it might seem. One reason for this is that the assignment of property rights handles the 'reward' and 'disclosure' effects discussed in Part I of this chapter by offering an expected reward to the rights holder. In many cases, this promised reward will not in fact materialise, as the innovation fails to find a profitable market or is rapidly pre-empted by further advances. In other cases, though, the innovation might prove significantly more profitable for a longer period than was initially thought. When investing in innovation, inventors usually do not have a very good idea of where their efforts might lead them on this continuum from bad to good fortune. What matters, then, is the reward that they can reasonably expect to obtain on average.[44] This has two important consequences. Firstly, *(intellectual) property law can achieve its goals even if competition law limits the extent to which the rights holder can benefit from the monopoly power that might be attached to her property rights.* This can be achieved by granting stronger (i.e. longer and/or broader) property rights initially if the ex post restrictions imposed by competition law are expected to be strong on average. The only requirement for this approach to succeed is that competition law does not essentially expropriate every right that results in some market power. Secondly, *there is no need for (intellectual) property law to react to small changes in competition law.* In particular, individual case decisions are of no consequence except if they herald a forthcoming sea-change in the enforcement of competition law.

Overall, then, all that is needed is for IPR law to adjust slowly over time to perceived changes in competition law. Faster adjustments are also possible. An example of this 'fast track' approach is the US Drug Price Competition and Patent Term Restoration Act of 1984 (also known as the Waxman–Hatch Act). The Act extended the duration of the patents granted on compounds that have to go through lengthy FDA approval procedures. The protection granted to other types of intellectual property could be similarly strengthened if, for some reason, there was a significant tightening of competition law in some sectors of activity.

Having discussed whether and how (intellectual) property law should accommodate changes in competition law, we now examine whether competition law should systematically revisit the trade-offs already considered in the design of (intellectual) property law. In particular, should arguments about the trade-off between 'static' and 'dynamic' efficiency be part and parcel of competition law cases – as they increasingly are? The short answer to this question is no. The main reason for this is precisely that the relevant trade-offs have already been embedded in the design of the various property rights regimes. As we saw in the first part, these regimes appear to accommodate the essential differences between various types of assets rather well. Moreover, the specific rules that apply to different kinds of *intellectual* property closely resemble the socially optimal mechanisms that economic theory would recommend.

One could object that, even though property rights regimes optimally balance static and dynamic efficiency considerations, they do this based on the information available at the time property rights are granted. As we have just seen, competition authorities are likely to have better information at the time of their own involvement. Shouldn't this additional information be used to 're-optimise' and adjust the balance called for by the reward and disclosure effects? For example, we know that market structure can affect the private returns to investment. Why, then, shouldn't we apply competition policy differentially across sectors in order to fine-tune the balance between investments incentives and efficiency losses? If, for example, we knew that less competitive markets increase private returns to investment (compared to their social return), then being tougher on firms operating in concentrated markets would in fact bring returns in such industries in line with returns in other more competitive sectors. The problem with this line of argument is that, in fact, *we do not know what the effect of market structure on investment incentives are*. Economic theory just does not have any robust prediction as to whether 'competition drives innovation' or invention is best nurtured – and financed – by large firms with significant monopoly power.[45]

A further reason not to allow competition law judges to systematically revisit the trade-offs already considered by (intellectual) property law is what economists refer to as the risk of regulatory opportunism. As we saw in Part I, once intellectual property is produced (and disclosed), the socially optimal allocation is for every economic agent to have free access to it. In other words, the optimal level of monopoly power ex post is none. As competition law only faces such ex post situations, there might be a strong temptation to limit the use of IP-based monopoly power so much that adequate rewards for investment in IP could no longer be provided. This temptation might even be stronger at the level of individual cases since, as we discussed above, a single case is unlikely to significantly affect the expected reward on which investors base their decisions. However, succumbing to this temptation would lead to a 'death of a thousand cuts', where the combined effect of apparently innocuous individual case decisions combine to wreck the delicate balance achieved by IP law.

The remedy against regulatory opportunism is commitment. In the case of competition law, commitment can only come from the clarity of how the law should be implemented. The clearer the rules, the stronger the commitment. It would therefore be advisable to explicitly state that competition law should respect the rights granted by (intellectual) property law and that the trade-off between static and dynamic efficiency is not a primary concern of competition law. This principle does not prevent the enforcement of (possibly strict) competition laws but it implies that conditions under which the use of monopoly power will be restricted must be as unambiguous as possible. The 'essential facility' doctrine can be seen as a good example of such an approach. On the one hand, it is entirely consistent with the general respect of property rights that we advocate and acknowledge that property rights can only be effective if they do imply some monopoly power. On the other hand, it allows for a clear exception when the monopoly power associated with the property right is so large as to result in an unacceptable loss of welfare.[46]

Before closing this section, we must point out that the arguments presented apply to investment in all types of economic assets, not just to intellectual property. This has a most important consequence: *As the distinct characteristics of various types of property are already adequately reflected in their specific property rights regimes, all types of assets should be treated equally by competition law.* From the point of view of competition law, the only relevant difference between assets is the degree of monopoly power that their ownership confers. For equal degrees of market power, further distinctions between asset is not only not required but counterproductive: by introducing artificial differences in the treatment of assets, competition law would only skew the relative returns that can be obtained from different types of investment and adversely affect the allocation of resources in the economy.

In particular then, claims that a firm with significant market power should be treated more benevolently because 'the source of its market power is intellectual property and being harsh would compromise innovation and the social benefits accruing from it' should be dismissed. The specificity of intellectual property, including the 'social benefits accruing from it', has already been taken into account in the special property rights regime that it enjoys.

The discussion in this section can be summarised in the following set of principles for competition policy:

(i) Restraint. If competition law focuses narrowly on monopoly power, it risks dissipating the expected rewards that are essential to provide adequate investment incentives. This principle applies to both intellectual and 'real' property.

(ii) Each individual competition law decision might seem to have (and does have) only a small effect on expectations of reward but their combined effect can be devastating. There is therefore a need for a clear commitment not to revisit ex post the rights granted by IP law.

(iii) There is no need to systematically revisit the trade-off between incentives and economic efficiency in competition law cases.

(iv) Only large changes in ex post regulation (for example competition policy) call for adjustment of property right regimes.

(v) It is important to treat all sources of monopoly power similarly.

C. Applications and specific issues

In this section, we discuss how the principles laid down in the previous section – The argument for independence – can be applied to patents, copyrights and trade marks. As above, the main line of argument is that intellectual assets should be treated like any other source of market power. This, however, does not mean that the interface between intellectual property and competition law does not have any special characteristics. In particular, we will argue that some types of (potentially) abusive practices are more likely to arise in the presence of IP-based dominance. We will also see that the competition authority's ability to detect abusive practices and to enforce an adequate remedy can be affected by some of the special features of intellectual assets.

1. Patents

Intellectual property is only a concern for competition policy if it is the source of significant market power. This raises the question of how relevant markets – and a firm's competitive position in these markets – should be determined. Do the traditional approaches to market definition, market power and dominance work well when intellectual property rights are involved? Subject to the caveats discussed below in the paragraph on mergers, the answer is yes. One should just be careful to identify all relevant markets. In the case of patents, one would generally expect both upstream and downstream markets to be involved. The downstream markets are all the product markets where the patented innovation can find a commercial use. The relevant upstream market is the market for 'knowledge' itself, where firms allow others to use their intellectual property through various forms of contractual arrangements.

In determining the relevant downstream markets, one should be mindful of the fact that there is no strict correspondence between the notion(s) of patent breadth and the market power that the patent confers. An example of a 'broad' patent is Agracetus' EPO patent covering any possible type of transformation of soybean through genetic engineering techniques. If GM products had proved to be a commercial success in Europe, this patent would likely have resulted in significant monopoly power in the soybean market. On the other hand, consider another patent that would grant exclusivity to all genetic engineering methods of conferring glyphosate resistance to plants. This is also a rather broad patent as it covers all types of plants, wheat as well as cotton or fruit trees. On the other hand, as glyphosate is not the only high-performance herbicide available, plants that are resistant to other herbicides are still likely to limit the market power of the patent holder in any of the relevant downstream markets. In other words, the legal 'breadth' of the patent is 'spread' across a large number of relevant product markets (say one per plant in a family of plants) so that the resulting market power need not be a concern.

1.1. Mergers In appraising a merger, competition authorities evaluate whether markets are likely to be significantly less competitive after the new entity is formed. This assessment involves both unilateral effects and coordinated effects. We will focus on the former. In practice, the first step of the competition authority's analysis is to determine the likely effect of the mergers on market shares in the relevant market. These shares need not be based solely on the sales of the merging party. Often the parties' share of industry-wide productive capacity is also considered because it is thought to be a good indicator of potential market shares.

As argued above, the same principles should be applied regardless of the source of potential monopoly power. In terms of mergers, this implies that, while shares in the relevant product markets are of course still relevant, one should also seriously scrutinise the merging partners intellectual property 'capacity'. As a first step, one should assess the firms' share in the upstream market for intellectual property. This involves a disclosure of all licensing agreements, i.e. of the actual 'sales' of IP. This, however, does not suffice: As for productive capacity, it is also necessary to assess the merging parties' share of the existing stock of intellectual assets. This share should be computed for each of the downstream markets. This presents two difficulties. Firstly, as discussed above, going from a specific patent to the markets that it can affect is not always straightforward. Secondly, it is not obvious how to weight the various patents in the firms' IP portfolio to obtain some aggregate measure of 'capacity'.

At the level of the EU at least, publicly available information and our own experience suggests that a thorough appraisal of merging parties' IP positions rarely takes place. Even considering the difficulties of measurement involved, we would argue that more rigorous assessments are both workable and highly desirable. By making IP-intensive mergers more likely to be approved than mergers involving other sources of market power, the current practice might artificially bias the allocation of resources toward IP-incentive sectors.

1.2 Licensing   In most jurisdictions, patent licensing is the object of a host of special competition law rules.[47] From the point of view of economic analysis, this is rather confusing as there is essentially no reason to treat patent licensing agreements differently from any other kind of vertical contract. Hence, in the EU for example, most aspects of licensing contracts can perfectly well – and should – be assessed according to the Commission's 'vertical guidelines'. Accordingly, special dispensations, such as the EU's block exemption on patent licensing, do not make much sense. In fact, by treating patent-based monopoly power differently (and, arguably, more leniently) than market power based on other types of assets, such a policy distorts the economy-wide allocation of resources (see Part I of this chapter).

One caveat to this general principle is that, because of the nature of the 'input' being sold, licensing contracts must often include clauses aimed at safeguarding the integrity of the innovation.[48] In other words, some contractual clauses might be indispensable as, without them, the value of the intellectual property right might be lost. Clearly such clauses can only justify a differential treatment of IP-based market power if they would not be necessary to protect the value of other types of contractable assets. The main source for such a discrepancy is the public good nature of intellectual property, i.e. the fact that it is an 'input' in the production process that is not effectively destroyed when used. This has several implications. The first issue is that of *resale.* A manufacturer purchasing ball bearings from a firm with market power cannot resell these inputs to another downstream customer without depriving itself of its use. By contrast, since knowledge is non-rival, a licensee can easily resell the knowledge acquired from the licensor to a third party without restricting its own use of the technology. In fact, if the licensee and the firm to which it resells the technology operate in distinct markets, the resale does not impose any cost at all on the licensee. Accordingly, it is perfectly legitimate to allow clauses that forbid the divulgation of the licensor's intellectual property to third parties, at least until that property has fallen into the public domain. Such clauses could include, for example, a ban on sublicensing or even assignment.

A second issue is that of the reputation of *the technology.* Even if licensees do not use the licensor's trade mark, their behaviour can damage the value of her intellectual property. Consider for example a new contraceptive device. Even if faulty products are clearly identified as being made by a given licensee, they can damage consumer confidence in the new contraceptive method itself. This would damage the profitability of all licensees and, therefore decrease the revenues of the licensor. In fact, when consumers are initially quite uncertain about the new technology, the behaviour of a few rogue licensees might affect the technology's very viability. One might therefore want to treat clauses aimed at ensuring some quality control (for example prohibition to deviate from the technology or prescribed production methods) rather leniently.

A somewhat different problem is that it is difficult to measure the 'intensity' with which the licensee uses the contracted input. The issue here is not that this difficulty might 'destroy' the value of the patent but rather that it might make patent-based monopoly inherently less profitable than other types of monopolies. When dealing with a physical input, the intensity of use can be assessed directly from the number of units purchased by the 'downstream' firm. The upstream firm can then easily vary the price of the input depending on the total quantities purchased. In order to duplicate such contracts, and therefore be able to 'extract surplus' as efficiently as the seller of physical inputs, a licensor must be able to condition the payments received from the licensee on some other measure of 'intensity', such as the relevant sales of the licensee. This can justify stricter clauses – such as some control over distribution channels downstream, aimed at making such measure reliable.

While patent-based monopoly power should not receive differential treatment, it gives rise to potentially abusive conducts that are rarely observed when market power comes from the ownership of other types of exclusive assets. The competitive implications of these types of conduct – not some broad theoretical 'conflict' between the two bodies of law – are the proper subject matter for those interested in the interface between IP law and competition law.

1.2.1 Cross-licensing

From the point of view of competition policy, cross-licensing and patent pools are probably the most significant IP-specific practices. Even in this case, though, one can think of non-IP equivalents. For example, a contract whereby two airlines which have a stranglehold on two different airports agree to give each other access to their gates, terminals and/or other ground facilities looks very much like an agreement to share various technologies. Still, patent pools and cross-licensing are observed much more often than their non-IP analogies. We will initially focus on cross-licensing, leaving some of the specific features of patent pools for the end of this section.

In assessing the antitrust implications of cross-licensing, it is vital to determine whether the technologies involved are (broadly) 'substitutes' or 'complements'. Technologies are 'substitutes' if they (potentially) compete with each other. This does not necessarily mean that the scientific principles on which the two technologies rely must be similar. For example, two patents on separate pain relievers are substitutes even though the chemical compounds and the physiological mechanisms involved might be very different. On the other hand, technologies are 'complements' if using them jointly enables a firm to improve the quality of its product and/or lower its cost of production. One might believe, for example, that combining the DVD patents held by a number of firms would allow each of the firms involved to present more attractive products to consumers. In fact, in cases where different parties hold 'blocking' patents on different aspects of a technology, cross-licensing might be the only way to ensure that the new technology is used at all. Because of this 'value-increasing' or 'cost-decreasing' effect, cross-licensing of complementary technologies should, as a rule, be given the benefit of the doubt: in the absence of some specific, documented, competitive concern, they should escape antitrust scrutiny. Quite the opposite principle applies to the case of substitute technologies: given the lack of any obvious benefit, they should generally be considered with suspicion.

There are two main reasons to be wary of cross-licensing agreements between firms. The first issue relates to the structure of the licensing payments. As Katz and Shapiro[49] and Fershtman and Kamien[50] have shown, competing firms can replicate the monopoly outcome by choosing appropriate levels of royalties. The intuition behind this result is relatively straightforward. Consider cross-licensing between two firms, A and B, that compete in the same market and assume that each firm actually uses the technology that it licenses from the other. Assume further that the royalty payment is linked to the volume or value of the sales made using the licensed technology. When deciding how hard to compete (i.e. how much to produce or what price to set), firm A considers two factors that would not be present without cross-licensing. Firstly, A must now pay a royalty to firm B. This effectively raises firm A's cost of production, leading to less aggressive behaviour.[51] Secondly, firm A also considers the effect of its behaviour on the flow of royalties that it is getting from firm B. As more aggressive behaviour on A's part reduces both the output and the profitability of its rival, it also decreases A's licensing income, leading it to adopt a less aggressive stance. Of course, the same reasoning also applies to B. The end result is that both firms compete less harshly, moving the industry closer to the monopoly outcome.

Notice that this collusive effect does not require any explicit or even tacit coordination of the two firms' actions: the cross-licensing agreement simply modifies the firms' incentives to ensure that the uncoordinated equilibrium is less competitive than before. In fact, this is very similar to the effect of cross-ownership of shares, to which several antitrust authorities are now paying increasing attention: a firm owning shares in a rival will compete less intensively since competition hurts its rival and, therefore, the value of the firm's shareholdings in its rival. As a matter of consistency then, it would make little sense to scrutinise cross-shareholdings and ignore cross-licensing agreements. It is also worth noting that the collusive effect of royalty payments arises irrespective of whether the technologies licensed are substitutes or complements. In the latter case, then, one would have to weight the potential benefits of cross-licensing (see above) against the resulting decrease in the intensity of competition. As a final remark, notice that the effect discussed above depends crucially on the structure of the royalty payments. Fixed payments, i.e. payments that are not linked in any way to the performance of the rival, would not affect the competitiveness of the industry. This suggests a possible remedy that would remove any ambiguity for the case of complementary technologies: if the parties are willing to rely mostly on lump sum licensing fees, then cross-licensing of such technologies would not raise any serious antitrust concern.

Cross-licensing agreements can also restrict competition through a very different channel by acting as facilitating practices, i.e. practices that facilitate 'tacit collusion' between rivals.[52] 'Tacit collusion' refers to an implicit agreement to keep prices high (or quantities low). They are enforced through implicit threats: as long as other firms hold their side of the bargain, everybody else does too. But as soon as one firm 'deviates' by setting a lower price or producing more, then the industry gets into a 'punishment' phase, where all members of the tacit agreement set much lower prices (or sell larger quantities). It is the threat of these costly punishment episodes that ensures that the firms prefer to abide by the implicit agreement. The more effective this threat, the more collusive (i.e. closer to the monopoly outcome) the industry equilibrium that can be sustained. It is precisely by making the punishment harsher that cross-licensing agreements can be anticompetitive. To explain how this comes about, it is worth considering a number of distinct situations.

Assume first that the two firms, A and B, *do not compete in the same market*. For example, A might have a patent for an antidepressant while B might have a patent for a drug that fights stomach ulcers. In the absence of cross-licensing, each firm might be tempted to develop its own drug in order to enter the other firm's market. The firms could try to keep their rival out of their market by threatening to invade the rival's own turf if and only if the rival invades first. Unfortunately, this threat is unlikely to be very effective: If A does in fact move into the other firm's market, it will take time for its rival to react by developing an antidepressant of its own. During that time, A enjoys monopoly profits in antidepressants and gets a share of the anti-ulcer market. If B's reaction time is long enough, this prospect would prove too attractive and both firms would in fact get onto each other's turf, increasing competition. Suppose now that the two firms have a cross-licensing agreement. This means that each firm could now react much more quickly if its rival decided to breach the implicit agreement. Anticipating this quicker reaction, both firms find it more profitable to stay in their own market and respect the monopoly of the other firm. This anticompetitive effect of cross-licensing has two notable features. Firstly, it applies to firms which *do not compete in the same market*. Secondly, the firms *do not actually use the technologies that they obtain from the other firm*. This is an important feature and strongly suggests that, when tacit collusion is a concern, the actual use of cross-licensed technologies should be closely monitored.

Now assume that the two firms actually compete in the same market, say the market for pain relievers. Their products are substitutes, but not perfectly so. For example, firm A's product might be aspirin-based while B's relies on paracetamol. The two firms might already be able to support some level of tacit collusion even in the absence of cross-licensing: firm B knows that if it lowers its price, A will retaliate by starting a price war. As the products are substitutes, A's retaliation would hurt B significantly. However, as before, the retaliation would be even more effective if A could retaliate by selling a product that is an even closer substitute to B's product. This is precisely what cross-licensing would make possible. As firms would fear retaliation more, they would be able to further decrease the intensity of competition in the market. In this context, the firms do compete in the same market but, as above, they do not actually use the technology obtained from their rivals.[53]

Overall then, cross-licensing is likely to facilitate tacit collusion irrespective of whether they involve competing technologies or technologies that find their applications in distinct markets. The fact that the firms do not broadly use the licensed technologies should be seen as prima facie evidence for this collusive effect. Importantly, this concern does not apply to the cross-licensing of complementary technologies.[54]

1.2.2 Patent pools

From the point of view of economic analysis, patent pools are very similar to cross-licensing: a number of firms give each other access to a number of their patents. The payments schemes involved vary widely. Some pools grant free access to all members, others involve elaborate royalty schemes. In this respect, as discussed above, the main concern would be a systematic reliance on output or sales-related royalties. Like cross-licensing, patent pools also facilitate tacit collusion. They are, if anything, even more suspicious in this respect, for two reasons. Firstly, given that pools typically include a large number of patents, one would not expect all members to use all technologies anyway. This makes it harder to distinguish 'innocuous' pools from those meant to reduce competition between members. Secondly, the number of patents involved also multiplies the potential for 'multi-market contact' between pool members, making tacit agreements even easier to support.

A distinct feature of patent pools is the conditions of access that they set for non-members. The potential for abuse is obvious. For example, refusal to grant access to third parties on terms resembling those available to members would, if the pool members have sufficient monopoly power, amount to collective foreclosure. There would in this case be absolutely no difference between a patent pool and discriminatory access arrangements among a group of powerful airlines. Another common practice has more subtle anti-trust implications. Often, third parties are only offered access to the whole set of patents in the pool, i.e. they are charged a single price for what is effectively a 'bundle' of intellectual property rights. Such tactics could be used to leverage the monopoly power that pool members enjoy in one market into another. The precise economic argument can be found in Whinston.[55] Its basic flavour can be obtained from the following example. A firm (or a patent pool) has patents on two types of vaccines, one against polio, the other against German measles. Assume further that the firm's polio vaccine is the only one available, i.e. the firm is a monopolist in the market for polio vaccines. On the other hand, it faces (potential) competition in the market for the other vaccine. The firm licenses its patents to companies that actually make the vaccine. Suppose that instead of licensing the vaccine separately, the firm only offers the two licences jointly. What this means is that, in order to realise the profits corresponding to its polio monopoly, the firm now must also induce its customers to buy its German measles vaccine. This makes the

firm much more aggressive in the market for German measles vaccines than it would have been, had it decided to licence its two technologies separately. In particular, the firm might be willing to sell its German measles vaccine at an implicit price[56] that is below the cost of its main (potential) rivals. The prospect of such fierce competition would discourage potential entrants and might even induce existing competitors to exit. If this occurs, the firm will have successfully used its monopoly power in the polio market to enhance its position in the market for its other vaccine.

A subtlety of this argument is that it does not apply when the two patents involved are strict complements. Suppose that firm A had a patent-based monopoly on a medical diagnostic machine that uses films but that various types of films could be used on the machine. Because the machine cannot be used without films and vice-versa, the firm could extend its monopoly in the 'machine' market into the market for film without selling machine and films jointly. Since the customers must use the two products together anyway, the firm could charge a very low price for its film, driving out the competition, and simply recoup this by selling the machine at a price in excess of its stand-alone monopoly price.[57] This is therefore a further reason for looking less favourably on pooling of patents that are not strong complements.

Overall, then, there are overwhelming reasons to be suspicious of patent pools. There is a strong argument for requiring that all patent pool agreements be notified to the antitrust authority, if not for banning them outright.

1.2.3 Settlements[58]

Patent pools and cross-licensing agreements often arise as part of litigation settlements. In such cases, their welfare properties cannot be properly assessed without considering the potential benefits and costs of having firms reach such a settlement rather than proceed with litigation. Moreover, this also means that agreements to settle patent litigation should not be the sole province of patent law and IP courts: They should be subjected to antitrust scrutiny. Since more than 95 per cent of US patent litigation cases are settled[59] this issue is of more than academic interest.

Clearly, settlements are only reached if they are privately beneficial to each of the contracting parties. Social costs and benefits are those affecting parties that are not involved in the agreement, mostly consumers, the government and, possibly, other firms. On the benefit side, avoiding litigation saves on direct court costs and helps relieve court congestion. On the cost side, are the fact that settling a case might prevent the establishment of a socially useful precedent on a point of law and any potential loss of competition. The resulting decrease in competition can take three forms. Firstly, market rivalry between parties would presumably have persisted over the period of litigation. Secondly, there is a chance that the outcome of continued litigation would have been to invalidate or seriously limit the contested patent, eliminating or reducing the monopoly power of the patent-holder. Finally, as discussed in the previous section, the settlement itself might support more collusive behaviour in the post-settlement market.

Given these costs and benefits, how can we distinguish between 'collusive' and 'pro-competitive' settlements. Shapiro[60] proposes to rely on a principle of consumer neutrality: an agreement will be deemed to be pro-competitive if it leaves consumers at least as well off as they would have been had the parties seen the litigation to its bitter end. Shapiro's core result is that, under quite general conditions, there always exists a settlement that makes the litigating parties better off without hurting consumers. In other words, respecting the principle of consumer neutrality should not prevent litigating parties from reaching a settlement; it only imposes restrictions on the types of settlements that might be reached. In practice, however, the information required to determine which agreements pass this test might be hard to obtain. In particular, since one must compare the outcome of the agreement to what would have occurred, had litigation proceeded, one needs to assess the strength of the contested patent and this must be done without the benefit of a full trial on the issue.

1.2.4 Grant-backs

As part of the conditions for licensing their technology, many companies require their licensees to 'grant back' to them any improvements that they make. The precise agreement can take a variety of forms. The grant-back can be free or involve some payments from the original licensor and the licensor might or might not enjoy the exclusive benefit of the improvements. The grant-back can also be unilateral, in which case improvements only flow from the licensee to the licensor, or mutual, in which case the licensee also receives the further improvements discovered by the licensor.

To discuss the economics of grant-back, it is useful to take EU competition law as a point of reference. In a nutshell[61] under Article 85(1), the Commission has no objection to grant-back clauses that are both non-exclusive and mutual. The Commission further distinguishes between severable improvements, which are those that can be used independently of the original licensed technology and non-severable improvements which can only be exploited jointly with the original licensed technology. The Commission's position on severable improvements is strong: the licensee has the right to use and license this improvement both during and after the term of the initial licensing contract. The Commission also takes a dim view of any attempt by the original licensor to obtain rights over the severable improvement *beyond the term of the original licensing agreement* without an appropriate quid pro quo. What constitutes an 'appropriate' quid pro quo is, however, not clear. There seems to be some preference for continuing reciprocal exchange of the right to use each other's technology over the simple payment of royalties by the former licensor.

The treatment of non-severable improvements differ mostly during the term of the initial licensing contract, as an exclusive – but still mutual – licensing of improvements would not be deemed to raise significant competitive concerns.

The most obvious effect of grant-back clauses is that they tend to decrease the parties' incentives to invest resources in seeking to improve the technology. To see this, consider the simple case where the licensee must grant back its improvements to the licensor for free. Compared to a situation where the licensee could negotiate ex post a reward for transferring its new know-how, the grant-back clause decreases the returns that the licensee can obtain, discouraging investment. Requiring that grant-back clauses ensure the mutual exchange of improvement does not help. On the contrary, this also discourages innovation as it decreases the licensor's own incentive to improve the technology. Also, by guaranteeing that the licensee gets some technology improvements anyway mutual grant-back clauses might[62] also dull the licensee's own incentives to innovate even further. The Commission's preference for reciprocal exchange is not therefore particularly well-founded.

One should add that, in terms of economic analysis, the idea that 'less innovation is bad' is not particularly compelling either. While consumers are likely to benefit from more innovation, society as a whole might not as the firms might be investing too heavily in R&D. The reason for this goes back to the 'business stealing' effect discussed at the beginning of this chapter: while some of a firm's reward from innovation comes from the greater social value that it creates, another part comes from the profits that it diverts from other firms. The first part is socially useful, the second part is not.[63]

The disincentive effect of grant-back clauses could of course be avoided if each party agreed to make an appropriate payment for the new know-how that it receives. In that sense, the Commission's preference for a 'quid pro quo' appears to be justified. However, in order to be effective, such a quid pro quo must be conditional, i.e. the contract should be such that each party only receives something from the other *if it does indeed produce improvements and make them available to the other party*. Hence, a broad agreement to exchange all improvements without payment would not help at all since a party would receive the other party's improvements regardless of whether or not it comes up with improvements of its own. Another issue is that conditional payments are hard to determine ex ante. By definition, future improvements cannot be described – and therefore valued – accurately before they have been obtained. This makes the inclusion of pre-set tariffs in a grant-back clause unlikely. The alternative, then, is simply to negotiate the price of the transfer ex post, i.e. once an improvement has actually been made. This approach seems quite feasible in the case of severable improvements: as the number of potential users is not limited by the availability of the original technology, the licensee should be able to obtain a reasonable return on its investment. If the

improvements were non-severable, then the parties would run into a traditional hold up problem. This is clearest in the case where the licensor only has
one licensee. Since the two parties are the only ones who can actually use the
non-severable improvements, these innovations have no value outside of the
specific licensor–licensee relationship. This makes it easy for the 'buying'
party to obtain the improvement at a price much below its actual value. This
in turn means that the two parties would have insufficient incentives to
pursue non-severable improvements.

Overall, then, economic analysis appears to provide little support for the
Commission's preference for the mutual exchange of improvements.
Furthermore, the arguments presented suggest that there is no benefit to
agreeing ex ante to the exchange of severable improvements. On the other
hand agreeing on ex ante conditional payments for non-severable improvements might help resolve a hold up problem, increasing the firms' incentives
to innovate.

The issue of exclusivity is relatively straightforward. There is absolutely no
reason to let the licensor obtain through the grant-back more 'exclusivity'
than already conferred by her patent on the initial technology. One implication of this principle is that the licensor should never be allowed to demand ex
ante that the grant-back of severable improvements be exclusive.[64] The
implications for non-severable improvements are rather different. During
the validity of the initial licensing agreement, the licensor already has the
power to prevent any party that is not authorised to use the main technology
from using the improvement. A clause requiring exclusivity for the licensor
and all of its licensees would therefore be redundant and, as such, would not
further damage competition. On the other hand, one should take a dim view
of exclusivity clauses that prevent the licensee from using its own improvement or from making them available (at a price) to all licensees of the original
licensor.

The previous arguments assume that the original technology has already
been licensed. Choi[65] examines the effect of grant-back clauses on the original
inventor's incentive to license in the first place. Choi's model has several
important features. There are two firms that are involved in a repeated
innovation race. These two firms only compete in the market for technologies, i.e. they sell their technology to the same potential customers. The two
firms do not compete in the same product market(s). Initially, one of the two
firms has a technology that it considers licensing to its rival. The benefit from
licensing is the revenues that it generates. The cost is that, by licensing its
technology, the licensor essentially gives its rival a leg up in the race for
further innovations. Still Choi shows that *if the two firms can write complete
contracts* then the licensor always sells its highest quality technology to its
rival. In practice, however, parties are unlikely to be able to write complete
contracts. Choi assumes that the initial licensing contract between the two

firms involves moral hazard. More precisely, the quality of the technology licensed is not 'contract-able': while the two firms may be able to observe this quality, a third party could not make any contractual clause based on observed quality unenforceable. If payments cannot be linked explicitly to quality, how then can the licensor ensure that it gets higher revenues from licensing a higher quality technology? The answer lies in royalties that are tied to the output of the licensee: as better technology will result in greater sales, the licensor's revenues are tied indirectly to the quality of the licensed technology. Unfortunately, royalties are imperfect instruments: They do not extract the full value added by the licensed technology. There will therefore be situations where the revenues actually obtained through 'per unit' royalties do not cover the cost from increasing the rival's ability to compete, even though the true value of the technology transfers would exceed this cost. In such cases, the licensor would not licence its best technology even though this is the socially optimal thing to do. Choi's key result is that, in the presence of this moral hazard problem, including grant-back clauses in the licensing contract can ensure that the best technology is always licensed.

Choi's analysis can therefore be seen as providing a rationale for a more lenient antitrust treatment of grant-back clauses. However, one should consider the following caveats. Firstly, while grant-back clauses ensure that the best technology gets licensed in the first place, it also affects the rest of the repeated R&D race between the two firms. These effects, as Choi admits, have ambiguous welfare consequences. Secondly, the model is a little too favourable to grant-back clauses as it assumes that they can be enforced without facing a *moral hazard* problem of their own. This seems extreme as, in practice, enforcing grant-back clauses also requires that the parties make sure that they are getting 'the best' improvement obtained by their rival. If the quality of the initial technology could not be contracted upon, why should we assume that the quality of improvements can be?

1.2.5 Compulsory licensing
(i) Refusal to license
As we have argued, a patent provides temporary property rights on an intellectual asset. This asset might prove useful in the production of a number of goods and services to which various downstream markets correspond. While the patent confers exclusive property rights it does not necessarily confer monopoly power. If it does, subject to the caveats discussed above, it should then be treated like any other source of market power. In particular, any refusal to grant access to the protected intellectual asset should be assessed in a manner consistent with the competition authority's policy on vertical restraints. In the EU, for example, this would mean that a refusal to license the intellectual property to a (potential) downstream competitor

would be deemed unlawful if the patent holder has significant market power in both the upstream and downstream markets. In other words, licensing could be made compulsory even if the patent is not absolutely essential to compete in the downstream market. The correct test in the upstream market is whether the number, type and ownership of alternative technologies are such that the patent-holder enjoys significant market power. Hence the exclusive nature of the property rights granted by a patent should not automatically translate into a right to use the patent exclusively.

The issue of compulsory licensing also arises in a rather different context where another firm comes up with an innovation that cannot be used without access to the original patent. This can be because the production of a commercially viable product requires that both innovations be combined or because the second innovation infringes the original patent. This situation is different from the 'vertical restraint' case considered in the previous paragraph because the potential licensee (potentially) competes with the patent owner in the upstream market, i.e. in the market for innovations. It is useful to distinguish between two scenarios, one where the two innovations are complements and one where they are substitutes.

The original patent and the new innovation are complements if both are needed in order to serve the relevant downstream market(s). In the field of genetically modified crops, for example, one might need to combine a patent on a specific DNA sequence (and its use) with a patent on a manner of introducing the DNA in a cell in order to produce a genetically modified seed. From an economic perspective, this does not give rise to any specific competition policy concern.[66] In particular, one would not expect the original patent holder to refuse to enter into some form of licensing agreement with the new innovator: since the patent holder could not in any case enter the relevant downstream markets on its own, any kind of licensing deal must be better than none. Still, such theoretical certainty is cold comfort if a refusal to license is actually observed. If this is the case, it is important to try to understand what motivates the refusal. A possible explanation is that the technologies are in fact not complementary. In practice, telling complements from substitutes is not necessarily easy. In the recent EU *Microsoft* case, for example, operating systems for PCs and operating systems for servers might have been construed as complements but the Commission argued that, in a dynamic perspective, they were actually substitutes.

Let us now consider a situation where the new innovation represents an (infringing) improvement on the original patent. As in the case of complementary technologies, the improvement represents an additional source of 'value' that the original patent holder should be eager to share through some form of licensing. However, *unless the licensing agreement can be designed to effectively enforce collusion between the two firms*, allowing the new invention to be introduced also increases competition in the downstream market(s).[67] If this pro-competitive effect dominates, then the patent holder would refuse to license even though licensing would be socially desirable ex post. Since competition policy will (and should) often frown on collusive licensing agreements, refusals to license are likely to be rather frequent. Does it mean that compulsory licensing should be imposed? As we will see, the answer depends on the terms of the compulsory licence.

(ii) Conditions of the compulsory licence

As we have just seen, compulsory licensing is most likely to be called for in two types of situations: When the patent holder has significant market power in both the upstream and downstream market and when another firm develops an infringing innovation. However, these two cases call for different principles when it comes to setting the terms of the licensing contract.

In the infringing innovation case, the object of compulsory licensing is to ensure that a socially useful innovation actually gets introduced, not to increase competition downstream. This objective can be achieved by choosing the royalty according to Baumol and Willig's ECPR formula. This formula sets the 'access charge' paid by the licensee as equal to the marginal cost of granting access (likely to be close to zero in the case of IPR) plus an amount reflecting the profits lost by the licensor because of increased competition downstream. In other words, the licence contract would be such that the original patent holder is made (at least) as well off as if it refused to grant a licence. Licence terms that are less favourable to the licensor would amount to an ex post revision of the scope of the property right initially granted. As we have discussed above, such revisions are undesirable as they undermine the implicit 'contract between society and innovators'.[68]

In the 'vertical restraint' scenario, the point of compulsory licensing is to ensure sufficient competition in the downstream markets. IPRs are, in this respect, treated like any other source of monopoly power. The terms of the compulsory licensing agreement can be determined in two manners. In the first approach, the competition authority would undertake to set the level of royalty, assuming therefore a quasi-regulatory role. Since the main concern is to promote downstream competition, the level of royalty should not be too high. In particular, it should be significantly below the level determined by the Baumol–Willig ECPR formula. The drawback of this system is that it can only work well if the competition authority has quite accurate information about the industry. Alternatively, the competition authority could simply decide how many downstream competitors are needed in order to insure sufficient competition. The rights to obtain one of the licences can then be auctioned to the bidders offering the highest levels of compensation to the patent holder.[69] Of course, the competition authority should make clear that only agreements that would pass traditional antitrust scrutiny are permissible.

1.2.6 Extending the legal patent 'monopoly' beyond the life of the patent

Several practices raise the question of whether the patent holder is effectively trying to extend its monopoly power beyond the length of the patent. Examples include licensing contracts that require grant-backs or payments even after the licensor's legal protection has expired. Such practices are surely an issue at the level of intellectual property law since they might be seen as violating the implicit contract whereby inventors receive protection for a predetermined period of time as reward for their innovative efforts and as incentives to divulge economically useful information (see Part I of this chapter). But should these practices raise antitrust concerns?

We will limit ourselves to the case of post-patent payments. On the positive side, this can be seen as deferred payments that reduce the immediate financial burden of the licensee. In other words, the practice is equivalent to a loan from the licensor to the licensee that is paid back in instalments after the patent (or the licensing agreement) expires. Of course, this raises the question of why the licensee should receive this 'loan' from the licensor rather than from some standard financial institution. A possible reason is that the licensor has privileged information about the quality of the technology licensed. A bank might be reluctant to finance the acquisition of a technology of uncertain quality. The licensor should have no such qualm.

To qualify as pure deferred payments, the fees paid after the expiry of the patent should be independent of the licensee's post-patent use of the technology, i.e. they should either be pre-set lump sum payments or they should be linked to the licensee's use of the technology while the patent was valid. Royalties that are linked to the output of the licensee in the post-patent period are potentially more problematic since they make the licensee less competitive even after the patent has expired. If the licensor competes in the same product market as the licensee, these continuing royalties can be seen as a way to raise the costs of a rival. One should however refrain from concluding that such royalties are undesirable. After all, such royalty schemes must be agreed by the licensee. Since the licensee knows that it will be legally able to access the technology for free once the patent has expired, it will never agree to a total payment that exceeds its willingness to pay in order to get access to the technology while the patent is valid. The relevant question then is whether, for a given total (discounted) payment, lower per unit royalties over a longer period are preferable to higher per unit royalties that stop at the end of the patent's life. This problem is remarkably similar to Gilbert and Shapiro's comparison of patent's breadth and length. In fact, we already mentioned in Part I that the size of the 'per unit' royalty that can be charged was one possible example of patent 'breadth'. Applying Gilbert and Shapiro's result, we can therefore conclude that deferred 'per unit' period will actually improve welfare if the 'per period' deadweight loss increases more quickly than the licensor's per period revenues as the rate of 'per unit' royalty increases.[70] If it does not, then deferred 'per unit' royalties are undesirable. In practice then, there seems to be little cause for systematically looking at such extended royalty scheme with alarm.

A further concern might be that the patent holder is leveraging its mono-poly power during the patent period to increase its monopoly power in the post-patent period. This claim would rely on the foreclosure argument of Whinston,[71] which we already discussed in the section on patent pools. In this case, the 'monopoly market' would be a relevant product market while the patent is valid, while the market to be foreclosed would be the same market after the patent has expired. By asking for payments in both periods, the licensor would essentially be 'tying' the sale of its technology in both markets. This analogy is in fact incorrect. In Whinston, tying works because it eliminates actual or potential competitors from the potentially competitive market. Here, however, there is one fundamental source of 'competition' that cannot be discarded: the fact that, in the post-patent period, the licensee can simply use the technology for free. In other words since the licensee does not need to obtain the technology from any other 'supplier' in the post-patent 'market' there is no room for the licensor to artificially expand its patent-based monopoly power.

2. Copyrights

Many of the arguments presented in the section on patents also apply to copyrights. We will therefore be brief and concentrate on a few distinctive aspects of copyrighted intellectual property as a source of monopoly power.

A significant difference is that individual copyrighted material is rarely the source of significant monopoly power. This is a direct consequence of the smaller breadth of copyright protection. From genetically modified crops to laser technology or prescription drugs, there are numerous examples of patents that have allowed a firm to dominate important markets. One would struggle to find any equivalent example among traditional copyrighted products. Even copyrights on such blockbuster items as 'Harry Potter' or 'Lord of the Rings', hardly help their holder corner the market for fantasy movies, let alone the broader market for movies aimed at children and young adults. Hence copyright-based market power will usually stem from a sig-nificant concentration of copyrighted materials.[72] As such, it might be some-what easier to detect than patent-based market power, where a detailed understanding of individual patent scope is required.

Mergers between firms that hold significant intellectual property portfolios should carefully consider the potential effects of an increase in the concentration of ownership of copyrighted material. Such an evaluation is likely to be easier than in the case of patents as the relevant markets in which the intellectual property might confer monopoly power is more readily identified.

The copyright protection of software raises additional issues. Foremost among them is the protection of interfaces, i.e. the parts of code that ensure the interoperability between a piece of software and other software packages or peripheral equipment. This has been a crucial aspect of the recent string of competition law cases involving Microsoft. In particular, the issue of inter-operability was central to the latest EC complaint where Microsoft was alleged to be withholding information necessary to ensure that computer servers using non-Microsoft operating systems would work well with per-sonal computers, for which Microsoft 's family of 'Windows' operating systems are dominant.

Reviewing the relevant economic theory on compatibility would require a paper in itself. We will therefore limit ourselves to roughly summarising its main points. Two situations must be considered depending on whether the products involved are substitute or complements.

The case of rival technologies is discussed in detail in Farrell and Katz.[73] The key mechanism is that of network externalities. As explained in Part I of this chapter, there are network externalities when the value of a product increases with the number of its users. If two technologies are compatible, then they share the same network: if files can be transferred easily between two word processing packages, then consumers do not care whether more potential co-workers use one of the two. On the other hand, if two rival products are incompatible then the 'network' of each product is limited to its own customers. This creates intense competition aimed at 'building an installed base' of users in order to offer a more attractive product than the rival. If the product or technology purchased consists of durable goods then consumers will also rely on their expectation as to what the network size of the two products are likely to be, giving firms huge incentives to manipulate these expectations through product pre-announcements or, more simply, the diffusion of incorrect information.[74] Incompatibility is also likely to lead to market dominance as rivals might find an early lead in network size to be an insurmountable advantage. Incompatibility also favours incumbents, not only because they might already have a significant installed base but also because consumers might simply expect that a big successful firm entering a new market is more likely to attract a large network of consumers.[75]

Because of this, most economists would agree that overall, ensuring compatibility between rival technologies strengthens market competition. As shown in Farrell and Katz,[76] the effect of compatibility on the firms' incentives to innovate is more ambiguous. On the one hand, compatibility dilutes the reward from innovation as new consumers attracted by the better product also increase the network size – and therefore the value – of rival products. On the other hand, compatibility opens up R&D competition to firms that could not enter otherwise because of their small expected network sizes.

If technologies are (possibly imperfect) complements, then the openness of interfaces allows consumers to use the two technologies or products together. A natural antitrust concern – strongly evoked in the *Microsoft* cases – is that a firm with significant monopoly power in one of the two markets will use its control of interfaces to also monopolise the potentially competitive second market. Such deliberate control of interfaces should be seen with great suspicion as a more competitive second market actually enhances the profitability of the firm's monopoly market. In other words, the benefits from preventing the interoperability of complementary products cannot arise in the original monopoly market. Incentives to prevent interoperability must therefore be found in the firm's desire to use its position in the monopoly market to also dominate the second market.

Overall then, it seems that opening up interfaces is generally the better policy. One should however remain open to a showing that, in particular cases, ensuring interoperability would have too large a negative effect on innovation incentives. The following principles – adapted from Farrell and Katz[77] – should be helpful in deciding which cases deserve more careful consideration:

(i) Opening up the interface is likely to be a better policy when the interface itself contributes little relative to obvious ex ante alternatives. In other words, ensuring access to proprietary interfaces is more likely to be innocuous if the interface itself – as opposed to the main body of the software – is not particularly innovative. The other side of the coin is that one should be more suspicious of the motives of the copyright holder the more arbitrary the interfaces appear to be.[78]

(ii) Forcing the disclosure of sufficient information to ensure interoperability is less attractive when such disclosure cannot be effected without at the same time revealing proprietary information about the innovative aspects of the body of the software itself. However, this argument can also be seen as further support for the claim that such innovative aspects of software products ought to be protected by a patent rather than under copyright law. If they were, then the fact that opening interfaces would also reveal the main innovations would be irrelevant since rivals still could not *use* them without infringing the patent.

3. Trade marks

As discussed in Part I, the main economic function of trade marks is to facilitate reputation building. Like other intellectual property assets, trade marks can be the source of significant monopoly power. What sets trade marks apart is the essential fragility of the advantage that they might confer. While reputations take a long time to build they can be seriously damaged by a single incident. Even the largest firms with the strongest 'brands' are not immune. A few years ago, Coca-Cola took almost a year to get over the fact that a number of European users were apparently affected by a foreign substance found in Coke bottles.[79] Union Carbide never recovered from the Bhopal tragedy and Exxon clearly suffered from the Valdez pollution. This fragility has two main consequences for competition policy.

The first implication is that one should expect firms with strong trade marks to keep a tight control over the production and sales of goods or services bearing their name. If they did not, then the risk would be great that another party allowed to use their trade name would 'free ride' on their reputation to sell shoddy (and therefore cheaper) products at the premium price commanded by the brand's reputation. Such behaviour could easily ruin the valuable goodwill associated with the brand. Hence competition policies forcing companies to license their trade mark or preventing them from including clauses to control the behaviour of their licensee would ultimately be counterproductive as they would remove the firm's incentive to provide consumers with high quality goods.[80] In our opinion, competition authorities should take a lenient view of refusal to license trade marks as well as of most restrictive clauses found in trade mark licensing agreements.[81]

The fragility of reputations also affects our view of the practice of umbrella branding (also known as brand extension) whereby a company uses a trade mark made famous by the sale of one product to enter into another market. Perhaps the most famous recent example is *Virgin*, which has now been used to brand products as different as airlines, train services, electricity supply and cola drinks. Other examples abound, from *Easy(jet)* to *Dior*. Such brand extension strategies raise legitimate competition policy issues as a firm is essentially using an advantage acquired in one market to enhance its position in another. We believe however, that there is little room for concern – and even less room for appropriate antitrust intervention. This position is based on two main arguments. The first one is that the 'foreclosure' mechanism described in Whinston[82] does not apply. That mechanism relies on the fact that the firm only sells its two products as a bundle. This is not the case with umbrella branding as consumers are still completely free to buy the firm's original product without also purchasing the new good or service that it offers under the same name. The second argument is that the firm's brand name is not separable from the quality of the product that it sells in its new market. While the brand name might provide an initial advantage, it will be useless if the quality of the new product does not meet consumer expectations. In fact, because bad performance would likely also affect the firm's sales in its original market, the firm will have greater incentives to maintain quality in its new market than if it were not using the same brand name.[83]

These two arguments do not mean that umbrella branding cannot have anticompetitive effects. The very fact that consumers understand that a well-known brand has 'more at stake' will convince them to give it the benefit of the doubt and try its product. This means that, provided the brand-extension firm delivers on quality, a new company offering a product of similar quality might find it hard to get a foothold into the market.[84] Still, it is hard to see what would constitute an effective remedy. Compulsory trade mark licensing would run into the difficulties described above: if tight controls are required to preserve quality, can we be sure that the licensee would provide effective competition? One could of course simply prevent a company with a dominant trade mark from using it in new markets. However, as we have explained, such a remedy would reduce the firm's incentive to provide a high-quality product both in the new market and in the markets where it is currently dominant.

Conclusion

We have tried to provide a consistent economic view of the legal protection of intellectual property and its interface with competition policy. We made two main points. Firstly, the protection granted under patent, copyright and trade mark laws is broadly consistent with the principles of the economic theory of property rights. In particular, the specificity of intellectual property assets (as opposed to other forms of investment) is accounted for in the type of property rights attached to them. This leads to our second conclusion: since the main distinguishing features of various types of assets are handled effectively by their respective property rights regime, all sources of monopoly power should be treated equally under competition law. In particular, intellectual property should not receive special consideration because of its 'contribution to the creation and diffusion of knowledge'.

Equal treatment of monopoly power, regardless of its source does not mean that the interface between intellectual property and competition law does not have any special characteristics. In fact, we argue that some types of (potentially) abusive practices are more likely to arise in the presence of IP-based dominance. We then provide an economic analysis for a number of these practices, including cross-licensing, patent pools, grant-backs, the copyright protection of software interfaces and the practice of 'umbrella' branding. We also address the role of intellectual property portfolios in merger reviews.

Notes

1. We have assumed that there are no direct externalities. Direct externalities are costs (or benefits) imposed by one economic agent on others. Examples include pollution – you breathe the exhaust of my car; or the fact that you get some enjoyment from living in a well-maintained neighbourhood – you enjoy some of the benefits from my maintenance work. Direct externalities drive a wedge

between private opportunity cost – i.e. the cost taken into account by the agents making the decisions – and social opportunity cost – the cost that should be taken into account from the point of view of society as a whole. With externalities, the principles discussed above still hold as long as opportunity cost is understood as the 'social opportunity cost' that incorporates all relevant external effects.

2. We do not use the term 'scope' to define how the property right owner can, or cannot, use her asset. We focus instead on the exclusionary aspect of property rights. In this sense, the scope of the property right is the precise asset that others can be precluded from using.

3. We refer here to the rights of the owner of the asset, not to the temporary rights that this owner might grant to others. These latter rights are best seen as a use of the owner's original property right.

4. There are of course exceptions such as the rights given to prospectors – from gold diggers to oil companies – which are typically for a limited duration. One of the reasons for this is that, in most cases, the useful life of the asset is itself rather short. Such 'real' assets have other 'intellectual asset' characteristics such as the fact the scope of the rights is not always unambiguous (for example adjacent natural gas fields might be linked geologically) or the fact that the very location of the find provides information about the type of terrains where similar assets might be found.

5. W. Nordhaus, *Invention, Growth and Welfare: A Theoretical Treatment of Technological Change* (Cambridge, MA: MIT Press, 1969) and F. Scherer, 'Nordhaus' Theory of Optimal Patent Life: A Geometric Reinterpretation' (1972) 62 *American Economic Review* 422–7.

6. P. Tandon, 'Optimal Patents with Compulsory Licensing' (1982) 90:3 *Journal of Political Economy* 470–86.

7. R. J. Gilbert and C. Shapiro, 'Optimal Patent Length and Breadth' (1990) 21:1 *Rand Journal of Economics* 106–12.

8. This is satisfied by relatively standard assumptions that demand and marginal revenue slope down while marginal cost slopes up and goods are homogeneous.

9. Their results also require that there be no uncertainty about profits, that the underlying environment is stationary, and that no further improvements to the technology will occur. In the conclusion to their paper, they note that their extreme conclusions on breadth could easily be overturned by relaxing either of these assumptions.

10. P. Klemperer, 'How Broad Should the Scope of Patent Protection Be?' (1990) 21:1 *Rand Journal of Economics* 113–30.

11. T. O'Donoghue, 'A Patentability Requirement for Sequential Innovation' (1998) 29:4 *Rand Journal of Economics* 654–79.

12. This benchmark is easily defined if the innovation consists of a new product. For process innovation, the equivalent assumption is that it is licensed to all.

13. J. R. Green and S. Scotchmer, 'On the Division of Profit in Sequential Innovation' (1995) 26:1 *Rand Journal of Economics* 20–33.

14. Note 11 above.
15. V. DeNicolo, 'Two Stage Patent Races and Patent Policy' (2000) 31:3 *Rand Journal of Economics* 488–501.
16. Ibid.
17. Note 13 above.
18. T. O'Donoghue, S. Scotchmer and J. Thisse, 'Patent Breadth, Patent Life and the Pace of Technological Progress' 7:1 (1998) *Journal of Economics and Management Strategy* 1–32.
19. Note 11 above.
20. Eswaran and Gallini also investigate the effects of patents on the *type* of research conducted, focusing on whether product or process innovation will occur. In the absence of patents, too much product innovation occurs, as this tends to attenuate competitive pressures, while too little process innovation occurs as this tends to increase competitive pressures. This bias can be rectified by modifying the relative patent breadth appropriately on process and product innovations: M. Eswaran and N. Gallini, 'Patent Policy and the Direction of Technological Change' (1996) 27:4 *Rand Journal of Economics* 722–46.
21. S. Scotchmer and J. Green, 'Novelty and Disclosure in Patent Law', (1990) 21 *Rand Journal of Economics* 131–47.
22. C. Matutes, P. Régibeau and K. Rockett, 'Optimal Patent Design and the Diffusion of Innovation' (1996) 27:1 *Rand Journal of Economics* 60–83.
23. Ibid.
24. Referring to the United States, the *Gottschalk* v. *Benson* decision (S. Ct. 175 U.S.P.Q. 673) established in 1972 that a pure algorithm is not patentable in the sense that one cannot pre-empt all uses of a mathematical formula. The *Diamond* v. *Diehr* case (In re *Diehr* (1979) C.C.P.A.: 203 U.S.P.Q. 44, *Diamond* v. *Diehr* (1981) S. Ct. 209 U.S.P.Q. 1) further clarified this by finding that the algorithm in question was patentable because it was applied to a particular process that was specified as part of the patent claims. More recent patents (such as US 4,405,829) seem to have gone against this 'narrow' interpretation. In terms of this model, a broad scope would be equivalent to allowing a patent on the formula itself in the *Benson* case, or on very loosely defined applications of the algorithm. A narrow patent would amount to following the philosophy of the *Diehr* decision that very few applications that are already well-developed would be protected by the patent for the period of its duration.
25. B. Wright, 'The Economics of Invention Incentives: Patents, Prizes and Research Contracts' (1983) 73:4 *American Economic Review* 691–707.
26. M. Kremer, 'Patent Buyouts: A Mechanism for Encouraging Innovation' (1998) CXIII:4 Q*uarterly Journal of Economics* 1137–67.
27. We focus on the protection granted to *published* material. For a discussion of the protection of *unpublished* works, see W. M. Landes, 'Copyright Protection of Letters, Diaries, and Other Unpublished Works: An Economic Approach' (1992) XXI *Journal of Legal Studies* 79–113.

28. See K-L. Hui and I. P. L. Png, 'On the Supply of Creative Work: Evidence from the Movies' 92:2 (2002) *American Economic Review* 217–20.

29. One need only think of the various 'schools' or 'movements' that have characterised literature or painting over the last two centuries.

30. In fact, further works might even enhance the value of earlier works to the extent that they help 'cement' the legitimacy of the movement. In economic terms, such an effect would be seen as a form of 'network externality'.

31. The doctrine of 'fair use' can be seen as an example.

32. Notice that, as obsolescence is not a significant issue, 'length' and 'effective length' essentially coincide.

33. Hui and Png, note 28 above. They suggest that, in the USA at least, copyrighted materials actually receive the maximum effective length of protection. They find that the extension of the length of protection following the Sonny Bono Copyright Extension Act of 1998, adding 20 years to the previous length, had no significant effect on the production of copyrighted movie material.

34. Other examples rely on a price-discrimination mechanism. See L. N. Takeyama, 'The Intertemporal Consequences of Unauthorized Reproduction of Intellectual Property' (1997) XL *Journal of Law and Economics* 511–22 or Y. Bakos et al, 'Shared Information Goods' XLII (1999) *Journal of Law and Economics* 117–55.

35. See L. N.Takeyama, 'The Welfare Implications of Unauthorized Reproduction of Intellectual Property in the Presence of Demand Network Externalities' (1994) 58 *Journal of Industrial Economics* 155–66.

36. I. E. Novos and M. Waldman, 'The Effects of Increased Copyright Protection: An Analytic Approach' (1984) 92 *Journal of Political Economy* 236–46.

37. Total welfare is the sum of consumer surplus and profits.

38. See L. De Alessi and R. Staaf, 'What Does Reputation Really Assure? The Relationship of Trademarks to Expectations and Legal Remedies' 32:3 (1994) *Economic Inquiry* 477–85 for a review of the empirical evidence.

39. See W. M. Landes and R. Posner, 'Trademark Law – An Economic Perspective' 30:2 (1987) *Journal of Law and Economics* 265–309 for a discussion and examples of cases where functional elements, specifically shaped, have not been permitted trademark protection.

40. Trade marks clearly can contribute to the image of a product, which can serve to differentiate the product. To the extent that this creates variety, quality, or disseminates information about the product, it may create a static welfare gain. To the extent that a protected image creates a barrier to entry by raising the entry cost potentially borne by entrants, this could create a static welfare loss. As the economics of this role of advertising creates ambiguous recommendations, it will not be considered as a factor here.

41. See note 39 above for more discussion.

42. This is, in fact, the legal scope. Details and an application to the case of geographically remote users is discussed at length in Landes and Posner, note 39 above.

43. Examples of (ab)uses controlled by IPR law include practices that deceive consumers (for example deceptive pricing or advertising) and, more generally any form of competition that is not 'on the merits'. Broadly understood, this could be (and has sometimes been) construed as including some abuses of monopoly power. In practice, we would argue that there is much to be gained by keeping issues of monopoly power out of IP courts, leaving then to be dealt with under competition law.

44. This argument is similar to the view taken in I. Ayres and P. Klemperer, 'Limiting Patentees' Market Power without Reducing Innovation Incentives: The Perverse Benefits of Uncertainty and Non-injunctive Remedies' 97 (1999) *Michigan Law Review* 985–1033 and in C. Shapiro, 'Antitrust Limits to Patent Settlements' (2003) 34:2 *Rand Journal of Economics* 391–411. Shapiro sees patents as conferring partial property rights. Shapiro elaborates as follows: 'Nothing in the patent grant guarantees that the patent will be declared valid, or that the defendant in the patent suit will be found to have infringed. In other words, all real patents are *less strong* than the idealised patent grant usually imagined in economic theory' (p. 395). We simply extend this approach by adding that there is no guarantee that the right to exclude granted to a patent holder, for example, will not be limited ex post by competition law. What matters is the expected monopoly power associated with IPRs ex ante.

45. For a summary of this debate, see M. I. Kamien and N. L. Schwartz, *Market Structure and Innovation* (Cambridge University Press, 1982) p. 241. Although not recent, this reference is not dated: the debate has not progressed significantly over the last two decades.

46. The economic logic behind this argument is similar to Gilbert and Shapiro's argument discussed in Part I of this chapter: if increased monopoly power increases the deadweight loss faster than profits, then extreme monopoly power can be very damaging without necessarily adding much to the ex ante incentives to invest.

47. See S. D. Anderman, *EC Competition Law and Intellectual Property Rights* (Oxford: Oxford University Press, 1998) p. 320 for the EU and both the old 'No Nos' of licensing and the more recent 1995 DOJ/FTC *Antitrust Guidelines for the Licensing of Intellectual Property* in the US.

48. Anderman, *EC Competition Law and Intellectual Property Rights*, pp. 102–29.

49. M. Katz and C. Shapiro, 'On the Licensing of Innovations' (1985) 16 *Rand Journal of Economics* 505–20.

50. C. Fershtman and M. I. Kamien, 'Cross-Licensing of Complementary Technologies' 10 (1992) *International Journal of Industrial Organization* 329–48.

51. This is straightforward for the case of 'per unit' royalties as they directly increase marginal cost. If the royalty is on the value of sale, they reduce the firm's marginal revenue while leaving its marginal cost unchanged. This too leads the firm to behave less aggressively.

52. See M. Eswaran, 'Cross-Licensing of Competing Patents as a Facilitating Device' 27:3 (1994) *Canadian Journal of Economics* 698–708 for a formal analysis.

53. Theoretically at least, cross-licensing can facilitate tacit collusion even if the firms actually use the technologies that they acquire from one another. This is especially likely in a situation where technologies apply to different markets. As Bernheim and Whinston have shown, under some conditions, extending the number of markets where the same firms compete increase their ability to support collusive outcomes: D. Bernheim and M. D. Whinston, 'Multimarket Contact and Collusive Behaviour' 21 (1990) *Rand Journal of Economics* 1–26.

54. It might apply if cross-licensing the two complementary technologies helps make the products of the two firms more similar. This, however, is a much less robust effect than in the case of independent or substitutable technologies.

55. This argument was amply discussed in the context of the *Microsoft* cases, both in the USA and in the EU. M. D.Whinston, 'Tying, Foreclosure, and Exclusion' 80:4 (1990) *American Economic Review* 837–59.

56. Suppose that the royalty that the firm would charge for the polio vaccine, were the patents to be licensed separately, is r^M and that the royalty that it charges for the two licences jointly is r^B. The implicit royalty charged for the German measles vaccine as part of the bundle is simply $r^B - r^M$.

57. Strictly speaking, this argument only applies exactly when the two complementary products – or licences – must be consumed in fixed proportions. It is only in that case that the traditional Chicago-school claim that foreclosure cannot occur 'because there is only one monopoly profit' applies with full force.

58. This section is based on Shapiro, 'Antitrust Limits to Patent Settlements'.

59. J. O. Lanjouw and M. Schankerman, 'Enforcing Intellectual Property Rights: Suits, Settlements and the Explosion in Patent Litigation' (2002) mimeo, Department of Economics, Yale University.

60. Shapiro, 'Antitrust Limits to Patent Settlements'.

61. For more details, see Anderman, *EC Competition Law and Intellectual Property Rights* pp. 109–18.

62. This second effect can actually go either way: getting better technology from its rival might induce lesser effort from the licensee or might, on the contrary, both increase the licensee's incentives to forge ahead and its ability to do so. See J. P. Choi, 'A Dynamic Analysis of Licensing: The "Boomerang" Effect and Grant-back Clauses' 43:3 (2002) *International Economic Review* 817–18.

63. Van Dijk develops a model where the firms' private incentives to innovate are too large. In such a case, grant-back clauses might be desirable since they help scale R&D back. T.Van Dijk, 'License Contracts, Future Exchange Clauses and Technological Competition' (2002) 44:8 *European Economic Review* 1431–48. Choi also points out the possibility that grant-backs can reduce socially excessive R&D. One could however take the following pragmatic attitude. Whether

or not R&D is indeed insufficient, public policy makers certainly act as if they believe that it is: measures aimed at *increasing* innovation are many and they receive a great deal of publicity. On the other hand, examples of measures that are publicly advertised as aiming at reducing innovation are rare (in fact, we do not know of any). As a matter of *revealed preference*, then, one might be justified to assume that privately financed innovation tends in fact to fall short of what would be socially desirable. Choi, 'A Dynamic Analysis of Licensing: The "Boomerang" Effect and Grant-back Clauses' pp. 803–29.

64. Licensee and licensor should of course be free – subject to the usual antitrust limits – to voluntarily reach an exclusive agreement ex post.

65. Choi, 'A Dynamic Analysis of Licensing: The "Boomerang" Effect and Grant-back Clauses' pp. 803–29.

66. The 'vertical restraint' concerns discussed above would of course remain. If the two innovators jointly have significant market power in the upstream market, they might still be required to license both of their technologies to some downstream competitors.

67. For a similar idea see Scotchmer and Green, 'Novelty and Disclosure in Patent Law' pp. 131–47.

68. Of course, such ex post revisions are fully justified if they are aimed at preventing abuse of monopoly power, as in our 'vertical restraint' case. Not doing so would amount to treating IPRs more favourably than other sources of monopoly power, which, as we have already argued, would distort the allocation of resources.

69. To avoid the progressive disappearance of downstream competitors as some of them might fail, one might want to insist that these licensing agreements be potentially transferable to an alternative licensee.

70. This is only an approximation. A formal analysis would also need to consider the fact that competitive conditions, and thus the profits and deadweight losses associated with a given royalty, are likely to be different in the post-patent period.

71. M. D. Whinston, 'Tying, Foreclosure, and Exclusion' 80:4 (1990) *American Economic Review* 837–59.

72. Indeed, recent competition law cases involving copyright-based monopoly power have focused on such concentrations. See for example the AOL–Time Warner merger, the OFT's review of BskyB or the recent EC review of the acquisition of Telepiu by Stream (i.e. Sky Italy).

73. J. Farrell and M. L. Katz, 'The Effect of Antitrust and Intellectual Property Law on Compatibility and Innovation', *Working Paper*, University of California, Berkeley, Department of Economics (April 1998).

74. Disputes between producers of spreadsheet software as to the accuracy of their published sales figures are a case in point.

75. This is not the same as the 'reputation' mechanism that underlies the economic theory of trade marks. Here it is sufficient that consumers expect the firm to

'get big' in a new market just because it is already big in another. These expectations do not need to be backed by any objected or expected differences in product quality.

76. Note 73 above.

77. Ibid.

78. And the more often they are changed without a substantial technical reason.

79. See Landes and Posner, 'Trademark Law – An Economic Perspective' pp. 265–309 for more examples and a similar view.

80. M. K. Perry and R. Groff, 'Trademark Licensing in a Monopolistically Competitive Industry', *Rand Journal of Economics* 17:2 (1986) 189–200. Perry and Groff also show that trade mark licensing reduces the variety of products available to consumers and that, in most cases, this decreases overall welfare.

81. Franchising agreements often include strict clauses as to how the product should be made and displayed, territorial restrictions aimed at linking products sold back to specific franchisees and 'tie-ins' whereby the franchisee must purchase some inputs from the franchisors.

82. Note 71 above.

83. B. Wernerfelt, 'Umbrella Branding as a Signal of New Product Quality – An Example of Signalling by Posting a Bond' (1988) 19:3 *Rand Journal of Economics* 458–66.

84. On the other hand, a firm already established in that market should have no such problem as it has already demonstrated its quality to customers.

INDEX

Abbott, F., 488, 490
abuse of dominance (Art 82EC)
  biological inventions, 18
  concept of abuse
    burden of proof, 48
    excessive pricing, 39, 47, 49–54
    excessive pricing of IPRs, 51–3
    generally, 46
    pricing by collecting societies, 54
    proportionality, 48
    refusal to supply, 46, 48, 54–71,
      101–2
    self-defence, 48
    tie-ins, 46, 47, 48, 72
  concept of dominance
    barriers to entry, 44–5
    collective dominance, 46
    essential facilities, 45–6, 60
    generally, 44–6, 107–8
    single firm dominance, 44–6
  designs, 18
  determination of relevant markets
    generally, 41–4
    geographic market, 43–4
    substitutes test, 42
  examples, 40
  exceptional circumstances test,
    37, 41, 46, 57–8, 59–71,
    107
  generally, 39–76
  parallel imports, 447
  plant variety rights, 18
  remedies, 100–3
    Commission powers, 100–1
    ECJ case law, 101–2
    fines, 100
acquisitions. *See* mergers

advertising, comparative advertising,
  398–9
agency agreements, 77, 361
Agenda 21, 472
Andean Group, 481
Anderman, S., 480
anti-competitive agreements (Art 81EC)
  appreciable quantitative effect,
    77–9
  block exemptions, 79–81
    research and development, 80, 84
    technology transfer. *See*
      technology transfer
    vertical agreements, 84–5
  competition prevention objective, 78
  concept of undertaking, 77
  convergence with US, 109
  exemptions, 79
    de minimis agreements, 80
  generally, 76–81
  licensing agreements, 81–100
    assessment of non-exempted
      agreements, 92–5
    legislative development, 82
  prohibited agreements, 76–7
  remedies, 103–5
anti-trust law (US)
  ancillary restraints, 180
  Business Review Letters, 185
  cease and desist orders, 185
  economics, 171, 177
    classical economics, 172
    dynamic approaches, 175
    innovation economics, 175
    neo-classical price reprise, 174–5
    neo-classical price theory, 172–3,
      188–9